The Imperial Japanese Navy

Andris J. Kursietis

The Imperial Japanese Navy

(Nihon Kaigun)

1900 - 1945

Uitgeverij Aspekt

THE IMPERIAL JAPANESE NAVY
© Andris J. Kursietis
© 2015 Uitgeverij ASPEKT
Amersfoortsestraat 27, 3769 AD Soesterberg, Nederland
info@uitgeverijaspekt.nl-http://www.uitgeverijaspekt.nl

Omslagontwerp: Mark Heuveling
Binnenwerk: Thomas Wunderink

ISBN: 9789461536044
NUR: 680

Alle rechten voorbehouden. Niets van deze uitgave mag worden verveelvoudigd, opgeslagen in een geautomatiseerd gegevensbestand of openbaar gemaakt, in enige vorm of op enige wijze, hetzij elektronisch, mechanisch, door fotokopieën, opnamen of enig andere manier, zonder voorafgaande toestemming van de uitgever.

Voorzover het maken van kopieën uit deze uitgave is toegestaan op grond van artikel 16B Auteurswet 1912 j° het Besluit van 20 juni 1974, St.b. 351, zoals gewijzigd bij het Besluit van 23 augustus 1985, St.b. 471 en artikel 17 Auteurswet 1912, dient men de daarvoor wettelijk verschuldigde vergoedingen te voldoen aan de Stichting Reprorecht (postbus 882, 1180 AW, Amstelveen). Voor het overnemen van gedeelte(n) van deze uitgave in bloemlezingen, readers, en andere compilatiewerken (artikel 16 Auteurswet 1912), dient men zich tot de uitgever te wenden.

My thanks go especially to my wife, Rosemarie, for her patience during the long hours that I was at my computer, researching and writing this book.

Above all, I have to recognize Hiroshi Nishida, who has tirelessly constructed an excellent website on the Imperial Japanese Navy that has made information about this force accessible to non-Japanese speakers: http://homepage2.nifty.com/nishidah/e/index.htm .Without this goldmine of information, this book would not have been possible.

Table of contents

Introduction	**9**
Admirals of the Imperial Japanese Navy	**11**
- Table of Ranks	11
- Admirals	11
Illustrations of Admirals	**418**
Order of Battle	**433**
- Ministry of the Navy	433
- High Command	439
- Fleets	443
- Air Fleets	450
- Naval Districts	451
- Guard Districts	458
- Naval College, Academies and Schools	465
Major Ships of the Imperial Japanese Navy	**474**
- Aircraft Carriers	474
- Battleships/Battlecruisers	483
- Cruisers	496

Introduction

The Imperial Japanese Navy (IJN) was formally established in July 1869, combining the ships from the previously privately-held navies of the various Japanese warlords. A Ministry of Military Affairs had already been set up in 1868, and in February 1872 this was split up into separate Army and Navy Ministries.

The early fleet was small in both numbers and tonnage, and limited to coastal defense activities, but plans were in the works for modernization and expansion. The First Naval Expansion bill in 1882 envisaged the construction of 48 warships, 22 of which were to be torpedo boats.

Japan's naval expansion was to pay off during the Sino-Japanese War (1894 - 1895), when the IJN gained a decisive victory over the Chinese fleet. Following this conflict, Japan recognized the need for even further expansion, and during the next ten years commissioned a further 109 warships. The strength of the Japanese fleet was evident during the Russo-Japanese War (1904 -1905), with Admiral Togo's victory over the Russians at the Battle of Tsushima.

By 1920, Japan owned the third largest navy in the world. Although it had fought on the side of the Allies during World War I, Japan's relations with the west began to deteriorate post-war. By 1937, when Japan launched the Second Sino-Japanese War, tensions with the USA had grown to particularly high levels, and relations between the two countries continued to deteriorate over the next few years, culminating in the IJN's attack on the US Pacific Fleet at Pearl Harbor in December 1941.

Japan in 1941 had the largest and most heavily-armed battleship ever built (Yamato), and the largest and most modern carrier fleet of any of the combatants in the war, yet following the early successes of 1941 and 1942, the IJN began to suffer increasing losses at the hands of the numerically superior US Navy. The war of attrition in the Pacific during the next three years took its toll on the IJN, both in terms of vessels and their crew, many of whom went down with their ships. It is interesting to note that many ships' captains that lost with their commands were posthumously promoted to Rear-Admiral (and in some instances promoted two grades to Vice-Admiral), in recognition of their sacrifice.

The remnants of the once-proud IJN were dissolved following Japan's surrender in August 1945, ending 76 years of activity. The force has never been rebuilt.

This book provides brief career biographies of over 2100 Imperial Japanese Navy Admirals. This includes information about those officers promoted prior to 1900, but who were still serving in 1900 and beyond. Also included is a chapter with the order of battle of the IJN, showing who led the major commands during the 1900-1945 period, and a chapter listing the major vessels (aircraft carriers, battleships, battlecruisers, cruisers) of the IJN, with brief information about their birth and fates.

TABLE OF RANKS

Grand Marshal   *Dai-Gensui*
Fleet Admiral   *Gensui*
Admiral   *Taisho*
Vice-Admiral   *Chujo*
Rear-Admiral   *Shosho*

Rear-Admiral (Surgeon) **Bungoro ABE** (1 May 1881 - 2 Jul 1955)
10 Dec 1928 - 25 Feb 1932:   Director, Minato Naval Hospital
1 Dec 1931:   Promoted to *Rear-Admiral (Surgeon)*
25 Feb 1932 - 15 Nov 1933:   Medical Officer, Yokosuka Naval District
15 Nov 1933 - 11 Dec 1933:   Attached to the Naval General Staff
15 Dec 1933:   Transferred to the reserve

Vice-Admiral **Hiroaki ABE**   (15 Mar 1889 - 6 Feb 1949)
15 Nov 1938:   Promoted to *Rear-Admiral*
15 Dec 1938 - 1 Nov 1940:   Chief Instructor, Naval Academy
1 Nov 1940 - 15 Nov 1940:   Assistant Chief of Staff, 4th Fleet
15 Nov 1940 - 21 Jul 1941:   Commander, 6th Destroyer Flotilla
21 Jul 1941 - 1 Aug 1941:   Attached to the Naval General Staff
1 Aug 1941 - 14 Jul 1942:   Commander, 8th Cruiser Division
14 Jul 1942 - 20 Dec 1942:   Commander, 11th Battleship Division
1 Nov 1942:   Promoted to *Vice-Admiral*
20 Dec 1942 - 15 Mar 1943:   Attached to the Naval General Staff
20 Mar 1943:   Transferred to the reserve

Vice-Admiral **Kasuke ABE**   (7 Apr 1890 - 21 Jan 1976)
15 Nov 1938:   Promoted to *Rear-Admiral*
15 Nov 1938 - 15 Nov 1939:   Attached to the Naval General Staff
15 Nov 1939 - 22 Aug 1940:   Director of Section B2, Navy Ministry
22 Aug 1940 - 15 Nov 1940:   Attached to the Naval General Staff
15 Nov 1940 - 20 Sep 1941:   Chief Instructor, Naval College
10 Apr 1941 - 6 Sep 1941:   Commandant of the Naval College
20 Sep 1941 - 1 Oct 1941:   Attached to Yokosuka Naval District
1 Oct 1941 - 10 Apr 1942:   Commander, 7th Auxiliary Base Force
10 Apr 1942 - 20 Apr 1943:   Commandant, Naval Navigation School
1 Nov 1942:   Promoted to *Vice-Admiral*
20 Apr 1943 - 21 Jun 1943:   Attached to the Naval General Staff
21 Jun 1943 - 1 May 1945:   Chief of Naval Hydrography Command
1 May 1945 - 15 May 1945:   Attached to the Naval General Staff
21 May 1945:   Transferred to the reserve

Vice-Admiral **Katsuo ABE**	(18 Apr 1891 - 26 May 1948)
25 Apr 1938 - 10 Oct 1939:	Chief of Section N3, Naval General Staff
15 Nov 1938:	Promoted to *Rear-Admiral*
10 Oct 1939 - 18 Oct 1939:	Attached to the Naval General Staff
18 Oct 1939 - 15 Oct 1940:	Chief, Bureau of Naval Affairs
15 Oct 1940 - 13 Nov 1940:	Attached to the Naval General Staff
13 Nov 1940 - 20 Sep 1944:	Chief of Military Mission to Berlin
1 Nov 1942:	Promoted to *Vice-Admiral*
20 Sep 1944 - May 1945:	Naval Attache, Italy
May 1945 - Oct 1945:	Unassigned
Vice-Admiral **Koso ABE**	(24 Mar 1892 - 19 Jun 1947)
15 Oct 1940 - 1 Jun 1941:	Attached to Yokosuka Naval District
15 Nov 1940:	Promoted to *Rear-Admiral*
1 Jun 1941 - 2 Feb 1942:	Chief of Tateyama Gunnery School
2 Feb 1942 - 5 Feb 1942:	Attached to 4th Fleet
5 Feb 1942 - 29 Nov 1943:	Commander, 6th Auxiliary Base Force
29 Nov 1943 - 27 Dec 1943:	Attached to the Naval General Staff
27 Dec 1943 - 25 Apr 1945:	Chief of Tateyama Gunnery School
1 May 1944:	Promoted to *Vice-Admiral*
25 Apr 1945 - 1 May 1945:	Attached to Sasebo Naval District
1 May 1945 - 15 Oct 1945:	Commander, Sasebo Guard Unit & Sailor Corps
Rear-Admiral **Koun ABE**	(3 Aug 1891 - 8 Jun 1945)
22 Mar 1945 - 8 Jun 1945:	Captain, Auxiliary Ship *"Hakusa"*
8 Jun 1945:	Posthumously promoted to *Rear-Admiral*
Rear-Admiral **Toshio ABE**	(27 Apr 1896 - 29 Nov 1944)
1 Oct 1944 - 29 Nov 1944:	Captain, Aircraft Carrier *"Shinano"*
29 Nov 1944:	Posthumously promoted to *Rear-Admiral*
Admiral **Baron Kiyokazu ABO**	(15 Oct 1870 - 8 Jun 1948)
1 Dec 1916:	Promoted to *Rear-Admiral*
1 Dec 1916 - 1 Dec 1920:	Chief of Bureau 1, Naval General Staff
1 Dec 1920:	Promoted to *Vice-Admiral*
1 Dec 1920 - 1 May 1922:	Deputy Chief of the Naval General Staff
1 Dec 1922 - 10 May 1922:	Member, Admirals Committee
10 May 1922 - 25 May 1923:	Naval Attache
25 May 1923 - 11 Jun 1924:	Director, Naval Shipbuilding Command
11 Jun 1924 - 15 Apr 1925:	Deputy Minister of the Navy
15 Apr 1925 - 10 Dec 1926:	Admiral Commanding, Kure Naval District
10 Dec 1926 - 20 Apr 1927:	Navy Councillor
1 Apr 1927:	Promoted to *Admiral*

20 Apr 1927 - 16 May 1928:	Admiral Commanding, Yokosuka Naval District
16 May 1928 - 3 Oct 1930:	Navy Councillor
3 Oct 1930 - 13 Dec 1931:	Minister of the Navy
13 Dec 1931 - 1 Jun 1933:	Navy Councillor
1 Jun 1933 - 15 Jan 1934:	Unassigned
15 Jan 1934:	Transferred to the reserve

Rear-Admiral **Kichihei ADACHI** (10 Nov 1889 - 23 Sep 1961)

15 Nov 1935 - 15 Nov 1939:	Chief of Electronic Division, Kure Navy Yard
1 Dec 1926:	Promoted to *Rear-Admiral*
15 Nov 1939 - 15 Dec 1939:	Attached to the Naval General Staff
21 Dec 1939:	Transferred to the reserve

Rear-Admiral (Paymaster) **Matahiko ADACHI** (22 Mar 1894 - 14 Jul 1958)

13 Apr 1943 - 1 Sep 1943:	Attached to Yokosuka Naval District
1 May 1943:	Promoted to *Rear-Admiral (Paymaster)*
1 Sep 1943 - 10 Jun 1944:	Chief, 102nd Supply Bureau
10 Jun 1944 - 1 Apr 1945:	Chief, Maizuru Supply & Transport Bureaus
1 Apr 1945 - 15 Sep 1945:	Director, 3rd Clothing & Food Depot
15 Sep 1945 - 5 Oct 1945:	Attached to the Naval General Staff

Rear-Admiral **Sukezo ADACHI** (19 Sep 1894 - 14 Jun 1974)

1 Nov 1943:	Promoted to *Rear-Admiral*
1 Nov 1943 - 10 Mar 1944:	Chief of Steel Division, Air Technical Arsenal
10 Mar 1944 - 25 Jul 1944:	Attached to Naval Air Command
25 Jul 1944 - 25 Dec 1944:	Chief of Explosives Division, Department of Military Supply
25 Dec 1944 - 15 Sep 1945:	Director, Tsu Navy Yard
15 Sep 1945 - 15 Oct 1945:	Attached to Naval Air Command

Rear-Admiral (Surgeon) **Tsuneji AIDA** (4 Jul 1881 - 11 Jan 1943)

1 May 1928 - 15 Nov 1933:	Chief Medical Officer, Yokosuka Navy Yard
15 Nov 1933:	Promoted to *Rear-Admiral (Surgeon)*
15 Nov 1933 - 11 Dec 1933:	Attached to Yokosuka Naval District
15 Dec 1933:	Transferred to the reserve

Rear-Admiral **Aritaka AIHARA** (8 Aug 1889 - 4 Sep 1950)

4 Nov 1943:	Promoted to *Rear-Admiral*
5 Nov 1943 - 28 Mar 1946:	Chief of Eastern Branch, Southern Islands Agency
1 Jun 1944 - 20 Mar 1946:	Attached to the staff, 4th Fleet

Rear-Admiral (Paymaster) **Bunshiro AIHARA** (23 Dec 1870 - 9 Sep 1926)

1 Dec 1918 - 1 Dec 1921:	Paymaster-General, Sasebo Naval District

1 Jun 1919:	Promoted to *General (Paymaster)*
23 Sep 1919:	Redesignated *Rear-Admiral (Paymaster)*
1 Dec 1921 - 10 Dec 1921:	Attached to Sasebo Naval District
10 Dec 1921 - 31 Mar 1923:	Unassigned
31 Mar 1923:	Transferred to the reserve

Vice-Admiral (Paymaster) **Masukatsu AIHARA** (1 Oct 1855 - 6 Jun 1930)

10 Nov 1903 - 15 Aug 1908:	Paymaster-General, Sasebo Naval District
1 Sep 1904:	Promoted to *General (Paymaster)*
15 Aug 1908 - 1 Dec 1909:	Paymaster-General, Yokosuka Naval District
1 Dec 1909 - 17 Apr 1911:	Unassigned
17 Apr 1911:	Transferred to the reserve
23 Sep 1919:	Redesignated *Vice-Admiral (Paymaster)*

Rear-Admiral **Ichiro AITOKU** (17 Dec 1896 - 4 Feb 1974)

1 Oct 1944 - 1 Apr 1945:	Chief of Research Division, Anti-Submarine School
15 Oct 1944:	Promoted to *Rear-Admiral*
1 Apr 1945 - 20 Nov 1945:	Chief of Administration Division, Yokosuka Navy Yard

Rear-Admiral (Paymaster) **Jiro AIURA** (20 Aug 1893 - 12 May 1946)

1 Oct 1941 - 25 Sep 1943:	Chief of Accounting Division, 21st Air Arsenal
1 May 1943:	Promoted to *Rear-Admiral (Paymaster)*
25 Sep 1943 - 10 Oct 1943:	Attached to Sasebo Naval District
10 Oct 1943 - 8 Apr 1944:	Chief of Accounting Division, Sasebo Naval District
8 Apr 1944 - 25 Nov 1944:	Attached to the Naval General Staff
25 Nov 1944 - 5 Sep 1945:	Unassigned
5 Sep 1945:	Transferred to the reserve

Vice-Admiral **Baron Norimichi AIURA** (23 Jun 1841 - 1 Apr 1911)

28 Dec 1885:	Promoted to *Rear-Admiral*
28 Dec 1885 - 17 Jun 1886:	Commander, Readiness Flotilla
17 Jun 1886 - 28 Sep 1887:	Chairman, Ordnance Committee, Admirals Committee
28 Sep 1887 - 22 Jan 1889:	Chairman, Ordnance & Shipbuilding Committees, Admirals Committee
22 Jan 1889 - 23 May 1890:	Chairman, Technical Committee, Admirals Committee
23 May 1890 - 12 Dec 1892:	Director of Bureau 2, Department of the Navy
12 Dec 1892 - 20 May 1893:	Commander-in-Chief, Readiness Fleet
20 May 1893 - 13 Jul 1894:	Admiral Commanding, Sasebo Naval District
13 Jul 1894 - 19 Jul 1894:	Commander-in-Chief, Patrol Fleet
19 Jul 1894 - 16 Feb 1895:	Commander-in-Chief, West Fleet

16 Feb 1895:	Promoted to *Vice-Admiral*
16 Feb 1895 - 9 Apr 1897:	Admiral Commanding, Yokosuka Naval District
9 Apr 1897 - 8 Oct 1897:	Commander-in-Chief, Readiness Fleet
8 Oct 1897 - 19 Jan 1899:	Admiral Commanding, Sasebo Naval District
19 Jan 1899 - 20 May 1900:	Admiral Commanding, Yokosuka Naval District
31 May 1900:	Transferred to the reserve

Rear-Admiral **Kenkichi AKABORI** (30 Nov 1882 - 17 Apr 1971)

10 Dec 1928 - 1 Dec 1930:	Chief of Shipping Bureau, Kure Naval District
30 Nov 1929:	Promoted to *Rear-Admiral*
1 Dec 1930 - 15 Dec 1930:	Attached to the Naval General Staff
24 Dec 1930:	Transferred to the reserve

Rear-Admiral **Yoshiichiro AKAMATSU** (25 Feb 1894 - 29 Dec 1944)

20 Jul 1944 - 29 Dec 1944:	Attached to Osaka Guard District
29 Dec 1944:	Posthumously promoted to *Rear-Admiral*

Vice-Admiral **Isao AKASAKA** (29 Nov 1890 - 11 Nov 1949)

15 Nov 1939 - 15 Dec 1941:	Chief of Engine Construction Division, Sasebo Navy Yard
15 Nov 1940:	Promoted to *Rear-Admiral*
15 Dec 1941 - 1 May 1943:	Commander, 101st Naval Facility
30 Dec 1941 - 1 May 1943:	Supervisor for Construction & Ordnance, Naval Shipbuilding Command
1 May 1943 - 20 Jun 1943:	Attached to Naval Shipbuilding Command
20 Jun 1943 - 10 May 1944:	Commandant, Naval Engineering School
1 Nov 1943:	Promoted to *Vice-Admiral*
10 May 1944 - 20 Apr 1945:	Chief of Bureau 5, Naval Shipbuilding Command
20 Apr 1945 - 1 Jun 1945:	Director, Hiro Navy Yard
20 Apr 1945 - 1 Nov 1945:	Director, 11th Air Arsenal

Rear-Admiral **Unosuke AKASAKA** (9 Sep 1891 - 11 Feb 1954)

1 Dec 1928 - 15 Nov 1939:	Supervisor for Construction & Ordnance, Naval Shipbuilding Command, Supervisor for Ordnance, Naval Air Command
15 Nov 1939:	Promoted to *Rear-Admiral*
15 Nov 1939 - 15 Dec 1939:	Attached to the Naval General Staff
21 Dec 1939:	Transferred to the reserve

Rear-Admiral **Shizuo AKAZAWA** (8 Jun 1899 - 8 Jun 1944)

20 Mar 1944 - 8 Jun 1944:	Commander, 10th Destroyer Division
8 Jun 1944:	Posthumously promoted to *Rear-Admiral*

Rear-Admiral (Paymaster) **Kotaro AKIBA** (27 Oct 1870 - 26 Jan 1931)
1 Dec 1919:	Promoted to *Rear-Admiral (Paymaster)*
1 Dec 1919 - 10 Aug 1920:	Paymaster-General, Maizuru Navy Yard
10 Aug 1920 - 20 Aug 1920:	Attached to Maizuru Navy Yard
20 Aug 1920 - 1 May 1921:	Unassigned
1 May 1921:	Transferred to the reserve

Rear-Admiral (Engineer) **Takeshiro AKIMOTO** (12 Jan 1879 - 1 Sep 1957)
10 Nov 1923 - 1 Dec 1923:	Attached to Naval Shipbuilding Command
1 Dec 1923:	Promoted to *Rear-Admiral (Engineer)*
1 Dec 1923 - 12 Jan 1924:	Unassigned
12 Jan 1924:	Transferred to the reserve

Rear-Admiral **Moriichi AKINAGA** (11 Oct 1892 - 27 Jan 1945)
26 Jan 1945 - 27 Jan 1945:	Supervisor for Construction & Ordnance, Naval Shipbuilding Command
27 Jan 1945:	Posthumously promoted to *Rear-Admiral*

Rear-Admiral **Jitsue AKISHIGE** (13 Jul 1897 - 7 Sep 1988)
20 Sep 1944 - 15 Nov 1945:	Chief of the Supply Bureau, Auxiliary Fuel Yard
1 May 1945:	Promoted to *Rear-Admiral*
5 May 1945 - 15 Nov 1945:	Chief of Division 2, Supply Bureau, Department of the Navy
22 Jun 1945 - 15 Nov 1945:	Chief of Division 4, Supply Bureau, Department of the Navy
1 Oct 1945 - 15 Nov 1945:	Chief of Administration Division, Supply Bureau, Department of the Navy
15 Nov 1945 - 30 Nov 1945:	Chief of Supply Bureau, Department of the Navy

Rear-Admiral **Katsuzo AKIYAMA** (18 Feb 1891 - 9 Dec 1962)
20 Apr 1942 - 15 Sep 1942:	Attached to Yokosuka Naval District
1 May 1942:	Promoted to *Rear-Admiral*
15 Sep 1942 - 5 Aug 1943:	Commander, 51st Auxiliary Base Force
5 Aug 1943 - 17 Aug 1943:	Attached to the Naval General Staff
17 Aug 1943 - 1 Sep 1943:	Attached to Yokosuka Naval District
1 Sep 1943 - 10 Oct 1945:	Chief of Personnel, Yokosuka Naval District

Vice-Admiral **Monzo AKIYAMA** (30 Dec 1891 - 6 Feb 1944)
10 Aug 1942 - 15 Nov 1943:	Chief of Administration, Kure Navy Yard
1 May 1943:	Promoted to *Rear-Admiral*
15 Nov 1943 - 29 Nov 1943:	Attached to the staff, 4th Fleet
29 Nov 1943 - 6 Feb 1944:	Commander, 6th Auxiliary Base Force
6 Feb 1944:	Posthumously promoted to *Vice-Admiral*

Vice-Admiral **Saneyuki AKIYAMA** (20 Mar 1868 - 4 Feb 1918)
1 Dec 1912 - 17 Apr 1914:	Chief of Bureau 1, Naval General Staff
1 Dec 1913:	Promoted to *Rear-Admiral*
17 Apr 1914 - 21 Feb 1916:	Director, Bureau of Naval Affairs, Department of the Navy
21 Feb 1916 - 1 Dec 1916:	Attached to the Naval General Staff
1 Dec 1916 - 16 Jul 1917:	Commander, 2nd Destroyer Flotilla
16 Jul 1917 - 1 Dec 1917:	Member, Admirals Committee
1 Dec 1917:	Promoted to *Vice-Admiral*
1 Dec 1917 - 4 Feb 1918:	Unassigned

Vice-Admiral **Teruo AKIYAMA** (16 Sep 1891 - 6 Jul 1943)
20 Sep 1942 - 11 Nov 1942:	Attached to Kure Naval District
1 Nov 1942:	Promoted to *Rear-Admiral*
11 Nov 1942 - 23 Mar 1943:	Commander, 2nd Sasebo Sailor Corps
23 Mar 1943 - 6 Jul 1943:	Commander, 3rd Destroyer Flotilla
6 Jul 1943:	Posthumously promoted to *Vice-Admiral*

Vice-Admiral (Paymaster) **Tokichi AKIYAMA** (13 Nov 1863 - 5 Dec 1931)
19 Sep 1911 - 8 Aug 1914:	Paymaster-General, Sasebo Naval District
1 Dec 1911:	Promoted to *General (Paymaster)*
8 Aug 1914 - 1 Dec 1916:	Paymaster-General, Kure Naval District
1 Dec 1916 - 1 Dec 1917:	Unassigned
1 Jun 1917:	Promoted to *General (Paymaster), Senior Grade*
1 Dec 1917:	Transferred to the reserve
23 Sep 1919:	Redesignated *Vice-Admiral (Paymaster)*

Rear-Admiral **Toraroku AKIYAMA** (2 Aug 1883 - 28 Apr 1952)
1 Dec 1931:	Promoted to *Rear-Admiral*
1 Dec 1931 - 18 Sep 1933:	Commander, Yokosuka Sailor Corps
18 Sep 1933 - 15 Nov 1934:	Commander, Yokosuka Defense Force
15 Nov 1934 - 10 Dec 1934:	Attached to the Naval General Staff
15 Dec 1934:	Transferred to the reserve

Rear-Admiral **Toshio AKIYOSHI** (18 Nov 1889 - 23 Mar 1947)
20 Mar 1942 - 5 Aug 1943:	Chief of Division 2, Naval Hydrography Command
1 Nov 1942:	Promoted to *Rear-Admiral*
5 Aug 1943 - 1 Dec 1943:	Attached to the Naval General Staff
1 Dec 1943 - 20 Sep 1945:	Chief of Division 2, Naval Hydrography Command
10 Jan 1944 - 1 Apr 1945:	Chief of Division 1, Naval Hydrography Command

Rear-Admiral **Yoshima AKIZAWA** (29 Nov 1869 - 20 Jul 1971)
17 Dec 1917 - 1 Dec 1918:	Captain, Battleship *"Ise"*

1 Dec 1918: Promoted to *Rear-Admiral*
1 Dec 1918 - 1 Aug 1919: Unassigned
1 Aug 1919: Transferred to the reserve

Rear-Admiral (Surgeon) **Mutsumi AKUNE** (23 Apr 1894 - 11 Mar 1984)
1 Apr 1939 - 22 Dec 1941: Professor, University of Nagoya
15 Oct 1941: Promoted to *Rear-Admiral (Surgeon)*
22 Dec 1941: Transferred to the reserve

Vice-Admiral (Surgeon) **Ryoshichiro AMAMIYA** (26 Feb 1874 - Feb 1965)
16 Feb 1921 - 10 Nov 1922: Chief Instructor, Naval Medical School
1 Dec 1921: Promoted to *Rear-Admiral (Surgeon)*
10 Nov 1922 - 1 Dec 1923: Director, Sasebo Naval Hospital
1 Dec 1923 - 1 Dec 1924: Director, Kure Naval Hospital
1 Dec 1924 - 1 Dec 1925: Commandant, Naval Medical School
1 Dec 1925: Promoted to *Vice-Admiral (Surgeon)*
1 Dec 1925 - 1 Dec 1927: Chief of Naval Medical Service
1 Dec 1927 - 15 Dec 1927: Attached to the Naval General Staff
25 Dec 1927: Transferred to the reserve

Rear-Admiral (Surgeon) **Naoe AMANO** (28 Jun 1897 - 5 Mar 1945)
15 Dec 1944 - 5 Mar 1945: Attached to Yokosuka Naval District
5 Mar 1945: Posthumously promoted to *Rear-Admiral (Surgeon)*

Rear-Admiral (Surgeon) **Senkichi AMANO** (1 Dec 1890 - 19 Apr 1944)
3 Dec 1943 - 19 Apr 1944: Attached to Maizuru Naval District
19 Apr 1944: Posthumously promoted to *Rear-Admiral (Surgeon)*

Rear-Admiral **Shigetaka AMANO** (2 Feb 1897 - 25 Oct 1944)
20 Mar 1944 - 25 Oct 1944: Commander, 61st Destroyer Division
25 Oct 1944: Posthumously promoted to *Rear-Admiral*

Rear-Admiral **Tsuneo AMARI** (22 Dec 1886 - 13 Aug 1955)
1 Dec 1936: Promoted to *Rear-Admiral*
1 Dec 1936 - 15 Dec 1936: Attached to the Naval General Staff
22 Dec 1936: Transferred to the reserve

Rear-Admiral **Yoshiyuki AMARI** (9 Nov 1897 - ?)
20 Jan 1944 - 25 Aug 1944: Chief of Engine Construction, Sasebo Navy Yard
1 May 1944: Promoted to *Rear-Admiral*
25 Aug 1944 - 20 Sep 1945: Attached to Naval Shipbuilding Command
20 Feb 1945 - 20 Sep 1945: Staff supervisor, Department of Military Supply

Rear-Admiral **Yoshishige AMAYA** (? - 26 Dec 1944)
26 Apr 1943 - 26 Dec 1944:	Commander, 4th Survey Force
26 Dec 1944:	Posthumously promoted to *Rear-Admiral*

Vice-Admiral **Masataka ANDO** (28 May 1880 - 7 Apr 1956)
1 Dec 1924:	Promoted to *Rear-Admiral*
1 Dec 1924 - 20 Oct 1925:	Chief of Bureau 2, Naval General Staff
20 Oct 1925 - 1 Dec 1927:	Commander, Kasumigaura Flying Division
1 Dec 1927 - 10 Dec 1928:	Attached to the Naval General Staff
10 Dec 1928:	Promoted to *Vice-Admiral*
10 Dec 1928 - 10 Oct 1931:	Chief of Naval Air Command
10 Oct 1931 - 1 Dec 1931:	Attached to the Naval General Staff
25 Dec 1931:	Transferred to the reserve

Rear-Admiral **Norihide ANDO** (16 Aug 1903 - 25 Oct 1944)
10 Sep 1944 - 25 Oct 1944:	Attached to the staff, 2nd Flotilla
25 Oct 1944:	Posthumously promoted to *Rear-Admiral*

Rear-Admiral **Shigeki ANDO** (9 Apr 1895 - 21 Aug 1943)
25 Sep 1942 - 21 Aug 1943:	Attached to Yokosuka Naval District
21 Aug 1943:	Posthumously promoted to *Rear-Admiral*

Rear-Admiral **Takashi ANDO** (6 Jun 1884 - 19 May 1961)
15 Nov 1933:	Promoted to *Rear-Admiral*
15 Nov 1933 - 15 Dec 1934:	Commander, Kure Sailors Corps
15 Dec 1934 - 15 Nov 1935:	Commander, Kure Defense Flotilla
15 Nov 1935 - 1 Dec 1936:	Commander, Sasebo Guard Division
1 Dec 1936 - 15 Dec 1936:	Attached to the Naval General Staff
22 Dec 1936:	Transferred to the reserve

Rear-Admiral **Shoichi ANJU** (10 Sep 1878 - 10 Jul 1945)
11 Oct 1921 - 1 Dec 1922:	Supervisor for Construction and Ordnance, Yokosuka Navy Yard
1 Dec 1922:	Promoted to *Rear-Admiral*
1 Dec 1922 - 10 Dec 1922:	Attached to Naval Shipbuilding Command
10 Dec 1922 - 31 Mar 1923:	Unassigned
31 Mar 1923:	Transferred to the reserve

Rear-Admiral **Eitaro ANKYU** (5 Jun 1901 - 12 Apr 1945)
15 Mar 1945 - 12 Apr 1945:	Commander, 33rd Submarine Division
12 Apr 1945:	Posthumously promoted to *Rear-Admiral*

Vice-Admiral **Kiyoshi ANNO** (12 May 1886 - 6 Apr 1935)
1 Dec 1930:	Promoted to *Rear-Admiral*
1 Dec 1930 - 15 Nov 1933:	Chief of Naval Personnel, Department of the Navy
15 Nov 1933 - 15 Nov 1934:	Commander, 2nd Destroyer Flotilla
15 Nov 1934 - 20 Feb 1935:	Attached to the Naval General Staff
20 Feb 1935 - 6 Apr 1935:	Chief of Bureau 1, Naval General Staff
6 Apr 1935:	Posthumously promoted to *Vice-Admiral*

Rear-Admiral **Susumu ANZAWA** (20 Mar 1892 - ?)
15 Dec 1939 - 1 Oct 1943:	Chief of Machine Gun Division, Toyokawa Navy Yard
1 May 1943:	Promoted to *Rear-Admiral*
1 Oct 1943 - 25 Mar 1945:	Chief of Gunnery Division, Hikari Navy Yard
25 Mar 1945 - 20 Sep 1945:	Chief of Gunnery & Bomb Divisions, Hikari Navy Yard

Rear-Admiral **Masao AOKI** (18 Mar 1893 - 31 Dec 1957)
1 Nov 1943:	Promoted to *Rear-Admiral*
1 Nov 1943 - 10 May 1944:	Director, 4th Naval Facility
10 May 1944 - 1 Jun 1944:	Attached to Yokosuka Naval District
1 Jun 1944 - 16 Sep 1944:	Commandant, Numazu Naval Construction School
16 Sep 1944 - 15 Feb 1945:	Attached to Naval Shipbuilding Command
15 Feb 1945 - 5 Aug 1945:	Chief of Administration, Kure Navy Yard
5 Aug 1945 - 15 Oct 1945:	Director, Chinkai Naval Facility

Rear-Admiral **Tamon AOKI** (? - 19 Dec 1944)
6 Aug 1944 - 19 Dec 1944:	Captain, Aircraft Carrier *"Unryu"*
19 Dec 1944:	Posthumously promoted to *Rear-Admiral*

Rear-Admiral **Tohei AOKI** (17 May 1878 - 3 Jun 1927)
10 Nov 1923 - 1 Dec 1923:	Attached to Yokosuka Naval District
1 Dec 1923:	Promoted to *Rear-Admiral*
1 Dec 1923 - 25 Feb 1924:	Unassigned
25 Feb 1924:	Transferred to the reserve

Rear-Admiral **Muneshige AOYAGI** (20 Aug 1888 - 24 May 1971)
25 Apr 1938 - 15 Nov 1938:	Captain, Battlecruiser *"Hiei"*
15 Nov 1938:	Promoted to *Rear-Admiral*
15 Nov 1938 - 15 Dec 1938:	Attached to the Naval General Staff
21 Dec 1938:	Transferred to the reserve

Rear-Admiral **Hideo AOYAMA** (? - 17 Feb 1944)
20 Dec 1943 - 17 Feb 1944: Commander, 68th Guard Unit
17 Feb 1944: Posthumously promoted to *Rear-Admiral*

Rear-Admiral **Tadashi ARA** (16 Apr 1884 - 3 Dec 1943)
25 May 1943 - 3 Dec 1943: Chief of Minesweeping, Tanker *"Azuma-maru"*
3 Dec 1943: Posthumously promoted to *Rear-Admiral*

Vice-Admiral **Aritsura ARAI** (10 Nov 1849 - 1 Dec 1909)
8 Oct 1897 - 20 May 1900: Chief of Harbor Bureau, Yokosuka Naval District
14 May 1898: Promoted to *Rear-Admiral*
20 May 1900 - 5 Jul 1901: Chief of Yokosuka Harbor,
 Chief of Reserve Bureau, Yokosuka Naval District
5 Jul 1901 - 16 Feb 1904: Unassigned
16 Feb 1904 - 20 Dec 1905: Attached to the Joint General Staff
23 Sep 1905: Promoted to *Vice-Admiral*
20 Dec 1905 - 14 Feb 1907: Unassigned
14 Feb 1907: Transferred to the reserve

Rear-Admiral (Surgeon) **Keizaburo ARAI** (18 Jun 1876 - 7 Jan 1936)
10 Nov 1923 - 1 Dec 1923: Attached to Kure Naval District
1 Dec 1923: Promoted to *Rear-Admiral (Surgeon)*
1 Dec 1923 - 25 Feb 1924: Unassigned
25 Feb 1924: Transferred to the reserve

Rear-Admiral **Seitaro ARAI** (12 Mar 1893 - 2 Feb 1978)
20 Jan 1940 - 15 Nov 1940: Supervisor for Construction & Ordnance,
 Naval Shipbuilding Command
15 Nov 1940: Promoted to *Rear-Admiral*
15 Nov 1940 - 16 Dec 1940: Attached to Naval Shipbuilding Command
21 Dec 1940: Transferred to the reserve

Rear-Admiral **Chugo ARAKAWA** (4 Sep 1868 - 15 Mar 1917)
1 Dec 1916: Promoted to *Rear-Admiral*
1 Dec 1916 - 7 Feb 1917: Commander, 3rd Destroyer Flotilla
7 Feb 1917 - 15 Mar 1917: Unassigned

Rear-Admiral **Kishi ARAKAWA** (5 Oct 1861 - 1 Dec 1934)
1 Dec 1909 - 1 Dec 1910: Commander, Sasebo Sailors Corps
1 Dec 1910 - 1 Dec 1912: Unassigned
1 Dec 1912: Promoted to *Rear-Admiral (Reserve)*
1 Dec 1912: Transferred to the reserve

Rear-Admiral (Paymaster) **Shin ARAKAWA** (12 Feb 1890 - 11 May 1977)

1 Apr 1939 - 10 Jul 1941:	Chief of Accounting Bureau, Air Technical Arsenal
15 Nov 1939:	Promoted to *Rear-Admiral (Paymaster)*
10 Jul 1941 - 1 Oct 1941:	Attached to Yokosuka Naval District
1 Oct 1941 - 1 Dec 1942:	Commander, 1st Air Arsenal
1 Dec 1942 - 1 Jul 1943:	Commander, 2nd Air Arsenal
1 Jul 1943 - 6 Sep 1943:	Attached to the Naval General Staff
10 Sep 1943:	Transferred to the reserve

Vice-Admiral (Paymaster) **Hikosuke ARAKI** (23 Dec 1883 - 8 Jun 1947)

15 Nov 1933:	Promoted to *Rear-Admiral (Paymaster)*
15 Nov 1933 - 1 Apr 1934:	Chief of Section 1, Accounting Bureau, Department of the Navy
1 Apr 1934 - 1 Nov 1934:	Attached to the Naval General Staff
1 Nov 1934 - 1 Feb 1935:	Chief of Section 2, Accounting Bureau, Naval Shipbuilding Command
1 Feb 1935 - 1 Dec 1936:	Chief of Accounting Bureau, Naval Shipbuilding Command
1 Dec 1936 - 15 Nov 1938:	Director, Hiro Navy Yard
1 Dec 1937:	Promoted to *Vice-Admiral (Paymaster)*
15 Nov 1938 - 15 Nov 1940:	Director, Yokosuka Navy Yard
15 Nov 1940 - 16 Dec 1940:	Attached to the Naval General Staff
21 Dec 1940:	Transferred to the reserve

Vice-Admiral **Jiro ARAKI** (6 Nov 1880 - 3 Jun 1952)

1 Dec 1925:	Promoted to *Rear-Admiral*
1 Dec 1925 - 20 Aug 1926:	Commander, 2nd Submarine Flotilla
20 Aug 1926 - 1 Dec 1927:	Commander, 1st Expeditionary Fleet
1 Dec 1927 - 1 Mar 1928:	Chief of Bureau 2, Naval Shipbuilding Command
1 Mar 1928 - 10 Jun 1930:	Chief of Bureau 5, Naval Shipbuilding Command
10 Jun 1930 - 15 Nov 1932:	Director, Yokosuka Navy Yard
1 Dec 1930:	Promoted to *Vice-Admiral*
15 Nov 1932 - 10 Dec 1932:	Attached to the Naval General Staff
15 Dec 1932:	Transferred to the reserve

Rear-Admiral **Keikichi ARAKI** (25 Feb 1896 - 15 Jan 1948)

7 Aug 1944 - 5 May 1945:	Commander, Takuma Flying Unit
1 May 1945:	Promoted to *Rear-Admiral*
5 May 1945 - 10 May 1945:	Attached to the staff, 5th Air Fleet
10 May 1945 - 15 Nov 1945:	Commander, Utsumi Flying Unit

Rear-Admiral **Sadaaki ARAKI** (5 May 1885 - 28 Apr 1961)

15 Nov 1934:	Promoted to *Rear-Admiral*

15 Nov 1934 - 2 Dec 1935:	Commander, Shanghai Marine Force
2 Dec 1935 - 1 Dec 1936:	Commander, Yokosuka Defense Flotilla
1 Dec 1936 - 15 Dec 1936:	Attached to the Naval General Staff
22 Dec 1936:	Transferred to the reserve

Rear-Admiral **Setsuzo ARAKI** (8 Nov 1888 - 6 Aug 1950)

15 Nov 1938:	Promoted to *Rear-Admiral*
15 Nov 1938 - 15 Dec 1938:	Attached to the Naval General Staff
21 Dec 1938:	Transferred to the reserve

Rear-Admiral (Paymaster) **Shinichi ARAKI** (27 Nov 1896 - 22 Jul 1974)

1 Sep 1943 - Oct 1945:	Paymaster-General, Southeastern Area Fleet, Paymaster-General, 11th Air Fleet
15 Oct 1944:	Promoted to *Rear-Admiral (Paymaster)*

Rear-Admiral **Tsuto ARAKI** (19 Mar 1897 - 22 Mar 1963)

15 Nov 1943 - 6 Nov 1944:	Captain, Heavy Cruiser *"Atago"*
15 Oct 1944:	Promoted to *Rear-Admiral*
6 Nov 1944 - 1 Dec 1944:	Attached to Yokosuka Naval District
1 Dec 1944 - 15 Jul 1945:	Chief of Research Bureau, Torpedo School
15 Jul 1945 - 6 Sep 1945:	Attached to Yokosuka Naval District
6 Sep 1945:	Transferred to the reserve

Rear-Admiral **Keijiro ARANISHI** (14 May 1865 - 19 Mar 1947)

17 Apr 1914 - 1 Dec 1916:	Captain, Battleship *"Fuji"*
1 Dec 1916:	Promoted to *Rear-Admiral*
1 Dec 1916 - 1 Dec 1917:	Unassigned
1 Dec 1917:	Transferred to the reserve

Rear-Admiral (Engineer) **Fumio ARAO** (14 Aug 1878 - 9 Oct 1932)

20 Nov 1919 - 1 Dec 1922:	Chief Engineer, Ryojun Guard District
1 Dec 1922:	Promoted to *Rear-Admiral (Engineer)*
1 Dec 1922 - 10 Dec 1922:	Attached to Kure Naval District
15 Dec 1922:	Transferred to the reserve

Vice-Admiral **Jugoro ARICHI** (22 Oct 1882 - 8 Nov 1947)

1 Dec 1931 - 15 Nov 1933:	Commander, 1st Destroyer Flotilla
1 Dec 1932:	Promoted to *Rear-Admiral*
15 Nov 1933 - 15 Nov 1934:	Chief of Staff, 2nd Fleet
15 Nov 1934 - 1 Aug 1936:	Director of the Torpedo School
1 Aug 1936 - 1 Dec 1936:	Commander, 4th Flotilla
1 Dec 1936:	Promoted to *Vice-Admiral*
1 Dec 1936 - 1 Dec 1937:	Commander, 3rd Flotilla

1 Dec 1937 - 15 Nov 1938:	Commander, Chinkai Guard District
15 Nov 1938 - 15 Mar 1939:	Attached to the Naval General Staff
21 Mar 1939:	Transferred to the reserve

Rear-Admiral **Tatsunosuke ARIIZUMI** (? - 29 Aug 1945)

15 Dec 1944 - 29 Aug 1945:	Commander, 1st Submarine Division, Commander, 631st Air Flotilla
29 Aug 1945:	Posthumously promoted to *Rear-Admiral*

Rear-Admiral **Sadashiro ARIKAWA** (? - 13 Jan 1944)

31 Aug 1905 - 30 Nov 1906:	Captain, *"Hongkong-maru"*
30 Nov 1906:	Promoted to *Rear-Admiral (Reserve)*
30 Nov 1906:	Transferred to the reserve

Vice-Admiral **Kaoru ARIMA** (15 Dec 1893 - 23 Jan 1956)

5 Aug 1942 - 9 Jun 1943:	Captain, Battleship *"Musashi"*
1 Nov 1942:	Promoted to *Rear-Admiral*
9 Jun 1943 - 21 Jun 1943:	Attached to the Naval General Staff
21 Jun 1943 - 19 Feb 1944:	Chief Instructor, Naval Academy
22 Sep 1943 - 19 Feb 1944:	Deputy Director, Naval Academy
1 Dec 1943 - 19 Feb 1944:	Commander, Kure Training Flotilla
19 Feb 1944 - 1 May 1944:	Commander, 4th Auxiliary Base Force
19 Feb 1944 - 1 Mar 1944:	Commander, 2nd Marine Escort Force
30 Mar 1944 - 12 Aug 1944:	Chief of Staff, 4th Fleet
12 Aug 1944 - 10 Sep 1944:	Attached to the staff, Southwestern Area Fleet
10 Sep 1944 - 17 Nov 1944:	Commander, 31st Base Force
1 Nov 1944 - 5 Feb 1945:	Chief of Staff, 13th Air Fleet
1 Nov 1944 - 1 Nov 1945:	Chief of Staff, Southwestern Area Fleet, Chief of Staff, Southern Expeditionary Fleet
1 Nov 1945:	Promoted to *Vice-Admiral*

Vice-Admiral **Masafumi ARIMA** (25 Sep 1895 - 15 Oct 1944)

16 Feb 1943 - 15 Mar 1944:	Chief of Training Bureau, Naval Air Command
1 May 1943:	Promoted to *Rear-Admiral*
15 Mar 1944 - 1 Apr 1944:	Attached to Naval Air Command
1 Apr 1944 - 9 Apr 1944:	Attached to the staff, Central Pacific Area Fleet
9 Apr 1944 - 15 Oct 1944:	Commander, 26th Air Flotilla
15 Oct 1944:	Posthumously promoted to *Vice-Admiral*

Admiral **Ryokitsu ARIMA** (15 Nov 1861 - 2 May 1944)

20 Nov 1908 - 1 Dec 1910:	Commandant, Naval Gunnery School
1 Dec 1909:	Promoted to *Rear-Admiral*
1 Dec 1910 - 1 Dec 1912:	Chief of Section 1, Naval General Staff

1 Dec 1912 - 19 Nov 1913:	C-in-C, 3rd Fleet
19 Nov 1913 - 28 Jan 1914:	Unassigned
1 Dec 1913:	Promoted to *Vice-Admiral*
28 Jan 1914 - 25 Mar 1914:	Member, Admirals Committee
25 Mar 1914 - 1 Dec 1916:	Commandant of the Naval Academy
1 Dec 1916 - 6 Apr 1917:	Chief of Naval Training Command
6 Apr 1917 - 1 Dec 1918:	C-in-C, 3rd Fleet
1 Dec 1918 - 1 Aug 1921:	Member, Admirals Committee
25 Nov 1919:	Promoted to *Admiral*
1 Dec 1919 - 1 Dec 1920:	Chief of Naval Training Command
1 Aug 1921 - 1 Apr 1922:	Unassigned
1 Apr 1922:	Transferred to the reserve

Rear-Admiral **Seiho ARIMA** (28 Nov 1884 - 24 Aug 1973)

1 Nov 1943 - 5 Jun 1945:	Chief of Fukuoka Area Personnel Bureau
1 May 1945:	Promoted to *Rear-Admiral*
5 Jun 1945 - 15 Jul 1945:	Attached to Sasebo Naval District
15 Jul 1945 - 1 Sep 1945:	Attached to Yokosuka Naval District

Vice-Admiral **Baron Shinichi ARIMA** (26 Jan 1851 - 6 Dec 1909)

27 Dec 1897 - 14 May 1898:	Commander, Takeshiki Guard District
27 Dec 1897:	Promoted to *Rear-Admiral*
14 May 1898 - 20 May 1900:	Admiral Commanding, Yokosuka Naval District
17 Juj 1899 - 20 May 1900:	Commander, Yokosuka District Fleet
20 May 1900 - 3 Jul 1901:	C-in-C, Readiness Fleet
3 Jul 1901 - 7 Jan 1905:	Chief of Naval Shipbuilding Command
24 May 1902:	Promoted to *Vice-Admiral*
27 Oct 1903 - 7 Jan 1905:	Chief of Naval Training Command
7 Jan 1905 - 2 Feb 1906:	Admiral Commanding, Kure Naval District
2 Feb 1906 - 22 Nov 1906:	Admiral Commanding, Sasebo Naval District
22 Nov 1906 - 26 May 1908:	C-in-C, 1st Fleet
26 May 1908 - 28 Aug 1908:	Chief of Naval Training Command
28 Aug 1908 - 1 Mar 1909:	Unassigned
1 Mar 1909 - 1 Dec 1909:	Admiral Commanding, Sasebo Naval District
1 Dec 1909 - 6 Dec 1909:	Member, Admirals Committee

Vice-Admiral **Yutaka ARIMA** (1885 - 31 Jan 1951)

1 May 1929 - 1 May 1931:	Naval Attache, USSR
1 Dec 1930:	Promoted to *Rear-Admiral*
1 May 1931 - 1 Dec 1931:	Attached to the Naval General Staff
1 Dec 1931 - 1 Dec 1932:	Chief Instructor, Naval College
1 Dec 1932 - 15 Nov 1934:	Chief of Shipping Bureau, Sasebo Naval District
15 Nov 1934:	Promoted to *Vice-Admiral*

15 Nov 1934 - 10 Dec 1934:	Attached to the Naval General Staff
15 Dec 1934:	Transferred to the reserve

Rear-Admiral **Fuji ARIMURA** (3 Jan 1898 - 10 May 1944)
18 Jan 1944 - 10 May 1944:	Traffic Controller, 2nd Marine Escort Flotilla
10 May 1944:	Posthumously promoted to *Rear-Admiral*

Vice-Admiral **Shozo ARISAKA** (11 Jan 1868 - 19 Jan 1941)
1 Nov 1915 - 1 Dec 1922:	Director of the Ordnance Arsenal
31 Dec 1915:	Promoted to *General (Ordnance)*
23 Sep 1919:	Redesignated *Rear-Admiral (Ordnance)*
1 Dec 1920:	Promoted to *Vice-Admiral*
1 Dec 1922 - 10 Dec 1922:	Attached to the Naval General Staff
10 Dec 1922 - 31 Mar 1923:	Unassigned
31 Mar 1923:	Transferred to the reserve

Fleet Admiral **Prince Takehito ARISUGAWA** (13 Jan 1862 - 10 Jul 1913)
5 Nov 1896:	Promoted to *Rear-Admiral*
5 Nov 1896 - 3 Mar 1898:	C-in-C, Readiness Fleet
3 Mar 1898 - 29 Nov 1901:	Member, Admirals Committee
26 Sep 1899:	Promoted to *Vice-Admiral*
29 Nov 1901 - 6 Mar 1904:	Unassigned
6 Mar 1904 - 19 Jan 1905:	Member, Joint General Staff
28 Jun 1904:	Promoted to *Admiral*
19 Jan 1905 - 10 Jul 1913:	Navy Councillor
7 Jul 1913:	Appointed *Fleet Admiral*

Rear-Admiral **Nobu ARITA** (2 Jan 1878 - 19 Oct 1944)
1 Apr 1923 - 1 Oct 1925:	Attached to the Research Bureau, Department of the Navy
1 Dec 1924:	Promoted to *Rear-Admiral*
1 Oct 1925 - 16 Dec 1925:	Unassigned
16 Dec 1925:	Transferred to the reserve

Vice-Admiral **Yoshitomo ARITSUKA** (4 Feb 1883 - 18 May 1945)
1 Dec 1930:	Promoted to *Rear-Admiral*
1 Dec 1930 - 1 Dec 1931:	Chief of Shipping Bureau, Yokosuka Naval District
1 Dec 1931 - 1 May 1934:	Supervisor for Construction & Ordnance, Naval Shipbuilding Command, Supervisor for Ordnance, Naval Air Command
1 May 1934 - 15 Nov 1934:	Chief Supervisor for Construction & Ordnance, Naval Shipbuilding Command
15 Nov 1934:	Promoted to *Vice-Admiral*

15 Nov 1934 - 10 Dec 1934:	Attached to the Naval Shipbuilding Command
15 Dec 1934:	Transferred to the reserve

Vice-Admiral **Kosaku ARUGA** (21 Aug 1897 - 7 Apr 1945)
25 Nov 1944 - 7 Apr 1945:	Captain, Battleship *"Yamato"*
7 Apr 1945:	Posthumously promoted 2 grades to *Vice-Admiral*

Rear-Admiral **Takeo ARUGA** (1 Dec 1893 - 28 Aug 1973)
1 Mar 1943 - 18 Nov 1943:	Chief, Southern Hydrographic Office
1 May 1943:	Promoted to *Rear-Admiral*
18 Nov 1943 - 15 Oct 1945:	Chief of Bureau 6, Naval Shipbuilding Command
1 Mar 1945 - 15 Oct 1945:	Chief of Bureau 6, Naval Air Command

Rear-Admiral **Kenji ASAI** (20 Jul 1884 - 31 Jan 1943)
5 Oct 1942 - 31 Jan 1943:	Commander of Minesweeping, *"Iwashiro-maru"*
31 Jan 1945:	Posthumously promoted to *Rear-Admiral*

Rear-Admiral **Shojiro ASAI** (5 Nov 1856 - 2 Sep 1923)
14 Jun 1905 - 12 Dec 1905:	Commander, Sasebo Torpedo Corps
12 Dec 1905 - 27 Dec 1906:	Unassigned
30 Nov 1906:	Promoted to *Rear-Admiral*
27 Dec 1906:	Transferred to the reserve

Vice-Admiral **Hikokichi ASAKUMA** (5 Jan 1887 - ?)
15 Nov 1935:	Promoted to *Rear-Admiral*
15 Nov 1935 - 1 Dec 1936:	Chief of Shipping Bureau, Kure Naval District
1 Dec 1936 - 15 Nov 1939:	Commandant, Naval Engineering School
15 Nov 1939:	Promoted to *Vice-Admiral*
15 Nov 1939 - 15 Mar 1940:	Attached to the Naval General Staff
21 Mar 1940:	Transferred to the reserve
15 Dec 1941 - 15 Mar 1943:	Recalled; Commandant, Naval Construction School
15 Mar 1943 - 20 Mar 1943:	Attached to the Naval General Staff
20 Mar 1943:	Demobilized

Vice-Admiral **Toshihide ASAKUMA** (12 Nov 1892 - 11 Jun 1987)
15 Nov 1940 - 1 Nov 1943:	Chief of Torpedo Bureau, Kure Navy Yard
15 Oct 1941:	Promoted to *Rear-Admiral*
1 Nov 1943 - 30 Oct 1945:	Commander, Kawatana Navy Yard
1 May 1945:	Promoted to *Vice-Admiral*

Rear-Admiral **Bunji ASAKURA** (6 Jul 1894 - 27 Jan 1966)
6 Dec 1943 - 2 Aug 1944:	Captain, Battleship *"Musashi"*

1 May 1944:	Promoted to *Rear-Admiral*
2 Aug 1944 - 16 Aug 1944:	Attached to the staff, 1st Southern Expeditionary Fleet
16 Aug 1944 - Oct 1945:	Chief of Staff, 1st Southern Expeditionary Fleet
8 Jan 1945 - Oct 1945:	Chief of Staff, 13th Air Fleet
5 Feb 1945 - Oct 1945:	Chief of Staff, 10th Area Fleet

Vice-Admiral **Masayasu ASANO** (28 Dec 1867 - 20 Oct 1945)

1 Dec 1914 - 1 Jun 1919:	Chief of Gunnery Bureau, Kure Navy Yard
13 Dec 1915:	Promoted to *Rear-Admiral*
1 Jun 1919 - 1 Dec 1919:	Attached to Naval Technical Command
1 Dec 1919:	Promoted to *Vice-Admiral*
1 Dec 1919 - 1 Aug 1920:	Unassigned
1 Aug 1920:	Transferred to the reserve

Rear-Admiral **Shinpei ASANO** (1 Dec 1895 - 13 Mar 1949)

20 Feb 1944 - Oct 1945:	Commander, 41st Guard Unit
15 Jul 1944 - Oct 1945:	Commander, 85th Submarine Base Force
1 May 1945:	Promoted to *Rear-Admiral*

Vice-Admiral (Constructor) **Mitsutoshi ASAOKA** (27 Nov 1861 - 26 Aug 1936)

24 May 1913 - 1 Dec 1914:	Chief of Shipbuilding Bureau, Yokosuka Navy Yard
1 Dec 1913:	Promoted to *General (Constructor)*
1 Dec 1914 - 1 Oct 1915:	Attached to Naval Shipbuilding Command
1 Oct 1915 - 26 Jul 1917:	Attached to Naval Technical Command
26 Jul 1917 - 1 Dec 1918:	Chief of Bureau 4, Naval Technical Command
1 Dec 1918:	Promoted to *General (Constructor), Senior Grade*
1 Dec 1918 - 1 Aug 1919:	Unassigned
1 Aug 1919:	Transferred to the reserve
23 Sep 1919:	Redesignated *Vice-Admiral (Constructor)*

Rear-Admiral **Saburo ASHINA** (5 Jan 1900 - 8 Jul 1944)

4 Mar 1944 - 8 Jul 1944:	Staff Officer, Central Pacific Area Fleet, Staff Officer, 14th Air Fleet
8 Jul 1944:	Posthumously promoted to *Rear-Admiral*

Rear-Admiral **Hitoshi AWANOHARA** (11 Dec 1900 - 2 Aug 1944)

1 Jan 1944 - 2 Aug 1944:	Commander, 121st Air Flotilla
2 Aug 1944:	Posthumously promoted to *Rear-Admiral*

Rear-Admiral **Kenzo AWANOHARA** (1 Oct 1883 - 16 Jan 1942)

15 Nov 1932 - 15 Nov 1935:	Chief of Explosives Bureau, Navy Powder Yard
15 Nov 1933:	Promoted to *Rear-Admiral*

15 Nov 1935 - 10 Dec 1935:	Attached to Naval Shipbuilding Command
15 Dec 1935:	Transferred to the reserve

Rear-Admiral **Makoto AWAYA** (12 Apr 1892 - 16 Mar 1982)
15 Nov 1940 - 30 Sep 1945:	Chief of Landing Gear Bureau, Air Technical Arsenal
1 May 1943:	Promoted to *Rear-Admiral*

Rear-Admiral **Sei AZUKIZAWA** (19 Oct 1892 - 17 Nov 1944)
1 Dec 1943 - 17 Nov 1944:	Traffic Controller, 1st Marine Escort Flotilla
17 Nov 1944:	Posthumously promoted to *Rear-Admiral*

Rear-Admiral **Giichi BAN** (9 Sep 1896 - 27 Jul 1964)
15 Sep 1944 - 10 Nov 1945:	Deputy Chief of Staff, Yokosuka Naval District
1 May 1945:	Promoted to *Rear-Admiral*

Rear-Admiral **Jiro BAN** (7 Mar 1884 - 9 May 1973)
15 Apr 1943 - 15 Oct 1945:	Chief, Takamatsu Area Personnel Bureau
15 Oct 1944:	Promoted to *Rear-Admiral*

Vice-Admiral **Masami BAN** (18 Oct 1893 - 25 Oct 1944)
23 Feb 1944 - 25 Oct 1944:	Captain, Battleship *"Fuso"*
15 Oct 1944:	Promoted to *Rear-Admiral*
25 Oct 1944:	Posthumously promoted to *Vice-Admiral*

Rear-Admiral **Akitomo BEPPU** (1 Jan 1889 - 16 Jan 1968)
15 Oct 1944:	Promoted to *Rear-Admiral*
15 Oct 1944 - 1 Nov 1944:	Attached to Kure Naval District
1 Nov 1944 - 1 Mar 1945:	Commander, Urato Air Flotilla
1 Mar 1945 - 30 Jun 1945:	Commander, 23rd Combined Air Flotilla
1 Mar 1945 - 15 Sep 1945:	Commander, Shiga Air Flotilla

Vice-Admiral **Ryozo BEPPU** (20 Jul 1892 - 18 Dec 1953)
15 Nov 1939:	Promoted to *Rear-Admiral*
15 Nov 1939 - 1 Feb 1941:	Attached to Yokosuka Naval District
1 Feb 1941 - 21 Apr 1941:	Chief of Oil Refining Bureau, Navy Fuel Yard
21 Apr 1941 - 1 Oct 1942:	Commander, 2nd Navy Fuel Yard
20 May 1942 - 1 Apr 1944:	Attached to Mako Guard District
1 Nov 1943:	Promoted to *Vice-Admiral*
1 Apr 1944 - 10 Jun 1944:	Commander, 6th Navy Fuel Yard
10 Jun 1944 - 5 Aug 1944:	Attached to the Naval General Staff
5 Aug 1944:	Transferred to the reserve

Rear-Admiral **Keizo CHIBA** (20 Mar 1889 - 9 Jul 1969)
15 Nov 1939:	Promoted to *Rear-Admiral*
15 Nov 1939 - 20 Nov 1941:	Commander, Sasebo Sailors Corps
20 Nov 1941 - 15 Sep 1942:	Commander, 1st Sasebo Sailors Corps, Commander, Sasebo Guard Unit
15 Sep 1942 - 10 Oct 1942:	Attached to the Naval General Staff
15 Oct 1942:	Transferred to the reserve

Vice-Admiral **Tomojiro CHISAKA** (15 Feb 1868 - 23 Feb 1936)
1 Dec 1913:	Promoted to *Rear-Admiral*
1 Dec 1913 - 25 Mar 1914:	Commander, Sasebo Torpedo Group
25 Mar 1914 - 1 Dec 1914:	Chief of Staff, Sasebo Naval District
1 Dec 1914 - 6 Dec 1915:	C-in-C, Training Fleet
6 Dec 1915 - 7 Feb 1917:	Chief of Bureau 1, Naval Training Command
7 Feb 1917 - 30 May 1917:	Chief of Bureau 2, Naval Training Command
30 May 1917 - 12 Dec 1917:	Commander, 2nd Division
1 Dec 1917:	Promoted to *Vice-Admiral*
12 Dec 1917 - 13 Jun 1918:	Commander, Mako Guard District
13 Jun 1918 - 1 Dec 1919:	C-in-C, 1st Special Task Fleet
1 Dec 1919 - 1 Dec 1920:	Commander, Chinkai Guard District
1 Dec 1920 - 1 Apr 1923:	Commandant of the Naval Academy
1 Apr 1923 - 1 Jun 1923:	Member of the Admirals Committee
1 Jul 1923:	Transferred to the reserve

Rear-Admiral **Sadae CHIYA** (6 Oct 1885 - 6 Jul 1944)
25 Jul 1943 - 6 Jul 1944:	Commander, Ise Base Force
6 Jul 1944:	Posthumously promoted to *Rear-Admiral*

Rear-Admiral **Kanei CHUDO** (27 Apr 1894 - 20 Oct 1985)
26 Aug 1943 - Oct 1945:	Staff Officer, Burma Area Army
21 Oct 1943 - 11 Feb 1945:	Chief of Staff, 13th Auxiliary Base Force
15 Oct 1944:	Promoted to *Rear-Admiral*
11 Feb 1945 - Oct 1945:	Deputy Chief of Staff, Southern Army

Vice-Admiral **Marquis Tadashige DAIGO** (15 Oct 1891 - 6 Dec 1947)
15 Dec 1938 - 20 Oct 1941:	Aide-de-Camp to the Emperor
15 Nov 1940:	Promoted to *Rear-Admiral*
20 Oct 1941 - 14 Jul 1942:	Commander, 5th Submarine Division
14 Jul 1942 - 20 Aug 1942:	Attached to the Naval General Staff
20 Aug 1942 - 31 Aug 1942:	Attached to Kure Naval District
31 Aug 1942 - 1 Apr 1943:	Commander, Kure Submarine Division
1 Apr 1943 - 20 Oct 1943:	Commander, 11th Submarine Division
20 Oct 1943 - 1 Nov 1943:	Attached to the Naval General Staff

1 Nov 1943:	Promoted to *Vice-Admiral*
1 Nov 1943 - 8 Nov 1943:	Attached to the staff, 2nd Southern Expeditionary Fleet
8 Nov 1943 - 23 Aug 1944:	Commander, 22nd Base Force, Commander, Eastern Attack Force
23 Aug 1944 - 1 May 1945:	Commandant, Submarine School, Commander, Kure Submarine Division
1 May 1945 - 15 Sep 1945:	C-in-C, 6th (Submarine) Fleet
15 Sep 1945 - 25 Sep 1945:	Attached to the Naval General Staff
25 Sep 1945:	Transferred to the reserve

Vice-Admiral (Engineer) **Tadakichi DATE** (9 Jun 1867 - 30 Mar 1920)

1 Dec 1912:	Promoted to *Rear-Admiral*
1 Dec 1912 - 1 Apr 1916:	Chief Engineer, Sasebo Naval District
1 Apr 1916 - 1 Dec 1918:	Chief Engineer, Yokosuka Naval District
1 Dec 1917:	Promoted to *Vice-Admiral*
1 Dec 1918 - 1 Aug 1919:	Unassigned
1 Aug 1919:	Transferred to the reserve

Admiral **Baron Shigeto DEWA** (10 Dec 1855 - 27 Jan 1930)

20 May 1900:	Promoted to *Rear-Admiral*
20 May 1900 - 3 Jul 1901:	C-in-C, Readiness Fleet
3 Jul 1901 - 29 Oct 1902:	Chief of Shipping Bureau, Yokosuka Naval District
29 Oct 1902 - 27 Oct 1903:	Director, Bureau of Naval Affairs, Department of the Navy, Member, Admirals Committee
29 Oct 1902 - 5 Sep 1903:	Deputy Chief of the Naval General Staff
27 Oct 1903 - 28 Dec 1903:	C-in-C, Readiness Fleet
28 Dec 1903 - 14 Jun 1905:	C-in-C, 1st Fleet
6 Jun 1904:	Promoted to *Vice-Admiral*
14 Jun 1905 - 20 Dec 1905:	C-in-C, 4th Fleet
20 Dec 1905 - 22 Nov 1906:	C-in-C, 2nd Fleet
22 Nov 1906 - 26 May 1908:	Chief of Naval Training Command
26 May 1908 - 1 Dec 1909:	C-in-C, 2nd Fleet
1 Dec 1909 - 1 Dec 1911:	Admiral Commanding, Sasebo Naval District
1 Dec 1911 - 1 Dec 1913:	C-in-C, 1st Fleet
9 Jul 1912:	Promoted to *Admiral*
1 Dec 1913 - 17 Dec 1920:	Navy Councillor

Rear-Admiral (Surgeon) **Sugizo DOBETA** (3 Mar 1893 - ?)

1 Jun 1943 - 10 Oct 1945:	Chief Medical Officer, Suzuka Navy Yard
1 May 1945:	Promoted to *Rear-Admiral (Surgeon)*

Paymaster General **Junnosuke DOI** (29 Sep 1858 - 23 Aug 1917)
2 Nov 1905:   Promoted to *Paymaster General*
2 Nov 1905 - 15 Aug 1908:   Paymaster-General, Kure Naval District
15 Aug 1908 - 15 Aug 1909:   Unassigned
15 Aug 1909:   Transferred to the reserve

Rear-Admiral **Naoji DOI**   (26 Mar 1894 - 12 Feb 1963)
25 Aug 1942 - 5 May 1944:   Chief of Administration, Toyokawa Navy Yard
1 May 1944:   Promoted to *Rear-Admiral*
5 May 1944 - 25 Jun 1944:   Attached to Yokosuka Naval District
25 Jun 1944 - 20 Sep 1944:   Commander, Rashin Area Base Force
20 Sep 1944 - 6 Oct 1944:   Attached to the staff,
                                    3rd Southern Expeditionary Fleet
6 Oct 1944 - Oct 1945:   Commander, 32nd Special Naval Base Force

Rear-Admiral **Takashi DOI**   (31 Dec 1892 - 12 Jan 1944)
8 Oct 1943 - 12 Jan 1944:   Commander of Auxiliaries, *"Yamabiko-maru"*
12 Jan 1944:   Posthumously promoted to *Rear-Admiral*

Rear-Admiral **Keizo DOMEN**   (6 Jan 1904 - 23 Oct 1944)
10 Nov 1943 - 23 Oct 1944:   Chief Engineer, Heavy Cruiser *"Atago"*
23 Oct 1944:   Posthumously promoted to *Rear-Admiral*

Rear-Admiral **Keiichi EBIHARA** (15 Apr 1872 - 7 Apr 1939)
20 Nov 1920 - 1 Dec 1920:   Attached to Kure Naval District
1 Dec 1920:   Promoted to *Rear-Admiral*
1 Dec 1920 - 1 Aug 1921:   Unassigned
1 Aug 1921:   Transferred to the reserve

Vice-Admiral **Yurikazu EDAHARA** (? - 28 Jun 1944)
1 Dec 1927:   Promoted to *Rear-Admiral*
1 Dec 1927 - 30 Nov 1929:   Commander, Kasumigaura Air Flotilla
30 Nov 1929 - 1 Dec 1930:   Commander, 1st Air Force
1 Dec 1930 - 8 Jun 1931:   Attached to Naval Air Command
8 Jun 1931 - 1 Apr 1932:   Attached to Yokosuka Naval District
1 Apr 1932 - 1 Sep 1933:   Commander of the Air Arsenal
1 Dec 1932:   Promoted to *Vice-Admiral*
1 Sep 1933 - 15 Nov 1934:   Commander, Ryojun Guard District
15 Nov 1934 - 25 Mar 1935:   Attached to the Naval General Staff
30 Mar 1935:   Transferred to the reserve

Vice-Admiral **Heitaro EDO**   (5 Jul 1890 - 25 Nov 1944)
1 Oct 1941 - 6 Mar 1943:   Commander, Kii Base Force

1 Nov 1942:	Promoted to *Rear-Admiral*
6 Mar 1943 - 23 Mar 1943:	Commander, 3rd Destroyer Flotilla
23 Mar 1943 - 8 Apr 1943:	Attached to Yokosuka Naval District
8 Apr 1943 - 24 Aug 1943:	Commander, 2nd Yokosuka Sailors Corps
24 Aug 1943 - 10 Aug 1944:	Commander, Yokosuka Guard Unit
24 Aug 1943 - 4 Jan 1944:	Commander, 1st Yokosuka Sailors Corps
4 Jan 1944 - 10 Aug 1944:	Commander, Yokosuka Sailors Corps
10 Aug 1944 - 15 Aug 1944:	Attached to the Naval General Staff
15 Aug 1944 - 20 Aug 1944:	Commander, 3rd Destroyer Flotilla
20 Aug 1944 - 25 Nov 1944:	Commander, 31st Cruiser Division
25 Nov 1944:	Posthumously promoted to *Vice-Admiral*

Vice-Admiral **Yasutaro EGASHIRA** (12 Feb 1865 - 23 Jan 1913)
28 Aug 1908:	Promoted to *Rear-Admiral*
28 Aug 1908 - 1 Dec 1909:	Chief of Staff, Ryojun Naval District
1 Dec 1909 - 11 Mar 1911:	Chief of Staff, Sasebo Naval District
11 Mar 1911 - 20 Apr 1912:	Chief of Naval Personnel, Department of the Navy
20 Apr 1912 - 10 Jan 1913:	Chief, Bureau of Naval Affairs
7 Jan 1913:	Promoted to *Vice-Admiral*
10 Jan 1913 - 23 Jan 1913:	Unassigned

Rear-Admiral **Kotaro EGOSHI** (11 Aug 1866 - 26 Jul 1924)
1 Apr 1916 - 1 Jun 1919:	Chief Engineer Officer, Sasebo Naval District
1 Dec 1917:	Promoted to *Rear-Admiral*
1 Jun 1919 - 1 Mar 1920:	Unassigned
1 Mar 1920:	Transferred to the reserve

Rear-Admiral **Kaname EGUCHI** (6 Nov 1877 - 5 Mar 1942)
10 May 1923 - 1 Dec 1923:	Captain, Battlecruiser *"Ikoma"*
1 Dec 1923:	Promoted to *Rear-Admiral*
1 Dec 1923 - 10 Dec 1923:	Attached to the Naval General Staff
10 Dec 1923 - 25 Feb 1924:	Unassigned
25 Feb 1924:	Transferred to the reserve

Rear-Admiral **Matsuro EGUCHI** (15 Sep 1890 - 23 Feb 1944)
29 Nov 1943 - 23 Feb 1944:	Commander, 60th Submarine Chaser Flotilla
23 Feb 1944:	Posthumously promoted to *Rear-Admiral*

Rear-Admiral **Nao EGUCHI** (? - 4 Jun 1945)
10 Oct 1944 - 4 Jun 1945:	Chief of Section 1, Supply Bureau, Kure Navy Yard
4 Jun 1945:	Posthumously promoted to *Rear-Admiral*

Vice-Admiral **Rinroku EGUCHI** (15 Apr 1865 - 19 Mar 1941)
21 Sep 1911 - 20 Apr 1912:	Chief of Staff, Sasebo Naval District
1 Dec 1911:	Promoted to *Rear-Admiral*
20 Apr 1912 - 1 Dec 1913:	Commandant, Naval Gunnery School
1 Dec 1913 - 1 Dec 1914:	Director, Naval Hydrography Command
1 Dec 1914 - 13 Dec 1915:	Commander, Mako Guard District
13 Dec 1915:	Promoted to *Vice-Admiral*
13 Dec 1915 - 1 Dec 1916:	Commander, Yokosuka Navy Yard
1 Dec 1916 - 1 Dec 1917:	Unassigned
1 Dec 1917:	Transferred to the reserve

Rear-Admiral **Tetsushiro EMI** (30 Jan 1901 - 31 May 1944)
? - 31 May 1944:	Attached to Naval Shipbuilding Command
26 Aug 1944:	Posthumously promoted to *Rear-Admiral*

Rear-Admiral **Denzaburo EMOTO** (7 Jun 1893 - 25 Apr 1980)
15 Jun 1942 - 1 Apr 1944:	Chief of Ordnance Bureau, Maizuru Navy Yard
1 May 1943:	Promoted to *Rear-Admiral*
1 Apr 1944 - 20 Apr 1944:	Attached to Naval Air Command
20 Apr 1944 - 15 Feb 1945:	Chief of Technical Bureau, Naval Radar Command
15 Feb 1945 - 10 May 1945:	Attached to 2nd Naval Technical Arsenal
10 May 1945 - 15 Oct 1945:	Chief of Bureau 3, Naval Shipbuilding Command, Chief of Bureau 5, Naval Air Command

Rear-Admiral **Kaku ENDO** (16 May 1880 - 11 Sep 1969)
1 Dec 1924:	Promoted to *Rear-Admiral*
1 Dec 1924 - 20 Dec 1924:	Attached to Sasebo Naval District
20 Dec 1924 - 1 Aug 1925:	Chief of Shipping Bureau, Sasebo Naval District
1 Aug 1925 - 1 Dec 1926:	Commander, Sasebo Defense Force
1 Dec 1926 - 20 Mar 1927:	Attached to the Naval General Staff
20 Mar 1927 - 10 Apr 1927:	Unassigned
10 Apr 1927:	Transferred to the reserve

Rear-Admiral **Kitaro ENDO** (16 Feb 1856 - 16 Jul 1902)
22 May 1900:	Promoted to *Rear-Admiral*
22 May 1900 - 20 Jun 1900:	Commander, Sasebo Naval District Fleet
20 Jun 1900 - 6 Jul 1901:	C-in-C, Readiness Fleet
6 Jul 1901 - 22 Apr 1902:	Chief of Bureau 3, Naval General Staff
22 Apr 1902 - 16 Jul 1902:	Unassigned

Rear-Admiral **Kuro ENDO** (20 Sep 1881 - 16 Jun 1948)
1 Dec 1927:	Promoted to *Rear-Admiral*
1 Dec 1927 - 1 Apr 1929:	Chief of Briquette Bureau, Navy Fuel Yard

1 Apr 1929 - 1 Dec 1930:	Attached to Kure Naval District
1 Dec 1930 - 10 Sep 1931:	Attached to Naval Shipbuilding Command
20 Sep 1931:	Transferred to the reserve

Admiral **Yoshikazu ENDO** (8 Aug 1891 - 3 May 1944)

15 Nov 1937 - 15 Dec 1938:	Aide-de-Camp to the Emperor
1 Dec 1937:	Promoted to *Rear-Admiral*
15 Dec 1938 - 24 Dec 1938:	Attached to the Naval General Staff
24 Dec 1938 - 2 Dec 1940:	Naval Attache, Germany
2 Dec 1940 - 15 Oct 1941:	Chief of Staff, Yokosuka Naval District
4 Dec 1940 - 15 Oct 1941:	Chief of Communications Bureau, Yokosuka Naval District
15 Oct 1941:	Promoted to *Vice-Admiral*
15 Oct 1941 - 1 Nov 1941:	Attached to the Naval General Staff
1 Nov 1941 - 9 Mar 1943:	Director, Total Warfare Research Laboratory
9 Mar 1943 - 20 Aug 1943:	C-in-C, 1st China Expeditionary Fleet
20 Aug 1943 - 15 Nov 1943:	Attached to the Naval General Staff
15 Nov 1943 - 3 May 1944:	C-in-C, 9th Fleet
3 May 1944:	Posthumously promoted to *Admiral*

Vice-Admiral **Takaichiro ENOMOTO** (8 Feb 1894 - 7 Feb 1987)

15 Nov 1938 - 10 Oct 1943:	Attached to the Bureau of Naval Affairs
1 Nov 1942:	Promoted to *Rear-Admiral*
10 Oct 1943 - 25 Oct 1943:	Attached to the Naval General Staff
25 Oct 1943 - 1 Jul 1944:	Director, 2nd Navy Fuel Yard
1 Jul 1944 - 6 Jun 1945:	Chief of Research Section, Fuel Bureau, Department of Military Supply
6 Jun 1945 - 26 Aug 1945:	Director of Fuel Bureau, Department of Military Supply
26 Aug 1945 - 10 Nov 1945:	Attached to the Naval General Staff
1 Nov 1945:	Promoted to *Vice-Admiral*

Rear-Admiral **Tokuzo ESAKA** (4 Oct 1885 - 14 Aug 1964)

15 Nov 1933:	Promoted to *Rear-Admiral*
15 Nov 1933 - 15 Nov 1935:	Chief of Mining Bureau, Navy Fuel Yard
15 Nov 1935 - 30 Mar 1936:	Attached to the Naval General Staff
30 Mar 1936:	Transferred to the reserve

Vice-Admiral **Iwakichi EZAKI** (1 Dec 1890 - 16 Jan 1986)

15 Nov 1938 - 15 Nov 1940:	Chief of Shipbuilding Bureau, Yokosuka Navy Yard
15 Nov 1940:	Promoted to *Rear-Admiral*
15 Nov 1940 - 14 Aug 1943:	Attached to Bureau 4, Naval Shipbuilding Command

14 Aug 1943 - 15 Oct 1945:	Chief of Bureau 4, Naval Shipbuilding Command
1 May 1944:	Promoted to *Vice-Admiral*

Rear-Admiral **Samakitsu EZURA** (11 Oct 1867 - 12 Mar 1924)

1 Apr 1913 - 13 Dec 1915:	Chief Engineer Officer, Maizuru Naval District
13 Dec 1915:	Promoted to *Rear-Admiral*
13 Dec 1915 - 1 Dec 1916:	Unassigned
1 Dec 1916:	Transferred to the reserve

Rear-Admiral (Engineer) **Itsushi FUJIE** (3 Dec 1875 - 11 Sep 1952)

1 Dec 1919 - 20 Nov 1920:	Chief Engineer, 2nd Fleet
20 Nov 1920 - 20 Nov 1922:	Chief Instructor, Naval Engineer Academy
1 Dec 1920:	Promoted to *Rear-Admiral*
20 Nov 1922 - 1 Dec 1922:	Attached to the Naval General Staff
1 Dec 1922 - 31 Mar 1923:	Unassigned
31 Mar 1923:	Transferred to the reserve

Rear-Admiral **Akiyoshi FUJII** (22 May 1899 - 15 Jun 1943)

31 Jul 1941 - 15 Jun 1943:	Captain, Submarine *I-9*
15 Jun 1943:	Posthumously promoted to *Rear-Admiral*

Rear-Admiral **Kensuke FUJII** (26 May 1880 - 16 Mar 1961)

1 Dec 1924 - 1 Feb 1927:	Chief of Personnel, Yokosuka Naval District
1 Dec 1926:	Promoted to *Rear-Admiral*
1 Feb 1927 - 20 Mar 1927:	Attached to the Naval General Staff
25 Mar 1927:	Transferred to the reserve

Admiral **Koichi FUJII** (18 Aug 1858 - 9 Jul 1926)

12 Jan 1905 - 20 Dec 1905:	Chief of Staff, 2nd Fleet
2 Nov 1905:	Promoted to *Rear-Admiral*
20 Dec 1905 - 22 Nov 1906:	Chief of Staff, 1st Fleet
22 Nov 1906 - 21 Oct 1907:	Chief of Staff, Yokosuka Naval District
21 Oct 1907 - 28 Aug 1908:	C-in-C, 1st Fleet
28 Aug 1908 - 1 Dec 1909:	Commander, Sasebo Navy Yard
1 Dec 1909:	Promoted to *Vice-Admiral*
1 Dec 1909 - 25 Mar 1914:	Deputy Chief of the Naval General Staff, Member, Admirals Committee
25 Mar 1914 - 10 Aug 1915:	Admiral Commanding, Sasebo Naval District
10 Aug 1915 - 23 Sep 1915:	C-in-C, 1st Fleet
23 Sep 1915 - 1 Dec 1916:	Admiral Commanding, Yokosuka Naval District, Member, Admirals Committee
1 Dec 1916:	Promoted to *Admiral*
1 Dec 1916 - 25 Nov 1919:	Navy Councillor

25 Nov 1919 - 1 Aug 1920:	Unassigned
1 Aug 1920:	Transferred to the reserve

Rear-Admiral (Engineer) **Terugoro FUJII** (22 Jun 1867 - ?)
1 Dec 1910:	Promoted to *Rear-Admiral (Engineer)*
1 Dec 1910 - 17 Feb 1914:	Chief of Bureau 4, Naval Shipbuilding Command
17 Feb 1914 - 14 Sep 1914:	Unassigned
14 Sep 1914:	Discharged

Rear-Admiral **Yoshiro FUJII** (8 Oct 1893 - 18 Jun 1979)
1 Apr 1942 - 20 Aug 1943:	Chief of Engine Construction Bureau, Hiro Navy Yard
1 Nov 1942:	Promoted to *Rear-Admiral*
20 Aug 1943 - 16 Sep 1944:	Commander, Hiro Navy Yard
16 Sep 1944 - 15 May 1945:	Attached to Kure Naval District
15 May 1945 - 1 Jun 1945:	Director, Osaka Naval Facility
1 Jun 1945 - 25 Sep 1945:	Attached to the Administration Bureau, Naval Air Command

Rear-Admiral **Seiichiro FUJIMORI** (10 Nov 1888 - 20 May 1975)
1 Dec 1936:	Promoted to *Rear-Admiral*
1 Dec 1936 - 1 Dec 1937:	Commander, Kure Defense Force
1 Dec 1937 - 15 Dec 1938:	Commander, 10th Escort Flotilla
15 Dec 1938 - 10 Mar 1939:	Attached to Kure Naval District
10 Mar 1939 - 15 Mar 1940:	Attached to the Naval General Staff
15 Mar 1940 - 21 Mar 1940:	Unassigned
21 Mar 1940:	Transferred to the reserve
6 Oct 1941 - 15 Oct 1941:	Recalled; Attached to Kure Naval District
15 Oct 1941 - 10 Jan 1942:	Commander, Kure Guard Division
10 Jan 1942 - 10 Apr 1942:	Commander, Yokosuka Guard Division
10 Apr 1942 - 15 Jun 1942:	Commander, 7th Auxiliary Base Force
15 Jun 1942 - 1 Nov 1942:	Commander, Chichijima Area Base Force
1 Nov 1942 - 1 Dec 1942:	Unassigned
1 Dec 1942:	Demobilized

Vice-Admiral **Hideshiro FUJIMOTO** (29 Sep 1862 - 20 Dec 1923)
1 Dec 1909 - 2 Sep 1911:	Commander, Kure Torpedo Corps
1 Dec 1910:	Promoted to *Rear-Admiral*
2 Sep 1911 - 9 Jul 1912:	Commander, Ominato Guard District
9 Jul 1912 - 1 Dec 1912:	C-in-C, 1st Fleet
1 Dec 1912 - 1 Apr 1913:	Commander, Sasebo Torpedo Corps
1 Apr 1913 - 10 Aug 1913:	Commander, Sasebo Torpedo Group
10 Aug 1913 - 10 Aug 1914:	Commander, Yokosuka Torpedo Group
10 Aug 1914 - 1 Dec 1914:	C-in-C, 1st Fleet

1 Dec 1914:	Promoted to *Vice-Admiral*
1 Dec 1914 - 1 Dec 1915:	Unassigned
1 Dec 1915:	Transferred to the reserve

Rear-Admiral **Kikuo FUJIMOTO** (12 Jan 1888 - 9 Jan 1935)
15 Nov 1933:	Promoted to *Rear-Admiral*
15 Nov 1933 - 9 Jan 1935:	Attached to Bureau 4, Naval Shipbuilding Command

Rear-Admiral **Shiro FUJINAGA** (1 Jan 1893 - 9 May 1979)
25 Jun 1943 - 6 Jan 1945:	Chief of Transport Bureau, Rabaul
15 Oct 1944:	Promoted to *Rear-Admiral*
1 Dec 1944 - Oct 1945:	Commander, 84th Guard Unit

Rear-Admiral **Iwao FUJISAWA** (Nov 1875 - 14 Feb 1947)
10 Nov 1922 - 1 Dec 1924:	Chief Engineer Officer, Sasebo Naval District
1 Dec 1923:	Promoted to *Rear-Admiral*
1 Dec 1924 - 2 Mar 1925:	Attached to the Naval General Staff
20 Mar 1925:	Transferred to the reserve

Admiral **Hisanori FUJITA** (30 Oct 1880 - 23 Jul 1970)
20 Oct 1925 - 1 Dec 1926:	Chief of Administration Bureau, Naval Shipbuilding Command
1 Dec 1925:	Promoted to *Rear-Admiral*
1 Dec 1926 - 10 Dec 1928:	Chief of Naval Personnel, Department of the Navy
10 Dec 1928 - 30 Nov 1929:	Commander, 3rd Escort Flotilla
30 Nov 1929:	Promoted to *Vice-Admiral*
30 Nov 1929 - 10 Jun 1930:	Commander, Yokosuka NavyYard
10 Jun 1930 - 1 Jun 1932:	Chief of Naval Shipbuilding Command, Member, Admirals Committee
1 Jun 1932 - 10 May 1934:	Deputy Minister of the Navy, Member, Admirals Committee
10 May 1934 - 1 Dec 1936:	Admiral Commanding, Kure Naval District
1 Apr 1936:	Promoted to *Admiral*
1 Dec 1936 - 1 Apr 1939:	Navy Councillor
5 Apr 1939:	Transferred to the reserve

Rear-Admiral **Kenroku FUJITA** (14 Jan 1893 - 6 Feb 1980)
20 Apr 1944 - 20 Nov 1945:	Chief of Administration Bureau, Technical Research
1 May 1944:	Promoted to *Rear-Admiral*

Rear-Admiral **Masuzo FUJITA** (12 Jun 1873 - 1950)
1 Dec 1918 - 13 Aug 1923:	Chief of Shipbuilding Bureau, Sasebo NavyYard

1 Dec 1920:	Promoted to *Rear-Admiral*
13 Aug 1923 - 1 Dec 1923:	Attached to the Naval General Staff
5 Dec 1923:	Transferred to the reserve

Vice-Admiral **Risaburo FUJITA** (4 Jan 1892 - 17 Apr 1958)

18 May 1939 - 23 Dec 1939:	Chief of Staff, Training Fleet
15 Nov 1939:	Promoted to *Rear-Admiral*
23 Dec 1939 - 25 Mar 1940:	Attached to the Naval General Staff
25 Mar 1940 - 20 Apr 1940:	Attached to the staff, China Area Fleet
20 Apr 1940 - 15 Nov 1941:	Naval Attache, China
15 Nov 1941 - 31 Dec 1941:	Chief Instructor, Naval College
31 Dec 1941 - 1 Sep 1943:	Chief of Staff, Yokosuka Naval District
1 May 1943:	Promoted to *Vice-Admiral*
1 Sep 1943 - 10 Sep 1943:	Attached to the staff, 1st Southern Expeditionary Fleet
10 Sep 1943 - 2 Jan 1945:	Commander, 11th Naval Base Force
2 Jan 1945 - 20 Jun 1945:	Attached to the Naval General Staff
20 Jun 1945 - 15 Oct 1945:	Chief, Tohoku Navy Office
10 Aug 1945 - 15 Oct 1945:	Tohoku area supervisor, Department of Military Supply

Vice-Admiral **Ruitaro FUJITA** (27 Oct 1887 - 15 Apr 1947)

15 Nov 1939:	Promoted to *Rear-Admiral*
15 Nov 1939 - 1 May 1940:	Attached to the Naval General Staff
1 May 1940 - 1 Sep 1941:	Commander, 3rd Destroyer Flotilla
1 Sep 1941 - 20 Jun 1942:	Commander, 11th Carrier Division
20 Jun 1942 - 14 Jul 1942:	Attached to Yokosuka Naval District
14 Jul 1942 - 9 Sep 1943:	Commander, 7th Auxiliary Base Force
1 May 1943:	Promoted to *Vice-Admiral*
9 Sep 1943 - 10 Nov 1943:	Attached to the Naval General Staff
10 Nov 1943 - 29 Jan 1945:	Commander, Seito Area Base Force
29 Jan 1945 - 10 Apr 1945:	Attached to the Naval General Staff
10 Apr 1945 - 25 Apr 1945:	C-in-C, South China Fleet
25 Apr 1925 - Sep 1945:	C-in-C, 2nd China Expeditionary Fleet

Rear-Admiral **Sachiemon FUJITA** (14 Feb 1849 - 26 Sep 1902)

17 Jun 1900 - 1 Feb 1902:	Unassigned
1 Feb 1902:	Promoted to *Rear-Admiral*, reserve status

Rear-Admiral (Paymaster) **Tsunetaka FUJITA** (1 Sep 1866 - 29 Jun 1924)

1 Dec 1913 - 1 Dec 1914:	Paymaster-General, Maizuru Naval District
1 Dec 1914:	Promoted to *General (Paymaster)*
1 Dec 1914 - 1 Dec 1915:	Unassigned

1 Dec 1915:	Transferred to the reserve
23 Sep 1919:	Redesignated *Rear-Admiral (Paymaster)*

Vice-Admiral **Eizaburo FUJIWARA** (26 Apr 1872 - 6 Nov 1949)
1 Dec 1919:	Promoted to *Rear-Admiral*
1 Dec 1919 - 1 Oct 1920:	Member, Admirals Committee
1 Oct 1920 - 10 Jun 1922:	Chief of Administration Bureau, Naval Shipbuilding Command
10 Jun 1922 - 11 Jun 1924:	Commander, Yokosuka Navy Yard
1 Dec 1923:	Promoted to *Vice-Admiral*
11 Jun 1924 - 20 Dec 1924:	Chief of Supply Bureau, Department of the Navy
20 Dec 1924 - 1 Aug 1925:	Commander, Mako Guard District
1 Aug 1925 - 1 Oct 1925:	Attached to the Naval General Staff
1 Oct 1925 - 16 Dec 1925:	Unassigned
16 Dec 1925:	Transferred to the reserve

Rear-Admiral **Kiyoma FUJIWARA** (8 Oct 1895 - 2 Feb 1980)
15 Oct 1944:	Promoted to *Rear-Admiral*
15 Oct 1944 - 1 Jul 1945:	Commander, 951st Air Flotilla
1 Jul 1945 - 10 Jul 1945:	Attached to the staff, 7th Fleet
10 Jul 1945 - 15 Sep 1945:	Chief of Staff, 7th Fleet
15 Sep 1945 - 30 Nov 1945:	Attached to the Naval General Staff

Vice-Admiral **Akira FUJIYOSHI** (2 May 1883 - 31 Mar 1970)
10 Dec 1928:	Promoted to *Rear-Admiral*
10 Dec 1928 - 1 Dec 1930:	Chief of Staff, Sasebo Naval District
1 Dec 1930 - 1 Dec 1931:	Commander, 1st Submarine Flotilla
1 Dec 1931 - 15 Nov 1932:	Commander, 1st Escort Flotilla
15 Nov 1932 - 11 Dec 1933:	Attached to the Naval General Staff
15 Nov 1933:	Promoted to *Vice-Admiral*
15 Dec 1933:	Transferred to the reserve

Rear-Admiral **Naoshiro FUJIYOSHI** (1 Mar 1895 - 17 Aug 1966)
19 Feb 1944 - 1 Mar 1945:	Commander, 12th Combined Air Flotilla
15 Mar 1944 - 1 Mar 1945:	Commander, Tsukuba Air Flotilla
17 Mar 1944 - 1 Jul 1944:	Commander, Hakata Air Flotilla
1 May 1944:	Promoted to *Rear-Admiral*
1 Mar 1945 - 30 Jun 1945:	Commander, 24th Combined Air Flotilla
30 Jun 1945 - 15 Sep 1945:	Commander, Tsuchiura Air Flotilla
15 Sep 1945:	Transferred to the reserve

Rear-Admiral (Surgeon) **Kanichi FUKADA** (20 Jul 1888 - 6 Feb 1959)
15 Nov 1934 - 1 Dec 1936:	Director, Minato Naval Hospital

1 Dec 1936:	Promoted to *Rear-Admiral (Surgeon)*
1 Dec 1936 - 15 Dec 1936:	Attached to the Naval General Staff
22 Dec 1936:	Transferred to the reserve

Rear-Admiral **Morio FUKAMI** (5 Dec 1901 - 8 Aug 1945)
1 Sep 1943 - 8 Aug 1945:	Commander, 13th Guard Unit
8 Aug 1945:	Posthumously promoted to *Rear-Admiral*

Rear-Admiral (Engineer) **Shosaburo FUKAMI** (4 Aug 1855 - 20 May 1906)
30 Mar 1904 - 2 Nov 1905:	Attached to Bureau 4, Naval Shipbuilding Command
2 Nov 1905:	Promoted to *General (Engineer)*
2 Nov 1905 - 12 Dec 1905:	Attached to Naval Shipbuilding Command
12 Dec 1905 - 20 May 1906:	Unassigned
26 Jan 1906:	Redesignated *Rear-Admiral (Engineer)*

Vice-Admiral (Paymaster) **Sadakichi FUKAMIZU** (28 Mar 1869 - 18 Oct 1962)
1 Jun 1919:	Promoted to *General (Paymaster)*
1 Jun 1919 - 1 Dec 1919:	Paymaster-General, Maizuru Naval District
23 Sep 1919:	Redesignated *Rear-Admiral (Paymaster)*
1 Dec 1919 - 25 May 1923:	Commandant, Paymaster Academy
25 May 1923 - 1 Aug 1925:	Chief of Naval Accounting Bureau
1 Dec 1923:	Promoted to *Vice-Admiral (Paymaster)*
1 Aug 1925 - 1 Oct 1925:	Attached to the Naval General Staff
1 Oct 1925 - 16 Dec 1925:	Unassigned
16 Dec 1925:	Transferred to the reserve

Rear-Admiral **Sokichi FUKAYA** (18 Nov 1895 - 17 Dec 1941)
28 Sep 1940 - 17 Dec 1941:	Commander, 27th Submarine Flotilla
17 Dec 1941:	Posthumously promoted to *Rear-Admiral*

Vice-Admiral **Hideo FUKUCHI** (9 Dec 1893 - 17 Aug 1945)
5 Oct 1942 - 25 Sep 1943:	Chief Instructor, Naval Engineer Academy
1 Nov 1942:	Promoted to *Rear-Admiral*
25 Sep 1943 - 10 Oct 1943:	Attached to Sasebo Naval District
10 Oct 1943 - 10 Jun 1944:	Chief of Supply & Transport Bureaus, Sasebo Naval District
10 Jun 1944 - 21 Apr 1945:	Commander, 6th Navy Fuel Yard
21 Apr 1945 - 10 May 1945:	Attached to the Naval General Staff
10 May 1945 - 10 Aug 1945:	Chief Supervisor for Construction & Ordnance, Naval Shipbuilding Command
10 Aug 1945 - 17 Aug 1945:	Chugoku area supervisor, Department of Military Supply
17 Aug 1945:	Posthumously promoted to *Vice-Admiral*

Rear-Admiral **Ichiro FUKUDA** (31 May 1878 - 10 Mar 1980)
1 Jul 1922 - 1 Dec 1922:	Attached to Yokosuka Naval District
1 Dec 1922:	Promoted to *Rear-Admiral*
1 Dec 1922 - 31 Mar 1923:	Unassigned
31 Mar 1923:	Transferred to the reserve

Vice-Admiral **Keiji FUKUDA** (1 Dec 1890 - 29 Mar 1964)
1 Dec 1936:	Promoted to *Rear-Admiral*
1 Dec 1936 - 15 Oct 1941:	Attached to Bureau 4, Naval Shipbuilding Command
15 Nov 1940:	Promoted to *Vice-Admiral*
15 Oct 1941 - 14 Aug 1943:	Chief of Bureau 4, Naval Shipbuilding Command
14 Aug 1943 - 15 Sep 1945:	Technical Chief, Naval Shipbuilding Command

Rear-Admiral (Surgeon) **Ryo FUKUDA** (21 May 1876 - 16 Mar 1938)
1 Dec 1923 - 1 Dec 1924:	Chief Medical Officer, 1st Fleet, Chief Medical Officer, Combined Fleet
1 Dec 1924:	Promoted to *Rear-Admiral (Surgeon)*
1 Dec 1924 - 1 Dec 1925:	Director, Kure Naval Hospital
1 Dec 1925 - 5 Dec 1925:	Attached to the Naval General Staff
10 Dec 1925:	Transferred to the reserve

Vice-Admiral **Ryozo FUKUDA** (1 Nov 1889 - 26 Mar 1980)
20 Apr 1938 - 15 Nov 1939:	Attached to Mako Guard District
15 Nov 1938:	Promoted to *Rear-Admiral*
15 Nov 1939 - 15 Nov 1940:	Commander, Kainan I. Auxiliary Base Force
15 Nov 1940 - 10 Apr 1941:	Attached to Kure Naval District
10 Apr 1941 - 25 Apr 1941:	Attached to the Naval General Staff
25 Apr 1941 - 1 Aug 1942:	Attached to the staff, 2nd China Expeditionary Fleet
1 May 1942:	Promoted to *Vice-Admiral*
1 Aug 1942 - 15 Oct 1942:	Attached to the Naval General Staff
15 Oct 1942 - 20 Oct 1942:	Attached to the staff, Southwestern Area Fleet
20 Oct 1942 - 8 Nov 1943:	Commander, 22nd Naval Base Force
8 Nov 1943 - 30 Nov 1943:	Attached to the Naval General Staff
30 Nov 1943 - 10 May 1945:	Commander, Takao Guard District
10 May 1945 - 15 May 1945:	Chief of Staff, China Area Fleet
15 May 1945 - Sep 1945:	C-in-C, China Area Fleet

Vice-Admiral **Tadashi FUKUDA** (26 Jan 1893 - 28 Aug 1967)
15 Nov 1940 - 15 Oct 1941:	Chief of Shipbuilding Bureau, Sasebo Navy Yard
15 Oct 1941:	Promoted to *Rear-Admiral*
15 Oct 1941 - 15 Sep 1942:	Attached to Naval Shipbuilding Command
15 Sep 1942 - 5 Aug 1945:	Chief of Shipbuilding Bureau, Kure Navy Yard

1 May 1945:	Promoted to *Vice-Admiral*
5 Aug 1945 - 15 Sep 1945:	Attached to Naval Air Command

Rear-Admiral **Teizaburo FUKUDA** (19 Jun 1891 - 25 Nov 1972)
25 Sep 1940 - 1 Nov 1941:	Attached to the staff, China Area Fleet,
15 Oct 1941:	Promoted to *Rear-Admiral*
1 Nov 1941 - 20 Nov 1941:	Attached to Kure Naval District
20 Nov 1941 - 15 Jan 1944:	Commander, Otake Sailors Corps
15 Jan 1944 - 1 Feb 1944:	Attached to the staff, 4th Southern Expeditionary Fleet
1 Feb 1944 - 10 Sep 1944:	Commander, 24th Auxiliary Base Force
10 Sep 1944 - 15 Dec 1944:	Attached to the Naval General Staff
20 Dec 1944:	Transferred to the reserve

Rear-Admiral **Teisuke FUKUDA** (3 Oct 1870 - 18 Feb 1940)
1 Dec 1916 - 10 Nov 1922:	Commander, Kure Defense Force
1 Dec 1920:	Promoted to *Rear-Admiral*
1 Dec 1921 - 10 Nov 1922:	Commandant, Submarine School
10 Nov 1922 - 1 Dec 1922:	Attached to Kure Naval District
1 Dec 1922 - 31 Mar 1923:	Unassigned
31 Mar 1923:	Transferred to the reserve

Vice-Admiral **Umanosuke FUKUDA** (24 Oct 1856 - 12 Apr 1936)
26 Dec 1906 - 1 Oct 1915:	Chief of Bureau 3, Naval Shipbuilding Command
13 Mar 1907:	Promoted to *General (Constructor)*
?:	Promoted to *General (Constructor), Senior grade*
1 Oct 1915 - 26 Jul 1917:	Chief of Bureau 4, Naval Technical Command
26 Jul 1917 - 26 Jul 1918:	Unassigned
26 Jul 1918:	Transferred to the reserve
23 Sep 1919:	Redesignated *Vice-Admiral*

Rear-Admiral **Junpei FUKUI** (6 Oct 1872 - 31 Jan 1940)
1 Dec 1924:	Promoted to *Rear-Admiral*
1 Dec 1924 - 1 Dec 1925:	Attached to Naval Shipbuilding Command
16 Dec 1925:	Transferred to the reserve

Rear-Admiral **Masayoshi FUKUI** (29 Nov 1858 - 12 May 1916)
1 Dec 1910:	Promoted to *Rear-Admiral*
1 Dec 1910 - 12 Apr 1911:	Commander, Yokosuka Torpedo Group
12 Apr 1911 - 12 Apr 1912:	Unassigned
12 Apr 1912:	Transferred to the reserve

Vice-Admiral (Surgeon) **Nobutatsu FUKUI** (25 Jun 1892 - 6 Jul 1975)
15 Nov 1939:	Promoted to *Rear-Admiral (Surgeon)*
15 Nov 1939 - 15 Nov 1940:	Chief Medical Officer, China Area Fleet
15 Nov 1940 - 15 Oct 1941:	Attached to Yokosuka Naval District
15 Oct 1941 - 25 Oct 1943:	Director, Beppu Naval Hospital
25 Oct 1943 - 1 Nov 1944:	Director, Kure Naval Hospital, Chief Medical Officer, Kure Naval District
1 Nov 1943:	Promoted to *Vice-Admiral (Surgeon)*
1 Nov 1944 - 15 Nov 1945:	Attached to Kure Naval District

Vice-Admiral **Tadayoshi FUKUMA** (24 Feb 1887 - ?)
1 Jun 1932 - 15 Nov 1935:	Chief of Engine Construction Bureau, Kure Navy Yard
15 Nov 1933:	Promoted to *Rear-Admiral*
15 Nov 1935 - 1 Dec 1936:	Commander, Hiro Navy Yard
1 Dec 1936 - 15 Oct 1941:	Chief of Bureau 5, Naval Shipbuilding Command
1 Dec 1937:	Promoted to *Vice-Admiral*
15 Oct 1941 - 20 Dec 1941:	Attached to Naval Shipbuilding Command
22 Dec 1941:	Transferred to the reserve

Rear-Admiral **Toshiaki FUKUMURA** (2 Oct 1905 - 15 May 1944)
23 Feb 1943 - 15 May 1944:	Captain, Submarine *I-27*
15 May 1944:	Posthumously promoted 2 grades to *Rear-Admiral*

Vice-Admiral (Paymaster) **Kichinosuke FUKUNAGA** (5 Dec 1856 - 31 Jul 1945)
10 Nov 1903 - 15 Aug 1908:	Paymaster-General, Yokosuka Naval District
13 Mar 1907:	Promoted to *General (Paymaster)*
15 Aug 1908 - 10 May 1912:	Chief of Naval Accounting Bureau
?:	Promoted to *General (Paymaster), Senior grade*
27 May 1912:	Transferred to the reserve
23 Sep 1919:	Redesignated *Vice-Admiral (Paymaster)*

Rear-Admiral **Tokujiro FUKUOKA** (6 May 1899 - 10 Mar 1945)
1 Mar 1945 - 10 Mar 1945:	Attached to the staff, 2nd Special Attack Division
10 Mar 1945:	Posthumously promoted to *Rear-Admiral*

Vice-Admiral (Surgeon) **Hisashi FUKUSHIMA** (8 Apr 1881 - Feb 1966)
30 Nov 1929:	Promoted to *Rear-Admiral (Surgeon)*
30 Nov 1929 - 1 Dec 1930:	Chief Instructor, Navy Medical School
1 Dec 1930 - 15 Nov 1933:	Director, Kure Naval Hospital, Chief Medical Officer, Kure Naval District
15 Nov 1933 - 15 Nov 1934:	Director, Yokosuka Naval Hospital, Chief Medical Officer, Yokosuka Naval District

15 Nov 1934:	Promoted to *Vice-Admiral (Surgeon)*
15 Nov 1934 - 10 Dec 1934:	Attached to Naval General Staff
15 Dec 1934:	Transferred to the reserve

Rear-Admiral **Kumataro FUKUSHIMA** (13 Feb 1873 - 15 Feb 1941)

3 Nov 1921 - 1 Jun 1922:	Attached to Yokosuka Naval District
1 Dec 1921:	Promoted to *Rear-Admiral*
1 Jun 1922 - 31 Mar 1923:	Unassigned
31 Mar 1923:	Transferred to the reserve

Vice-Admiral **Shigeru FUKUTOME** (1 Feb 1891 - 6 Feb 1971)

15 Nov 1939:	Promoted to *Rear-Admiral*
15 Nov 1939 - 10 Apr 1941:	Chief of Staff, Combined Fleet, Chief of Staff, 1st Fleet
10 Apr 1941 - 22 May 1943:	Chief of Bureau 1, Naval General Staff
1 Nov 1942:	Promoted to *Vice-Admiral*
22 May 1943 - 6 Apr 1944:	Chief of Staff, Combined Fleet
6 Apr 1944 - 15 Jun 1944:	Attached to the Naval General Staff
15 Jun 1944 - 8 Jan 1945:	C-in-C, 2nd Air Fleet
8 Jan 1945 - 13 Jan 1945:	Attached to the staff, Southwestern Area Fleet
13 Jan 1945 - Sep 1945:	C-in-C, 13th Air Fleet, C-in-C, 1st Southern Expeditionary Fleet
5 Feb 1945 - Sep 1945:	C-in-C, 10th Area Fleet

Rear-Admiral **Heizaburo FUKUYO** (18 Feb 1879 - 6 Feb 1952)

1 Dec 1923 - 1 Dec 1924:	Captain, Battleship *"Ise"*
1 Dec 1924:	Promoted to *Rear-Admiral*
1 Dec 1924 - 2 Mar 1925:	Attached to Kure Naval District
20 Mar 1925:	Transferred to the reserve

Rear-Admiral **Yasuo FUKUYOSHI** (1 Oct 1891 - 13 Jun 1945)

| 1 Sep 1944 - 13 Jun 1945: | Chief of Naha area Personnel Bureau |
| 13 Jun 1945: | Posthumously promoted to *Rear-Admiral* |

Rear-Admiral **Tetsushiro FUKUZAWA** (3 Mar 1886 - 2 Mar 1944)

| 25 May 1943 - 2 Mar 1944: | Commander of Minesweeping, *"Akashisan-maru"* |
| 2 Mar 1944: | Posthumously promoted to *Rear-Admiral* |

Rear-Admiral **Tsunekichi FUKUZAWA** (25 Sep 1892 - 30 Sep 1982)

25 Sep 1942 - 15 Jan 1943:	Attached to Chinkai Guard District
1 Nov 1942:	Promoted to *Rear-Admiral*
15 Jan 1943 - 12 Feb 1943:	Attached to Naval General Staff
12 Feb 1943 - 16 Feb 1943:	Attached to the staff, 4th Fleet

16 Feb 1943 - 1 Oct 1943:	Commander, 5th Naval Base Force
1 Oct 1943 - 10 Aug 1945:	Chief Supervisor for Construction & Ordnance, Naval Shipbuilding Command
10 Aug 1945 - 10 Oct 1945:	Korea area supervisor, Department of Military Supply

Vice-Admiral (Engineer) **Zenya FUNABASHI** (10 Jul 1866 - 14 Apr 1925)

1 Dec 1912:	Promoted to *Rear-Admiral*
1 Dec 1912 - 1 Apr 1916:	Chief Engineer, Kure Naval District
1 Apr 1916 - 1 Dec 1917:	Chief of Bureau 3, Naval Training Command
1 Dec 1917:	Promoted to *Vice-Admiral*
1 Dec 1917 - 1 Sep 1921:	Commandant, Naval Engineering Academy
1 Sep 1921 - 25 May 1923:	Chief of Naval Engineers, Department of the Navy
25 May 1923 - 1 Jun 1923:	Attached to Naval General Staff
1 Jun 1923 - 1 Jul 1923:	Unassigned
1 Jul 1923:	Transferred to the reserve

Rear-Admiral **Rentaro FUNAKI** (6 Jan 1856 - 20 Oct 1923)

6 Dec 1900 - 1 Oct 1901:	Captain, Battleship *"Fuji"*
1 Oct 1901 - 28 May 1902:	Unassigned
28 May 1902:	Promoted to *Rear-Admiral*, Transferred to the reserve

Vice-Admiral **Kajishiro FUNAKOSHI** (28 Aug 1870 - 29 Mar 1962)

13 Dec 1915:	Promoted to *Rear-Admiral*
13 Dec 1915 - 25 Dec 1915:	Attached to Naval General Staff
25 Dec 1915 - 1 Dec 1917:	Naval Attache, United Kingdom
1 Dec 1917 - 10 Jul 1918:	Supervisor for Construction & Ordnance, Naval Shipbuilding Command
10 Jul 1918 - 1 Dec 1918:	Chief of Staff, Yokosuka Naval District
1 Dec 1918 - 1 Dec 1919:	Chief of Staff, 1st Fleet
1 Jun 1919 - 1 Dec 1919:	Chief of Staff, Combined Fleet
1 Dec 1919:	Promoted to *Vice-Admiral*
1 Dec 1919 - 12 Jan 1920:	Commander, 2nd Expeditionary Fleet
12 Jan 1920 - 1 Jun 1920:	Member, Admirals Committee
1 Jun 1920 - 1 May 1921:	C-in-C, Training Fleet
1 May 1921 - 1 Sep 1921:	Member, Admirals Committee
1 Sep 1921 - 10 Jun 1922:	Commander, Yokosuka Navy Yard
10 Jun 1922 - 1 Sep 1922:	Unassigned
1 Sep 1922 - 1 Dec 1922:	Attached to Naval Shipbuilding Command
10 Dec 1922:	Transferred to the reserve

Vice-Admiral **Satoshi FURIHATA** (29 Mar 1885 - 1 Oct 1962)
20 Dec 1933 - 1 Dec 1936:	Commandant, Navy Communications School
15 Nov 1934:	Promoted to *Rear-Admiral*
1 Dec 1936 - 15 Nov 1938:	Chief of Bureau 4, Naval General Staff
20 Nov 1937 - 15 Nov 1938:	Chief of Communications Bureau, Joint General Staff
15 Nov 1938:	Promoted to *Vice-Admiral*
15 Nov 1938 - 15 Dec 1938:	Attached to Naval General Staff
15 Dec 1938 - 21 Dec 1938:	Unassigned
21 Dec 1938:	Transferred to the reserve
6 Oct 1941 - 10 Oct 1941:	Recalled; Attached to Yokosuka Naval District
10 Oct 1941 - 10 Mar 1943:	Commandant, Navy Communications School
10 Mar 1943 - 20 Mar 1943:	Attached to Naval General Staff
20 Mar 1943:	Demobilized

Vice-Admiral **Tatsuo FURUICHI** (15 Feb 1885 - 1 Feb 1966)
1 Dec 1931:	Promoted to *Rear-Admiral*
1 Dec 1931 - 1 Apr 1933:	Chief of Bureau 2, Naval Shipbuilding Command
1 Apr 1933 - 15 Nov 1935:	Chief of Bureau 3, Naval Shipbuilding Command
15 Nov 1935 - 1 Dec 1937:	Commander, Yokosuka Navy Yard
1 Dec 1936:	Promoted to *Vice-Admiral*
1 Dec 1937 - 15 Dec 1937:	Attached to Naval General Staff
21 Dec 1937:	Transferred to the reserve

Rear-Admiral **Bunji FURUKAWA** (12 Dec 1899 - 16 Jan 1944)
6 Dec 1943 - 16 Jan 1944:	Commander, 16th Destroyer Flotilla
16 Jan 1944:	Posthumously promoted to *Rear-Admiral*

Rear-Admiral **Hiroshi FURUKAWA** (13 Feb 1873 - ?)
1 Dec 1920:	Promoted to *Rear-Admiral*
1 Dec 1920 - 1 Aug 1922:	Commander, Kure Sailors Corps
1 Aug 1922 - 1 Dec 1922:	Attached to Yokosuka Naval District
1 Dec 1922 - 31 Mar 1923:	Unassigned
31 Mar 1923:	Transferred to the reserve

Rear-Admiral **Isami FURUKAWA** (16 Oct 1896 - 5 May 1946)
20 Jan 1944 - 20 Sep 1945:	Chief of Torpedo Bureau, Hikari Navy Yard
10 Jun 1944 - 25 Mar 1945:	Chief of Bomb Bureau, Hikari Navy Yard
1 May 1945:	Promoted to *Rear-Admiral*

Rear-Admiral (Paymaster) **Kaneyoshi FURUKAWA** (14 May 1901 - 8 Jul 1944)
20 Nov 1943 - 8 Jul 1944:	Paymaster-General, 4th Fleet
8 Jul 1944:	Posthumously promoted to *Rear-Admiral (Paymaster)*

Vice-Admiral **Shinzaburo FURUKAWA** (24 Oct 1872 - 1 Jan 1959)
1 Dec 1918 - 10 Jun 1919:	Chief of Staff, 3rd Fleet
1 Jun 1919:	Promoted to *Rear-Admiral*
10 Jun 1919 - 30 Mar 1920:	Chief of Staff, Yokosuka Naval District
30 Mar 1920 - 1 Dec 1920:	Unassigned
1 Dec 1920 - 1 Feb 1923:	Chief of Naval Personnel, Department of the Navy
1 Feb 1923 - 1 Apr 1923:	Attached to Naval General Staff
1 Apr 1923 - 10 Apr 1924:	Chief of Naval Training Bureau
1 Dec 1923:	Promoted to *Vice-Admiral*
10 Apr 1924 - 4 Oct 1924:	C-in-C, Training Fleet
4 Oct 1924 - 1 Jun 1925:	Attached to Naval General Staff
1 Jun 1925 - 10 Dec 1926:	Admiral Commanding, Maizuru Naval District
10 Dec 1926 - 10 Dec 1928:	Admiral Commanding, Sasebo Naval District
10 Dec 1928 - 15 Mar 1929:	Attached to Naval General Staff
25 Mar 1929:	Transferred to the reserve

Vice-Admiral **Shiro FURUKAWA** (4 Nov 1877 - 11 May 1958)
1 Dec 1923:	Promoted to *Rear-Admiral*
1 Dec 1923 - 1 Dec 1925:	Chief of Staff, Sasebo Naval District
1 Dec 1925 - 1 Dec 1926:	Commander, 3rd Escort Flotilla
1 Dec 1926 - 5 Apr 1927:	Chief of Bureau 2, Naval Shipbuilding Command
5 Apr 1927 - 1 Dec 1927:	Chief of Technical Bureau, Naval Air Command
1 Dec 1927:	Promoted to *Vice-Admiral*
1 Dec 1927 - 15 Dec 1927:	Attached to Naval General Staff
22 Dec 1927:	Transferred to the reserve

Rear-Admiral **Tamotsu FURUKAWA** (5 Sep 1894 - 25 Jan 1980)
16 Feb 1944 - 1 Sep 1944:	Commander, Kasumigaura Air Flotilla
1 May 1944:	Promoted to *Rear-Admiral*
1 Sep 1944 - 9 Sep 1944:	Attached to the staff, 1st Air Fleet
9 Sep 1944 - 15 May 1945:	Commander, 23rd Carrier Flotilla
15 May 1945 - 5 Aug 1945:	Attached to Yokosuka Naval District
5 Aug 1945 - 20 Oct 1945:	Chief of Transport Bureau, Chinkai Guard District

Rear-Admiral **Hiroshi FURUNO** (1 Apr 1897 - 26 Dec 1955)
3 Aug 1944 - 30 Sep 1945:	Chief of Aircraft Engine Bureau, Air Technical Arsenal
15 Oct 1944:	Promoted to *Rear-Admiral*

Vice-Admiral (Surgeon) **Tadao FUSEJIMA** (2 Apr 1884 - 18 Mar 1960)
1 Dec 1931:	Promoted to *Rear-Admiral (Surgeon)*
1 Dec 1931 - 15 Nov 1934:	Director, Sasebo Naval Hospital, Chief Medical Officer, Sasebo Naval District

15 Nov 1934 - 15 Nov 1935:	Director, Yokosuka Naval Hospital, Chief Medical Officer, Yokosuka Naval District
15 Nov 1935:	Promoted to *Vice-Admiral (Surgeon)*
15 Nov 1935 - 10 Dec 1935:	Attached to Naval General Staff
14 Dec 1935:	Transferred to the reserve

Fleet Admiral **Prince Hiroyasu FUSHIMI** (16 Oct 1875 - 16 Aug 1946)

31 Aug 1913:	Promoted to *Rear-Admiral*
31 Aug 1913 - 18 Aug 1914:	Commander, Yokosuka Naval District Fleet
18 Aug 1914 - 13 Dec 1915:	Commandant of the Naval College
13 Dec 1915 - 1 Dec 1916:	Commander, 2nd Escort Flotilla
1 Dec 1916:	Promoted to *Vice-Admiral*
1 Dec 1916 - 1 Dec 1919:	Member, Admirals Committee
1 Dec 1919 - 1 Dec 1920:	C-in-C, 2nd Fleet
1 Dec 1920 - 5 Feb 1924:	Navy Councillor
1 Dec 1922:	Promoted to *Admiral*
27 Oct 1923 - 9 Apr 1941:	Chairman, Supreme War Council
5 Feb 1924 - 15 Apr 1925:	Admiral Commanding, Sasebo Naval District
15 Apr 1925 - 2 Feb 1932:	Navy Councillor
2 Feb 1932 - 9 Apr 1941:	Chief of the Naval General Staff
27 May 1932:	Appointed *Fleet Admiral*

Rear-Admiral **Otomaru GEJO** (27 Sep 1861 - 28 Feb 1920)

28 Sep 1907 - 1 Dec 1910:	Chief of Bureau 3, Naval Training Command
28 Aug 1908:	Promoted to *Rear-Admiral*
1 Dec 1910 - 1 Dec 1911:	Commandant, Naval Engineering Academy
1 Dec 1911 - 1 Dec 1912:	Unassigned
1 Dec 1912:	Transferred to the reserve

Vice-Admiral **Takuo GODO** (23 Sep 1877 - 7 Apr 1956)

10 Jan 1921 - 11 Jun 1924:	Chief of Gunnery Bureau, Kure Navy Yard
1 Dec 1922:	Promoted to *Rear-Admiral*
11 Jun 1924 - 10 Dec 1928:	Commander, Kure Navy Yard
1 Dec 1926:	Promoted to *Vice-Admiral*
10 Dec 1928 - 27 Dec 1928:	Attached to Naval Shipbuilding Command
28 Dec 1928:	Transferred to the reserve
2 Feb 1937 - 4 Jun 1937:	Minister of Commerce and Industry / Minister of Railways
30 Aug 1939 - 16 Oct 1939:	Minister of Agriculture / Minister of Commerce and Industry
16 Oct 1939 - 16 Jan 1940:	Minister of Commerce and Industry

Vice-Admiral **Keijiro GOGA** (10 Apr 1889 - 8 Apr 1951)
15 Nov 1938: Promoted to *Rear-Admiral*
15 Nov 1938 - 15 Dec 1938: Attached to Naval General Staff
15 Dec 1938 - 15 Nov 1939: Commander, 1st Auxiliary Base Force
15 Nov 1939 - 15 Nov 1940: Chief of Torpedo Bureau, Kure Navy Yard
15 Nov 1940 - 15 Sep 1942: Chief of Bureau 2, Naval Shipbuilding Command
1 May 1942: Promoted to *Vice-Admiral*
15 Sep 1942 - 25 Sep 1942: Attached to the staff, Southwestern Area Fleet
25 Sep 1942 - 31 Sep 1943: Commander, 21st Base Force
13 Sep 1943 - 15 Dec 1943: Attached to Naval General Staff
20 Dec 1943: Transferred to the reserve
27 Dec 1943 - 1 Apr 1944: Recalled; Attached to the Bureau of Naval Affairs, Department of the Navy
1 Apr 1944 - 1 Nov 1944: Kanto area inspector, Department of Military Supply
1 Nov 1944 - 4 Nov 1944: Attached to Naval General Staff
4 Nov 1944 - Oct 1945: Commander, Kainan Guard District

Rear-Admiral **Mitsuru GOGA** (30 Sep 1885 - 8 Nov 1935)
15 Nov 1934: Promoted to *Rear-Admiral*
15 Nov 1934 - 8 Nov 1935: Instructor, Naval College

Rear-Admiral **Hiroshi GONDO** (25 Feb 1894 - 7 Apr 1975)
1 Aug 1942 - 15 Oct 1945: Chief of Bureau 1, Naval Facility Command
1 May 1943: Promoted to *Rear-Admiral*
15 May 1945 - 15 Oct 1945: Chief of Bureau 2, Naval Facility Command

Vice-Admiral **Shizuka GOSHO** (17 May 1888 - 14 Jul 1976)
1 Dec 1937: Promoted to *Rear-Admiral*
1 Dec 1937 - 15 Nov 1938: Chief of Shipping Bureau, Yokosuka Naval District
15 Nov 1938 - 15 Nov 1939: Chief of Supply Bureau, Sasebo Naval District
15 Nov 1939 - 10 Sep 1941: Commandant, Naval Engineering School
10 Sep 1941 - 1 May 1944: Commander, 3rd Navy Fuel Yard
15 Oct 1941: Promoted to *Vice-Admiral*
1 May 1944 - 10 May 1944: Attached to Naval General Staff
15 May 1944: Transferred to the reserve

Vice-Admiral **Akira GOTO** (24 Jan 1881 - 8 Jan 1956)
30 Nov 1929: Promoted to *Rear-Admiral*
30 Nov 1929 - 14 Oct 1930: Commander, 1st Destroyer Flotilla
14 Oct 1930 - 1 Dec 1930: Attached to Kure Naval District
1 Dec 1930 - 1 Dec 1931: Commander, 2nd Destroyer Flotilla
1 Dec 1931 - 1 Jan 1932: Attached to Naval General Staff

1 Jan 1932 - 16 Jun 1932:	Commander, Mako Guard District
16 Jun 1932 - 15 Nov 1933:	Chief of Naval Training Bureau, Department of the Navy
15 Nov 1933 - 15 Nov 1934:	Commander, 6th Division
15 Nov 1934:	Promoted to *Vice-Admiral*
15 Nov 1934 - 10 Dec 1934:	Attached to Naval General Staff
14 Dec 1934:	Transferred to the reserve

Vice-Admiral **Aritomo GOTO** (23 Jan 1888 - 12 Oct 1942)

15 Nov 1939:	Promoted to *Rear-Admiral*
15 Nov 1939 - 10 Sep 1941:	Commander, 2nd Destroyer Flotilla
10 Sep 1941 - 12 Oct 1942:	Commander, 6th Cruiser Division
12 Oct 1942:	Posthumously promoted to *Vice-Admiral*

Vice-Admiral **Eiji GOTO** (5 Nov 1887 - 24 Nov 1967)

1 Dec 1937:	Promoted to *Rear-Admiral*
1 Dec 1937 - 15 Nov 1938:	Commander, 5th Destroyer Flotilla
15 Nov 1938 - 15 Nov 1939:	Commander, 2nd Destroyer Flotilla
15 Nov 1939 - 28 Nov 1940:	Commander, 8th Division
28 Nov 1940 - 15 Mar 1941:	Attached to Yokosuka Naval District
15 Mar 1941 - 15 Apr 1941:	Attached to 11th Air Fleet
15 Apr 1941 - 1 Jun 1942:	Commander, 24th Air Flotilla
15 Oct 1941:	Promoted to *Vice-Admiral*
1 Jun 1942 - 15 Sep 1942:	Attached to Naval General Staff
15 Sep 1942 - 9 Sep 1944:	Commander, Chinkai Guard District
9 Sep 1944 - 15 Sep 1944:	Attached to Naval General Staff
15 Sep 1944 - 15 Mar 1945:	C-in-C, 12th Air Fleet
15 Sep 1944 - 5 Dec 1944:	C-in-C, Northeast Area Fleet
15 Feb 1945 - 15 Mar 1945:	Commander, Ominato Guard District
15 Mar 1945 - 15 May 1945:	Attached to Naval General Staff
21 May 1945:	Transferred to the reserve

Rear-Admiral **Kenzo GOTO** (15 Jun 1879 - 6 Feb 1937)

1 Apr 1923 - 1 Dec 1924:	Chief of Section 1, Engineering Bureau, Department of the Navy
1 Dec 1924:	Promoted to *Rear-Admiral*
1 Dec 1924 - 1 Jun 1925:	Attached to Naval General Staff
1 Jun 1925 - 16 Dec 1925:	Unassigned
16 Dec 1925:	Transferred to the reserve

Rear-Admiral (Surgeon) **Kosaburo GOTO** (18 Mar 1891 - 22 Jan 1973)

15 Nov 1939 - 5 Nov 1943:	Chief of Bureau 1, Sasebo Naval Hospital
1 Nov 1942:	Promoted to *Rear-Admiral (Surgeon)*

5 Nov 1943 - 14 Dec 1944:	Director, 102nd Naval Hospital
14 Dec 1944 - 1 Nov 1945:	Chief of the Medical Bureau, 11th Air Arsenal
20 Jan 1945 - 1 Nov 1945:	Chief of the Medical Bureau, Hiro Navy Yard

Rear-Admiral **Mitsutaro GOTO** (16 Apr 1897 - 24 Jul 1976)
10 Apr 1945 - 10 Jul 1945:	Chief of Staff, 7th Fleet,
	Chief of Staff, 1st Escort Fleet
1 May 1945:	Promoted to *Rear-Admiral*
10 Jul 1945 - 15 Sep 1945:	Deputy Chief of Staff, Maizuru Naval District
10 Jul 1945 - 25 Aug 1945:	Deputy Chief of Staff, 1st Escort Fleet
15 Sep 1945 - 30 Nov 1945:	Commander, Yokosuka Sailors Corps

Rear-Admiral **Shukichi GOTO** (7 Oct 1895 - 11 Jan 1966)
13 Aug 1944 - Oct 1945:	Commander, 30th Naval Facility
1 May 1945:	Promoted to *Rear-Admiral*

Vice-Admiral (Paymaster) **Hitoshi GYOBU** (14 Jun 1877 - ?)
18 Sep 1925 - 13 Apr 1927:	Paymaster-General, Yokosuka Naval District
1 Dec 1925:	Promoted to *Rear-Admiral (Paymaster)*
13 Apr 1927 - 1 Dec 1931:	Commandant, Naval Paymaster Academy
30 Nov 1929:	Promoted to *Vice-Admiral (Paymaster)*
1 Dec 1931 - 22 Mar 1922:	Attached to Naval General Staff
31 Mar 1922:	Transferred to the reserve

General (Paymaster) **Toru HACHISU** (3 Mar 1847 - 14 Oct 1917)
15 Jul 1898 - 7 Jul 1903:	Chief of Accounting Bureau,
	Yokosuka Naval District
20 May 1900:	Promoted to *General (Paymaster)*
7 Jul 1903 - 7 Jul 1906:	Unassigned
7 Jul 1906:	Transferred to the reserve

Rear-Admiral **Kanichi HAGIWARA** (12 Oct 1897 - 6 Feb 1944)
5 Feb 1944 - 6 Feb 1944:	Attached to the staff, 4th Fleet
6 Feb 1944:	Posthumously promoted to *Rear-Admiral*

Rear-Admiral **Kanshiro HAJI** (2 Oct 1870 - 12 May 1950)
20 Nov 1919 - 1 Dec 1919:	Attached to Kure Naval District
1 Dec 1919:	Promoted to *Rear-Admiral*
1 Dec 1919 - 1 Aug 1920:	Unassigned
1 Aug 1920:	Transferred to the reserve

Vice-Admiral **Kichijiro HAMADA** (11 Jan 1883 - 7 Mar 1967)
10 Oct 1931 - 15 Nov 1933:	Chief of Staff, Yokosuka Naval District

1 Dec 1931:	Promoted to *Rear-Admiral*
15 Nov 1933 - 15 Nov 1934:	Commander, 7th Escort Division
15 Nov 1934 - 15 Nov 1935:	Commander, Ryojun Guard District
15 Nov 1935:	Promoted to *Vice-Admiral*
15 Nov 1935 - 1 Dec 1936:	Commander, Manchuria Expeditionary Force
1 Dec 1936 - 15 Jan 1937:	Attached to Naval General Staff
25 Jan 1937:	Transferred to the reserve
13 Oct 1942 - 1 Feb 1944:	Naval Governor, New Guinea
1 Feb 1944 - 1 Dec 1944:	Naval Governor attached to 4th Southern Expeditionary Fleet

Rear-Admiral **Kiyoshi HAMADA** (16 Aug 1892 - 5 Dec 1962)

20 Jun 1942 - 27 Aug 1943:	Chief of Staff, 1st Southern Expeditionary Fleet
1 Nov 1942:	Promoted to *Rear-Admiral*
27 Aug 1943 - 15 Sep 1943:	Attached to Naval General Staff
15 Sep 1943 - 19 Dec 1944:	Commandant, Navigation School
19 Dec 1944 - 1 Jan 1945:	Attached to Naval General Staff
1 Jan 1945 - 5 Jul 1945:	Commander, 102nd Escort Flotilla
5 Jul 1945 - 25 Oct 1945:	Attached to Naval General Staff

Rear-Admiral **Kyoho HAMANAKA** (28 Aug 1893 - 23 Dec 1949)

1 Feb 1944 - 20 May 1944:	Chief, Manokwari Branch, 26th Construction Bureau
1 May 1944:	Promoted to *Rear-Admiral*
5 May 1944 - 29 Sep 1944:	Chief of Staff, 28th Auxiliary Base Force
29 Sep 1944 - 1 Dec 1944:	Attached to the staff, 4th Southern Expeditionary Fleet
1 Dec 1944 - Oct 1945:	Commander, 8th Guard Unit

Vice-Admiral **Eijiro HAMANO** (24 May 1880 - 2 Mar 1952)

1 Nov 1926 - 1 Dec 1927:	Chief of Bureau 2, Naval General Staff
1 Dec 1926:	Promoted to *Rear-Admiral*
1 Dec 1927 - 10 Dec 1928:	Chief of Staff, Combined Fleet, Chief of Staff, 1st Fleet
10 Dec 1928 - 1 Dec 1930:	Commander, Mako Guard District
1 Dec 1930 - 15 Dec 1931:	Attached to Naval General Staff
1 Dec 1931:	Promoted to *Vice-Admiral*
21 Dec 1931:	Transferred to the reserve

Rear-Admiral **Gunichi HAMANO** (8 Oct 1898 - 13 Jun 1945)

25 Aug 1944 - 13 Jun 1945:	Chief, Okinawa Branch, Bureau of Supply, Sasebo Naval District
13 Jun 1945:	Posthumously promoted to *Rear-Admiral*

Rear-Admiral **Tsutomu HAMANO** (30 Sep 1893 - 4 Mar 1957)
29 Apr 1940:	Promoted to *Rear-Admiral*
29 Apr 1940 - 15 Dec 1943:	Chief of Electronic Division, Air Technical Arsenal
15 Dec 1943 - 15 Feb 1945:	Attached to Technical Research Bureau
15 Feb 1945 - 30 Sep 1945:	Attached to 2nd Technical Arsenal

Rear-Admiral **Sukeshiro HANABUSA** (11 Sep 1866 - 15 Apr 1932)
1 Dec 1911:	Promoted to *Rear-Admiral*
1 Dec 1911 - 6 Dec 1911:	Chief of Staff, Ryojun Naval District
6 Dec 1911 - 31 Mar 1913:	Unassigned
31 Mar 1913:	Transferred to the reserve

Rear-Admiral **Taro HANABUSA** (19 Apr 1873 - 2 Aug 1932)
1 Sep 1921 - 1 Dec 1921:	Attached to Bureau 3, Naval General Staff
1 Dec 1921:	Promoted to *Rear-Admiral*
1 Dec 1921 - 31 Mar 1923:	Unassigned
31 Mar 1923:	Transferred to the reserve

Rear-Admiral **Masaaki HANADA** (10 Feb 1899 - 6 Feb 1989)
25 Feb 1945 - 30 Sep 1945:	Chief of Air Engineering Bureau, Tsy Navy Yard
1 May 1945:	Promoted to *Rear-Admiral*

Rear-Admiral **Yukitake HANADA** (4 May 1894 - 1 Jan 1954)
1 Oct 1943 - 10 Aug 1944:	Commander, Maizuru Guard Unit
1 May 1944:	Promoted to *Rear-Admiral*
10 Aug 1944 - 9 Sep 1944:	Attached to the staff, 2nd Southern Expeditionary Fleet
9 Sep 1944 - 10 Mar 1945:	Chief of Administration, Southwestern Area Fleet Civil Government
10 Mar 1945 - 5 Jul 1945:	Attached to Sasebo Naval District
5 Jul 1945 - 15 Sep 1945:	Chief of Transport Bureau, Yokosuka Naval District

Vice-Admiral **Koichi HANASHIMA** (18 Mar 1886 - 18 May 1965)
1 Apr 1932 - 15 Nov 1938:	Chief of Air Engineering Bureau, Air Arsenal
15 Nov 1934:	Promoted to *Rear-Admiral*
15 Nov 1938:	Promoted to *Vice-Admiral*
15 Nov 1938 - 1 Apr 1939:	Commander, Air Arsenal
1 Apr 1939 - 15 Nov 1939:	Commander, Air Technical Arsenal
15 Nov 1939 - 23 Dec 1939:	Attached to Naval General Staff
23 Dec 1939:	Transferred to the reserve

Rear-Admiral **Jiro HANEDA** (15 Mar 1897 - 13 Jun 1945)
15 Dec 1944 - 13 Jun 1945:	Attached to 951st Air Flotilla
13 Jun 1945:	Posthumously promoted to *Rear-Admiral*

Rear-Admiral **Rokuro HANI** (13 Apr 1885 - 15 Jun 1933)
28 Jun 1932 - 15 Jun 1933: Attached to Bureau 3, Naval General Staff
1 Dec 1932: Promoted to *Rear-Admiral*

Vice-Admiral **Chuichi HARA** (15 Mar 1889 - 17 Feb 1964)
15 Nov 1939: Promoted to *Rear-Admiral*
15 Nov 1939 - 13 Aug 1941: Chief of Staff, 2nd China Expeditionary Fleet
13 Aug 1941 - 1 Sep 1941: Commander, Detached Carrier Strike Force
1 Sep 1941 - 14 Jul 1942: Commander, 5th Carrier Division
14 Jul 1942 - 15 Mar 1943: Commander, 8th Cruiser Division
1 Nov 1942: Promoted to *Vice-Admiral*
15 Mar 1943 - 18 May 1943: Attached to Naval General Staff
18 May 1943 - 19 Feb 1944: Commander, Combined Training Air Units
19 Feb 1944 - 2 Sep 1944: C-in-C, 4th Fleet

Vice-Admiral **Goro HARA** (21 Jan 1886 - 31 Oct 1940)
15 Nov 1933: Promoted to *Rear-Admiral*
15 Nov 1933 - 1 May 1934: Supervisor for Construction & Ordnance, Naval Shipbuilding Command
1 May 1934 - 15 Nov 1935: Chief Supervisor for Construction & Ordnance, Naval Shipbuilding Command
15 Nov 1935 - 1 Dec 1936: Chief of Technical Bureau, Naval Air Command
1 Dec 1936 - 15 Nov 1938: Commander, Air Arsenal
1 Dec 1937: Promoted to *Vice-Admiral*
15 Nov 1938 - 15 Nov 1939: Commander, Mako Guard District
15 Nov 1939 - 1 Dec 1939: Commander, Maizuru Guard District
1 Dec 1939 - 15 Apr 1940: Admiral Commanding, Maizuru Naval District
15 Apr 1940 - 31 Oct 1940: Attached to Naval General Staff

Rear-Admiral (Surgeon) **Hayato HARA** (13 Feb 1889 - 21 Jul 1969)
20 May 1937 - 1 Dec 1939: Director, Maizuru Guard District Naval Hospital
15 Nov 1939: Promoted to *Rear-Admiral (Surgeon)*
1 Dec 1939 - 15 Nov 1940: Director, Maizuru Naval District Naval Hospital
15 Nov 1940 - 16 Dec 1940: Attached to Naval General Staff
21 Dec 1940: Transferred to the reserve

Vice-Admiral **Kanjiro HARA** (22 Nov 1880 - 26 Apr 1948)
10 Nov 1924 - 1 Dec 1925: Chief of Staff, Combined Fleet, Chief of Staff, 1st Fleet
1 Dec 1924: Promoted to *Rear-Admiral*
1 Dec 1925 - 1 Dec 1927: Chief of Bureau 1, Naval General Staff
1 Dec 1927 - 10 Dec 1928: Commander, 5th Escort Flotilla
10 Dec 1928: Promoted to *Vice-Admiral*

10 Dec 1928 - 1 Jul 1929:	Attached to Naval General Staff
1 Jul 1929 - 1 Dec 1930:	Commander, Chinkai Guard District
1 Dec 1930 - 20 Mar 1931:	Attached to Naval General Staff
31 Mar 1931:	Transferred to the reserve

Vice-Admiral **Keitaro HARA** (13 Oct 1885 - 13 Jan 1963)

1 Dec 1931:	Promoted to *Rear-Admiral*
1 Dec 1931 - 15 Nov 1934:	Commandant, Naval Gunnery School
15 Nov 1934 - 15 Nov 1935:	Commander, 6th Cruiser Division
15 Nov 1935:	Promoted to *Vice-Admiral*
15 Nov 1935 - 1 Jun 1936:	Commander, 1st Cruiser Division
1 Jun 1936 - 1 Dec 1936:	Commander, 3rd Cruiser Division
1 Dec 1936 - 1 Dec 1937:	Commander, Chinkai Guard District
1 Dec 1937 - 15 Mar 1938:	Attached to Naval General Staff
25 Mar 1938:	Transferred to the reserve

Vice-Admiral **Kenzaburo HARA** (15 Jul 1887 - 20 Sep 1971)

15 Nov 1939:	Promoted to *Rear-Admiral*
15 Nov 1939 - 15 Oct 1940:	Commander, Yokosuka Defense Force
15 Oct 1940 - 15 Nov 1940:	Attached to Maizuru Naval District
15 Nov 1940 - 10 Mar 1942:	Commander, 5th Destroyer Division
10 Mar 1942 - 3 Oct 1942:	Commander, 16th Cruiser Division
3 Oct 1942 - 15 Nov 1942:	Attached to Yokosuka Naval District
1 Nov 1942:	Promoted to *Vice-Admiral*
15 Nov 1942 - 15 Jan 1944:	Commander, Ryojun Area Base Force
15 Jan 1944 - 15 Mar 1944:	Attached to Naval General Staff
20 Mar 1944:	Transferred to the reserve

Vice-Admiral **Kiyoshi HARA** (2 May 1889 - 26 Aug 1976)

1 Dec 1936:	Promoted to *Rear-Admiral*
1 Dec 1936 - 25 Oct 1937:	Chief of Ordnance Bureau, Sasebo Navy Yard
25 Oct 1937 - 1 Jun 1938:	Director of the Transport Bureau, Planning Agency
1 Jun 1938 - 15 Nov 1939:	Attached to the Bureau of Naval Affairs, Department of the Navy
15 Nov 1939 - 5 Nov 1941:	Commander, Sasebo Navy Yard
15 Nov 1940:	Promoted to *Vice-Admiral*
5 Nov 1941 - 19 Dec 1941:	Attached to Naval General Staff
19 Dec 1941 - 14 Jul 1942:	Director of the Shipping Agency
14 Jul 1942 - 21 Jun 1943:	C-in-C, 2nd China Expeditionary Fleet
21 Jun 1943 - 6 Sep 1943:	Attached to Naval General Staff
10 Sep 1943:	Transferred to the reserve

Rear-Admiral **Sanekazu HARA**   (8 Mar 1950 - 23 Mar 1923)
28 Dec 1897 - 20 May 1900:   Commandant, Naval Engineer Training Center
20 May 1900 - 28 May 1902:   Unassigned
28 May 1902:   Promoted to *General (Engineer)*
28 May 1902:   Transferred to the reserve
26 Jan 1906:   Redesignated *Rear-Admiral*

Rear-Admiral **Seigo HARA**   (25 Sep 1865 - 12 Jan 1943)
17 Apr 1914 - 1 Dec 1916:   Commander, Yokosuka Harbor
1 Dec 1916:   Promoted to *Rear-Admiral*
1 Dec 1916 - 1 Dec 1917:   Unassigned
1 Dec 1917:   Transferred to the reserve

Rear-Admiral **Seitaro HARA**   (1 Sep 1884 - 29 May 1943)
26 Apr 1943 - 29 May 1943:   Captain, Seaplane Tender *"Kamikawa-maru"*
29 May 1943:   Posthumously promoted to *Rear-Admiral*

Rear-Admiral **Shigemasa HARA**   (28 Jan 1891 - 7 Jul 1970)
15 Apr 1942 - 1 Dec 1942:   Chief of Equipment Bureau, 21st Air Arsenal
1 May 1942:   Promoted to *Rear-Admiral*
1 Dec 1942 - 5 Apr 1943:   Commander, 1st Air Arsenal
5 Apr 1943 - 15 Apr 1943:   Attached to Naval Air Command
20 Apr 1943:   Transferred to the reserve

Vice-Admiral **Teizo HARA**   (6 Oct 1892 - 18 Jun 1946)
5 Mar 1941 - 30 Jan 1943:   Deputy Chief of Staff, China Area Fleet
15 Oct 1941:   Promoted to *Rear-Admiral*
30 Jan 1943 - 22 Feb 1943:   Attached to Naval General Staff
22 Feb 1943 - 1 Jun 1944:   Attached to the Bureau of Naval Affairs,
                             Department of the Navy
1 Nov 1943 - 1 Jun 1944:   Director of Planning Bureau, Department
                             of Transport & Communication
1 Jun 1944 - 15 Jun 1944:   Attached to Naval General Staff
15 Jun 1944 - 26 Jun 1944:   Attached to staff, 1st Southern Expeditionary Fleet
26 Jun 1944 - Oct 1945:   Commander, 12th Special Naval Base Force
15 Oct 1944:   Promoted to *Vice-Admiral*

Vice-Admiral (Paymaster) **Hiroshi HARADA** (10 Nov 1846 - 10 Apr 1921)
8 Oct 1897 - 2 Nov 1905:   Chief of Accounting Bureau, Kure Baval District
28 Dec 1897:   Promoted to *General (Paymaster)*
2 Nov 1905:   Promoted to *General (Paymaster), Senior grade*
2 Nov 1905 - 24 Feb 1907:   Unassigned
24 Feb 1907:   Transferred to the reserve
23 Sep 1919:   Redesignated *Vice-Admiral (Paymaster)*

Vice-Admiral **Kaku HARADA** (2 Oct 1890 - 25 Sep 1945)
20 Aug 1940 - 9 Jan 1943: Captain, Seaplane Tender *"Chiyoda"*
1 Nov 1942: Promoted to *Rear-Admiral*
9 Jan 1943 - 12 Jan 1943: Attached to Yokosuka Naval District
12 Jan 1943 - 4 Dec 1943: Commander, 7th Submarine Flotilla
4 Dec 1943 - 27 Dec 1943: Attached to Yokosuka Naval District
27 Dec 1943 - 5 Aug 1944: Commander, Yokosuka Defense Force
5 Aug 1944 - 25 Sep 1945: Commander, 33rd Naval Base Force
25 Sep 1945: Posthumously promoted to *Vice-Admiral*

Rear-Admiral **Kame HARADA** (28 Apr 1888 - 21 Feb 1944)
1 Mar 1943 - 21 Feb 1944: Commander, 24th Submarine Chaser Flotilla
21 Feb 1944: Posthumously promoted to *Rear-Admiral*

Vice-Admiral **Seiichi HARADA** (11 Jan 1890 - 20 Oct 1972)
15 Nov 1940: Promoted to *Rear-Admiral*
15 Nov 1940 - 15 Jul 1942: Chief of Naval Personnel, Sasebo Naval District
15 Jul 1942 - 1 Aug 1942: Attached to Naval General Staff
1 Aug 1942 - 1 Nov 1942: Chief, Communication Office, Asian Development Agency
1 Nov 1942 - Oct 1945: Commander, Amoi Area Base Force
1 May 1944: Promoted to *Vice-Admiral*

Rear-Admiral **Shosaku HARADA** (6 Oct 1874 - 6 Feb 1961)
1 Oct 1920 - 1 Nov 1921: Commander, Kure Harbor
1 Nov 1921 - 1 Dec 1921: Attached to Kure Naval District
1 Dec 1921: Promoted to *Rear-Admiral*
1 Dec 1921 - 31 Mar 1923: Unassigned
31 Mar 1923: Transferred to the reserve

General (Ordnance) **Sosuke HARADA** (9 Sep 1848 - 29 Sep 1909)
25 May 1897 - 20 May 1900: Commander, Tokyo Ordnance Arsenal
20 May 1900: Promoted to *General (Ordnance)*
20 May 1900 - 13 Dec 1901: Attached to Naval Shipbuilding Command
13 Dec 1901 - 18 Jul 1904: Unassigned
18 Jul 1904: Transferred to the reserve

Rear-Admiral **Fusataro HARAGUCHI** (10 Aug 1869 - 2 Feb 1936)
1 Dec 1916 - 1 Dec 1918: Commander, Sasebo Base Force
1 Dec 1918 - 1 Aug 1919: Unassigned
1 Aug 1919: Promoted to *Rear-Admiral*
1 Aug 1919: Transferred to the reserve

Rear-Admiral **Shinzaburo HASE** (28 Sep 1895 - 7 Apr 1985)
25 Apr 1943 - 25 Dec 1943:	Captain, Battleship *"Ise"*
1 Nov 1943:	Promoted to *Rear-Admiral*
25 Dec 1943 - 10 Jan 1944:	Attached to Naval General Staff
10 Jan 1944 - 24 Jan 1944:	Attached to staff, 4th Southern Expeditionary Fleet
24 Jan 1944 - 10 Jan 1945:	Commander, 25th Special Base Force
10 Jan 1945 - 19 Jan 1945:	Attached to staff, 2nd Southern Expeditionary Fleet
19 Jan 1945 - Oct 1945:	Chief of Staff, 2nd Southern Expeditionary Fleet

Rear-Admiral **Ryuzaburo HASEBE** (29 May 1892 - 5 Jan 1950)
21 Apr 1941 - 1 Nov 1942:	Chief of Production Bureau, 2nd Powder Yard
1 Nov 1942:	Promoted to *Rear-Admiral*
1 Nov 1942 - 10 Mar 1943:	Attached to Yokosuka Naval District
10 Mar 1943 - 30 Oct 1945:	Commander, 1st Powder Yard
1 Nov 1942:	Promoted to *Rear-Admiral*
1 Nov 1942 - 1 Sep 1943:	Attached to Naval Air Command
1 Sep 1943 - 1 Nov 1943:	Chief of Bureau 4, Naval Air Command
1 Nov 1943 - 15 Nov 1943:	Attached to Naval Air Command
15 Nov 1943 - 1 Jan 1944:	Commander, 50th Air Flotilla
1 Jan 1944 - 29 Mar 1944:	Commander, 22nd Air Flotilla
29 Mar 1944:	Posthumously promoted to *Vice-Admiral*

Admiral **Kiyoshi HASEGAWA** (7 May 1883 - 2 Sep 1970)
1 Dec 1927:	Promoted to *Rear-Admiral*
1 Dec 1927 - 30 Nov 1929:	Chief of Staff, Yokosuka Naval District
30 Nov 1929 - 1 Dec 1930:	Commander, 2nd Submarine Flotilla
1 Dec 1930 - 1 Dec 1931:	Chief of Bureau 5, Naval Shipbuilding Command
1 Dec 1931 - 10 Oct 1932:	Commander, Kure Navy Yard
10 Oct 1932 - 22 Oct 1932:	Attached to Naval General Staff
22 Oct 1932 - 25 Apr 1933:	Attached to the Plenipotentiary, Geneva Conference
1 Dec 1932:	Promoted to *Vice-Admiral*
25 Apr 1933 - 14 Feb 1934:	Plenipotentiary, Geneva Conference
14 Feb 1934 - 10 May 1934:	Attached to Naval General Staff
10 May 1934 - 1 Dec 1936:	Deputy Minister of the Navy
1 Dec 1936 - 25 Apr 1938:	C-in-C, 3rd Fleet
20 Oct 1937 - 25 Apr 1938:	C-in-C, China Area Fleet
25 Apr 1938 - 1 May 1940:	Admiral Commanding, Yokosuka Naval District, Member, Admirals Committee
1 Apr 1939:	Promoted to *Admiral*
1 May 1940 - 30 Nov 1945:	Navy Councillor
1 Jun 1945 - 30 Nov 1945:	Chairman, High Technical Committee

Rear-Admiral (Surgeon) **Seiichi HASEGAWA** (14 Feb 1895 - 12 Dec 1963)
20 Jan 1943 - 25 Mar 1944:	Director, 101st Naval Hospital
1 May 1943:	Promoted to *Rear-Admiral (Surgeon)*
25 Mar 1944 - 29 Nov 1945:	Attached to Yokosuka Naval District

Rear-Admiral **Yasutaka HASHIGUCHI** (28 Apr 1885 - 28 Mar 1948)
15 Nov 1935:	Promoted to *Rear-Admiral*
15 Nov 1935 - 28 Mar 1936:	Attached to Bureau 4, Naval Shipbuilding Command
30 Mar 1936:	Transferred to the reserve

Vice-Admiral **Baron Masaaki HASHIMOTO** (29 Dec 1853 - 31 Mar 1929)
24 May 1902:	Promoted to *Rear-Admiral*
24 May 1902 - 10 Nov 1903:	Chief of Shipping Bureau, Maizuru Naval District
10 Nov 1903 - 28 Dec 1903:	Commander, Maizuru Navy Yard
28 Dec 1903 - 13 Nov 1905:	Chief of Naval Personnel, Department of the Navy, Member, Admirals Committee
11 Feb 1904 - 20 Dec 1905:	Chief of Personnel Bureau, Joint General Staff, Member, Admirals Committee
13 Nov 1905:	Promoted to *Vice-Admiral*
20 Dec 1905 - 22 Nov 1906:	Commander, Mako Guard District
22 Nov 1906 - 28 Aug 1908:	Commander, Ryojun Guard District
28 Aug 1908 - 27 Aug 1909:	Unassigned
27 Aug 1909:	Transferred to the reserve

Rear-Admiral (Surgeon) **Masanao HASHIMOTO** (30 Mar 1880 - 1 May 1958)
1 Dec 1924 - 25 Sep 1926:	Director, Minato Naval Hospital
25 Sep 1926 - 1 Dec 1926:	Attached to Yokosuka Naval District
1 Dec 1926 - 25 Dec 1927:	Unassigned
1 Dec 1927:	Promoted to *Rear-Admiral (Surgeon)*
25 Dec 1927:	Transferred to the reserve

Rear-Admiral **Matakichiro HASHIMOTO** (15 Dec 1865 - 3 Jun 1928)
31 Jul 1912 - 3 Jun 1913:	Commander, Maizuru Harbor
3 Jun 1913 - 31 Mar 1914:	Unassigned
31 Mar 1914:	Promoted to *Rear-Admiral*
31 Mar 1914:	Transferred to the reserve

Rear-Admiral **Saisuke HASHIMOTO** (30 Jan 1883 - 8 Sep 1944)
1 Mar 1944 - 8 Sep 1944:	Supervisor for Construction, Naval Shipbuilding Command
8 Sep 1944:	Posthumously promoted to *Rear-Admiral*

Vice-Admiral **Shintaro HASHIMOTO** (11 May 1892 - 16 May 1945)
1 Sep 1941 - 12 Feb 1943:	Commander, 3rd Destroyer Flotilla
15 Oct 1941:	Promoted to *Rear-Admiral*
12 Feb 1943 - 15 Mar 1943:	Attached to Yokosuka Naval District
15 Mar 1943 - 25 Nov 1943:	Commandant, Torpedo School
25 Nov 1943 - 16 May 1945:	Commander, 5th Cruiser Flotilla

Rear-Admiral **Shozo HASHIMOTO** (31 Jan 1894 - 20 Aug 1973)
11 Jan 1943 - 27 Jul l944:	Chief of Staff, 3rd Southern Expeditionary Fleet
1 May 1943:	Promoted to *Rear-Admiral*
27 Jul 1944 - 7 Sep 1944:	Attached to Naval General Staff
7 Sep 1944 - 10 Sep 1944:	Attached to Kure Naval Department
10 Sep 1944 - 15 Oct 1945:	Chief of Staff, Kure Naval Department

Rear-Admiral **Uroku HASHIMOTO** (? - 25 Oct 1944)
1 Apr 1943 - 25 Oct 1944:	Executive Officer, Cruiser *"Mogami"*
25 Oct 1944:	Posthumously promoted to *Rear-Admiral*

Vice-Admiral **Koichiro HATAKEYAMA** (28 Jan 1889 - 15 Jan 1945)
15 Nov 1939:	Promoted to *Rear-Admiral*
15 Nov 1939 - 11 Aug 1941:	Commander, Kure Sailors Corps
11 Aug 1941 - 1 Sep 1941:	Attached to staff, China Area Fleet
1 Sep 1941 - 15 Jan 1942:	Commander, Amoi Area Base Force
15 Jan 1942 - 5 Feb 1942:	Commander, Ambon Island Invasion Force
5 Sep 1942 - 13 Mar 1943:	Commander 24th Naval Base Force
13 Mar 1943 - 25 May 1943:	Attached to Naval General Staff
1 May 1943:	Promoted to *Vice-Admiral*
25 May 1943 - 1 Jun 1943:	Attached to staff, China Area Fleet
1 Jun 1943 - 20 Mar 1944:	Commander, Shanghai Area Auxiliary Base Force, Commander, Shanghai Marine Force
20 Mar 1944 - 21 Nov 1944:	Commander, Yosuko Area Base Force
21 Nov 1944 - 6 Jan 1945:	Attached to Naval General Staff
6 Jan 1945 - 15 Jan 1945:	Attached to staff, China Area Fleet (KIA)

Vice-Admiral **Sadao HATAN** (21 May 1881 - 7 Jan 1942)
13 Aug 1923 - 10 Jun 1930:	Commander, Powder Yard
1 Dec 1923:	Promoted to *Rear-Admiral*
1 Dec 1927:	Promoted to *Vice-Admiral*
10 Jun 1930 - 25 Apr 1931:	Attached to Naval Shipbuilding Command
25 Apr 1931 - 22 Mar 1932:	Attached to Naval General Staff
31 Mat 1932:	Transferred to the reserve

Rear-Admiral **Katsuji HATTORI** (15 Mar 1895 - 16 Jun 1971)
15 Feb 1944 - 10 Jul 1944: Commander, Suzuka Air Flotilla
1 May 1944: Promoted to *Rear-Admiral*
10 Jul 1944 - 29 Sep 1944: Commander, Yokosuka Air Flotilla
29 Sep 1944 - 1 Mar 1945: Commander, 19th Combined Air Flotilla
1 Mar 1945 - 15 Nov 1945: Commander, Ominato Sailors Corps
10 Jul 1945 - 15 Nov 1945: Commander, Ominato Combined Marine Force

Rear-Admiral (Paymaster) **Kunimitsu HATTORI** (19 Oct 1876 - 19 Oct 1941)
1 Dec 1924 - 18 Sep 1925: Chief of Section 1, Accounting Bureau, Yokosuka Naval District
18 Sep 1925 - 1 Dec 1925: Attached to Naval General Staff
1 Dec 1925: Promoted to *Rear-Admiral (Paymaster)*
16 Dec 1925: Transferred to the reserve

Rear-Admiral **Masato HATTORI** (15 Mar 1883 - 27 Jul 1941)
1 Dec 1931: Promoted to *Rear-Admiral*
1 Dec 1931 - 15 Dec 1931: Attached to Naval Shipbuilding Command
21 Dec 1931: Transferred to the reserve

Rear-Admiral (Paymaster) **Masayuki HATTORI** (20 Nov 1878 - 8 Dec 1962)
20 Oct 1925 - 15 Mar 1927: Paymaster-General Sasebo Naval District
1 Dec 1925: Promoted to *Rear-Admiral (Paymaster)*
15 Mar 1927 - 20 Mar 1927: Attached to Naval General Staff
10 Apr 1927: Transferred to the reserve

Rear-Admiral (Surgeon) **Seiichi HATTORI** (12 Jul 1877 - 6 Mar 1945)
1 Dec 1922 - 1 Dec 1923: Chief of Bureau 1, Kure Naval Hospital
1 Dec 1923: Promoted to *Rear-Admiral (Surgeon)*
1 Dec 1923 - 10 Dec 1923: Attached to Kure Naval District
10 Dec 1923 - 25 Feb 1924: Unassigned
25 Feb 1924: Transferred to the reserve

Rear-Admiral **Kuraji HAYAKAWA** (30 Sep 1892 - 11 Feb 1990)
26 Aug 1941 - 25 Sep 1943: Chief of Submarine Bureau, Kure Navy Yard
1 Nov 1942: Promoted to *Rear-Admiral*
25 Sep 1943 - Oct 1945: Commander, 103rd Naval Facility, Supervisor for Construction & Ordnance, Naval Shipbuilding Command

Vice-Admiral **Mikio HAYAKAWA** (18 Apr 1894 - 11 Nov 1944)
1 Mar 1943 - 2 Aug 1943: Captain, Battleship *"Yamashiro"*
2 Aug 1943 - 15 Dec 1943: Captain, Battleship *"Nagato"*

1 Nov 1943:	Promoted to *Rear-Admiral*
15 Dec 1943 - 11 Nov 1944:	Commander, 2nd Destroyer Flotilla
11 Nov 1944:	Posthumously promoted to *Vice-Admiral*

Rear-Admiral (Paymaster) **Teikichi HAYAKAWA** (26 Apr 1891 - 8 Oct 1976)

15 Nov 1940 - 10 Jul 1943:	Chief of Section 3, Supply Bureau, Department of the Navy
1 May 1943:	Promoted to *Rear-Admiral (Paymaster)*
10 Jul 1943 - 1 Apr 1945:	Chief of Supply Bureau, Yokosuka Naval District
1 Apr 1945 - 29 Nov 1945:	Director, 1st Clothing & Food Depot

Rear-Admiral **Gengo HAYASAKI** (12 Dec 1853 - 20 Sep 1918)

1 May 1901 - 12 Jan 1903:	Captain, Battleship *"Mikasa"*
12 Jan 1903 - 4 Jun 1903:	Unassigned
4 Jun 1903:	Promoted to *Rear-Admiral*
4 Jun 1903:	Transferred to the reserve

Rear-Admiral **Hiroshi HAYASHI** (? - 27 May 1945)

20 Dec 1941 - 27 May 1945:	Commander, 54th Guard Unit
27 May 1945:	Posthumously promoted to *Rear-Admiral*

Rear-Admiral **Masao HAYASHI** (16 Jun 1880 - 27 Jul 1965)

10 May 1928 - 30 Nov 1929:	Supervisor for Ordnance, Naval Air Command
30 Nov 1929:	Promoted to *Rear-Admiral*
30 Nov 1929 - 15 Dec 1929:	Attached to Naval General Staff
15 Dec 1929:	Transferred to the reserve

Rear-Admiral **Shigechika HAYASHI** (1 Feb 1896 - 10 Apr 1968)

15 Oct 1944:	Promoted to *Rear-Admiral*
15 Oct 1944 - 30 Nov 1945:	Commander, Hario Sailors Corps
1 Mar 1945 - 15 Jul 1945:	Chief Instructor, Naval Academy
25 Sep 1945 - 30 Nov 1945:	Deputy Chief of Staff, Sasebo Naval District

Rear-Admiral **Shiro HAYASHI** (? - 7 Apr 1945)

1 Dec 1943 - 7 Apr 1945:	Chief Intendant, Battleship *"Yamato"*
7 Apr 1945:	Posthumously promoted to *Rear-Admiral*

Rear-Admiral (Paymaster) **Yoshiro HAYASHI** (22 Jun 1877 - 1 Feb 1944)

1 Oct 1920 - 1 Dec 1923:	Chief of Section 3, Bureau of Accounting, Department of the Navy
1 Dec 1923:	Promoted to *Rear-Admiral (Paymaster)*
1 Dec 1923 - 20 Dec 1923:	Attached to Naval General Staff
20 Dec 1923 - 25 Feb 1924:	Unassigned
25 Feb 1924:	Transferred to the reserve

Rear-Admiral **Tsuneo HAYASHIDA** (6 Jul 1888 - 26 Nov 1962)

5 Apr 1934 - 2 Dec 1935:	Chief of Engine Construction Bureau, Yokosuka Navy Yard
15 Nov 1934:	Promoted to *Rear-Admiral*
2 Dec 1935 - 1 Dec 1937:	Chief of Scientific Research Bureau, Technical Research
1 Dec 1937 - 15 Dec 1937:	Attached to Naval Shipbuilding Command
21 Dec 1937:	Transferred to the reserve

Vice-Admiral **Masaharu HIBINO** (2 Mar 1885 - 7 Mar 1947)

1 Dec 1932:	Promoted to *Rear-Admiral*
1 Dec 1932 - 15 Nov 1934:	Chief of Public Relations Bureau, Department of the Navy
15 Nov 1934 - 15 Nov 1935:	Commander, 1st Escort Flotilla
15 Nov 1935 - 2 Dec 1935:	Attached to Naval General Staff
2 Dec 1935 - 1 Dec 1936:	Commander, 11th Escort Flotilla
1 Dec 1936:	Promoted to *Vice-Admiral*
1 Dec 1936 - 1 Dec 1937:	Commander, Manchuria Expeditionary Force
1 Dec 1937 - 15 Nov 1938:	Director of the Naval College
15 Nov 1938 - 15 Nov 1939:	C-in-C, 4th Fleet
15 Nov 1939 - 15 Apr 1940:	Attached to Naval General Staff
15 Apr 1940 - 18 Sep 1941:	Admiral Commanding, Kure Naval District
18 Sep 1941 - 5 Jan 1942:	Navy Councillor
6 Jan 1942:	Transferred to the reserve

Rear-Admiral **Toraji HIDAI** (2 Dec 1886 - 5 Aug 1943)

10 Jan 1943 - 5 Aug 1943:	Chief of Traffic Control, 1st Maritime Escort Flotilla
5 Aug 1943:	Posthumously promoted to *Rear-Admiral*

Rear-Admiral **Kinji HIDAKA** (9 Mar 1877 - 16 Jan 1928)

25 Mar 1921 - 1 Dec 1922:	Attached to Naval General Staff
1 Dec 1922:	Promoted to *Rear-Admiral*
1 Dec 1922 - 31 Mar 1923:	Unassigned
31 Mar 1923:	Transferred to the reserve

Vice-Admiral **Koichi HIDAKA** (12 Apr 1887 - ?)

15 May 1929 - 1 Dec 1936:	Chief of Gunnery Bureau, Kure Navy Yard
15 Nov 1933:	Promoted to *Rear-Admiral*
1 Dec 1936 - 15 Nov 1939:	Director of Technical Research, Department of the Navy
1 Dec 1937:	Promoted to *Vice-Admiral*
15 Nov 1939 - 23 Dec 1939:	Attached to Naval Shipbuilding Command
3 Dec 1939:	Transferred to the reserve

Admiral **Baron Sonojo HIDAKA** (23 Mar 1848 - 24 Jul 1932)
25 Jul 1895 - 19 Jan 1899:	Director of the Naval Academy
5 Nov 1896:	Promoted to *Rear-Admiral*
19 Jan 1899 - 20 May 1900:	C-in-C, Readiness Fleet
20 May 1900:	Promoted to *Vice-Admiral*
20 May 1900 - 26 Jul 1902:	Commander, Takeshiki Guard District
26 Jul 1902 - 19 Oct 1903:	C-in-C, Readiness Fleet
19 Oct 1903 - 28 Aug 1908:	Admiral Commanding, Maizuru Naval District
7 Aug 1908:	Promoted to *Admiral*
28 Aug 1908 - 27 Aug 1909:	Unassigned
27 Aug 1909:	Transferred to the reserve

Rear-Admiral **Tamenori HIDAKA** (20 Feb 1894 - 11 Aug 1891)
20 Mar 1943 - 25 Sep 1943:	Chief Engineer, Yokosuka Naval District
1 May 1943:	Promoted to *Rear-Admiral*
25 Sep 1943 - 1 Oct 1944:	Chief Instructor, Naval Engineer Academy
1 Oct 1944 - 1 Oct 1945:	Commandant, Naval Engineer Academy

Rear-Admiral (Engineer) **Kumaroku HIDEJIMA** (18 Mar 1865 - 19 Oct 1934)
1 Dec 1912 - 1 Dec 1913:	Chief Engineer, 2nd Fleet
1 Dec 1913 - 13 Dec 1915:	Chief Engineer, 1st Fleet
1 Dec 1914:	Promoted to *Rear-Admiral*
1 Nov 1915 - 13 Dec 1915:	Chief Engineer, Combined Fleet
13 Dec 1915 - 1 Dec 1916:	Unassigned
1 Dec 1916:	Transferred to the reserve

Rear-Admiral **Shichisaburo HIDEJIMA** (14 Sep 1865 - 18 Jan 1936)
1 Dec 1911 - 1 Dec 1912:	Commander, Sasebo Torpedo Corps
1 Dec 1912:	Promoted to *Rear-Admiral*
1 Dec 1912 - 31 May 1913:	Unassigned
31 May 1913:	Transferred to the reserve

Rear-Admiral **Shigetada HIDEJIMA** (23 Nov 1865 - 2 Jul 1948)
18 Jun 1912 - 29 May 1914:	Naval Chief of Staff, Taiwan Government
29 May 1914:	Promoted to *Rear-Admiral*
29 May 1914 - 27 May 1915:	Unassigned
27 May 1915:	Transferred to the reserve

Fleet Admiral **Prince Yorihito HIGASHIFUSHIMI** (19 Sep 1867 - 27 Jun 1922)
24 Dec 1906 - 1 Dec 1912:	Attached to Naval General Staff
1 Dec 1909:	Promoted to *Rear-Admiral*
1 Dec 1912 - 1 Apr 1913:	Commander, Yokosuka Reserve Fleet
1 Apr 1913 - 31 Aug 1913:	Commander, Yokosuka Naval District Fleet

31 Aug 1913:	Promoted to *Vice-Admiral*
31 Aug 1913 - 1 Dec 1917:	Member, Admirals Committee
1 Dec 1916 - 1 Dec 1917:	Admiral Commanding, Yokosuka Naval District
1 Dec 1917 - 13 Jun 1918:	C-in-C, 2nd Fleet
13 Jun 1918 - 2 Jul 1918:	Member, Admirals Committee
2 Jul 1918:	Promoted to *Admiral*
2 Jul 1918 - 27 Jun 1922:	Navy Councillor
27 Jun 1922:	Posthumously appointed *Fleet Admiral*

Rear-Admiral **Ko HIGUCHI** (? - 25 Oct 1944)

1 Oct 1944 - 25 Oct 1944:	Commander, Kofuji Air Flotilla
25 Oct 1944:	Posthumously promoted to *Rear-Admiral*

Vice-Admiral **Shuichiro HIGUCHI** (18 Jan 1888 - 24 Nov 1949)

1 Dec 1937:	Promoted to *Rear-Admiral*
1 Dec 1937 - 15 Nov 1938:	Commander, Kure Defense Flotilla
15 Nov 1938 - 10 Mar 1939:	Attached to Naval General Staff
10 Mar 1939 - 1 Nov 1939:	Attached to Kure Naval District
1 Nov 1939 - 15 Nov 1939:	Attached to staff, 3rd Fleet
15 Nov 1939 - 15 Nov 1940:	Commander, Shanghai Area Auxiliary Base Force
15 Nov 1940 - 15 Jan 1941:	Attached to Naval General Staff
15 Jan 1941 - 10 Apr 1941:	Commander, 5th Auxiliary Base Force
10 Apr 1941 - 5 Jul 1941:	Attached to Naval General Staff
5 Jul 1941 - 15 Sep 1943:	Commandant, Submarine School
15 Oct 1941:	Promoted to *Vice-Admiral*
15 Sep 1943 - 25 Jan 1944:	Attached to Naval General Staff
31 Jan 1944:	Transferred to the reserve

Rear-Admiral **Teiji HIGUCHI** (29 Sep 1901 - 18 Jul 1945)

15 Jun 1945 - 18 Jul 1945:	Executive Officer, Battleship *"Nagato"*
18 Jul 1945:	Posthumously promoted to *Rear-Admiral*

Rear-Admiral (Judge) **Yoshikane HIGUCHI** (23 Sep 1890 - 27 Aug 1986)

1 Nov 1942 - 1 Nov 1944:	Chief Judge, Sasebo Naval District
1 Nov 1943:	Promoted to *Rear-Admiral (Judge)*
1 Nov 1944 - 20 Nov 1945:	Chief Judge, Kure Naval District

Rear-Admiral **Toshiu HIGURASHI** (19 Aug 1886 - 21 Apr 1946)

1 Dec 1932 - 15 Nov 1934:	Commandant, Torpedo School
1 Dec 1932 - 20 Dec 1933:	Commandant, Naval Communications School
15 Nov 1933:	Promoted to *Rear-Admiral*
15 Nov 1934 - 15 Nov 1935:	Commander, 2nd Destroyer Flotilla
15 Nov 1935 - 1 Dec 1936:	Commander, Kure Guard Squadron

1 Dec 1936 - 16 Jan 1937:	Attached to Naval General Staff
25 Jan 1937:	Transferred to the reserve

Rear-Admiral (Surgeon) **Yoshiyuki HIKI** (4 Feb 1884 - 17 Jan 1958)
15 Nov 1934 - 15 Dec 1937:	Chief of Medical Bureau, Kure Navy Yard
15 Nov 1935:	Promoted to *Rear-Admiral (Surgeon)*
21 Dec 1937:	Transferred to the reserve

Rear-Admiral **Kiyoshi HIO** (11 Feb 1889 - 5 Apr 1972)
15 Nov 1938:	Promoted to *Rear-Admiral*
15 Nov 1938 - 15 Oct 1941:	Chief of Shipping Bureau, Kure Naval District
15 Oct 1941 - 15 Dec 1941:	Attached to Naval General Staff
22 Dec 1941:	Transferred to the reserve

Rear-Admiral **Nagaaki HIOKA** (7 Feb 1894 - ?)
18 Aug 1943 - 20 Sep 1944:	Chief of Facility Bureau, Ominato
1 Sep 1943:	Promoted to *Rear-Admiral*
20 Sep 1944 - 7 Sep 1945:	Chief of Facility Bureau, Yokosuka
7 Sep 1945 - 30 Sep 1945:	Attached to Naval Facility Command

Rear-Admiral (Engineer) **Teiichi HIRABE** (11 Nov 1865 - 4 Oct 1928)
1 Dec 1911:	Promoted to *Rear-Admiral (Engineer)*
1 Dec 1911 - 1 Dec 1912:	Chief Engineer, Sasebo Naval District
1 Dec 1912 - 31 May 1913:	Unassigned
31 May 1913:	Transferred to the reserve

Rear-Admiral **Tokutaro HIRAGA** (6 Jan 1871 - 13 May 1919)
1 Aug 1916 - 19 Mar 1917:	Chief of Staff, 3rd Fleet
1 Dec 1916:	Promoted to *Rear-Admiral*
19 Mar 1917 - 30 May 1917:	Unassigned
30 May 1917 - 10 Nov 1918:	Chief of Bureau 1, Naval Training Command
10 Nov 1918 - 13 May 1919:	Unassigned

Vice-Admiral **Baron Dr. Yuzuru HIRAGA** (8 Mar 1878 - 17 Feb 1943)
1 Jun 1922:	Promoted to *Rear-Admiral*
1 Jun 1922 - 3 Jun 1925:	Attached to Naval Shipbuilding Command
3 Jun 1925 - 1 Nov 1926:	Chief of Shipbuilding Research Bureau, Department of the Navy
7 Dec 1925 - 1 Dec 1930:	Director, Naval Technical Research Laboratory
1 Dec 1926:	Promoted to *Vice-Admiral*
1 Dec 1930 - 20 Mar 1931:	Attached to Naval Shipbuilding Command
31 Mar 1931:	Transferred to the reserve

Vice-Admiral (Paymaster) **Hiroshi HIRAI** (29 Mar 1886 - ?)
15 Nov 1935:	Promoted to *Rear-Admiral (Paymaster)*
15 Nov 1935 - 1 Dec 1936:	Paymaster-General, Kure Navy Yard
1 Dec 1936 - 12 Apr 1939:	Paymaster-General, Kure Naval District
12 Apr 1939 - 15 Nov 1939:	Paymaster-General, Yokosuka Naval District
15 Nov 1939:	Promoted to *Vice-Admiral (Paymaster)*
15 Nov 1939 - 15 Dec 1939:	Attached to Naval General Staff
21 Dec 1939:	Transferred to the reserve

Rear-Admiral **Masahira HIRAI** (16 Feb 1897 - 3 Apr 1954)
1 Mar 1945 - 5 Aug 1945:	Chief of Section 1, Bureau 5, Naval Air Command, Chief of Section 1, Bureau 3, Naval Shipbuilding Command
1 May 1945:	Promoted to *Rear-Admiral*
5 Aug 1945 - 30 Nov 1945:	Chief of Administration Bureau, Kure Navy Yard

Rear-Admiral **Taiji HIRAI** (2 May 1893 - 20 Jun 1944)
5 May 1944 - 20 Jun 1944:	Commander, 30th Navy Harbor
20 Jun 1944:	Promoted to *Rear-Admiral*

Rear-Admiral **Hideo HIRAIDE** (9 Feb 1896 - 15 Dec 1948)
28 Dec 1943 - 25 Nov 1944:	Naval Attache, Philippines
1 May 1944:	Promoted to *Rear-Admiral*
15 Aug 1944 - 25 Nov 1944:	Deputy Chief of Staff, Southwest Area Fleet
25 Nov 1944 - 10 Aug 1945:	Attached to Naval General Staff
10 Aug 1945 - 15 Sep 1945:	Chief of Section 3, Hokkai area supervisory office, Department of Military Supply

Rear-Admiral **Motoo HIRAIWA** (14 Dec 1882 - 15 Mar 1934)
5 Aug 1919 - 10 Nov 1922:	Supervisor for Construction & Ordnance, Naval Shipbuilding Command
10 Nov 1922 - 1 Dec 1922:	Attached to Naval Shipbuilding Command
1 Dec 1922:	Promoted to *Rear-Admiral*
1 Dec 1922 - 31 Mar 1923:	Unassigned
31 Mar 1923:	Transferred to the reserve

Vice-Admiral (Surgeon) **Isamu HIRANO** (28 Feb 1870 - 24 Mar 1941)
1 Dec 1919:	Promoted to *Rear-Admiral (Surgeon)*
1 Dec 1919 - 1 Dec 1921:	Director, Sasebo Naval Hospital, Chief Surgeon, Sasebo Naval District
1 Dec 1921 - 1 Dec 1923:	Director, Yokosuka Naval Hospital, Chief Surgeon, Yokosuka Naval District
1 Dec 1923:	Promoted to *Vice-Admiral (Surgeon)*

1 Dec 1923 - 1 Dec 1925:	Chief of Naval Medical Service
1 Dec 1925 - 5 Dec 1925:	Attached to Naval General Staff
16 Dec 1925:	Transferred to the reserve

Rear-Admiral **Fukusaburo HIRAO** (18 Sep 1852 - 31 May 1917)

1 Feb 1899 - 20 May 1900:	Chief of Harbor Bureau, Sasebo Naval District
20 May 1900 - 28 May 1902:	Unassigned
29 May 1902:	Promoted to *Rear-Admiral*
28 May 1902:	Transferred to the reserve

Rear-Admiral **Matsuo HIRAO** (18 Dec 1896 - 31 Oct 1988)

1 Apr 1944 - 15 Oct 1945:	Chief of 1st Ordnance Bureau, Maizuru Navy Yard
1 May 1945:	Promoted to *Rear-Admiral*

Vice-Admiral **Iwao HIRAOKA** (10 Mar 1886 - 28 Mar 1965)

23 Jul 1934 - 15 Nov 1935:	Chief of Electronic Research Bureau, Technical Research Department
15 Nov 1934:	Promoted to *Rear-Admiral*
15 Nov 1935 - 15 Nov 1938:	Chief of Bureau 3, Naval Shipbuilding Command
15 Nov 1938:	Promoted to *Vice-Admiral*
15 Nov 1938 - 20 Nov 1941:	Commandant, Naval Engineering Academy
20 Nov 1941 - 14 Mar 1942:	Attached to Naval General Staff
20 Mar 1942:	Transferred to the reserve

Vice-Admiral **Kumeichi HIRAOKA** (5 Mar 1889 - ?)

15 Nov 1939:	Promoted to *Rear-Admiral*
15 Nov 1939 - 15 Oct 1940:	Attached to Naval General Staff
15 Oct 1940 - 10 Apr 1941:	Commander, Yokosuka Defense Squadron
10 Apr 1941 - 1 May 1941:	Attached to staff, China Area Fleet
1 May 1941 - 15 Sep 1941:	Commander, Shanghai Area Auxiliary Base Force
15 Sep 1941 - 31 Oct 1941:	Attached to Kure Naval District
31 Oct 1941 - 22 Feb 1944:	Commander, 9th Naval Base Force
1 May 1943:	Promoted to *Vice-Admiral*
22 Feb 1944 - 15 Mar 1944:	Attached to Naval General Staff
20 Mar 1944:	Transferred to the reserve

Rear-Admiral **Sadaichi HIRAOKA** (3 Feb 1868 - 5 Jan 1946)

18 Aug 1914 - 13 Dec 1915:	Chief of Ordnance Bureau, Sasebo Navy Yard
1 Dec 1914:	Promoted to *Rear-Admiral*
13 Dec 1915 - 1 Dec 1917:	Chief of Ordnance Bureau, Yokosuka Navy Yard
1 Dec 1917 - 1 Dec 1918:	Unassigned
1 Dec 1918:	Transferred to the reserve

Vice-Admiral **Noboru HIRATA** (1 Dec 1885 - 19 May 1958)
15 Nov 1933: Promoted to *Rear-Admiral*
15 Nov 1933 - 25 May 1935: Commander, 1st Submarine Flotilla
25 May 1935 - 5 Jun 1935: Attached to Naval General Staff
5 Jun 1935 - 15 Nov 1939: Aide-de-Camp to the Emperor
1 Dec 1937: Promoted to *Vice-Admiral*
15 Nov 1939 - 15 Oct 1940: Admiral Commanding, Sasebo Naval District
15 Oct 1940 - 15 Nov 1940: Attached to Naval General Staff
15 Nov 1940 - 21 Jul 1941: C-in-C, 6th (Submarine) Fleet
21 Jul 1941 - 31 Jul 1941: Attached to Naval General Staff
31 Jul 1941 - 18 Oct 1941: C-in-C, Southern Expeditionary Fleet
18 Oct 1941 - 1 Nov 1942: Admiral Commanding, Yokosuka Naval District, Member, Admirals Committee
1 Nov 1942 - 15 Mar 1943: Navy Councillor
20 Mar 1943: Transferred to the reserve

Rear-Admiral **Shuji HIRATA** (10 Jan 1892 - 3 Feb 1946)
1 Dec 1937 - 15 Nov 1939: Supervisor for Construction & Ordnance, Naval Shipbuilding Command, Supervisor for Ordnance, Naval Air Command
15 Nov 1939: Promoted to *Rear-Admiral*
15 Nov 1939 - 15 Dec 1939: Attached to Naval General Staff
21 Dec 1939: Transferred to the reserve

Rear-Admiral **Tsutomu HIRATA** (6 Nov 1899 - 25 Oct 1944)
15 Sep 1943 - 25 Oct 1944: Executive Officer, Battleship *"Fuso"*
25 Oct 1944: Posthumously promoted to *Rear-Admiral*

Rear-Admiral **Yoshiyuki HIRATA** (30 Dec 1888 - 21 Nov 1943)
25 May 1943 - 21 Nov 1943: Commander of Minesweepers, Transport *"Nichii-maru"*
21 Nov 1943: Posthumously promoted to *Rear-Admiral*

Vice-Admiral (Engineer) **Tamotsu HIRATSUKA** (25 Aug 1870 - 16 Apr 1926)
14 Oct 1916 - 1 Dec 1917: Chief Engineer, 1st Fleet
1 Dec 1916: Promoted to *Rear-Admiral (Engineer)*
1 Oct 1917 - 1 Dec 1917: Chief Engineer, Combined Fleet
1 Dec 1917 - 1 Dec 1920: Chief of Bureau 3, Naval Training Command
1 Dec 1920 - 1 Sep 1921: Commander, Maizuru Navy Yard
1 Sep 1921 - 25 May 1923: Commandant, Naval Engineering Academy
1 Dec 1921: Promoted to *Vice-Admiral (Engineer)*
25 May 1923 - 20 Dec 1924: Chief of Naval Engineers
20 Dec 1924 - 1 Aug 1925: Chief of Supply Bureau

1 Aug 1925 - 20 Oct 1925:	Attached to Naval General Staff
20 Oct 1925 - 16 Dec 1925:	Unassigned
16 Dec 1925:	Transferred to the reserve

Grand Marshal Emperor **HIROHITO** (Showa) (29 Apr 1901 - 7 Jan 1989)

25 Dec 1926 - 15 Aug 1945:	Supreme Commander-in-Chief of the Armed Forces

Rear-Admiral (Surgeon) **Wataru HIROKAWA** (16 Jan 1902 - 17 Mar 1945)

1 May 1944 - 24 Feb 1945:	Director, 104th Naval Hospital
24 Feb 1945 - 17 Mar 1945:	Attached to Kure Naval District
17 Mar 1945:	Posthumously promoted to *Rear-Admiral (Surgeon)*

Rear-Admiral **Juntaro HIROSE** (14 Jun 1868 - 26 Aug 1949)

11 Nov 1914 - 13 Dec 1915:	Acting Commander, Seito Base Force
13 Dec 1915:	Promoted to *Rear-Admiral*
13 Dec 1915 - 1 Dec 1916:	Unassigned
1 Dec 1916:	Transferred to the reserve

Rear-Admiral **Katsuhiko HIROSE** (27 Aug 1862 - 20 Oct 1920)

15 Sep 1908 - 1 Dec 1910:	Captain, Battlecruiser *"Tsukuba"*
1 Dec 1910 - 1 Dec 1911:	Unassigned
12 Apr 1911:	Promoted to *Rear-Admiral*
1 Dec 1911:	Transferred to the reserve

Rear-Admiral **Koki HIROSE** (5 Sep 1867 - 22 Jul 1944)

27 Oct 1914 - 1 Dec 1916:	Technical Inspector, Kure Navy Yard
1 Dec 1916:	Promoted to *Rear-Admiral*
1 Dec 1916 - 1 Dec 1917:	Unassigned
1 Dec 1917:	Transferred to the reserve

Vice-Admiral **Masatsune HIROSE** (15 Mar 1887 - 28 Jun 1953)

15 Nov 1935:	Promoted to *Rear-Admiral*
15 Nov 1935 - 15 Nov 1938:	Chief of Scientific Bureau, Air Arsenal
15 Nov 1938 - 15 Nov 1939:	Chief of Aircraft Bureau, Air Arsenal
15 Nov 1939:	Promoted to *Vice-Admiral*
15 Nov 1939 - 1 Oct 1940:	Commander, Hiro Navy Yard
1 Oct 1940 - 16 Dec 1940:	Attached to Naval General Staff
21 Dec 1940:	Transferred to the reserve

Vice-Admiral **Sueto HIROSE** (11 Nov 1888 - 9 Aug 1968)

15 Jan 1941 - 10 Mar 1942:	Commander, 2nd Auxiliary Base Force
15 Oct 1941:	Promoted to *Rear-Admiral*

10 Mar 1942 - 20 Oct 1942:	Commander, 22nd Naval Base Force
20 Oct 1942 - 15 Nov 1942:	Attached to Yokosuka Naval District
15 Nov 1942 - 5 Feb 1944:	Commander, Sasebo Defense Squadron
5 Feb 1944 - 22 Mar 1944:	Attached to staff, 1st Southern Expeditionary Fleet
22 Mar 1944 - Oct 1945:	Commander, 9th Naval Base Force
1 May 1945:	Promoted to *Vice-Admiral*

Rear-Admiral **Tozo HIROSE** (15 Dec 1895 - 7 Jun 1950)

1 Feb 1944 - 20 Sep 1945:	Chief of Submarine Bureau, Sasebo Naval District
1 May 1945:	Promoted to *Rear-Admiral*
20 Sep 1945 - 30 Nov 1945:	Chief of Supply Bureau, Sasebo Naval District

Rear-Admiral **Minoru HIROTA** (16 Jun 1884 - 4 Jun 1948)

1 Nov 1929 - 1 Dec 1930:	Chief of Supply Bureau, Kure Naval District
30 Nov 1929:	Promoted to *Rear-Admiral*
1 Dec 1930 - 15 Dec 1930:	Attached to Naval General Staff
24 Dec 1930:	Transferred to the reserve

Rear-Admiral **Ichiro HISAE** (5 Apr 1891 - 24 Jul 1987)

15 Oct 1940 - 15 Jul 1942:	Chief of Section 1, Supply Bureau, Department of the Navy
1 May 1942:	Promoted to *Rear-Admiral*
15 Jul 1942 - 20 Oct 1945:	Chief of Personnel Bureau, Sasebo Naval District

Rear-Admiral **Fukumatsu HISAHARA** (13 Oct 1882 - 24 Dec 1955)

30 Sep 1929 - 15 Nov 1932:	Chief of Administration Bureau, Sasebo Navy Yard
15 Nov 1932 - 15 Nov 1933:	Attached to Sasebo Naval District
15 Nov 1933:	Promoted to *Rear-Admiral*
15 Nov 1933 - 11 Dec 1933:	Attached to Naval General Staff
15 Dec 1933:	Transferred to the reserve

Rear-Admiral **Yonejiro HISAMUNE** (15 Feb 1892 - 4 Feb 1960)

2 Aug 1943 - 25 Dec 1943:	Captain, Battleship *"Yamashiro"*
1 Nov 1943:	Promoted to *Rear-Admiral*
25 Dec 1943 - 21 Dec 1944:	Commander, 22nd Escort Flotilla
21 Dec 1944 - 25 Dec 1944:	Attached to staff of 1st Escort Fleet
25 Dec 1944 - 20 Jan 1945:	Commander, 5th Convoy HQ
20 Jan 1945 - 15 Sep 1945:	Commander, 103rd Escort Flotilla

Vice-Admiral (Paymaster) **Takumi HISANO** (10 Nov 1874 - 3 Jun 1960)

1 Dec 1916 - 10 Aug 1920:	Chief of Section 1, Accounting Bureau, Department of the Navy
1 Dec 1919:	Promoted to *Rear-Admiral (Paymaster)*

10 Aug 1920 - 10 Nov 1922:	Paymaster-General, Maizuru Naval District
10 Nov 1922 - 1 Dec 1923:	Paymaster-General, Yokosuka Naval District
1 Dec 1923:	Promoted to *Vice-Admiral (Paymaster)*
1 Dec 1923 - 10 Dec 1923:	Attached to Naval General Staff
10 Dec 1923 - 12 Jan 1924:	Unassigned
12 Jan 1924:	Transferred to the reserve

Vice-Admiral (Paymaster) **Kaizo HISATAKE** (29 Aug 1888 - 11 Dec 1954)

15 Nov 1938:	Promoted to *Rear-Admiral (Paymaster)*
15 Nov 1938 - 15 Oct 1941:	Chief of Accounting Bureau, Kure Navy Yard
15 Oct 1941 - 1 Nov 1942:	Paymaster-General, Yokosuka Naval District
1 Nov 1942:	Promoted to *Vice-Admiral (Paymaster)*
1 Nov 1942 - 15 Dec 1942:	Attached to Naval General Staff
21 Dec 1942:	Transferred to the reserve

Vice-Admiral **Mansaburo HISHIKAWA** (1 Sep 1888 - 13 Jan 1973)

1 Dec 1936:	Promoted to *Rear-Admiral*
1 Dec 1936 - 15 Nov 1939:	Attached to Bureau 1, Naval Shipbuilding Command
15 Nov 1939 - 15 Nov 1940:	Chief of Gunnery Bureau, Kure Navy Yard
15 Nov 1940:	Promoted to *Vice-Admiral*
15 Nov 1940 - 1 Apr 1942:	Attached to Naval Shipbuilding Command
1 Apr 1942:	Transferred to the reserve

Rear-Admiral **Saburo HITOMI** (19 Dec 1878 - 1 Dec 1938)

1 Dec 1918 - 10 Nov 1922:	Commander, Sasebo Harbor
10 Nov 1922 - 1 Dec 1922:	Attached to Sasebo Naval District
1 Dec 1922:	Promoted to *Rear-Admiral*
1 Dec 1922 - 31 Mar 1923:	Unassigned
31 Mar 1923:	Transferred to the reserve

Rear-Admiral **Soichiro HITOMI** (16 Sep 1899 - 25 Nov 1944)

29 Mar 1944 - 25 Nov 1944:	Captain, Heavy Cruiser *"Kumano"*
25 Nov 1944:	Posthumously promoted to *Rear-Admiral*

Rear-Admiral **Kesaichi HITSUDA** (22 Apr 1880 - 4 Jul 1956)

20 Apr 1925 - 20 Aug 1926:	Commander, Kure Base Force
1 Dec 1925:	Promoted to *Rear-Admiral*
20 Aug 1926 - 1 Dec 1927:	Commander, 2nd Submarine Flotilla
1 Dec 1927 - 10 Dec 1928:	Commander, Mako Guard District
10 Dec 1928 - 15 Mar 1929:	Attached to Naval General Staff
25 Mar 1929:	Transferred to the reserve

Vice-Admiral **Kinya HOKOTATE** (12 Jun 1890 - ?)
1 Dec 1937:	Promoted to *Rear-Admiral*
1 Dec 1937 - 1 Apr 1938:	Attached to Naval Air Command
1 Apr 1938 - 15 Nov 1940:	Chief of Supply Bureau, Naval Air Command
15 Nov 1940 - 1 Oct 1941:	Attached to Kure Naval District
1 Oct 1941 - 1 Aug 1944:	Commander, 11th Air Arsenal
15 Oct 1941:	Promoted to *Vice-Admiral*
20 Nov 1941 - 15 Dec 1941:	Commander, Hiro Navy Yard
1 Aug 1944 - 12 Aug 1944:	Attached to Naval Air Command
12 Aug 1944 - 10 Mar 1945:	Kyushu Area Inspector, Department of Military Supply
10 Mar 1945 - 26 Aug 1945:	Kyushu Area Deputy Inspector, Department of Military Supply
26 Aug 1945 - 15 Sep 1945:	Attached to Naval Air Command

Rear-Admiral **Chikatami HONDA** (26 Jan 1868 - 15 Jul 1947)
1 Dec 1916 - 1 Dec 1917:	Captain, Battleship *"Settsu"*
1 Dec 1917:	Promoted to *Rear-Admiral*
1 Dec 1917 - 1 Dec 1918:	Unassigned
1 Dec 1918:	Transferred to the reserve

Rear-Admiral **Keitaro HONDA** (13 Jun 1881 - 1 Sep 1961)
10 Dec 1928 - 30 Nov 1929:	Chief Engineer, Combined Fleet, Chief Engineer, 1st Fleet
30 Nov 1929:	Promoted to *Rear-Admiral*
30 Nov 1929 - 1 Dec 1930:	Chief of Shipping Bureau, Yokosuka Naval District
1 Dec 1930 - 1 Dec 1932:	Chief of Supply Bureau, Sasebo Naval District
1 Dec 1932 - 10 Dec 1932:	Attached to Naval General Staff
15 Dec 1932:	Transferred to the reserve

Rear-Admiral **Kiichiro HONDA** (29 Jun 1885 - 18 Dec 1960)
15 Nov 1934:	Promoted to *Rear-Admiral*
15 Nov 1934 - 1 Dec 1936:	Chief of Ordnance Bureau, Yokosuka Navy Yard
1 Dec 1936 - 1 Dec 1937:	Commander, Maizuru Navy Yard
1 Dec 1937 - 15 Dec 1937:	Attached to Naval General Staff
21 Dec 1937:	Transferred to the reserve

Vice-Admiral (Paymaster) **Masuzo HONDA** (18 Dec 1886 - 4 Nov 1971)
20 Oct 1933 - 15 Nov 1934:	Chief Finance Officer, Combined Fleet, Chief Finance Officer, 1st Fleet
15 Nov 1934 - 12 Apr 1939:	Chief of Accounting Bureau, Yokosuka Navy Yard
1 Dec 1936:	Promoted to *Rear-Admiral (Paymaster)*
12 Apr 1939 - 1 Apr 1941:	Chief of Accounting Bureau, Naval Shipbuilding Command

15 Nov 1940:	Promoted to *Vice-Admiral (Paymaster)*
1 Apr 1941 - 16 Mar 1942:	Commandant, Paymaster Academy
16 Mar 1942 - 26 Mar 1943:	Attached to Naval General Staff
30 Mar 1943:	Transferred to the reserve

Vice-Admiral (Surgeon) **Tadao HONDA** (27 Jul 1858 - 13 Dec 1928)

4 Jan 1906 - 13 Dec 1915:	Commandant, Navy Medical School
24 Nov 1906:	Promoted to *Surgeon-General*
1 Dec 1913:	Promoted to *Surgeon-General, Senior grade*
13 Dec 1915 - 1 Dec 1919:	Chief of the Naval Medical Service
23 Sep 1919:	Redesignated *Vice-Admiral (Surgeon)*
1 Dec 1919 - 10 Dec 1919:	Attached to Department of the Navy
10 Dec 1919 - 27 Jul 1920:	Unassigned
27 Jul 1920:	Transferred to the reserve

Rear-Admiral **Tadao HONDA** (17 Mar 1888 - 10 Oct 1946)

1 Dec 1936:	Promoted to *Rear-Admiral*
1 Dec 1936 - 25 Apr 1938:	Naval Attache, China
9 Dec 1937 - 25 Apr 1938:	Chief of Navy Special Purposes Office
25 Apr 1938 - 15 Dec 1939:	Chief of Military History Bureau, Naval General Staff
21 Dec 1939:	Transferred to the reserve

Rear-Admiral **Teijiro HONJO** (13 Apr 1877 - 5 Apr 1964)

1 Apr 1923 - 1 Dec 1923:	Chief Engineer, Maizuru Guard District
1 Dec 1923:	Promoted to *Rear-Admiral*
1 Dec 1923 - 10 Dec 1923:	Attached to Kure Naval District
10 Dec 1923 - 25 Feb 1924:	Unassigned
25 Feb 1924:	Transferred to the reserve

Rear-Admiral (Surgeon) **Masato HONMA** (24 Jul 1897 - 8 Aug 1979)

1 Nov 1944 - 10 Oct 1945:	Director, Ureshino Naval Hospital
1 May 1945:	Promoted to *Rear-Admiral (Surgeon)*

Rear-Admiral **Yutaka HONMA** (1 Jul 1900 - 25 Jan 1945)

15 Oct 1944 - 25 Jan 1945:	Chief Engineer, 2nd Air Fleet
25 Jan 1945:	Posthumously promoted to *Rear-Admiral*

Rear-Admiral **Naojiro HONSHUKU** (15 Jan 1882 - 6 Nov 1933)

1 Dec 1926 - 1 Dec 1927:	Captain, Battlecruiser *"Kirishima"*
1 Dec 1927:	Promoted to *Rear-Admiral*
1 Dec 1927 - 15 Dec 1927:	Attached to Naval General Staff
25 Dec 1927:	Transferred to the reserve

Rear-Admiral **Masasyuki HORI** (16 Jul 1881 - 30 Aug 1960)
30 Nov 1929:	Promoted to *Rear-Admiral*
30 Nov 1929 - 1 Dec 1930:	Chief of Aircraft Research Bureau, Technical Research Department
1 Dec 1930 - 15 Dec 1930:	Attached to Naval General Staff
24 Dec 1930:	Transferred to the reserve

Vice-Admiral (Surgeon) **Nobuaki HORI** (28 Mar 1889 - 22 Nov 1967)
1 Dec 1937:	Promoted to *Rear-Admiral (Surgeon)*
1 Dec 1937 - 15 Nov 1938:	Chief Medical Officer, Combined Fleet, Chief Medical Officer, 1st Fleet
15 Nov 1938 - 1 Mar 1939:	Director, Beppu Naval Hospital
1 Mar 1939 - 15 Nov 1939:	Director, Kure Naval Hospital, Chief Medical Officer, Kure Naval District
15 Nov 1939 - 15 Oct 1941:	Director, Yokosuka Naval Hospital, Chief Medical Officer, Yokosuka Naval District
15 Oct 1941:	Promoted to *Vice-Admiral (Surgeon)*
15 Oct 1941 - 25 Oct 1943:	Commandant, Navy Medical School
25 Oct 1943 - 29 Nov 1945:	Chief of Naval Medical Service

Vice-Admiral **Teikichi HORI** (16 Aug 1883 - 12 May 1959)
10 Dec 1928:	Promoted to *Rear-Admiral*
10 Dec 1928 - 6 Sep 1929:	Chief of Staff, 2nd Fleet
6 Sep 1929 - 2 Nov 1931:	Chief, Bureau of Naval Affairs, Member, Admirals Committee
2 Nov 1931 - 1 Dec 1931:	Attached to Naval General Staff
1 Dec 1931 - 15 Nov 1932:	Commander, 3rd Escort Flotilla
15 Nov 1932 - 15 Nov 1933:	Commander, 1st Escort Flotilla
15 Nov 1933:	Promoted to *Vice-Admiral*
15 Nov 1933 - 10 Dec 1934:	Attached to Naval General Staff
15 Dec 1934:	Transferred to the reserve

Rear-Admiral **Terufusa HORI** (1 Nov 1868 - 4 Jan 1948)
1 Dec 1916 - 1 Dec 1917:	Captain, Battlecruiser *"Hiei"*
1 Dec 1917:	Promoted to *Rear-Admiral*
1 Dec 1917 - 1 Dec 1918:	Unassigned
1 Dec 1918:	Transferred to the reserve

Rear-Admiral **Yugoro HORI** (15 Mar 1893 - 8 Jan 1973)
15 Nov 1940 - 5 Aug 1943:	Commander, Yokosuka Harbor
1 May 1942:	Promoted to *Rear-Admiral*
5 Aug 1943 - 1 Dec 1943:	Chief of Bureau 2, Naval Hydrographic Command
1 Dec 1943 - 15 Jan 1945:	Chief of Southern Hydrographic Office

15 Jan 1945 - 20 Mar 1945:	Attached to Naval General Staff
20 Mar 1945 - Oct 1945:	Commander, Rashin Area Base Force

Rear-Admiral **Giichiro HORIE** (15 Jan 1895 - 18 Jul 1963)
21 Jan 1943 - 18 May 1944:	Chief of Staff, 1st Escort Flotilla
1 May 1943:	Promoted to *Rear-Admiral*
18 May 1944 - 25 Jun 1944:	Attached to Department of the Navy
20 May 1944 - 15 Nov 1944:	Chief of Reinforcement Division, Joint General Staff
25 Jun 1944 - 15 Nov 1944:	Chief of Naval Transportation Command
15 Nov 1944 - 15 Oct 1945:	Chief Instructor, Naval Academy
20 Nov 1944 - 10 May 1945:	Commander, Kure Training Squadron

Vice-Admiral **Rokuro HORIE** (25 Aug 1886 - 14 Feb 1968)
15 Nov 1935 - 1 Dec 1937:	Commander, 2nd Air Flotilla
1 Dec 1936:	Promoted to *Rear-Admiral*
1 Dec 1937 - 15 Dec 1938:	Commander, Kasumigaura Air Flotilla
15 Dec 1938 - 15 Nov 1940:	Commander, 11th Combined Air Flotilla
15 Nov 1940:	Promoted to *Vice-Admiral*
15 Nov 1940 - 15 Mar 1941:	Attached to Naval General Staff
20 Mar 1941:	Transferred to the reserve

Rear-Admiral **Ryusuke HORIE** (15 Feb 1899 - 12 Aug 1945)
10 Aug 1945 - 12 Aug 1945:	Chief of Administration Bureau, Department of Military Supply
12 Aug 1945:	Posthumously promoted to *Rear-Admiral*

Rear-Admiral **Miyoshi HORINOUCHI** (1 May 1902 - 8 Jul 1944)
15 Jan 1944 - 8 Jul 1944:	Chief of Operations, 6th Fleet
8 Jul 1944:	Posthumously promoted to *Rear-Admiral*

Rear-Admiral **Kazuo HORIUCHI** (16 Jul 1895 - 11 Oct 1982)
1 May 1943:	Promoted to *Rear-Admiral*
1 May 1943 - 25 May 1944:	Chief of Ordnance Bureau, Sasebo Navy Yard
25 May 1944 - 20 Dec 1944:	Chief of Bureau 4, Naval Air Command
20 Dec 1944 - 10 May 1945:	Chief Supervisor for Construction & Ordnance, Naval Shipbuilding Command
10 May 1945 - 10 Aug 1945:	Supervisor for Construction & Ordnance, Naval Shipbuilding Command, Supervisor for Ordnance, Naval Air Command
10 Aug 1945 - 25 Sep 1945:	Chief of Toyama Branch, Department of Military Supply

Vice-Admiral **Saburo HORIUCHI** (6 Dec 1869 - 20 Dec 1933)

13 Dec 1915:	Promoted to *Rear-Admiral*
13 Dec 1915 - 1 Dec 1917:	Chief of Staff, 1st Fleet
1 Sep 1916 - 14 Oct 1916:	Chief of Staff, Combined Fleet
1 Oct 1917 - 22 Oct 1917:	Chief of Staff, Combined Fleet
1 Dec 1917 - 10 Jul 1918:	Chief of Staff, Yokosuka Naval District
10 Jul 1918 - 10 Sep 1919:	Commandant, Naval Gunnery School
4 Sep 1918 - 1 Dec 1918:	Commandant, Torpedo School
10 Sep 1919 - 1 Jun 1920:	Commander, Training Fleet
1 Dec 1919:	Promoted to *Vice-Admiral*
1 Jun 1920 - 1 May 1922:	Member, Admirals Committee
16 Aug 1920 - 1 May 1922:	Chief, Bureau of Naval Affairs
1 May 1922 - 1 Jun 1923:	Commandant of the Naval College
1 Jun 1923 - 5 Feb 1924:	Deputy Chief of the Naval General Staff, Member, Admirals Committee
5 Feb 1924 - 1 Dec 1924:	Admiral Commanding, Yokosuka Naval District, Member, Admirals Committee
1 Dec 1924 - 2 Mar 1925:	Attached to Naval General Staff
20 Mar 1925:	Transferred to the reserve

Vice-Admiral **Shigenori HORIUCHI** (14 Jun 1891 - ?)

15 Nov 1938:	Promoted to *Rear-Admiral*
15 Nov 1938 - 15 Nov 1939:	Commander, Yokosuka Defense Squadron
15 Nov 1939 - 15 Oct 1940:	Chief of Staff, 1st China Expeditionary Fleet
15 Oct 1940 - 10 Oct 1941:	Chief of Staff, Sasebo Naval District
10 Oct 1941 - 15 Oct 1941:	Attached to Kure Naval District
15 Oct 1941 - 15 Nov 1942:	Commander, 22nd Escort Flotilla
1 Nov 1942:	Promoted to *Vice-Admiral*
15 Nov 1942 - 29 Nov 1942:	Attached to Naval General Staff
29 Nov 1942 - 4 Dec 1942:	Attached to staff, 1st Southern Expeditionary Fleet
4 Dec 1942 - 1 Sep 1943:	Commander, 11th Naval Base Force
1 Sep 1943 - 15 Dec 1943:	Attached to Naval General Staff
15 Dec 1943 - 20 Dec 1943:	Unassigned
20 Dec 1943:	Transferred to the reserve
20 Dec 1943 - 27 Nov 1943:	Recalled; Attached to Department of the Navy
27 Nov 1943 - 1 Apr 1944:	Fukuoka Area Inspector, Department of Military Supply
1 Apr 1944 - 12 Aug 1944:	Kyushu Area Inspector, Department of Military Supply
12 Aug 1944 - 20 Oct 1944:	Attached to Naval General Staff
20 Oct 1944:	Demobilized

Rear-Admiral **Shigetada HORIUCHI** (6 Aug 1897 - 18 Apr 1984)
18 May 1944 - 10 Dec 1944:	Chief of Staff, 1st Escort Flotilla
15 Oct 1944:	Promoted to *Rear-Admiral*
10 Dec 1944 - 1 Jan 1945:	Chief of Staff, 1st Escort Fleet
1 Jan 1945 - 15 Sep 1945:	Commander, 901st Air Flotilla
15 Sep 1945 - 25 Sep 1945:	Attached to Maizuru Naval District
25 Sep 1945 - 30 Nov 1945:	Deputy Chief of Staff, Osaka Guard District

Vice-Admiral **Zenshiro HOSHINA** (8 Mar 1891 - 25 Dec 1991)
15 Nov 1940:	Promoted to *Rear-Admiral*
15 Nov 1940 - 1 Mar 1945:	Chief of Naval Readiness Bureau
3 Dec 1941 - 25 Jun 1943:	Chief of Transportation Bureau, Department of the Navy
25 Jun 1943 - 25 Jun 1944:	Chief of Naval Transporation Command
1 Nov 1943:	Promoted to *Vice-Admiral*
1 Mar 1945 - 15 May 1945:	Deputy Chief of the Naval Affairs Bureau
20 Mar 1945 - 15 May 1945:	Chief of Shipping Safety Command, Department of the Navy
1 Apr 1945 - 15 May 1945:	Chief of Chemical Warfare Division, Department of the Navy
15 May 1945 - 17 Nov 1945:	Chief of the Naval Affairs Bureau
1 Sep 1945 - 17 Nov 1945:	Chief of Transportation Bureau, Department of the Navy

Rear-Admiral **Masatsugu HOSHINO** (14 Oct 1890 - 6 Jan 1965)
26 Jul 1941 - 1 Sep 1942:	Chief of Administration Bureau, Sasebo Navy Yard
1 May 1942:	Promoted to *Rear-Admiral*
1 Sep 1942 - 15 Sep 1942:	Attached to Yokosuka Naval District
15 Sep 1942 - 1 Sep 1943:	Chief of Personnel Bureau, Yokosuka Naval District
1 Sep 1943 - 13 Sep 1943:	Attached to staff, 2nd Southern Expeditionary Fleet
13 Sep 1943 - 17 Nov 1944:	Commander, 21st Naval Base Force
17 Nov 1944 - 20 Mar 1945:	Attached to Naval General Staff
20 Mar 1945 - 15 May 1945:	Chief of Osaka branch, Shipping Guard Division, Joint General Staff
15 May 1945 - 10 Oct 1945:	Commander, Osaka Harbor Guard Force

Vice-Admiral **Shuichi HOSHINO** (1 Aug 1886 - 26 Mar 1947)
15 Nov 1934:	Promoted to *Rear-Admiral*
15 Nov 1934 - 15 Jul 1935:	Chief of Supply Bureau Kure Naval District
15 Jul 1935 - 1 Aug 1935:	Attached to Naval General Staff
1 Aug 1935 - 29 May 1937:	Chief of Planning Division, Materiel Bureau, Department of Commerce & Industry
29 May 1937 - 1 Dec 1937:	Attached to Naval General Staff
1 Dec 1937 - 15 Nov 1938:	Commander, Yokosuka Navy Yard

15 Nov 1938:	Promoted to *Vice-Admiral*
15 Nov 1938 - 15 Nov 1940:	Commander, Ominato Guard District
15 Nov 1940 - 18 Dec 1940:	Attached to Naval General Staff
21 Dec 1940:	Transferred to the reserve

Vice-Admiral **Boshiro HOSOGAYA** (24 Jun 1888 - 8 Feb 1964)

15 Nov 1935:	Promoted to *Rear-Admiral*
15 Nov 1935 - 1 Dec 1936:	Commander, 5th Destroyer Flotilla
1 Dec 1936 - 28 Jul 1937:	Commandant, Navy Communications School
10 Mar 1937 - 28 Jul 1937:	Commandant, Torpedo School
28 Jul 1937 - 19 Apr 1938:	Commander, 4th Destroyer Flotilla
19 Apr 1938 - 25 Apr 1938:	Attached to Naval General Staff
25 Apr 1938 - 15 Nov 1939:	Commander, 1st Carrier Flotilla
15 Nov 1939:	Promoted to *Vice-Admiral*
15 Nov 1939 - 15 Nov 1940:	Commander, Ryojun Guard District
15 Nov 1940 - 5 Jul 1941:	C-in-C, 1st China Expeditionary Fleet
5 Jul 1941 - 25 Jul 1941:	Attached to Naval General Staff
25 Jul 1941 - 1 Apr 1943:	C-in-C, 5th Fleet
1 Apr 1943 - 3 Nov 1943:	Attached to Naval General Staff
4 Nov 1943:	Transferred to the reserve

Vice-Admiral **Shinzaburo HOSOTANI** (12 Jan 1893 - 18 Nov 1970)

15 Nov 1940:	Promoted to *Rear-Admiral*
15 Nov 1940 - 20 Dec 1944:	Chief of Administration Bureau, Naval Shipbuilding Command
1 Nov 1943:	Promoted to *Vice-Admiral*
20 Dec 1944 - 1 Nov 1945:	Commander, Yokosuka Navy Yard

Rear-Admiral **Sukehiko HOSOYA** (13 Jun 1897 - 12 Sep 1944)

25 Dec 1943 - 12 Sep 1944:	Chief of Traffic Control, 1st Escort Flotilla
12 Sep 1944:	Posthumously promoted to *Rear-Admiral*

Rear-Admiral **Sukeuji HOSOYA** (? - 2 Feb 1944)

22 Apr 1902 - 26 Dec 1903:	Chief of Bureau 3, Naval General Staff
7 Jul 1903:	Promoted to *Rear-Admiral*
26 Dec 1903 - 31 Jan 1905:	C-in-C, 3rd Fleet
31 Jan 1905 - 14 Jun 1905:	C-in-C, Special Task Fleet
14 Jun 1905 - 14 Feb 1907:	Unassigned
14 Feb 1907:	Transferred to the reserve

Rear-Admiral **Sukeyoshi HOSOYA** (8 Oct 1900 - 8 May 1945)

5 May 1945 - 8 May 1945:	Commander, Takuma Air Flotilla
8 May 1945:	Posthumously promoted to *Rear-Admiral*

Rear-Admiral (Surgeon) **Chikayuki HOTTA** (13 Feb 1890 - 2 Oct 1969)
15 Nov 1939:	Promoted to *Rear-Admiral (Surgeon)*
15 Nov 1939 - 15 Oct 1941:	Chief of Medical Bureau, Kure Navy Yard
15 Oct 1941 - 1 Nov 1942:	Director, Maizuru Naval Hospital, Chief Surgeon, Maizuru Naval District
1 Nov 1942 - 15 Dec 1942:	Attached to Naval General Staff
21 Dec 1942:	Transferred to the reserve

Rear-Admiral **Ritsunosuke HOZUMI** (13 Aug 1884 - 23 Feb 1959)
8 Sep 1932 - 8 May 1933:	Attached to Bureau 3, Naval Shipbuilding Command
1 Dec 1932:	Promoted to *Rear-Admiral*
8 May 1933 - 15 Nov 1933:	Chief of Shipbuilding Research Bureau, Technical Research Department
15 Nov 1933 - 11 Dec 1933:	Attached to Naval Shipbuilding Command
15 Dec 1933:	Transferred to the reserve

Admiral **Gengo HYAKUTAKE** (28 Jan 1882 - 15 Jan 1976)
19 Jun 1925 - 15 Apr 1926:	Naval Attache, League of Nations
1 Dec 1925:	Promoted to *Rear-Admiral*
15 Apr 1926 - 1 Dec 1927:	Chief Instructor, Naval College
1 Dec 1927 - 30 Nov 1929:	Chief of Bureau 1, Naval General Staff
30 Nov 1929 - 1 Dec 1930:	Commander, 5th Escort Flotilla
1 Dec 1930:	Promoted to *Vice-Admiral*
1 Dec 1930 - 10 Oct 1931:	Attached to Naval General Staff
10 Oct 1931 - 8 Feb 1932:	Deputy Chief of the Naval General Staff
8 Feb 1932 - 1 Oct 1932:	Commandant of the Naval College
1 Oct 1932 - 15 Sep 1933:	C-in-C, Training Fleet
15 Sep 1933 - 15 Nov 1934:	Admiral Commanding, Maizuru Naval District
15 Nov 1934 - 2 Dec 1935:	C-in-C, 3rd Fleet
2 Dec 1935 - 16 Mar 1936:	Admiral Commanding, Sasebo Naval District
16 Mar 1936 - 1 Dec 1936:	Chief of Naval Shipbuilding Command
1 Dec 1936 - 25 Apr 1938:	Admiral Commanding, Yokosuka Naval District, Member, Admirals Committee
1 Apr 1937:	Promoted to *Admiral*
25 Apr 1938 - 13 Jul 1942:	Navy Councillor
9 Apr 1941 - 13 Jul 1942:	Chairman, High Technical Committee
15 Jul 1942:	Transferred to the reserve

Admiral **Saburo HYAKUTAKE** (28 Apr 1872 - 30 Oct 1963)
15 Sep 1917 - 10 Nov 1918:	Chief of Staff, 2nd Fleet
1 Dec 1917:	Promoted to *Rear-Admiral*
10 Nov 1918 - 1 Dec 1919:	Chief of Staff, Sasebo Naval District

1 Dec 1919 - 1 Dec 1921:	Chief of Bureau 2, Naval Training Command
1 Dec 1921:	Promoted to *Vice-Admiral*
1 Dec 1921 - 26 Dec 1921:	Member, Admirals Committee
26 Dec 1921 - 1 Dec 1922:	Commander, 3rd Escort Flotilla
1 Dec 1922 - 1 Jun 1923:	Commander, Chinkai Guard District
1 Jun 1923 - 4 Oct 1924:	Commander, Maizuru Naval District
4 Oct 1924 - 15 Apr 1925:	C-in-C, Training Fleet
15 Apr 1925 - 10 Dec 1926:	Admiral Commanding, Sasebo Naval District
16 Sep 1925 - 10 Dec 1926:	C-in-C, 2nd Fleet
10 Dec 1926 - 16 May 1928:	Navy Councillor
10 Dec 1926 - 10 Dec 1928:	Admiral Commanding, Kure Naval District
1 Apr 1928:	Promoted to *Admiral*
10 Dec 1928 - 11 Nov 1929:	C-in-C, Combined Fleet, C-in-C, 1st Fleet
11 Nov 1929 - 11 Jun 1930:	Admiral Commanding, Kure Naval District
?:	Transferred to the reserve

Rear-Admiral **Fujio IBUSUKI** (13 Aug 1895 - 10 May 1985)

25 Apr 1945 - 20 Nov 1945:	Chief of Administration Bureau, 1st Technical Arsenal
1 May 1945:	Promoted to *Rear-Admiral*

Rear-Admiral (Apothecary) **Shoichi ICHIJO** (13 Mar 1898 - ?)

28 Apr 1945 - 15 Sep 1945:	Attached to 1st Medical Depot
1 May 1945:	Promoted to *Rear-Admiral (Apothecary)*

Rear-Admiral **Daijiro ICHIKAWA** (10 Mar 1885 - 6 Mar 1958)

1 Dec 1931:	Promoted to *Rear-Admiral*
1 Dec 1931 - 1 Apr 1932:	Chief of Aircraft Research Bureau, Yokosuka Navy Yard
1 Apr 1932 - 3 Oct 1933:	Chief of Aircraft Research Bureau, Air Arsenal
3 Oct 1933 - 15 Nov 1934:	Chief of Aircraft Bureau, Air Arsenal
15 Nov 1934 - 10 Dec 1934:	Attached to Naval General Staff
15 Dec 1934:	Transferred to the reserve

Vice-Admiral (Engineer) **Kiyojiro ICHIKAWA** (3 Oct 1865 - 16 Oct 1936)

1 Dec 1909 - 15 Jun 1911:	Chief Engineer, Kure Naval District
1 Apr 1910:	Promoted to *Rear-Admiral (Engineer)*
15 Jun 1911 - 1 Dec 1911:	Chief Engineer, Yokosuka Naval District
1 Dec 1911 - 1 Dec 1913:	Commandant, Naval Engineer Academy
1 Dec 1913 - 17 Feb 1914:	Chief of Bureau 3, Naval Training Command
17 Feb 1914 - 1 Oct 1915:	Chief of Bureau 4, Naval Shipbuilding Command
1 Dec 1914:	Promoted to *Vice-Admiral (Engineer)*

1 Oct 1915 - 1 Apr 1916:	Chief of Bureau 5, Naval Transportation Command
1 Apr 1916 - 1 Sep 1921:	Chief of Naval Engineers, Department of the Navy
1 Sep 1921 - 1 Dec 1921:	Attached to Naval Shipbuilding Command
1 Dec 1921 - 31 Mar 1923:	Unassigned
31 Mar 1923:	Transferred to the reserve

Rear-Admiral **Keiichi ICHIKIZAKI** (7 Aug 1882 - 14 Feb 1944)

1 Dec 1927 - 30 Nov 1929:	Commander, Sasebo Defense Force
30 Nov 1929:	Promoted to *Rear-Admiral*
30 Nov 1929 - 15 Dec 1929:	Attached to Naval General Staff
24 Dec 1929:	Transferred to the reserve

Vice-Admiral **Rinosuke ICHIMARU** (20 Sep 1891 - 17 Mar 1945)

15 Nov 1940 - 20 Aug 1942:	Commander, Suzuka Air Group
1 May 1942:	Promoted to *Rear-Admiral*
20 Aug 1942 - 1 Sep 1942:	Attached to staff, Southwestern Area Fleet
1 Sep 1942 - 1 Sep 1943:	Commander, 21st Air Flotilla
1 Sep 1943 - 15 Nov 1943:	Attached to Naval General Staff
15 Nov 1943 - 5 Aug 1944:	Commander, 13th Combined Air Flotilla
5 Aug 1944 - 10 Aug 1944:	Attached to staff, 3rd Air Fleet
10 Aug 1944 - 17 Mar 1945:	Commander, 27th Air Flotilla
17 Mar 1945:	Posthumously promoted to *Vice-Admiral*

Rear-Admiral **Yoshiyuki ICHIMIYA** (1 Jan 1897 - 12 Nov 1948)

19 Mar 1943 - 18 May 1943:	Attached to Readiness Bureau, Department of the Navy
1 May 1943:	Promoted to *Rear-Admiral*
18 May 1943 - 6 Feb 1945:	Chief of Staff, 12th Air Fleet
5 Aug 1943 - 5 Dec 1944:	Chief of Staff, Northeastern Area Fleet
6 Feb 1945 - 5 May 1945:	Attached to Naval General Staff
5 May 1945 - 25 Oct 1945:	Chief of Administration Section, Supply Bureau, Department of the Navy

Vice-Admiral **Hisao ICHIMURA** (14 Apr 1883 - 24 Dec 1962)

10 Dec 1928:	Promoted to *Rear-Admiral*
10 Dec 1928 - 30 Nov 1929:	Commander, 1st Destroyer Flotilla
30 Nov 1929 - 1 Dec 1930:	Commander, 2nd Destroyer Flotilla
1 Dec 1930 - 1 Dec 1932:	Commandant, Torpedo School, Commandant, Navy Communications School
1 Dec 1932 - 20 May 1933:	Commander, 5th Escort Flotilla
20 May 1933 - 15 Nov 1933:	Commander, 6th Escort Flotilla
15 Nov 1933:	Promoted to *Vice-Admiral*
15 Nov 1933 - 17 Jan 1934:	Attached to Naval General Staff

17 Jan 1934 - 15 Nov 1934:	Commander, Chinkai Guard District
15 Nov 1934 - 25 Mar 1935:	Attached to Naval General Staff
30 Mar 1935:	Transferred to the reserve

Rear-Admiral **Josuke ICHIMURA** (2 Aug 1890 - 10 Jun 1944)

5 Apr 1944 - 10 Jun 1944:	Staff Officer, 101st Supply Bureau
10 Jun 1944:	Posthumously promoted to *Rear-Admiral*

Rear-Admiral **Shigematsu ICHIMURA** (? - 8 Dec 1946)

?:	Promoted to *Rear-Admiral*

Vice-Admiral **Hisashi ICHIOKA** (26 May 1893 - 14 Feb 1963)

25 Mar 1941 - 5 Feb 1942:	Chief Instructor, Naval Academy
15 Oct 1941:	Promoted to *Rear-Admiral*
5 Feb 1942 - 20 Aug 1942:	Commander, 2nd Submarine Flotilla
20 Aug 1942 - 15 Sep 1942:	Attached to Naval General Staff
15 Sep 1942 - 9 Aug 1943:	Chief Instructor, Naval College
9 Aug 1943 - 19 Aug 1943:	Attached to staff, 6th Fleet
19 Aug 1943 - 4 Aug 1944:	Commander, 8th Submarine Flotilla
20 Jun 1944 - 4 Aug 1944:	Commander, 15th Auxiliary Base Force
4 Aug 1944 - 10 Sep 1944:	Attached to Naval General Staff
10 Sep 1944 - 17 Sep 1944:	Attached to staff, Maritime Escort Fleet
17 Sep 1944 - 1 May 1945:	Deputy Chief of Staff, Maritime Escort Fleet
1 May 1945:	Promoted to *Vice-Admiral*
1 May 1945 - 15 Sep 1945:	Commandant, Submarine School, Commander, Kure Submarine Flotilla

Vice-Admiral **Shinichi ICHISE** (10 Sep 1890 - 13 Jan 1994)

15 Oct 1940 - 25 Jul 1942:	Chief of Staff, 1st China Expeditionary Fleet
15 Nov 1940:	Promoted to *Rear-Admiral*
11 Aug 1941 - 15 Jan 1942:	Commander, Hanko Area Base Force
25 Jul 1942 - 28 Sep 1942:	Attached to Naval General Staff
28 Sep 1942 - 5 Feb 1943:	Commander, Yokosuka Defense Squadron
5 Feb 1943 - 19 Feb 1943:	Attached to Kainan Guard District
19 Feb 1943 - 10 Mar 1944:	Chief of Staff, Kainan Guard District
10 Mar 1944 - 15 May 1944:	Attached to Naval General Staff
1 May 1944:	Promoted to *Vice-Admiral*
15 May 1944 - 25 May 1944:	Attached to staff, 4th Southern Expeditionary Fleet
25 May 1944 - 29 May 1945:	Commander, 26th Naval Base Force
29 May 1945 - 9 Jun 1945:	Attached to staff, 10th Area Fleet
9 Jun 1945 - Oct 1945:	Commander, 25th Auxiliary Base Force

Rear-Admiral **Genji IDE** (13 Oct 1875 - 10 Jan 1948)
20 Nov 1921 - 10 Nov 1922: Captain, Battleship *"Hyuga"*
10 Nov 1922 - 1 Dec 1922: Attached to Sasebo Naval District
1 Dec 1922: Promoted to *Rear-Admiral*
1 Dec 1922 - 31 Mar 1923: Unassigned
31 Mar 1923: Transferred to the reserve

Admiral **Kenji IDE** (9 May 1870 - 30 Oct 1946)
1 Dec 1913: Promoted to *Rear-Admiral*
1 Dec 1913 - 17 Apr 1914: Commander, Kure Torpedo Group
17 Apr 1914 - 13 Dec 1915: Chief of Staff, Kure Naval District
13 Dec 1915 - 1 Dec 1916: Commander, 4th Escort Flotilla
1 Dec 1916 - 16 Aug 1920: Chief, Bureau of Naval Affairs,
 Member, Admirals Committee
1 Dec 1917: Promoted to *Vice-Admiral*
16 Aug 1920 - 25 May 1923: Deputy Minister of the Navy,
 Member, Admirals Committee
16 Aug 1920 - 1 Apr 1924: Chief of Temporary Construction Bureau,
 Department of the Navy,
 Member, Admirals Committee
1 Apr 1924 - 11 Jun 1924: Attached to Naval General Staff
11 Jun 1924: Promoted to *Admiral*
11 Jun 1924 - 5 Dec 1925: Navy Councillor
16 Dec 1925: Transferred to the reserve

Rear-Admiral **Mitsuteru IDE** (28 Aug 1878 - 9 Feb 1937)
13 Aug 1923 - 1 Dec 1924: Chief of Section 6/3, Naval General Staff
1 Dec 1924: Promoted to *Rear-Admiral*
1 Dec 1924 - 1 Sep 1925: Attached to Naval General Staff
1 Sep 1925 - 16 Dec 1925: Unassigned
16 Dec 1925: Transferred to the reserve

Rear-Admiral **Rinroku IDE** (14 Dec 1856 - 27 Apr 1939)
15 May 1908 - 10 Dec 1908: Chief of Reserve Bureau, Yokosuka Naval District
28 Aug 1908: Promoted to *Rear-Admiral*
10 Dec 1908 - 1 Dec 1911: Commander, Sasebo Reserve Fleet
1 Dec 1911 - 1 Dec 1912: Unassigned
1 Dec 1912: Transferred to the reserve

Rear-Admiral **Tatsumi IDEBUCHI** (4 Jun 1895 - 27 Aug 1969)
1 Nov 1942 - 15 Oct 1945: Chief of Shipbuilding Research Bureau,
 Technical Research Department
1 May 1943: Promoted to *Rear-Admiral*

Vice-Admiral **Manbei IDEMITSU** (9 Nov 1882 - 16 Jul 1964)
1 Jun 1930 - 1 May 1931:	Chief Instructor, Navy Communications School
1 Dec 1930:	Promoted to *Rear-Admiral*
1 May 1931 - 5 Jun 1935:	Aide-de-Camp to the Emperor
5 Jun 1935 - 15 Nov 1935:	Commander, 1st Submarine Flotilla
15 Nov 1935:	Promoted to *Vice-Admiral*
15 Nov 1935 - 1 Dec 1937:	Commandant of the Naval Academy
1 Dec 1937 - 15 Nov 1938:	Admiral Commanding, Maizuru Naval District
15 Nov 1938 - 15 Mar 1939:	Attached to Naval General Staff
25 Mar 1939:	Transferred to the reserve

Rear-Admiral (Paymaster) **Kazuo IGAWA** (15 Apr 1894 - 17 Jan 1982)
10 Jul 1943 - 15 Nov 1945:	Chief of Section 3, Supply Bureau, Department of the Navy
1 May 1945:	Promoted to *Rear-Admiral (Paymaster)*

Rear-Admiral **Daijiro IGUCHI** (1 Sep 1876 - 3 Aug 1959)
21 Nov 1921 - 10 Dec 1922:	Supervisor of Ordnance, Naval Shipbuilding Command
1 Dec 1922:	Promoted to *Rear-Admiral*
10 Dec 1922 - 1 Apr 1923:	Attached to Naval Shipbuilding Command
1 Apr 1923 - 1 May 1923:	Unassigned
1 May 1923:	Transferred to the reserve

Rear-Admiral **Mikio IHARA** (? - 25 Nov 1942)
15 Jan 1942 - 25 Nov 1942:	Commander, Amoi Guard Force
25 Nov 1942:	Posthumously promoted to *Rear-Admiral*

Vice-Admiral **Hisatsune IIDA** (10 Oct 1869 - 16 Oct 1956)
1 Dec 1917:	Promoted to *Rear-Admiral*
1 Dec 1917 - 25 Oct 1920:	Naval Attache, United Kingdom
25 Oct 1920 - 1 Dec 1921:	Commander, 4th Escort Flotilla
1 Dec 1921:	Promoted to *Vice-Admiral*
1 Dec 1921 - 26 Dec 1921:	Commander, 3rd Escort Flotilla
26 Dec 1921 - 1 Jun 1923:	Commander, Mako Guard District
1 Jun 1923 - 1 Dec 1923:	Member, Admirals Committee
1 Dec 1923 - 25 Feb 1924:	Unassigned
25 Feb 1924:	Transferred to the reserve

Rear-Admiral (Paymaster) **Kyutaro IIDA** (4 Mar 1872 - ?)
1 Dec 1921 - 10 Nov 1922:	Paymaster, Ominato Guard District
10 Nov 1922 - 1 Dec 1922:	Attached to Yokosuka Naval District
1 Dec 1922:	Promoted to *Rear-Admiral (Paymaster)*

1 Dec 1922 - 31 Mar 1923:	Unassigned
31 Mar 1923:	Transferred to the reserve

Vice-Admiral **Nobutaro IIDA** (13 Feb 1875 - 3 Nov 1938)
1 Dec 1921:	Promoted to *Rear-Admiral*
1 Dec 1921 - 1 Aug 1922:	Attached to Naval General Staff
1 Aug 1922 - 1 Dec 1922:	Commander, Sasebo Defense Force
1 Dec 1922 - 1 Dec 1924:	Commander, 2nd Destroyer Flotilla
1 Dec 1924 - 1 Aug 1925:	Commandant, Torpedo School
1 Aug 1925 - 1 Dec 1927:	Commander, Mako Guard District
1 Dec 1925:	Promoted to *Vice-Admiral*
1 Dec 1927 - 16 May 1928:	Attached to Naval General Staff
16 May 1928 - 10 Dec 1928:	Admiral Commanding, Maizuru Naval District
10 Dec 1928 - 11 Nov 1929:	Admiral Commanding, Sasebo Naval District
11 Nov 1929 - 1 Dec 1930:	C-in-C, 2nd Fleet
1 Dec 1930 - 20 Mar 1931:	Attached to Naval General Staff
31 Mar 1931:	Transferred to the reserve

Rear-Admiral **Teizo IIKURA** (23 Nov 1886 - 20 Apr 1970)
1 Oct 1937 - 15 Nov 1938:	Chief of Aircraft Bureau, Air Arsenal
15 Nov 1938:	Promoted to *Rear-Admiral*
15 Nov 1938 - 15 Dec 1938:	Attached to Naval General Staff
21 Dec 1938:	Transferred to the reserve

Vice-Admiral **Hikojiro IJICHI** (14 Dec 1859 - 4 Jan 1912)
7 Apr 1906 - 28 Aug 1908:	Chief of Bureau 1, Naval Training Command
22 Nov 1906:	Promoted to *Rear-Admiral*
28 Aug 1908 - 16 Jul 1910:	C-in-C, Training Fleet
16 Jul 1910 - 1 Dec 1910:	Member, Admirals Committee
1 Dec 1910:	Promoted to *Vice-Admiral*
1 Dec 1910 - 1 Dec 1911:	Commander, Mako Guard District
1 Dec 1911 - 4 Jan 1912:	Member, Admirals Committee

Vice-Admiral **Kiyohiro IJICHI** (7 Jun 1881 - ?)
1 Dec 1926:	Promoted to *Rear-Admiral*
1 Dec 1926 - 10 Dec 1928:	Chief of Staff, Kure Naval District
10 Dec 1928 - 21 May 1930:	C-in-C, 2nd Expeditionary Fleet
21 May 1930 - 1 Mar 1931:	Attached to Naval General Staff
1 Mar 1931 - 1 Dec 1931:	Commander, Ominato Guard District
1 Dec 1931:	Promoted to *Vice-Admiral*
1 Dec 1931 - 22 Mar 1932:	Attached to Naval General Staff
31 Mar 1932:	Transferred to the reserve

Rear-Admiral **Shiro IJICHI**   (18 Nov 1879 - 19 May 1965)
10 Dec 1928 - 1 Dec 1931:   Chief of Mining Bureau, Navy Fuel Yard
30 Nov 1929:   Promoted to *Rear-Admiral*
1 Dec 1931 - 15 Dec 1931:   Attached to Naval General Staff
21 Dec 1931:   Transferred to the reserve

Vice-Admiral **Suetaka IJICHI**   (26 Mar 1857 - 7 Apr 1935)
22 Nov 1906 - 15 May 1908:   Chief of Staff, Maizuru Naval District
12 Mar 1907:   Promoted to *Rear-Admiral*
15 May 1908 - 1 Dec 1912:   Commander, Kure Navy Yard
5 Jun 1911:   Promoted to *Vice-Admiral*
1 Dec 1912 - 1 Dec 1913:   C-in-C, 2nd Fleet
1 Dec 1913 - 23 May 1914:   Chief of Naval Shipbuilding Command,
    Member, Admirals Committee
23 May 1914 - 23 Sep 1915:   Admiral Commanding, Yokosuka Naval District,
    Member, Admirals Committee
23 Sep 1915 - 1 Dec 1916:   Admiral Commanding, Kure Naval District
1 Dec 1916 - 26 Mar 1917:   Member, Admirals Committee
26 Mar 1917:   Transferred to the reserve

Fleet Admiral **Baron Goro IJUIN** (27 Sep 1852 - 13 Jan 1921)
10 Nov 1898 - 17 Mar 1902:   Deputy Chief of the Naval General Staff,
    Member, Admirals Committee
26 Sep 1899:   Promoted to *Rear-Admiral*
17 Mar 1902 - 5 Sep 1903:   C-in-C, Readiness Fleet
5 Sep 1903:   Promoted to *Vice-Admiral*
5 Sep 1903 - 9 Jan 1906:   Deputy Chief of the Naval General Staff,
    Member, Admirals Committee
9 Jan 1906 - 22 Nov 1906:   Chief of Naval Shipbuilding Command
22 Nov 1906 - 26 May 1908:   C-in-C, 2nd Fleet
26 May 1908 - 1 Dec 1909:   C-in-C, 1st Fleet
8 Oct 1908 - 20 Nov 1908:   C-in-C, Combined Fleet
1 Dec 1909 - 22 Apr 1914:   Chief of the Naval General Staff,
    Member, Admirals Committee
1 Dec 1910:   Promoted to *Admiral*
22 Apr 1914 - 13 Jan 1921:   Navy Councillor
26 May 1917:   Appointed *Fleet Admiral*

Vice-Admiral **Matsuji IJUIN**   (21 Apr 1893 - 24 May 1944)
7 Jul 1943 - 16 Dec 1943:   Commander, 3rd Destroyer Flotilla
1 Nov 1943:   Promoted to *Rear-Admiral*
16 Dec 1943 - 7 Mar 1944:   Attached to Naval General Staff
7 Mar 1944 - 8 Apr 1944:   Attached to staff, Maritime Escort Fleet

8 Apr 1944 - 24 May 1944:	Commander, 1st Convoy HQ
24 May 1944:	Posthumously promoted to *Vice-Admiral*

Rear-Admiral **Shun IJUIN** (15 Nov 1871 - 4 Feb 1925)
10 May 1919 - 1 Oct 1920:	Attached to Naval General Staff
1 Dec 1919:	Promoted to *Rear-Admiral*
1 Oct 1920 - 1 Aug 1922:	Commander, Sasebo Defense Force
1 Aug 1922 - 1 Dec 1922:	Attached to Naval General Staff
1 Dec 1922 - 31 Mar 1923:	Unassigned
31 Mar 1923:	Transferred to the reserve

Vice-Admiral (Paymaster) **Yasuo IKEBE** (10 Jan 1881 - 22 Apr 1946)
10 Dec 1928 - 1 Dec 1932:	Chief of Supply Bureau, Yokosuka Naval District
30 Nov 1929:	Promoted to *Rear-Admiral (Paymaster)*
1 Dec 1932 - 10 Oct 1933:	Paymaster-General, Yokosuka Naval District
10 Oct 1933 - 15 Nov 1935:	Commandant, Navy Paymaster Academy
15 Nov 1934:	Promoted to *Vice-Admiral (Paymaster)*
15 Nov 1935 - 28 Mar 1936:	Attached to Naval General Staff
30 Mar 1936:	Transferred to the reserve

Rear-Admiral **Akira IKEDA** (? - 14 Apr 1945)
? - 14 Apr 1945:	Commander, 1st Surface Escort Division
14 Apr 1945:	Posthumously promoted to *Rear-Admiral*

Rear-Admiral (Paymaster) **Heisaku IKEDA** (12 Apr 1885 - 21 Sep 1935)
15 Nov 1934:	Promoted to *Rear-Admiral (Paymaster)*
15 Nov 1934 - 21 Sep 1935:	Chief of Supply Bureau, Yokosuka Naval District

Vice-Admiral **Iwasaburo IKEDA** (23 Aug 1874 - 10 Feb 1937)
1 Dec 1920:	Promoted to *Rear-Admiral*
1 Dec 1920 - 1 Dec 1921:	Chief Engineer Officer, 1st Fleet
1 May 1921 - 31 Oct 1921:	Chief Engineer Officer, Combined Fleet
1 Dec 1921 - 1 Apr 1923:	Chief of Bureau 3, Naval Training Command
1 Apr 1923 - 25 May 1923:	Attached to Naval General Staff
25 May 1923 - 25 Jul 1924:	Commandant, Naval Engineering Academy
25 Jul 1924 - 1 Aug 1925:	Commander, Sasebo Navy Yard
1 Dec 1924:	Promoted to *Vice-Admiral*
1 Aug 1925 - 10 Dec 1928:	Chief of Supply Bureau, Department of the Navy
10 Dec 1928 - 5 Jul 1929:	Attached to Naval General Staff
10 Jul 1929:	Transferred to the reserve

Rear-Admiral **Keinosuke IKEDA** (17 Apr 1884 - 14 Aug 1945)
5 Mar 1944 - 14 Aug 1945:	Commander, 33rd Guard Force
1 May 1945:	Promoted to *Rear-Admiral*

Vice-Admiral **Taiichi IKEDA** (10 Mar 1885 - 18 Dec 1971)
15 Nov 1932 - 1 Dec 1936: Chief of Shipbuilding Bureau, Yokosuka Navy Yard
1 Dec 1932: Promoted to *Rear-Admiral*
1 Dec 1936: Promoted to *Vice-Admiral*
1 Dec 1936 - 15 Dec 1936: Attached to Naval Shipbuilding Command
20 Dec 1936: Transferred to the reserve

Rear-Admiral **Tanin IKEDA** (18 Nov 1881 - 1 Apr 1944)
1 Dec 1925 - 1 Dec 1926: Captain, Battleship *"Mutsu"*
1 Dec 1926: Promoted to *Rear-Admiral*
1 Dec 1926 - 20 Mar 1927: Attached to Naval General Staff
20 Mar 1927 - 10 Apr 1927: Unassigned
10 Apr 1927: Transferred to the reserve

Rear-Admiral (Surgeon) **Masao IKEGAMI** (2 Mar 1898 - 3 Jun 1945)
1 Aug 1943 - 3 Jun 1945: Attached to staff, Southeastern Area Fleet
3 Jun 1945: Posthumously promoted to *Rear-Admiral (Surgeon)*

Rear-Admiral **Kenichi IKENAKA** (20 Oct 1882 - 21 Aug 1954)
10 Dec 1928 - 1 Dec 1930: Captain, Battlecruiser *"Kongo"*
1 Dec 1930: Promoted to *Rear-Admiral*
1 Dec 1930 - 15 Dec 1930: Attached to Naval General Staff
24 Dec 1930: Transferred to the reserve

Rear-Admiral **Masamichi IKEUCHI** (31 Aug 1890 - 4 Aug 1974)
15 Apr 1944 - 1 Aug 1944: Attached to Yokosuka Naval District
1 May 1944: Promoted to *Rear-Admiral*
1 Aug 1944 - 21 Aug 1944: Supervisor of Ordnance, Naval Shipbuilding Command, Supervisor of Ordnance, Naval Air Command
21 Aug 1944 - 20 Dec 1944: Chief Supervisor for Construction & Ordnance, Naval Shipbuilding Command
20 Dec 1944 - 20 Mar 1945: Chief Supervisor, Muroran
20 Mar 1945 - 10 May 1945: Chief of Sapporo office, Ominato Guard District
10 May 1945 - 25 May 1945: Chief Supervisor, Hokkai
25 May 1945 - 28 Jul 1945: Attached to Yokosuka Naval District
28 Jul 1945 - 28 Aug 1945: Recalled; Captain, Battleship *"Nagato"*
1 Sep 1945: Demobilized

Rear-Admiral **Masuta IKEYA** (3 Feb 1894 - 15 Jul 1963)
15 Feb 1945 - 30 Sep 1945: Chief of Electronic Bureau, 2nd Technical Arsenal
1 May 1945: Promoted to *Rear-Admiral*

Rear-Admiral (Surgeon) **Zenji IKUTA** (15 Nov 1887 - 2 Jul 1972)
1 Dec 1932 - 15 Nov 1933:	Director, Maizuru Guard District Naval Hospital, Chief Surgeon, Maizuru Guard District
15 Nov 1933:	Promoted to *Rear-Admiral (Surgeon)*
15 Nov 1933 - 11 Dec 1933:	Attached to Yokosuka Naval District
15 Dec 1933:	Transferred to the reserve

Vice-Admiral (Surgeon) **Ibuo IMADA** (9 Feb 1892 - 14 Sep 1967)
22 Sep 1941 - 10 Nov 1942:	Chief Surgeon, Combined Fleet
1 Nov 1942:	Promoted to *Rear-Admiral (Surgeon)*
10 Nov 1942 - 25 Oct 1943:	Attached to Kure Naval District
25 Oct 1943 - 1 Nov 1944:	Director, Ureshino Naval Hospital
1 Nov 1944 - 1 Nov 1945:	Chief of Medical Bureau, Sasebo Navy Yard
1 Nov 1945:	Promoted to *Vice-Admiral (Surgeon)*

Rear-Admiral **Satoshi IMADA** (23 Mar 1900 - 18 Jun 1945)
5 Oct 1944 - 18 Jun 1945:	Chief of Administration Bureau, Southwest Area Air Depot
18 Jun 1945:	Posthumously promoted to *Rear-Admiral*

Rear-Admiral **Hiroshige IMAI** (1 Dec 1885 - 29 Jul 1935)
15 Nov 1934 - 29 Jul 1935:	Chief of Ordnance Bureau, Sasebo Navy Yard
29 Jul 1935:	Posthumously promoted to *Rear-Admiral*

Rear-Admiral **Kanemasa IMAI** (14 Nov 1858 - 25 Jul 1907)
12 Dec 1905 - 22 Nov 1906:	Commander, Yokosuka Sailors Corps
22 Nov 1906:	Promoted to *Rear-Admiral*
22 Nov 1906 - 12 Mar 1907:	Commander, Yokosuka Torpedo Corps
12 Mar 1907 - 25 Jul 1907:	Unassigned

Rear-Admiral **Kanetane IMAI** (7 Mar 1867 - 27 Dec 1928)
1 Dec 1912 - 29 May 1914:	Commander, Yokosuka Sailors Corps
29 May 1914:	Promoted to *Rear-Admiral*
29 May 1914 - 27 May 1915:	Unassigned
27 May 1915:	Transferred to the reserve

Rear-Admiral (Surgeon) **Kinsaburo IMAI** (13 Oct 1877 - 24 Jul 1967)
1 May 1927 - 30 Nov 1929:	Chief of Medical Section, Technical Research Department
30 Nov 1929:	Promoted to *Rear-Admiral*
30 Nov 1929 - 15 Dec 1929:	Attached to Naval General Staff
25 Dec 1929:	Transferred to the reserve

Rear-Admiral **Eizo IMAIZUMI** (8 Jan 1895 - 30 May 1984)
1 May 1943:	Promoted to *Rear-Admiral*
1 May 1943 - 15 Oct 1945:	Chief of Scientific Research Bureau, Technical Research Department

Rear-Admiral **Tetsutaro IMAIZUMI** (12 Sep 1877 - 8 Feb 1945)
15 Sep 1920 - 1 Dec 1921:	Acting Commandant, Submarine School
1 Dec 1921:	Promoted to *Rear-Admiral*
1 Dec 1921 - 1 Dec 1922:	Commander, 1st Submarine Flotilla
1 Dec 1922 - 1 Dec 1923:	Commander, 2nd Submarine Flotilla
1 Dec 1923 - 5 Feb 1924:	Attached to Kure Naval District
25 Feb 1924:	Transferred to the reserve

Rear-Admiral **Toshiyoshi IMAIZUMI** (7 May 1858 - 23 Dec 1936)
4 Sep 1902 - 28 Aug 1908:	Chief of Documents Section, Naval Hydrographic Command
28 Aug 1908:	Promoted to *Rear-Admiral*
28 Aug 1908 - 27 Aug 1909:	Unassigned
27 Aug 1909:	Transferred to the reserve

Rear-Admiral **Yoshijiro IMAIZUMI**
20 Feb 1945 - 1 Nov 1945:	Commander, Yokosuka Submarine Base Force
20 Mar 1945 - 1 Nov 1945:	Commander, 16th Submarine Flotilla
1 Nov 1945:	Promoted to *Rear-Admiral*

Vice-Admiral **Osamu IMAMURA** (16 Oct 1891 - 31 Mar 1978)
10 Apr 1941 - 1 Feb 1942:	Commander, 12th Air Flotilla
15 Oct 1941:	Promoted to *Rear-Admiral*
1 Feb 1942 - 1 Apr 1942:	Attached to Yokosuka Naval District
1 Apr 1942 - 15 Nov 1943:	Commander, 13th Combined Air Flotilla
15 Nov 1943 - 25 Nov 1943:	Attached to staff, 1st Southern Expeditionary Fleet
25 Nov 1943 - Oct 1945:	Commander, 10th Special Naval Base Force
15 Oct 1944:	Promoted to *Vice-Admiral*

Vice-Admiral **Shinjiro IMAMURA** (4 Dec 1880 - 1 Sep 1969)
20 Oct 1925 - 25 Dec 1926:	Aide-de-Camp to the Crown Prince
1 Dec 1925:	Promoted to *Rear-Admiral*
25 Dec 1926 - 1 May 1931:	Aide-de-Camp to the Emperor
1 Dec 1930:	Promoted to *Vice-Admiral*
1 May 1931 - 1 Oct 1931:	Attached to Naval General Staff
1 Oct 1931 - 1 Oct 1932:	C-in-C, Training Fleet
1 Oct 1932 - 1 Dec 1932:	Attached to Naval General Staff
1 Dec 1932 - 15 Sep 1933:	Admiral Commanding, Maizuru Naval District

15 Sep 1933 - 15 Nov 1934:	C-in-C, 3rd Fleet
15 Nov 1934 - 2 Dec 1935:	Admiral Commanding, Sasebo Naval District
2 Dec 1935 - 28 Mar 1936:	Attached to Naval General Staff
30 Mar 1936:	Transferred to the reserve

Rear-Admiral (Surgeon) **Masakichi IMAYOSHI** (23 Feb 1884 - 18 Mar 1940)

30 Nov 1929:	Promoted to *Rear-Admiral (Surgeon)*
30 Nov 1929 - 1 Dec 1931:	Director, Sasebo Naval Hospital, Chief Surgeon, Sasebo Naval District
1 Dec 1931 - 15 Dec 1931:	Attached to Naval General Staff
21 Dec 1931:	Transferred to the reserve

Rear-Admiral **Hiroshi IMAZATO** (24 Sep 1896 - 11 Nov 1942)

25 Aug 1942 - 11 Nov 1942:	Captain, Auxiliary Cruiser *"Hokoku-maru"*
11 Nov 1942:	Posthumously promoted to *Rear-Admiral*

Rear-Admiral (Surgeon) **Masafuyu IMAZAWA** (11 May 1882 - 29 Jan 1963)

16 May 1927 - 10 Dec 1928:	Director, Minato Naval Hospital
10 Dec 1928:	Promoted to *Rear-Admiral (Surgeon)*
10 Dec 1928 - 20 Dec 1928:	Attached to Naval General Staff
25 Dec 1928:	Transferred to the reserve

Rear-Admiral (Surgeon) **Chiaki IMOKAWA** (1891 - 4 Jan 1964)

1 Dec 1937 - 15 Nov 1939:	Chief of Medical Bureau, Yokosuka Navy Yard
15 Nov 1938:	Promoted to *Rear-Admiral (Surgeon)*
15 Nov 1939 - 15 Nov 1940:	Director, Beppu Naval Hospital
15 Nov 1940 - 15 Oct 1941:	Director, Maizuru Naval Hospital, Chief Surgeon, Maizuru Naval District
15 Oct 1941 - 15 Dec 1941:	Attached to Naval General Staff
22 Dec 1941:	Transferred to the reserve

Rear-Admiral **Torahiko INADA** (17 Nov 1890 - 15 Nov 1970)

1 Oct 1938 - 15 Nov 1939:	Chief of Communication Research Bureau, Yokosuka Navy Yard
15 Nov 1939:	Promoted to *Rear-Admiral*
15 Nov 1939 - 15 Dec 1939:	Attached to Naval Shipbuilding Command
21 Dec 1939:	Transferred to the reserve

Vice-Admiral **Ayao INAGAKI** (20 Feb 1890 - 15 Sep 1942)

1 Dec 1937:	Promoted to *Rear-Admiral*
1 Dec 1937 - 1 Dec 1939:	Chief of Administration Bureau, Naval Air Command
1 Dec 1939 - 1 Apr 1941:	Attached to Naval General Staff

1 Apr 1941 - 30 Dec 1941:	Unassigned
30 Dec 1941 - 1 Jun 1942:	Attached to Naval General Staff
1 Jun 1942 - 15 Sep 1942:	Commandant of the Naval College
15 Sep 1942:	Posthumously promoted to *Vice-Admiral*

Rear-Admiral **Yoichi INAGAWA** (12 Jun 1876 - 24 Jun 1943)

1 Oct 1920 - 2 Mar 1925:	Attached to Bureau 5, Naval Shipbuilding Command
1 Dec 1922:	Promoted to *Rear-Admiral*
10 Apr 1924 - 1 Dec 1924:	Chief of Research Bureau, Technical Research Department
20 Mar 1925:	Transferred to the reserve

Rear-Admiral (Paymaster) **Arata INAOKA** (23 Feb 1895 - 7 Apr 1968)

30 May 1941 - 1 May 1943:	Chief of Section 1, Accounting Bureau, Department of the Navy
1 May 1943:	Promoted to *Rear-Admiral (Paymaster)*
1 May 1943 - 17 Mar 1945:	Attached to the Department of the Navy
17 Mar 1945 - 30 Nov 1945:	Chief of Contracts Division, Accounting Bureau, Department of the Navy

Vice-Admiral **Toshihira INOGUCHI** (11 Aug 1896 - 24 Oct 1944)

12 Aug 1944 - 24 Oct 1944:	Captain, Battleship *"Musashi"*
15 Oct 1944:	Promoted to *Rear-Admiral*
24 Oct 1944:	Posthumously promoted to *Vice-Admiral*

Rear-Admiral **Noboru INOMATA** (14 Aug 1896 - 2 Mar 1969)

10 Jan 1945 - Oct 1945:	Commander, 4th Navy Fuel Yard
1 May 1945:	Promoted to *Rear-Admiral*

Rear-Admiral **Masamori INOSE** (? - 22 Jul 1944)

8 Nov 1943 - 22 Jul 1944:	Captain, Auxiliary Cruiser *"Hakkai-maru"*
22 Jul 1944:	Posthumously promoted to *Rear-Admiral*

Rear-Admiral **Kintaro INOUCHI** (18 May 1866 - 18 May 1931)

1 Dec 1910 - 29 May 1914:	Chief of Survey Section, Naval Hydrographic Command
29 May 1914:	Promoted to *Rear-Admiral*
29 May 1914 - 27 May 1915:	Unassigned
27 May 1915:	Transferred to the reserve

Vice-Admiral **Choji INOUE** (23 Jan 1886 - 26 Sep 1938)

1 Dec 1931:	Promoted to *Rear-Admiral*

1 Dec 1931 - 15 Nov 1932:	Chief of Staff, Kure Naval District
15 Nov 1932 - 15 Nov 1933:	Commander, 1st Submarine Flotilla
15 Nov 1933 - 15 Nov 1934:	Commander, Ominato Guard District
15 Nov 1934 - 15 Nov 1935:	Chief of Bureau 6, Naval Shipbuilding Command
15 Nov 1935:	Promoted to *Vice-Admiral*
15 Nov 1935 - 10 Dec 1935:	Attached to Naval Shipbuilding Command
15 Dec 1935:	Transferred to the reserve

Rear-Admiral **Samaji INOUE** (13 Mar 1895 - 17 Mar 1945)

10 Jul 1944 - 17 Mar 1945:	Commander, Southern Islands Air Flotilla
17 Mar 1945:	Posthumously promoted to *Rear-Admiral*

Admiral **Shigeyoshi INOUE** (9 Dec 1889 - 15 Dec 1975)

15 Nov 1935:	Promoted to *Rear-Admiral*
15 Nov 1935 - 16 Nov 1936:	Chief of Staff, Yokosuka Naval District
16 Nov 1936 - 20 Oct 1937:	Attached to Naval General Staff
20 Oct 1937 - 18 Oct 1939:	Chief of the Naval Affairs Bureau, Member, Admirals Committee
18 Oct 1939 - 23 Oct 1939:	Attached to Naval General Staff
23 Oct 1939 - 15 Nov 1939:	Chief of Staff, 3rd Fleet
23 Oct 1939 - 1 Oct 1940:	Chief of Staff, China Area Fleet
15 Nov 1939:	Promoted to *Vice-Admiral*
1 Oct 1940 - 11 Aug 1941:	Chief of Naval Air Command
11 Aug 1941 - 26 Oct 1942:	C-in-C, 4th Fleet
26 Oct 1942 - 5 Aug 1944:	Commandant, Etajima Naval Academy
5 Aug 1944 - 15 May 1945:	Deputy Minister of the Navy, Member, Admirals Committee
4 Nov 1944 - 18 Nov 1944:	Chief of Naval Shipbuilding Command
1 May 1945 - 15 May 1945:	Chief of Naval Air Command
15 May 1945:	Promoted to *Admiral*
15 May 1945 - 10 Oct 1945:	Navy Councillor

Rear-Admiral **Shiro INOUE** (15 Apr 1881 - 12 May 1960)

1 Dec 1925 - 10 Dec 1928:	Chief of Personnel Bureau, Sasebo Naval District
1 Dec 1927:	Promoted to *Rear-Admiral*
10 Dec 1928 - 20 Dec 1928:	Attached to Naval General Staff
25 Dec 1928:	Transferred to the reserve

Rear-Admiral **Toshio INOUE** (12 Aug 1857 - 9 Mar 1924)

14 Jun 1905:	Promoted to *Rear-Admiral*
14 Jun 1905 - 4 Nov 1905:	C-in-C, Special Task Fleet
4 Nov 1905 - 13 Nov 1905:	Unassigned
13 Nov 1905 - 28 May 1906:	Chief of Reserve Bureau, Kure Naval District
28 May 1906:	Transferred to the reserve

Vice-Admiral **Tsugumatsu INOUE** (1883 - 24 Dec 1966)

30 Nov 1929:	Promoted to *Rear-Admiral*
30 Nov 1929 - 1 Dec 1931:	Chief Instructor, Naval College
1 Dec 1931 - 4 Feb 1932:	Attached to Naval General Staff
4 Feb 1932 - 15 Nov 1933:	Commander, 2nd Destroyer Flotilla
15 Nov 1933 - 2 Dec 1935:	Commandant of the Naval College
15 Nov 1934:	Promoted to *Vice-Admiral*
2 Dec 1935 - 16 Mar 1936:	Attached to Naval General Staff
16 Mar 1936 - 1 Dec 1936:	Commander, Chinkai Guard District
1 Dec 1936 - 15 Mar 1937:	Attached to Naval General Staff
25 Mar 1937:	Transferred to the reserve

Vice-Admiral **Yasuo INOUE** (6 Oct 1888 - 29 Sep 1981)

1 Dec 1937:	Promoted to *Rear-Admiral*
1 Dec 1937 - 1 Feb 1938:	Commander, Yokosuka Defense Squadron
1 Feb 1938 - 15 Nov 1938:	Commander, Yokosuka Sailors Corps
15 Nov 1938 - 15 Nov 1940:	Chief of Personnel Bureau, Yokosuka Naval District
15 Nov 1940 - 10 Apr 1941:	Commander, Kainan Auxiliary Base Force
10 Apr 1941 - 1 Sep 1941:	Chief of Staff, Kaina Guard District
1 Sep 1941 - 10 Mar 1942:	Commander, Kanton Area Base Force
15 Oct 1941:	Promoted to *Vice-Admiral*
10 Mar 1942 - 10 Apr 1942:	Attached to Naval General Staff
10 Apr 1942 - 14 Jan 1943:	Commander, 1st Escort Flotilla
14 Jan 1943 - 1 Apr 1943:	Attached to Naval General Staff
1 Apr 1943 - 15 Feb 1945:	Commander, Ominato Guard District
15 Feb 1945 - 15 Mar 1945:	Attached to Naval General Staff
20 Mar 1945:	Transferred to the reserve

Fleet Admiral **Viscount Yoshika INOUE** (3 Nov 1845 - 22 Mar 1929)

29 Jan 1886 - 17 Jun 1886:	Deputy Chief of the Naval Affairs Bureau
15 Jun 1886:	Promoted to *Rear-Admiral*
17 Jun 1886 - 8 Mar 1889:	Chief of the Naval Affairs Bureau
16 Aug 1888 - 8 Mar 1889:	Commandant of the Naval College
8 Mar 1889 - 15 May 1889:	Chief of Bureau 1, Department of the Navy
15 May 1889 - 29 Jul 1889:	Commander, Readiness Flotilla
29 Jul 1889 - 17 Jun 1891:	C-in-C, Readiness Fleet
17 Jun 1891 - 12 Dec 1892:	Chief of the Naval General Staff
12 Dec 1892:	Promoted to *Vice-Admiral*
12 Dec 1892 - 20 May 1893:	Admiral Commanding, Sasebo Naval District
20 May 1893 - 16 Feb 1895:	Admiral Commanding, Yokosuka Naval District
16 Feb 1895 - 16 Nov 1895:	C-in-C, West Fleet
16 Nov 1895 - 26 Feb 1896:	C-in-C, Readiness Fleet
26 Feb 1896 - 20 May 1900:	Admiral Commanding, Kure Naval District

20 May 1900 - 20 Dec 1905:	Admiral Commanding, Yokosuka Naval District
24 Dec 1901:	Promoted to *Admiral*
14 Jan 1904 - 22 Mar 1929:	Navy Councillor
31 Oct 1911:	Appointed *Fleet Admiral*

Rear-Admiral **Yoshio INOUE** (22 Jan 1898 - 27 Oct 1944)
31 Mar 1944 - 27 Oct 1944:	Commander, 18th Destroyer Division
27 Oct 1944:	Posthumously promoted to *Rear-Admiral*

Vice-Admiral **Baron Yoshitomo INOUE** (11 Jun 1851 - 4 Jan 1913)
23 May 1898 - 26 May 1908:	Aide-de-Camp to the Emperor
26 May 1902:	Promoted to *Rear-Admiral*
13 Nov 1905:	Promoted to *Vice-Admiral*
26 May 1908 - 28 Aug 1908:	Member, Admirals Committee
28 Aug 1908 - 27 Aug 1909:	Unassigned
27 Aug 1909:	Transferred to the reserve

Rear-Admiral (Paymaster) **Toshitaka INUI** (5 Apr 1893 - 10 Feb 1946)
15 Mar 1941 - 10 Oct 1943:	Chief of Accounting Bureau, Yokosuka Navy Yard
15 Oct 1941:	Promoted to *Rear-Admiral (Paymaster)*
10 Oct 1943 - 10 Jun 1945:	Paymaster-General, Sasebo Naval District
10 Jun 1945 - 10 Aug 1945:	Attached to Naval General Staff
15 Aug 1945:	Transferred to the reserve

Rear-Admiral **Sukejiro INUTSUKA** (2 Sep 1871 - 29 Jul 1947)
1 Oct 1920 - 1 Jun 1923:	Chief of Naval Hydrographic Command
1 Dec 1920:	Promoted to *Rear-Admiral*
1 Jun 1923 - 1 Dec 1923:	Attached to Naval General Staff
1 Dec 1923 - 25 Feb 1924:	Unassigned
25 Feb 1924:	Transferred to the reserve

Vice-Admiral **Taro INUTSUKA** (23 Oct 1875 - 17 Jul 1936)
22 Nov 1917 - 5 Feb 1924:	Aide-de-Camp to the Crown Prince
1 Dec 1921:	Promoted to *Rear-Admiral*
5 Feb 1924 - 1 Dec 1924:	Commander, 5th Escort Flotilla
1 Dec 1924 - 15 Apr 1925:	Attached to Naval General Staff
15 Apr 1925 - 1 Dec 1926:	Commander, Chinkai Guard District
1 Dec 1925:	Promoted to *Vice-Admiral*
1 Dec 1926 - 15 Dec 1927:	Attached to Naval General Staff
25 Dec 1927:	Transferred to the reserve

Vice-Admiral **Kei IOKIBE** (18 Aug 1891 - 1 Mar 1945)
15 Oct 1941:	Promoted to *Rear-Admiral*

15 Oct 1941 - 10 May 1944:	Chief of Material Research Bureau, Technical Research Department
10 May 1944 - 1 Oct 1944:	Attached to Naval Shipbuilding Command
1 Oct 1944 - 10 Feb 1945:	Chief of Material Research Bureau, Technical Research Department
10 Feb 1945 - 1 Mar 1945:	Attached to Naval Shipbuilding Command
1 Mar 1945:	Posthumously promoted to *Vice-Admiral*

Rear-Admiral **Itaru IRIE** (? - 25 Oct 1944)
1 Dec 1943 - 25 Oct 1944:	Chief Engineer, Heavy Cruiser *"Chikuma"*
25 Oct 1944:	KIA; Posthumously promoted to *Rear-Admiral*

Vice-Admiral **Naosaburo IRIFUNE** (27 Feb 1891 - 24 Dec 1953)
15 Nov 1940:	Promoted to *Rear-Admiral*
15 Nov 1940 - 17 Nov 1941:	Commandant, Naval Gunnery School
17 Nov 1941 - 20 Nov 1941:	Attached to staff, 3rd Fleet
20 Nov 1941 - 15 Mar 1943:	Commander, 32nd Special Naval Base Force
15 Mar 1943 - 1 Nov 1943:	Commandant, Naval Gunnery School
1 Nov 1943 - 8 Nov 1943:	Attached to staff, 8th Fleet
8 Nov 1943 - 1 Dec 1944:	Commander, 8th Naval Base Force
1 May 1944:	Promoted to *Vice-Admiral*
7 Nov 1944 - Oct 1945:	Chief of Staff, Southeastern Area Fleet, Chief of Staff, 11th Air Fleet

Rear-Admiral **Toshiie IRISA** (26 Apr 1902 - 19 Jun 1944)
15 Feb 1944 - 19 Jun 1944:	Commander, 601st Air Flotilla
19 Jun 1944:	Posthumously promoted 2 grades to *Rear-Admiral*

Vice-Admiral **Toshio IRISAWA** (11 Feb 1868 - 1 Jan 1939)
15 Jun 1911 - 1 Dec 1912:	Chief Engineer Officer, Kure Naval District
3 Feb 1912:	Promoted to *Rear-Admiral*
1 Dec 1912 - 1 Apr 1916:	Chief Engineer Officer, Yokosuka Naval District
1 Apr 1916 - 1 Jul 1916:	Chief of Engine Construction Bureau, Yokosuka Navy Yard
1 Jul 1916 - 1 Jul 1917:	Unassigned
1 Dec 1916:	Promoted to *Vice-Admiral*

Vice-Admiral (Paymaster) **Kiyonaga IRITANI** (12 Apr 1877 - 16 Jul 1948)
8 Oct 1925 - 1 Dec 1926:	Chief of Section 2, Administration Bureau, Naval Shipbuilding Command
1 Dec 1926:	Promoted to *Rear-Admiral (Paymaster)*
1 Dec 1926 - 13 Apr 1927:	Attached to Naval Shipbuilding Command

13 Apr 1927 - 1 Dec 1931:	Paymaster-General, Kure Naval District
1 Dec 1931:	Promoted to *Vice-Admiral (Paymaster)*
1 Dec 1931 - 1 Dec 1932:	Commandant, Naval Paymaster Academy
1 Dec 1932 - 10 Dec 1932:	Attached to Naval General Staff
15 Dec 1932:	Transferred to the reserve

Vice-Admiral **Shunji ISAKI** (5 Feb 1892 - 12 Jul 1943)

1 Nov 1941 - 21 Jan 1943:	Commander, Kure Harbor
1 Nov 1942:	Promoted to *Rear-Admiral*
21 Jan 1943 - 12 Jul 1943:	Commander, 2nd Destroyer Flotilla
12 Jul 1943:	Posthumously promoted to *Vice-Admiral*

Rear-Admiral **Sadayoshi ISE** (20 Apr 1896 - 25 Jan 1957)

12 Feb 1945 - 25 Apr 1945:	Chief of Administration Bureau, Air Technical Arsenal
25 Apr 1945 - 20 Sep 1945:	Attached to Yokosuka Naval District
1 May 1945:	Promoted to *Rear-Admiral*

Vice-Admiral **Hajime ISHIBASHI** (2 Jul 1862 - 11 Jan 1942)

22 Jun 1910 - 10 Mar 1923:	Commandant, Merchant Navy High School
16 Jul 1910:	Promoted to *Rear-Admiral*
1 Dec 1914:	Promoted to *Vice-Admiral*
1 Dec 1914:	Transferred to the reserve

Rear-Admiral **Masakazu ISHIBASHI** (11 Jan 1889 - 15 Nov 1980)

1 May 1943:	Promoted to *Rear-Admiral*
1 May 1943 - 5 Apr 1944:	Chief of 2nd Pyrotechnical Bureau, Sagami Navy Yard
1 Oct 1943 - 1 Aug 1944:	Chief of 1st Pyrotechnical Bureau, Sagami Navy Yard
1 Aug 1944 - 1 Jun 1945:	Commander, 3rd Navy Powder Yard
1 Jun 1945 - 2 Jul 1945:	Attached to Naval Shipbuilding Yard
3 Jul 1945:	Transferred to the reserve

Rear-Admiral **Ichiro ISHIDA** (15 Nov 1862 - 1 Jan 1934)

1 Dec 1910:	Promoted to *Rear-Admiral*
1 Dec 1910 - 21 Sep 1911:	Commander, Sasebo Torpedo Corps
21 Sep 1911 - 21 Sep 1912:	Transferred to the reserve

Rear-Admiral **Yuzo ISHIDO** (15 Oct 1886 - 16 Dec 1952)

8 Apr 1943 - 10 Jul 1945:	Commander, 4th Naval Guard Force
1 May 1943:	Promoted to *Rear-Admiral*
10 Jul 1945 - Oct 1945:	Attached to staff, 2nd Southern Expeditionary Fleet

Rear-Admiral **Hirosuke ISHIGURO** (23 Jun 1890 - 5 May 1947)
15 Nov 1940:	Promoted to *Rear-Admiral*
15 Nov 1940 - 15 Jan 1941:	Attached to Yokosuka Naval District
15 Jan 1941 - 15 Aug 1941:	Chief of Aircraft Bureau, Hiro Navy Yard
15 Aug 1941 - 1 Oct 1941:	Attached to Mako Guard District
1 Oct 1941 - 1 Feb 1943:	Commander, 61st Air Arsenal
1 Feb 1943 - 15 Feb 1943:	Attached to Naval General Staff
17 Feb 1943:	Transferred to the reserve

Rear-Admiral **Torao ISHIGURO** (8 Jul 1888 - 18 Jan 1944)
4 Dec 1943 - 18 Jan 1944:	Attached to Yokosuka Naval District
18 Jan 1944:	Posthumously promoted to *Rear-Admiral*

Rear-Admiral (Paymaster) **Toshiyoshi ISHIGURO** (9 Feb 1886 - 29 Jan 1945)
1 Dec 1936:	Promoted to *Rear-Admiral (Paymaster)*
1 Dec 1936 - 15 Nov 1938:	Paymaster-General, Sasebo Naval District
15 Nov 1938 - 16 Dec 1938:	Attached to Naval General Staff
21 Dec 1938:	Transferred to the reserve

Rear-Admiral (Surgeon) **Uchuji ISHIGURO** (7 Feb 1854 - 5 Sep 1923)
13 Dec 1905 - 24 Nov 1906:	Director, Maizuru Naval Hospital, Chief Surgeon, Maizuru Naval District
6 Jul 1906:	Promoted to *General (Surgeon)*
30 Nov 1906:	Transferred to the reserve
23 Sep 1919:	Redesignated *Rear-Admiral (Surgeon)*

Vice-Admiral (Surgeon) **Yoshio ISHIGURO** (26 Aug 1893 - 5 Aug 1969)
1 Apr 1939 - 1 Nov 1944:	Chief of Medical Bureau, Air Technical Arsenal
15 Nov 1940:	Promoted to *Rear-Admiral (Surgeon)*
1 May 1944:	Promoted to *Vice-Admiral (Surgeon)*
1 Nov 1944 - 15 Oct 1945:	Director, Sasebo Naval Hospital, Chief Surgeon, Sasebo Naval District

Rear-Admiral **Itsu ISHIHARA** (2 Sep 1897 - 19 Feb 1975)
5 Dec 1943 - 15 Jan 1945:	Captain, Heavy Cruiser *"Myoko"*
15 Oct 1944:	Promoted to *Rear-Admiral*
15 Jan 1945 - 10 Feb 1945:	Attached to Yokosuka Naval District
10 Feb 1945 - 15 Oct 1945:	Deputy Chief of Staff, Sasebo Naval District
1 Sep 1945 - 15 Oct 1945:	Chief of Transport Bureau, Sasebo Naval District

Rear-Admiral (Surgeon) **Ryo ISHIHARA** (1 Apr 1884 - 11 Apr 1957)
1 Dec 1930:	Promoted to *Rear-Admiral (Surgeon)*
1 Dec 1930 - 1 Dec 1931:	Chief Instructor, Navy Medical School

1 Dec 1931 - 15 Dec 1931:	Attached to Naval General Staff
21 Dec 1931:	Transferred to the reserve

Rear-Admiral (Surgeon) **Sumikata ISHIHARA** (15 Jul 1862 - 10 Mar 1945)
20 Apr 1912:	Promoted to *General (Surgeon)*
20 Apr 1912 - 1 Apr 1913:	Director, Maizuru Naval Hospital, Chief Surgeon, Maizuru Naval District
1 Apr 1913 - 1 Dec 1913:	Unassigned
1 Dec 1913:	Transferred to the reserve
23 Sep 1919:	Redesignated *Rear-Admiral (Surgeon)*

Rear-Admiral **Gitaro ISHII** (27 Jul 1866 - 16 Feb 1927)
1 Dec 1911:	Promoted to *Rear-Admiral*
1 Dec 1911 - 1 Dec 1912:	Chief of Bureau 1, Naval Training Command
1 Dec 1912 - 31 May 1913:	Unassigned
31 May 1913:	Transferred to the reserve

Rear-Admiral **Keishi ISHII** (18 Dec 1893 - 3 Apr 1975)
20 Jun 1942 - 14 Jun 1943:	Captain, Battlecruiser *"Haruna"*
1 May 1943:	Promoted to *Rear-Admiral*
14 Jun 1943 - 17 Jul 1943:	Attached to Naval General Staff
17 Jul 1943 - 1 Nov 1943:	Chief of Sailor Bureau, Shipping Agency
1 Nov 1943 - 19 Dec 1944:	Chief of Sailor Bureau, Sealift Agency, Department of Transport & Communication
19 Dec 1944 - 29 Jan 1945:	Attached to Naval General Staff
29 Jan 1945 - 30 Nov 1945:	Chief of Staff, Sasebo Naval District

Rear-Admiral **Masao ISHII** (31 Oct 1893 - 4 Jun 1967)
1 Apr 1942 - 6 Sep 1943:	Chief of Oita Branch, 11th Air Arsenal
1 May 1943:	Promoted to *Rear-Admiral*
10 Sep 1943:	Transferred to the reserve

Vice-Admiral **Shizue ISHII** (20 Dec 1888 - 17 Nov 1944)
15 Dec 1943 - 17 Nov 1944:	Captain, Aircraft Carrier *"Shinyo"*
15 Oct 1944:	Promoted to *Rear-Admiral*
17 Nov 1944:	Posthumously promoted to *Vice-Admiral*

Vice-Admiral **Tsunejiro ISHII** (18 Nov 1887 - 16 Jan 1951)
1 Dec 1936:	Promoted to *Rear-Admiral*
1 Dec 1936 - 15 Nov 1938:	Chief of Mining Bureau, Navy Fuel Yard
15 Nov 1938 - 15 Nov 1940:	Chief Supervisor for Construction & Ordnance, Naval Shipbuilding Command
15 Nov 1940:	Promoted to *Vice-Admiral*

15 Nov 1940 - 15 Oct 1941:	Commander, Maizuru Navy Yard
25 Oct 1941:	Transferred to the reserve

Rear-Admiral **Hidesaburo ISHIKAWA** (20 Dec 1876 - 28 Dec 1967)

20 Nov 1920 - 20 Nov 1921:	Captain, Battleship *"Hyuga"*
20 Nov 1921 - 1 Dec 1921:	Attached to Sasebo Naval District
1 Dec 1921:	Promoted to *Rear-Admiral*
1 Dec 1921 - 31 Mar 1923:	Unassigned
31 Mar 1923:	Transferred to the reserve

Rear-Admiral **Kiyoshi ISHIKAWA** (27 Apr 1882 - 13 Oct 1934)

10 Jul 1925 - 1 Dec 1926:	Captain, Battlecruiser *"Haruna"*
1 Dec 1926:	Promoted to *Rear-Admiral*
1 Dec 1926 - 1 Dec 1927:	Commander, Yokosuka Defense Force
1 Dec 1927 - 15 Dec 1927:	Attached to Naval General Staff
25 Dec 1927:	Transferred to the reserve

Vice-Admiral **Shigeru ISHIKAWA** (3 Oct 1889 - 21 Feb 1947)

20 Apr 1941 - 2 Feb 1942:	Commander, Kure Defense Flotilla
15 Oct 1941:	Promoted to *Rear-Admiral*
2 Feb 1942 - 15 Feb 1942:	Attached to staff, 1st Southern Expeditionary Fleet
15 Feb 1942 - 26 Jun 1944:	Commander, 12th Naval Base Force
26 Jun 1944 - 5 Aug 1944:	Attached to Naval General Staff
5 Aug 1944 - 15 Jul 1945:	Commander, Yokosuka Defense Flotilla
15 Oct 1944:	Promoted to *Vice-Admiral*
15 Jul 1945 - 6 Sep 1945:	Attached to Naval General Staff

Rear-Admiral **Shingo ISHIKAWA** (1 Jan 1894 - 17 Dec 1964)

10 Jun 1942 - 20 Jan 1943:	Deputy Chief of Staff, Southwestern Area Fleet
1 Nov 1942:	Promoted to *Rear-Admiral*
20 Jan 1943 - 25 Jan 1943:	Attached to staff, Southwestern Area Fleet
25 Jan 1943 - 20 Aug 1943:	Commander, 23rd Naval Air Flotilla
20 Aug 1943 - 1 Nov 1943:	Attached to Naval General Staff
1 Nov 1943 - 10 Nov 1944:	Chief of Administration Section/Mobilization Bureau, Department of Military Supply
10 Nov 1944 - 15 Nov 1944:	Attached to Naval General Staff
15 Nov 1944 - 1 Sep 1945:	Chief of Naval Transportation Command, Chief of Reinforcement Section, Joint General Staff
1 Sep 1945 - 30 Sep 1945:	Attached to Naval General Staff

Rear-Admiral **Tetsushiro ISHIKAWA** (8 Nov 1882 - 1 Mar 1942)

1 Dec 1941 - 1 Mar 1942:	Chief of Minesweeping, Tanker *"No.2 Kaijo-maru"*
1 Mar 1942:	Posthumously promoted to *Rear-Admiral*

Vice-Admiral **Tokiji ISHIKAWA** (30 Jun 1879 - 23 Jun 1964)
5 Feb 1924 - 11 Apr 1927:	Chief of Engine Construction Bureau, Hiro Navy Yard
1 Dec 1925:	Promoted to *Rear-Admiral*
11 Apr 1927 - 1 Dec 1930:	Chief of Scientific Research Bureau, Technical Research Department
1 Dec 1930:	Promoted to *Vice-Admiral*
1 Dec 1930 - 15 Dec 1930:	Attached to Naval General Staff
24 Dec 1930:	Transferred to the reserve

Rear-Admiral **Yuzo ISHIKAWA** (4 Feb 1895 - 9 Mar 1972)
15 Dec 1941 - 20 Jan 1944:	Chief of Engine Construction Bureau, Sasebo Navy Yard
1 May 1943:	Promoted to *Rear-Admiral*
20 Jan 1944 - 1 Feb 1944:	Attached to staff, 1st Southern Expeditionary Fleet
1 Feb 1944 - 5 Apr 1945:	Commander, 101st Naval Facility
5 Apr 1945 - 12 May 1945:	Attached to Naval Air Command
12 May 1945 - 30 Sep 1945:	Chief of Rocket Bureau, 1st Technical Arsenal

Rear-Admiral **Eikichi ISHIKO** (8 Aug 1884 - 18 Apr 1953)
1 Dec 1923 - 30 Nov 1929:	Chief of Electriconics Bureau, Kure Navy Yard
30 Nov 1929:	Promoted to *Rear-Admiral*
30 Nov 1929 - 15 Dec 1929:	Attached to Naval Shipbuilding Command
25 Dec 1929:	Transferred to the reserve

Rear-Admiral (Paymaster) **Shunkan ISHIKURA** (18 Feb 1880 - 20 Mar 1975)
1 Dec 1924 - 1 Dec 1926:	Chief of Section 1, Accounting Bureau, Kure Naval District
1 Dec 1926:	Promoted to *Rear-Admiral (Paymaster)*
1 Dec 1926 - 20 Mar 1927:	Attached to Naval General Staff
20 Mar 1927 - 10 Apr 1927:	Unassigned
10 Apr 1927:	Transferred to the reserve

Rear-Admiral **Saburo ISHISE** (24 Sep 1898 - 8 Jul 1944)
1 Mar 1944 - 8 Jul 1944:	Staff officer, 5th Construction Bureau
8 Jul 1944:	Posthumously promoted to *Rear-Admiral*

Rear-Admiral **Noboru ISHIZAKI** (20 Oct 1893 - 9 Aug 1959)
10 Mar 1942 - 19 Aug 1943:	Commander, 8th Submarine Flotilla
1 Nov 1942:	Promoted to *Rear-Admiral*
19 Aug 1943 - 20 Oct 1943:	Attached to Naval General Staff
20 Oct 1943 - 21 Dec 1944:	Commander, 11th Submarine Flotilla
21 Dec 1944 - 10 Aug 1945:	Commander, 22nd Escort Flotilla
10 Aug 1945 - 6 Sep 1945:	Attached to Naval General Staff

Rear-Admiral **Chitoshi ISHIZUKA** (15 Apr 1896 - 11 Nov 1946)
15 Aug 1944 - 15 Apr 1945: Chief of Staff, Chinkai Guard District
15 Apr 1945 - 1 Nov 1945: Attached to Chinkai Guard District
1 May 1945: Promoted to *Rear-Admiral*

Rear-Admiral **Megumi ISO** (18 Oct 1895 - 20 Feb 1986)
10 Dec 1943 - 20 Jul 1945: Chief of Gunnery Research & Pyrotechnic Bureaus, Kure Navy Yard
1 May 1945: Promoted to *Rear-Admiral*
20 Jul 1945 - 1 Nov 1945: Commander, Sagami Navy Yard

Rear-Admiral **Jun ISOBE** (21 Jul 1893 - 2 Apr 1975)
17 Dec 1942 - 10 Sep 1944: Commander, 4th Communications Unit
1 May 1944: Promoted to *Rear-Admiral*
10 Sep 1944 - 15 Oct 1944: Attached to Naval General Staff
15 Oct 1944 - 20 Nov 1945: Chief of Personnel Bureau, Chinkai Guard District

Rear-Admiral **Kenma ISOHISA** (13 Feb 1898 - 17 Feb 1944)
17 Nov 1943 - 17 Feb 1944: Commander, 4th Destroyer Division
17 Feb 1944: Posthumously promoted to *Rear-Admiral*

Rear-Admiral (Apothecary) **Shuhei ISONO** (13 Oct 1878 - 16 Oct 1933)
1 Dec 1917 - 30 Nov 1929: Instructor, Navy Medical School
1 Dec 1926: Promoted to *Rear-Admiral (Apothecary)*
30 Nov 1929 - 10 Jun 1930: Attached to Naval General Staff
20 Jun 1930: Transferred to the reserve

Vice-Admiral **Seikichi ISOZAKI** (15 Oct 1877 - ?)
13 Aug 1923 - 1 Dec 1927: Chief of Shipbuilding Bureau, Yokosuka Navy Yard
1 Dec 1923: Promoted to *Rear-Admiral*
1 Dec 1927: Promoted to *Vice-Admiral*
1 Dec 1927 - 15 Dec 1927: Attached to Naval Shipbuilding Command
25 Dec 1927: Transferred to the reserve

Rear-Admiral **Kizo ISUMI** (23 Sep 1880 - 10 Mar 1964)
10 Dec 1928 - 1 Dec 1931: Chief of Personnel, Yokosuka Naval District
30 Nov 1929: Promoted to *Rear-Admiral*
1 Dec 1931 - 15 Dec 1931: Attached to Naval General Staff
21 Dec 1931: Transferred to the reserve

Rear-Admiral **Akira ITAGAKI** (20 Jun 1897 - 17 Feb 1945)
10 Sep 1944 - 17 Feb 1945: Executive Officer, 31st Naval Base Force
17 Feb 1945: Posthumously promoted to *Rear-Admiral*

Rear-Admiral **Koichi ITAGAKI** (9 Apr 1889 - 15 Sep 1942)
20 Sep 1941 - 15 Sep 1942: Chief of Minesweeping, Transport *"Nojima-maru"*
15 Sep 1942: Posthumously promoted to *Rear-Admiral*

Rear-Admiral **Sakan ITAGAKI** (18 Jul 1889 - 28 Jan 1980)
20 Nov 1941 - 10 Aug 1942: Commander, 2nd Sasebo Sailors Corps
1 May 1942: Promoted to *Rear-Admiral*
10 Aug 1942 - 1 Oct 1942: Commander, Chinkai Defense Force
1 Oct 1942 - 10 Oct 1942: Attached to Naval General Staff
10 Oct 1942 - 31 Oct 1942: Attached to staff, 8th Fleet
31 Oct 1942 - 1 Nov 1943: Commander, 1st Auxiliary Base Force
1 Nov 1943 - 20 Nov 1943: Attached to Kure Naval District
20 Nov 1943 - 20 Jul 1945: Commander, Kure Naval Guard Force
20 Jul 1945 - 6 Sep 1945: Attached to Naval General Staff

Rear-Admiral (Surgeon) **Shun ITAKURA** (29 Mar 1897 - 14 Jun 1952)
15 Nov 1944 - 30 Nov 1945: Director, Iwakuni Naval Hospital
1 May 1945: Promoted to *Rear-Admiral (Surgeon)*

Rear-Admiral **Tokushi ITAKURA** (17 Mar 1893 - 20 Mar 1984)
1 Apr 1945 - 10 Oct 1945: Commander, Ise Defense Force
15 Apr 1945 - 5 Nov 1945: Commander, 13th Assault Force
1 May 1945: Promoted to *Rear-Admiral*

Rear-Admiral **Jotaro ITO** (15 Jul 1892 - 22 Jul 1943)
5 Dec 1942 - 22 Jul 1943: Captain, Seaplane Tender *"Nisshin"*
22 Jul 1943: Posthumously promoted to *Rear-Admiral*

Vice-Admiral **Kenzo ITO** (6 Mar 1894 - 12 May 1974)
1 Oct 1940 - 6 Dec 1940: Chief of Press Bureau, Joint General Staff
15 Nov 1940: Promoted to *Rear-Admiral*
6 Dec 1940 - 2 Jun 1942: Chief of Bureau 1, Cabinet Intelligence Agency
2 Jun 1942 - 1 Mar 1943: Chief of Administration Bureau, Southwestern Area Fleet Civil Government
1 Mar 1943 - 1 Apr 1943: Attached to Naval General Staff
1 Apr 1943 - 10 Jan 1944: Commander, 14th Escort Flotilla
10 Jan 1944 - 1 Mar 1944: Commander, 30th Naval Base Force
1 Mar 1944 - Oct 1945: Commander, 30th Area Base Force
1 May 1944: Promoted to *Vice-Admiral*

Vice-Admiral **Koji ITO** (8 Jun 1878 - 24 Mar 1936)
1 Jul 1925 - 30 Nov 1929: Supervisor for Construction & Ordnance, Naval Shipbuilding Command

1 Dec 1925:	Promoted to *Rear-Admiral*
30 Nov 1929:	Promoted to *Vice-Admiral*
30 Nov 1929 - 1 Dec 1930:	Commander, Hiro Navy Yard
1 Dec 1930 - 15 Nov 1933:	Director of Navy Technical Research
15 Nov 1933 - 26 Mar 1934:	Attached to Naval Shipbuilding Command
31 Mar 1934:	Transferred to the reserve

Vice-Admiral **Otojiro ITO** (26 Oct 1866 - 27 Mar 1941)

1 Dec 1911:	Promoted to *Rear-Admiral*
1 Dec 1911 - 20 Apr 1912:	Chief of Naval Hydrographic Command
20 Apr 1912 - 1 Dec 1913:	Chief of Staff, Sasebo Naval District
1 Dec 1913 - 13 Dec 1915:	Commander, Sasebo Navy Yard
13 Dec 1915:	Promoted to *Vice-Admiral*
13 Dec 1915 - 12 Dec 1917:	Commander, Kure Navy Yard
12 Dec 1917 - 1 Oct 1920:	Chief of Naval Technical Command
12 Dec 1917 - 27 Nov 1920:	Member, Admirals Committee
1 Dec 1920:	Transferred to the reserve

Rear-Admiral **Risaburo ITO** (19 Jan 1885 - 14 Mar 1963)

1 Dec 1930 - 15 Nov 1934:	Chief of Communications Section, Department of the Navy
15 Nov 1934 - 10 Dec 1935:	Attached to Naval General Staff
15 Nov 1935:	Promoted to *Rear-Admiral*
14 Dec 1935:	Transferred to the reserve

Admiral **Seiichi ITO** (26 Jul 1890 - 7 Apr 1945)

15 Nov 1937 - 15 Nov 1938:	Chief of Staff, 2nd Fleet
1 Dec 1937:	Promoted to *Rear-Admiral*
15 Nov 1938 - 15 Dec 1938:	Attached to Naval General Staff
15 Dec 1938 - 28 Nov 1940:	Chief of Naval Personnel, Department of the Navy
28 Nov 1940 - 10 Apr 1941:	Commander, 8th Cruiser Division
10 Apr 1941 - 1 Aug 1941:	Chief of Staff, Combined Fleet, Chief of Staff, 1st Fleet
1 Aug 1941 - 1 Sep 1941:	Attached to Naval General Staff
1 Sep 1941 - 18 Nov 1944:	Deputy Chief of the Naval General Staff
15 Oct 1941:	Promoted to *Vice-Admiral*
22 May 1943 - 15 Jun 1943:	Acting Chief of Bureau 1, Naval General Staff
15 Mar 1944 - 18 Nov 1944:	Commandant of the Naval College
18 Nov 1944 - 23 Dec 1944:	Attached to Naval General Staff
23 Dec 1944 - 7 Apr 1945:	C-in-C, 2nd Fleet
1 Apr 1945 - 7 Apr 1945:	Commander, 1st Special Attack Force
7 Apr 1945:	Posthumously promoted to *Admiral*

Rear-Admiral (Engineer) **Shigeji ITO** (10 Mar 1862 - 11 Jan 1940)
21 Feb 1908 - 1 Dec 1911:	Commandant, Naval Engineering School
1 Dec 1909:	Promoted to *Rear-Admiral (Engineer)*
1 Dec 1911 - 1 Dec 1912:	Unassigned
1 Dec 1912:	Transferred to the reserve

Rear-Admiral (Surgeon) **Shinichi ITO** (29 Oct 1894 - 26 Jan 1957)
15 Nov 1943 - 28 Nov 1944:	Director, 1st Naval Hospital, Chief Surgeon, China Area Fleet
1 May 1944:	Promoted to *Rear-Admiral (Surgeon)*
28 Nov 1944 - 25 Jun 1945:	Attached to Maizuru Naval District
25 Jun 1945 - 1 Nov 1945:	Chief of the Medical Bureau, Maizuru Navy Yard

Rear-Admiral (Surgeon) **Shunkichi ITO** (2 Jun 1894 - 27 Oct 1946)
15 Nov 1943 - 11 May 1945:	Attached to Kure Naval Department
1 May 1945:	Promoted to *Rear-Admiral (Surgeon)*
11 May 1945 - 25 Jun 1945:	Director, Osaka Naval Hospital, Chief Surgeon, Osaka Guard District
25 Jun 1945 - 6 Sep 1945:	Attached to Kure Naval Department

Fleet Admiral **Count Sukeyuki ITO** (20 May 1843 - 16 Jan 1914)
20 Nov 1885 - 17 Jun 1886:	Captain, Armored Cruiser *"Naniwa"*
15 Jun 1886:	Promoted to *Rear-Admiral*
17 Jun 1886 - 15 May 1889:	Commander, Readiness Flotilla
15 May 1889 - 24 Sep 1890:	Commandant of the Naval College
15 May 1889 - 12 Dec 1892:	Chief of Bureau 1, Department of the Navy
12 Dec 1892:	Promoted to *Vice-Admiral*
12 Dec 1892 - 20 May 1893:	Admiral Commanding, Yokosuka Naval District
20 May 1893 - 18 Jul 1894:	C-in-C, Readiness Fleet
18 Jul 1894 - 11 May 1895:	C-in-C, Combined Fleet
11 May 1895 - 20 Dec 1905:	Chief of the Naval General Staff
28 Sep 1898:	Promoted to *Admiral*
20 Dec 1905 - 16 Jan 1914:	Navy Councillor
31 Jan 1906:	Appointed *Fleet Admiral*

Rear-Admiral **Tadahide ITO** (22 Jan 1895 - 30 Jun 1947)
1 Oct 1943 - 20 Sep 1945:	Chief of Machine Gun Bureau, Tagajo Navy Yard
1 May 1945:	Promoted to *Rear-Admiral*

Rear-Admiral **Tsunesaku ITO** (16 Feb 1849 - 2 Dec 1911)
17 May 1898 - 29 Sep 1899:	Commander, Navy Gunnery Training Center
29 Sep 1899 - 1 Feb 1902:	Unassigned
1 Feb 1902:	Promoted to *Rear-Admiral*
1 Feb 1902:	Transferred to the reserve

Rear-Admiral **Yasukichi ITO** (14 May 1873 - 15 Sep 1951)
1 Jun 1917 - 15 Jun 1921: Chief of Engine Construction Bureau, Yokosuka Navy Yard
1 Jun 1919: Promoted to *General (Engine Constructor)*
23 Sep 1919: Redesignated *Rear-Admiral*
15 Jun 1921 - 10 Apr 1922: Attached to Bureau 5, Naval Shipbuilding Command
10 Apr 1922 - 31 Mar 1923: Unassigned
31 Mar 1923: Transferred to the reserve

Vice-Admiral **Yasunoshin ITO** (1894 - 8 Jul 1944)
1 Nov 1941 - 25 Oct 1943: Chief Supervisor, Taihoku
1 Nov 1942: Promoted to *Rear-Admiral*
25 Oct 1943 - 5 Nov 1943: Attached to Naval General Staff
5 Nov 1943 - 11 Nov 1943: Attached to the staff, Combined Fleet
11 Nov 1943 - 8 Jul 1944: Commander, 1st Combined Communications Unit
8 Jul 1944: Posthumously promoted to *Vice-Admiral*

Rear-Admiral **Yoshiaki ITO** (25 Sep 1893 - 30 Jul 1972)
20 Aug 1943 - 9 Sep 1944: Commander, 23rd Naval Air Flotilla
1 Nov 1943: Promoted to *Rear-Admiral*
9 Sep 1944 - 7 Oct 1944: Attached to Naval General Staff
7 Oct 1944 - 5 May 1945: Commander, 13th Combined Air Flotilla
5 May 1945 - 15 Sep 1945: Commander, 13th Naval Air Flotilla

Vice-Admiral **Baron Yoshigoro ITO** (16 May 1858 - 22 Feb 1919)
6 Jul 1901: Promoted to *Rear-Admiral*
6 Jul 1901 - 12 Apr 1902: C-in-C, Readiness Fleet
12 Apr 1902 - 9 Nov 1903: Chief of Shipping Bureau, Yokosuka Naval District
9 Nov 1903 - 22 Nov 1906: Commander, Yokosuka Naval Yard
13 Nov 1905: Promoted to *Vice-Admiral*
22 Nov 1906 - 21 Oct 1907: Commander, Takeshiki Guard District
21 Oct 1907 - 10 Dec 1907: Member, Admirals Committee
10 Dec 1907 - 31 May 1909: Unassigned
31 May 1909: Transferred to the reserve

Rear-Admiral **Suetada ITOKAWA** (11 Dec 1887 - 18 Mar 1944)
1 Dec 1943 - 18 Mar 1944: Attached to staff, Transport *"Hokuriku-maru"*
18 Mar 1944: Posthumously promoted to *Rear-Admiral*

Vice-Admiral **Suetaka IWABE** (17 Feb 1872 - 24 Apr 1955)
1 Dec 1917 - 1 Dec 1919: Chief Engineer Officer, 1st Fleet
1 Jun 1919: Promoted to *Rear-Admiral*

1 Jun 1919 - 1 Dec 1919:	Chief Engineer Officer, Combined Fleet
1 Dec 1919 - 1 Dec 1923:	Chief Engineer Officer, Yokosuka Naval District
1 Dec 1923:	Promoted to *Vice-Admiral*
1 Dec 1923 - 10 Dec 1923:	Attached to Yokosuka Naval District
10 Dec 1923 - 25 Feb 1924:	Unassigned
25 Feb 1924:	Transferred to the reserve

Vice-Admiral **Sanji IWABUCHI** (2 Mar 1895 - 26 Feb 1945)

10 Feb 1943 - 5 May 1943:	Attached to Yokosuka Naval District
1 May 1943:	Promoted to *Rear-Admiral*
5 May 1943 - 1 Nov 1944:	Chief of Personnel, Maizuru Naval District
1 Nov 1944 - 17 Nov 1944:	Attached to staff of 3rd Southern Expeditionary Fleet
17 Nov 1944 - 26 Feb 1945:	Commander, 31st Naval Special Base Force
26 Feb 1945:	Posthumously promoted to *Vice-Admiral*

Rear-Admiral **Eiju IWAGAMI** (14 Sep 1896 - 2 Feb 1944)

23 Sep 1943 - 2 Feb 1944:	Commander, 2nd Submarine Division
2 Feb 1944:	Posthumously promoted to *Rear-Admiral*

Rear-Admiral **Jiichi IWAGAMI** (10 Apr 1900 - 8 Jan 1945)

29 Nov 1944 - 8 Jun 1945:	Commander, 52nd Destroyer Division
8 Jan 1945:	Posthumously promoted to *Rear-Admiral*

Rear-Admiral **Kanki IWAGOE** (25 Jan 1889 - 15 Jan 1954)

15 Nov 1940:	Promoted to *Rear-Admiral*
15 Nov 1940 - 10 Mar 1942:	Chief of South China Naval Special Task Office
10 Mar 1942 - 15 Aug 1942:	Attached to Sasebo Naval District
15 Aug 1942 - 25 Aug 1942:	Attached to Naval General Staff
1 Sep 1942:	Transferred to the reserve
10 Aug 1944 - 25 Oct 1945:	Recalled; Commander, Otake Sailors Corps

Rear-Admiral **Fuchina IWAIHARA** (15 May 1886 - 2 Dec 1969)

15 Nov 1934 - 1 Dec 1937:	Chief of Personnel, Sasebo Naval District
15 Nov 1935:	Promoted to *Rear-Admiral*
1 Dec 1937 - 20 Apr 1938:	Commander, Yokosuka Guard Flotilla
20 Apr 1938 - 15 Dec 1938:	Attached to Naval General Staff
21 Dec 1938:	Transferred to the reserve

Vice-Admiral **Kanae IWAMOTO** (19 Feb 1891 - 12 May 1970)

15 Nov 1939:	Promoted to *Rear-Admiral*
15 Nov 1939 - 15 Nov 1940:	Chief of Oil Bureau, Navy Fuel Yard
15 Nov 1940 - 1 Oct 1941:	Attached to Yokosuka Naval District

1 Oct 1941 - 15 Mar 1943:	Commander, 2nd Air Arsenal
15 Mar 1943 - 15 Apr 1943:	Attached to Naval Air Command
15 Apr 1943 - 1 Aug 1944:	Chief of Bureau 1, Naval Air Command
1 May 1943:	Promoted to *Vice-Admiral*
1 Aug 1944 - 20 Apr 1945:	Commander, 11th Air Arsenal
20 Apr 1945 - 15 Jun 1945:	Attached to Naval Air Command
20 Jun 1945:	Transferred to the reserve

Rear-Admiral **Kosaku IWAMOTO** (12 Jul 1861 - 27 Nov 1929)

13 Jun 1905 - 28 Dec 1907:	Chief of Ordnance Bureau, Kure Navy Yard
28 Dec 1907:	Promoted to *Rear-Admiral*
28 Dec 1907:	Transferred to the reserve

Rear-Admiral **Kanekoto IWAMURA** (18 Oct 1880 - 11 Mar 1946)

14 Oct 1930 - 1 Dec 1931:	Commander, 1st Destroyer Flotilla
1 Dec 1930:	Promoted to *Rear-Admiral*
1 Dec 1931 - 20 Jul 1932:	Attached to Naval General Staff
30 Jul 1932:	Transferred to the reserve
18 Jul 1934 - 24 Oct 1934:	Recalled; Attached to Sasebo Naval District
24 Oct 1934:	Demobilized

Rear-Admiral (Paymaster) **Kaneyoshi IWAMURA** (4 Nov 1845 - 27 Nov 1919)

13 Feb 1894 - 15 Mar 1897:	Chief of Accounting Bureau, Yokosuka Naval District
15 Mar 1897 - 16 May 1900:	Unassigned
16 May 1900:	Promoted to *General (Paymaster)*
16 May 1900:	Transferred to the reserve
23 Sep 1919:	Redesignated *Rear-Admiral (Paymaster)*

Vice-Admiral **Seiichi IWAMURA** (14 Sep 1889 - 9 Feb 1970)

15 Nov 1935:	Promoted to *Rear-Admiral*
15 Nov 1935 - 2 Dec 1935:	Attached to the staff, 3rd Fleet
2 Dec 1935 - 16 Nov 1936:	Chief of Staff, 3rd Fleet
16 Nov 1936 - 1 Dec 1937:	Chief of Staff, Yokosuka Naval District
1 Dec 1937 - 30 Sep 1939:	Chief of Administration Bureau, Naval Shipbuilding Command
30 Sep 1939 - 26 Oct 1939:	Attached to the staff, 3rd Fleet
26 Oct 1939 - 15 Oct 1940:	Naval Attache, China
15 Nov 1939:	Promoted to *Vice-Admiral*
15 Oct 1940 - 15 Nov 1940:	Attached to the staff, 1st Fleet
15 Nov 1940 - 11 Aug 1941:	Commander, 2nd Escort Flotilla
11 Aug 1941 - 18 Sep 1941:	Attached to Naval General Staff
18 Sep 1941 - 15 Apr 1943:	Chief of Naval Shipbuilding Command, Member, Admirals Committee

15 Apr 1943 - 3 Sep 1943:	C-in-C, 2nd Southern Expeditionary Fleet
3 Sep 1943 - 15 Mar 1944:	Attached to Naval General Staff
20 Mar 1944:	Transferred to the reserve

Vice-Admiral **Toshitake IWAMURA** (Aug 1866 - 9 Nov 1943)

1 Dec 1913:	Promoted to *Rear-Admiral*
1 Dec 1913 - 11 Nov 1914:	Attached to the Governor of Korea
11 Nov 1914 - 30 Jun 1915:	Commander, Tsingtao Guard District
30 Jun 1915 - 13 Dec 1915:	Commander, 4th Destroyer Flotilla
13 Dec 1915 - 1 Sep 1916:	Commander, 1st Destroyer Flotilla
1 Sep 1916 - 1 Sep 1917:	C-in-C, Training Fleet
1 Sep 1917 - 1 Dec 1917:	Member, Admirals Committee
1 Dec 1917:	Promoted to *Vice-Admiral*
1 Dec 1917 - 1 Dec 1919:	Commander, Ominato Guard District
1 Dec 1919 - 1 Aug 1920:	Member, Admirals Committee
1 Aug 1920 - 1 Apr 1921:	Unassigned
1 Apr 1921:	Transferred to the reserve

Rear-Admiral (Paymaster) **Yoshimitsu IWANARI** (9 Apr 1895 - 29 Nov 1978)

8 Apr 1944 - 1 Nov 1945:	Chief of Accounting Bureau, Sasebo Navy Yard
1 May 1944:	Promoted to *Rear-Admiral (Paymaster)*

Rear-Admiral **Naohide IWANO** (28 Aug 1871 - 2 May 1943)

1 Apr 1919 - 20 Nov 1919:	Chief of Civil Engineer Torpedo Corps
20 Nov 1919 - 1 Dec 1919:	Attached to Yokosuka Naval District
1 Dec 1919:	Promoted to *Rear-Admiral*
1 Dec 1919 - 1 Apr 1920:	Unassigned
1 Apr 1920:	Transferred to the reserve

Rear-Admiral **Seiichiro IWANO** (20 Mar 1874 - ?)

1 Aug 1919 - 1 Dec 1922:	Instructor, Naval College
1 Dec 1922:	Promoted to *Rear-Admiral*
1 Dec 1922 - 10 Dec 1922:	Attached to Naval Shipbuilding Command
10 Dec 1922 - 31 Mar 1923:	Unassigned
31 Mar 1923:	Transferred to the reserve

Rear-Admiral **Shoichi IWASA** (11 Apr 1876 - 13 Feb 1958)

13 Aug 1923 - 2 Feb 1925:	Chief of Shipbuilding Bureau, Sasebo Navy Yard
1 Dec 1924:	Promoted to *Rear-Admiral*
2 Feb 1925 - 2 Mar 1925:	Attached to Naval Shipbuilding Command
20 Mar 1925:	Transferred to the reserve

Rear-Admiral (Paymaster) **Mitsu IWASAKI** (22 Oct 1893 - 14 Mar 1973)
20 Oct 1943 - 15 Feb 1945:	Chief of Accounting Bureau, Takao
15 Oct 1944:	Promoted to *Rear-Admiral (Paymaster)*
15 Feb 1945 - 1 Apr 1945:	Attached to Naval General Staff
1 Apr 1945 - 30 Sep 1945:	Chief of Supply Bureau, Yokosuka Naval District

Rear-Admiral **Moshiro IWASAKI** (15 Feb 1872 - 5 Oct 1924)
1 Dec 1920:	Promoted to *Rear-Admiral*
1 Dec 1920 - 10 Nov 1922:	Commander, Maizuru Defense Unit
10 Nov 1922 - 1 Dec 1922:	Attached to Naval General Staff
1 Dec 1922 - 31 Mar 1923:	Unassigned
31 Mar 1923:	Transferred to the reserve

Rear-Admiral **Tatsuto IWASAKI** (21 Nov 1858 - 1 Nov 1941)
2 Feb 1906 - 21 Oct 1907:	Chief of Bureau 1, Naval Shipbuilding Command
3 Apr 1906:	Promoted to *Rear-Admiral*
21 Oct 1907 - 25 Sep 1908:	Attached to the Department of the Navy
25 Sep 1908 - 27 Aug 1909:	Unassigned
27 Aug 1909:	Transferred to the reserve

Rear-Admiral **Wasaburo IWASAKI** (18 Jul 1893 - 9 Jun 1945)
15 Nov 1940 - 17 Oct 1944:	Chief of Engine Construction Bureau, Yokosuka Navy Yard
15 Oct 1941:	Promoted to *Rear-Admiral*
17 Oct 1944 - 10 Jan 1945:	Attached to Naval Shipbuilding Command
10 Jan 1945 - 25 Feb 1945:	Attached to Naval Air Command
26 Feb 1945:	Transferred to the reserve

Rear-Admiral **Yasutaro IWASHITA** (10 Jun 1887 - 18 Feb 1937)
5 Nov 1935 - 16 Nov 1936:	Attached to the Plenipotentiary, London Conference
15 Nov 1935:	Promoted to *Rear-Admiral*
16 Nov 1936 - 18 Feb 1937:	Chief of Staff, Combined Fleet, Chief of Staff, 1st Fleet

Rear-Admiral **Shunji IZAKI** (? - 13 Jul 1943)
Jun 1943 - 13 Jul 1943:	Commander, 2nd Destroyer Flotilla
13 Jul 1943:	Posthumously promoted to *Rear-Admiral*

Rear-Admiral **Haruma IZAWA** (2 Dec 1885 - 5 Mar 1975)
20 Sep 1934 - 15 Nov 1935:	Chief of Staff, Yokosuka Naval District
15 Nov 1934:	Promoted to *Rear-Admiral*
15 Nov 1935 - 1 Dec 1936:	Chief Instructor, Naval College

1 Dec 1936 - 1 Dec 1937:	Commander, Ominato Guard District
1 Dec 1937 - 15 Mar 1938:	Attached to Naval General Staff
25 Mar 1938:	Transferred to the reserve

Rear-Admiral **Ishinosuke IZAWA** (26 Jan 1893 - 18 Jul 1947)

7 Oct 1944 - 1 Apr 1945:	Attached to Yokosuka Naval District
15 Oct 1944:	Promoted to *Rear-Admiral*
1 Apr 1945 - 13 Apr 1945:	Unassigned
13 Apr 1945 - 8 Aug 1945:	Attached to Yokosuka Naval District
8 Aug 1945 - 15 Sep 1945:	Commander, Yokosuka Guard Force
15 Sep 1945 - 20 Sep 1945:	Attached to Yokosuka Naval District

Rear-Admiral **Masuzo IZUCHI** (25 Apr 1898 - 19 Aug 1979)

15 Feb 1945 - 30 Sep 1945:	Chief of Bomb Bureau, 1st Technical Arsenal
1 May 1945:	Promoted to *Rear-Admiral*

Rear-Admiral **Fukujiro IZUMI** (26 Nov 1902 - 18 Jul 1945)

15 Nov 1943 - 3 May 1945:	Instructor, Naval Navigation School
3 May 1945 - 28 Jul 1945:	Executive Officer, Aircraft Carrier *"Katsuragi"*
28 Jul 1945:	Posthumously promoted to *Rear-Admiral*

Vice-Admiral **Benichi JINBO** (1 Jan 1892 - ?)

1 Jun 1938 - 15 Dec 1939:	Attached to Naval Shipbuilding Command
15 Nov 1939:	Promoted to *Rear-Admiral*
15 Dec 1939 - 21 Apr 1941:	Commander, Toyokawa Navy Yard
21 Apr 1941 - 1 May 1943:	Commander, 3rd Powder Yard
1 May 1943:	Promoted to *Vice-Admiral*
1 May 1943 - 20 Jun 1943:	Attached to Naval General Staff
25 Jun 1943:	Transferred to the reserve

Rear-Admiral **Eiichiro JO** (1 Apr 1899 - 25 Oct 1944)

15 Feb 1944 - 25 Oct 1944:	Captain, Aircraft Carrier *"Chiyoda"*
25 Oct 1944:	Posthumously promoted to *Rear-Admiral*

Rear-Admiral **Takatsugu JOJIMA** (20 Jun 1890 - 9 Oct 1967)

17 Apr 1941 - 25 May 1942:	Captain, Aircraft Carrier *"Shokaku"*
1 May 1942:	Promoted to *Rear-Admiral*
25 May 1942 - 15 Jun 1942:	Attached to Sasebo Naval District
15 Jun 1942 - 20 Jun 1942:	Attached to the staff, Combined Fleet
20 Jun 1942 - 15 Apr 1943:	Commander, 11th Carrier Division
15 Apr 1943 - 10 May 1943:	Attached to Yokosuka Naval District
10 May 1943 - 1 Sep 1943:	Commander, 50th Carrier Division
1 Sep 1943 - 10 Jul 1944:	Commander, 2nd Carrier Flotilla

10 Jul 1944 - 20 Dec 1944:	Commander, 21st Carrier Flotilla
20 Dec 1944 - 1 Mar 1945:	Commander, 11th Combined Flying Division
1 Mar 1945 - 5 May 1945:	Commander, 12th Combined Flying Division
5 May 1945 - 30 Sep 1945:	Commander, 12th Carrier Flotilla

Vice-Admiral **Setsuo KABASHIMA** (5 Nov 1887 - 11 Feb 1973)

1 Dec 1932 - 15 Dec 1938:	Commander, Yokosuka Harbor
15 Nov 1938:	Promoted to *Rear-Admiral*
15 Dec 1938 - 15 Jan 1939:	Attached to Naval General Staff
15 Jan 1939 - 25 Dec 1941:	Attached to Mako Guard District
25 Dec 1941 - 10 Mar 1943:	Commander, 11th Auxiliary Naval Facility
1 May 1942:	Promoted to *Vice-Admiral*
10 Mar 1943 - 20 Jun 1943:	Attached to Naval General Staff
25 Jun 1943:	Transferred to the reserve

Rear-Admiral **Bekinari KABAYAMA** (14 Oct 1877 - 27 Oct 1932)

20 Nov 1922 - 1 Apr 1923:	Commander, Yokosuka Defense Force
1 Dec 1922:	Promoted to *Rear-Admiral*
1 Apr 1923 - 1 Dec 1923:	Commandant, Naval Gunnery School
1 Dec 1923 - 10 Nov 1924:	Chief of Staff, Combined Fkeet, Chief of Staff, 1st Fleet
10 Nov 1924 - 1 Dec 1924:	Attached to Kure Naval District
1 Dec 1924 - 16 Dec 1924:	Chief of Staff, Kure Naval District
16 Dec 1924 - 20 Nov 1925:	Attached to Naval General Staff
20 Nov 1925 - 16 Dec 1925:	Unassigned
16 Dec 1925:	Transferred to the reserve

Admiral **Count Sukenori KABAYAMA** (20 Nov 1837 - 8 Feb 1922)

7 Feb 1881:	Promoted to *Major-General (Army)*
7 Feb 1881 - 13 Dec 1883:	Chief of the Metropolitan Police
13 Dec 1883 - 1 Apr 1886:	Vice-Lord of the Navy
6 Feb 1884:	Redesignated *Rear-Admiral*
29 Jun 1885:	Promoted to *Vice-Admiral*
29 Jan 1886 - 15 Jun 1886:	Chief, Bureau of Naval Affairs
1 Apr 1886 - 17 May 1890:	Deputy Minister of the Navy
17 May 1890 - 8 Aug 1892:	Minister of the Navy
8 Aug 1892:	Transferred to the reserve
18 Jul 1894 - 10 May 1895:	Recalled; Chief of the Naval General Staff, Member, Admirals Committee
10 May 1895:	Promoted to *Admiral*
10 May 1895 - 2 Jun 1896:	Governor of Taiwan
2 Jun 1896 - 20 Sep 1896:	Councilor of the Court
20 Sep 1896 - 12 Jan 1898:	Minister of the Interior

12 Jan 1898 - 8 Nov 1898:	Unassigned
8 Nov 1898 - 19 Oct 1900:	Minister of Education
19 Oct 1900 - 20 Nov 1905:	Councilor of the Court
20 Nov 1905:	Transferred to the reserve

Rear-Admiral (Surgeon) **Tamezo KABEJIMA** (13 Jan 1881 - 27 Dec 1952)
1 Dec 1927 - 10 Dec 1928:	Chief Medical Officer, Combined Fleet, Chief Medical Officer, 1st Fleet
10 Dec 1928:	Promoted to *Rear-Admiral (Surgeon)*
10 Dec 1928 - 15 Mar 1929:	Attached to Naval General Staff
25 Mar 1929:	Transferred to the reserve

Vice-Admiral (Surgeon) **Kihei KABURAGI** (11 Jan 1892 - 3 Nov 1961)
22 Sep 1941 - 1 Oct 1942:	Director, Minato Naval Hospital
15 Oct 1941:	Promoted to *Rear-Admiral (Surgeon)*
1 Oct 1942 - 13 Oct 1942:	Attached to Naval General Staff
13 Oct 1942 - 1 Feb 1944:	Chief of Health Bureau, New Guinea Civil Government
1 Feb 1944 - 10 Mar 1944:	Attached to Yokosuka Naval District
10 Mar 1944 - 1 Nov 1944:	Instructor, Navy Medical School
1 Nov 1944 - 10 Oct 1945:	Director, Beppu Naval Hospital
1 May 1945:	Promoted to *Vice-Admiral (Surgeon)*

Rear-Admiral **Makoto KABURAGI** (20 Aug 1857 - 9 Apr 1919)
28 May 1906:	Promoted to *Rear-Admiral*
28 May 1906 - 22 Nov 1906:	Chief of Reserve Bureau, Kure Naval District
22 Nov 1906 - 12 Mar 1907:	Commander, Kure Torpedo Group
12 Mar 1907 - 15 May 1908:	Commander, Sasebo Torpedo Group
15 May 1908 - 31 May 1909:	Unassigned
31 May 1909:	Transferred to the reserve

Rear-Admiral **Otohiko KAGARA** (12 Aug 1879 - 4 Jun 1962)
1 Dec 1922 - 1 Dec 1923:	Captain, Battleship *"Fuso"*
1 Dec 1923:	Promoted to *Rear-Admiral*
1 Dec 1923 - 10 Dec 1923:	Attached to Naval General Staff
10 Dec 1923 - 25 Feb 1924:	Unassigned
25 Feb 1924:	Transferred to the reserve

Rear-Admiral **Kiyoto KAGAWA** (11 Dec 1895 - 24 Nov 1943)
12 Feb 1943 - 24 Nov 1943:	Commander, 31st Destroyer Division
24 Nov 1943:	Posthumously promoted to *Rear-Admiral*

Vice-Admiral **Takeo KAIZUKA** (3 Jan 1898 - 25 Oct 1944)
18 Dec 1943 - 25 Oct 1944:	Captain, Aircraft Carrier *"Zuikaku"*
15 Oct 1944:	Promoted to *Rear-Admiral*
25 Oct 1944:	Posthumously promoted to *Vice-Admiral*

Rear-Admiral **Ryokichi KAJIKAWA** (13 Aug 1858 - 6 Oct 1909)
12 Mar 1907:	Promoted to *Rear-Admiral*
12 Mar 1907 - 28 Aug 1908:	Chief of Reserve Bureau, Maizuru Naval District
28 Aug 1908 - 6 Oct 1909:	Unassigned

Vice-Admiral **Kinpei KAJIMOTO** (25 Apr 1887 - 13 May 1969)
1 Dec 1932 - 15 Nov 1934:	Chief of Supply Bureau, Sasebo Naval District
15 Nov 1933:	Promoted to *Rear-Admiral*
15 Nov 1934 - 1 Dec 1937:	Chief Supervisor for Construction & Ordnance, Naval Shipbuilding Command
1 Dec 1937:	Promoted to *Vice-Admiral*
1 Dec 1937 - 15 Dec 1937:	Attached to Naval General Staff
21 Dec 1937:	Transferred to the reserve

Vice-Admiral **Sadamichi KAJIOKA** (18 May 1891 - 12 Sep 1944)
15 Nov 1940:	Promoted to *Rear-Admiral*
15 Nov 1940 - 10 Apr 1941:	Commander, Sasebo Defense Flotilla
10 Apr 1941 - 1 Jul 1941:	Commander, Yokosuka Defense Flotilla
1 Jul 1941 - 21 Jul 1941:	Attached to staff, 4th Fleet
21 Jul 1941 - 11 Jul 1942:	Commander, 6th Destroyer Flotilla
11 Jul 1942 - 14 Jul 1942:	Attached to Yokosuka Naval District
14 Jul 1942 - 1 Sep 1942:	Commander, 18th Escort Flotilla
1 Sep 1942 - 10 Oct 1943:	Commander, Rashin Area Base Force
10 Oct 1943 - 20 Oct 1943:	Attached to Naval General Staff
25 Oct 1943:	Transferred to the reserve
10 Jan 1944 - 8 Apr 1944:	Recalled; Attached to Naval General Staff
8 Apr 1944 - 12 Sep 1944:	Commander, 6th Convoy HQ
12 Sep 1944:	Posthumously promoted to *Vice-Admiral*

Rear-Admiral **Masami KAJIWARA** (16 Feb 1901 - 4 Mar 1945)
5 Mar 1943 - 4 Mar 1945:	Commander, 11th Submarine Chaser Division
4 Mar 1945:	Posthumously promoted to *Rear-Admiral*

Rear-Admiral **Hideo KAKEHASHI** (4 Mar 1889 - 20 Apr 1967)
15 Nov 1935 - 1 Dec 1937:	Supervisor for Construction & Ordnance, Naval Shipbuilding Command
1 Dec 1937:	Promoted to *Rear-Admiral*
1 Dec 1937 - 15 Dec 1937:	Attached to Naval General Staff
21 Dec 1937:	Transferred to the reserve

Rear-Admiral **Gonichiro KAKIMOTO** (18 Mar 1891 - 28 Feb 1977)
15 May 1941 - 30 Jan 1943:	Commander, 1st Combined Communications Unit
15 Oct 1941:	Promoted to *Rear-Admiral*
30 Jan 1943 - 1 Dec 1944:	Chief of Decipher Group, Communications Bureau, Joint General Staff
1 Dec 1944 - 15 Dec 1944:	Attached to Naval General Staff
20 Dec 1944:	Transferred to the reserve

Rear-Admiral **Tomeo KAKU** (8 Nov 1893 - 6 Jun 1942)
5 Sep 1941 - 6 Jun 1942:	Captain, Aircraft Carrier *"Hiryu"*
6 Jun 1942:	Posthumously promoted to *Rear-Admiral*

Vice-Admiral **Kakuji KAKUTA** (23 Sep 1890 - 2 Aug 1944)
15 Nov 1939:	Promoted to *Rear-Admiral*
15 Nov 1939 - 15 Oct 1940:	Chief of Staff, Sasebo Naval District
15 Oct 1940 - 15 Nov 1940:	Attached to staff, 1st Fleet
15 Nov 1940 - 1 Sep 1941:	Commander, 3rd Carrier Division
1 Sep 1941 - 14 Jul 1942:	Commander, 4th Carrier Division
14 Jul 1942 - 22 May 1943:	Commander, 2nd Carrier Division
1 Nov 1942:	Promoted to *Vice-Admiral*
22 May 1943 - 1 Jul 1943:	Attached to Naval General Staff
1 Jul 1943 - 2 Aug 1944:	C-in-C, 1st Air Fleet

Vice-Admiral **Michiaki KAMATA** (15 Jan 1890 - 18 Oct 1947)
1 Jul 1941 - 28 Sep 1942:	Commander, Yokosuka Defense Flotilla
15 Oct 1941:	Promoted to *Rear-Admiral*
28 Sep 1942 - 5 Oct 1942:	Attached to Naval General Staff
5 Oct 1942 - 25 Nov 1942:	Attached to staff, 8th Fleet
25 Nov 1942 - 10 Dec 1943:	Chief of 8th Construction Bureau
29 Dec 1942 - 10 Dec 1943:	Commander, 2nd Special Naval Base Force
10 Dec 1943 - 15 Jan 1944:	Attached to Naval General Staff
15 Jan 1944 - 10 Aug 1944:	Commander, Otake Sailors Corps
10 Aug 1944 - 23 Aug 1944:	Attached to staff, 2nd Southern Expeditionary Fleet
23 Aug 1944 - Oct 1945:	Commander, 22nd Special Naval Base Force
1 May 1945:	Promoted to *Vice-Admiral*

Rear-Admiral **Shoichi KAMATA** (16 Sep 1892 - 12 Dec 1986)
18 Oct 1943 - Oct 1945:	Commander, 63rd Guard Unit
15 Oct 1944:	Promoted to *Rear-Admiral*

Vice-Admiral **Rokuro KAMAYA** (13 Jan 1868 - 15 Aug 1940)
13 Dec 1915:	Promoted to *Rear-Admiral*
13 Dec 1915 - 1 Dec 1916:	Director, Naval Hydrographic Command

1 Dec 1916 - 18 Oct 1918:	Attached to the Governor of Korea
18 Oct 1918 - 1 Dec 1919:	Commander, 2nd Destroyer Flotilla
1 Dec 1919:	Promoted to *Vice-Admiral*
1 Dec 1919 - 10 Dec 1919:	Member, Admirals Committee
10 Dec 1919 - 1 Aug 1920:	Unassigned
1 Aug 1920:	Transferred to the reserve

Vice-Admiral **Tadamichi KAMAYA** (13 Sep 1862 - 19 Jan 1939)

1 Dec 1910:	Promoted to *Rear-Admiral*
1 Dec 1910 - 1 Dec 1911:	Chief of Staff, Ryojun Naval District
1 Dec 1911 - 9 Jul 1912:	Chief of Staff, Yokosuka Naval District
9 Jul 1912 - 1 Apr 1913:	C-in-C, Sasebo Reserve Fleet
1 Apr 1913 - 1 Dec 1913:	C-in-C, Sasebo Naval District Reserve Fleet
1 Dec 1913 - 1 Dec 1914:	Commander, Mako Guard District
1 Dec 1914:	Promoted to *Vice-Admiral*
1 Dec 1914 - 1 Dec 1915:	Unassigned
1 Dec 1915:	Transferred to the reserve

Rear-Admiral **Yoshio KAMEI** (21 Mar 1896 - 10 Aug 1944)

10 Jul 1944 - 10 Aug 1944:	Commander, Mariana Air Division
10 Aug 1944:	Posthumously promoted to *Rear-Admiral*

Rear-Admiral **Minegoro KAMEYAMA** (20 Feb 1894 - 18 Sep 1944)

15 Aug 1944 - 18 Sep 1944:	Captain, Tanker *"Saigon-maru"*
18 Sep 1944:	Posthumously promoted to *Rear-Admiral*

Rear-Admiral **Shigenori KAMI** (23 Jan 1900 - 15 Sep 1945)

20 Jun 1945 - 15 Sep 1945:	Chief of Staff, 10th Air Fleet
15 Sep 1945:	Posthumously promoted to *Rear-Admiral*

Vice-Admiral **Tokuya KAMIIZUMI** (25 Sep 1865 - 27 Nov 1946)

1 Dec 1909:	Promoted to *Rear-Admiral*
1 Dec 1909 - 2 Sep 1911:	Commander, Ominato Guard District
2 Sep 1911 - 9 Jul 1912:	Commander, Chinkai Guard Force
9 Jul 1912 - 1 Apr 1913:	Commander, Yokosuka Torpedo Corps
1 Apr 1913 - 10 Aug 1913:	Commander, Yokosuka Torpedo Group
10 Aug 1913 - 15 Nov 1913:	Acting C-in-C, 1st Fleet
15 Nov 1913 - 1 Dec 1913:	Commander, Sasebo Torpedo Group
1 Dec 1913 - 1 Dec 1914:	Unassigned
1 Dec 1914:	Promoted to *Vice-Admiral*
1 Dec 1914:	Transferred to the reserve

Rear-Admiral **Fukashi KAMIJO** (20 Oct 1888 - 8 Dec 1943)
26 May 1943 - 8 Dec 1943:	Chief of Traffic Control, 2nd Maritime Escort Force
8 Dec 1943:	Posthumously promoted to *Rear-Admiral*

Rear-Admiral **Takeo KAMIKAWA** (15 Nov 1899 - 25 Oct 1944)
1 Jun 1944 - 25 Oct 1944:	Executive Officer, Heavy Cruiser *"Chokai"*
25 Oct 1944:	Posthumously promoted to *Rear-Admiral*

Admiral **Baron Hikonojo KAMIMURA** (1 May 1849 - 8 Aug 1916)
26 Sep 1899:	Promoted to *Rear-Admiral*
26 Sep 1899 - 25 Oct 1900:	Supervisor for Construction & Ordnance, Naval Shipbuilding Command
25 Oct 1900 - 29 Oct 1902:	Chief, Bureau of Naval Affairs
17 Mar 1902 - 29 Oct 1902:	Deputy Chief of the Naval General Staff
29 Oct 1902 - 5 Sep 1903:	C-in-C, Readiness Fleet
5 Sep 1903:	Promoted to *Vice-Admiral*
5 Sep 1903 - 27 Oct 1903:	Chief of Naval Training Command, Member, Admirals Committee
27 Oct 1903 - 28 Dec 1903:	C-in-C, Readiness Fleet
28 Dec 1903 - 20 Dec 1905:	Cin-C, 2nd Fleet
20 Dec 1905 - 1 Dec 1909:	Admiral Commanding, Yokosuka Naval District, Member, Admirals Committee
1 Dec 1909 - 1 Dec 1911:	C-in-C, 1st Fleet
1 Dec 1910:	Promoted to *Admiral*
?:	Deputy C-in-C, Combined Fleet
1 Dec 1911 - 1 May 1914:	Navy Councillor

Vice-Admiral **Osuke KAMIMURA** (20 Jan 1869 - 16 Aug 1920)
1 Dec 1912:	Promoted to *Rear-Admiral*
1 Dec 1912 - 18 Aug 1914:	Chief of Staff, Yokosuka Naval District
18 Aug 1914 - 1 Oct 1914:	Acting C-in-C, 2nd Fleet
1 Oct 1914 - 1 Dec 1914:	Commander, 4th Escort Flotilla
1 Dec 1914 - 1 Feb 1915:	Commander, 3rd Escort Flotilla
1 Feb 1915 - 6 Aug 1915:	Commander, 2nd Escort Flotilla
6 Aug 1915 - 13 Dec 1915:	Commander, 4th Escort Flotilla
13 Dec 1915 - 1 Dec 1916:	Commander, Maizuru Navy Yard
1 Dec 1916:	Promoted to *Vice-Admiral*
1 Dec 1916 - 1 Dec 1917:	Unassigned
1 Dec 1917:	Transferred to the reserve

Vice-Admiral **Shonojo KAMIMURA** (9 May 1851 - 13 Mar 1908)
4 Jul 1901:	Promoted to *Rear-Admiral*
4 Jul 1901 - 23 Sep 1903:	Commander, Mako Guard District

23 Sep 1903 - 10 Nov 1903:	Chief of Shipping Bureau, Sasebo Naval District
10 Nov 1903 - 10 May 1905:	Commander, Sasebo Naval Yard
10 May 1905 - 14 Feb 1907:	Unassigned
13 Nov 1905:	Promoted to *Vice-Admiral*
14 Feb 1907:	Transferred to the reserve

Rear-Admiral **Kohyo KAMIOKA** (12 Dec 1897 - 28 Jan 1945)

5 Aug 1944 - 28 Jan 1945:	Captain, Seaplane Tender *"Sanuki-maru"*
28 Jan 1945:	Posthumously promoted to *Rear-Admiral*

Rear-Admiral (Paymaster) **Masayoshi KAMIYAMA** (23 Jul 1857 - 21 Jun 1924)

1 Oct 1901 - 7 Jul 1903:	Chief of Accounting Bureau, Maizuru Naval District
7 Jul 1903 - 7 Jul 1906:	Unassigned
7 Jul 1906:	Promoted to *General (Paymaster)*
7 Jul 1906:	Transferred to the reserve
23 Sep 1919:	Redesignated *Rear-Admiral (Paymaster)*

Vice-Admiral **Iwao KAMO** (7 Jun 1867 - ?)

1 Dec 1910:	Promoted to *Rear-Admiral*
1 Dec 1910 - 1 Dec 1911:	Chief Engineer Officer, Sasebo Naval District
1 Dec 1911 - 1 Dec 1913:	Commandant, Naval Engineering School
1 Dec 1913 - 18 Feb 1914:	Attached to Naval Training Command
18 Feb 1914 - 1 Apr 1914:	Chief of Bureau 3, Naval Training Command
1 Apr 1914 - 1 Apr 1916:	Commandant, Navy Engineer Academy
1 Apr 1916:	Promoted to *Vice-Admiral*
1 Apr 1916 - 1 Apr 1917:	Unassigned
1 Apr 1917:	Transferred to the reserve

Rear-Admiral **Yuhao KAMO** (22 Feb 1898 - 13 Feb 1944)

25 Oct 1943 - 13 Feb 1944:	Commander, 802nd Air Group
13 Feb 1944:	Posthumously promoted to *Rear-Admiral*

Rear-Admiral (Surgeon) **Izumi KANAI** (12 Jan 1896 - 26 Dec 1992)

10 Jul 1943 - 5 Feb 1945:	Instructor, Navy Medical School
1 May 1944:	Promoted to *Rear-Admiral (Surgeon)*
5 Feb 1945 - 15 Mar 1945:	Chief Instructor, Navy Medical School
15 Mar 1945 - 1 Apr 1945:	Director, Totsuka Naval Hospital
1 Apr 1945 - 11 Sep 1945:	Commandant, Totsuka Sanitary School
11 Sep 1945 - 22 Oct 1945:	Attached to Naval General Staff
22 Oct 1945 - 30 Nov 1945:	Director, Yokosuka Naval Hospital, Chief Surgeon, Yokosuka Naval District
30 Nov 1945:	Transferred to the reserve

Rear-Admiral **Sanmatsu KANAYA** (7 Dec 1884 - 8 Feb 1953)
1 Dec 1930:	Promoted to *Rear-Admiral*
1 Dec 1930 - 1 Dec 1931:	Chief of Shipping Bureau, Kure Naval District
1 Dec 1931 - 15 Dec 1931:	Attached to Naval General Staff
21 Dec 1931:	Transferred to the reserve

Vice-Admiral (Paymaster) **Takaichi KANAYA** (4 May 1884 - ?)
10 Oct 1935 - 15 Nov 1937:	Chief of Coalmining Bureau, Navy Fuel Yard
15 Nov 1935:	Promoted to *Rear-Admiral (Paymaster)*
15 Nov 1937 - 12 Apr 1939:	Paymaster-General, Yokosuka Naval District
12 Apr 1939 - 10 Apr 1941:	Commandant, Naval Paymaster Academy
15 Nov 1939:	Promoted to *Vice-Admiral (Paymaster)*
10 Apr 1941 - 1 Jul 1941:	Attached to Naval General Staff
5 Jul 1941:	Transferred to the reserve

Vice-Admiral **Masao KANAZAWA** (25 Oct 1889 - 24 Jun 1969)
15 Nov 1938:	Promoted to *Rear-Admiral*
15 Nov 1938 - 1 Oct 1940:	Chief of Press Bureau, Joint General Staff, Chief of Press Bureau, Department of the Navy
1 Oct 1940 - 15 Oct 1940:	Attached to the staff, China Area Fleet
15 Oct 1940 - 15 Oct 1941:	Naval Attache, China
15 Oct 1941 - 31 Dec 1941:	Chief of Staff, Yokosuka Naval District
31 Dec 1941 - 1 Feb 1942:	Attached to staff, 4th Fleet
1 Feb 1942 - 10 Apr 1942:	Commander, 8th Naval Base Force
10 Apr 1942 - 29 Nov 1942:	Commander, 8th Auxiliary Naval Base Force
1 May 1942:	Promoted to *Vice-Admiral*
29 Nov 1942 - 15 Dec 1942:	Attached to Naval General Staff
15 Dec 1942 - 1 May 1945:	Chief of Naval Facility Command
1 May 1945 - 15 Nov 1945:	Admiral Commanding, Kure Naval District

Rear-Admiral (Surgeon) **Shintaro KANAZAWA** (3 May 1894 - 28 Aug 1967)
1 Nov 1942:	Promoted to *Rear-Admiral (Surgeon)*
1 Nov 1942 - 10 Nov 1944:	Chief of Medical Bureau, 11th Air Arsenal
10 Nov 1944 - 28 Nov 1944:	Attached to the staff, China Area Fleet
28 Nov 1944 - Oct 1945:	Director, 1st Naval Hospital, Chief Surgeon, China Area Fleet

Vice-Admiral (Surgeon) **Yoshiharu KANBAYASHI** (8 Dec 1890 - 27 Feb 1979)
15 Nov 1939:	Promoted to *Rear-Admiral (Surgeon)*
15 Nov 1939 - 15 Nov 1940:	Chief Surgeon, Combined Fleet, Chief Surgeon, 1st Fleet
15 Nov 1940 - 15 Oct 1941:	Director, Beppu Naval Hospital
15 Oct 1941 - 1 Nov 1942:	Chief Instructor, Navy Medical School
1 Nov 1942 - 25 Oct 1943:	Director, Kure, Naval Hospital, Chief Surgeon, Kure Naval District

25 Oct 1943 - 1 Nov 1945:	Commandant, Navy Medical School
1 Nov 1943:	Promoted to *Vice-Admiral (Surgeon)*

Rear-Admiral (Surgeon) **Kinsaku KANDATSU** (25 Oct 1894 - 11 Jan 1966)

1 Nov 1942 - 6 Apr 1944:	Director, Kasumigaura Naval Hospital
1 May 1943:	Promoted to *Rear-Admiral (Surgeon)*
6 Apr 1944 - 30 Apr 1944:	Attached to Naval General Staff
30 Apr 1944 - 22 May 1945:	Chief Surgeon, Combined Fleet
25 Apr 1945 - 22 May 1945:	Chief Surgeon, Navy Supreme HQ
22 May 1945 - 10 Oct 1945:	Director, Nobi Naval Hospital
10 Oct 1945 - 20 Oct 1945:	Chief of Medical Bureau, 1st Technical Arsenal
20 Oct 1945 - 20 Nov 1945:	Attached to Department of the Navy
20 Nov 1945 - 30 Nov 1945:	Attached to Kure Naval District
30 Nov 1945:	Transferred to the reserve

Vice-Admiral **Hidetaro KANEDA** (28 Jan 1873 - 11 Jun 1925)

4 Sep 1918 - 1 Dec 1921:	Chief of Ordnance Bureau, Yokosuka Navy Yard
1 Dec 1919:	Promoted to *Rear-Admiral*
1 Dec 1921 - 1 Dec 1922:	Chief of Bureau 1, Naval Shipbuilding Command
1 Dec 1922 - 13 Aug 1923:	Commander, Kure Navy Yard
13 Aug 1923 - 25 Feb 1924:	Unassigned
1 Dec 1923:	Promoted to *Vice-Admiral*

Vice-Admiral **Ichiro KANEDA** (16 Jan 1885 - 23 Jan 1953)

1 Dec 1931 - 1 Dec 1933:	Chief of Scientific Research Bureau, Technical Research Department
15 Nov 1933:	Promoted to *Rear-Admiral*
1 Dec 1933 - 15 Nov 1934:	Instructor, Naval College
23 Jul 1934 - 2 Dec 1935:	Chief of Scientific Research Bureau, Technical Research Department
2 Dec 1935 - 15 Nov 1938:	Commandant, Naval Engineering Academy
1 Dec 1937:	Promoted to *Vice-Admiral*
15 Nov 1938 - 15 Mar 1939:	Attached to Naval General Staff
21 Mar 1939:	Transferred to the reserve

Rear-Admiral (Engineer) **Bunsaku KANEKO** (14 Jan 1874 - 4 Apr 1945)

1 Dec 1920:	Promoted to *Rear-Admiral*
1 Dec 1920 - 1 Dec 1922:	Instructor, Naval College
1 Sep 1921 - 1 Dec 1921:	Chief of Bureau 3, Naval Training Command
1 Dec 1922 - 10 Dec 1922:	Attached to Naval General Staff
10 Dec 1922 - 31 Mar 1923:	Unassigned
31 Mar 1923:	Transferred to the reserve

Rear-Admiral **Mitsuki KANEKO** (11 Jan 1868 - 2 Feb 1938)
1 Dec 1913 - 1 Dec 1917:	Chief of Documentation Section, Naval Hydrographic Command
1 Dec 1917:	Promoted to *Rear-Admiral*
1 Dec 1917 - 1 Dec 1918:	Unassigned
1 Dec 1918:	Transferred to the reserve

Vice-Admiral **Shigeji KANEKO** (1894 - 19 Feb 1981)
1 Jul 1941 - 25 Jan 1943:	Chief of Bureau 4, Naval General Staff, Chief of Communications Bureau, Joint General Staff
15 Oct 1941:	Promoted to *Rear-Admiral*
25 Jan 1943 - 30 Jan 1943:	Attached to the staff, Combined Fleet
30 Jan 1943 - 11 Nov 1943:	Commander, 1st Combined Communications Unit
11 Nov 1943 - 15 Nov 1943:	Attached to Naval General Staff
15 Nov 1943 - 29 Jan 1945:	Chief of Staff, Sasebo Naval District
29 Jan 1945 - Oct 1945:	Commander, Seito Area Base Force
1 May 1945:	Promoted to *Vice-Admiral*

Rear-Admiral **Toyokichi KANEKO** (8 Feb 1888 - 15 Aug 1952)
15 Nov 1939:	Promoted to *Rear-Admiral*
15 Nov 1939 - 5 Apr 1940:	Attached to Technical Research Department
5 Apr 1940 - 15 Sep 1942:	Chief of Sonic Research Bureau, Technical Research Department
15 Sep 1942 - 10 Oct 1942:	Attached to Naval General Staff
15 Oct 1942:	Transferred to the reserve

Rear-Admiral **Yoshitada KANEKO** (3 Apr 1895 - 6 Aug 1989)
1 Apr 1942 - 1 May 1943:	Chief of Chemical Research Bureau, Technical Research Department
1 Nov 1942:	Promoted to *Rear-Admiral*
1 May 1943 - 20 Jul 1945:	Commander, Sagami Navy Yard
20 Jul 1945 - 6 Sep 1945:	Attached to Naval Shipbuilding Command

Rear-Admiral **Yozo KANEKO** (11 Jun 1882 - 27 Dec 1941)
1 Dec 1925 - 1 Dec 1926:	Instructor, Naval College
1 Dec 1926:	Promoted to *Rear-Admiral*
1 Dec 1926 - 20 Mar 1927:	Attached to Naval General Staff
20 Mar 1927 - 10 Apr 1927:	Unassigned
10 Apr 1927:	Transferred to the reserve

Rear-Admiral **Kiyotsugu KANEMARU** (20 May 1871 - 21 Feb 1943)
1 Dec 1918 - 20 Nov 1919:	Chief of Survey Section, Naval Hydrographic Command

20 Nov 1919 - 1 Dec 1919:	Attached to Yokosuka Naval District
1 Dec 1919:	Promoted to *Rear-Admiral*
1 Dec 1919 - 1 Aug 1920:	Unassigned
1 Aug 1920:	Transferred to the reserve

Rear-Admiral **Yoshio KANEMASU** (1 Aug 1890 - 17 Feb 1944)

15 Dec 1943 - 17 Feb 1944:	Commander of Minesweepers, Transport *"Rio de Janeiro-maru"*
17 Feb 1944:	Posthumously promoted to *Rear-Admiral*

Rear-Admiral **Tomojiro KANEOKA** (1 Jan 1899 - 8 Jul 1944)

1 Mar 1944 - 8 Jul 1944:	Chief of Staff, 5th Auxiliary Base Force
8 Jul 1944:	Posthumously promoted to *Rear-Admiral*

Vice-Admiral **Takashi KANESAKA** (25 Sep 1877 - 16 Dec 1961)

1 Dec 1923:	Promoted to *Rear-Admiral*
1 Dec 1923 - 1 Dec 1925:	Commandant, Naval Gunnery School
1 Dec 1925 - 1 Dec 1927:	Commander, Ominato Guard District
1 Dec 1927:	Promoted to *Vice-Admiral*
1 Dec 1927 - 15 Mar 1928:	Attached to Naval General Staff
25 Mar 1928:	Transferred to the reserve

Rear-Admiral **Norikazu KANNA** (6 Sep 1877 - 25 Jul 1950)

1 Dec 1923:	Promoted to *Rear-Admiral*
1 Dec 1923 - 1 Dec 1924:	Commander, Yokosuka Defense Force
1 Dec 1924 - 1 Aug 1925:	Attached to Naval General Staff
1 Aug 1925 - 5 Dec 1925:	Unassigned
5 Dec 1925:	Transferred to the reserve

Rear-Admiral **Yushichi KANNO** (22 Jun 1869 - 9 Apr 1943)

1 Apr 1916 - 1 Dec 1917:	Chief of Staff, Maizuru Naval District
1 Dec 1917:	Promoted to *Rear-Admiral*
1 Dec 1917 - 1 Apr 1919:	Commander, 4th Destroyer Flotilla
1 Apr 1919 - 1 Dec 1919:	Commander, 1st Submarine Flotilla
1 Dec 1919 - 10 Dec 1919:	Member, Admirals Committee
10 Dec 1919 - 1 Aug 1920:	Unassigned
1 Aug 1920:	Transferred to the reserve

Rear-Admiral (Paymaster) **Kinzaburo KANO** (8 May 1891 - 7 Oct 1963)

15 Dec 1937 - 15 Nov 1938:	Chief of Coal Mining Bureau, Navy Fuel Yard
15 Nov 1938:	Promoted to *Rear-Admiral (Paymaster)*
15 Nov 1938 - 15 Dec 1938:	Attached to Naval General Staff
21 Nov 1938:	Transferred to the reserve

Vice-Admiral **Baron Yunoshin KANO** (14 Sep 1851 - 7 Apr 1914)
7 Jul 1903:	Promoted to *Rear-Admiral*
7 Jul 1903 - 28 May 1906:	Chief of Reserve Bureau, Sasebo Naval District, Commander, Sasebo Harbor
28 May 1906 - 12 Mar 1907:	Chief of Reserve Bureau, Yokosuka Naval District, Commander, Yokosuka Harbor
12 Mar 1907:	Promoted to *Vice-Admiral*
12 Mar 1907 - 1 Dec 1909:	Commander, Mako Guard District
1 Dec 1909 - 17 Apr 1911:	Unassigned
17 Apr 1911:	Transferred to the reserve

Rear-Admiral **Saburo KANOE** (6 Oct 1881 - 1 Apr 1944)
15 Apr 1925 - 1 Dec 1927:	Commander, Yokosuka Sailors Corps
1 Dec 1926:	Promoted to *Rear-Admiral*
1 Dec 1927 - 30 Nov 1929:	Commandant, Naval Gunnery School
30 Nov 1929 - 10 Jun 1930:	Attached to Naval General Staff
20 Jun 1930:	Transferred to the reserve

Rear-Admiral **Zensuke KANOME** (22 Nov 1893 - 21 Sep 1960)
1 Jul 1943 - 30 Nov 1945:	Chief of Staff, Ominato Guard District
15 Oct 1944:	Promoted to *Rear-Admiral*
15 Feb 1945 - 30 Nov 1945:	Chief of Staff, 12th Air Fleet

Rear-Admiral **Enpei KANOOKA** (11 Apr 1901 - 5 Nov 1944)
20 Aug 1944 - 5 Nov 1944:	Captain, Heavy Cruiser *"Nachi"*
5 Nov 1944:	Posthumously promoted to *Rear-Admiral*

Rear-Admiral **Tamotsu KANZAKI** (4 Nov 1879 - 31 Aug 1934)
15 Apr 1925 - 1 Dec 1927:	Chief of Shipping Bureau, Kure Naval District
1 Dec 1925:	Promoted to *Rear-Admiral*
1 Dec 1927 - 15 Dec 1927:	Attached to Naval General Staff
25 Dec 1927:	Transferred to the reserve

Rear-Admiral **Minoru KARIYA** (1 Sep 1905 - 24 Oct 1944)
20 Apr 1944 - 24 Oct 1944:	Navigation Officer, Battleship *"Musashi"*
24 Oct 1944:	Posthumously promoted to *Rear-Admiral*

Rear-Admiral **Saburo KASE** (17 Mar 1894 - 21 Dec 1944)
29 Aug 1944 - 21 Dec 1944:	Captain, Supply Ship *"Mamiya"*
21 Dec 1944:	Posthumously promoted to *Rear-Admiral*

Rear-Admiral **Ei KASHIWAGI** (3 Apr 1886 - 22 Feb 1944)
20 Mar 1943 - 22 Feb 1944:	Captain, Transport Ship *"Yamashimo-maru"*
22 Feb 1944:	Posthumously promoted to *Rear-Admiral*

Vice-Admiral (Paymaster) **Masafumi KASHIWAGI** (25 May 1871 - 11 Nov 1962)
1 Dec 1918 - 1 Dec 1922:	Chief of Accounting Bureau, Kure Navy Yard
1 Dec 1920:	Promoted to *Rear-Admiral (Paymaster)*
1 Dec 1922 - 18 Sep 1925:	Paymaster-General, Kure Naval District
1 Dec 1924:	Promoted to *Vice-Admiral (Paymaster)*
18 Sep 1925 - 1 Dec 1925:	Attached to Naval General Staff
16 Dec 1925:	Transferred to the reserve

Rear-Admiral (Surgeon) **Osamu KASHIWAZAKI** (7 Dec 1884 - ?)
1 Dec 1931 - 15 Nov 1933:	Chief of Medical Bureau, Kure Navy Yard
15 Nov 1933:	Promoted to *Rear-Admiral (Surgeon)*
15 Nov 1933 - 11 Dec 1933:	Attached to Kure Naval District
15 Dec 1933:	Transferred to the reserve

Rear-Admiral **Atsushi KASUGA** (4 Oct 1887 - 11 Feb 1976)
1 Dec 1937:	Promoted to *Rear-Admiral*
1 Dec 1937 - 20 Apr 1938:	Commander, Sasebo Defense Flotilla
20 Apr 1938 - 15 Nov 1938:	Chief of Ordnance Bureau, Sasebo Navy Yard
15 Nov 1938 - 15 Nov 1939:	Commander, 1st Submarine Flotilla
15 Nov 1939 - 15 Mar 1940:	Attached to Naval General Staff
21 Mar 1940:	Transferred to the reserve
25 Jul 1941 - 11 Aug 1941:	Recalled; Attached to Naval General Staff
11 Aug 1941 - 10 Apr 1942:	Commander, 5th Auxiliary Base Force
10 Apr 1942 - 15 Sep 1942:	Commander, 5th Naval Base Force
15 Sep 1942 - 15 Oct 1942:	Attached to Naval General Staff
15 Oct 1942:	Demobilized

Rear-Admiral **Soichi KASUYA** (14 Jul 1885 - 23 Jan 1942)
15 Nov 1934:	Promoted to *Rear-Admiral*
15 Nov 1934 - 15 Dec 1934:	Commander, Yokosuka Defense Force
15 Dec 1934 - 2 Dec 1935:	Commander, Yokosuka Defense Flotilla
2 Dec 1935 - 28 Mar 1936:	Attached to Naval General Staff
30 Mar 1936:	Transferred to the reserve

Vice-Admiral **Eikichi KATAGIRI** (24 Sep 1885 - 16 Aug 1972)
15 Nov 1933:	Promoted to *Rear-Admiral*
15 Nov 1933 - 15 Nov 1934:	Chief of Staff, Sasebo Naval District
15 Nov 1934 - 15 Nov 1935:	Commander, 2nd Air Flotilla
15 Nov 1935 - 1 Dec 1937:	Commander, Kasumigaura Air Division
1 Dec 1937:	Promoted to *Vice-Admiral*
1 Dec 1937 - 15 Nov 1938:	Commander, 3rd Escort Flotilla
15 Nov 1938 - 15 Nov 1939:	Admiral Commanding, Maizuru Naval District
15 Nov 1939 - 15 Nov 1940:	C-in-C, 4th Fleet

15 Nov 1940 - 15 Jan 1941:	Attached to Naval General Staff
15 Jan 1941 - 10 Sep 1941:	C-in-C, 11th Air Fleet
10 Sep 1941 - 1 Dec 1942:	Chief of Naval Air Command
1 Dec 1942 - 15 Mar 1943:	Navy Councillor
20 Mar 1943:	Transferred to the reserve

Rear-Admiral **Tsunejiro KATAHARA** (21 Sep 1886 - 8 Aug 1946)

15 Apr 1943 - 15 Jul 1945:	Commander, Mako Area Base Force
1 May 1943:	Promoted to *Rear-Admiral*
15 Jul 1945 - 1 Sep 1945:	Attached to Kure Naval District

Rear-Admiral **Takuji KATAHIRA** (20 Dec 1893 - 15 Mar 1956)

1 Jul 1943 - 30 Jun 1945:	Commander, 61st Air Arsenal
1 Nov 1943:	Promoted to *Rear-Admiral*
30 Jun 1945 - 30 Sep 1945:	Attached to Naval Air Command

Rear-Admiral **Eitaro KATAOKA** (29 Dec 1867 - 31 Aug 1924)

1 Apr 1915 - 13 Dec 1915:	Captain, Battlecruiser *"Tsukuba"*
13 Dec 1915:	Promoted to *Rear-Admiral*
13 Dec 1915 - 1 Dec 1916:	Unassigned
1 Dec 1916:	Transferred to the reserve

Vice-Admiral (Paymaster) **Kakutaro KATAOKA** (18 Feb 1888 - 16 Dec 1959)

15 Nov 1938:	Promoted to *Rear-Admiral (Paymaster)*
15 Nov 1938 - 15 Nov 1939:	Chief of Coal Mining Bureau, Navy Fuel Yard
15 Nov 1939 - 15 Oct 1941:	Chief of Supply Bureau, Kure Navy Yard
15 Oct 1941 - 15 Jan 1942:	Attached to Naval General Staff
15 Jan 1942 - 26 Mar 1942:	Attached to Naval Air Command
26 Mar 1942 - 1 Jun 1943:	Commandant, Navy Paymaster Academy
1 Nov 1942:	Promoted to *Vice-Admiral (Paymaster)*
1 Jun 1943 - 20 Oct 1943:	Attached to Naval General Staff
25 Oct 1943:	Transferred to the reserve

Rear-Admiral (Surgeon) **Katsumi KATAOKA** (1 Feb 1897 - 13 Apr 1977)

1 May 1944 - 5 Oct 1945:	Director, Kasumigaura Naval Hospital
1 May 1945:	Promoted to *Rear-Admiral (Surgeon)*

Admiral **Baron Shichiro KATAOKA** (14 Dec 1853 - 11 Jan 1920)

17 Jun 1899:	Promoted to *Rear-Admiral*
17 Jun 1899 - 20 May 1900:	C-in-C, Kure Naval District Fleet, Admiral Commanding, Kure Naval District
20 May 1900 - 26 Jul 1902:	Chief of Shipping Bureau, Kure Naval District
26 Jul 1902 - 28 Dec 1903:	Commander, Takeshiki Guard District

5 Sep 1903:	Promoted to *Vice-Admiral*
28 Dec 1903 - 20 Dec 1905:	C-in-C, 3rd Fleet
20 Dec 1905 - 22 Nov 1906:	C-in-C, 1st Fleet
22 Nov 1906 - 28 Aug 1908:	Chief of Naval Shipbuilding Command, Member, Admirals Committee
28 Aug 1908 - 18 Jan 1911:	Admiral Commanding, Maizuru Naval District
1 Dec 1910:	Promoted to *Admiral*
18 Jan 1911 - 1 Dec 1911:	Unassigned
1 Dec 1911 - 26 Apr 1917:	Navy Councillor
26 Apr 1917 - 10 May 1917:	Unassigned
10 May 1917:	Transferred to the reserve

Rear-Admiral **Tashiro KATAOKA** 4 Dec 1888 - 11 Nov 1956)

1 Dec 1936 - 20 Nov 1944:	Chief of Optics Research Bureau, Yokosuka Navy Yard
15 Oct 1941:	Promoted to *Rear-Admiral*
20 Nov 1944 - 15 Dec 1944:	Attached to Naval Shipbuilding Command
20 Dec 1944:	Transferred to the reserve
10 Feb 1945 - 15 Feb 1945:	Recalled; Attached to Yokosuka Naval District
15 Feb 1945 - 15 Sep 1945:	Chief of Optics Research Bureau, Toyokawa Navy Yard

Rear-Admiral **Ariki KATAYAMA** (19 Aug 1894 - 22 Dec 1985)

1 Nov 1942:	Promoted to *Rear-Admiral*
1 Nov 1942 - 5 Dec 1942:	Attached to Bureau 4, Naval Shipbuilding Command
5 Dec 1942 - 28 Jul 1943:	Chief of Shipbuilding Research Bureau, Kure Navy Yard
28 Jul 1943 - 2 Oct 1944:	Attached to Bureau 4, Naval Shipbuilding Command
2 Oct 1944 - 15 Sep 1945:	Professor, University of Tokyo

Rear-Admiral **Noboru KATAYAMA** (1 Apr 1884 - 23 Feb 1957)

1 Dec 1927 - 1 Dec 1930:	Commander, Kure Harbor
1 Dec 1930:	Promoted to *Rear-Admiral*
1 Dec 1930 - 20 May 1931:	Attached to Naval General Staff
25 May 1931:	Transferred to the reserve

Rear-Admiral **Seiji KATAYAMA** (1 Dec 1885 - 30 Apr 1944)

15 Nov 1934:	Promoted to *Rear-Admiral*
15 Nov 1934 - 1 Dec 1936:	Chief of Supply Bureau, Sasebo Naval District
1 Dec 1936 - 15 Dec 1936:	Attached to Naval General Staff
22 Dec 1936:	Transferred to the reserve

Rear-Admiral (Paymaster) **Hachitaro KATO** (18 Sep 1863 - 16 Feb 1932)
1 Dec 1909 - 1 Dec 1912:	Paymaster-General, Yokosuka Naval District
5 Jun 1911:	Promoted to *General (Paymaster)*
1 Dec 1912 - 31 May 1913:	Unassigned
31 May 1913:	Transferred to the reserve
23 Sep 1919:	Redesignated *Rear-Admiral (Paymaster)*

Rear-Admiral **Hideyoshi KATO** (? - 30 Aug 1945)
10 Jul 1944 - 30 Aug 1945:	Commander, Kochi Air Division
30 Aug 1945:	Posthumously promoted to *Rear-Admiral*

Admiral **Hiroharu KATO** (2 Nov 1870 - 9 Apr 1939)
1 Dec 1916:	Promoted to *Rear-Admiral*
1 Dec 1916 - 6 Jan 1918:	Commandant, Naval Gunnery School
6 Jan 1918 - 4 Sep 1918:	Commander, 5th Escort Flotilla
4 Sep 1918 - 1 Dec 1918:	Member, Admirals Committee
1 Dec 1918 - 10 Jun 1919:	Chief of Staff, Yokosuka Naval District
10 Jun 1919 - 10 Aug 1920:	Attached to Naval General Staff
10 Aug 1920 - 27 Sep 1921:	Commandant of the Naval College
1 Dec 1920:	Promoted to *Vice-Admiral*
27 Sep 1921 - 1 May 1922:	Assistant to the Plenipotentiary, Washington Conference
1 May 1922 - 1 Jun 1923:	Deputy Chief of the Naval General Staff, Member, Admirals Committee
1 Jun 1923 - 1 Dec 1924:	C-in-C, 2nd Fleet
1 Dec 1924 - 10 Dec 1926:	Admiral Commanding, Yokosuka Naval District, Member, Admirals Committee
10 Dec 1926 - 10 Dec 1928:	C-in-C, Combined Fleet, C-in-C, 1st Fleet
1 Apr 1927:	Promoted to *Admiral*
10 Dec 1928 - 22 Jan 1929:	Navy Councillor
22 Jan 1929 - 11 Jun 1930:	Chief of the Naval General Staff, Member, Admirals Committee
11 Jun 1930 - 2 Nov 1935:	Navy Councillor
2 Nov 1935:	Transferred to the reserve

Rear-Admiral **Hisao KATO** (21 Aug 1893 - 20 Mar 1967)
1 Oct 1941 - 1 Apr 1942:	Chief of Armaments Bureau, 21st Air Arsenal
15 Oct 1941:	Promoted to *Rear-Admiral*
1 Apr 1942 - 10 Mar 1945:	Chief of Optics Bureau, Air Technical Arsenal
10 Mar 1945 - 18 Mar 1945:	Attached to Yokosuka Naval District
20 Mar 1945:	Transferred to the reserve
11 Apr 1945 - 15 Sep 1945:	Recalled; Commander, Mie Air Division

Rear-Admiral **Nitaro KATO** (27 Oct 1886 - 31 Jul 1938)
16 Aug 1937 - 31 Jul 1938: Commander, 1st Harbor
31 Jul 1938: Posthumously promoted to *Rear-Admiral*

Rear-Admiral (Paymaster) **Nobuo KATO** (15 Oct 1893 - 7 Jan 1964)
1 Nov 1942: Promoted to *Rear-Admiral (Paymaster)*
1 Nov 1942 - 1 Nov 1945: Chief of Accounting Bureau, Kure Navy Yard

Vice-Admiral (Paymaster) **Ryoichi KATO** (2 Sep 1877 - 25 Dec 1946)
25 May 1923 - 1 Dec 1924: Commandant, Naval Paymaster Academy
1 Dec 1923: Promoted to *Rear-Admiral (Paymaster)*
1 Dec 1924 - 18 Sep 1925: Paymaster-General, Yokosuka Naval District
18 Sep 1925 - 13 Apr 1927: Paymaster-General, Kure Naval District
13 Apr 1927 - 20 May 1933: Chief of Naval Accounting Bureau
1 Dec 1927: Promoted to *Vice-Admiral (Paymaster)*
20 May 1933 - 1 Dec 1933: Attached to Naval General Staff
15 Dec 1933: Transferred to the reserve

Rear-Admiral **Ryonosuke KATO** (1 Jan 1901 - 25 Jun 1944)
1 Sep 1943 - 25 Jun 1944: Commander, 51st Submarine Division
25 Jun 1944: Posthumously promoted to *Rear-Admiral*

Admiral **Baron Sadakichi KATO** (18 Nov 1861 - 5 Sep 1927)
15 May 1908 - 9 Apr 1910: Chief of Staff, Maizuru Naval District
28 Aug 1908: Promoted to *Rear-Admiral*
9 Apr 1910 - 11 Mar 1911: Commander, Maizuru Navy Yard
11 Mar 1911 - 20 Apr 1912: C-in-C, Training Fleet
20 Apr 1912 - 1 Dec 1912: Commander, Sasebo Navy Yard
1 Dec 1912: Promoted to *Vice-Admiral*
1 Dec 1912 - 1 Dec 1913: Commander, Yokosuka Navy Yard
1 Dec 1913 - 5 Feb 1915: C-in-C, 2nd Fleet
5 Feb 1915 - 1 Dec 1916: Chief of Naval Training Command
1 Dec 1916 - 1 Dec 1919: Admiral Commanding, Kure Naval District
2 Jul 1918: Promoted to *Admiral*
1 Dec 1919 - 10 Dec 1922: Navy Councillor
10 Dec 1922 - 21 Jan 1923: Unassigned
21 Jan 1923: Transferred to the reserve

Rear-Admiral **Shigeyoshi KATO** (9 Jul 1890 - 27 Feb 1976)
15 Nov 1939 - 15 Nov 1940: Supervisor of Ordnance, Naval Air Command
15 Nov 1940: Promoted to *Rear-Admiral*
15 Nov 1940 - 15 Jun 1941: Attached to Yokosuka Naval District
15 Jun 1941 - 1 Jul 1941: Attached to Naval Air Command
5 Jul 1941: Transferred to the reserve

Rear-Admiral **Tadao KATO** (16 Nov 1894 - 5 Feb 1976)
29 Sep 1944 - 20 Mar 1945:	Commander, Yokosuka Air Division
15 Oct 1944:	Promoted to *Rear-Admiral*
20 Mar 1945 - 30 Jul 1945:	Chief of Staff, Okinawa Area Auxiliary Base Force
30 Jul 1945 - Oct 1945:	Attached to Yokosuka Naval District

Admiral **Viscount Takayoshi KATO** (30 Nov 1886 - 10 Feb 1955)
13 Jul 1927 - 30 Nov 1929:	Naval Attache, League of Nations
1 Dec 1927:	Promoted to *Rear-Admiral*
30 Nov 1929 - 18 Jun 1930:	Chief of Bureau 1, Naval General Staff
18 Jun 1930 - 1 Dec 1930:	Attached to Naval Air Command
1 Dec 1930 - 15 Nov 1932:	Commander, 1st Air Flotilla
15 Nov 1932 - 15 Nov 1933:	Commandant of the Naval College
1 Dec 1932:	Promoted to *Vice-Admiral*
15 Nov 1933 - 17 Jan 1934:	Chief of Naval Air Command
17 Jan 1934 - 2 Dec 1935:	Deputy Chief of the Naval General Staff
2 Dec 1935 - 1 Dec 1936:	C-in-C, 2nd Fleet
1 Dec 1936 - 15 Nov 1938:	Admiral Commanding, Kure Naval District
15 Nov 1938 - 1 Jun 1945:	Navy Councillor
1 Apr 1939:	Promoted to *Admiral*
1 Jun 1945:	Transferred to the reserve

Fleet Admiral **Viscount Tomozaburo KATO** (22 Feb 1861 - 25 Aug 1923)
28 Dec 1903 - 12 Jan 1905:	Chief of Staff, 2nd Fleet
1 Sep 1904:	Promoted to *Rear-Admiral*
12 Jan 1905 - 20 Dec 1905:	Chief of Staff, Combined Fleet, Chief of Staff, 1st Fleet
20 Dec 1905 - 22 Nov 1906:	Chief, Bureau of Naval Affairs, Member, Admirals Committee
8 Jan 1906 - 1 Dec 1909:	Deputy Minister of the Navy, Member, Admirals Committee
28 Aug 1908:	Promoted to *Vice-Admiral*
1 Dec 1909 - 1 Dec 1913:	Admiral Commanding, Kure Naval District
1 Dec 1913 - 10 Aug 1915:	C-in-C, 1st Fleet
10 Aug 1915 - 25 Aug 1923:	Minister of the Navy
28 Aug 1915:	Promoted to *Admiral*
12 Jun 1922 - 25 Aug 1923:	Prime Minister
24 Aug 1923:	Appointed *Fleet Admiral*

Rear-Admiral (Surgeon) **Yasukichi KATO** (15 Sep 1873 - 26 May 1945)
1 Dec 1921:	Promoted to *Rear-Admiral (Surgeon)*
1 Dec 1921 - 10 Nov 1922:	Chief of Bureau 1, Kure Naval Hospital
10 Nov 1922 - 1 Dec 1922:	Attached to Kure Naval District

1 Dec 1922 - 31 Mar 1923:	Unassigned
31 Mar 1923:	Transferred to the reserve

Rear-Admiral **Yoshio KATO** (26 Aug 1892 - 20 Mar 1974)
15 Dec 1941 - 20 Apr 1943:	Chief of Engine Construction Bureau, Kure Navy Yard
1 Nov 1942:	Promoted to *Rear-Admiral*
20 Apr 1943 - 1 May 1943:	Attached to the staff, 1st Southern Expeditionary Fleet
1 May 1943 - 1 Feb 1944:	Commander, 101st Naval Facility
1 Feb 1944 - 1 Mar 1944:	Attached to Naval General Staff
1 Mar 1944 - 15 Nov 1944:	Chief Supervisor for Construction & Ordnance, Naval Shipbuilding Command
17 Nov 1944:	Transferred to the reserve

Rear-Admiral **Yoshio KATO** (28 Mar 1894 - 25 Feb 1945)
10 Dec 1944 - 25 Feb 1945:	Chief of Traffic Control, 1st Escort Fleet
25 Feb 1945:	Posthumously promoted to *Rear-Admiral*

Rear-Admiral **Yujiro KATO** (6 Dec 1870 - 6 Aug 1945)
1 Dec 1917 - 20 Nov 1919:	Captain, Battleship *"Yamashiro"*
20 Nov 1919 - 1 Dec 1919:	Attached to Yokosuka Naval District
1 Dec 1919:	Promoted to *Rear-Admiral*
1 Dec 1919 - 1 Aug 1920:	Unassigned
1 Aug 1920:	Transferred to the reserve

Rear-Admiral **Yukio KATO** (25 Oct 1898 - 17 Jan 1942)
10 Nov 1941 - 17 Jan 1942:	Commander, 28th Submarine Division
17 Jan 1942:	Posthumously promoted to *Rear-Admiral*

Rear-Admiral (Surgeon) **Shokichi KATSU** (15 Oct 1885 - 16 Mar 1941)
14 Nov 1931 - 20 Oct 1935:	Director, Kamekawa Naval Hospital
15 Nov 1934:	Promoted to *Rear-Admiral (Surgeon)*
20 Oct 1935 - 15 Nov 1935:	Director, Beppu Naval Hospital
15 Nov 1935 - 10 Dec 1935:	Attached to Naval General Staff
14 Dec 1935:	Transferred to the reserve

Rear-Admiral **Genjiro KATSUKI** (8 Jan 1872 - 3 Jun 1948)
20 Nov 1920 - 1 Aug 1922:	Commander, Yokosuka Sailors Corps
1 Dec 1920:	Promoted to *Rear-Admiral*
1 Aug 1922 - 1 Dec 1922:	Attached to Yokosuka Naval District
1 Dec 1922 - 31 Mar 1923:	Unassigned
31 Mar 1923:	Transferred to the reserve

Rear-Admiral **Seizo KATSUMATA** (1894 - 5 Sep 1968)
1 Apr 1944 - 1 Mar 1945:	Commander, 18th Combined Air Division
1 May 1944:	Promoted to *Rear-Admiral*
1 Mar 1945 - 10 Jul 1945:	Commander, 22nd Combined Air Division
10 Jul 1945 - 20 Jul 1945:	Attached to Yokosuka Naval District
20 Jul 1945 - 10 Oct 1945:	Commander, 101st Air Flotilla

Rear-Admiral **Minoru KATSUNO** (17 Jun 1891 - 1 Aug 1957)
15 Sep 1942 - 8 Apr 1943:	Commander, 2nd Yokosuka Sailors Corps
1 Nov 1942:	Promoted to *Rear-Admiral*
8 Apr 1943 - 20 Apr 1943:	Attached to staff, 8th Fleet
20 Apr 1943 - 1 Sep 1943:	Commander, 7th Combined Marine Force
1 Sep 1943 - 20 Sep 1943:	Attached to Yokosuka Naval District
20 Sep 1943 - 4 Jan 1944:	Commander, 2nd Yokosuka Sailors Corps
4 Jan 1944 - 10 Aug 1944:	Commander, Buzan Sailors Corps
10 Aug 1944 - 18 Aug 1944:	Attached to staff, China Area Fleet
18 Aug 1944 - Oct 1945:	Commander, Shanghai Marine Force

Rear-Admiral **Haruo KATSUTA** (26 Oct 1896 - 12 Oct 1955)
15 Apr 1945 - 29 Nov 1945:	Chief of Staff, Chinkai Guard District
1 May 1945:	Promoted to *Rear-Admiral*

Rear-Admiral **Kaneshige KATSUTA** (24 Feb 1894 - 4 Jan 1961)
1 Sep 1942 - 1 Oct 1943:	Attached to Yokosuka Naval District
1 Nov 1942:	Promoted to *Rear-Admiral*
1 Oct 1943 - 10 Mar 1944:	Director, Tagajo Navy Yard
10 Mar 1944 - 19 Mar 1944:	Attached to Naval Air Command
20 Mar 1944:	Transferred to the reserve

Rear-Admiral **Masaharu KAWABATA** (6 May 1898 - 29 Apr 1947)
1 Apr 1945 - 29 Nov 1945:	Deputy Chief of Staff, Yokosuka Naval District
1 May 1945:	Promoted to *Rear-Admiral*

Vice-Admiral **Katsuji KAWADA** (11 Jun 1868 - 19 Feb 1943)
1 Dec 1917:	Promoted to *Rear-Admiral*
1 Dec 1917 - 1 Dec 1918:	Chief of Ordnance Bureau, Sasebo Navy Yard
1 Dec 1918 - 1 Oct 1920:	Chief of Bureau 2, Naval Technical Command
1 Oct 1920 - 1 Sep 1921:	Chief of Bureau 2, Naval Shipbuilding Command
1 Sep 1921 - 1 Dec 1922:	Director, Sasebo Navy Yard
1 Jun 1922:	Promoted to *Vice-Admiral*
1 Dec 1922 - 10 Dec 1922:	Attached to Naval Shipbuilding Command
10 Dec 1922 - 31 Mar 1923:	Unassigned
31 Mar 1923:	Transferred to the reserve

Rear-Admiral (Paymaster) **Kosaburo KAWADA** (24 Feb 1883 - 3 Nov 1955)
1 Dec 1931 - 15 Nov 1933:	Paymaster-General, Maizuru Guard District
15 Nov 1933:	Promoted to *Rear-Admiral (Paymaster)*
15 Nov 1933 - 11 Dec 1933:	Attached to Naval General Staff
15 Dec 1933:	Transferred to the reserve

Rear-Admiral (Surgeon) **Masashi KAWADA** (12 Jul 1895 - 25 Apr 1945)
4 Mar 1944 - 25 Apr 1945:	Chief of Section 1, Medical Bureau, Department of the Navy
25 Apr 1945:	Posthumously promoted to *Rear-Admiral (Surgeon)*

Rear-Admiral **Tadamitsu KAWAGOE** (6 Oct 1882 - 13 Nov 1943)
25 May 1943 - 13 Nov 1943:	Chief of Minesweeping, Troop Transport *"Nachisan-maru"*
13 Nov 1943:	Posthumously promoted to *Rear-Admiral*

Rear-Admiral **Masao KAWAGUCHI** (19 Feb 1898 - 5 Jun 1942)
1 Sep 1941 - 5 Jun 1942:	Executive Officer, Aircraft Carrier *"Kaga"*
5 Jun 1942:	Posthumously promoted to *Rear-Admiral*

Vice-Admiral **Hiroshi KAWAHARA** (27 Feb 1883 - 22 Jul 1961)
1 Dec 1932:	Promoted to *Rear-Admiral*
1 Dec 1932 - 15 Nov 1934:	Chief of Shipping Bureau, Yokosuka Naval District
15 Nov 1934 - 1 Dec 1936:	Commandant, Naval Engineering School
1 Dec 1936:	Promoted to *Vice-Admiral*
1 Dec 1936 - 15 Mar 1937:	Attached to the Naval General Staff
25 Mar 1937:	Transferred to the reserve

Vice-Admiral **Kesataro KAWAHARA** (1 Dec 1869 - 6 Sep 1933)
1 Dec 1916:	Promoted to *Rear-Admiral*
1 Dec 1916 - 4 Sep 1918:	Commandant, Torpedo School
9 Jan 1918 - 10 Jul 1918:	Commandant, Naval Gunnery School
4 Sep 1918 - 1 Dec 1920:	Commander, 5th Escort Flotilla
1 Dec 1920:	Promoted to *Vice-Admiral*
1 Dec 1920 - 1 May 1921:	Member, Admirals Committee
1 May 1921 - 1 Dec 1921:	Commander, 2nd Escort Flotilla
1 Dec 1921 - 1 Dec 1922:	Commander, Ryojun Guard District
1 Dec 1922 - 10 Dec 1922:	Member, Admirals Committee
10 Dec 1922 - 31 Mar 1923:	Unassigned
31 Mar 1923:	Transferred to the reserve

Vice-Admiral **Yoichi KAWAHARA** (28 May 1850 - 17 Dec 1926)
27 Dec 1897:	Promoted to *Rear-Admiral*

27 Dec 1897 - 19 Jan 1899:	C-in-C, Readiness Fleet
19 Jan 1899 - 24 May 1902:	Commandant of the Naval Academy
24 May 1902 - 7 Jul 1903:	Unassigned
7 Jul 1903 - 5 Sep 1903:	Member, Admirals Committee
5 Sep 1903:	Promoted to *Vice-Admiral*
5 Sep 1903 - 5 Sep 1906:	Unassigned
5 Sep 1906:	Transferred to the reserve

Vice-Admiral **Takushiro KAWAHIGASHI** (10 Mar 1885 - 9 May 1947)

1 Dec 1931:	Promoted to *Rear-Admiral*
1 Dec 1931 - 15 Nov 1933:	Chief of Shipbuilding Bureau, Sasebo Navy Yard
15 Nov 1933 - 10 Oct 1935:	Chief of Shipbuilding Research Bureau, Technical Research Department
10 Oct 1935 - 15 Dec 1936:	Attached to Naval Shipbuilding Command
1 Dec 1936:	Promoted to *Vice-Admiral*
2 Dec 1936:	Transferred to the reserve

Rear-Admiral **Fukashi KAWAI** (1 Oct 1897 - 8 Aug 1944)

10 Mar 1944 - 8 Aug 1944:	Commander, 30th Naval Facility
8 Aug 1944:	Posthumously promoted to *Rear-Admiral*

Rear-Admiral **Iwao KAWAI** (2 Sep 1896 - 15 May 1972)

18 Nov 1943 - 1 Dec 1945:	Chief of Section 1, Personnel Bureau, Department of the Navy
1 May 1945:	Promoted to *Rear-Admiral*
24 Nov 1945 - 1 Dec 1945:	Chief of Naval Personnel

Rear-Admiral **Shigezo KAWAI** (12 Apr 1896 - 28 Jan 1968)

1 Mar 1944 - Oct 1945:	Chief of Staff, 30th Auxiliary Base Force
25 Apr 1944 - 1 Sep 1944:	Commander, 30th Submarine Base Force
1 May 1945:	Promoted to *Rear-Admiral*

Vice-Admiral **Shuntaro KAWAI** (1 Jun 1880 - 4 Dec 1939)

1 Dec 1923:	Promoted to *Rear-Admiral*
1 Dec 1923 - 1 Dec 1924:	Chief Engineer Officer, 2nd Fleet
1 Dec 1924 - 10 Dec 1924:	Attached to Naval General Staff
10 Dec 1924 - 1 Apr 1925:	Supervisor for Construction & Ordnance, Naval Shipbuilding Command
1 Apr 1925 - 1 Dec 1926:	Commander, Hiro Navy Yard
1 Dec 1926 - 1 Dec 1927:	Commander, Sasebo Navy Yard
1 Dec 1927:	Promoted to *Vice-Admiral*
1 Dec 1927 - 15 Dec 1927:	Attached to Naval General Staff
20 Dec 1927:	Transferred to the reserve

Rear-Admiral **Taizo KAWAI** (7 Oct 1877 - 4 Mar 1940)
1 Dec 1923:	Promoted to *Rear-Admiral*
1 Dec 1923 - 1 Apr 1924:	Attached to Naval General Staff
1 Apr 1924 - 1 Dec 1925:	Commander, 2nd Submarine Flotilla
1 Dec 1925 - 1 Dec 1926:	Chief of Bureau 3, Naval Shipbuilding Command
1 Dec 1926 - 20 Mar 1927:	Attached to Kure Naval District
20 Mar 1927 - 10 Apr 1927:	Unassigned
10 Apr 1927:	Transferred to the reserve

Rear-Admiral **Toshinori KAWAJI** (24 Apr 1880 - 22 Dec 1975)
1 Dec 1922:	Promoted to *Rear-Admiral*
1 Dec 1922 - 1 Dec 1923:	Chief Engineer Officer, Combined Fleet, Chief Engineer Officer, 1st Fleet
1 Dec 1923 - 20 Dec 1924:	Chief Engineer Officer, Kure Naval District
20 Dec 1924 - 15 Apr 1925:	Chief of Shipping Bureau, Kure Naval District
15 Apr 1925 - 20 Nov 1925:	Attached to Naval General Staff
20 Nov 1925 - 16 Dec 1925:	Unassigned
16 Dec 1925:	Transferred to the reserve

Rear-Admiral **Tekizo KAWAKAMI** (15 Sep 1878 - 30 Jan 1944)
1 Dec 1920 - 20 Nov 1922:	Chief Engineer Officer, Chinkai Guard District
20 Nov 1922 - 1 Dec 1922:	Attached to Yokosuka Naval District
1 Dec 1922:	Promoted to *Rear-Admiral*
1 Dec 1922 - 31 Mar 1923:	Unassigned
31 Mar 1923:	Transferred to the reserve

Vice-Admiral **Giichiro KAWAMURA** (8 Feb 1883 - 7 Jan 1957)
1 Dec 1930:	Promoted to *Rear-Admiral*
1 Dec 1930 - 1 Dec 1931:	Chief of Staff, Sasebo Naval District
1 Dec 1931 - 1 Jun 1934:	Chief of Administration Bureau, Naval Shipbuilding Command
1 Jun 1934 - 15 Nov 1936:	Commander, Kasumigaura Air Division
15 Nov 1935:	Promoted to *Vice-Admiral*
15 Nov 1935 - 10 Dec 1935:	Attached to Naval General Staff
14 Dec 1935:	Transferred to the reserve

Rear-Admiral (Surgeon) **Hoshu KAWAMURA** (26 Jan 1849 - 8 Nov 1933)
8 Oct 1897 - 29 Nov 1900:	Chief of Medical Bureau, Yokosuka Naval District
28 Dec 1897:	Promoted to *General (Surgeon)*
29 Nov 1900 - 1 Oct 1901:	Chief of Medical Bureau, Kure Naval District
1 Oct 1901 - 27 May 1902:	Unassigned
27 May 1902:	Transferred to the reserve
23 Sep 1919:	Redesignated *Rear-Admiral (Surgeon)*

Rear-Admiral (Paymaster) **Ko KAWAMURA** (29 Sep 1893 - 21 Mar 1976)
1 Oct 1942 - 15 Nov 1945: Director, 2nd Clothing & Food Depot
1 Nov 1942: Promoted to *Rear-Admiral*

Rear-Admiral **Shigemoto KAWAMURA** (10 Apr 1884 - 26 Aug 1937)
15 Sep 1930 - 1 Jun 1931: Attached to Yokosuka Naval District
1 Jun 1931 - 21 Dec 1931: Unassigned
1 Dec 1931: Promoted to *Rear-Admiral*
21 Dec 1931: Transferred to the reserve

Rear-Admiral **Tatsuzo KAWAMURA** (30 Aug 1882 - 18 Feb 1968)
10 Nov 1923 - 15 Jun 1926: Chief of Section 1, Naval Hydrographic Command
15 Jun 1926 - 15 Jun 1927: Attached to Naval General Staff
1 Dec 1926: Promoted to *Rear-Admiral*
15 Jun 1927 - 1 Jul 1927: Unassigned
1 Jul 1927: Transferred to the reserve

Rear-Admiral **Takeo KAWANA** (21 Dec 1883 - 4 May 1942)
1 Oct 1941 - 4 May 1942: Captain, Gunboat *"Kongosan-maru"*
4 May 1942: Posthumously promoted to *Rear-Admiral*

Vice-Admiral **Chimaki KAWANO** (22 Apr 1892 - 25 Jan 1966)
15 Sep 1941 - 10 Apr 1942: Commander, 6th Submarine Flotilla
15 Oct 1941: Promoted to *Rear-Admiral*
10 Apr 1942 - 26 Apr 1942: Attached to Yokosuka Naval District
26 Apr 1942 - 5 Dec 1942: Commander, 3rd Submarine Flotilla
5 Dec 1942 - 25 Jan 1943: Attached to Naval General Staff
25 Jan 1943 - 30 Jan 1943: Chief of Communications Bureau, Joint General Staff
25 Jan 1943 - 15 Feb 1944: Chief of Section 4, Naval General Staff
15 Feb 1944 - 15 Jul 1945: Commandant, Yokosuka Naval Communications School
20 Jul 1944 - 15 Jul 1945: Commander, Kurihama 2nd Guard Force
1 May 1945: Promoted to *Vice-Admiral*
1 May 1945 - 1 Jun 1945: Commandant, Anti-Submarine School
15 Jul 1945 - 20 Jul 1945: Attached to Naval General Staff
20 Jul 1945 - 10 Aug 1945: Chief Supervisor for Construction & Ordnance, Naval Shipbuilding Command
10 Aug 1945 - 15 Oct 1945: Kanto & Shinetsu Area Supervisor, Department of Military Supply

Rear-Admiral **Hideo KAWANO** (8 Mar 1894 - 15 Nov 1988)
1 Apr 1944 - 25 Dec 1944: Commander, Tsu Navy Yard

1 May 1944:	Promoted to *Rear-Admiral*
25 Dec 1944 - 20 Aug 1945:	Supervisor for Construction & Ordnance, Naval Shipbuilding Command
27 Dec 1944 - 20 Aug 1945:	Supervisor for Ordnance, Naval Air Command
20 Aug 1945 - 25 Oct 1945:	Chief, Kobe Branch, Department of Military Supply

Rear-Admiral **Katsuji KAWANO** (6 Jul 1887 - 3 Sep 1936)
15 Nov 1934 - 15 Nov 1935:	Chief Engineer Officer, Kure Naval District
15 Nov 1935 - 3 Sep 1936:	Attached to Yokosuka Naval District
3 Sep 1936:	Posthumously promoted to *Rear-Admiral*

Rear-Admiral **Sakinta KAWANO** (1 Sep 1965 - 8 Apr 1932)
13 Sep 1915 - 1 Dec 1916:	Commander, Sasebo Harbor
1 Dec 1916:	Promoted to *Rear-Admiral*
1 Dec 1916 - 1 Dec 1917:	Unassigned
1 Dec 1917:	Transferred to the reserve

Vice-Admiral **Togo KAWANO** (7 Dec 1881 - 10 Sep 1940)
1 Dec 1927:	Promoted to *Rear-Admiral*
1 Dec 1927 - 10 Dec 1928:	Chief of Staff, Sasebo Naval District
10 Dec 1928 - 1 Apr 1931:	Chief of Section 3, Naval General Staff
1 Apr 1931 - 10 Oct 1931:	Attached to Naval General Staff
10 Oct 1931 - 1 Dec 1931:	Commander, 5th Escort Flotilla
1 Dec 1931 - 15 Nov 1932:	Commander, Ominato Guard District
15 Nov 1932 - 1 Dec 1932:	Attached to Naval General Staff
1 Dec 1932:	Promoted to *Vice-Admiral*
15 Dec 1932:	Transferred to the reserve

Rear-Admiral **Yasushi KAWANO** (26 Nov 1897 - 12 Apr 1945)
| 6 Jun 1944 - 12 Apr 1945: | Commander, 12th Guard Force |
| 12 Apr 1945: | Posthumously promoted to *Rear-Admiral* |

Rear-Admiral **Chinae KAWASAKI** (25 Sep 1897 - 9 Jul 1945)
15 Jan 1945 - 10 Jun 1945:	Commander, 101st Air Arsenal
10 Jun 1945 - 9 Jul 1945:	Attached to Naval Air Command
9 Jul 1945:	Posthumously promoted to *Rear-Admiral*

Rear-Admiral **Shigeharu KAWASAKI** (28 Nov 1891 - 20 Aug 1945)
20 Dec 1944 - 15 Feb 1945:	Staff Officer, Shipping Safety Division, Joint General Staff
15 Feb 1945 - 20 Aug 1945:	Attached to Yokosuka Naval District
20 Aug 1945:	Posthumously promoted to *Rear-Admiral*

Rear-Admiral **Takashi KAWASAKI** (? - 5 Nov 1944)
25 Oct 1944 - 5 Nov 1944:	Chief Engineer Officer, Heavy Cruiser *"Nachi"*
5 Nov 1944:	Posthumously promoted to *Rear-Admiral*

Rear-Admiral **Makoto KAWASE** (21 Sep 1883 - 24 Jan 1953)
1 Jul 1925 - 15 Nov 1933:	Chief of Research Bureau, Navy Fuel Yard
1 Dec 1931:	Promoted to *Rear-Admiral*
15 Nov 1933 - 11 Dec 1933:	Attached to Naval General Staff
15 Dec 1933:	Transferred to the reserve

Vice-Admiral **Shiro KAWASE** (7 Jul 1889 - 20 Jul 1946)
1 Dec 1937:	Promoted to *Rear-Admiral*
1 Dec 1937 - 15 Nov 1938:	Chief of Bureau 2, Naval Shipbuilding Command
15 Nov 1938 - 25 Nov 1939:	Commander, 5th Destroyer Flotilla
25 Nov 1939 - 15 Oct 1940:	Commander, 1st Destroyer Flotilla
15 Oct 1940 - 15 Nov 1940:	Attached to the staff, 1st Fleet
15 Nov 1940 - 10 Apr 1941:	Commander, 7th Air Flotilla
10 Apr 1941 - 1 Sep 1941:	Commander 11th Air Flotilla
1 Sep 1941 - 26 Dec 1941:	Commandant, Torpedo School
15 Oct 1941:	Promoted to *Vice-Admiral*
26 Dec 1941 - 10 Apr 1942:	C-in-C, 3rd China Expeditionary Fleet
10 Apr 1942 - 15 Sep 1942:	Attached to Naval General Staff
15 Sep 1942 - 1 Apr 1943:	Commander, Ominato Guard District
1 Apr 1943 - 15 Feb 1944:	C-in-C, 5th Fleet
15 Feb 1944 - 5 Jun 1944:	Attached to Naval General Staff
5 Jun 1944 - 18 Jun 1944:	Attached to the staff, Southwestern Area Fleet
18 Jun 1944 - 29 Jan 1945:	C-in-C, 2nd Southern Expeditionary Fleet
29 Jan 1945 - 15 Mar 1945:	Attached to Naval General Staff
20 Mar 1945:	Transferred to the reserve

Vice-Admiral **Yoshishige KAWASE** (21 Feb 1886 - 14 Oct 1970)
30 Nov 1929 - 15 Nov 1935:	Chief of Gunnery Research Bureau, Kure Navy Yard
15 Nov 1934:	Promoted to *Rear-Admiral*
15 Nov 1935 - 1 Dec 1937:	Chief of Explosives Bureau, Navy Powder Yard
1 Dec 1937 - 15 Nov 1939:	Attached to the Technical Research Department
15 Nov 1938:	Promoted to *Vice-Admiral*
15 Nov 1939 - 15 Dec 1939:	Attached to Naval General Staff
21 Dec 1939:	Transferred to the reserve

Rear-Admiral (Surgeon) **Hideshi KAWASHIMA** (29 Sep 1895 - Apr 1975)
25 Oct 1943 - 10 Nov 1944:	Attached to Sasebo Naval District
1 May 1944:	Promoted to *Rear-Admiral (Surgeon)*

10 Nov 1944 - 16 Dec 1944:   Attached to the staff,
                                                          1st Southern Expeditionary Fleet
16 Dec 1944 - 2 Feb 1945:   Director, 101st Naval Hospital
2 Feb 1945 - 10 Jul 1945:   Attached to Sasebo Naval District
10 Jul 1945 - 6 Sep 1945:   Attached to Naval General Staff

Vice-Admiral **Reijiro KAWASHIMA** (14 Sep 1864 - 22 Nov 1947)

21 Oct 1907 - 4 Mar 1909:   Chief of Bureau 1, Naval Shipbuilding Command
28 Aug 1908:   Promoted to *Rear-Admiral*
4 Mar 1909 - 1 Dec 1909:   Chief of Bureau 1, Naval General Staff
1 Dec 1909 - 1 Dec 1910:   Commandant of the Naval College,
                                                         Member, Admirals Committee
1 Dec 1910 - 20 Apr 1912:   C-in-C, 3rd Fleet
20 Apr 1912 - 1 Dec 1913:   Chief of Naval Hydrographic Command
7 Jan 1913:   Promoted to *Vice-Admiral*
1 Dec 1913 - 1 Apr 1914:   Unassigned
1 Apr 1914 - 13 Dec 1915:   Commander, Ryojun Guard District
13 Dec 1915 - 1 Apr 1916:   Member, Admirals Committee
1 Apr 1916 - 27 Jun 1916:   Unassigned
27 Jun 1916:   Transferred to the reserve

Rear-Admiral **Yoshio KAWASHIMA** (6 Apr 1899 - 9 Apr 1945)

5 Dec 1943 - 9 Apr 1945:   Commander, 1st Minesweeper Division
9 Apr 1945:   Posthumously promoted to *Rear-Admiral*

Rear-Admiral **Yasuchika KAYABARA** (21 Oct 1899 - 12 Jul 1944)

31 Jan 1944 - 12 Jul 1944:   Commander, 22nd Submarine Division
12 Jul 1944:   Posthumously promoted to *Rear-Admiral*

Rear-Admiral (Engineer) **Tokujiro KAZAMA** (23 Oct 1874 - 16 May 1947)

1 Oct 1920 - 1 Sep 1921:   Attached to Bureau 5,
                                                       Naval Shipbuilding Command
1 Dec 1920:   Promoted to *Rear-Admiral*
1 Sep 1921 - 1 Dec 1922:   Chief of Engine Construction Bureau,
                                                        Kure Navy Yard
1 Dec 1922 - 10 Dec 1922:   Attached to Naval Shipbuilding Command
10 Dec 1922 - 31 Mar 1923:   Unassigned
31 Mar 1923:   Transferred to the reserve

Rear-Admiral **Toyohei KAZAMA** (15 Aug 1883 - 6 Feb 1941)

1 Apr 1929 - 15 Nov 1932:   Chief of Engine Construction Bureau, Hiro Navy Yard
15 Nov 1932 - 10 Dec 1932:   Attached to Naval Shipbuilding Command
1 Dec 1932:   Promoted to *Rear-Admiral*
15 Dec 1932:   Transferred to the reserve

Rear-Admiral **Shinpei KIDA** (? - 17 Jan 1944)
1 Dec 1927 - 1 Dec 1930: Commander, Sasebo Harbor
1 Dec 1930: Promoted to *Rear-Admiral*
1 Dec 1930 - 24 Dec 1930: Attached to Sasebo Naval District
24 Dec 1930: Transferred to the reserve

Rear-Admiral (Paymaster) **Kanji KIDERA** (29 Nov 1892 - 29 Mar 1961)
1 Nov 1942: Promoted to *Rear-Admiral (Paymaster)*
1 Nov 1942 - 25 Sep 1943: Chief of 1st Accounting Bureau,
 Chief of 1st Supply Bureau
15 Aug 1943 - 25 Sep 1943: Paymaster-General, China Area Fleet
25 Sep 1943 - 10 Oct 1943: Attached to Yokosuka Naval District
10 Oct 1943 - 1 Nov 1945: Chief of Accounting Bureau, Yokosuka Navy Yard

Rear-Admiral **Tadahiko KIDO** (25 Aug 1881 - 26 Apr 1971)
1 Feb 1928 - 30 Nov 1929: Chief of Electronics Bureau, Kure Navy Yard
10 Dec 1928: Promoted to *Rear-Admiral*
30 Nov 1929 - 10 Jun 1930: Attached to Naval Shipbuilding Command
20 Jun 1930: Transferred to the reserve

Rear-Admiral **Haruju KIKKAWA** (6 Aug 1885 - ?)
5 Dec 1927 - 1 Apr 1932: Chief of Steel Bureau, Kure Navy Yard
1 Apr 1932 - 12 Jan 1933: Attached to Naval Shipbuilding Command
1 Dec 1932: Promoted to *Rear-Admiral*
14 Jan 1933: Transferred to the reserve

Rear-Admiral **Kiyoshi KIKKAWA** (24 Nov 1900 - 25 Nov 1943)
20 Dec 1942 - 25 Nov 1943: Captain, Destroyer *"Onami"*
25 Nov 1943: Posthumously promoted to *Rear-Admiral*

Rear-Admiral (Surgeon) **Mitsugu KIKUCHI** (17 Sep 1882 - 1 Jul 1950)
25 Feb 1932 - 15 Nov 1934: Chief Instructor, Navy Medical School
1 Dec 1932: Promoted to *Rear-Admiral (Surgeon)*
15 Nov 1934 - 10 Dec 1935: Attached to Naval General Staff
14 Dec 1935: Transferred to the reserve

Rear-Admiral **Tomozo KIKUCHI** (22 Nov 1896 - 31 Jan 1988)
10 Jul 1944 - 24 Oct 1944: Commander, 25th Air Flotilla
15 Oct 1944: Promoted to *Rear-Admiral*
24 Oct 1944 - 27 Oct 1944: Attached to the staff, 2nd Air Fleet
27 Oct 1944 - 8 Jan 1945: Chief of Staff, 2nd Air Fleet
8 Jan 1945 - 10 May 1945: Chief of Staff, 1st Air Fleet
10 May 1945 - 5 Jun 1945: Deputy Chief of Staff, 1st Air Fleet,
 Deputy Chief of Staff, Takao Guard District

5 Jun 1945 - 25 Jun 1945:	Attached to the staff, Combined Fleet
25 Jun 1945 - 15 Sep 1945:	Deputy Chief of Staff, Supreme Naval HQ, Deputy Chief of Staff, Combined Fleet
15 Sep 1945 - 15 Oct 1945:	Attached to Naval General Staff

Rear-Admiral **Tsuruji KIKUCHI** (30 Mar 1892 - 14 Oct 1977)

10 Apr 1943 - 1 Aug 1944:	Supervisor of Ordnance, Naval Shipbuilding Command, Supervisor of Ordnance, Naval Air Command
1 May 1944:	Promoted to *Rear-Admiral*
1 Aug 1944 - 25 May 1945:	Chief of Transport Bureau, Yokosuka Naval District
25 May 1945 - 10 Aug 1945:	Chief Supervisor for Construction & Ordnance, Naval Shipbuilding Command
10 Aug 1945 - 7 Nov 1945:	Hokkai Area Supervisor, Department of Military Supply

Rear-Admiral **Nobuyoshi KIKUI** (17 May 1882 - 24 Oct 1937)

1 Dec 1927 - 30 Nov 1929:	Chief of Shipping Bureau, Sasebo Naval District
30 Nov 1929:	Promoted to *Rear-Admiral*
30 Nov 1929 - 15 Dec 1929:	Attached to Naval General Staff
25 Dec 1929:	Transferred to the reserve

Vice-Admiral **Shigeru KIKUNO** (22 Dec 1885 - 16 Nov 1961)

28 Jun 1932 - 1 Apr 1933:	Chief of Staff, 3rd Fleet
1 Dec 1932:	Promoted to *Rear-Admiral*
1 Apr 1933 - 15 Nov 1935:	Chief of Bureau 2, Naval Shipbuilding Command
15 Nov 1935 - 1 Dec 1937:	Commander, Sasebo Navy Yard
1 Dec 1936:	Promoted to *Vice-Admiral*
1 Dec 1937 - 15 Dec 1937:	Attached to Naval General Staff
21 Dec 1937:	Transferred to the reserve

Rear-Admiral **Goroku KIMOTO** (9 Nov 1895 - 22 Oct 1989)

20 Jan 1944 - 5 Aug 1945:	Chief of Torpedo Bureau, Kure Navy Yard
1 May 1944:	Promoted to *Rear-Admiral*
5 Aug 1945 - 10 Aug 1945:	Attached to Naval Shipbuilding Command
10 Aug 1945 - 15 Sep 1945:	Chief of Section 1, Kinki Area Supervisor's office, Department of Military Supply

Vice-Admiral **Baron Kaneyuki KIMOTSUKE** (16 Mar 1853 - 13 Jan 1922)

27 Jun 1894 - 2 Nov 1905:	Chief of Naval Hydrographic Command
14 May 1898:	Promoted to *Rear-Admiral*
3 Feb 1904 - 2 Nov 1905:	Commandant of the Naval College
23 Sep 1905:	Promoted to *Vice-Admiral*

2 Nov 1905 - 28 May 1906: Unassigned
28 May 1906: Transferred to the reserve

Rear-Admiral **Gunji KIMURA** (22 Feb 1904 - 25 Oct 1944)
29 Mar 1944 - 25 Oct 1944: Commander, 653rd Air Division
25 Oct 1944: Posthumously promoted to *Rear-Admiral*

Rear-Admiral **Jin KIMURA** (3 Dec 1888 - 9 Dec 1967)
15 Nov 1938: Promoted to *Rear-Admiral*
15 Nov 1938 - 15 Nov 1940: Chief of Shipping Bureau, Sasebo Naval District
15 Nov 1940 - 15 Oct 1941: Chief of Shipping Bureau, Yokosuka Naval District
15 Oct 1941 - 15 Dec 1941: Attached to Naval General Staff
22 Dec 1941: Transferred to the reserve

Rear-Admiral (Engineer) **Kanichi KIMURA** (15 Mar 1875 - 10 Jan 1965)
1 Dec 1920: Promoted to *Rear-Admiral (Engineer)*
1 Dec 1920 - 10 Nov 1922: Chief Engineer Officer, Sasebo Naval District
10 Nov 1922 - 1 Dec 1923: Chief Engineer Officer, Kure Naval District
1 Dec 1923 - 10 Dec 1923: Attached to Naval General Staff
10 Dec 1923 - 25 Feb 1924: Unassigned
25 Feb 1924: Transferred to the reserve

Rear-Admiral **Kokichi KIMURA** (23 Jul 1861 - 14 Jan 1940)
28 Aug 1908 - 1 Dec 1910: Commander, Sasebo Torpedo Corps
1 Dec 1909: Promoted to *Rear-Admiral*
1 Dec 1910 - 1 Dec 1911: Commander, Maizuru Torpedo Corps
1 Dec 1911 - 1 Dec 1912: Unassigned
1 Dec 1912: Transferred to the reserve

Rear-Admiral **Kozo KIMURA** (12 Oct 1899 - 17 Sep 1944)
1 Jul 1944 - 17 Sep 1944: Captain, Aircraft Carrier *"Unyo"*
17 Sep 1944: Posthumously promoted to *Rear-Admiral*

Rear-Admiral (Surgeon) **Masao KIMURA** (? - 21 Nov 1944)
1 Mar 1944 - 21 Nov 1944: Chief Surgeon, 1st Task Fleet,
 Chief Surgeon, 3rd Fleet
21 Nov 1944: Posthumously promoted to *Rear-Admiral (Surgeon)*

Vice-Admiral **Masatomi KIMURA** (6 Dec 1891 - 14 Feb 1960)
15 Oct 1940 - 24 Nov 1942: Captain, Heavy Cruiser *"Suzuya"*
1 Nov 1942: Promoted to *Rear-Admiral*
24 Nov 1942 - 5 Dec 1942: Attached to Yokosuka Naval District
5 Dec 1942 - 5 Feb 1943: Commander, Maizuru Guard Force

5 Feb 1943 - 14 Feb 1943:	Attached to the staff, 1st Fleet
14 Feb 1943 - 6 Mar 1943:	Commander, 3rd Destroyer Flotilla
6 Mar 1943 - 8 Jun 1943:	Attached to Yokosuka Naval District
8 Jun 1943 - 20 Nov 1944:	Commander, 1st Destroyer Flotilla
20 Nov 1944 - 3 Jan 1945:	Commander, 2nd Destroyer Flotilla
3 Jan 1945 - 18 Feb 1945:	Attached to Naval General Staff
18 Feb 1945 - 1 Jun 1945:	Attached to the staff, Combined Fleet
1 Jun 1945 - 15 Jul 1945:	Commandant, Anti-Submarine School
15 Jul 1945 - 1 Oct 1945:	Commandant, Hofu Naval Communications School
1 Oct 1945 - 11 Nov 1945:	Attached to Yokosuka Naval District
1 Nov 1945:	Promoted to *Vice-Admiral*

Rear-Admiral (Surgeon) **Ritsuo KIMURA** (21 Feb 1883 - 7 Aug 1948)

30 Nov 1929 - 1 Dec 1930:	Chief of Medical Bureau, Kure Navy Yard
1 Dec 1930:	Promoted to *Rear-Admiral (Surgeon)*
1 Dec 1930 - 15 Dec 1930:	Attached to Kure Naval District
24 Dec 1930:	Transferred to the reserve

Vice-Admiral (Surgeon) **Sosuke KIMURA** (28 Mar 1857 - 28 Mar 1939)

9 Aug 1902 - 4 Jan 1906:	Commandant, Navy Medical School
12 Jan 1905:	Promoted to *General (Surgeon)*
13 Dec 1905 - 13 Dec 1915:	Chief of Naval Medical Service
13 Dec 1915 - 1 Dec 1916:	Unassigned
1 Dec 1916:	Transferred to the reserve
23 Sep 1919:	Redesignated *Vice-Admiral (Surgeon)*

Vice-Admiral **Susumu KIMURA** (1 Jun 1891 - 16 Mar 1980)

10 Apr 1942 - 21 Jan 1943:	Commander, 10th Escort Flotilla
1 May 1942:	Promoted to *Rear-Admiral*
21 Jan 1943 - 1 Apr 1943:	Attached to Yokosuka Naval District
1 Apr 1943 - 20 Nov 1943:	Commander, 11th Destroyer Flotilla
20 Nov 1943 - 3 Dec 1943:	Attached to the staff, 3rd Fleet
3 Dec 1943 - 15 Nov 1944:	Commander, 10th Escort Flotilla
15 Nov 1944 - 19 Dec 1944:	Attached to Naval General Staff
19 Dec 1944 - 1 May 1945:	Commandant, Navigation School
1 May 1945:	Promoted to *Vice-Admiral*
1 May 1945 - 29 Nov 1945:	Chief of Naval Hydrographic Command

Rear-Admiral **Takashi KIMURA** (21 Sep 1888 - 6 Dec 1945)

1 Mar 1944 - 10 Nov 1945:	Chief of Facilities Bureau, Maizuru Naval District
1 May 1945:	Promoted to *Rear-Admiral*

Vice-Admiral **Takeshi KIMURA** (24 Jan 1867 - 23 Sep 1929)
1 Dec 1914:	Promoted to *Rear-Admiral*
1 Dec 1914 - 1 Dec 1916:	Chief of Staff, Yokosuka Naval District
1 Dec 1916 - 4 Sep 1918:	Commander, Maizuru Navy Yard
4 Sep 1918 - 1 Sep 1921:	Commander, Sasebo Navy Yard
1 Dec 1918:	Promoted to *Vice-Admiral*
1 Sep 1921 - 1 Dec 1921:	Member, Admirals Committee
1 Dec 1921 - 31 Mar 1923:	Unassigned
31 Mar 1923:	Transferred to the reserve

Rear-Admiral **Ritsuma KINASHI** (23 Jul 1888 - 18 Jun 1951)
1 Dec 1936:	Promoted to *Rear-Admiral*
1 Dec 1936 - 1 Dec 1937:	Chief of Shipping Bureau, Yokosuka Naval District
1 Dec 1937 - 15 Dec 1937:	Attached to Naval General Staff
21 Dec 1937:	Transferred to the reserve

Rear-Admiral **Takakazu KINASHI** (7 Mar 1902 - 26 Jul 1944)
10 Oct 1943 - 26 Jul 1944:	Captain, Submarine *"I-29"*
26 Jul 1944:	Posthumously promoted 2 grades to *Rear-Admiral*

Rear-Admiral **Mitsuo KINOSHITA** (7 Aug 1893 - 3 Jul 1959)
10 Dec 1942 - 20 Aug 1943:	Chief, Gunnery Research Bureau, Kure Navy Yard
1 May 1943:	Promoted to *Rear-Admiral*
20 Aug 1943 - 27 Aug 1943:	Attached to Naval Shipbuilding Command
27 Aug 1943 - 20 Dec 1944:	Chief of Bureau 1, Naval Shipbuilding Command
20 Dec 1944 - 1 Nov 1945:	Commander, Tagajo Navy Yard

Vice-Admiral **Shunichi KIRA** (9 Sep 1889 - 30 Apr 1947)
1 Nov 1940 - 15 May 1942:	Commander, 12th Combined Air Division
15 Nov 1940:	Promoted to *Rear-Admiral*
15 May 1942 - 1 Jan 1944:	Commander, 22nd Air Flotilla
1 Nov 1943:	Promoted to *Vice-Admiral*
1 Jan 1944 - 19 Feb 1944:	Attached to Naval General Staff
19 Feb 1944 - 15 Mar 1944:	Commander, 51st Air Flotilla
15 Mar 1944 - 10 Jul 1944:	Commander, Yokosuka Air Division
10 Jul 1944 - 11 Nov 1944:	C-in-C, 3rd Air Fleet
11 Nov 1944 - 6 Sep 1945:	Attached to Naval General Staff

Rear-Admiral **Yoshitane KISAKA** (1 Jan 1904 - 8 Nov 1944)
10 May 1943 - 8 Nov 1944:	Staff Officer, 8th Fleet
8 Nov 1944:	Posthumously promoted to *Rear-Admiral*

Vice-Admiral **Kosuke KISAKI** (23 Jul 1867 - 12 Feb 1944)
24 May 1913: Promoted to *Rear-Admiral*
24 May 1913 - 26 Sep 1913: Attached to Naval Training Command
26 Sep 1913 - 29 May 1914: Unassigned
29 May 1914 - 1 Apr 1916: Chief of Bureau 3, Naval Training Command
1 Apr 1916 - 1 Dec 1917: Commandant, Naval Engineering Academy
1 Dec 1917 - 1 Apr 1921: Chief Engineer Officer, Kure Naval District
1 Dec 1918: Promoted to *Vice-Admiral*
1 Apr 1921 - 10 Nov 1922: Commander, Navy Fuel Yard
10 Nov 1922 - 10 Dec 1922: Attached to Naval Shipbuilding Command
10 Dec 1922 - 31 Mar 1923: Unassigned
31 Mar 1923: Transferred to the reserve

Vice-Admiral **Fukuji KISHI** (30 Apr 1891 - 10 Jul 1949)
15 Nov 1939: Promoted to *Rear-Admiral*
15 Nov 1939 - 10 Oct 1941: Chief of Staff, 4th Fleet
10 Oct 1941 - 20 Nov 1941: Attached to Naval General Staff
20 Nov 1941 - 15 Mar 1943: Commander, 9th Cruiser Division
15 Mar 1943 - 1 Jan 1944: Commander, 8th Cruiser Division
1 May 1943: Promoted to *Vice-Admiral*
1 Jan 1944 - 23 Feb 1944: Attached to Naval General Staff
23 Feb 1944 - 4 Nov 1944: Chief of Staff, Escort Fleet
4 Nov 1944 - 10 Dec 1944: Commander, 1st Escort Force
10 Dec 1944 - 10 Jul 1945: C-in-C, 1st Escort Fleet
15 Apr 1945 - 20 Aug 1945: C-in-C, 7th Fleet
20 Aug 1945 - 15 Sep 1945: Attached to Naval General Staff

Rear-Admiral **Yoshiyuki KISHI** (24 Apr 1898 - 25 Oct 1944)
7 Apr 1944 - 25 Oct 1944: Captain, Aircraft Carrier *"Chitose"*
25 Oct 1944: Posthumously promoted to *Rear-Admiral*

Rear-Admiral **Tojiro KISHIDA** (23 Mar 1880 - 11 May 1973)
20 May 1926 - 1 Dec 1927: Chief of Oil Bureau, Navy Fuel Yard
1 Dec 1926: Promoted to *Rear-Admiral*
1 Dec 1927 - 15 Dec 1927: Attached to Naval General Staff
25 Dec 1927: Transferred to the reserve

Rear-Admiral **Koichi KISHII** (21 Nov 1879 - 23 Mar 1960)
1 Dec 1924: Promoted to *Rear-Admiral*
1 Dec 1924 - 1 Dec 1925: Commandant, Submarine School
1 Dec 1925 - 10 Mar 1926: Commander, 1st Submarine Flotilla
10 Mar 1926 - 1 May 1926: Attached to Kure Naval District
1 May 1926 - 20 May 1926: Attached to Naval General Staff

20 May 1926 - 1 Aug 1926:	Unassigned
1 Aug 1926 - 1 Dec 1926:	Attached to Naval General Staff
1 Dec 1926 - 5 Apr 1927:	Chief of Bureau 3, Naval Shipbuilding Command
5 Apr 1927 - 1 Dec 1927:	Chief of Bureau 2, Naval Shipbuilding Command
1 Dec 1927 - 15 Jan 1928:	Attached to Naval General Staff
25 Jan 1928:	Transferred to the reserve

Rear-Admiral **Kakuo KISHIKAWA** (28 Apr 1897 - 8 Jul 1944)

4 Mar 1944 - 8 Jul 1944 :	Chief Engineer Officer, Central Pacific Area Fleet,
20 May 1944 - 8 Jul 1944:	Deputy Chief of Staff, Central Pacific Area Fleet
8 Jul 1944:	Posthumously promoted to *Rear-Admiral*

Vice-Admiral **Hajime KISHIMOTO** (8 Apr 1885 - 25 Nov 1976)

30 Nov 1929:	Promoted to *Rear-Admiral*
30 Nov 1929 - 10 Jun 1930:	Attached to Naval Shipbuilding Command
10 Jun 1930 - 15 Nov 1935:	Commander, Navy Powder Yard
15 Nov 1934:	Promoted to *Vice-Admiral*
15 Nov 1935 - 10 Dec 1935:	Attached to Naval Shipbuilding Command
20 Dec 1935:	Transferred to the reserve

Rear-Admiral **Kaneji KISHIMOTO** (14 Apr 1888 - 1 Jan 1981)

1 Dec 1936:	Promoted to *Rear-Admiral*
1 Dec 1936 - 15 Nov 1939:	Chief of Torpedo Bureau, Kure Navy Yard
15 Nov 1939 - 16 Jan 1940:	Attached to Naval General Staff
21 Jan 1940:	Transferred to the reserve

Vice-Admiral **Nobuta KISHIMOTO** (18 Jan 1881 - 14 Jul 1962)

1 Dec 1925:	Promoted to *Rear-Admiral*
1 Dec 1925 - 25 Jun 1928:	Chief of Education, Naval Engineering Academy
25 Jun 1928 - 10 Dec 1928:	Commandant, Naval Engineering School
10 Dec 1928 - 1 Dec 1931:	Commander, Navy Fuel Yard
30 Nov 1929:	Promoted to *Vice-Admiral*
1 Dec 1931 - 15 Dec 1931:	Attached to Naval General Staff
21 Dec 1931:	Transferred to the reserve

Vice-Admiral **Masao KISHINA** (27 Feb 1878 - 1 Dec 1938)

1 Dec 1925:	Promoted to *Rear-Admiral*
1 Dec 1925 - 10 Dec 1928:	Chief of Torpedo Bureau, Kure Navy Yard
10 Dec 1928 - 15 Dec 1929:	Attached to Naval Shipbuilding Command
30 Nov 1929:	Promoted to *Vice-Admiral*
25 Dec 1929:	Transferred to the reserve

Rear-Admiral **Saburo KISHINDO** (21 Jul 1890 - 14 Sep 1959)
14 Sep 1943 - Oct 1945:   Commander, 3rd Weather Unit
15 Oct 1944:   Promoted to *Rear-Admiral*

Rear-Admiral **Kiyoshi KITAGAWA** (2 Apr 1883 - 18 Mar 1952)
26 Oct 1930 - 15 Nov 1933: Commander, Kure Defense Force
1 Feb 1932 - 28 Jun 1932:   Acting Commandant, Submarine School
1 Dec 1932:   Promoted to *Rear-Admiral*
15 Nov 1933 - 11 Dec 1933: Attached to Kure Naval District
11 Dec 1933 - 15 Nov 1934: Commander, Kure Guard Flotilla
15 Nov 1934 - 25 Mar 1935: Attached to Naval General Staff
30 Mar 1935:   Transferred to the reserve

Rear-Admiral **Masa KITAGAWA** (19 Jun 1898 - 14 Oct 1987)
20 May 1944 - 8 Jan 1945:   Deputy Chief of Staff, Southwestern Area Fleet
15 Oct 1944:   Promoted to *Rear-Admiral*
8 Jan 1945 - 1 Aug 1945:   Attached to Yokosuka Naval District
1 Aug 1945 - 25 Aug 1945:   Attached to Naval General Staff
25 Aug 1945 - 5 Nov 1945:   Commandant, Dainan Naval Engineering School
5 Nov 1945 - 30 Nov 1945:   Attached to Sasebo Naval District

Rear-Admiral **Shigeharu KITAGAWA**
6 Jan 1945 - Oct 1945:   Chief of Indicator Bureau, Air Technical Arsenal
1 May 1945:   Promoted to *Rear-Admiral*

Vice-Admiral **Takeichiro KITAKOGA** (4 Aug 1858 - 14 Aug 1926)
20 May 1900 - 2 Jun 1906:   Chief of Bureau 1, Naval Shipbuilding Command
2 Nov 1905:   Promoted to *Rear-Admiral*
2 Jun 1906 - 15 May 1908:   Commander, Kure Navy Yard
15 May 1908 - 28 Aug 1908: Commander, Maizuru Navy Yard
28 Aug 1908 - 1 Dec 1909:   Commander, Yokosuka Torpedo Corps
28 Aug 1908 - 25 Sep 1908: Commandant, Torpedo School
1 Dec 1909:   Promoted to *Vice-Admiral*
1 Dec 1909 - 17 Apr 1911:   Unassigned
17 Apr 1911:   Transferred to the reserve

Rear-Admiral **Fumio KITAMURA** (1 Apr 1897 - 30 Mar 1944)
27 Apr 1943 - 30 Mar 1944: Commander of Auxiliary Forces, Oiler *"Iro"*
30 Mar 1944:   Posthumously promoted to *Rear-Admiral*

Rear-Admiral **Masayuki KITAMURA** (3 Oct 1894 - 9 Sep 1944)
7 Apr 1944 - 9 Sep 1944:   Chief of Traffic Control, 1st Maritime Escort Force
9 Sep 1944:   Posthumously promoted to *Rear-Admiral*

Rear-Admiral (Paymaster) **Motoharu KITAMURA** (10 Aug 1893 - 24 Nov 1957)
25 Sep 1943 - 1 Apr 1945:	Chief of Accounting Bureau, 21st Air Arsenal
1 May 1944:	Promoted to *Rear-Admiral (Paymaster)*
1 Apr 1945 - 1 Nov 1945:	Chief of Accounting Bureau, Maizuru Navy Yard

Rear-Admiral **Katsuya KITANO** (4 Apr 1862 - 20 Jul 1923)
25 Mar 1914:	Promoted to *Rear-Admiral*
25 Mar 1914 - 7 Apr 1914:	Attached to Kure Naval District
7 Apr 1914 - 27 May 1914:	Commander, Kure Harbor
27 May 1914 - 27 May 1915:	Unassigned
27 May 1915:	Transferred to the reserve

Rear-Admiral **Tsunao KITANO** (12 Jan 1890 - 25 Mar 1946)
10 Feb 1939 - 15 Nov 1939:	Supervisor for Construction & Ordnance, Naval Shipbuilding Command
15 Nov 1939:	Promoted to *Rear-Admiral*
15 Nov 1939 - 15 Dec 1939:	Attached to Naval General Staff
21 Dec 1939:	Transferred to the reserve

Rear-Admiral **Haruo KITAOKA** (2 Apr 1884 - 22 Apr 1947)
15 Nov 1933:	Promoted to *Rear-Admiral*
15 Nov 1933 - 1 Mar 1934:	Attached to Naval General Staff
1 Mar 1934 - 15 Nov 1934:	Commander, Kure Guard Force
15 Nov 1934 - 10 Dec 1934:	Attached to Naval General Staff
15 Dec 1934:	Transferred to the reserve

Rear-Admiral (Paymaster) **Kitaru KITAZAKI** (27 Mar 1893 - 20 Oct 1942)
15 Feb 1942 - 20 Oct 1942:	Chief of Davao Branch, 103rd Accounting Bureau
20 Oct 1942:	Posthumously promoted to *Rear-Admiral*

Rear-Admiral **Tatsuo KIYAMA** (11 Apr 1892 - 22 Dec 1949)
15 Feb 1943 - Oct 1945:	Commander, 81st Guard Force
1 May 1944:	Promoted to *Rear-Admiral*

Rear-Admiral (Paymaster) **Katsuji KIYOFUJI** (13 Feb 1894 - 27 Mar 1973)
10 Jun 1944 - Oct 1945:	Paymaster-General, Southwestern Area Fleet
8 Jan 1945 - Oct 1945:	Paymaster-General, 3rd Southern Expeditionary Fleet
1 May 1945:	Promoted to *Rear-Admiral (Paymaster)*

Vice-Admiral **Junichi KIYOKAWA** (7 Jan 1878 - 1 Mar 1935)
13 Sep 1920 - 28 May 1923:	Deputy Naval Attache, League of Nations
1 Dec 1922:	Promoted to *Rear-Admiral*
28 May 1923 - 19 Jun 1925:	Naval Attache, League of Nations

19 Jun 1925 - 1 Sep 1925:	Attached to Naval General Staff
1 Sep 1925 - 1 Dec 1926:	Instructor, Naval College
1 Dec 1926:	Promoted to *Vice-Admiral*
1 Dec 1926 - 1 Dec 1927:	Commander, 5th Escort Flotilla
1 Dec 1927 - 1 Jul 1929:	Commander, Chinkai Guard District
1 Jul 1929 - 11 Nov 1929:	Attached to Naval General Staff
11 Nov 1929 - 1 Dec 1930:	Admiral Commanding, Maizuru Naval District
1 Dec 1930 - 20 Mar 1931:	Attached to Naval General Staff
31 Mar 1931:	Transferred to the reserve

Rear-Admiral **Ko KIYOMIYA** (19 Jun 1889 - 5 Feb 1969)

10 Sep 1936 - 15 Nov 1938:	Chief of Section 3, Administration Bureau, Naval Shipbuilding Command
15 Nov 1938:	Promoted to *Rear-Admiral*
15 Nov 1938 - 15 Dec 1938:	Attached to Naval General Staff
21 Dec 1938:	Transferred to the reserve

Rear-Admiral **Takahiko KIYOTA** (28 Nov 1892 - 17 Jul 1961)

20 Aug 1941 - 16 Nov 1942:	Captain, Heavy Cruiser *"Nachi"*
1 Nov 1942:	Promoted to *Rear-Admiral*
16 Nov 1942 - 10 Jan 1944:	Chief of Bureau 1, Naval Hydrographic Command
25 Jan 1943 - 10 Jan 1944:	Chief of Administration Bureau, Naval Hydrographic Command
10 Jan 1944 - 4 Mar 1944:	Commander, 14th Escort Flotilla
4 Mar 1944 - 15 Mar 1944:	Attached to Yokosuka Naval District
15 Mar 1944 - 8 Apr 1944:	Attached to Naval General Staff
8 Apr 1944 - 8 Jul 1944:	Commander, 2nd Convoy HQ
8 Jul 1944 - 20 Jul 1945:	Commander, Kure Defense Flotilla
20 Jul 1945 - 5 Nov 1945:	Commander, 8th Special Attack Flotilla

Rear-Admiral **Tokuya KIYOTO** (25 Apr 1882 - 1953)

1 Dec 1927 - 10 Dec 1928:	Chief of Shipping Bureau, Yokosuka Naval District
10 Dec 1928:	Promoted to *Rear-Admiral*
10 Dec 1928 - 20 Dec 1928:	Attached to Naval General Staff
25 Dec 1928:	Transferred to the reserve

Rear-Admiral (Surgeon) **Einosuke KIZU** (8 Mar 1896 - 30 Jun 1946)

15 Dec 1943 - 1 Nov 1944:	Director, Totsuka Naval Hospital
1 May 1944:	Promoted to *Rear-Admiral (Surgeon)*
1 Nov 1944 - 15 Feb 1945:	Chief of Medical Bureau, Air Technical Arsenal
15 Feb 1945 - 10 Oct 1945:	Chief of Medical Bureau, 1st Technical Arsenal
10 Oct 1945 - 29 Nov 1945:	Attached to the Department of the Navy
29 Nov 1945 - 30 Nov 1945:	Director, Totsuka Naval Hospital

Rear-Admiral **Yasuo KO** (31 Oct 1885 - 11 Jan 1963)
5 Jul 1932 - 28 Dec 1933:	Air & Naval Attahce, League of Nations
1 Dec 1932:	Promoted to *Rear-Admiral*
28 Dec 1933 - 10 Dec 1935:	Attached to Naval General Staff
14 Dec 1935:	Transferred to the reserve

Rear-Admiral **Yoriharu KO** (29 Sep 1897 - ?)
15 Apr 1944 - 1 Nov 1944:	Chief of the Legal Service, Takao Guard District
15 Oct 1944:	Promoted to *Rear-Admiral*
1 Nov 1944 - 10 Jul 1945:	Chief of the Legal Service, Sasebo Naval District
10 Jul 1945 - 20 Oct 1945:	Attached to Yokosuka Naval District

Rear-Admiral **Tsuyoshi KOBATA** (2 Jun 1887 - 10 Aug 1977)
1 Dec 1936 - 1 Dec 1937:	Commander, Yokosuka Defense Force
1 Dec 1937:	Promoted to *Rear-Admiral*
1 Dec 1937 - 15 Dec 1937:	Attached to Naval General Staff
21 Dec 1937:	Transferred to the reserve

Rear-Admiral **Hajime KOBAYASHI** (13 Jul 1898 - 26 Mar 1944)
28 Dec 1942 - 26 Mar 1944:	Commander, 12th Submarine Division
26 Mar 1944:	Posthumously promoted to *Rear-Admiral*

Vice-Admiral **Kengo KOBAYASHI** (22 Mar 1893 - 23 Apr 1948)
11 Aug 1941 - 16 Jan 1943:	Chief of Staff, 1st Fleet
15 Oct 1941:	Promoted to *Rear-Admiral*
16 Jan 1943 - 11 Jun 1943:	Chief of Staff, Kure Naval District
11 Jun 1943 - 10 Sep 1944:	Deputy Chief of Staff, Combined Fleet
10 Sep 1944 - 20 Apr 1945:	Attached to Naval General Staff
15 Oct 1944:	Promoted to *Vice-Admiral*
20 Apr 1945 - Oct 1945:	Commander, Ryojun Area Base Force

Rear-Admiral (Surgeon) **Kengo KOBAYASHI** (30 Nov 1889 - 30 Jan 1940)
15 Nov 1935 - 15 Nov 1939:	Chief of Bureau 2, Yokosuka Naval Hospital
15 Nov 1939:	Promoted to *Rear-Admiral (Surgeon)*
15 Nov 1939 - 30 Jan 1940:	Attached to Yokosuka Naval District

Vice-Admiral **Kenzo KOBAYASHI** (11 Mar 1872 - 26 Oct 1942)
10 Nov 1918 - 1 Nov 1919:	Commander, 3rd Destroyer Flotilla
1 Jun 1919:	Promoted to *Rear-Admiral*
1 Nov 1919 - 1 May 1922:	Chief of Staff, Sasebo Naval District
1 May 1922 - 15 Sep 1923:	C-in-C, 1st Expeditionary Fleet
15 Sep 1923 - 5 Feb 1924:	Member, Admirals Committee
1 Dec 1923:	Promoted to *Vice-Admiral*
25 Feb 1924:	Transferred to the reserve

Vice-Admiral **Masami KOBAYASHI** (18 Jun 1890 - 7 Aug 1977)
20 Oct 1937 - 1 Sep 1938:	Chief of Staff, 4th Fleet
1 Dec 1937:	Promoted to *Rear-Admiral*
1 Sep 1938 - 15 Nov 1939:	Chief of Staff, Sasebo Naval District
15 Nov 1939 - 15 Nov 1940:	Commander, Kanko Area Base Force
15 Nov 1940 - 1 May 1941:	Commander, Shanghai Area Auxiliary Base Force
1 May 1941 - 2 Jun 1941:	Attached to Naval General Staff
2 Jun 1941 - 20 Nov 1941:	Chief of Naval Hydrographic Command
15 Oct 1941:	Promoted to *Vice-Admiral*
20 Nov 1941 - 9 Mar 1943:	Commander, Osaka Guard District
9 Mar 1943 - 1 Apr 1943:	Attached to Naval General Staff
1 Apr 1943 - 19 Feb 1944:	C-in-C, 4th Fleet
19 Feb 1944 - 30 May 1944:	Attached to Naval General Staff
31 May 1944:	Transferred to the reserve

Rear-Admiral (Surgeon) **Mikio KOBAYASHI** (4 Mar 1875 - 5 Sep 1934)
1 Dec 1923:	Promoted to *Rear-Admiral (Surgeon)*
1 Dec 1923 - 1 Dec 1925:	Chief Instructor, Navy Medical School
1 Dec 1925 - 1 Dec 1926:	Director, Kure Naval Hospital,
	Chief Surgeon, Kure Naval District
1 Dec 1926 - 20 Mar 1927:	Attached to Naval General Staff
20 Mar 1927 - 25 Dec 1927:	Unassigned
25 Dec 1927:	Transferred to the reserve

Vice-Admiral **Seizaburo KOBAYASHI** (5 Sep 1883 - 22 Apr 1956)
30 Nov 192:	Promoted to *Rear-Admiral*
30 Nov 1929 - 1 Dec 1931:	Commander, Kasumigaura Air Division
1 Dec 1931 - 8 Feb 1932:	Attached to Naval General Staff
8 Feb 1932 - 15 Sep 1932:	Government Representative, China
15 Sep 1932 - 1 Apr 1933:	Government Representative, Manchuria
1 Apr 1933 - 15 Nov 1934:	Commander, Manchuria Expeditionary Force
15 Nov 1934:	Promoted to *Vice-Admiral*
15 Nov 1934 - 16 Mar 1936:	Commander, Chinkai Guard District
16 Mar 1936 - 28 Mar 1936:	Attached to Naval General Staff
30 Mar 1936:	Transferred to the reserve

Admiral **Seizo KOBAYASHI** (1 Oct 1877 - 4 Jul 1962)
1 Apr 1920 - 1 Dec 1922:	Military Attache, United Kingdom
1 Jun 1922:	Promoted to *Rear-Admiral*
1 Dec 1922 - 1 Dec 1923:	Commander, 3rd Escort Flotilla
1 Dec 1923 - 25 Mar 1927:	Chief, Bureau of Naval Affairs,
	Member, Admirals Committee
1 Dec 1926:	Promoted to *Vice-Admiral*

25 Mar 1927 - 15 Apr 1927:	Attached to Naval General Staff
15 Apr 1927 - 15 Jan 1928:	Attached to the Plenipotentiary, Geneva Conference
15 Jan 1928 - 1 Feb 1929:	C-in-C, Training Fleet
1 Feb 1929 - 10 Jun 1930:	Chief of Naval Shipbuilding Command, Member, Admirals Committee
10 Jun 1930 - 1 Dec 1931:	Deputy Minister of the Navy, Member, Admirals Committee
1 Dec 1931 - 15 Nov 1933:	C-in-C, Combined Fleet, C-in-C, 1st Fleet
1 Mar 1933:	Promoted to *Admiral*
15 Nov 1933 - 28 Mar 1936:	Navy Councillor
30 Mar 1936:	Transferred to the reserve
2 Sep 1936 - 27 Nov 1940:	Governor-General of Taiwan

Rear-Admiral **Shozo KOBAYASHI** (7 Nov 1898 - 9 Dec 1945)

10 Jul 1944 - Oct 1945	Commander, 214th Construction Battalion
9 Dec 1945:	Posthumously promoted to *Rear-Admiral*

Vice-Admiral **Sonosuke KOBAYASHI** (2 Oct 1886 - 17 Mar 1975)

15 Nov 1933:	Promoted to *Rear-Admiral*
15 Nov 1933 - 1 Dec 1936:	Chief of Naval Personnel
1 Dec 1936 - 10 Mar 1937:	Commander, 5th Escort Flotilla
10 Mar 1937 - 15 Jul 1937:	Commander, 4th Escort Flotilla
15 Jul 1937 - 28 Jul 1937:	Attached to Naval General Staff
28 Jul 1937 - 1 Feb 1938:	Commander, 9th Escort Flotilla
1 Dec 1937:	Promoted to *Vice-Admiral*
1 Feb 1938 - 15 Nov 1938:	Attached to Naval General Staff
15 Nov 1938 - 15 Apr 1940:	Commander, Chinkai Guard District
15 Apr 1940 - 14 Jul 1942:	Admiral Commanding, Maizuru Naval District
14 Jul 1942 - 10 Nov 1942:	Attached to Naval General Staff
16 Nov 1942:	Transferred to the reserve

Rear-Admiral **Tadashi KOBAYASHI** (5 Nov 1894 - 11 Dec 1974)

15 Sep 1944 - 21 Apr 1945:	Chief of Chemical Bureau, 6th Navy Fuel Yard, Chief of Maintenance Bureau, 6th Navy Fuel Yard
15 Oct 1944:	Promoted to *Rear-Admiral*
1 Apr 1945 - 21 Apr 1945:	Chief of Administration Bureau, 6th Navy Fuel Yard
21 Apr 1945 - Oct 1945:	Commander, 6th Navy Fuel Yard

Vice-Admiral **Tetsuri KOBAYASHI** (20 May 1888 - 23 Sep 1954)

15 Nov 1938:	Promoted to *Rear-Admiral*
15 Nov 1938 - 19 Oct 1940:	Commander, Kure Defense Flotilla
19 Oct 1940 - 15 Nov 1940:	Attached to the staff, Combined Fleet

15 Nov 1940 - 3 Jan 1942:	Commander, 17th Minelayer Flotilla
3 Jan 1942 - 20 Feb 1943:	Commander, 31st Naval Base Force
1 May 1942:	Promoted to *Vice-Admiral*
20 Feb 1943 - 20 Jun 1943:	Attached to Naval General Staff
25 Jun 1943:	Transferred to the reserve

Vice-Admiral **Yoshiharu KOBAYASHI** (25 Nov 1892 - 27 Jul 1982)

1 Oct 1940 - 15 Dec 1941:	Chief of Engine Construction Bureau, Kure Navy Yard
15 Nov 1940:	Promoted to *Rear-Admiral*
15 Dec 1941 - 20 Aug 1943:	Commander, Hiro Navy Yard
20 Aug 1943 - 15 Sep 1943:	Attached to Naval Shipbuilding Command
15 Sep 1943 - 10 May 1944:	Chief of Bureau 5, Naval Shipbuilding Command
1 May 1944:	Promoted to *Vice-Admiral*
10 May 1944 - 15 Nov 1944:	Attached to Naval Shipbuilding Command
15 Nov 1944 - 1 May 1945:	Chief Supervisor for Construction & Ordnance, Naval Shipbuilding Command
1 May 1945 - 1 Nov 1945:	Commander, Maizuru Navy Yard

Rear-Admiral **Yuji KOBE** (8 Oct 1895 - 21 Jan 1989)

15 Dec 1943 - 20 Dec 1944:	Captain, Battleship *"Nagato"*
15 Oct 1944:	Promoted to *Rear-Admiral*
20 Dec 1944 - 27 Dec 1944:	Attached to Yokosuka Naval District
27 Dec 1944 - 15 Feb 1945:	Attached to Naval General Staff
15 Feb 1945 - 29 Nov 1945:	Chief of Administration Bureau, 2nd Technical Arsenal

Vice-Admiral (Surgeon) **Naka KODA** (15 Mar 1878 - 27 Feb 1947)

1 Dec 1927:	Promoted to *Rear-Admiral (Surgeon)*
1 Dec 1927 - 30 Nov 1929:	Director, Yokosuka Naval Hospital, Chief Surgeon, Yokosuka Naval District
30 Nov 1929 - 25 Feb 1932:	Commandant, Navy Medical School
25 Feb 1932 - 15 Nov 1934:	Chief of Naval Medical Service
1 Dec 1932:	Promoted to *Vice-Admiral (Surgeon)*
15 Nov 1934 - 25 Mar 1935:	Attached to Naval General Staff
30 Mar 1935:	Transferred to the reserve

Rear-Admiral **Takero KODA** (15 May 1891 - 23 Mar 1982)

20 May 1942 - 10 Mar 1943:	Commander, Shanghai Harbor
1 Nov 1942:	Promoted to *Rear-Admiral*
10 Mar 1943 - 29 Mar 1943:	Attached to the staff, 6th Fleet
29 Mar 1943 - 15 Jan 1944:	Commander, 1st Submarine Flotilla
15 Jan 1944 - 1 Feb 1944:	Attached to Naval General Staff

1 Feb 1944 - 15 Aug 1945:	Chief of Submarine Bureau, Kure Navy Yard
15 Aug 1945 - 6 Sep 1945:	Attached to Kure Naval District

Rear-Admiral **Tokichi KODACHI** (24 Aug 1882 - 1 Sep 1944)
1 Apr 1926 - 1 Dec 1927:	Chief of Electronics Bureau, Kure Navy Yard
1 Dec 1926:	Promoted to *Rear-Admiral*
1 Dec 1927 - 15 Dec 1927:	Attached to Naval General Staff
15 Dec 1927:	Transferred to the reserve

Rear-Admiral **Toshikata KODAMA** (6 Oct 1851 - 21 Dec 1928)
10 Nov 1903 - 12 Dec 1905:	Chief of Ordnance Bureau, Sasebo Navy Yard
1 Sep 1904:	Promoted to *General (Ordnance)*
12 Dec 1905 - 14 Feb 1907:	Unassigned
14 Feb 1907:	Transferred to the reserve
23 Sep 1919:	Redesignated *Rear-Admiral*

Fleet Admiral **Mineichi KOGA** (25 Sep 1885 - 31 Mar 1944)
1 Dec 1932:	Promoted to *Rear-Admiral*
1 Dec 1932 - 1 Sep 1933:	Chief of Bureau 3, Naval General Staff
1 Sep 1933 - 15 Sep 1933:	Attached to Naval General Staff
15 Sep 1933 - 15 Nov 1935:	Chief of Bureau 2, Naval General Staff
15 Nov 1935 - 1 Dec 1936:	Commander, 7th Escort Flotilla
1 Dec 1936:	Promoted to *Vice-Admiral*
1 Dec 1936 - 1 Dec 1937:	C-in-C, Training Fleet
1 Dec 1937 - 21 Oct 1939:	Deputy Chief of the Naval General Staff
21 Oct 1939 - 1 Sep 1941:	C-in-C, 2nd Fleet
1 Sep 1941 - 10 Nov 1942:	C-in-C, China Area Fleet
1 May 1942:	Promoted to *Admiral*
10 Nov 1942 - 21 Apr 1943:	Admiral Commanding, Yokosuka Naval District, Member, Admirals Committee
21 Apr 1943 - 31 Mar 1944:	C-in-C, Combined Fleet
31 Mar 1944:	Posthumously appointed *Fleet Admiral*

Rear-Admiral (Surgeon) **Ryoichi KOGANEI** (6 Aug 1889 - 9 Dec 1970)
20 May 1937 - 15 Dec 1939:	Chief of Medical Bureau, Kure Navy Yard
1 Dec 1937:	Promoted to *Rear-Admiral (Surgeon)*
21 Dec 1939:	Transferred to the reserve

Vice-Admiral **Gunji KOGURE** (15 Nov 1890 - 21 Apr 1975)
11 Aug 1941 - 20 Jun 1942:	Captain, Battleship *"Mutsu"*
1 May 1942:	Promoted to *Rear-Admiral*
20 Jun 1942 - 11 Jul 1942:	Attached to Naval General Staff
11 Jul 1942 - 25 Jul 1942:	Staff Officer, China Area Fleet

25 Jul 1942 - 20 Aug 1943:	Chief of Staff, 1st Southern Expeditionary Fleet
20 Aug 1943 - 1 Sep 1943:	Attached to Naval General Staff
1 Sep 1943 - Oct 1945:	Commander, 28th Air Flotilla
1 May 1945:	Promoted to *Vice-Admiral*

Vice-Admiral **Shiro KOIKE** (30 Aug 1886 - 19 Jun 1961)

15 Nov 1935:	Promoted to *Rear-Admiral*
15 Nov 1935 - 1 Dec 1937:	Commandant, Navigation School
1 Dec 1937 - 1 Jun 1941:	Chief of Naval Hydrographic Command
15 Nov 1939:	Promoted to *Vice-Admiral*
1 Jun 1941 - 1 Aug 1941:	Attached to Naval General Staff
1 Aug 1941 - 15 Dec 1942:	Chief of Naval Facility Command
15 Dec 1942 - 1 Oct 1943:	Commander, Kainan Guard District
1 Oct 1943 - 15 Mar 1944:	Attached to Naval General Staff
20 Mar 1944:	Transferred to the reserve

Rear-Admiral **Chikaharu KOIZUMI** (6 Nov 1878 - 30 Aug 1943)

1 Dec 1922 - 1 Dec 1923:	Captain, Battlecruiser *"Haruna"*
1 Dec 1923:	Promoted to *Rear-Admiral*
1 Dec 1923 - 10 Dec 1923:	Attached to Yokosuka Naval District
10 Dec 1923 - 25 Feb 1924:	Unassigned
25 Feb 1924:	Transferred to the reserve

Rear-Admiral **Hisao KOIZUMI** (2 Sep 1885 - 8 Aug 1942)

20 Sep 1941 - 8 Aug 1942:	Chief of Minesweeping, Transport *"Meiyo-maru"*
8 Aug 1942:	Posthumously promoted to *Rear-Admiral*

Vice-Admiral **Kotaro KOIZUMI** (2 Feb 1858 - 13 Mar 1925)

15 Nov 1907 - 16 Jul 1910:	Chief of Staff, Yokosuka Naval District
28 Aug 1908:	Promoted to *Rear-Admiral*
16 Jul 1910 - 11 Mar 1911:	C-in-C, Yokosuka Reserve Fleet
11 Mar 1911 - 1 Dec 1911:	Commander, Maizuru Navy Yard
1 Dec 1911 - 14 Apr 1913:	Commander, Mako Guard District
1 Dec 1912:	Promoted to *Vice-Admiral*
14 Apr 1913 - 1 Dec 1913:	Unassigned
1 Dec 1913:	Transferred to the reserve

Rear-Admiral **Takezo KOIZUMI** (3 Apr 1881 - 26 Feb 1948)

1 Dec 1927:	Promoted to *Rear-Admiral*
1 Dec 1927 - 10 Dec 1928:	Chief of Shipping Bureau, Kure Naval District
10 Dec 1928 - 20 Dec 1928:	Attached to Naval General Staff
25 Dec 1928:	Transferred to the reserve

Rear-Admiral **Hideo KOJIMA** (5 Apr 1896 - 22 Mar 1982)
1 May 1943:	Promoted to *Rear-Admiral*
1 May 1943 - 1 Sep 1943:	Attached to Naval General Staff
1 Sep 1943 - 9 May 1945:	Naval Attaché, Berlin
1 Sep 1943 - 7 Jun 1944:	Naval Attaché, Finland
7 Jun 1944 - Aug 1944:	Naval Attaché, France
9 May 1945 - 6 Dec 1945:	Chief Supervisor for Construction & Ordnance, Naval Shipbuilding Command

Rear-Admiral **Hitoshi KOJIMA** (11 Mar 1893 - 13 Feb 1959)
1 Dec 1944 - Oct 1945:	Commander, 43rd Guard Force
1 May 1945:	Promoted to *Rear-Admiral*

Rear-Admiral **Kentaro KOJIMA** (26 Apr 1886 - 30 Aug 1968)
15 Dec 1934 - 15 Nov 1935:	Commander, Yokosuka Defense Force
15 Nov 1935:	Promoted to *Rear-Admiral*
15 Nov 1934 - 10 Dec 1935:	Attached to Naval General Staff
15 Dec 1935:	Transferred to the reserve

Rear-Admiral (Paymaster) **Ryokichi KOKOBU** (14 Sep 1882 - 24 Oct 1941)
1 Dec 1924 - 1 Dec 1926:	Paymaster-General, Maizuru Guard District
1 Dec 1926:	Promoted to *Rear-Admiral (Paymaster)*
1 Dec 1926 - 20 Mar 1927:	Attached to Naval General Staff
10 Apr 1927:	Transferred to the reserve

Rear-Admiral **Shizen KOMAKI** (23 Mar 1873 - 8 Jun 1939)
1 Dec 1921:	Promoted to *Rear-Admiral*
1 Dec 1921 - 1 Dec 1923:	Chief of Bureau 2, Naval General Staff
1 Dec 1923 - 10 Dec 1923:	Attached to Naval General Staff
10 Dec 1923 - 25 Feb 1924:	Unassigned
25 Feb 1924:	Transferred to the reserve

Rear-Admiral **Wasuke KOMAKI** (10 Dec 1884 - 20 Aug 1932)
1 Dec 1930:	Promoted to *Rear-Admiral*
1 Dec 1930 - 10 Oct 1931:	Chief of Staff, 2nd Fleet
10 Oct 1931 - 9 Dec 1931:	Attached to Naval General Staff
9 Dec 1931 - 20 Aug 1932:	Attached to the Plenipotentiary, Geneva Conference

Vice-Admiral **Naomoto KOMATSU** (19 Oct 1875 - 12 Sep 1932)
1 Dec 1921:	Promoted to *Rear-Admiral*
1 Dec 1921 - 1 Dec 1922:	Chief of Staff, 3rd Fleet
1 Dec 1922 - 6 Nov 1923:	Chief of Staff, Kure Naval District
6 Nov 1923 - 20 Oct 1925:	Commander, Kasumigaura Air Division

20 Oct 1925 - 1 Dec 1925:	Attached to Naval General Staff
1 Dec 1925:	Promoted to *Vice-Admiral*
16 Dec 1925:	Transferred to the reserve

Vice-Admiral **Marquis Teruhisa KOMATSU** (12 Aug 1888 - 5 Nov 1970)

1 Dec 1936:	Promoted to *Rear-Admiral*
1 Dec 1936 - 1 Dec 1937:	Commander, 1st Submarine Flotilla
1 Dec 1937 - 15 Nov 1938:	Commandant, Submarine School
15 Nov 1938 - 15 Nov 1940:	Chief Instructor, Naval College
15 Nov 1940:	Promoted to *Vice-Admiral*
15 Nov 1940 - 5 Jul 1941:	Commander, Ryojun Guard District
5 Jul 1941 - 14 Feb 1942:	C-in-C, 1st China Expeditionary Fleet
14 Feb 1942 - 16 Mar 1942:	Attached to Naval General Staff
16 Mar 1942 - 21 Jun 1943:	C-in-C, 6th (Submarine) Fleet
21 Jun 1943 - 4 Nov 1944:	Admiral Commanding, Sasebo Naval District
4 Nov 1944 - 15 Jan 1945:	Commandant of the Naval Academy
15 Jan 1945 - 15 May 1945:	Unassigned
21 May 1945:	Transferred to the reserve

Rear-Admiral **Katsumi KOMAZAWA** (23 Feb 1892 - 12 Jan 1955)

28 Jan 1942 - 5 Dec 1942:	Captain, Seaplane Tender *"Nisshin"*
1 Nov 1942:	Promoted to *Rear-Admiral*
5 Dec 1942 - 15 Sep 1943:	Commander, 3rd Submarine Flotilla
15 Sep 1943 - 25 Sep 1943:	Attached to Kure Naval District
25 Sep 1943 - 1 Feb 1944:	Chief of Submarine Bureau, Kure Navy Yard
1 Feb 1944 - 23 Dec 1944:	Chief of Bureau 2, Naval Shipbuilding Command
23 Dec 1944 - 25 Feb 1945:	Commander, 7th Convoy HQ
25 Feb 1945 - 10 May 1945:	Commander, 4th Maritime Escort Force
10 May 1945 - 15 Nov 1945:	Commander, 5th Special Attack Flotilla

Rear-Admiral **Kichisuke KOMORI** (23 May 1882 - 2 Oct 1959)

1 Apr 1928 - 10 Dec 1928:	Chief of Personnel Bureau, Kure Naval District
10 Dec 1928:	Promoted to *Rear-Admiral*
10 Dec 1928 - 20 Dec 1925:	Attached to Naval General Staff
15 Dec 1925:	Transferred to the reserve

Rear-Admiral **Keizo KOMURA** (20 Jul 1896 - 7 Feb 1978)

9 Jun 1943 - 6 Dec 1943:	Captain, Battleship *"Musashi"*
1 Nov 1943:	Promoted to *Rear-Admiral*
6 Dec 1943 - 1 Oct 1944:	Chief of Staff, 3rd Fleet
1 Mar 1944 - 1 Oct 1944:	Chief of Staff, 1st Task Fleet
1 Oct 1944 - 10 Dec 1944:	Commander, 1st Air Flotilla
10 Dec 1944 - 3 Jan 1945:	Attached to the staff, Southwestern Area Fleet

3 Jan 1945 - 20 Apr 1945:	Commander, 2nd Destroyer Flotilla
20 Apr 1945 - 20 May 1945:	Attached to Naval General Staff
20 May 1945 - 30 Nov 1945:	Chief of Staff, Yokosuka Naval District

Vice-Admiral **Eijiro KONDO** (12 Sep 1887 - 27 Dec 1955)

15 Nov 1934 - 2 Dec 1935:	Chief of Staff, 3rd Fleet
15 Nov 1935:	Promoted to *Rear-Admiral*
2 Dec 1935 - 16 Nov 1936:	Commander, Shanghai Marine Force
16 Nov 1936 - 1 Dec 1936:	Attached to Naval General Staff
1 Dec 1936 - 28 Jul 1937:	Commander, Yokosuka Guard Flotilla
28 Jul 1937 - 1 Dec 1937:	Commander, 3rd Destroyer Flotilla
1 Dec 1937 - 15 Dec 1938:	Commander, 11th Cruiser Flotilla
15 Dec 1938 - 15 Nov 1939:	Attached to Yokosuka Naval District
15 Nov 1939:	Promoted to *Vice-Admiral*
15 Nov 1939 - 15 Dec 1939:	Unassigned
21 Dec 1939:	Transferred to the reserve

Rear-Admiral **Ichiro KONDO** (2 Apr 1895 - ?)

1 May 1943:	Promoted to *Rear-Admiral*
1 May 1943 - 15 Oct 1945:	Chief of Engine Construction Bureau, Yokosuka Navy Yard

Rear-Admiral **Katsuji KONDO** (11 Jun 1897 - 28 Jan 1955)

1 Oct 1944 - 10 Jun 1945:	Attached to Yokosuka Air Division
1 May 1945:	Promoted to *Rear-Admiral*
10 Jun 1945 - 3 Nov 1945:	Commander, Chosen Air Division

Vice-Admiral **Kazuma KONDO** (1 Mar 1890 - 29 Apr 1945)

15 Oct 1941:	Promoted to *Rear-Admiral*
15 Oct 1941 - 15 Oct 1942:	Chief Supervisor for Construction & Ordnance, Naval Shipbuilding Command
15 Oct 1942 - 1 Nov 1942:	Attached to Yokosuka Navy Yard
1 Nov 1942 - 1 Apr 1944:	Commander, 18th Combined Air Division
1 Apr 1944 - 12 Apr 1944:	Attached to the staff, Southwestern Area Fleet
12 Apr 1944 - 29 Apr 1945:	Commander, Southwest Area Air Depot
15 Oct 1944:	Promoted to *Vice-Admiral*

Vice-Admiral **Motoki KONDO** (11 Mar 1864 - 8 Mar 1930)

10 Dec 1908:	Promoted to *General (Constructor)*
10 Dec 1908 - 15 May 1911:	Attached to Naval Shipbuilding Command
15 May 1911 - 30 May 1913:	Chief of Ship Design Research, Naval Shipbuilding Command
30 May 1913 - 1 Oct 1915:	Unassigned

29 May 1914:	Promoted to *General (Constructor), Senior grade*
1 Oct 1915 - 1 Dec 1922:	Chief of Ship Design Research, Naval Shipbuilding Command
23 Sep 1919:	Redesignated *Vice-Admiral*
1 Dec 1922 - 10 Dec 1922:	Attached to Naval Shipbuilding Command
10 Dec 1922 - 31 Mar 1923:	Unassigned
31 Mar 1923:	Transferred to the reserve

Rear-Admiral **Naokata KONDO** (19 Dec 1880 - 16 Apr 1954)

10 Jul 1925 - 1 Dec 1927:	Commander, Kure Sailors Corps
1 Dec 1927:	Promoted to *Rear-Admiral*
1 Dec 1927 - 15 Dec 1927:	Attached to Kure Naval District
25 Dec 1927:	Transferred to the reserve

Admiral **Nobutake KONDO** (25 Sep 1886 - 19 Feb 1953)

15 Nov 1933:	Promoted to *Rear-Admiral*
15 Nov 1933 - 15 Mar 1935:	Chief Instructor, Naval College
15 Mar 1935 - 15 Nov 1935:	Chief of Staff, Combined Fleet, Chief of Staff, 1st Fleet
15 Nov 1935 - 2 Dec 1935:	Attached to Naval General Staff
2 Dec 1935 - 15 Dec 1938:	Chief of Bureau 1, Naval General Staff
1 Dec 1937:	Promoted to *Vice-Admiral*
15 Dec 1938 - 29 Sep 1939:	C-in-C, 5th Fleet
29 Sep 1939 - 21 Oct 1939:	Attached to Naval General Staff
21 Oct 1939 - 1 Sep 1941:	Deputy Chief of the Naval General Staff
1 Sep 1941 - 9 Aug 1943:	C-in-C, 2nd Fleet
29 Apr 1943:	Promoted to *Admiral*
9 Aug 1943 - 1 Dec 1943:	Navy Councillor
1 Dec 1943 - 15 May 1945:	C-in-C, China Area Fleet
15 May 1945 - 5 Sep 1945:	Navy Councillor

Rear-Admiral **Saburo KONDO** (5 Aug 1897 - 8 Jul 1944)

18 Jan 1944 - 8 Jul 1944:	Commander of Minesweeping, Aircraft Transport *"Keiyo-maru"*
8 Jul 1944:	Posthumously promoted to *Rear-Admiral*

Rear-Admiral **Tojiro KONDO** (12 Jul 1890 - 22 Apr 1980)

10 Jan 1942 - 15 Apr 1943:	Chief of 101st Supply Bureau
1 Nov 1942:	Promoted to *Rear-Admiral*
15 Apr 1943 - 20 Apr 1943:	Attached to Maizuru Naval District
20 Apr 1943 - 10 Jun 1944:	Chief of Supply Bureau, Maizuru Naval District
10 Jun 1944 - 1 May 1945:	Chief of Supply Bureau, Sasebo Naval District
1 May 1945 - 15 Jun 1945:	Attached to Naval General Staff
20 Jun 1945:	Transferred to the reserve

Rear-Admiral **Tsunematsu KONDO** (3 Feb 1867 - 21 Feb 1944)
1 Dec 1914:	Promoted to *Rear-Admiral*
1 Dec 1914 - 13 Dec 1915:	Commander, 2nd Destroyer Flotilla
13 Dec 1915 - 1 Dec 1916:	Commandant, Torpedo School
1 Dec 1916 - 1 Dec 1917:	Unassigned
1 Dec 1917:	Transferred to the reserve

Rear-Admiral **Yasuhira KONDO** (19 Jul 1902 - 19 Dec 1944)
6 Nov 1943 - 12 Dec 1944:	Deputy Captain, Battleship *"Nagato"*
12 Dec 1944 - 19 Dec 1944:	Staff Officer, Aircraft Carrier *"Hiryu"*
19 Dec 1944:	Posthumously promoted to *Rear-Admiral*

Vice-Admiral **Yasuichiro KONDO** (1 Jan 1893 - 24 Dec 1975)
10 Feb 1939 - 26 Aug 1941:	Naval Attache, United Kingdom
26 Aug 1941 - 26 Dec 1941:	Attached to Naval General Staff
15 Oct 1941:	Promoted to *Rear-Admiral*
26 Dec 1941 - 3 Jan 1942:	Attached to the staff, 3rd Fleet
3 Jan 1942 - 25 Jan 1943:	Chief of Staff, 3rd Southern Expeditionary Fleet
25 Jan 1943 - 30 Jan 1943:	Attached to the staff, China Area Fleet
30 Jan 1943 - 7 Nov 1944:	Deputy Chief of Staff, China Area Fleet
15 Oct 1944:	Promoted to *Vice-Admiral*
7 Nov 1944 - 25 Dec 1944:	Attached to Naval General Staff
25 Dec 1944 - 2 Jan 1945:	Attached to the staff, 1st Southern Expeditionary Fleet
2 Jan 1945 - 1 May 1945:	Commander, 11th Base Force
1 May 1945 - Oct 1945:	Commander, 11th Auxiliary Base Force

Rear-Admiral **Kaname KONISHI** (8 May 1895 - 19 Dec 1944)
6 Aug 1944 - 19 Dec 1944:	Captain, Aircraft Carrier *"Uryu"*
19 Dec 1944:	Posthumously promoted to *Rear-Admiral*

Rear-Admiral **Seizo KONISHI** (20 Aug 1897 - 5 Jun 1945)
16 Oct 1944 - 5 Jun 1945:	Commander, 3rd Patrol Boat Division
5 Jun 1945:	Posthumously promoted to *Rear-Admiral*

Rear-Admiral **Yukie KONISHI** (? - 30 Aug 1942)
15 May 1942 - 30 Aug 1942:	Commander, 85th Submarine Base Force
30 Aug 1942:	Posthumously promoted to *Rear-Admiral*

Vice-Admiral (Paymaster) **Itsuya KONNO** (19 Mar 1891 - 25 Mar 1973)
15 Nov 1939:	Promoted to *Rear-Admiral (Paymaster)*
15 Nov 1939 - 1 Dec 1939:	Paymaster-General, Maizuru Guard District
1 Dec 1939 - 15 Nov 1940:	Paymaster-General, Maizuru Naval District

15 Nov 1940 - 21 Apr 1941:	Chief of Mining Bureau, Navy Fuel Yard
21 Apr 1941 - 20 Apr 1943:	Commander, 5th Fuel Yard
20 Apr 1943 - 1 Jun 1943:	Attached to Naval General Staff
1 Jun 1943 - 1 Oct 1945:	Commandant, Naval Paymaster Academy
1 Nov 1943:	Promoted to *Vice-Admiral (Paymaster)*

Rear-Admiral **Nobuo KONNO** (23 Jul 1899 - 13 Mar 1944)

7 Mar 1944 - 13 Mar 1944:	Staff Officer, Maritime Escort Fleet
13 Mar 1944:	Posthumously promoted to *Rear-Admiral*

Rear-Admiral **Rokuro KONO** (16 Jul 1898 - 3 May 1944)

10 Jan 1944 - 1 May 1944:	Staff Officer, 8th Construction Bureau
1 May 1944 - 3 May 1944:	Attached to Yokosuka Naval District
3 May 1944:	Posthumously promoted to *Rear-Admiral*

Vice-Admiral **Hidesaburo KOORI** (21 Dec 1887 - 19 Dec 1977)

16 Nov 1936 - 1 Sep 1938:	Chief of Staff, Sasebo Naval District
1 Dec 1936:	Promoted to *Rear-Admiral*
1 Sep 1938 - 15 Dec 1938:	Commander, 13th Escort Flotilla
15 Dec 1938 - 2 Oct 1939:	Commander, 1st Combined Marine Force
2 Oct 1939 - 15 Nov 1940:	Naval Attache, Manchuria
15 Nov 1940:	Promoted to *Vice-Admiral*
15 Nov 1940 - 17 Dec 1940:	Attached to Naval General Staff
17 Dec 1940:	Transferred to the reserve

Rear-Admiral (Paymaster) **Junosuke KOREKAWA** (19 Feb 1890 - 23 May 1964)

15 Oct 1941:	Promoted to *Rear-Admiral (Paymaster)*
15 Oct 1941 - 10 Oct 1943:	Paymaster-General, Sasebo Naval District
10 Oct 1943 - 20 Oct 1943:	Attached to Naval General Staff
25 Oct 1943:	Transferred to the reserve

Rear-Admiral **Kanae KOSAKA** (8 Oct 1892 - 10 Dec 1974)

12 Sep 1941 - 16 Feb 1943:	Chief of Training Bureau, Naval Air Command
1 Nov 1942:	Promoted to *Rear-Admiral*
16 Feb 1943 - 25 Feb 1943:	Staff officer, Combined Fleet
25 Feb 1943 - 1 Sep 1943:	Commander, 26th Air Flotilla
1 Sep 1943 - 15 Nov 1943:	Commander, 50th Air Flotilla
15 Nov 1943 - 15 Mar 1944:	Chief of Administration Bureau, Naval Air Command
15 Mar 1943 - 20 Aug 1945:	Chief of Training Bureau, Naval Air Command
1 Sep 1944 - 20 Aug 1945:	Chief of Staff, Combined Flying Division
7 Apr 1945 - 20 Aug 1945:	Deputy Chief of Training Sectoin, Joint General Staff

| 20 Aug 1945 - 1 Oct 1945: | Chief of Naval Training Bureau, Department of the Navy, Chief of Training Section, Joint General Staff |

Rear-Admiral **Taihachi KOSE** (11 Nov 1879 - 1 Dec 1969)
10 Nov 1923 - 1 Dec 1927:	Commander, Sasebo Harbor
1 Dec 1927:	Promoted to *Rear-Admiral*
1 Dec 1927 - 15 Dec 1927:	Attached to Naval General Staff
25 Dec 1927:	Transferred to the reserve

Rear-Admiral **Takasue KOSE** (9 Apr 1893 - 4 Feb 1960)
| 15 Nov 1944 - Oct 1945: | Commander, North Philippines Air Division |
| 1 May 1945: | Promoted to *Rear-Admiral* |

Rear-Admiral **Kimitake KOSHINO** (13 May 1903 - 24 Oct 1944)
| 25 Jun 1944 - 24 Oct 1944: | Chief Gunnery Officer, Battleship *"Musashi"* |
| 24 Oct 1944: | Posthumously promoted to *Rear-Admiral* |

Rear-Admiral **Hisao KOTAKI** (11 Jul 1901 - 7 Apr 1945)
| 25 Mar 1945 - 7 Apr 1945: | Commander, 21st Destroyer Division |
| 7 Apr 1945: | Posthumously promoted to *Rear-Admiral* |

Vice-Admiral **Katsutaka KOTARI** (20 Oct 1891 - 11 Aug 1979)
1 Dec 1937 - 1 Aug 1939:	Chief of Explosives Bureau, Navy Powder Yard
15 Nov 1938:	Promoted to *Rear-Admiral*
1 Aug 1939 - 15 Nov 1940:	Chief of Explosives Bureau, Navy Main Powder Yard
15 Nov 1940 - 21 Apr 1941:	Commander, Navy Main Powder Yard
21 Apr 1941 - 1 Aug 1944:	Commander, 2nd Navy Powder Yard
1 Nov 1942:	Promoted to *Vice-Admiral*
1 Aug 1944 - 15 Nov 1944:	Attached to the Department of the Navy
15 Nov 1944 - 15 Sep 1945:	Technical Supervisor, Naval Shipbuilding Command

Rear-Admiral (Surgeon) **Kappei KOTATSU** (14 Feb 1895 - 27 Mar 1981)
| 2 Feb 1945 - Oct 1945: | Director, 101st Naval Hospital |
| 1 May 1945: | Promoted to *Rear-Admiral (Surgeon)* |

Rear-Admiral **Kichiro KOYAMA** (1 Mar 1860 - 25 Feb 1929)
24 Apr 1908 - 18 Jan 1911:	Chief of Shipbuilding Bureau, Maizuru Navy Yard
10 Dec 1908:	Promoted to *General (Constructor)*
18 Jan 1911 - 24 May 1913:	Chief of Shipbuilding Bureau, Yokosuka Navy Yard
13 May 1913 - 1 Dec 1913:	Unassigned
1 Dec 1913:	Transferred to the reserve
23 Sep 1919:	Redesignated *Rear-Admiral*

Rear-Admiral **Takeshi KOYAMA** (21 Nov 1878 - 30 Jun 1945)
1 Jul 1922 - 10 Nov 1922:	Captain, Battlecruiser *"Haruna"*
10 Nov 1922 - 1 Dec 1922:	Attached to Yokosuka Naval District
1 Dec 1922:	Promoted to *Rear-Admiral*
1 Dec 1922 - 31 Mar 1923:	Unassigned
31 Mar 1923:	Transferred to the reserve

Rear-Admiral **Chunojo KOYAMADA** (6 Aug 1869 - 5 Feb 1951)
13 Dec 1915 - 1 Dec 1917:	Captain, Battleship *"Kawachi"*
1 Dec 1917:	Promoted to *Rear-Admiral*
1 Dec 1917 - 1 Dec 1918:	Unassigned
1 Dec 1918:	Transferred to the reserve

Vice-Admiral **Tomiji KOYANAGI** (16 Jul 1893 - 6 Aug 1978)
15 Aug 1941 - 26 Dec 1942:	Captain, Battlecruiser *"Kongo"*
1 Nov 1942:	Promoted to *Rear-Admiral*
26 Dec 1942 - 29 Dec 1942:	Attached to the staff, 2nd Fleet
29 Dec 1942 - 21 Jan 1943:	Commander, 2nd Destroyer Flotilla
21 Jan 1943 - 21 Jun 1943:	Commander, 10th Destroyer Flotilla
21 Jun 1943 - 2 Jul 1943:	Attached to the staff, 2nd Fleet
2 Jul 1943 - 25 Nov 1944:	Chief of Staff, 2nd Fleet
25 Nov 1944 - 1 Feb 1945:	Attached to the staff, Combined Fleet
1 Feb 1945 - 10 Aug 1945:	Attached to Yokosuka Naval District
10 Aug 1945 - 10 Nov 1945:	Commandant, Torpedo School, Commander, Taura Guard Force
1 Nov 1945:	Promoted to *Vice-Admiral*

Rear-Admiral **Kimata KUBO** (8 Nov 1867 - 26 Jan 1950)
1 Dec 1916 - 1 Dec 1917:	Commander, Yokosuka Harbor
1 Dec 1917:	Promoted to *Rear-Admiral*
1 Dec 1917 - 1 Dec 1918:	Unassigned
1 Dec 1918:	Transferred to the reserve

Vice-Admiral **Kyuji KUBO** (15 Oct 1888 - 12 Sep 1958)
15 Nov 1940:	Promoted to *Rear-Admiral*
15 Nov 1940 - 11 Feb 1942:	Commander, 1st Auxiliary Base Force
11 Feb 1942 - 10 Mar 1942:	Attached to the staff, 1st Southern Expeditionary Fleet
10 Mar 1942 - 25 Sep 1942:	Commander, 21st Naval Base Force
25 Sep 1942 - 9 Nov 1942:	Attached to Yokosuka Naval District
9 Nov 1942 - 13 Nov 1942:	Attached to the staff, 5th Fleet
13 Nov 1942- 25 Dec 1943:	Commander, 22nd Escort Flotilla
25 Dec 1943 - 1 Jan 1944:	Attached to Ominato Guard District

1 Jan 1944 - 15 Jun 1945:	Commander, Chishima Area Auxiliary Base Force
1 May 1944:	Promoted to *Vice-Admiral*
15 Jun 1945 - 20 Jul 1945:	Attached to Naval General Staff
20 Jul 1945 - 15 Sep 1945:	Commander, Kure Combined Marine Force
15 Sep 1945 - 20 Sep 1945:	Attached to Kure Naval District

Vice-Admiral **Satoshi KUBO** (18 Apr 1893 - 17 Dec 1980)

15 Mar 1941 - 10 Jan 1942:	Attached to Bureau 1, Naval Shipbuilding Command
15 Oct 1941:	Promoted to *Rear-Admiral*
10 Jan 1942 - 1 May 1943:	Chief of Ordnance Bureau, Sasebo Navy Yard
1 May 1943 - 10 Aug 1945:	Chief of Gunnery Bureau, Kure Navy Yard
1 May 1945:	Promoted to *Vice-Admiral*
10 Aug 1945 - 5 Nov 1945:	Commander, Suzuka Navy Yard

Rear-Admiral **Tsunahiko KUBO** (12 Jan 1881 - 1961)

1 Dec 1927 - 1 Dec 1930:	Chief of Shipbuilding Bureau, Sasebo Navy Yard
10 Dec 1928:	Promoted to *Rear-Admiral*
1 Dec 1930 - 1 Dec 1931:	Chief of Shipbuilding Bureau, Kure Navy Yard
1 Dec 1931 - 15 Dec 1931:	Attached to Naval Shipbuilding Command
21 Dec 1931:	Transferred to the reserve

Rear-Admiral **Hikoshichi KUBOTA** (6 Jun 1866 - 10 May 1922)

1 Dec 1910 - 23 May 1911:	Commander, Yokosuka Sailors Corps
23 May 1911 - 31 Mar 1913:	Unassigned
31 Mar 1913:	Promoted to *Rear-Admiral*
31 Mar 1913:	Transferred to the reserve

Rear-Admiral **Hisaharu KUBOTA** (5 Oct 1885 - 15 Jul 1962)

20 Apr 1933 - 15 Nov 1935:	Chief of Staff, Ryojun Guard District
15 Nov 1935 - 15 Dec 1937:	Attached to Naval General Staff
1 Dec 1937:	Promoted to *Rear-Admiral*
21 Dec 1937:	Transferred to the reserve
1 Aug 1941 - 15 Aug 1941:	Recalled; Attached to Naval General Staff
15 Aug 1941 - 25 Oct 1943:	Military Representative, Beijing
25 Oct 1943 - 26 Dec 1944:	Attached to Naval General Staff
26 Dec 1944:	Demobilized

Rear-Admiral **Toshi KUBOTA** (22 Nov 1896 - 18 Aug 1944)

18 Mar 1944 - 18 Aug 1944:	Captain, Light Cruiser *"Natori"*
18 Aug 1944:	Posthumously promoted to *Rear-Admiral*

Rear-Admiral **Yoshio KUBOTA**   (27 Sep 1895 - 16 Feb 1991)
4 Jan 1943 - 5 Sep 1943:	Chief Engineer Officer, Combined Fleet
1 May 1943:	Promoted to *Rear-Admiral*
5 Sep 1943 - 1 Nov 1943:	Chief of Air Engine Bureau, Air Technical Arsenal
1 Nov 1943 - 26 Aug 1945:	Chief of Bureau 3, Warplane Agency, Department of Military Supply
26 Aug 1945 - 15 Nov 1945:	Attached to Naval Air Command
15 Nov 1945 - 30 Nov 1945:	Attached to Department of the Navy

Vice-Admiral **Kyuhachi KUDO**   (21 May 1889 - 17 Jul 1984)
15 Oct 1941:	Promoted to *Rear-Admiral*
15 Oct 1941 - 20 Nov 1941:	Attached to Yokosuka Naval District
20 Nov 1941 - 15 Sep 1942:	Commander, 2nd Yokosuka Sailors Corps
15 Sep 1942 - 20 Oct 1943:	Commander, Sasebo Guard Force
20 Oct 1943 - 25 Oct 1943:	Attached to the staff, 8th Fleet
25 Oct 1943 - 25 Mar 1944:	Commander, 7th Auxiliary Base Force
25 Mar 1944 - 10 Aug 1944:	Attached to Naval General Staff
10 Aug 1944 - 15 Sep 1945:	Commander, Yokosuka Guard Force
1 May 1945:	Promoted to *Vice-Admiral*
1 Jul 1945 - 15 Sep 1945:	Commander, Yokosuka Combined Marine Force

Rear-Admiral **Fujio KUMABE**   (1 Nov 1888 - 19 Feb 1950)
25 Oct 1937 - 15 Nov 1938:	Chief of Shipping Bureau, Kure Naval District
1 Dec 1937:	Promoted to *Rear-Admiral*
15 Nov 1938 - 30 Aug 1939:	Chief of Research Bureau, Navy Fuel Yard
30 Aug 1939 - 15 Dec 1939:	Attached to Naval General Staff
21 Dec 1939:	Transferred to the reserve

Rear-Admiral **Hideo KUMAGAYA** (? - 3 Dec 1943)
20 Dec 1942 - 3 Dec 1943:	Commander, 31st Submarine Chaser Division
3 Dec 1943:	Posthumously promoted to *Rear-Admiral*

Rear-Admiral (Surgeon) **Motoi KUMAKAWA**   (17 Aug 1874 - 2 Nov 1939)
16 Feb 1921 - 1 Dec 1921:	Instructor, Navy Medical School
1 Dec 1921 - 1 Dec 1922:	Attached to Section 3, Naval General Staff
1 Dec 1922:	Promoted to *Rear-Admiral (Surgeon)*
1 Dec 1922 - 31 Mar 1923:	Unassigned
31 Mar 1923:	Transferred to the reserve

Rear-Admiral (Paymaster) **Sakae KUMAO**   (4 May 1882 - 14 Oct 1965)
1 Dec 1933 - 15 Nov 1934:	Paymaster-General, Maizuru Guard District
15 Nov 1934:	Promoted to *Rear-Admiral (Paymaster)*
15 Nov 1934 - 15 Nov 1935:	Chief of Accounting Bureau, Kure Navy Yard

15 Nov 1935 - 1 Dec 1936:	Paymaster-General, Sasebo Naval District
1 Dec 1936 - 15 Dec 1936:	Attached to Naval General Staff
22 Dec 1936:	Transferred to the reserve

Vice-Admiral **Yuzuru KUMAOKA** (Dec 1887 - 16 Jun 1945)

15 Nov 1935:	Promoted to *Rear-Admiral*
15 Nov 1935 - 1 Aug 1936:	Chief of Bureau 6, Naval Shipbuilding Command
1 Aug 1936 - 1 Dec 1937:	Commander, 3rd Submarine Flotilla
1 Dec 1937 - 15 Nov 1938:	Commander, 1st Submarine Flotilla
15 Nov 1938 - 15 Nov 1939:	Commandant, Submarine School
15 Nov 1939:	Promoted to *Vice-Admiral*
15 Nov 1939 - 15 Mar 1940:	Attached to Naval General Staff
21 Mar 1940:	Transferred to the reserve

Rear-Admiral **Moritsugu KUMASHIRO** (12 Jun 1876 - 21 Dec 1940)

30 Aug 1923 - 1 Dec 1924:	Captain, Submarine Tender *"Jingei"*
1 Dec 1924:	Promoted to *Rear-Admiral*
1 Dec 1924 - 15 Apr 1925:	Attached to Kure Naval District
15 Apr 1925 - 1 Jun 1925:	Attached to Naval General Staff
1 Jun 1925 - 16 Dec 1925:	Unassigned
16 Dec 1925:	Transferred to the reserve

Rear-Admiral **Shigenori KUMON** (1 Feb 1899 - 25 Oct 1944)

1 Oct 1944 - 25 Oct 1944:	Deputy Commander, Aircraft Carrier *"Chiyoda"*
25 Oct 1944:	Posthumously promoted to *Rear-Admiral*

Vice-Admiral **Prince Asaakira KUNI** (2 Feb 1901 - 7 Dec 1959)

21 Oct 1942 - 1 Apr 1943:	Attached to Naval General Staff
1 Nov 1942:	Promoted to *Rear-Admiral*
1 Apr 1943 - 29 Sep 1944:	Commander, 19th Combined Air Division
29 Sep 1944 - 1 Oct 1944:	Staff Officer, Combined Air Division
1 Oct 1944 - 25 Aug 1945:	Commander, 20th Combined Air Division
1 May 1945:	Promoted to *Vice-Admiral*
25 Aug 1945 - 15 Oct 1945:	Attached to Naval General Staff

Rear-Admiral **Akira KURAGANO** (13 Aug 1885 - 28 Sep 1962)

1 Dec 1931:	Promoted to *Rear-Admiral*
1 Dec 1931 - 1 Dec 1932:	Chief of Supply Bureau, Kure Naval District
1 Dec 1932 - 10 Dec 1932:	Attached to Naval General Staff
15 Dec 1932:	Transferred to the reserve

Rear-Admiral **Tadashi KURATA** (1 Apr 1885 - 5 Oct 1969)

1 Dec 1930 - 15 Nov 1933:	Commander, Kure Sailors Corps

1 Dec 1932:	Promoted to *Rear-Admiral*
15 Nov 1933 - 11 Dec 1933:	Attached to Naval General Staff
15 Dec 1933:	Transferred to the reserve

Rear-Admiral (Paymaster) **Tomogoro KURATOMI** (14 Jun 1891 - 29 Mar 1957)
1 Apr 1943 - 10 Jan 1945:	Commander, 4th Navy Fuel Yard
1 May 1943:	Promoted to *Rear-Admiral (Paymaster)*
10 Jan 1945 - 14 Jan 1945:	Attached to Naval General Staff
15 Jan 1945:	Transferred to the reserve

Rear-Admiral **Etsuzo KURIHARA** (31 Mar 1894 - 18 Sep 1987)
1 Mar 1945 - 15 May 1945:	Chief of Section 4, Bureau of Naval Affairs, Department of the Navy
1 May 1945:	Promoted to *Rear-Admiral*
15 May 1945 - 5 Sep 1945:	Deputy Chief of the Press Bureau, Joint General Staff
5 Sep 1945 - 30 Nov 1945:	Attached to Naval General Staff

Rear-Admiral (Surgeon) **Shunzo KURITA** (1 Feb 1876 - 8 Jan 1940)
7 Jun 1921 - 1 Dec 1921:	Chief of Bureau 2, Yokosuka Naval Hospital
1 Dec 1921:	Promoted to *Rear-Admiral (Surgeon)*
1 Dec 1921 - 10 Dec 1921:	Attached to Yokosuka Naval District
10 Dec 1921 - 1 Dec 1922:	Unassigned
1 Dec 1922:	Transferred to the reserve

Vice-Admiral **Takeo KURITA** (18 Apr 1889 - 19 Dec 1977)
15 Nov 1938:	Promoted to *Rear-Admiral*
15 Nov 1938 - 25 Nov 1939:	Commander, 1st Destroyer Flotilla
25 Nov 1939 - 1 Nov 1940:	Commander, 4th Destroyer Flotilla
1 Nov 1940 - 25 Jun 1942:	Commander 7th Cruiser Division
1 May 1942:	Promoted to *Vice-Admiral*
25 Jun 1942 - 12 Jul 1942:	Attached to the staff, Combined Fleet
12 Jul 1942 - 22 Jul 1943:	Commander, 3rd Battleship Flotilla
22 Jul 1943 - 9 Aug 1943:	Attached to Naval General Staff
9 Aug 1943 - 23 Dec 1944:	C-in-C, 2nd Fleet
23 Dec 1944 - 15 Jan 1945:	Attached to Naval General Staff
15 Jan 1945 - 1 Oct 1945:	Commandant of the Naval Academy

Rear-Admiral (Engineer) **Tomitaro KURITA** (11 Nov 1872 - 9 Nov 1932)
1 May 1920 - 1 Dec 1920:	Chief Engineer Officer, Combined Fleet, Chief Engineer Officer, 1st Fleet
1 Dec 1920:	Promoted to *Rear-Admiral*
1 Dec 1920 - 10 Nov 1922:	Chief Engineer Officer, Maizuru Naval District

10 Nov 1922 - 1 Dec 1922:	Attached to Naval General Staff
1 Dec 1922 - 31 Mar 1923:	Unassigned
31 Mar 1923:	Transferred to the reserve

General (Constructor) **Hiroki KUROBE** (13 Nov 1857 - 22 Apr 1913)

10 Nov 1903 - 6 Mar 1908:	Chief of Engine Construction Bureau, Yokosuka Navy Yard
1 Sep 1904:	Promoted to *General (Constructor)*
6 Mar 1908 - 28 Aug 1908:	Attached to Bureau 4, Naval Shipbuilding Command
28 Aug 1908 - 27 Aug 1909:	Unassigned
27 Aug 1909:	Transferred to the reserve

Rear-Admiral **Akira KURODA** (7 Jan 1894 - 20 Dec 1976)

20 Dec 1943 - 10 May 1945:	Chief of Pyrotechnical Bureau, Suzuka Navy Yard
1 May 1944:	Promoted to *Rear-Admiral*
10 May 1945 - 1 Jun 1945:	Attached to Naval Shipbuilding Command
1 Jun 1945 - 15 Sep 1945:	Chief of Chemical Research Bureau, Technical Research Department

Vice-Admiral **Takuma KURODA** (11 Sep 1882 - ?)

1 Dec 1925:	Promoted to *Rear-Admiral*
1 Dec 1925 - 1 Dec 1927:	Chief of Naval Facilities, Maizuru Guard District
1 Dec 1927 - 30 Nov 1929:	Commander, Hiro Navy Yard
30 Nov 1929 - 1 Dec 1931:	Commandant of the Naval Engineering Academy
1 Dec 1930:	Promoted to *Vice-Admiral*
1 Dec 1931 - 15 Nov 1932:	Commander, Sasebo Navy Yard
15 Nov 1932 - 10 Dec 1932:	Attached to Naval General Staff
15 Dec 1932:	Transferred to the reserve

Rear-Admiral **Taizo KUROHARA** (6 Dec 1891 - 13 Mar 1956)

15 Oct 1941:	Promoted to *Rear-Admiral*
15 Oct 1941 - 25 Aug 1942:	Chief of Shipping Bureau, Maizuru Naval District
25 Aug 1942 - 25 Mar 1944:	Chief of Oil Refining Bureau, 3rd Navy Fuel Yard
25 Mar 1944 - 1 Apr 1944:	Attached to the staff, 2nd Southern Expeditionary Fleet
1 Apr 1944 - Oct 1945:	Commander, 101st Navy Fuel Yard

Admiral **Teijiro KUROI** (22 May 1866 - 29 Apr 1937)

1 Dec 1909:	Promoted to *Rear-Admiral*
1 Dec 1909 - 20 Apr 1912:	Commander, Sasebo Navy Yard
20 Apr 1912 - 1 Apr 1913:	C-in-C, Maizuru Reserve Fleet
1 Apr 1913 - 24 May 1913:	C-in-C, Maizuru Naval District Fleet

24 May 1913 - 1 Dec 1913:	Member, Admirals Committee
1 Dec 1913 - 18 Aug 1914:	C-in-C, Training Fleet
29 May 1914:	Promoted to *Vice-Admiral*
18 Aug 1914 - 13 Dec 1915:	Commander, Yokosuka Navy Yard, C-in-C, Yokosuka Naval District Fleet
13 Dec 1915 - 1 Dec 1916:	Commander, Mako Guard District
1 Dec 1916 - 1 Dec 1918:	Commander, Ryojun Guard District
1 Dec 1918 - 1 Dec 1919:	C-in-C, 3rd Fleet
1 Dec 1919 - 16 Aug 1920:	Admiral Commanding, Maizuru Naval District
16 Aug 1920:	Promoted to *Admiral*
16 Aug 1920 - 1 Apr 1921:	Member, Admirals Committee
1 Apr 1921 - 1 Dec 1921:	Unassigned
1 Dec 1921:	Transferred to the reserve

Rear-Admiral (Surgeon) **Kenzo KUROIWA** (31 Aug 1882 - 1 Feb 1964)

1 Dec 1925 - 1 Dec 1926:	Chief Medical Officer, Combined Fleet, Chief Medical Officer, 1st Fleet
1 Dec 1926:	Promoted to *Rear-Admiral (Surgeon)*
1 Dec 1926 - 1 Dec 1927:	Director, Kure Naval Hospital, Chief Medical Officer, Kure Naval District
1 Dec 1927 - 15 Dec 1927:	Attached to Naval General Staff
15 Dec 1927:	Transferred to the reserve

Rear-Admiral **Yukuma KUROKAWA** (9 Sep 1852 - 13 Sep 1931)

11 Mar 1901 - 5 Apr 1902:	Commander, Kure Submarine Yard
6 Jul 1901:	Promoted to *General (Constructor)*
5 Apr 1902 - 18 Sep 1904:	Unassigned
18 Sep 1904:	Transferred to the reserve
23 Sep 1919:	Redesignated *Rear-Admiral*

Rear-Admiral **Goichi KUROKI** (16 Feb 1894 - 21 May 1972)

5 Oct 1943 - 6 Mar 1945:	Attached to the Ambassador Extraordinary to French Indochina
1 May 1944:	Promoted to *Rear-Admiral*
6 Mar 1945 - 1 Jun 1945:	Attached to Naval General Staff
1 Jun 1945 - Oct 1945:	Military Representative, Toyohara
9 Aug 1945 - Oct 1945:	Attached to the staff, 12th Air Fleet

Rear-Admiral (Surgeon) **Morihide KUROKI** (8 Jan 1893 - 13 Jan 1969)

10 Oct 1942 - 1 Dec 1944:	Chief of Medical Bureau, 21st Air Arsenal
1 May 1943:	Promoted to *Rear-Admiral (Surgeon)*
1 Dec 1944 - Oct 1945:	Director, Takao Naval Hospital, Chief Medical Officer, Takao Guard District

Rear-Admiral (Surgeon) **Takeichi KUROKI** (23 Oct 1894 - ?)
1 Oct 1943 - 1 Dec 1943:	Director, Hayato Naval Hospital
1 Dec 1943 - 17 Nov 1944:	Director, Kirishima Naval Hospital
1 May 1944:	Promoted to *Rear-Admiral (Surgeon)*
17 Nov 1944 - 6 Sep 1945:	Attached to Sasebo Naval District

Vice-Admiral **Tatewaki KUROOKA** (2 Aug 1851 - 19 Dec 1927)
27 Dec 1897:	Promoted to *Rear-Admiral*
27 Dec 1897 - 4 Jul 1901:	Chief of Naval Staff, Taiwan Government
4 Jul 1901 - 5 Sep 1905:	Unassigned
5 Sep 1905:	Promoted to *Vice-Admiral*
5 Sep 1905:	Transferred to the reserve

Rear-Admiral **Rinzo KUROSAKI** (25 Mar 1887 - 2 Mar 1944)
2 Mar 1943 - 2 Mar 1944:	Captain, Auxiliary Cruiser *"Akagi-maru"*
2 Mar 1944:	Posthumously promoted to *Rear-Admiral*

Rear-Admiral **Hiroshi KUROSE** (22 Sep 1892 - 20 Oct 1975)
10 Apr 1941 - 1 Apr 1943:	Chief of Administration Bureau, Yokosuka Navy Yard
1 May 1942:	Promoted to *Rear-Admiral*
1 Apr 1943 - 1 May 1943:	Attached to Kure Naval District
1 May 1943 - 15 Aug 1944:	Commandant, Hofu Naval Communication School
15 Aug 1944 - 1 May 1945:	Chief of Staff, Takao Guard District
1 May 1945 - Oct 1945:	Commander, Takao Area Auxiliary Base Force

Rear-Admiral **Seiichi KUROSE** (22 Nov 1876 - 9 Jun 1946)
1 Dec 1922:	Promoted to *Rear-Admiral*
1 Dec 1922 - 1 Dec 1923:	Commander, 1st Submarine Flotilla
1 Dec 1923 - 5 Feb 1924:	Attached to Naval General Staff
25 Feb 1924:	Transferred to the reserve

Rear-Admiral **Kameto KUROSHIMA** (10 Oct 1893 - 20 Oct 1965)
19 Jul 1943 - 27 May 1945:	Chief of Bureau 2, Naval General Staff
1 Nov 1943:	Promoted to *Rear-Admiral*
15 Feb 1944 - 20 Aug 1944:	Chief of Bureau 4, Naval General Staff
27 May 1945 - 6 Sep 1945:	Attached to Naval General Staff
6 Sep 1945 - 1 Oct 1945:	Staff Officer, Pacific War Research Committee
1 Oct 1945 - 1 Nov 1945:	Attached to the Department of the Navy

Rear-Admiral **Miozo KUROYANAGI** (28 Sep 1883 - 9 Jul 1950)
15 Nov 1926 - 30 Nov 1929:	Chief of Ordnance Bureau, Sasebo Navy Yard

1 Dec 1927:	Promoted to *Rear-Admiral*
30 Nov 1929 - 15 Dec 1930:	Attached to Naval Shipbuilding Command
25 Dec 1930:	Transferred to the reserve

Vice-Admiral **Jinichi KUSAKA** (7 Dec 1888 - 24 Aug 1972)

1 Dec 1936:	Promoted to *Rear-Admiral*
1 Dec 1936 - 1 Dec 1937:	Commandant, Naval Gunnery School
1 Dec 1937 - 25 Apr 1938:	Commander, 1st Air Flotilla
25 Apr 1938 - 23 Oct 1939:	Chief of Staff, China Area Fleet, Chief of Staff, 3rd Fleet
23 Oct 1939 - 15 Nov 1939:	Attached to the staff, China Area Fleet
15 Nov 1939 - 4 Apr 1941:	Chief of Naval Training Bureau
15 Nov 1940:	Promoted to *Vice-Admiral*
4 Apr 1941 - 1 Oct 1942:	Commandant of the Naval Academy
1 Oct 1942 - Sep 1945:	C-in-C, 11th Air Fleet
24 Dec 1942 - Sep 1945:	C-in-C, Southeast Area Fleet

Vice-Admiral **Ryunosuke KUSAKA** (25 Sep 1892 - 23 Nov 1971)

15 Nov 1940:	Promoted to *Rear-Admiral*
15 Nov 1940 - 15 Jan 1941:	Commander, 4th Combined Air Division
15 Jan 1941 - 15 Apr 1941:	Commander, 24th Air Flotilla
15 Apr 1941 - 14 Jul 1942:	Chief of Staff, 1st Air Fleet
14 Jul 1942 - 23 Nov 1942:	Chief of Staff, 3rd Fleet
23 Nov 1942 - 20 Nov 1943:	Commander, Yokosuka Air Division
20 Nov 1943 - 29 Nov 1943:	Attached to the staff, Southeastern Area Fleet
29 Nov 1943 - 6 Apr 1944:	Chief of Staff, Southeastern Area Fleet, Chief of Staff, 11th Air Force
6 Apr 1944 - 24 Jun 1945:	Chief of Staff, Combined Fleet
1 May 1944:	Promoted to *Vice-Admiral*
25 Apr 1945 - 24 Jun 1945:	Chief of Staff, Navy Supreme HQ
24 Jun 1945 - 10 Aug 1945:	Attached to Naval General Staff
10 Aug 1945 - 17 Aug 1945:	Attached to the staff, Navy Supreme HQ
17 Aug 1945 - 10 Oct 1945:	C-in-C, 5th Air Fleet

Rear-Admiral **Enjiro KUSAKABE** (27 Jul 1889 - 3 Apr 1964)

4 Aug 1944 - 1 Sep 1945:	Staff Supervisor, Department of Military Supply
15 Oct 1944:	Promoted to *Rear-Admiral*
1 Sep 1945:	Demobilized

Vice-Admiral **Kiyoshi KUSAKAWA** (22 Apr 1890 - 24 Jul 1945)

10 Aug 1944 - 1 Mar 1945:	Captain, Armored Cruiser *"Izumo"*
15 Oct 1944:	Promoted to *Rear-Admiral*
1 Mar 1945 - 24 Jul 1945:	Captain, Battleship *"Hyuga"*
24 Jul 1945:	Posthumously promoted to *Vice-Admiral*

Rear-Admiral (Surgeon) **Tadao KUSANO** (13 Nov 1879 - 14 Sep 1944)
1 Dec 1926 - 1 Dec 1927:	Chief Medical Officer, Combined Fleet, Chief Medical Officer, 1st Fleet
1 Dec 1927:	Promoted to *Rear-Admiral (Surgeon)*
1 Dec 1927 - 10 Dec 1928:	Director, Kure Naval Hospital, Chief Medical Officer, Kure Naval District
10 Dec 1928 - 20 Dec 1928:	Attached to Naval General Staff
25 Dec 1928:	Transferred to the reserve

Rear-Admiral (Judge) **Naokata KUSUDA** (19 Apr 1897 - ?)
1 Nov 1944 - 10 Jul 1945:	Judge, China Area Fleet Court Martial
1 May 1945:	Promoted to *Rear-Admiral (Judge)*
10 Jul 1945 - 20 Nov 1945:	Chief Legal Officer, Sasebo Naval District

Vice-Admiral **Kumaji KUSUSE** (15 May 1865 - 17 Jun 1933)
1 Dec 1916:	Promoted to *General (Ordnance)*
1 Dec 1916 - 1 Apr 1919:	Instructor, Naval College
1 Apr 1919 - 8 Oct 1920:	Commander, Navy Powder Yard
23 Sep 1919:	Redesignated *Rear-Admiral*
8 Oct 1920 - 1 Apr 1921:	Unassigned
1 Apr 1921 - 9 Jul 1921:	Attached to Naval Shipbuilding Command
9 Jul 1921 - 13 Aug 1923:	Commander, Navy Powder Yard
1 Dec 1921:	Promoted to *Vice-Admiral*
13 Aug 1923 - 1 Dec 1923:	Attached to Naval Shipbuilding Command
1 Dec 1923 - 25 Feb 1925:	Unassigned
25 Feb 1925:	Transferred to the reserve

Rear-Admiral (Paymaster) **Hideo KUWABARA** (30 Aug 1892 - 8 Feb 1989)
1 Nov 1942 - 1 Apr 1945:	Chief Instructor, Navy Paymaster Academy
1 May 1943:	Promoted to *Rear-Admiral (Paymaster)*
1 Apr 1945 - 29 Nov 1945:	Chief of Supply Bureau, Maizuru Naval District

Vice-Admiral **Shigeharu KUWABARA** (10 May 1886 - ?)
8 Sep 1932 - 1 Dec 1937:	Chief of Shipbuilding Bureau, Kure Navy Yard
15 Nov 1933:	Promoted to *Rear-Admiral*
1 Dec 1937:	Promoted to *Vice-Admiral*
1 Dec 1937 - 15 Oct 1941:	Chief of Bureau 4, Naval Shipbuilding Command
15 Oct 1941 - 20 Dec 1941:	Attached to Naval Shipbuilding Command
22 Dec 1941:	Transferred to the reserve

Rear-Admiral (Surgeon) **Sokichi KUWABARA** (8 Jun 1861 - 20 Jul 1945)
9 Apr 1910 - 1 Dec 1910:	Director, Ryojun Naval Hospital, Chief Medical Officer, Ryojun Naval District

1 Dec 1910 - 1 Dec 1913:	Director, Kure Naval Hospital, Chief Medical Officer, Kure Naval District
5 Jun 1911:	Promoted to *General (Surgeon)*
1 Dec 1913 - 1 Dec 1914:	Unassigned
1 Dec 1914:	Transferred to the reserve
23 Sep 1919:	Redesignated *Rear-Admiral (Surgeon)*

Vice-Admiral **Torao KUWABARA** (26 Oct 1887 - 5 Jun 1975)

15 Nov 1938:	Promoted to *Rear-Admiral*
15 Nov 1938 - 19 Oct 1939:	Commander, 2nd Combined Air Division
19 Oct 1939 - 15 Jan 1940:	Commander, 1st Combined Air Division
15 Jan 1940 - 15 Nov 1940:	Commander, Yokosuka Air Division
15 Nov 1940 - 10 Apr 1941:	Commander, 11th Combined Air Division
10 Apr 1941 - 1 Sep 1941:	Commander, 4th Air Flotilla
1 Sep 1941 - 1 Apr 1942:	Commander, 3rd Air Flotilla
1 Apr 1942 - 5 Apr 1942:	Attached to Naval General Staff
5 Apr 1942 - 10 Apr 1942:	Attached to the staff, China Area Fleet
10 Apr 1942 - 10 Nov 1943:	Commander, Seito Area Base Force
1 May 1942:	Promoted to *Vice-Admiral*
10 Nov 1943 - 15 Dec 1943:	Attached to Naval General Staff
15 Dec 1943 - 20 Dec 1943:	Unassigned
20 Dec 1943:	Transferred to the reserve
20 Dec 1943 - 27 Dec 1943:	Recalled; Attached to Naval General Staff
27 Dec 1943 - 1 Apr 1944:	Niigata Area Inspector, Department of Military Supply
1 Apr 1944 - 1 Sep 1945:	Hokuriku Area Inspector, Department of Military Supply
1 Sep 1945:	Demobilized

Rear-Admiral (Surgeon) **Kataaki KUWAHARA** (27 May 1874 - Mar 1952)

20 Nov 1921 - 1 Dec 1923:	Chief of Bureau 1, Sasebo Naval Hospital
1 Dec 1923:	Promoted to *Rear-Admiral (Surgeon)*
1 Dec 1923 - 10 Dec 1923:	Attached to Sasebo Naval District
10 Dec 1923 - 25 Feb 1924:	Unassigned
25 Feb 1924:	Transferred to the reserve

Rear-Admiral (Paymaster) **Ken KUWAHARA** (31 Jul 1890 - 1 May 1941)

1 Dec 1936 - 15 Nov 1939:	Chief of Section 4, Administration Bureau, Naval Shipbuilding Command
15 Nov 1939:	Promoted to *Rear-Admiral (Paymaster)*
15 Nov 1939 - 15 Dec 1939:	Attached to Naval Shipbuilding Command
21 Dec 1939:	Transferred to the reserve

Rear-Admiral (Paymaster) **Toshitsugu KUWAKUBO** (18 Nov 1886 - 24 May 1980)
1 Dec 1937:	Promoted to *Rear-Admiral (Paymaster)*
1 Dec 1937 - 15 Nov 1938:	Chief of Accounting Bureau, Air Arsenal
15 Nov 1938 - 15 Dec 1938:	Attached to Naval General Staff
21 Dec 1938:	Transferred to the reserve

Vice-Admiral **Shozo KUWASHIMA** (27 Apr 1870 - 4 Aug 1925)
1 Dec 1919:	Promoted to *Rear-Admiral*
1 Dec 1919 - 1 Dec 1920:	Commander, 3rd Destroyer Flotilla
1 Dec 1920 - 1 Dec 1921:	Commander, 2nd Destroyer Flotilla
1 Dec 1921 - 1 Jun 1923:	Commandant, Torpedo School
1 Apr 1923 - 1 May 1923:	Commander, Yokosuka Defense Division
1 Jun 1923 - 5 Feb 1924:	Commander, Chinkai Guard District
1 Dec 1923:	Promoted to *Vice-Admiral*
5 Feb 1924 - 10 Mar 1924:	Member, Admirals Committee
20 Mar 1924:	Transferred to the reserve

Rear-Admiral **Tsuneo KUZUMI** (16 Nov 1866 - 25 Jul 1943)
1 Dec 1914 - 1 Nov 1918:	Commander, Kure Harbor
1 Nov 1918 - 1 Dec 1918:	Attached to Kure Naval District
1 Dec 1918:	Promoted to *Rear-Admiral*
1 Dec 1918 - 1 Aug 1919:	Unassigned
1 Aug 1919:	Transferred to the reserve

Rear-Admiral **Komajiro MACHIDA** (6 Feb 1870 - 7 Feb 1959)
1 Dec 1913 - 13 Dec 1915:	Captain, Battleship *"Kawachi"*
13 Dec 1915:	Promoted to *Rear-Admiral*
13 Dec 1915 - 1 Dec 1916:	Unassigned
1 Dec 1916:	Transferred to the reserve

Rear-Admiral **Shinichiro MACHIDA** (13 Dec 1884 - 29 Mar 1936)
15 Nov 1933 - 15 Nov 1935:	Commander, 1st Destroyer Flotilla
15 Nov 1934:	Promoted to *Rear-Admiral*
15 Nov 1935 - 29 Mar 1936:	Attached to Naval General Staff

Vice-Admiral **Kenji MAEBARA** (15 Jun 1882 - 7 Mar 1963)
5 Apr 1927 - 1 Dec 1931:	Chief of Administration Bureau, Naval Air Corps
30 Nov 1929:	Promoted to *Rear-Admiral*
1 Dec 1931 - 1 Sep 1933:	Chief of Ordnance Bureau, Yokosuka Navy Yard
1 Sep 1933 - 1 Dec 1936:	Commander, Air Arsenal
15 Nov 1934:	Promoted to *Vice-Admiral*
1 Dec 1936 - 15 Apr 1937:	Attached to Naval General Staff
20 Apr 1937:	Transferred to the reserve

Vice-Admiral **Masaichi MAEDA** (4 May 1886 - 21 Nov 1945)
23 Feb 1933 - 1 Dec 1936:   Chief of Bureau 4, Naval General Staff
15 Nov 1933:   Promoted to *Rear-Admiral*
1 Dec 1936 - 15 Nov 1938:   Commander, Ryojun Guard District
1 Dec 1937:   Promoted to *Vice-Admiral*
15 Nov 1938 - 15 Mar 1939:   Attached to Naval General Staff
21 Mar 1939:   Transferred to the reserve

Vice-Admiral **Minoru MAEDA** (10 Feb 1893 - 3 Apr 1990)
15 Oct 1940 - 15 May 1942:   Chief of Bureau 3, Naval General Staff
15 Nov 1940:   Promoted to *Rear-Admiral*
15 May 1942 - 1 Jun 1942:   Attached to the staff, 11th Air Force
1 Jun 1942 - 20 Jan 1943:   Commander, 24th Air Flotilla
20 Jan 1943 - 1 Feb 1943:   Attached to Naval General Staff
1 Feb 1943 - 10 Feb 1943:   Staff Officer, China Area Fleet
10 Feb 1943 - 14 Jan 1944:   Naval Attache, China
1 Nov 1943:   Promoted to *Vice-Admiral*
14 Jan 1944 - 10 Feb 1945:   Staff Officer, China Area Fleet
20 Jul 1944 - 10 Fev 1945:   Naval Attache, China
10 Feb 1945 - 1 Mar 1945:   Attached to Naval Air Command
1 Mar 1945 - 1 Oct 1945:   C-in-C, 10th Air Fleet
1 Oct 1945 - 10 Oct 1945:   Attached to Department of the Navy

Rear-Admiral **Tadashi MAEDA** (3 Mar 1898 - 13 Dec 1977)
15 Aug 1942 - 12 May 1945:   Staff Officer, Southwestern Area Fleet
1 May 1945:   Promoted to *Rear-Admiral*
12 May 1945 - Oct 1945:   Commander, 5th Guard Force

Rear-Admiral **Toshihide MAEJIMA** (22 Mar 1898 - 1 Mar 1944)
31 Jan 1944 - 1 Mar 1944:   Staff Officer, 6th Fleet
1 Mar 1944:   Posthumously promoted to *Rear-Admiral*

Rear-Admiral **Shinichiro MAEKAWA** (6 Jul 1900 - 13 Jun 1945)
20 Dec 1944 - 13 Jun 1945:   Attached to Okinawa Area Auxiliary Base Force
13 Jun 1945:   Posthumously promoted to *Rear-Admiral*

Rear-Admiral (Paymaster) **Chikaji MAIDA** (3 Jun 1894 - 24 Jun 1976)
1 Apr 1945 - 10 Aug 1945:   Accounting Supervisor for Construction &
                             Ordnance, Naval Shipbuilding Command
1 May 1945:   Promoted to *Rear-Admiral (Paymaster)*
10 Aug 1945 - 1 Nov 1945:   Chief of Economics Bureau,
                             Kanto & Shinetsu Area Supervision Office,
                             Department of Military Supply

Rear-Admiral **Kikuta MAKI** (23 Dec 1884 - 17 Feb 1944)
1 Oct 1943 - 17 Feb 1944: Commander of Minesweepers, Auxiliary Cruiser *"Kiyosumi-maru"*
17 Feb 1944: Posthumously promoted to *Rear-Admiral*

Vice-Admiral (Paymaster) **Mitsuyoshi MAKI** (1 Nov 1875 - 26 Sep 1928)
1 Dec 1921 - 1 Dec 1923: Chief of Accounting Bureau, Yokosuka Navy Yard
1 Dec 1922: Promoted to *Rear-Admiral (Paymaster)*
1 Dec 1923 - 20 Oct 1925: Paymaster-General, Sasebo Naval District
20 Oct 1925 - 13 Apr 1927: Director of the Naval Paymaster Academy
1 Dec 1926: Promoted to *Vice-Admiral (Paymaster)*
13 Apr 1927 - 25 May 1927: Attached to Naval General Staff
1 Jun 1927: Transferred to the reserve

Rear-Admiral **Shunkai MAKI** (17 Aug 1880 - 1 May 1965)
10 Jul 1924 - 1 Dec 1924: Chief of Briquette Bureau, Navy Fuel Yard
1 Dec 1924: Promoted to *Rear-Admiral*
1 Dec 1924 - 2 Mar 1925: Attached to Naval General Staff
20 Mar 1925: Transferred to the reserve

Rear-Admiral **Toyosuke MAKINO** (1 Sep 1880 - 4 Feb 1952)
15 Jun 1921 - 1 Apr 1923: Chief of Engine Construction Bureau, Maizuru Navy Yard
1 Apr 1923 - 1 Dec 1923: Attached to Bureau 5, Naval Shipbuilding Command
1 Dec 1923: Promoted to *Rear-Admiral*
1 Dec 1923 - 25 Feb 1924: Unassigned
25 Feb 1924: Transferred to the reserve

Vice-Admiral **Kakusaburo MAKITA** (1 Dec 1889 - 31 May 1964)
1 Dec 1937: Promoted to *Rear-Admiral*
1 Dec 1937 - 15 Nov 1939: Commandant, Naval Communications School
15 Nov 1939 - 15 Oct 1940: Commander, Amoi Area Base Force
15 Oct 1940 - 15 Nov 1940: Attached to the staff, 1st Fleet
15 Nov 1940 - 15 Sep 1941: Commander, 6th Escort Flotilla
15 Sep 1941 - 14 Feb 1942: Commander, Shanghai Area Auxiliary Base Force
15 Oct 1941: Promoted to *Vice-Admiral*
14 Feb 1942 - 9 Mar 1943: C-in-C, 1st China Expeditionary Fleet
9 Mar 1943 - 1 Apr 1944: Commander, Osaka Guard District
1 Apr 1944 - 1 Mar 1945: Admiral Commanding, Maizuru Naval District
1 Mar 1945 - 15 Mar 1945: Attached to Naval General Staff
20 Mar 1945: Transferred to the reserve

Rear-Admiral (Paymaster) **Hideo MANO** (22 Aug 1855 -26 Feb 1920)
24 Dec 1907 - 16 Jun 1910:	Paymaster-General, Ryojun Naval District
16 Jun 1910 - 2 Aug 1910:	Attached to Yokosuka Naval District
2 Aug 1910 - 22 Aug 1910:	Unassigned
22 Aug 1910:	Promoted to *Rear-Admiral (Paymaster)*
22 Aug 1910:	Transferred to the reserve

Rear-Admiral **Iwajiro MANO** (14 Dec 1863 - 24 Feb 1924)
1 Dec 1912:	Promoted to *Rear-Admiral*
1 Dec 1912 - 1 Apr 1913:	Commander, Kure Torpedo Corps
1 Apr 1913 - 24 May 1913:	Commander, Kure Torpedo Group
24 May 1913 - 1 Dec 1913:	Unassigned
1 Dec 1913:	Transferred to the reserve

Rear-Admiral **Hikosaburo MARUHASHI** (16 Feb 1867 - 9 Mar 1928)
13 Dec 1915 - 1 Dec 1918:	Chief of Survey Section, Naval Hydrographic Command
1 Dec 1918:	Promoted to *Rear-Admiral*
1 Dec 1918 - 1 Aug 1919:	Unassigned
1 Aug 1919:	Transferred to the reserve

Vice-Admiral **Kuninori MARUMO** (2 Oct 1891 - 24 Jun 1985)
22 Oct 1938 - 5 Nov 1941:	Chief of Personnel Bureau, Kure Naval District
15 Nov 1939:	Promoted to *Rear-Admiral*
5 Nov 1941 - 20 Nov 1941:	Attached to Naval General Staff
20 Nov 1941 - 1 Dec 1941:	Commander, Support Group, 4th Fleet
1 Dec 1941 - 11 Jun 1942:	Commander, 18th Escort Flotilla
11 Jun 1942 - 1 Sep 1942:	Attached to Maizuru Naval District
1 Sep 1942 - 21 Dec 1942:	Commander, Yokosuka Guard Force
21 Dec 1942 - Oct 1945:	Naval Attache, Manchuria
1 Nov 1943:	Promoted to *Vice-Admiral*

Rear-Admiral (Surgeon) **Koji MARUTA** (10 Feb 1880 - 28 Aug 1945)
1 May 1927 - 1 May 1928:	Chief Medical Officer, 2nd Fleet
1 May 1928 - 1 Dec 1931:	Instructor, Navy Medical School
1 Dec 1931:	Promoted to *Rear-Admiral (Surgeon)*
1 Dec 1931 - 15 Dec 1931:	Attached to Naval General Staff
21 Dec 1931:	Transferred to the reserve

Rear-Admiral **Hidenori MARUYAMA** (13 Mar 1892 - 16 Jun 1942)
1 Feb 1942 - 10 Apr 1942:	Commander, Sasebo Communications Unit
10 Apr 1942 - 16 Jun 1942:	Attached to Yokosuka Naval District
16 Jun 1942:	Posthumously promoted to *Rear-Admiral*

Rear-Admiral **Misao MARUYAMA** (? - 21 Nov 1944)
10 Feb 1944 - 21 Nov 1944:	Chief Engineer Officer, Battlecruiser *"Kongo"*
21 Nov 1944:	Posthumously promoted to *Rear-Admiral*

Rear-Admiral **Katsuji MASAKI** (22 Dec 1884 - 15 Oct 1966)
15 Nov 1933:	Promoted to *Rear-Admiral*
15 Nov 1933 - 15 Nov 1934:	Chief of Personnel Bureau, Yokosuka Naval District
15 Nov 1934 - 7 Oct 1935:	Commander, Yokosuka Guard Flotilla
7 Oct 1935 - 16 Mar 1936:	Commander, Ominato Guard District
16 Mar 1936 - 28 Mar 1936:	Attached to Naval General Staff
30 Mar 1936:	Transferred to the reserve

Vice-Admiral **Nobutsune MASAKI** (9 Jun 1886 - 30 Jun 1957)
25 Oct 1935 - 15 Dec 1937:	Chief of Shipbuilding Bureau, Sasebo Navy Yard
15 Nov 1935:	Promoted to *Rear-Admiral*
15 Dec 1937 - 10 Nov 1939:	Chief of Shipbuilding Bureau, Kure Navy Yard
10 Nov 1939:	Promoted to *Vice-Admiral*
10 Nov 1939 - 15 Mar 1940:	Attached to Naval Shipbuilding Command
21 Mar 1940:	Transferred to the reserve

Vice-Admiral **Yoshimoto MASAKI** (25 Oct 1871 - 29 Oct 1934)
1 Dec 1920:	Promoted to *Rear-Admiral*
1 Dec 1920 - 1 Dec 1922:	Chief of Staff, Kure Naval District
1 Dec 1922 - 1 Apr 1923:	Commander, Maizuru Navy Yard
1 Apr 1923 - 11 Jun 1924:	Chief of Naval Facilities, Maizuru Guard District
11 Jun 1924 - 15 Apr 1925:	Commander, Yokosuka Navy Yard
1 Dec 1924:	Promoted to *Vice-Admiral*
15 Apr 1925 - 1 Jul 1925:	Attached to Naval General Staff
1 Jul 1925 - 16 Dec 1925:	Unassigned
16 Dec 1925:	Transferred to the reserve

Rear-Admiral **Rokuya MASHIKO** (1 Oct 1880 - 11 Jan 1950)
1 Mar 1927 - 1 Dec 1927:	Captain, Battlecruiser *"Haruna"*
1 Dec 1927:	Promoted to *Rear-Admiral*
1 Dec 1927 - 15 Dec 1927:	Attached to Kure Naval District
25 Dec 1927:	Transferred to the reserve

Rear-Admiral (Surgeon) **Rokusaburo MASHITA** (31 Mar 1887 - ?)
15 Nov 1933 - 15 Nov 1935:	Chief Medical Officer, Combined Fleet, Chief Medical Officer, 1st Fleet
15 Nov 1935:	Promoted to *Rear-Admiral (Surgeon)*
15 Nov 1935 - 1 Dec 1936:	Director, Sasebo Naval Hospital, Chief Medical Officer, Sasebo Naval District

1 Dec 1936 - 15 Dec 1936:	Attached to Naval General Staff
22 Dec 1936:	Transferred to the reserve

Rear-Admiral **Jinpei MASUDA** (1 Nov 1894 - ?)
1 Nov 1944 - 7 Aug 1945:	Commander, 2nd Naval Facility
1 May 1945:	Promoted to *Rear-Admiral*
7 Aug 1945:	Transferred to the reserve

Rear-Admiral (Paymaster) **Jiro MASUDA** (1 Mar 1878 - 5 Dec 1963)
1 Dec 1927:	Promoted to *Rear-Admiral (Paymaster)*
1 Dec 1927 - 30 Nov 1929:	Paymaster-General, Sasebo Naval District
30 Nov 1929 - 10 Jun 1930:	Attached to Naval General Staff
20 Jun 1930:	Transferred to the reserve

Rear-Admiral **Koichi MASUDA** (23 Nov 1873 - 19 Dec 1925)
20 Nov 1920 - 20 Nov 1921:	Captain, Battleship *"Yamashiro"*
20 Nov 1921 - 1 Dec 1921:	Attached to Yokosuka Naval District
1 Dec 1921:	Promoted to *Rear-Admiral*
1 Dec 1921 - 31 Mar 1923:	Unassigned
31 Mar 1923:	Transferred to the reserve

Rear-Admiral **Nisuke MASUDA** (25 Oct 1891 - 5 Oct 1945)
12 Sep 1942 - 5 Oct 1945:	Commander, 62nd Guard Force
1 May 1944:	Promoted to *Rear-Admiral*

Rear-Admiral **Otsusaburo MASUDA** (3 Dec 1884 - 20 Dec 1937)
1 Dec 1927 - 30 Nov 1929:	Supervisor for Construction & Ordnance, Naval Shipbuilding Command
30 Nov 1929:	Promoted to *Rear-Admiral*
30 Nov 1929 - 15 Dec 1929:	Attached to Naval Shipbuilding Command
25 Dec 1929:	Transferred to the reserve

Rear-Admiral **Takayori MASUDA** (5 Jun 1868 - 19 Feb 1929)
3 May 1918 - 20 Aug 1919:	Chief of Naval Staff, Taiwan Government
20 Aug 1919 - 1 Dec 1919:	Attached to Sasebo Naval District
1 Dec 1919:	Promoted to *Rear-Admiral*
1 Dec 1919 - 1 Aug 1920:	Unassigned
1 Aug 1920:	Transferred to the reserve

Vice-Admiral (Engineer) **Keijiro MASUI** (20 Feb 1872 - 2 Sep 1963)
1 Jun 1919:	Promoted to *Rear-Admiral*
1 Jun 1919 - 1 Sep 1921:	Chief of Engine Construction Bureau, Kure Navy Yard

1 Sep 1921 - 13 Aug 1923:	Chief of Bureau 5, Naval Shipbuilding Command
13 Aug 1923 - 10 Dec 1923:	Attached to Naval Shipbuilding Command
1 Dec 1923:	Promoted to *Vice-Admiral*
10 Dec 1923 - 25 Feb 1924:	Unassigned
25 Feb 1924:	Transferred to the reserve

Rear-Admiral **Narazaburo MASAKATA** (5 Sep 1895 - 1967)
1 May 1944:	Promoted to *Rear-Admiral*
1 May 1944 - 1 Jun 1945:	Supervisor for Construction, Naval Shipbuilding Command
1 Jun 1945 - 10 Aug 1945:	Commander, Osaka Naval Facility
10 Aug 1945 - 15 Sep 1945:	Attached to Osaka Guard District

Rear-Admiral **Kiroku MATAGA** (12 Feb 1895 - 14 Dec 1964)
1 Jul 1943 - 5 Aug 1944:	Chief of Electronics Research Bureau, Kure Navy Yard
1 May 1944:	Promoted to *Rear-Admiral*
5 Aug 1944 - 6 Sep 1945:	Attached to Naval Shipbuilding Command

Rear-Admiral **Hikoshichi MATSUBARA** (30 May 1881 - 18 Jul 1946)
15 Nov 1923 - 1 Nov 1925:	Chief of Mining Bureau, Navy Fuel Yard
1 Nov 1925 - 1 Dec 1925:	Attached to Naval General Staff
1 Dec 1925:	Promoted to *Rear-Admiral*
16 Dec 1925:	Transferred to the reserve

Rear-Admiral **Hiroshi MATSUBARA** (30 Aug 1896 - 29 Oct 1965)
15 Sep 1944 - 1 Mar 1945:	Commander, Kawatana Guard Force
15 Oct 1944:	Promoted to *Rear-Admiral*
1 Mar 1945 - 20 May 1945:	Commander, 3rd Special Attack Flotilla
20 May 1945 - 10 Jun 1945:	Staff Officer, Combined Fleet
10 Jun 1945 - 15 Sep 1945:	Deputy Chief of Staff, Naval High Command, Deputy Chief of Staff, Combined Fleet
15 Sep 1945 - 10 Oct 1945:	Attached to Naval General Staff
10 Oct 1945 - 30 Nov 1945:	Chief of Personnel Bureau, Yokosuka Naval District

Rear-Admiral **Masata MATSUBARA** (13 Jan 1886 - 22 Mar 1961)
10 Apr 1943 - Oct 1945:	Commander, Minamitorishima Guard Force
1 May 1943:	Promoted to *Rear-Admiral*

Rear-Admiral **Chiaki MATSUDA** (29 Sep 1896 - ?)
17 Dec 1942 - 7 Sep 1943:	Captain, Battleship *"Yamato"*
1 May 1943:	Promoted to *Rear-Admiral*
7 Sep 1943 - 1 May 1944:	Attached to Naval General Staff

1 May 1944 - 1 Mar 1945:	Commander, 4th Carrier Division
1 Mar 1945 - 10 Mar 1945:	Attached to Naval General Staff
10 Mar 1945 - 20 Mar 1945:	Attached to Naval Air Command
20 Mar 1945 - 1 Nov 1945:	Commander, Yokosuka Air Division

Rear-Admiral **Takatomo MATSUDA** (23 Dec 1894 - 18 Feb 1944)

17 Nov 1943 - 18 Feb 1944:	Commander, Light Cruiser *"Agano"*
18 Feb 1944:	Posthumously promoted to *Rear-Admiral*

Rear-Admiral **Taketaro MATSUDA** (16 Jan 1887 - 8 May 1944)

10 Oct 1927 - 15 Nov 1932:	Supervisor for Construction & Ordnance, Naval Shipbuilding Command
15 Nov 1932 - 10 Dec 1932:	Attached to Naval Shipbuilding Command
1 Dec 1932:	Promoted to *Rear-Admiral*
15 Dec 1932:	Transferred to the reserve

Rear-Admiral **Morio MATSUDAIRA** (6 Dec 1878 - 19 Jan 1944)

1 Dec 1923 - 15 Apr 1925:	Commander, Yokosuka Sailors Corps
15 Apr 1925 - 1 Sep 1925:	Attached to Naval General Staff
1 Sep 1925 - 15 Dec 1925:	Unassigned
1 Dec 1925:	Promoted to *Rear-Admiral*
15 Dec 1925:	Transferred to the reserve

Rear-Admiral **Kiyoshi MATSUKASA** (5 Jul 1893 - 4 Apr 1975)

21 May 1940 - 5 Apr 1943:	Chief of Air Engine Bureau, Air Technical Arsenal
1 Nov 1942:	Promoted to *Rear-Admiral*
5 Apr 1943 - 15 Feb 1944:	Commander, 1st Air Arsenal
15 Feb 1944 - 19 Feb 1944:	Attached to Naval Air Command
21 Feb 1944:	Transferred to the reserve

Vice-Admiral **Masukichi MATSUKI** (5 Feb 1887 - 30 Mar 1963)

1 Dec 1937:	Promoted to *Rear-Admiral*
1 Dec 1937 - 20 Sep 1939:	Commander, Maizuru Navy Yard
20 Sep 1939 - 30 Sep 1939:	Attached to Naval Shipbuilding Command
30 Sep 1939 - 15 Nov 1940:	Chief of Administration Bureau, Naval Shipbuilding Command
15 Nov 1940 - 14 Jul 1942:	Chief of Bureau 1, Naval Shipbuilding Command
15 Oct 1941:	Promoted to *Vice-Admiral*
14 Jul 1942 - 1 Oct 1943:	Director, Shipping Agency, Department of the Navy
1 Oct 1943 - 4 Nov 1944:	Commander, Kainan Guard District
4 Nov 1944 - 19 Dec 1944:	Attached to Naval General Staff
20 Dec 1944:	Transferred to the reserve

Rear-Admiral **Arinobu MATSUMOTO** (23 Jan 1860 - 14 Dec 1930)
22 Nov 1906 - 15 May 1908:	Commander, Maizuru Torpedo Corps
12 Mar 1907:	Promoted to *Rear-Admiral*
15 May 1908 - 31 May 1909:	Unassigned
31 May 1909:	Transferred to the reserve

Vice-Admiral (Surgeon) **Cho MATSUMOTO** (18 Sep 1890 - ?)
15 Nov 1938 - 1 Nov 1942:	Director, Ureshino Naval Hospital
15 Nov 1940:	Promoted to *Rear-Admiral (Surgeon)*
1 Nov 1942 - 1 Nov 1943:	Chief of Medical Bureau, Yokosuka Navy Yard
1 Nov 1943 - 1 Nov 1944:	Director, Sasebo Naval Hospital, Chief Medical Officer, Sasebo Naval District
1 May 1944:	Promoted to *Vice-Admiral (Surgeon)*
1 Nov 1944 - 20 Jan 1945:	Attached to Naval General Staff
22 Jan 1945:	Transferred to the reserve

Rear-Admiral **Chuza MATSUMOTO** (2 Oct 1882 - 10 Jan 1946)
5 Jun 1930 - 1 Dec 1931:	Commander, Yokosuka Sailors Corps
1 Dec 1931:	Promoted to *Rear-Admiral*
1 Dec 1931 - 15 Dec 1931:	Attached to Naval General Staff
21 Dec 1931:	Transferred to the reserve

Vice-Admiral **Inokichi MATSUMOTO** (20 Dec 1893 - ?)
15 Oct 1942 - 18 Aug 1943:	Chief of Construction Bureau, Kure Naval District
1 Nov 1942:	Promoted to *Rear-Admiral*
18 Aug 1943 - 1 Mar 1944:	Chief of Facilities Bureau, Kure Naval District
1 Mar 1944 - Oct 1945:	Chief of 103rd Facility Bureau
1 May 1945:	Promoted to *Vice-Admiral*

Vice-Admiral **Kazu MATSUMOTO** (23 Feb 1860 - 20 Jan 1940)
2 Nov 1905:	Promoted to *Rear-Admiral*
2 Nov 1905 - 22 Nov 1906:	Chief of Naval Hydrographic Command
22 Nov 1906 - 28 Aug 1908:	Commander, Yokosuka Navy Yard
28 Aug 1908 - 1 Dec 1913:	Chief of Naval Shipbuilding Command
1 Dec 1909:	Promoted to *Vice-Admiral*
1 Dec 1913 - 25 Mar 1914:	Admiral Commanding, Kure Naval District
25 Mar 1914 - 29 May 1914:	Unassigned
29 May 1914:	Discharged

Rear-Admiral **Shojiro MATSUMOTO** (27 Sep 1889 - 12 May 1942)
11 Aug 1941 - 12 May 1942:	Captain, Auxiliary Gunboat *"Shoei-maru"*
12 May 1942:	Posthumously promoted to *Rear-Admiral*

Rear-Admiral **Takeshi MATSUMOTO** (14 Apr 1896 - 14 May 1962)
17 Nov 1943 - 5 Feb 1945:	Chief of Staff, 5th Fleet
15 Oct 1944:	Promoted to *Rear-Admiral*
5 Feb 1945 - 6 Feb 1945:	Attached to Naval General Staff
6 Feb 1945 - 15 Feb 1945:	Chief of Staff, 12th Air Fleet
15 Feb 1945 - 1 Jul 1945:	Deputy Chief of Staff, Ominato Guard District
	Deputy Chief of Staff, 12th Air Fleet
1 Jul 1945 - 15 Jul 1945:	Commander, 11th Destroyer Flotilla
15 Jul 1945 - 22 Jul 1945:	Attached to Kure Naval District
22 Jul 1945 - 15 Aug 1945:	Attached to Naval General Staff
15 Aug 1945 - 30 Sep 1945:	Commander, 31st Escort Flotilla
30 Sep 1945 - 25 Oct 1945:	Attached to Kure Naval District

Rear-Admiral **Takumi MATSUMOTO** (23 Sep 1880 - 4 Nov 1953)
15 Apr 1925 - 1 Jun 1925:	Attached to Yokosuka Naval District
1 Jun 1925 - 16 Dec 1925:	Unassigned
1 Dec 1925:	Promoted to *Rear-Admiral*
16 Dec 1925:	Transferred to the reserve

Vice-Admiral **Junichi MATSUMURA** (3 Jul 1871 - 17 Apr 1935)
18 Jul 1917 - 1 Dec 1918:	Chief of Staff, Kure Naval District
1 Dec 1917:	Promoted to *Rear-Admiral*
1 Dec 1918 - 1 Dec 1919:	Attached to Naval General Staff
1 Dec 1919 - 1 Dec 1921:	Commander, 1st Submarine Flotilla
1 Dec 1921:	Promoted to *Vice-Admiral*
1 Dec 1921 - 10 Apr 1922:	Member, Admirals Committee
10 Apr 1922 - 31 Mar 1923:	Unassigned
31 Mar 1923:	Transferred to the reserve

Vice-Admiral **Kanji MATSUMURA** (5 Nov 1899 - 18 Nov 1944)
12 Sep 1944 - 18 Nov 1945:	Commander, 24th Submarine Division
18 Nov 1944:	Posthumously promoted 2 grades to *Vice-Admiral*

Vice-Admiral **Kikuo MATSUMURA** (23 Oct 1874 - 4 Apr 1941)
1 Dec 1920:	Promoted to *Rear-Admiral*
1 Dec 1920 - 1 Dec 1921:	Chief of Staff, 2nd Fleet
1 Dec 1921 - 1 Apr 1923:	Chief of Bureau 1, Naval Training Command
1 Apr 1923 - 1 Jun 1923:	Attached to Naval General Staff
1 Jun 1923 - 5 Feb 1924:	Commander, 5th Escort Flotilla
5 Feb 1924 - 15 Apr 1925:	Commander, Chinkai Guard District
1 Dec 1924:	Promoted to *Vice-Admiral*
15 Apr 1925 - 20 Nov 1925:	Attached to Naval General Staff
20 Nov 1925 - 16 Dec 1925:	Unassigned
16 Dec 1925:	Transferred to the reserve

Rear-Admiral **Midori MATSUMURA** (16 Jul 1900 - 12 Jan 1945)
5 Mar 1944 - 12 Jan 1945:	Captain, Training Cruiser *"Kashii"*
12 Jan 1945:	Posthumously promoted to *Rear-Admiral*

Rear-Admiral **Naoomi MATSUMURA** (13 Mar 1860 - 3 Nov 1941)
28 Aug 1908 - 12 Apr 1911:	Commander, Sasebo Harbor
12 Apr 1911:	Promoted to *Rear-Admiral*
12 Apr 1911 - 22 May 1911:	Attached to Sasebo Naval District
22 May 1911 - 22 May 1912:	Unassigned
22 May 1912:	Transferred to the reserve

Vice-Admiral **Tatsuo MATSUMURA** (3 Feb 1868 - 18 Jul 1932)
1 Dec 1912:	Promoted to *Rear-Admiral*
1 Dec 1912 - 27 Sep 1914:	Chief of Bureaus 1 & 2, Naval Training Command
27 Sep 1914 - 1 Oct 1914:	Acting C-in-C, 1st Fleet
1 Oct 1914 - 28 Dec 1914:	Commander, 2nd Southern Detachment
28 Dec 1914 - 6 Aug 1915:	Commander, Southern Islands Defense Force
6 Aug 1915 - 6 Dec 1915:	Commander, 1st Escort Flotilla
6 Dec 1915 - 1 Sep 1916:	C-in-C, Training Fleet
1 Sep 1916 - 1 Dec 1916:	Commander, 1st Destroyer Flotilla
1 Dec 1916:	Promoted to *Vice-Admiral*
1 Dec 1916 - 12 Dec 1917:	Commander, Mako Guard District
12 Dec 1917 - 1 Dec 1918:	Member, Admirals Committee
1 Dec 1918 - 1 Oct 1920:	Commander, Ryojun Guard District
1 Oct 1920 - 1 Aug 1921:	Member, Admirals Committee
1 Aug 1921 - 1 Apr 1922:	Unassigned
1 Apr 1922:	Transferred to the reserve

Vice-Admiral **Jiro MATSUNAGA** (18 Nov 1888 - 8 Jul 1953)
1 Dec 1937 - 15 Nov 1940:	Chief of Personnel Bureau, Sasebo Naval District
15 Nov 1938:	Promoted to *Rear-Admiral*
15 Nov 1940 - 11 Aug 1941:	Commander, Kanko Area Base Force
11 Aug 1941 - 15 Oct 1941:	Attached to Sasebo Naval District
15 Oct 1941 - 21 Dec 1942:	Naval Attache, Manchuria
1 May 1942:	Promoted to *Vice-Admiral*
21 Dec 1942 - 1 Apr 1943:	Attached to Naval General Staff
1 Apr 1943 - 1 Nov 1944:	Commandant, Shimizu Merchant Navy College
1 Nov 1944 - 15 Dec 1944:	Attached to Training Bureau, Department of the Navy
20 Dec 1944:	Transferred to the reserve

Rear-Admiral **Koichi MATSUNAGA** (3 Apr 1888 - ?)
1 Mar 1944 - 5 Aug 1945:	Chief of Facilities Bureau, Kainan

1 Jul 1944:	Promoted to *Rear-Admiral*
5 Aug 1945 - 20 Sep 1945:	Attached to Naval Facilities Command

Rear-Admiral **Saburo MATSUNAGA** (? - 17 Mar 1945)
1 Nov 1942 - 17 Mar 1945:	Chief of Chemical Bureau, 3rd Navy Fuel Yard
17 Mar 1945:	Posthumously promoted to *Rear-Admiral*

Vice-Admiral **Sadaichi MATSUNAGA** (25 Apr 1892 - 2 Dec 1965)
1 Nov 1940 - 15 Jan 1941:	Commander, 2nd Combined Air Division
15 Nov 1940:	Promoted to *Rear-Admiral*
15 Jan 1941 - 15 May 1942:	Commander, 22nd Air Flotilla
15 May 1942 - 25 Jun 1943:	Commander, 12th Combined Air Division
25 Jun 1943 - 1 Sep 1943:	Attached to Naval General Staff
1 Sep 1943 - 1 Mar 1944:	Chief of Staff, Yokosuka Naval District
1 Nov 1943:	Promoted to *Vice-Admiral*
1 Mar 1944 - 10 Aug 1944:	Commander, 27th Air Flotilla
10 Aug 1944 - 15 Aug 1944:	Attached to Naval Air Command
15 Aug 1944 - 1 Sep 1944:	Commander, 11th Combined Air Division
15 Aug 1944 - 1 Mar 1945:	Commander, Combined Air Training Units
1 Mar 1945 - 10 Jun 1945:	Attached to Naval General Staff
10 Jun 1945 - 30 Sep 1945:	Commander, 2nd Technical Arsenal

Rear-Admiral **Toshio MATSUNAGA** (15 Jan 1888 - 10 Dec 1955)
15 Nov 1935 - 1 Dec 1936:	Captain, Aircraft Carrier *"Akagi"*
1 Dec 1936:	Promoted to *Rear-Admiral*
1 Dec 1936 - 15 Dec 1936:	Attached to Naval General Staff
21 Dec 1936:	Transferred to the reserve

Vice-Admiral **Yuju MATSUNAGA** (18 Aug 1849 - 3 Nov 1926)
27 Dec 1897:	Promoted to *Rear-Admiral*
27 Dec 1897 - 14 May 1898:	Admiral Commanding, Kure Naval District
14 May 1898 - 12 Jan 1900:	Chief Supervisor for Construction & Ordnance, Naval Shipbuilding Command
12 Jan 1900 - 20 May 1900:	C-in-C, Sasebo Naval District Fleet, Admiral Commanding, Sasebo Naval District
20 May 1900 - 3 Jul 1901:	Chief of Shipping Bureau, Yokosuka Naval District
3 Jul 1901 - 5 Sep 1903:	Chief of Naval Training Command, Member, Admirals Committee
5 Sep 1903:	Promoted to *Vice-Admiral*
5 Sep 1903 - 13 Feb 1905:	Unassigned
13 Feb 1905 - 13 Jun 1905:	Commander, Mako Guard District
13 Jun 1905 - 14 Feb 1907:	Unassigned
14 Feb 1907:	Transferred to the reserve

Rear-Admiral (Surgeon) **Kinji MATSUNO** (19 Mar 1893 - 22 Sep 1963)
1 Apr 1945 - 30 Sep 1945:	Director, Totsuka Naval Hospital
1 May 1945:	Promoted to *Rear-Admiral (Surgeon)*
30 Sep 1945 - 5 Oct 1945:	Attached to Yokosuka Naval District

Rear-Admiral **Seizo MATSUNO** (1 May 1886 - 15 Mar 1955)
15 Nov 1935 - 1 Dec 1936:	Commander, Sasebo Defense Flotilla
1 Dec 1936:	Promoted to *Rear-Admiral*
1 Dec 1936 - 28 Jul 1937:	Attached to Naval General Staff
28 Jul 1937 - 1 Dec 1937:	Commander, Yokosuka Guard Flotilla
1 Dec 1937 - 15 Dec 1937:	Attached to Naval General Staff
21 Dec 1937:	Transferred to the reserve

Rear-Admiral (Surgeon) **Masamichi MATSUO** (15 Sep 1892 - 6 Jun 1959)
1 Dec 1944 - 20 Nov 1945:	Chief of the Medical Bureau, 21st Air Arsenal
1 May 1945:	Promoted to *Rear-Admiral (Surgeon)*

Rear-Admiral **Minoru MATSUO** (13 Feb 1897 - 13 Mar 1980)
1 Apr 1942 - 20 Dec 1944:	Chief of Section 1, Bureau 1, Naval Shipbuilding Command
15 Oct 1944:	Promoted to *Rear-Admiral*
20 Dec 1944 - 1 Mar 1945:	Chief of Bureau 1, Naval Shipbuilding Command
1 Mar 1945 - 15 Oct 1945:	Chief of Bureau 3, Naval Air Command

Rear-Admiral **Teizo MATSUO** (9 Jul 1894 - 29 Jun 1940)
1 Oct 1939 - 29 Jun 1940:	Commander, Chitose Air Division
29 Jun 1940:	Posthumously promoted to *Rear-Admiral*

General (Constructor) **Tsurutaro MATSUO** (23 Aug 1864 - 1945)
20 May 1904 - 8 May 1907:	Chief of Shipbuilding Bureau, Yokosuka Navy Yard
13 Mar 1907:	Promoted to *General (Constructor)*
8 May 1907 - 6 Nov 1907:	Unassigned
6 Nov 1907 - 6 Feb 1908:	Attached to Bureau 3, Naval Shipbuilding Command
6 Feb 1908:	Transferred to the reserve

Rear-Admiral (Paymaster) **Kaichi MATSUOKA** (5 Jul 1898 - 25 Oct 1944)
1 Jul 1944 - 25 Oct 1944:	Paymaster-General, 1st Task Fleet, Paymaster-General, 3rd Fleet
25 Oct 1944:	Posthumously promoted to *Rear-Admiral (Paymaster)*

Rear-Admiral **Shuzo MATSUOKA** (11 Dec 1867 - 28 Oct 1927)
13 Dec 1915:	Promoted to *Rear-Admiral*
13 Dec 1915 - 1 Apr 1917:	Commander, 4th Destroyer Flotilla
1 Apr 1917 - 1 Dec 1917:	Chief of Ordnance Bureau, Sasebo Navy Yard
1 Dec 1917 - 1 Dec 1918:	Unassigned
1 Dec 1918:	Transferred to the reserve

Rear-Admiral **Tomoyuki MATSUOKA** (4 Apr 1894 - 11 Nov 1943)
1 Nov 1942:	Promoted to *Rear-Admiral*
1 Nov 1942 - 1 Mar 1943:	Commander, Tsuchiura Air Division
1 Mar 1943 - 23 Mar 1943:	Attached to Yokosuka Naval District
23 Mar 1943 - 1 Sep 1943:	Commander, 2nd Sasebo Sailors Corps
1 Sep 1943 - 12 Sep 1943:	Attached to Sasebo Naval District
12 Sep 1943 - 11 Nov 1943:	Attached to Yokosuka Naval District

Vice-Admiral **Yoshimi MATSUOKA** (10 Jan 1885 - ?)
11 Jun 1930 - 1 Dec 1937:	Chief of Powder Bureau, Navy Powder Yard
15 Nov 1935:	Promoted to *Rear-Admiral*
1 Dec 1937 - 1 Aug 1939:	Commander, Navy Powder Yard
1 Aug 1939 - 15 Nov 1940:	Commander, Navy Main Powder Yard
15 Nov 1939:	Promoted to *Vice-Admiral*
15 Nov 1940 - 16 Dec 1940:	Attached to Naval Shipbuilding Command
21 Dec 1940:	Transferred to the reserve

Rear-Admiral **Tadayuki MATSURA** (29 Nov 1890 - 16 Dec 1969)
10 Sep 1944 - Oct 1945:	Commander, 31st Harbor
1 May 1945:	Promoted to *Rear-Admiral*

Vice-Admiral **Hajime MATSUSHITA** (10 Aug 1884 - 1 Dec 1953)
1 Dec 1927:	Promoted to *Rear-Admiral*
1 Dec 1927 - 10 Dec 1928:	Attached to Naval General Staff
10 Dec 1928 - 1 Dec 1930:	Chief of Naval Personnel, Department of the Navy
1 Dec 1930 - 1 Dec 1931:	Commander, 3rd Escort Flotilla
1 Dec 1931 - 3 Oct 1933:	Commandant of the Navy Academy
1 Dec 1932:	Promoted to *Vice-Admiral*
3 Oct 1933 - 20 Sep 1934:	C-in-C, Training Fleet
20 Sep 1934 - 15 Nov 1934:	Attached to Naval General Staff
15 Nov 1934 - 2 Dec 1935:	Admiral Commanding, Maizuru Guard District
2 Dec 1935 - 16 Mar 1936:	Attached to Naval General Staff
16 Mar 1936 - 1 Dec 1936:	Admiral Commanding, Sasebo Naval District
1 Dec 1936 - 15 Mar 1937:	Attached to Naval General Staff
25 Mar 1937:	Transferred to the reserve

Vice-Admiral **Shigeru MATSUSHITA** (4 Sep 1883 - 30 Sep 1973)
10 Dec 1928:	Promoted to *Rear-Admiral*
10 Dec 1928 - 30 Nov 1929:	Chief of Naval Facilities, Maizuru Guard District
30 Nov 1929 - 10 Oct 1932:	Chief of Administration Bureau, Naval Shipbuilding Command
10 Oct 1932 - 15 Feb 1936:	Commander, Kure Navy Yard
15 Nov 1933:	Promoted to *Vice-Admiral*
15 Feb 1936 - 28 Mar 1936:	Attached to Naval General Staff
30 Mar 1936:	Transferred to the reserve

Vice-Admiral **Tojiro MATSUSHITA** (Apr 1876 - 19 May 1944)
3 Aug 1918 - 20 Dec 1924:	Aide-de-Camp to the Emperor
1 Dec 1920:	Promoted to *Rear-Admiral*
1 Dec 1924:	Promoted to *Vice-Admiral*
20 Dec 1924 - 2 Mar 1925:	Attached to Naval General Staff
20 Mar 1925:	Transferred to the reserve

Vice-Admiral **Eijiro MATSUURA** (5 Mar 1889 - 8 Nov 1976)
1 Dec 1937:	Promoted to *Rear-Admiral*
1 Dec 1937 - 15 Nov 1938:	Chief of Shipbuilding Bureau, Sasebo Naval District
15 Nov 1938 - 15 Oct 1941:	Chief of Bureau 6, Naval Shipbuilding Command
15 Oct 1941:	Promoted to *Vice-Admiral*
15 Oct 1941 - 1 Nov 1943:	Commander, Sasebo Navy Yard
1 May 1943 - 1 Nov 1943:	Commander, Kawatana Navy Yard
1 Nov 1943 - 15 Dec 1943:	Attached to Naval General Staff
20 Dec 1943:	Transferred to the reserve

Vice-Admiral **Matsumi MATSUURA** (23 Nov 1880 - 4 Jun 1948)
15 Nov 1926 - 1 Dec 1927:	Chief of Ordnance Bureau, Yokosuka Navy Yard
1 Dec 1926:	Promoted to *Rear-Admiral*
1 Dec 1927 - 10 Dec 1928:	Chief of Gunnery Bureau, Kure Navy Yard
10 Dec 1928 - 15 Nov 1932:	Chief of Bureau 1, Naval Shipbuilding Command
1 Dec 1931:	Promoted to *Vice-Admiral*
15 Nov 1932 - 10 Dec 1932:	Attached to Naval General Staff
15 Dec 1932:	Transferred to the reserve

Rear-Admiral **Kanji MATSUYAMA** (26 Aug 1895 - ?)
1 May 1943 - 14 Oct 1944:	Chief of Materiel Bureau, Air Technical Arsenal
1 May 1944:	Promoted to *Rear-Admiral*
14 Oct 1944 - 25 Aug 1945:	Chief of Productivity Bureau, Technological Agency
25 Aug 1945 - 15 Sep 1945:	Attached to Naval Shipbuilding Command

Rear-Admiral **Mitsuharu MATSUYAMA** (12 Jan 1891 - 21 Sep 1959)

15 Nov 1940:	Promoted to *Rear-Admiral*
15 Nov 1940 - 1 Aug 1941:	Commander, Maizuru Sailors Corps
1 Aug 1941 - 11 Jun 1942:	Commander, Kure Sailors Corps
20 Nov 1941 - 11 Jun 1942:	Commander, Kure Guard Force
11 Jun 1942 - 10 Dec 1942:	Commander, 18th Cruiser Division
10 Dec 1942 - 6 Jan 1943:	Attached to Yokosuka Naval District
6 Jan 1943 - 27 Dec 1943:	Commandant, Tateyama Naval Gunnery School
27 Dec 1943 - 25 Jan 1944:	Attached to Naval General Staff
25 Jan 1944 - 31 Jan 1944:	Unassigned
31 Jan 1944 - 8 Apr 1944:	Attached to Naval General Staff
8 Apr 1944 - 23 Dec 1944:	Commander, 7th Convoy HQ
23 Dec 1944 - 5 May 1945:	Staff Officer, Maritime Escort Fleet
5 May 1945 - 15 Sep 1945:	Commander, 105th Escort Flotilla

Vice-Admiral **Shigeru MATSUYAMA** (14 Jul 1881 - 29 Dec 1937)

20 Nov 1925 - 1 Dec 1926:	Chief of Staff, Maizuru Naval District
1 Dec 1926:	Promoted to *Rear-Admiral*
1 Dec 1926 - 1 Dec 1927:	Chief of Staff, 2nd Fleet
1 Dec 1927 - 12 Sep 1929:	Chief of Bureau 2, Naval General Staff
12 Sep 1929 - 1 Dec 1930:	Commandant, Torpedo School
1 Jun 1930 - 1 Dec 1930:	Commandant, Navay Communications School
1 Dec 1930 - 10 Oct 1931:	Commander, 5th Escort Flotilla
10 Oct 1931 - 15 Nov 1933:	Chief of Naval Air Command
1 Dec 1931:	Promoted to *Vice-Admiral*
15 Nov 1933 - 17 Jan 1934:	Deputy Chief of the Naval General Staff
17 Jan 1934 - 10 Dec 1935:	Attached to Naval General Staff
14 Dec 1935:	Transferred to the reserve

Rear-Admiral **Akira MATSUZAKI** (25 Aug 1893 - 8 Feb 1981)

15 Apr 1943 - 19 Jan 1945:	Chief of Staff, 2nd Southern Expeditionary Fleet
1 May 1943:	Promoted to *Rear-Admiral*
19 Jan 1945 - 26 Feb 1945:	Attached to Naval General Staff
26 Feb 1945 - 30 Nov 1945:	Chief of Staff, Osaka Guard District

Vice-Admiral **Iori MATSUZAKI** (27 Feb 1886 - 17 Aug 1966)

10 Mar 1932 - 15 Nov 1935:	Chief of Personnel, Kure Naval District
15 Nov 1934:	Promoted to *Rear-Admiral*
15 Nov 1935 - 15 Nov 1938:	Chief Supervisor for Construction & Ordnance, Naval Shipbuilding Command
15 Nov 1938:	Promoted to *Vice-Admiral*
15 Nov 1938 - 15 Dec 1938:	Attached to Naval General Staff
21 Dec 1938:	Transferred to the reserve

Rear-Admiral **Sunao MATSUZAKI** (23 Jan 1881 - 27 Jul 1940)
1 Dec 1926 - 10 Dec 1928:	Chief of Staff, Chinkai Guard District
10 Dec 1928:	Promoted to *Rear-Admiral*
10 Dec 1928 - 20 Dec 1928:	Attached to Naval General Staff
25 Dec 1928:	Transferred to the reserve

Rear-Admiral **Kumagoro MIGITA** (8 Dec 1880 - 11 Feb 1955)
20 Apr 1925 - 1 Jul 1925:	Attached to Yokosuka Naval District
1 Jul 1925 - 16 Dec 1925:	Unassigned
1 Dec 1925:	Promoted to *Rear-Admiral*
16 Dec 1925:	Transferred to the reserve

Rear-Admiral **Taizo MIHARA** (17 Nov 1892 - 2 May 1979)
15 Oct 1941 - 1 Nov 1942:	Chief Engineer Officer, Sasebo Naval District
1 May 1942:	Promoted to *Rear-Admiral*
1 Nov 1942 - 22 Feb 1943:	Chief of Shipbuilding Bureau, Yokosuka Naval District
22 Feb 1943 - 4 Mar 1944:	Chief of Supply Bureau, Kure Naval District
4 Mar 1944 - 1 Jun 1944:	Commandant, Naval Construction School
1 Jun 1944 - 15 Oct 1945:	Commandant, Yokosuka Naval Construction School

Rear-Admiral **Denzo MIHORI** (3 Sep 1881 - 23 Mar 1947)
10 Dec 1928 - 10 Mar 1932:	Chief of Personnel Bureau, Kure Naval District
1 Dec 1930:	Promoted to *Rear-Admiral*
10 Mar 1932 - 22 Mar 1932:	Attached to Naval General Staff
31 Mar 1932:	Transferred to the reserve

Rear-Admiral **Yoshitada MIKAMI** (30 Nov 1880 - 12 Jan 1947)
1 Aug 1922 - 1 Dec 1923:	Commander, Kure Sailors Corps
1 Dec 1923:	Promoted to *Rear-Admiral*
1 Dec 1923 - 10 Dec 1923:	Attached to Kure Naval District
10 Dec 1923 - 25 Feb 1924:	Unassigned
25 Feb 1924:	Transferred to the reserve

Vice-Admiral **Gunichi MIKAWA** (29 Aug 1888 - 25 Feb 1981)
1 Dec 1936:	Promoted to *Rear-Admiral*
1 Dec 1936 - 15 Nov 1937:	Chief of Staff, 2nd Fleet
15 Nov 1937 - 15 Nov 1939:	Chief of Bureau 2, Naval General Staff
15 Nov 1939 - 1 Nov 1940:	Commander, 7th Escort Flotilla
1 Nov 1940 - 6 Sep 1941:	Commander, 5th Escort Flotilla
15 Nov 1940:	Promoted to *Vice-Admiral*
6 Sep 1941 - 12 Jul 1942:	Commander, 3rd Escort Flotilla
12 Jul 1942 - 14 Jul 1942:	Attached to Naval General Staff

14 Jul 1942 - 1 Apr 1943:	C-in-C, 8th Fleet
1 Apr 1943 - 20 Apr 1943:	Attached to Naval General Staff
20 Apr 1943 - 3 Sep 1943:	Commandant, Navigation School
3 Sep 1943 - 18 Jun 1944:	C-in-C, 2nd Southern Expeditionary Fleet
18 Jun 1944 - 1 Nov 1944:	C-in-C, Southwest Area Fleet, C-in-C, 13th Air Fleet
15 Aug 1944 - 1 Nov 1944:	C-in-C, 3rd Southern Expeditionary Fleet
1 Nov 1944 - 15 May 1945:	Attached to Naval General Staff
21 May 1945:	Transferred to the reserve

Rear-Admiral **Morihiko MIKI** (21 May 1890 - 6 Jul 1973)

20 Apr 1943 - 9 Aug 1943:	Attached to Administration Bureau, Naval Air Command
1 May 1943:	Promoted to *Rear-Admiral*
9 Aug 1943 - 1 Feb 1944:	Commander, Kasumigaura Air Division
15 Nov 1943 - 1 Feb 1944:	Commander, Yatabe Air Division
1 Feb 1944 - 1 Mar 1944:	Commander, 27th Air Flotilla
1 Mar 1944 - 1 Dec 1944:	Commander, 14th Combined Air Division
15 May 1944 - 1 Jul 1944:	Commander, Tainan Air Division
1 Dec 1944 - 1 Mar 1945:	Attached to Naval General Staff
1 Mar 1945 - 15 Jul 1945:	Commander, 21st Combined Air Division
15 Jul 1945 - 3 Aug 1945:	Attached to Kure Naval District
3 Aug 1945 - 15 Sep 1945:	Commander, 15th Combined Air Division

Rear-Admiral **Taichi MIKI** (31 Aug 1886 - 17 Feb 1956)

15 Nov 1934:	Promoted to *Rear-Admiral*
15 Nov 1934 - 15 Nov 1935:	Chief of Staff, 2nd Fleet
15 Nov 1935 - 1 Dec 1936:	Commander, 2nd Destroyer Flotilla
1 Dec 1936 - 10 Mar 1937:	Commandant, Torpedo School
10 Mar 1937 - 1 Dec 1937:	Commander, 5th Escort Flotilla
1 Dec 1937 - 15 Mar 1938:	Attached to Naval General Staff
25 Mar 1938:	Transferred to the reserve
6 Oct 1941 - 15 Oct 1941:	Recalled; Attached to Yokosuka Naval District
15 Oct 1941 - 10 Jan 1942:	Commander, Yokosuka Guard Flotilla
10 Jan 1942 - 15 Mar 1943:	Commandant, Torpedo School
20 Mar 1943:	Demobilized

Rear-Admiral **Takahide MIKI** (20 Dec 1897 - 31 Aug 1944)

13 Apr 1943 - 31 Aug 1944:	Captain, Minelayer *"Shirataka"*
31 Aug 1944:	Posthumously promoted to *Rear-Admiral*

Rear-Admiral **Hayato MIKOSHIBA** (18 May 1893 - 30 Aug 1977)

5 Oct 1942 - 10 Oct 1943:	Chief Engineer Officer, China Area Fleet

1 May 1943:	Promoted to *Rear-Admiral*
10 Oct 1943 - 25 Oct 1943:	Attached to Naval General Staff
25 Oct 1943 - 20 Apr 1944:	Chief of Administration Bureau, Technical Research Department
20 Apr 1944 - 25 Jan 1945:	Chief of Shipping Bureau, Kure Naval District
20 Apr 1944 - 11 Sep 1944:	Chief Engineer Officer, Kure Naval District
11 Sep 1944 - 25 Jan 1945:	Deputy Chief of Staff, Kure Naval District
25 Jan 1945 - 10 Aug 1945:	Supervisor for Construction & Ordnance, Naval Shipbuilding Command
10 Aug 1945 - 20 Sep 1945:	Chief of Yokohama Branch, Kanto and Shinetsu Area Supervision Office, Department of Military Supply

Rear-Admiral **Kinsaburo MIMURA** (16 Jun 1868 - 5 Apr 1932)

1 Dec 1919:	Promoted to *Rear-Admiral*
1 Dec 1919 - 1 Dec 1920:	Commander, 2nd Destroyer Flotilla
1 Dec 1920 - 10 Dec 1920:	Attached to Yokosuka Naval District
10 Dec 1920 - 1 Aug 1921:	Unassigned
1 Aug 1921:	Transferred to the reserve

Rear-Admiral **Takayasu MINAGAWA** (5 Jul 1894 - 13 Feb 1957)

10 Sep 1941 - 8 Aug 1942:	Chief Engineer, 2nd Fleet
8 Aug 1942 - 22 Oct 1943:	Chief Supervisor for Construction & Ordnance, Naval Shipbuilding Command
1 Nov 1942:	Promoted to *Rear-Admiral*
22 Oct 1943 - 1 Nov 1943:	Attached to Naval General Staff
1 Nov 1943 - 26 Aug 1945:	Chief of Steel Bureau, Department of Military Supply
26 Aug 1945 - 20 Sep 1945:	Attached to Naval Shipbuilding Command

Rear-Admiral **Seijiro MINAMIDE** (? - 31 Mar 1945)

25 Oct 1944 - 31 Mar 1945:	Chief Engineer Officer, Aircraft Carrier *"Amagi"*
31 Mar 1945:	Posthumously promoted to *Rear-Admiral*

Rear-Admiral **Keijo MINATO** (30 Aug 1896 - 19 Oct 1982)

1 Nov 1943 - 23 Oct 1944:	Chief Instructor, Naval Academy
1 May 1944:	Promoted to *Rear-Admiral*
23 Oct 1944 - 7 Nov 1944:	Staff Officer, China Area Fleet
7 Nov 1944 - Oct 1945:	Deputy Chief of Staff, China Area Fleet

Rear-Admiral **Sadakatsu MINOBE** (10 Aug 1892 - 29 Nov 1960)

10 Dec 1944 - 25 Aug 1945:	Area Supervisor, 1st Escort Fleet
1 May 1945:	Promoted to *Rear-Admiral*
25 Aug 1945 - Oct 1945:	Staff Officer, Southwestern Area Fleet

Vice-Admiral **Tsutsumu MINOHARA** (28 Aug 1882 - 15 Dec 1964)
3 Jun 1925 - 15 Nov 1933:	Chief of Electrical Research Bureau, Technical Research Department
10 Dec 1928:	Promoted to *Rear-Admiral*
15 Nov 1933:	Promoted to *Vice-Admiral*
15 Nov 1933 - 15 Nov 1935:	Chief of Technical Research Department
15 Nov 1935 - 15 Dec 1936:	Attached to Naval General Staff, Member, High Technical Committee
22 Dec 1936:	Transferred to the reserve

Vice-Admiral **Konomu MISHUKU** (22 May 1887 - 3 Apr 1950)
15 Nov 1935:	Promoted to *Rear-Admiral*
15 Nov 1935 - 1 Dec 1937:	Instructor, Naval College
1 Dec 1937 - 30 Aug 1939:	Commander, Navy Fuel Yard
30 Aug 1939 - 25 Oct 1943:	Chief of Supply Bureau
15 Nov 1939:	Promoted to *Vice-Admiral*
25 Oct 1943 - 13 Dec 1943:	Attached to Naval General Staff
14 Dec 1943:	Transferred to the reserve

Admiral **Baron Sotaro MISU** (6 Aug 1855 - 24 Dec 1921)
3 Jul 1901:	Promoted to *Rear-Admiral*
3 Jul 1901 - 28 Dec 1903:	Chief of Naval Personnel, Member, Admirals Committee
28 Dec 1903 - 12 Jan 1905:	C-in-C, 2nd Fleet
12 Jan 1905:	Promoted to *Vice-Admiral*
12 Jan 1905 - 7 Nov 1905:	C-in-C, 1st Fleet
7 Nov 1905 - 2 Feb 1906:	Chief of Naval Training Command, Member, Admirals Committee
2 Feb 1906 - 22 Nov 1906:	Commander, Ryojun Guard District
22 Nov 1906 - 1 Dec 1909:	Deputy Chief of the Naval General Staff
22 Nov 1906 - 18 Jan 1911:	Member, Admirals Committee
1 Apr 1910 - 18 Jan 1911:	Acting Chief of Construction Bureau, Department of the Navy
18 Jan 1911 - 25 Sep 1913:	Admiral Commanding, Maizuru Naval District
25 Sep 1913:	Promoted to *Admiral*
25 Sep 1913 - 1 Dec 1913:	Member, Admirals Committee
1 Dec 1913 - 1 Dec 1914:	Unassigned
1 Dec 1914:	Transferred to the reserve

General (Surgeon) **Tadakuni MITAMURA** (1 Dec 1846 - 3 Dec 1912)
8 Oct 1897 - 14 Sep 1898:	Chief of Medical Bureau, Kure Naval District
14 Sep 1898 - 15 Sep 1901:	Unassigned
15 Sep 1901:	Promoted to *General (Surgeon)*
15 Sep 1901:	Transferred to the reserve

Vice-Admiral **Hisashi MITO** (9 Nov 1891 - 17 May 1967)
6 Jan 1941 - 22 Oct 1942: Chief of Staff, 6th Fleet
22 Oct 1942 - 29 Mar 1943: Commander, 1st Submarine Flotilla
1 Nov 1942: Promoted to *Rear-Admiral*
29 Mar 1943 - 15 Jun 1943: Attached to Naval General Staff
15 Jun 1943 - 7 May 1945: Chief of Naval Personnel
7 May 1945 - 15 Sep 1945: Commander, 4th Special Attack Flotilla
15 Sep 1945 - 20 Nov 1945: Attached to Naval General Staff
20 Nov 1945 - 30 Sep 1945: Deputy Minister of the Navy
1 Nov 1945: Promoted to *Vice-Admiral*

Rear-Admiral **Motosuke MITO** (12 Apr 1882 - 16 Jul 1971)
1 Dec 1927 - 1 Dec 1930: Commander, Yokosuka Harbor
1 Dec 1930: Promoted to *Rear-Admiral*
1 Dec 1930 - 15 Dec 1930: Attached to Naval General Staff
24 Dec 1930: Transferred to the reserve

Vice-Admiral **Shunzo MITO** (1 Mar 1886 - 26 Oct 1965)
15 Nov 1935: Promoted to *Rear-Admiral*
15 Nov 1935 - 1 Apr 1936: Chief of Staff, 2nd Fleet
1 Apr 1936 - 1 Dec 1936: Attached to Kure Naval District
1 Dec 1936 - 1 Dec 1937: Commander, Kure Guard Flotilla
1 Dec 1937 - 15 Nov 1938: Commander, Mako Guard District
15 Nov 1938 - 10 Mar 1939: Attached to Naval General Staff
10 Mar 1939 - 1 Jul 1940: Chief of Communication Office, Asian Development Agency
15 Nov 1939: Promoted to *Vice-Admiral*
1 Jul 1940 - 16 Dec 1940: Attached to Naval General Staff
21 Dec 1940: Transferred to the reserve

Vice-Admiral **Yoshihiko MITO** (9 Nov 1888 - 16 Sep 1966)
1 Dec 1937: Promoted to *Rear-Admiral*
1 Dec 1937 - 15 Nov 1940: Chief of Engine Construction Bureau, Yokosuka Navy Yard
15 Nov 1940 - 15 Oct 1941: Attached to Naval General Staff
15 Oct 1941: Promoted to *Vice-Admiral*
15 Oct 1941 - 15 Sep 1943: Chief of Bureau 5, Naval Shipbuilding Command
15 Sep 1943 - 1 May 1945: Commander, Kure Navy Yard
1 May 1945 - 15 Sep 1945: Attached to Naval Shipbuilding Command

Rear-Admiral **Seizaburo MITSUI** (15 Sep 1885 - 31 May 1956)
15 May 1931 - 1 Apr 1933: Commander, Sasebo Sailors Corps
1 Dec 1932: Promoted to *Rear-Admiral*

1 Apr 1933 - 15 Nov 1933:	Chief of Staff, 3rd Fleet
15 Nov 1933 - 26 Mar 1934:	Attached to Naval General Staff
31 Mar 1934:	Transferred to the reserve

Rear-Admiral **Teizo MITSUNAMI** (26 Apr 1889 - 17 Jul 1964)

11 Jul 1937 - 15 Dec 1937:	Commander, 2nd Combined Air Division
1 Dec 1937:	Promoted to *Rear-Admiral*
15 Dec 1937 - 1 Sep 1938:	Commander, 2nd Air Flotilla
1 Sep 1938 - 15 Nov 1939:	Attached to Naval General Staff
15 Nov 1939 - 15 Sep 1940:	Chief Supervisor for Construction & Ordnance, Naval Shipbuilding Command
15 Sep 1940 - 16 Dec 1940:	Attached to Naval General Staff
21 Dec 1940:	Transferred to the reserve
20 Dec 1943 - 1 Sep 1945:	Recalled; Attached to Naval General Staff

Rear-Admiral **Toyo MITSUNOBU** (9 Oct 1897 - 9 Jun 1944)

7 Feb 1940 - 9 Jun 1944:	Naval Attache, Italy
9 Jun 1944:	Posthumously promoted to *Rear-Admiral*

Rear-Admiral **Ryoji MITSUOKA** (30 Nov 1882 - 27 Aug 1947)

1 Feb 1929 - 30 Nov 1929:	Chief Engineer Officer, Yokosuka Naval District
30 Nov 1929:	Promoted to *Rear-Admiral*
30 Nov 1929 - 15 Dec 1929:	Attached to Naval General Staff
25 Dec 1929:	Transferred to the reserve

Rear-Admiral **Hayao MIURA** (21 Jul 1895 - 27 Jun 1958)

30 Jan 1944 - 20 Jun 1945:	Captain, Heavy Cruiser *"Ashigara"*
1 May 1945:	Promoted to *Rear-Admiral*
20 Jun 1945 - Oct 1945:	Deputy Chief of Staff, 2nd Southern Expeditionary Fleet

Vice-Admiral **Isao MIURA** (8 May 1850 - 26 Apr 1919)

14 May 1898:	Promoted to *Rear-Admiral*
14 May 1898 - 20 May 1900:	Chief of Harbor Bureau, Kure Naval District
20 May 1900 - 7 Jul 1903:	Chief of Reserve Bureau, Kure Naval District
7 Jul 1903 - 1 Aug 1904:	Unassigned
1 Aug 1904 - 12 Jan 1905:	Commander, Wartime Fleet Anchorage Harbor
12 Jan 1905 - 15 Mar 1905:	Attached to Sasebo Naval District
15 Mar 1905 - 24 May 1905:	Unassigned
24 May 1905 - 13 Jun 1905:	Attached to Ryojun Naval District
13 Jun 1905 - 20 Dec 1905:	Commander, Ryojun Harbor
23 Sep 1905:	Promoted to *Vice-Admiral*
20 Dec 1905 - 20 Dec 1906:	Unassigned
20 Dec 1906:	Transferred to the reserve

Rear-Admiral **Kanzo MIURA** (3 Apr 1900 - 30 Jul 1944)
10 Jul 1944 - 30 Jul 1944: Chief of Staff, 3rd Air Fleet
30 Jul 1944: Posthumously promoted to *Rear-Admiral*

Rear-Admiral **Tomosaburo MIURA** (24 May 1889 - 21 Aug 1965)
16 Oct 1943 - Oct 1945: Commander, 4th Harbor
1 May 1945: Promoted to *Rear-Admiral*
1 May 1945 - Oct 1945: Commander, 49th Guard Force

Rear-Admiral (Paymaster) **Hiroshi MIWA** (4 Apr 1882 - 28 Apr 1960)
1 Dec 1930 - 1 Dec 1931: Paymaster-General, Maizuru Naval District
1 Dec 1931: Promoted to *Rear-Admiral (Paymaster)*
1 Dec 1931 - 1 Dec 1932: Accounting Supervisor for Construction & Ordnance, Naval Shipbuilding Command
1 Dec 1932 - 10 Dec 1932: Attached to Naval General Staff
15 Dec 1932: Transferred to the reserve

Vice-Admiral **Shigeyoshi MIWA** (15 May 1892 - 27 Feb 1959)
1 Dec 1936 - 15 Dec 1938: Chief of Staff, Mako Guard District
15 Nov 1938: Promoted to *Rear-Admiral*
15 Dec 1938 - 15 Nov 1939: Commander, Sasebo Defense Flotilla
15 Nov 1939 - 26 Apr 1942: Commander, 3rd Submarine Flotilla
26 Apr 1942 - 1 Nov 1942: Attached to Naval General Staff
1 Nov 1942: Promoted to *Vice-Admiral*
1 Nov 1942 - 1 May 1943: Chief of Bureau 7, Naval Shipbuilding Command
1 May 1943 - 10 Jul 1944: Chief of Submarine Division, Department of the Navy
10 Jul 1944 - 1 May 1945: C-in-C, 6th (Submarine) Fleet
1 May 1945 - 6 Sep 1945: Attached to Naval General Staff

Rear-Admiral **Yoshitake MIWA** (26 Apr 1899 - 2 Aug 1944)
1 Jul 1943 - 2 Aug 1944: Chief of Staff, 1st Air Fleet
2 Aug 1944: Posthumously promoted to *Rear-Admiral*

Rear-Admiral **Yujiro MIYA** (25 Mar 1900 - 13 May 1945)
? - 13 May 1945: Commander, 5th Special Attack Flotilla
13 May 1945: Posthumously promoted to *Rear-Admiral*

Vice-Admiral (Engineer) **Baron Jiro MIYAHARA** (7 Jul 1858 - 15 Jan 1918)
22 May 1900: Promoted to *General (Engineer)*
22 May 1900 - 28 Aug 1908: Chief of Bureau 4, Naval Shipbuilding Command
26 Jan 1906: Redesignated *Rear-Admiral (Engineer)*
8 Nov 1906: Promoted to *Vice-Admiral (Engineer)*

28 Aug 1908 - 27 Aug 1909:	Unassigned
27 Aug 1909:	Transferred to the reserve

Rear-Admiral **Sadatoki MIYAJI** (3 Jul 1861 - 26 Dec 1937)
10 Dec 1908 - 1 Dec 1910:	Commander, Kure Harbor
1 Dec 1910 - 17 Apr 1911:	Unassigned
17 Apr 1911:	Promoted to *Rear-Admiral*
17 Apr 1911:	Transferred to the reserve

Rear-Admiral **Tamisaburo MIYAJI** (21 Feb 1876 - 8 Feb 1961)
1 Oct 1920 - 1 Dec 1922:	Chief of Bureau 7, Naval Shipbuilding Command
1 Dec 1921:	Promoted to *Rear-Admiral*
1 Dec 1922 - 1 Oct 1923:	Commandant, Submarine School
1 Oct 1923 - 1 Dec 1923:	Attached to Naval General Staff
1 Dec 1923 - 25 Feb 1924:	Unassigned
25 Feb 1924:	Transferred to the reserve

Rear-Admiral (Paymaster) **Goro MIYAKAWA** (18 Aug 1893 - 8 Jul 1944)
4 May 1944 - 8 Jul 1944:	Paymaster-General, Central Pacific Area Fleet
	Paymaster-General, 14th Air Fleet
8 Jul 1944:	Posthumously promoted to *Rear-Admiral (Paymaster)*

Vice-Admiral **Kunimoto MIYAKAWA** (17 Sep 1871 - 13 Mar 1952)
1 Dec 1916 - 1 Jun 1919:	Chief of Engine Construction Bureau, Kure Navy Yard
1 Dec 1918:	Promoted to *Rear-Admiral*
1 Jun 1919 - 1 Oct 1919:	Attached to Naval Technical Command
1 Oct 1919 - 1 Apr 1921:	Attached to Naval Shipbuilding Command
1 Apr 1921 - 10 Nov 1922:	Chief Engineer Officer, Kure Naval District
10 Nov 1922 - 1 Dec 1922:	Attached to Naval General Staff
1 Dec 1922:	Promoted to *Vice-Admiral*
1 Dec 1922 - 31 Mar 1923:	Unassigned
31 Mar 1923:	Transferred to the reserve

Rear-Admiral (Surgeon) **Masao MIYAKAWA** (3 Jun 1880 - 3 May 1960)
1 Dec 1924 - 1 Dec 1925:	Chief Medical Officer, Combined Fleet, Chief Medical Officer, 1st Fleet
1 Dec 1925 - 10 Dec 1928:	Director, Sasebo Naval Hospital, Chief Surgeon, Sasebo Naval District
1 Dec 1926:	Promoted to *Rear-Admiral (Surgeon)*
10 Dec 1928 - 20 Dec 1928:	Attached to Naval General Staff
25 Dec 1928:	Transferred to the reserve

Rear-Admiral **Kozo MIYAKE** (7 May 1863 - 15 Jun 1929)
10 Dec 1908 - 3 Feb 1909: Chief Engineer Officer, Ryojun Naval District
3 Feb 1909 - 3 Feb 1912: Unassigned
3 Feb 1912: Promoted to *Rear-Admiral*
3 Feb 1912: Transferred to the reserve

Rear-Admiral (Paymaster) **Masamitsu MIYAMOTO** (30 Nov 1895 -1 Apr 1944)
25 Sep 1943 - 1 Apr 1944: Paymaster-General, Combined Fleet
1 Apr 1944: Posthumously promoted to
Rear-Admiral (Paymaster)

Rear-Admiral **Sadachika MIYAMOTO** (31 Oct 1888 - 6 Aug 1945)
24 Aug 1943 - 6 Aug 1945: Commander, Chinkai Defense Force
6 Aug 1945: Posthumously promoted to *Rear-Admiral*

Rear-Admiral **Rekizo MIYAMURA** (3 Nov 1879 - 26 Jan 1958)
1 Dec 1923: Promoted to *Rear-Admiral*
1 Dec 1923 - 20 Apr 1925: Commander, Kure Defense Force
20 Apr 1925 - 20 Jul 1925: Attached to Kure Naval District
20 Jul 1925 - 20 Nov 1925: Attached to Naval General Staff
20 Nov 1925 - 16 Dec 1925: Unassigned
16 Dec 1925: Transferred to the reserve

Rear-Admiral (Surgeon) **Nobuharu MIYAO** (28 Apr 1872 - 26 May 1935)
7 Jun 1921 - 1 Dec 1922: Chief of Bureau 2, Sasebo Naval Hospital
1 Dec 1922: Promoted to *Rear-Admiral (Surgeon)*
1 Dec 1922 - 10 Dec 1922: Attached to Yokosuka Naval District
10 Dec 1922 - 31 Mar 1923: Unassigned
31 Mar 1923: Transferred to the reserve

Vice-Admiral **Naoki MIYAOKA** (3 Jul 1857 - 14 Aug 1930)
5 Feb 1906 - 9 Sep 1907: Adjutant, Inspector for Korea
28 May 1906: Promoted to *Rear-Admiral*
9 Sep 1907 - 1 Dec 1910: Commander, Chinkai Defense Force
1 Dec 1910 - 1 Dec 1911: Unassigned
1 Dec 1911: Promoted to *Vice-Admiral*
1 Dec 1911: Transferred to the reserve

Rear-Admiral **Sukejiro MIYASAKA** (1 Jul 1880 - 2 Apr 1960)
1 Dec 1926: Promoted to *Rear-Admiral*
1 Dec 1926 - 11 Apr 1927: Chief of Scientific Research Bureau, Technical Research Department
11 Apr 1927 - 30 Nov 1929: Chief of Aircraft Research Bureau, Technical Research Department

30 Nov 1929 - 15 Dec 1929:	Attached to Naval Shipbuilding Command
25 Dec 1929:	Transferred to the reserve

Vice-Admiral **Giichi MIYATA** (5 Feb 1889 - 27 Nov 1960)

15 Nov 1935:	Promoted to *Rear-Admiral*
15 Nov 1935 - 1 Aug 1936:	Commander, Yokosuka Guard Flotilla
1 Aug 1936 - 1 Dec 1936:	Commander, 9th Escort Flotilla
1 Dec 1936 - 1 Dec 1937:	Commander, 12th Escort Flotilla
1 Dec 1937 - 18 Apr 1938:	Commandant, Naval Gunnery School
18 Apr 1938 - 20 Apr 1938:	Attached to Naval General Staff
20 Apr 1938 - 15 Nov 1938:	Commander, 2nd Combined Marine Division
15 Nov 1938 - 15 Nov 1939:	Commander, 3rd Auxiliary Base Force
15 Nov 1939:	Promoted to *Vice-Admiral*
15 Nov 1939 - 15 Mar 1940:	Attached to Naval General Staff
31 Mar 1940:	Transferred to the reserve
15 Nov 1941 - 17 Nov 1941:	Recalled; Attached to Yokosuka Naval District
17 Nov 1941 - 15 Mar 1943:	Commandant, Yokosuka Naval Gunnery School
20 Mar 1943:	Demobilized

Rear-Admiral **Hajime MIYATA** (9 Jul 1890 - 6 Jul 1982)

15 Nov 1938:	Promoted to *Rear-Admiral*
15 Nov 1938 - 15 Nov 1939:	Chief of Mining Bureau, Navy Fuel Yard
15 Nov 1939 - 15 Oct 1941:	Chief of Supply Bureau, Yokosuka Naval District
15 Oct 1941 - 25 Oct 1941:	Attached to Naval General Staff
27 Oct 1941:	Transferred to the reserve

Rear-Admiral **Shigetoshi MIYAZAKI** (29 Apr 1897 - 7 Aug 1942)

20 Apr 1942 - 7 Aug 1942:	Commander, Yokohama Defense Force
7 Aug 1942:	Posthumously promoted to *Rear-Admiral*

Rear-Admiral **Takeji MIYAZAKI** (9 Jan 1896 - 24 Oct 1943)

20 Jul 1943 - 25 Sep 1943:	Commander, 2nd Submarine Division
25 Sep 1943 - 24 Oct 1943:	Staff Officer, 6th (Submarine) Fleet
24 Oct 1943:	Posthumously promoted to *Rear-Admiral*

Rear-Admiral **Torakichi MIYAZAKI** (16 Aug 1877 - 31 Jan 1926)

13 Aug 1923 - 1 Apr 1925:	Commander, Hiro Navy Yard
20 Dec 1924:	Promoted to *Rear-Admiral*
1 Apr 1925 - 25 May 1925:	Attached to Kure Naval District
25 May 1925 - 16 Dec 1925:	Unassigned
16 Dec 1925:	Transferred to the reserve

Vice-Admiral **Shutoku MIYAZATO** (4 Dec 1889 - 7 Jun 1952)
5 Sep 1941 - 1 Nov 1941:	Captain, Battleship *"Yamato"*
15 Oct 1941:	Promoted to *Rear-Admiral*
1 Nov 1941 - 5 Nov 1941:	Attached to Kure Naval District
5 Nov 1941 - 10 Mar 1943:	Chief of Personnel, Kure Naval District
10 Mar 1943 - 30 Dec 1944:	Commander, 11th Auxiliary Naval Facility
15 Oct 1944:	Promoted to *Vice-Admiral*
30 Dec 1944 - 20 Mar 1945:	Chief of Shipping Safety Command, Department of the Navy
20 Mar 1945 - 15 Sep 1945:	Chief of Shipping Safety Division, Joint General Staff

Rear-Admiral **Takezo MIYAZAWA** (1 Feb 1895 - 14 Jan 1947)
15 Sep 1942 - 1 Feb 1944:	Chief of Sonic Research Bureau, Technical Research Department
1 May 1943:	Promoted to *Rear-Admiral*
1 Feb 1944 - 15 Feb 1945:	Attached to Technical Research Department
15 Feb 1945 - 30 Sep 1945:	Attached to 2nd Technical Arsenal

Rear-Admiral **Hisashi MIYOSHI** (1 Oct 1895 - 30 Oct 1987)
1 May 1944 - 15 May 1945:	Commander, 13th Air Division
1 May 1945:	Promoted to *Rear-Admiral*
15 May 1945 - 17 Aug 1945:	Attached to Yokosuka Naval District
17 Aug 1945 - 1 Sep 1945:	Commander, Tokyo Guard Division
1 Sep 1945 - 15 Oct 1945:	Attached to Naval General Staff
15 Oct 1945 - 30 Nov 1945:	Deputy Chief of Staff, Yokosuka Naval District

Rear-Admiral **Katsumi MIYOSHI** (4 Feb 1854 - 7 Feb 1901)
20 May 1900:	Promoted to *Rear-Admiral*
20 May 1900 - 1 Aug 1900:	C-in-C, Yokosuka Naval District Fleet
1 Aug 1900 - 7 Feb 1901:	Member, Admirals Committee

Rear-Admiral **Teruhiko MIYOSHI** (15 Nov 1893 - 8 Jun 1943)
10 Mar 1943- 5 Jun 1943:	Captain, Battleship *"Mutsu"*
5 Jun 1943 - 8 Jun 1943:	Staff officer, Combined Fleet
8 Jun 1943:	Posthumously promoted to *Rear-Admiral*

Rear-Admiral **Tadasu MIZOGUCHI** (22 Aug 1895 - 1 Dec 1945)
27 Oct 1943 - 1 Dec 1945:	Chief of Politics Bureau, Kainan I Naval Special Task Office
1 Dec 1945:	Posthumously promoted to *Rear-Admiral*

Rear-Admiral **Seiji MIZUI** (8 Sep 1889 - 27 Apr 1963)
25 Sep 1941 - 10 Aug 1942:	Supervisor for Construction & Ordnance, Naval Shipbuilding Command
1 May 1942:	Promoted to *Rear-Admiral*
10 Aug 1942 - 10 Sep 1942:	Commander, Maizuru Defense Flotilla
10 Sep 1942 - 25 Apr 1943:	Commander, Kure Defense Flotilla
25 Apr 1943 - 1 May 1943:	Attached to Yokosuka Naval District
1 May 1943 - 20 Jan 1944:	Commander, 52nd Auxiliary Base Force
20 Jan 1944 - 5 Jun 1945:	Commander, 18th Escort Flotilla
5 Jun 1945 - 10 Jun 1945:	Attached to Kure Naval District
10 Jun 1945 - 1 Nov 1945:	Commander, 81st Escort Flotilla

Rear-Admiral **Hajime MIZUMACHI** (24 Oct 1867 - 18 Nov 1936)
1 Dec 1913 - 1 Dec 1914:	Captain, Battleship *"Kashima"*
1 Dec 1914 - 1 Dec 1915:	Unassigned
1 Dec 1915:	Promoted to *Rear-Admiral*
1 Dec 1915:	Transferred to the reserve

Rear-Admiral **Akiyoshi MIZUMOTO** (? - 8 Jul 1944)
10 Sep 1943 - 8 Jul 1944:	Chief of Saipan Branch, 4th Supply Bureau
8 Jul 1944:	Posthumously promoted to *Rear-Admiral*

Rear-Admiral **Eiichi MIZUNO** (12 Sep 1889 - 26 Apr 1961)
1 Dec 1939 - 15 Oct 1941:	Chief of Shipping Bureau, Maizuru Naval District
15 Nov 1940:	Promoted to *Rear-Admiral*
15 Oct 1941 - 15 Dec 1941:	Chief of Shipping Bureau, Kure Naval District
15 Dec 1941 - 10 Nov 1942:	Commander, 2nd Naval Facility
10 Nov 1942 - 1 Jun 1943:	Chief Supervisor for Construction & Ordnance, Naval Shipbuilding Command
1 Jun 1943 - 20 Jun 1943:	Attached to Naval General Staff
25 Jun 1943:	Transferred to the reserve

Rear-Admiral **Junichi MIZUNO** (26 Mar 1887 - 9 Jan 1957)
15 Nov 1939:	Promoted to *Rear-Admiral*
15 Nov 1939 - 20 Nov 1941:	Commander, Yokosuka Sailors Corps
20 Nov 1941 - 1 Sep 1942:	Commander, Yokosuka Guard Force
1 Sep 1942 - 10 Oct 1942:	Attached to Naval General Staff
15 Oct 1942:	Transferred to the reserve
10 Aug 1944 - 15 Sep 1945:	Recalled; Commander, Buzan Sailors Corps

Rear-Admiral **Kokichi MIZUNO** (23 Mar 1886 - 10 Nov 1944)
1 Oct 1943 - 10 Nov 1944:	Commander of Minesweeping, Auxiliary Cruiser *"Gokoku-maru"*
10 Nov 1944:	Posthumously promoted to *Rear-Admiral*

Rear-Admiral **Kyosuke MIZUNO** (9 Sep 1893 - 28 Aug 1943)
20 Aug 1943 - 29 Aug 1943:	Staff officer, 8th Fleet
28 Aug 1943:	Posthumously promoted to *Rear-Admiral*

Rear-Admiral **Shojiro MIZUSAKI** (14 Jan 1889 - 13 Dec 1960)
10 Oct 1943 - 1 Sep 1944:	Chief of Osaka Area Personnel Bureau
1 May 1944:	Promoted to *Rear-Admiral*
1 Sep 1944 - 10 Nov 1945:	Chief of Personnel Bureau, Osaka Guard District

Vice-Admiral (Engineer) **Chimakichi MIZUTANI** (3 Nov 1867 - 22 Aug 1942)
9 May 1911 - 1 Apr 1922:	Chief of Mining Station, Government of Korea
1 Jun 1917:	Promoted to *Rear-Admiral*
1 Apr 1922 - 10 Nov 1922:	Chief of Mining Bureau, Navy Fuel Yard
10 Nov 1922 - 1 Dec 1922:	Attached to Naval General Staff
1 Dec 1922:	Promoted to *Vice-Admiral*
1 Dec 1922 - 31 Mar 1923:	Unassigned
31 Mar 1923:	Transferred to the reserve

Vice-Admiral **Mitsutaro MIZUTANI** (7 Sep 1876 - 26 Mar 1962)
1 Apr 1921 - 10 Nov 1922:	Chief of Briquette Bureau, Navy Fuel Yard
1 Jun 1922:	Promoted to *Rear-Admiral*
10 Nov 1922 - 10 Nov 1923:	Chief of Mining Bureau, Navy Fuel Yard
10 Nov 1923 - 1 Dec 1923:	Attached to Kure Naval District
1 Dec 1923 - 1 Dec 1924:	Commander, Navy Fuel Yard
1 Dec 1924 - 1 Jun 1925:	Attached to Naval General Staff
1 Jun 1925 - 16 Dec 1925:	Unassigned
15 Dec 1925:	Promoted to *Vice-Admiral*
16 Dec 1925:	Transferred to the reserve

Rear-Admiral **Yoshihiko MIZUTANI** (28 Dec 1866 - 20 Aug 1943)
10 Nov 1903 - 29 Jun 1912:	Chief of Engine Construction Bureau, Kure Navy Yard
1 Dec 1910:	Promoted to *Rear-Admiral*
29 Jun 1912 - 10 Feb 1913:	Unassigned
10 Feb 1913:	Transferred to the reserve

Vice-Admiral **Baron Heiji MOCHIHARA** (12 Dec 1851 - 25 Feb 1920)
7 Jul 1903:	Promoted to *Rear-Admiral*
7 Jul 1903 - 12 Jan 1904:	Chief of Reserve Bureau, Maizuru Naval District
12 Jan 1904 - 12 Dec 1905:	Commander, Chinkai Defense Force
12 Dec 1905 - 12 Mar 1907:	Commander, Ominato Guard District
12 Mar 1907:	Promoted to *Vice-Admiral*
12 Mar 1907 - 8 May 1907:	Member, Admirals Committee

8 May 1907 - 31 Oct 1907:   Unassigned
31 Oct 1907:   Transferred to the reserve

Vice-Admiral (Paymaster) **Tomokazu MOGI** (1 Nov 1889 - 29 Mar 1960)
1 Dec 1936:   Promoted to *Rear-Admiral (Paymaster)*
1 Dec 1936 - 15 Nov 1938:   Chief of Accounting Bureau, Kure Navy Yard
15 Nov 1938 - 15 Nov 1940:   Paymaster-General, Sasebo Naval District
15 Nov 1940:   Promoted to *Vice-Admiral (Paymaster)*
15 Nov 1940 - 16 Dec 1940:   Attached to Naval General Staff
21 Dec 1940:   Transferred to the reserve

Vice-Admiral **Shinichi MOIZUMI** (5 Apr 1888 - 26 Nov 1969)
1 Dec 1937:   Promoted to *Rear-Admiral*
1 Dec 1937 - 15 Nov 1940:   Commandant, Naval Navigation School
15 Nov 1940 - 10 Apr 1941:   Attached to Naval General Staff
10 Apr 1941 - 11 Aug 1941:   Commander, 5th Naval Base Force
11 Aug 1941 - 15 Jun 1942:   Commander, 4th Naval Base Force
15 Oct 1941:   Promoted to *Vice-Admiral*
10 Apr 1942 - 15 Jun 1942:   Commander, 2nd Maritime Escort Force
15 Jun 1942 - 25 Aug 1942:   Attached to Naval General Staff
1 Sep 1942:   Transferred to the reserve

Rear-Admiral **Isao MONAI**   (12 Oct 1884 - 16 May 1936)
1 Dec 1931:   Promoted to *Rear-Admiral*
1 Dec 1931 - 1 Dec 1932:   Chief of Shipping Bureau, Sasebo Naval District
1 Dec 1932 - 10 Dec 1932:   Attached to Naval General Staff
15 Dec 1932:   Transferred to the reserve

Vice-Admiral **Tei MONZEN**   (15 Apr 1892 - 9 Jun 1944)
20 Jul 1943 - 20 May 1944:   Commander, Maizuru Defense Force
1 May 1944:   Promoted to *Rear-Admiral*
20 May 1944 - 1 Jun 1944:   Staff Officer, Maritime Escort Fleet
1 Jun 1944 - 9 Jun 1944:   Commander, 3rd Convoy HQ
9 Jun 1944:   Posthumously promoted to *Vice-Admiral*

Vice-Admiral **Etsutaro MORI**   (14 Sep 1867 - 3 Nov 1957)
1 Dec 1914:   Promoted to *Rear-Admiral*
1 Dec 1914 - 1 Dec 1918:   Chief of Bureau 2, Naval Technical Command
13 Dec 1915 - 1 Dec 1916:   Chief of Bureau 3, Naval Technical Command
1 Dec 1918:   Promoted to *Vice-Admiral*
1 Dec 1918 - 15 Jan 1919:   Member, Admirals Committee
15 Jan 1919 - 4 Feb 1919:   Unassigned
4 Feb 1919:   Transferred to the reserve

Rear-Admiral **Hatsuji MORI** (5 Jun 1878 - 30 Apr 1963)
1 Dec 1922 - 1 Sep 1923: Captain, Battleship *"Aki"*
1 Sep 1923 - 1 Dec 1923: Attached to Yokosuka Naval District
1 Dec 1923: Promoted to *Rear-Admiral*
1 Dec 1923 - 25 Mar 1924: Unassigned
25 Mar 1924: Transferred to the reserve

Rear-Admiral **Ichibei MORI** (24 Jul 1858 - 2 Jun 1915)
22 Nov 1906 - 10 Dec 1908: Chief of Reserve Bureau, Kure Naval District
28 Aug 1908: Promoted to *Rear-Admiral*
10 Dec 1908 - 1 Dec 1909: Commander, Kure Torpedo Corps
1 Dec 1909 - 2 Sep 1911: C-in-C, Kure Reserve Fleet
2 Sep 1911 - 2 Sep 1912: Unassigned
2 Sep 1912: Transferred to the reserve

Rear-Admiral **Kan MORI** (18 Feb 1898 - 7 May 1944)
28 Jan 1944 - 7 May 1944: Chief, 1st Mobilization Bureau
7 May 1944: Posthumously promoted to *Rear-Admiral*

Vice-Admiral **Kunizo MORI** (18 Dec 1890 - 22 Apr 1949)
10 Mar 1942 - 25 Nov 1942: Commander, 23rd Naval Base Force
1 May 1942: Promoted to *Rear-Admiral*
25 Nov 1942 - 21 Dec 1942: Attached to Yokosuka Naval District
21 Dec 1942 - 24 Aug 1943: Commander, Yokosuka Guard Force
24 Aug 1943 - 9 Sep 1943: Staff officer, 8th Fleet
9 Sep 1943 - 25 Oct 1943: Commander, 7th Auxiliary Base Force
25 Oct 1943 - 15 Nov 1943: Staff officer, 8th Fleet
15 Nov 1943 - 15 Feb 1944: Attached to Yokosuka Naval District
15 Feb 1944 - Oct 1945: Commander, Chichijima Area Base Force
1 May 1945: Promoted to *Vice-Admiral*

Rear-Admiral **Raizo MORI** (15 Mar 1881 - 1 Apr 1945)
1 Dec 1922 - 1 Oct 1923: Captain, Light Cruiser *"Kiso"*
1 Oct 1923 - 15 Feb 1924: Attached to Yokosuka Naval District
15 Feb 1924 - 2 Mar 1925: Attached to Naval General Staff
1 Dec 1924: Promoted to *Rear-Admiral*
20 Mar 1925: Transferred to the reserve

Rear-Admiral **Ryo MORI** (25 Oct 1893 - 8 Jul 1944)
15 Dec 1943 - 8 Jul 1944: Commander of Minesweeping, Seaplane Tender *"Sanyo-maru"*
8 Jul 1944: Posthumously promoted to *Rear-Admiral*

Rear-Admiral **Takeo MORI** (4 Feb 1894 - 26 Oct 1981)
20 Oct 1942 - 10 Feb 1944: Chief of Chemical Bureau, 2nd Navy Fuel Yard
1 Nov 1943: Promoted to *Rear-Admiral*
10 Feb 1944 - 4 Mar 1944: Staff officer, 2nd Southern Expeditionary Fleet
4 Mar 1944 - Oct 1945: Commander, 102nd Naval Facility

Rear-Admiral **Tokuji MORI** (24 Sep 1891 - 3 Jun 1983)
10 Sep 1941 - 5 May 1943: Chief of Personnel, Maizuru Naval District
1 May 1942: Promoted to *Rear-Admiral*
5 May 1943 - 18 Aug 1944: Staff officer, China Area Fleet
18 Aug 1944 - Oct 1945: Commander, Shanghai Area Auxiliary Base Force

Rear-Admiral **Tomoichi MORI** (28 Feb 1893 - 23 Jan 1959)
20 Oct 1942 - 4 Nov 1942: Attached to Naval General Staff
1 Nov 1942: Promoted to *Rear-Admiral*
4 Nov 1942 - 5 Nov 1942: Staff officer, 5th Fleet
5 Nov 1942 - 8 Jun 1943: Commander, 1st Destroyer Flotilla
8 Jun 1943 - 2 May 1944: Attached to Yokosuka Naval District
2 May 1944 - 10 May 1945: Chief of Mine Research Bureau, Yokosuka Navy Yard
10 May 1945 - 10 Jul 1945: Commander, Kure Training Flotilla
10 Jul 1945 - 6 Sep 1945: Attached to Yokosuka Naval District

Rear-Admiral **Yoshiomi MORI** (25 Mar 1868 - 7 Oct 1949)
30 Oct 1914 - 1 Dec 1916: Adjutant, Governor of Korea
1 Dec 1914: Promoted to *Rear-Admiral*
1 Dec 1916 - 1 Jun 1917: Member, Admirals Committee
1 Jun 1917 - 1 Jun 1918: Unassigned
1 Jun 1918: Transferred to the reserve

Vice-Admiral **Yoshitaro MORI** (3 Feb 1863 - 24 Jun 1929)
23 May 1910 - 29 May 1914: Naval Attache, China
1 Dec 1910: Promoted to *Rear-Admiral*
29 May 1914 - 1 Dec 1914: Unassigned
1 Dec 1914: Promoted to *Vice-Admiral*
1 Dec 1914: Transferred to the reserve

Rear-Admiral **Akira MORIKAWA** (23 Jun 1892 - 8 Jun 1950)
15 Oct 1942 - 5 May 1945: Commander, 41st Air Arsenal
1 May 1944: Promoted to *Rear-Admiral*
5 May 1945 - 1 Jun 1945: Attached to Yokosuka Naval District
1 Jun 1945 - 15 Sep 1945: Attached to Naval Air Command

Rear-Admiral **Matao MORIKAWA** (? - 7 Sep 1942)
10 Sep 1941 - 7 Sep 1942:	Captain, Minelayer *"Itsukushima"*
7 Sep 1942:	Posthumously promoted to *Rear-Admiral*

Rear-Admiral **Jo MORIMOTO** (23 Jul 1886 - 1 Nov 1969)
14 Feb 1933 - 15 Nov 1933:	Captain, Heavy Cruiser *"Haguro"*
15 Nov 1933 - 15 Nov 1934:	Attached to Yokosuka Naval District
15 Nov 1934:	Promoted to *Rear-Admiral*
15 Nov 1934 - 10 Dec 1934:	Attached to Naval General Staff
15 Dec 1934:	Transferred to the reserve
10 Aug 1944 - 15 Aug 1944:	Recalled; Staff officer, Combined Air Division
15 Aug 1944 - 1 Mar 1945:	Commander, Shiga Air Division
1 Mar 1945 - 15 Mar 1945:	Attached to Yokosuka Naval District
15 Mar 1945 - 10 Jul 1945:	Commander, Kagoshima Air Division
10 Jul 1945 - 15 Sep 1945:	Commander, Kurashiki Air Division

Rear-Admiral **Yoshihiro MORIMOTO** (8 Oct 1871 - 28 Oct 1926)
7 Nov 1919 - 20 Nov 1920:	Captain, Battleship *"Satsuma"*
20 Nov 1920 - 1 Dec 1920:	Attached to Maizuru Naval District
1 Dec 1920:	Promoted to *Rear-Admiral*
1 Dec 1920 - 1 Aug 1921:	Unassigned
1 Aug 1921:	Transferred to the reserve

Rear-Admiral **Sorokuro MORINO** (18 May 1890 - 6 Feb 1944)
20 Dec 1943 - 6 Feb 1944:	Commander, 63rd Submarine Chaser Division
6 Feb 1944:	Posthumously promoted to *Rear-Admiral*

Vice-Admiral (Paymaster) **Taneo MORISHIMA** (14 Mar 1891 - 18 Oct 1945)
1 Apr 1940 - 10 May 1941:	Chief of Section 4, Accounting Bureau, Department of the Navy
15 Nov 1940:	Promoted to *Rear-Admiral (Paymaster)*
10 May 1941 - 15 May 1941:	Attached to Naval General Staff
15 May 1941 - 1 May 1943:	Attached to Accounting Bureau, Department of the Navy
1 May 1943 - 10 Dec 1944:	Paymaster-General, Yokosuka Naval District
1 May 1944:	Promoted to *Vice-Admiral (Paymaster)*
10 Dec 1944 - 15 Dec 1944:	Attached to Naval General Staff
20 Dec 1944:	Transferred to the reserve

Rear-Admiral **Nobuei MORISHITA** (2 Feb 1895 - 17 Jun 1960)
15 Jan 1944 - 25 Nov 1944:	Captain, Battleship *"Yamato"*
15 Oct 1944:	Promoted to *Rear-Admiral*
25 Nov 1944 - 20 Apr 1945:	Chief of Staff, 2nd Fleet

20 Apr 1945 - 1 May 1945:	Attached to Naval General Staff
1 May 1945 - 15 Sep 1945:	Deputy Chief of Staff, Shipping Supervisor, Joint General Staff
15 Sep 1945 - 30 Nov 1945:	Commander, Kure Sailors Corps
25 Oct 1945 - 30 Nov 1945:	Commander, Otake Sailors Corps

Vice-Admiral **Kanichi MORITA** (31 Aug 1894 - 28 Apr 1987)

1 Oct 1941 - 25 Aug 1942:	Chief of Oil Refining Bureau, 3rd Navy Fuel Yard
15 Oct 1941:	Promoted to *Rear-Admiral*
25 Aug 1942 - 1 Sep 1942:	Attached to Naval General Staff
1 Sep 1942 - 26 Jun 1944:	Commander, 102nd Navy Fuel Yard
26 Jun 1944 - 15 Jan 1945:	Commandant, Naval Engineering School
15 Oct 1944:	Promoted to *Vice-Admiral*
15 Jan 1945 - 1 May 1945:	Chief Supervisor for Construction & Ordnance, Naval Shipbuilding Command
1 May 1945 - 15 Nov 1945:	Chief of Supply Bureau

Rear-Admiral **Minoru MORITA** (8 Oct 1882 - 30 Aug 1942)

1 Dec 1925 - 1 Dec 1926:	Chief of Section 1, Supply Bureau, Department of the Navy
1 Dec 1926:	Promoted to *Rear-Admiral*
1 Dec 1926 - 20 Mar 1927:	Attached to Naval General Staff
20 Mar 1927 - 10 Apr 1927:	Unassigned
10 Apr 1927:	Transferred to the reserve

Rear-Admiral **Teizo MORITA** (27 Feb 1896 - 8 Nov 1973)

1 Jul 1944 - Oct 1945:	Commander, 4th Naval Facility
10 Oct 1944 - Oct 1945:	Chief Engineer, 4th Fleet
1 May 1945:	Promoted to *Rear-Admiral*

Rear-Admiral **Setsuji MORIYA** (25 Jan 1903 - 25 Oct 1944)

25 Dec 1943 - 25 Oct 1944:	Captain, Destroyer *"Nowaki"*
25 Oct 1944:	Posthumously promoted to *Rear-Admiral*

Vice-Admiral **Keizaburo MORIYAMA** (20 Jun 1870 - 24 May 1944)

19 Nov 1914 - 7 May 1915:	Commander, American Detachment
1 Dec 1914:	Promoted to *Rear-Admiral*
7 May 1915 - 6 Aug 1915:	Attached to Naval General Staff
6 Aug 1915 - 13 Dec 1915:	Commander, 2nd Escort Flotilla
13 Dec 1915 - 1 Nov 1916:	Chief of Bureau 4, Naval General Staff
1 Nov 1916 - 13 Jun 1918:	Chief of Bureau 3, Naval General Staff
13 Jun 1918 - 21 Jul 1918:	Commander, 2nd Escort Flotilla
21 Jul 1918 - 20 Aug 1918:	Commander, 1st Escort Flotilla

20 Aug 1918 - 1 Dec 1919:	Commander, 2nd Escort Flotilla
1 Dec 1918:	Promoted to *Vice-Admiral*
1 Dec 1919 - 1 Oct 1920:	Commander, Ominato Guard District
1 Oct 1920 - 1 Dec 1922:	Commander, Kure Navy Yard
1 Dec 1922 - 10 Dec 1922:	Member, Admirals Committee
10 Dec 1922 - 1 Apr 1923:	Unassigned
1 Apr 1923:	Transferred to the reserve

Vice-Admiral **Matsuo MORIZUMI** (24 May 1891 - 2 Sep 1945)

15 Nov 1940:	Promoted to *Rear-Admiral*
15 Nov 1940 - 10 Nov 1942:	Chief Supervisor for Construction & Ordnance, Naval Shipbuilding Command
10 Nov 1942 - 10 Mar 1944:	Chief of Electronic Research Bureau, Technical Research Department
10 Mar 1944 - 1 May 1944:	Commander, Maizuru Navy Yard
1 May 1944:	Promoted to *Vice-Admiral*
1 May 1944 - 10 Aug 1945:	Chief Supervisor for Construction & Ordnance, Naval Shipbuilding Command
10 Aug 1945 - 2 Sep 1945:	Kinki Area Supervisor, Department of Military Supply

Vice-Admiral **Yoriyuki MOROOKA** (19 Mar 1851 - 14 Aug 1914)

27 Dec 1897:	Promoted to *Rear-Admiral*
27 Dec 1897 - 10 Nov 1898:	Deputy Chief of the Naval General Staff, Member, Admirals Committee
10 Nov 1898 - 20 May 1900:	Chief of Bureau of Naval Affairs, Department of the Navy, Member, Admirals Committee
20 May 1900 - 3 Jul 1901:	Chief of Naval Training Command
3 Jul 1901 - 24 Apr 1902:	C-in-C, Readiness Fleet
24 Apr 1902:	Promoted to *Vice-Admiral*
24 Apr 1902 - 27 Nov 1904:	Unassigned
27 Nov 1904:	Transferred to the reserve

Rear-Admiral **Takeshi MOTOIZUMI** (12 Oct 1888 - 24 Jul 1965)

4 Nov 1939 - 15 Oct 1940:	Attached to Naval General Staff
15 Nov 1939:	Promoted to *Rear-Admiral*
15 Oct 1940 - 15 Nov 1940:	Staff officer, 4th Fleet
15 Nov 1940 - 15 Jan 1941:	Commander, 5th Naval Base Force
15 Jan 1941 - 21 Dec 1942:	Attached to Naval General Staff
21 Dec 1942:	Transferred to the reserve

Rear-Admiral (Paymaster) **Naoto MOTOMATSU** (1 Feb 1883 - 22 May 1954)
1 Dec 1932 - 1 Dec 1933:	Accounting Supervisor for Construction & Ordnance, Naval Shipbuilding Command
15 Nov 1933:	Promoted to *Rear-Admiral (Paymaster)*
1 Dec 1933 - 1 Dec 1936:	Paymaster-General, Kure Naval District
1 Dec 1936 - 15 Dec 1936:	Attached to Naval General Staff
22 Dec 1936:	Transferred to the reserve

Rear-Admiral **Hanzo MOTOZAWA** (? - 25 Oct 1944)
10 Feb 1944 - 25 Oct 1944:	Chief Engineer Officer, Battleship *"Yamashiro"*
25 Oct 1944:	Posthumously promoted to *Rear-Admiral*

Vice-Admiral **Yaichi MUKAI** (8 Jul 1867 - 4 Nov 1941)
27 May 1914 - 13 Dec 1915:	Acting Chief of Naval Personnel
13 Dec 1915 - 1 Dec 1916:	Captain, Battleship *"Fuso"*
1 Dec 1916:	Promoted to *Rear-Admiral*
1 Dec 1916 - 10 Feb 1923:	Aide-de-camp to the Emperor
1 Dec 1920:	Promoted to *Vice-Admiral*
10 Feb 1923 - 1 Mar 1923:	Member, Admirals Committee
31 Mar 1923:	Transferred to the reserve

Vice-Admiral **Hitoshi MUKAIYAMA** (29 Oct 1891 - 5 Jul 1978)
15 Nov 1935 - 15 Nov 1938:	Chief of Electronic Research Bureau, Technical Research Department
1 Dec 1936:	Promoted to *Rear-Admiral*
15 Nov 1938 - 15 Nov 1940:	Chief of Ordnance Bureau, Yokosuka Navy Yard
15 Nov 1940:	Promoted to *Vice-Admiral*
15 Nov 1940 - 16 Dec 1940:	Attached to Naval Shipbuilding Command
21 Dec 1940:	Transferred to the reserve

Vice-Admiral **Baron Shinkichi MUKAIYAMA** (14 Sep 1856 - 18 Dec 1910)
6 Dec 1900 - 28 Dec 1903:	Chief of Staff, Yokosuka Naval District
24 May 1902:	Promoted to *Rear-Admiral*
28 Dec 1903 - 10 May 1905:	Commander, Maizuru Naval Yard
10 May 1905 - 28 Aug 1908:	Commander, Sasebo Naval Yard
13 Nov 1905:	Promoted to *Vice-Admiral*
28 Aug 1908 - 1 Dec 1909:	Commander, Takeshiki Guard District
1 Dec 1909 - 18 Dec 1910:	Unassigned

Rear-Admiral **Kinichi MUKODA** (6 Oct 1881 - 5 May 1953)
1 Dec 1926:	Promoted to *Rear-Admiral*
1 Dec 1926 - 1 Apr 1928:	Chief of Personnel Bureau, Kure Naval District
1 Apr 1928 - 10 Dec 1928:	C-in-C, 2nd Expeditionary Fleet

10 Dec 1928 - 15 Sep 1929:	Attached to Naval General Staff
30 Sep 1929:	Transferred to the reserve

Vice-Admiral (Surgeon) **Yoshihiro MUKOYAMA** (9 Oct 1882 - 17 Jul 1955)
15 Nov 1933:	Promoted to *Rear-Admiral (Surgeon)*
15 Nov 1933 - 15 Nov 1934:	Director, Kure Naval Hospital, Chief Surgeon, Kure Naval District
15 Nov 1934 - 1 Dec 1937:	Commandant, Naval Medical School
1 Dec 1927:	Promoted to *Vice-Admiral (Surgeon)*
1 Dec 1937 - 15 Mar 1938:	Attached to Naval General Staff
25 Mar 1938:	Transferred to the reserve

Rear-Admiral **Hajime MUKUNO** (19 Dec 1893 - 22 Jun 1973)
20 Mar 1943 - 25 Jun 1943:	Chief of Shipping Bureau, Yokosuka Naval District
1 May 1943:	Promoted to *Rear-Admiral*
25 Jun 1943 - 1 Aug 1944:	Chief of Transport Bureau, Yokosuka Naval District
20 May 1944 - 1 Aug 1944:	Chief of Supply Bureau, Yokosuka Naval District
1 Aug 1944 - 15 Dec 1944:	Attached to Naval General Staff
20 Dec 1944:	Transferred to the reserve

Rear-Admiral **Shinnosuke MUNEYUKI** (22 Oct 1895 - 1 Mar 1941)
1 Oct 1940 - 1 Mar 1941:	Commander, Bihoro Air Division
1 Mar 1941:	Posthumously promoted to *Rear-Admiral*

Rear-Admiral **Chonosuke MURAKAMI** (20 Apr 1894 - 6 Oct 1944)
1 Apr 1943 - 20 May 1943:	Captain, Gunboat *"Eifuku-maru"*
20 May 1943 - 1 May 1944:	Attached to Yokosuka Naval District
1 May 1944 - 6 Oct 1944:	Unassigned
6 Oct 1944:	Posthumously promoted to *Rear-Admiral*

Rear-Admiral **Fusazo MURAKAMI** (1 Apr 1890 - 1 Jan 1967)
1 Apr 1942 - 1 May 1943:	Chief of Gunnery Bureau, Kure Navy Yard
1 May 1942:	Promoted to *Rear-Admiral*
1 May 1943 - 1 Aug 1944:	Commander, 3rd Navy Powder Yard
1 Aug 1944 - 1 Nov 1945:	Commander, 2nd Navy Powder Yard

Vice-Admiral (Paymaster) **Haruichi MURAKAMI** (25 Feb 1880 - 5 Jan 1945)
20 Apr 1928 - 30 Nov 1929:	Accounting Supervisor for Construction & Ordnance, Naval Shipbuilding Command
10 Dec 1928:	Promoted to *Rear-Admiral (Paymaster)*
30 Nov 1929 - 1 Dec 1932:	Paymaster-General, Yokosuka Naval District
1 Dec 1932 - 20 May 1933:	Commandant, Naval Paymaster Academy
20 May 1933 - 2 May 1938:	Chief of Naval Accounting Bureau

15 Nov 1933:	Promoted to *Vice-Admiral (Paymaster)*
2 May 1938 - 15 Oct 1938:	Attached to Naval General Staff
15 Oct 1938 - 21 Dec 1938:	Unassigned
21 Dec 1938:	Transferred to the reserve

Admiral **Kakuichi MURAKAMI** (1 Nov 1862 - 15 Nov 1927)

28 Aug 1908:	Promoted to *Rear-Admiral*
28 Aug 1908 - 1 Dec 1909:	Chief of Bureaus 1 & 2, Naval Training Command
19 Jul 1909 - 1 Dec 1912:	Chief of Bureau 1, Naval Shipbuilding Command
1 Dec 1912:	Promoted to *Vice-Admiral*
1 Dec 1912 - 17 Apr 1914:	Commander, Kure Navy Yard
17 Apr 1914 - 23 May 1914:	Unassigned
23 May 1914 - 1 Oct 1915:	Chief of Naval Shipbuilding Command, Member, Admirals Committee
1 Oct 1915 - 13 Dec 1915:	Chief of Naval Technical Command
13 Dec 1915 - 6 Apr 1917:	C-in-C, 3rd Fleet
6 Apr 1917 - 1 Dec 1919:	Chief of Naval Training Command
2 Jul 1918:	Promoted to *Admiral*
1 Dec 1919 - 27 Jul 1922:	Admiral Commanding, Kure Naval District
27 Jul 1922 - 7 Jan 1924:	Navy Councillor
7 Jan 1924 - 11 Jun 1924:	Minister of the Navy
11 Jun 1924 - 10 Dec 1924:	Navy Councillor
16 Dec 1924:	Transferred to the reserve

Rear-Admiral **Kanji MURAKAMI** (10 Feb 1875 - 3 Jun 1949)

20 Nov 1919 - 20 Nov 1920:	Chief Engineer Officer, 3rd Fleet
20 Nov 1920 - 1 Dec 1920:	Attached to Kure Naval District
1 Dec 1920:	Promoted to *Rear-Admiral*
1 Dec 1920 - 1 Aug 1921:	Unassigned
1 Aug 1921:	Transferred to the reserve

Vice-Admiral (Paymaster) **Baron Keijiro MURAKAMI** (4 Sep 1853 - 15 Feb 1929)

5 Jun 1897:	Promoted to *General (Paymaster)*
5 Jun 1897 - 15 Aug 1908:	Chief of Naval Accounting Bureau
26 May 1902:	Promoted to *General (Paymaster), Senior grade*
23 Sep 1919:	Redesignated *Vice-Admiral (Paymaster)*

Rear-Admiral **Sanji MURAKAMI** (7 Nov 1893 - 26 Jun 1980)

1 Sep 1942 - 1 Jun 1943:	Attached to Yokosuka Naval District
1 Nov 1942:	Promoted to *Rear-Admiral*
1 Jun 1943 - 30 Sep 1945:	Chief of Aviation Radio Bureau, Numazu Navy Yard

Rear-Admiral **Shinkichi MURAKAMI** (19 May 1868 - 30 Jan 1943)
1 Dec 1918 - 20 Nov 1919:	Captain, Armored Cruiser *"Hashidate"*
20 Nov 1919 - 1 Dec 1919:	Attached to Yokosuka Naval District
1 Dec 1919:	Promoted to *Rear-Admiral*
1 Dec 1919 - 1 Aug 1920:	Unassigned
1 Aug 1920:	Transferred to the reserve

Rear-Admiral **Takeo MURAKAMI** (20 Nov 1893 - 18 Feb 1988)
15 Nov 1939 - 10 Aug 1945:	Chief of Electronic Cell Research Bureau, Yokosuka Navy Yard
1 May 1943:	Promoted to *Rear-Admiral*
10 Aug 1945 - 1 Nov 1945:	Chief of Section 1, Kyushu Area Supervisor Office, Department of Military Supply

Rear-Admiral **Tasuku MURAKAMI** (25 Feb 1884 - 7 Oct 1947)
10 Jan 1930 - 15 Nov 1933:	Chief of Torpedo Research Bureau, Kure Navy Yard
15 Nov 1933:	Promoted to *Rear-Admiral*
15 Nov 1933 - 11 Dec 1933:	Attached to Naval General Staff
15 Dec 1933:	Transferred to the reserve

Rear-Admiral **Yoshitsugu MURAKAMI** (28 Mar 1890 - 22 May 1938)
1 Dec 1937 - 15 Dec 1937:	Chief of Shipbuilding Bureau, Kure Navy Yard
15 Dec 1937 - 15 Apr 1938:	Attached to Naval Shipbuilding Command
15 Apr 1938 - 22 May 1938:	Unassigned
22 May 1938:	Posthumously promoted to *Rear-Admiral*

Rear-Admiral **Hachiro MURAKOSHI** (6 May 1876 - 8 Aug 1969)
10 Jun 1922 - 1 Sep 1924:	Chief of Administration Bureau, Naval Shipbuilding Command
1 Dec 1923:	Promoted to *Rear-Admiral*
1 Sep 1924 - 1 Dec 1924:	Chief of Mine Research Bureau, Yokosuka Navy Yard
1 Sep 1924 - 1 Aug 1925:	Chief of Ordnance Bureau, Yokosuka Navy Yard
1 Aug 1925 - 1 Dec 1926:	Commander, Sasebo Navy Yard
1 Dec 1926 - 26 May 1927:	Attached to Naval General Staff
1 Jun 1927:	Transferred to the reserve

Rear-Admiral **Teijiro MURASE** (23 Jan 1879 - 9 May 1966)
1 Aug 1925 - 1 Dec 1927:	Chief of Shipping Bureau, Sasebo Naval District
1 Dec 1925:	Promoted to *Rear-Admiral*
1 Dec 1927 - 15 Dec 1927:	Attached to Naval General Staff
25 Dec 1927:	Transferred to the reserve

Rear-Admiral **Tojuro MURASE** (9 Sep 1890 - 16 Jan 1975)
1 Jul 1936 - 1 Dec 1937: Chief of Electronic Cell Research Bureau, Yokosuka Navy Yard
1 Dec 1937: Promoted to *Rear-Admiral*
1 Dec 1937 - 15 Dec 1937: Attached to Naval Shipbuilding Command
21 Dec 1937: Transferred to the reserve

Rear-Admiral (Engineer) **Aikichi MURATA** (25 Oct 1867 - 27 Jul 1917)
19 Feb 1914 - 1 Dec 1914: Technical Inspector, Yokosuka Navy Yard
1 Dec 1914: Promoted to *Rear-Admiral*
1 Dec 1914 - 1 Dec 1915: Unassigned
1 Dec 1915: Transferred to the reserve

Rear-Admiral (Surgeon) **Saburo MURATA** (1 Sep 1895 - 16 Aug 1944)
15 May 1944 - 16 Aug 1944: Director, 5th Naval Hospital
16 Aug 1944: Posthumously promoted to *Rear-Admiral*

Rear-Admiral (Apothecary) **Suguru MURATA** (9 Oct 1895 - 22 Dec 1974)
1 May 1944: Promoted to *Rear-Admiral (Apothecary)*
1 May 1944 - 20 Jun 1944: Attached to Naval General Staff
20 Jun 1944 - 15 Oct 1945: Commander, 1st Medical Depot

Rear-Admiral **Toshio MURATA** (25 Jul 1898 - 6 Feb 1944)
20 Jul 1943 - 6 Feb 1944: Chief of Kwajerin Branch, 4th Supply Bureau
6 Feb 1944: Posthumously promoted to *Rear-Admiral*

Vice-Admiral **Toyotaro MURATA** (15 Oct 1882 - 9 Dec 1952)
1 Dec 1927: Promoted to *Rear-Admiral*
1 Dec 1927 - 10 Dec 1928: Commander of Naval Facility, Maizuru Guard District
10 Dec 1928 - 15 Nov 1932: Commandant, Naval Engineering School
15 Nov 1932 - 15 Nov 1935: Commander, Yokosuka Navy Yard
1 Dec 1932: Promoted to *Vice-Admiral*
15 Nov 1935 - 10 Dec 1935: Attached to Naval General Staff
14 Dec 1935: Transferred to the reserve

Rear-Admiral **Kametaro MUTA** (15 Feb 1875 - 10 Aug 1955)
20 Nov 1921 - 1 May 1922: Commander, Sasebo Sailors Corps
1 Dec 1921: Promoted to *Rear-Admiral*
1 May 1922 - 1 Dec 1923: Chief of Staff, Sasebo Naval District
1 Dec 1923 - 10 Dec 1923: Attached to Sasebo Naval District
10 Dec 1923 - 25 Feb 1924: Unassigned
25 Feb 1924: Transferred to the reserve

Rear-Admiral **Kakuro MUTAGUCHI** (2 Jan 1894 - 24 Jul 1945)
20 Feb 1945 - 24 Jul 1945: Captain, Battleship *"Ise"*
24 Jul 1945: Posthumously promoted to *Rear-Admiral*

Vice-Admiral **Inetaro MUTO** (6 Jul 1877 -19 Oct 1954)
1 Jun 1922: Promoted to *Rear-Admiral*
1 Jun 1922 - 1 Dec 1922: Attached to Bureau 1, Naval Shipbuilding Command
1 Dec 1922 - 10 Dec 1928: Chief of Bureau 1, Naval Shipbuilding Command
1 Dec 1926: Promoted to *Vice-Admiral*
10 Dec 1928 - 15 Jan 1929: Attached to Naval Shipbuilding Command
15 Jan 1929 - 15 Dec 1929: Supervisor of Ordnance, Naval Shipbuilding Command
15 Dec 1929: Transferred to the reserve

Grand Marshal Emperor **MUTSUSHITO** (Meiji) (3 Nov 1852 - 30 Jul 1912)
3 Feb 1867 - 30 Jul 1912: Supreme Commander-in-Chief of the Armed Forces

Vice-Admiral **Hideo MYOGA** (8 Jan 1887 - 28 Mar 1951)
1 Dec 1936: Promoted to *Rear-Admiral*
1 Dec 1936 - 15 Nov 1939: Chief of Gunnery Bureau, Kure Navy Yard
15 Nov 1939 - 15 Nov 1940: Attached to Naval Shipbuilding Command
15 Nov 1940: Promoted to *Vice-Admiral*
15 Nov 1940 - 16 Dec 1940: Attached to Naval General Staff
21 Dec 1940: Transferred to the reserve

Vice-Admiral **Shigeaki NABESHIMA** (29 Mar 1889 - 13 Jan 1976)
1 Dec 1937: Promoted to *Rear-Admiral*
1 Dec 1937 - 30 Aug 1939: Instructor, Naval College
30 Aug 1939 - 21 Apr 1941: Commander, Navy Fuel Yard
21 Apr 1941 - 10 Sep 1941: Commander, 3rd Navy Fuel Yard
10 Sep 1941 - 20 Nov 1941: Attached to Naval General Staff
15 Oct 1941: Promoted to *Vice-Admiral*
20 Nov 1941 - 25 Oct 1943: Commandant, Naval Engineering Academy
25 Oct 1943 - 1 May 1945: Chief of Supply Bureau, Department of the Navy
1 May 1945 - 1 Nov 1945: Chief of Naval Facility Command

Rear-Admiral **Shunsaku NABESHIMA** (10 Sep 1892 - 28 Apr 1948)
1 Nov 1942: Promoted to *Rear-Admiral*
1 Nov 1942 - 6 Jan 1944: Chief of Staff, 4th Fleet
6 Jan 1944 - 20 Jan 1944: Attached to Naval General Staff
20 Jan 1944 - 25 Mar 1944: Commandant, Mine School
25 Mar 1944 - 1 May 1945: Commandant, Anti-Submarine School

1 May 1945 - 20 Jun 1945: Attached to Naval General Staff
20 Jun 1945 - 15 Oct 1945: Chief, Shikoku Navy Office

Rear-Admiral (Apothecary) **Toyota NABESHIMA** (30 Oct 1883 - 24 Jul 1962)
1 Dec 1925 - 1 Dec 1932: Attached to Medical Bureau, Department of the Navy
1 Dec 1932: Promoted to *Rear-Admiral (Apothecary)*
1 Dec 1932 - 10 Dec 1932: Attached to Naval General Staff
15 Dec 1932: Transferred to the reserve

Rear-Admiral **Gunkichi NAGAI** (18 May 1857 - 21 May 1927)
15 Sep 1908 - 10 Dec 1908: Commander, Kure Torpedo Corps
10 Dec 1908 - 4 Apr 1910: Unassigned
1 Dec 1909: Promoted to *Rear-Admiral*
4 Apr 1910: Transferred to the reserve

Rear-Admiral **Minoru NAGAI** (21 Mar 1884 - 19 Dec 1936)
1 Dec 1927 - 30 Nov 1929: Commander, Kure Defense Force
30 Nov 1929: Promoted to *Rear-Admiral*
30 Nov 1929 - 15 Dec 1929: Attached to Naval General Staff
25 Dec 1929: Transferred to the reserve

Rear-Admiral **Mitsuru NAGAI** (16 Jan 1895 - 13 Dec 1978)
25 Dec 1943 - 7 Jul 1944: Commander, Saiki Air Division
1 May 1944: Promoted to *Rear-Admiral*
7 Jul 1944 - 10 Jul 1944: Attached to Kure Naval District
10 Jul 1944 - 1 Mar 1945: Commander, 1st Special Base Force
1 Mar 1945 - Oct 1945: Commander, 2nd Special Attack Flotilla

Rear-Admiral **Teizo NAGAI** (? - 24 Oct 1944)
10 Apr 1944 - 24 Oct 1944: Executive Officer, Heavy Cruiser *"Maya"*
24 Oct 1944: Posthumously promoted to *Rear-Admiral*

Rear-Admiral **Masaru NAGAMATSU** (8 Sep 1891 - 26 Oct 1945)
15 Nov 1940: Promoted to *Rear-Admiral*
15 Nov 1940 - 25 Jan 1942: Chief of Shipping Bureau, Sasebo Naval District
25 Jan 1942 - 15 Apr 1943: Commander, 102nd Naval Facility
15 Apr 1943 - 1 Jun 1943: Attached to Naval General Staff
1 Jun 1943 - 5 Dec 1943: Chief Supervisor for Construction & Ordnance, Naval Shipbuilding Command
5 Dec 1943 - 15 Dec 1943: Attached to Naval General Staff
20 Dec 1943: Transferred to the reserve

Rear-Admiral **Kimikata NAGAMINE** (20 Dec 1900 - 17 Mar 1945)
30 Nov 1943 - 10 Jan 1945:	Chief Engineer Officer, 4th Southern Expeditionary Fleet
10 Jan 1945 - 17 Mar 1945:	Attached to Yokosuka Naval District
17 Mar 1945:	Posthumously promoted to *Rear-Admiral*

Rear-Admiral (Engineer) **Yoshimitsu NAGAMINE** (8 Aug 1857 - 7 Feb 1921)
28 Sep 1907:	Promoted to *Rear-Admiral*
28 Sep 1907 - 1 Dec 1910:	Commandant, Naval Engineering Academy
1 Dec 1910 - 1 Dec 1911:	Unassigned
1 Dec 1911:	Transferred to the reserve

Rear-Admiral (Paymaster) **Niozo NAGAMIYA** (12 Dec 1881 - 6 Jan 1946)
30 Nov 1929:	Promoted to *Rear-Admiral*
30 Nov 1929 - 1 Dec 1931:	Accounting Supervisor for Construction & Ordnance, Naval Shipbuilding Command
1 Dec 1931 - 1 Dec 1932:	Paymaster-General, Kure Naval District
1 Dec 1932 - 10 Dec 1932:	Attached to Naval General Staff
15 Dec 1932:	Transferred to the reserve

Vice-Admiral **Kiyoshi NAGAMURA** (6 Oct 1878 - 14 Mar 1966)
13 Aug 1923 - 1 Dec 1927:	Chief of Shipbuilding Bureau, Kure Navy Yard
1 Dec 1925:	Promoted to *Rear-Admiral*
1 Dec 1927 - 16 May 1928:	Chief of Shipbuilding Bureau, Yokosuka Navy Yard
16 May 1928 - 1 Dec 1930:	Chief of Bureau 3, Naval Shipbuilding Command
30 Nov 1929:	Promoted to *Vice-Admiral*
1 Dec 1930 - 20 Mar 1931:	Attached to Naval Shipbuilding Command
31 Mar 1931:	Transferred to the reserve

Rear-Admiral **Kensuke NAGANO** (10 Sep 1890 - 28 Oct 1959)
1 Apr 1939 - 15 Oct 1942:	Chief of Materiel Bureau, Air Technical Arsenal
15 Oct 1940:	Promoted to *Rear-Admiral*
15 Oct 1942 - 25 Apr 1944:	Chief Supervisor for Construction & Ordnance, Naval Shipbuilding Command
25 Apr 1944 - 10 May 1944:	Attached to Naval Air Command
15 May 1944:	Transferred to the reserve

Rear-Admiral (Paymaster) **Masatoshi NAGANO** (20 Feb 1893 - 15 Sep 1964)
15 Feb 1945 - Oct 1945:	Paymaster-General, Takao Guard District
1 May 1945:	Promoted to *Rear-Admiral (Paymaster)*

Fleet Admiral **Osami NAGANO** (15 Jun 1880 - 5 Jan 1947)
1 Dec 1920 - 5 Feb 1924:	Military Attache, USA

1 Dec 1923:	Promoted to *Rear-Admiral*
5 Feb 1924 - 1 Dec 1924:	Chief of Bureau 3, Naval General Staff
1 Dec 1924 - 20 Apr 1925:	Commander, 3rd Escort Flotilla
20 Apr 1925 - 20 Aug 1926:	C-in-C, 1st Expeditionary Fleet
20 Aug 1926 - 1 Feb 1927:	Attached to Naval General Staff
1 Feb 1927 - 15 Jan 1928:	C-in-C, Training Fleet
1 Dec 1927:	Promoted to *Vice-Admiral*
15 Jan 1928 - 10 Dec 1928:	Attached to Naval General Staff
10 Dec 1928 - 10 Jun 1930:	Commandant of the Naval Academy
10 Jun 1930 - 10 Oct 1931:	Deputy Chief of the Naval General Staff
10 Oct 1931 - 15 Nov 1933:	Attached to Naval General Staff
9 Dec 1931 - 25 Apr 1933:	Plenipotentiary, Geneva Conference
15 Nov 1933 - 15 Nov 1934:	Admiral Commanding, Yokosuka Naval District, Member, Admirals Committee
1 Mar 1934:	Promoted to *Admiral*
15 Nov 1934 - 9 Mar 1936:	Navy Councillor
9 Mar 1936 - 2 Feb 1937:	Minister of the Navy
2 Feb 1937 - 1 Dec 1937:	C-in-C, Combined Fleet, C-in-C, 1st Fleet
1 Dec 1937 - 9 Apr 1941:	Navy Councillor
13 Feb 1941 - 9 Apr 1941:	Chairman, High Technical Committee
9 Apr 1941 - 21 Feb 1944:	Chief of the Naval General Staff, Member, Admirals Committee
21 Jun 1943:	Appointed *Fleet Admiral*

Rear-Admiral **Hideji NAGAO** (25 Nov 1881 - 5 Jan 1966)
1 Dec 1931:	Promoted to *Rear-Admiral*
1 Dec 1931 - 1 Dec 1932:	Chief of Shipping Bureau, Yokosuka Naval District
1 Dec 1932 - 10 Dec 1932:	Attached to Naval General Staff
15 Dec 1932:	Transferred to the reserve

Rear-Admiral **Motoo NAGAO** (14 Feb 1894 - 13 Nov 1943)
20 May 1943 - 7 Jun 1943:	Attached to Yokosuka Naval District
7 Jun 1943 - 13 Nov 1943:	Unassigned
13 Nov 1943:	Posthumously promoted to *Rear-Admiral*

Rear-Admiral (Surgeon) **Moriyasu NAGAOKI** (21 Aug 1896 - 3 May 1944)
15 Nov 1943 - 3 May 1944:	Chief Surgeon, 9th Fleet
3 May 1944:	Posthumously promoted to *Rear-Admiral (Surgeon)*

Vice-Admiral **Naotaro NAGASAWA** (3 Dec 1877 - 26 Dec 1967)
1 Dec 1922:	Promoted to *Rear-Admiral*
1 Dec 1922 - 6 Nov 1923:	Commander, 1st Destroyer Flotilla

6 Nov 1923 - 1 Dec 1924:	Chief of Staff, Kure Naval District
1 Dec 1924 - 20 Oct 1925:	Commander, 2nd Destroyer Flotilla
20 Oct 1925 - 1 Dec 1926:	Commandant, Torpedo School
1 Dec 1926:	Promoted to *Vice-Admiral*
1 Dec 1926 - 1 Dec 1927:	Commander, Chinkai Guard District
1 Dec 1927 - 15 Mar 1928:	Attached to Naval General Staff
25 Mar 1928:	Transferred to the reserve

Vice-Admiral **Yasujiro NAGATA** (21 Dec 1866 - 19 Jan 1923)

13 Dec 1915:	Promoted to *Rear-Admiral*
13 Dec 1915 - 1 Dec 1916:	Chief of Staff, 2nd Fleet
1 Dec 1916 - 1 Dec 1917:	Chief of Staff, Yokosuka Naval District
1 Dec 1917 - 1 Dec 1919:	Commander, Southern Islands Defense Force
1 Dec 1919:	Promoted to *Vice-Admiral*
1 Dec 1919 - 1 Aug 1920:	Member, Admirals Committee
10 Aug 1920:	Transferred to the reserve

Rear-Admiral (Surgeon) **Chiyosaku NAGAYAMA** (15 Feb 1901 - 25 Jan 1945)

1 Aug 1944 - 25 Jan 1945:	Chief Surgeon, 2nd Air Fleet
25 Jan 1945:	Posthumously promoted to *Rear-Admiral (Surgeon)*

Vice-Admiral (Paymaster) **Shinjiro NAGAYASU** (6 Jan 1873 - 19 Feb 1935)

1 Dec 1921:	Promoted to *Rear-Admiral (Paymaster)*
1 Dec 1921 - 10 Nov 1922:	Chief of Section 3, Accounting Bureau, Naval Shipbuilding Command
10 Nov 1922 - 1 Dec 1923:	Paymaster-General, Sasebo Naval District
1 Dec 1923 - 1 Dec 1924:	Paymaster-General, Yokosuka Naval District
1 Dec 1924 - 1 Aug 1925:	Commandant, Naval Paymaster Academy
1 Aug 1925 - 13 Apr 1927:	Chief of Naval Accounting Bureau
1 Dec 1925:	Promoted to *Vice-Admiral (Paymaster)*
13 Apr 1927 - 15 Dec 1927:	Attached to Naval General Staff
25 Dec 1927:	Transferred to the reserve

Rear-Admiral **Juro NAGOYA** (6 Nov 1885 - 20 Oct 1961)

1 Dec 1932 - 15 Nov 1934:	Chief of Supply Bureau, Kure Naval District
15 Nov 1933:	Promoted to *Rear-Admiral*

Admiral **Chuichi NAGUMO** (25 Mar 1887 - 8 Jul 1944)

15 Nov 1935:	Promoted to *Rear-Admiral*
15 Nov 1935 - 1 Dec 1936:	Commander, 1st Destroyer Flotilla
1 Dec 1936 - 15 Nov 1937:	Commander, 8th Escort Flotilla
15 Nov 1937 - 15 Nov 1938:	Commandant, Torpedo School
15 Nov 1938 - 1 Nov 1940:	Commander, 3rd Escort Flotilla

15 Nov 1939:	Promoted to *Vice-Admiral*
1 Nov 1940 - 10 Apr 1941:	Commandant of the Naval College
10 Apr 1941 - 14 Jul 1942:	C-in-C, 1st Air Fleet
14 Jul 1942 - 11 Nov 1942:	C-in-C, 3rd Fleet
11 Nov 1942 - 21 Jun 1943:	Admiral Commanding, Sasebo Naval District
21 Jun 1943 - 20 Oct 1943:	Admiral Commanding, Kure Naval District
20 Oct 1943 - 25 Feb 1944:	C-in-C, 1st Fleet
25 Feb 1944 - 4 Mar 1944:	Attached to Naval General Staff
4 Mar 1944 - 8 Jul 1944:	C-in-C, Central Pacific Area Fleet, C-in-C, 14th Air Fleet
8 Jul 1944:	Posthumously promoted to *Admiral*

Vice-Admiral (Paymaster) **Junkichi NAKADAI** (23 Sep 1863 - 30 Jan 1934)

15 Aug 1908 - 1 Dec 1912:	Paymaster-General, Kure Naval District
1 Apr 1910:	Promoted to *General (Paymaster)*
1 Dec 1912 - 13 Dec 1915:	Paymaster-General, Yokosuka Naval District
13 Dec 1915:	Promoted to *General (Paymaster), Senior grade*
13 Dec 1915 - 1 Dec 1916:	Unassigned
1 Dec 1916:	Transferred to the reserve
23 Sep 1919:	Redesignated *Vice-Admiral (Paymaster)*

Rear-Admiral (Paymaster) **Sengoro NAKAGAKI** (27 Mar 1896 - 11 Sep 1985)

30 Apr 1944 - 9 Sep 1945:	Paymaster-General, Combined Fleet
25 Apr 1945 - 9 Sep 1945:	Paymaster-General, Supreme Naval HQ
1 May 1945:	Promoted to *Rear-Admiral (Paymaster)*
9 Sep 1945 - 15 Sep 1945:	Attached to Naval General Staff

Rear-Admiral (Surgeon) **Heihachi NAKAGAWA** (2 Feb 1870 - ?)

1 Jun 1919 - 1 Dec 1921:	Director, Maizuru Naval Hospital, Chief Surgeon, Maizuru Naval District
1 Dec 1919:	Promoted to *Rear-Admiral (Surgeon)*
1 Dec 1921 - 2 Nov 1922:	Director, Sasebo Naval Hospital, Chief Surgeon, Sasebo Naval District
2 Nov 1922 - 1 Dec 1922:	Attached to Naval General Staff
1 Dec 1922 - 31 Mar 1923:	Unassigned
31 Mar 1923:	Transferred to the reserve

Vice-Admiral **Ko NAKAGAWA** (22 Jan 1892 - 8 Jul 1944)

1 Sep 1943 - 5 Dec 1943:	Captain, Battleship *"Hyuga"*
1 Nov 1943:	Promoted to *Rear-Admiral*
5 Dec 1943 - 16 Dec 1943:	Staff officer, Southeastern Area Fleet
16 Dec 1943 - 8 Jul 1944:	Commander, 3rd Destroyer Flotilla
8 Jul 1944:	Posthumously promoted to *Vice-Admiral*

Rear-Admiral **Shigeushi NAKAGAWA** (10 Dec 1869 - 24 Oct 1957)
10 Nov 1918 - 1 Dec 1919:	Chief of Staff, 2nd Fleet
1 Dec 1918:	Promoted to *Rear-Admiral*
1 Dec 1919 - 1 Dec 1920:	Commander, Mako Guard District
1 Dec 1920 - 1 Dec 1921:	Member, Admirals Committee
1 Dec 1921 - 31 Mar 1923:	Unassigned
31 Mar 1923:	Transferred to the reserve

Rear-Admiral **Susumu NAKAGAWA** (12 Aug 1882 - 13 Dec 1960)
1 Dec 1930:	Promoted to *Rear-Admiral*
1 Dec 1930 - 1 Dec 1931:	Chief of Shipbuilding Bureau, Sasebo Navy Yard
1 Dec 1931 - 15 Dec 1931:	Attached to Naval Shipbuilding Command
21 Dec 1931:	Transferred to the reserve

Vice-Admiral **Giichiro NAKAHARA** (29 Mar 1900 - 7 Aug 1944)
8 May 1944 - 7 Aug 1944:	Captain, Light Cruiser *"Nagara"*
7 Aug 1944:	Posthumously promoted 2 grades to *Vice-Admiral*

Vice-Admiral **Yoshimasa NAKAHARA** (3 Apr 1892 - 23 Feb 1944)
20 May 1940 - 28 Nov 1940:	Attached to Naval General Staff
15 Nov 1940:	Promoted to *Rear-Admiral*
28 Nov 1940 - 10 Dec 1942:	Chief of Naval Personnel
10 Dec 1942 - 17 Dec 1942:	Attached to Naval General Staff
17 Dec 1942- 24 Dec 1942:	Staff officer, Combined Fleet
24 Dec 1942 - 29 Nov 1943:	Chief of Staff, Southeastern Area Fleet, Chief of Staff, 11th Air Force
1 Nov 1943:	Promoted to *Vice-Admiral*
29 Nov 1943 - 1 Dec 1943:	Staff officer, Southeastern Area Fleet
1 Dec 1943 - 23 Feb 1944:	Attached to Naval General Staff

Rear-Admiral **Akira NAKAJIMA** (4 Oct 1878 - Jan 1947)
1 Dec 1918 - 13 Aug 1923:	Chief of Ordnance Bureau, Sasebo Navy Yard
1 Dec 1922:	Promoted to *Rear-Admiral*
13 Aug 1923 - 15 Oct 1923:	Attached to Naval Shipbuilding Command
15 Oct 1923 - 1 Dec 1923:	Attached to Sasebo Naval District
1 Dec 1923 - 25 Feb 1924:	Unassigned
25 Feb 1924:	Transferred to the reserve

Rear-Admiral **Chihiro NAKAJIMA** (23 Dec 1893 - 1 Jul 1971)
15 Jan 1945 - 5 May 1945:	Staff officer, Kure Defense Flotilla
1 May 1945:	Promoted to *Rear-Admiral*
5 May 1945 - 25 May 1945:	Staff officer, 51st Escort Flotilla
25 May 1945 - 5 Jul 1945:	Chief of Transport Bureau, Yokosuka Naval District
5 Jul 1945 - 30 Nov 1945:	Commander, Niigata Harbor Guard Force

Rear-Admiral (Surgeon) **Etsuro NAKAJIMA** (2 May 1874 - 1 May 1946)
1 Dec 1921 - 1 Dec 1923:	Chief of Bureau 2, Yokosuka Naval Hospital
1 Dec 1923:	Promoted to *Rear-Admiral (Surgeon)*
1 Dec 1923 - 10 Dec 1923:	Attached to Yokosuka Naval District
10 Dec 1923 - 25 Feb 1924:	Unassigned
25 Feb 1924:	Transferred to the reserve

Rear-Admiral **Gonkichi NAKAJIMA** (20 Dec 1882 - 22 Dec 1946)
1 Dec 1927:	Promoted to *Rear-Admiral*
1 Dec 1927 - 30 Nov 1929:	Chief Instructor, Naval College
30 Nov 1929 - 1 Oct 1930:	Attached to Naval General Staff
10 Oct 1930:	Transferred to the reserve

Rear-Admiral (Engineer) **Ichiemon NAKAJIMA** (11 Sep 1867 - 1 Aug 1934)
1 Dec 1911 - 1 Dec 1912:	Chief Engineer Officer, 2nd Fleet
1 Dec 1912 - 1 Dec 1913:	Chief Engineer Officer, 1st Fleet
1 Dec 1913:	Promoted to *Rear-Admiral*
1 Dec 1913 - 1 Apr 1914:	Commandant, Engineering School
1 Apr 1914 - 31 Mar 1915:	Transferred to the reserve

Rear-Admiral **Ichitaro NAKAJIMA** (3 Jun 1868 - 5 Jul 1957)
1 Dec 1913:	Promoted to *Rear-Admiral*
1 Dec 1913 - 25 Mar 1914:	Chief of Staff, Sasebo Naval District
25 Mar 1914 - 17 Dec 1914:	C-in-C, Kure Naval District Fleet
17 Dec 1914 - 1 Apr 1916:	Commander, Ominato Guard District
1 Apr 1916 - 1 Apr 1917:	Unassigned
1 Apr 1917:	Transferred to the reserve

Rear-Admiral **Kiyonobu NAKAJIMA** (10 Jun 1887 - 22 Oct 1942)
25 Jul 1942 - 22 Oct 1942:	Captain, Gunboat *"Hakkaisan-maru"*
22 Oct 1942:	Posthumously promoted to *Rear-Admiral*

Rear-Admiral **Ryukichi NAKAJIMA** (17 Jan 1885 - 23 Jan 1948)
15 Nov 1934 - 15 Nov 1935:	Chief Supervisor for Construction & Ordnance, Naval Shipbuilding Command
15 Nov 1935:	Promoted to *Rear-Admiral*
15 Nov 1935 - 10 Dec 1935:	Attached to Naval Shipbuilding Command
14 Dec 1935:	Transferred to the reserve

Vice-Admiral **Seizaburo NAKAJIMA** (24 Jun 1892 - 23 Feb 1978)
15 Nov 1940:	Promoted to *Rear-Admiral*
15 Nov 1940 - 1 Apr 1941:	Chief of Armaments Bureau, Air Technical Arsenal
1 Apr 1941 - 1 Nov 1942:	Chief of Electronics Bureau, Air Technical Arsenal

1 Nov 1942 - 1 Jun 1943:	Attached to Yokosuka Naval District
1 Jun 1943 - 15 Oct 1945:	Commander, Numazu Navy Yard
1 Nov 1943:	Promoted to *Vice-Admiral*

Rear-Admiral **Shiro NAKAJIMA** (6 Aug 1899 - 30 Sep 1944)

20 May 1944 - 30 Sep 1944:	Chief of Administration Bureau, 102nd Navy Fuel Yard
30 Sep 1944:	Posthumously promoted to *Rear-Admiral*

Vice-Admiral **Suketomo NAKAJIMA** (10 Oct 1871 - 12 Jun 1942)

1 Dec 1917:	Promoted to *Rear-Admiral*
1 Dec 1917 - 25 Apr 1918:	Attached to Naval General Staff
25 Apr 1918 - 1 Dec 1919:	Commander, 1st Destroyer Flotilla
1 Dec 1919 - 16 Jul 1920:	Attached to Naval General Staff
16 Jul 1920 - 1 Dec 1921:	Commander, Yokosuka Defense Force
1 Dec 1921:	Promoted to *Vice-Admiral*
1 Dec 1921 - 10 Apr 1922:	Member, Admirals Committee
10 Apr 1922 - 31 Mar 1923:	Unassigned
31 Mar 1923:	Transferred to the reserve

Rear-Admiral **Susumu NAKAJIMA** (23 May 1882 - 14 Jun 1951)

22 Aug 1925 - 1 Dec 1926:	Commander, Yokosuka Defense Force
1 Dec 1925:	Promoted to *Rear-Admiral*
1 Dec 1926 - 16 May 1927:	Attached to Naval General Staff
16 May 1927 - 1 Apr 1928:	C-in-C, 2nd Expeditionary Fleet
1 Apr 1928 - 25 Jul 1928:	Attached to Naval General Staff
30 Jul 1928:	Transferred to the reserve

Vice-Admiral **Torahiko NAKAJIMA** (4 Jan 1890 - 31 Dec 1946)

15 Nov 1938:	Promoted to *Rear-Admiral*
15 Nov 1938 - 1 Jul 1941:	Chief of Bureau 4, Naval General Staff
1 Jul 1941 - 20 Aug 1941:	Attached to Naval General Staff
20 Aug 1941 - 6 Jan 1943:	Chief of Staff, Kure Naval District
1 Nov 1942:	Promoted to *Vice-Admiral*
6 Jan 1943 - 14 Jan 1943:	Staff officer, Southwestern Area Fleet
14 Jan 1943 - 4 Nov 1944:	Commander, 1st Maritime Escort Force
4 Nov 1944 - 15 Feb 1945:	Chief of Naval Radar Command
15 Feb 1945 - 10 Jun 1945:	Commander, 2nd Naval Technical Arsenal
10 Jun 1945 - 6 Sep 1945:	Attached to Naval General Staff

Vice-Admiral **Yosohachi NAKAJIMA** (19 Feb 1868 - 6 Oct 1929)

1 Dec 1910 - 29 Jun 1912:	Chief of Engine Construction Bureau, Yokosuka Navy Yard

3 Feb 1912:	Promoted to *Rear-Admiral*
29 Jun 1912 - 1 Dec 1913:	Chief of Engine Construction Bureau, Kure Navy Yard
1 Dec 1913 - 1 Apr 1916:	Chief of Engine Construction Bureau, Yokosuka Navy Yard
1 Apr 1916 - 1 Oct 1920:	Chief of Bureau 5, Naval Technical Command
1 Dec 1916:	Promoted to *Vice-Admiral*
1 Oct 1920 - 1 Sep 1921:	Chief of Bureau 5, Naval Shipbuilding Command
1 Sep 1921 - 1 Dec 1921:	Attached to Naval Shipbuilding Command
1 Dec 1921 - 31 Mar 1923:	Unassigned
31 Mar 1923:	Transferred to the reserve

Rear-Admiral **Torai NAKAJO** (13 Jul 1880 - 14 Feb 1952)

1 Oct 1923 - 1 Dec 1924:	Acting Commandant, Submarine School
1 Dec 1924:	Promoted to *Rear-Admiral*
1 Dec 1924 - 2 Mar 1925:	Attached to Kure Naval District
20 Mar 1925:	Transferred to the reserve

Rear-Admiral **Yoshizo NAKAMARUO** (24 Apr 1886 - 17 Feb 1944)

20 Oct 1943 - 17 Feb 1944:	Commander of Minesweeping, Auxiliary Cruiser *"Aikoku-maru"*
17 Feb 1944:	Posthumously promoted to *Rear-Admiral*

Rear-Admiral **Tadao NAKAMICHI** (10 Dec 1886 - 25 Feb 1972)

15 Nov 1933:	Promoted to *Rear-Admiral*
15 Nov 1933 - 15 Nov 1934:	Chief of Shipping Bureau, Kure Naval District
15 Nov 1934 - 10 Dec 1934:	Attached to Naval General Staff
15 Dec 1934:	Transferred to the reserve

Vice-Admiral **Baron Tokutaro NAKAMIZO** (22 Dec 1857 - 13 Feb 1923)

7 Jul 1903:	Promoted to *Rear-Admiral*
7 Jul 1903 - 27 Oct 1903:	C-in-C, Readiness Fleet
27 Oct 1903 - 3 Feb 1904:	Chief, Bureau of Naval Affairs, Member, Admirals Committee
3 Feb 1904 - 10 May 1905:	Chief of Staff, Kure Naval District
10 May 1905 - 15 May 1908:	Commander, Maizuru Navy Yard
12 Mar 1907:	Promoted to *Vice-Admiral*
15 May 1908 - 1 Dec 1909:	Chief, Bureau of Naval Affairs, Member, Admirals Committee
1 Dec 1909 - 17 Apr 1911:	Unassigned
17 Apr 1911:	Transferred to the reserve

Rear-Admiral **Shigeo NAKAMORI** (14 Sep 1893 - 7 Aug 1970)
20 Jun 1942 - 1 Jul 1943:	Chief of Electronic Research Bureau, Kure Navy Yard
1 May 1943:	Promoted to *Rear-Admiral*
1 Jul 1943 - 1 Nov 1945:	Chief of Electronics Bureau, Kure Navy Yard

Vice-Admiral **Goro NAKAMURA** (2 Dec 1891 - 6 Jul 1983)
1 Oct 1941 - 4 Jan 1943:	Chief Engineer Officer, Combined Fleet
1 Nov 1942:	Promoted to *Rear-Admiral*
4 Jan 1943 - 1 Feb 1943:	Attached to Naval Air Command
1 Feb 1943 - 1 Jul 1943:	Commander, 61st Air Arsenal
1 Jul 1943 - 15 Jun 1944:	Commander, 21st Air Arsenal
15 Jun 1944 - 1 Aug 1944:	Attached to Naval Air Command
1 Aug 1944 - 15 Nov 1945:	Chief of Bureau 1, Naval Air Command
1 Mar 1945 - 5 Sep 1945:	Chief of Bureau 7, Naval Air Command
5 Sep 1945 - 15 Nov 1945:	Chief of Administration Bureau, Naval Air Command
1 Nov 1945:	Promoted to *Vice-Admiral*

Vice-Admiral **Kamezaburo NAKAMURA** (28 Jan 1884 - 2 Nov 1944)
10 Oct 1931 - 15 Nov 1933:	Chief of Staff, 2nd Fleet
1 Dec 1931:	Promoted to *Rear-Admiral*
15 Nov 1933 - 20 Sep 1934:	Chief of Naval Training Bureau
20 Sep 1934 - 1 Aug 1935:	C-in-C, Training Fleet
1 Aug 1935 - 2 Dec 1935:	Chief of Bureau 1, Naval General Staff
15 Nov 1935:	Promoted to *Vice-Admiral*
2 Dec 1935 - 1 Dec 1936:	Commandant of the Naval College
1 Dec 1936 - 1 Dec 1937:	Admiral Commanding, Maizuru Guard District
1 Dec 1937 - 15 Nov 1938:	Attached to Naval General Staff
15 Nov 1938 - 15 Nov 1939:	Admiral Commanding, Sasebo Naval District
15 Nov 1939 - 16 Dec 1940:	Attached to Naval General Staff
21 Dec 1940:	Transferred to the reserve

Rear-Admiral **Katsuhei NAKAMURA** (5 Dec 1894 - 29 Jun 1971)
2 Mar 1943 - 5 Dec 1943:	Captain, Cruiser *"Myoko"*
1 Nov 1943:	Promoted to *Rear-Admiral*
5 Dec 1943 - 4 Jan 1944:	Attached to Naval General Staff
4 Jan 1944 - 20 Jul 1944:	Naval Attache, China
20 May 1944 - 20 Jul 1944:	Deputy Chief of Staff, China Area Fleet
20 Jul 1944 - 7 Aug 1944:	Attached to Naval General Staff
7 Aug 1944 - 5 Sep 1945:	Chief of Administration Bureau, Naval Air Command
5 Sep 1945 - 30 Nov 1945:	Attached to Naval General Staff

Rear-Admiral **Kazuo NAKAMURA** (25 Jul 1887 - 12 Aug 1979)
10 Nov 1939 - 15 Oct 1940:	Attached to Naval General Staff
15 Nov 1939:	Promoted to *Rear-Admiral*
15 Oct 1940 - 15 Nov 1940:	Staff officer, 4th Fleet
15 Nov 1940 - 20 Mar 1942:	Commander, 3rd Auxiliary Base Force
20 Mar 1942 - 20 Mar 1945:	Attached to Naval General Staff
20 Mar 1945 - 15 Sep 1945:	Chief of Psychological Research Bureau, Technical Research Department

Rear-Admiral **Masaki NAKAMURA** (12 Nov 1872 - 21 Jun 1943)
25 Sep 1918 - 23 Jul 1920:	Commander, Temporary Expeditionary Force
1 Dec 1919:	Promoted to *Rear-Admiral*
23 Jul 1920 - 1 Dec 1920:	Attached to Maizuru Naval District
1 Dec 1920 - 15 Nov 1921:	Commander, 5th Escort Flotilla
15 Nov 1921 - 10 Apr 1922:	Member, Admirals Committee
10 Apr 1922 - 31 Mar 1923:`	Unassigned
31 Mar 1923:	Transferred to the reserve

Rear-Admiral **Masao NAKAMURA** (11 Dec 1888 - 22 Jul 1943)
10 Jun 1942 - 22 Jul 1943:	Commander, 4th Navy Harbor
22 Jul 1943:	Posthumously promoted to *Rear-Admiral*

Rear-Admiral (Surgeon) **Michitaka NAKAMURA** (2 Jul 1894 - 27 May 1990)
1 Oct 1942 - 10 Mar 1944:	Director, Omura Naval Hospital
1 May 1943:	Promoted to *Rear-Admiral (Surgeon)*
10 Mar 1944 - 9 Dec 1944:	Chief of Health Bureau, Kainan I Naval Special Task Office
9 Dec 1944 - 15 Oct 1945:	Instructor, Naval Medical School

Rear-Admiral **Motoji NAKAMURA** (2 Jan 1890 - 2 May 1946)
20 Apr 1941 - 20 May 1942:	Commander, Shanghai Harbor
1 May 1942:	Promoted to *Rear-Admiral*
20 May 1942 - 1 Jun 1942:	Staff officer, China Area Fleet
1 Jun 1942 - 1 Nov 1942:	Attached to Sasebo Naval District
1 Nov 1942 - 15 Feb 1944:	Commander, Chichijima Area Base Force
15 Feb 1944 - 20 Mar 1944:	Attached to Kure Naval District
20 Mar 1944 - 8 Apr 1944:	Staff officer, Maritime Escort Fleet
8 Apr 1944 - 20 May 1944:	Commander, 4th Convoy HQ
20 May 1944 - 15 Apr 1945:	Commander, 3rd Maritime Escort Division
15 Apr 1945 - 7 May 1945:	Commander, 4th Special Attack Flotilla
7 May 1945 - 15 Jun 1945:	Attached to Naval General Staff
20 Jun 1945:	Transferred to the reserve

Rear-Admiral **Nenosuke NAKAMURA** (6 Jan 1901 - 10 Jun 1945)
15 Nov 1944 - 10 Jun 1945:	Commander, 141st Air Division
10 Jun 1945:	Posthumously promoted to *Rear-Admiral*

Rear-Admiral **Noboru NAKAMURA** (11 Feb 1904 - 29 Nov 1944)
1 Oct 1944 - 29 Nov 1944:	Chief Navigation Officer, Aircraft Carrier *"Shinano"*
29 Nov 1944:	Posthumously promoted to *Rear-Admiral*

Admiral **Ryozo NAKAMURA** (26 Jul 1878 - 1 Mar 1945)
6 Nov 1923 - 1 Dec 1924:	Commander, 1st Destroyer Flotilla
1 Dec 1923:	Promoted to *Rear-Admiral*
1 Dec 1924 - 1 Dec 1926:	Chief of Bureau 3, Naval General Staff
1 Dec 1926 - 10 Dec 1926:	Attached to Naval General Staff
10 Dec 1926 - 30 Nov 1929:	Commandant of the Naval College
1 Dec 1927:	Promoted to *Vice-Admiral*
30 Nov 1929 - 1 Dec 1930:	Attached to Naval General Staff
1 Dec 1930 - 1 Dec 1931:	C-in-C, 2nd Fleet
1 Dec 1931 - 1 Dec 1932:	Admiral Commanding, Sasebo Naval District
1 Dec 1932 - 10 May 1934:	Admiral Commanding, Kure Naval District
1 Mar 1934:	Promoted to *Admiral*
10 May 1934 - 16 Mar 1934:	Chief of Naval Shipbuilding Command
10 May 1934 - 28 Mar 1936:	Navy Councillor
30 Mar 1936:	Transferred to the reserve

Rear-Admiral **Shigekazu NAKAMURA** (4 Dec 1887 - 7 Dec 1945)
16 Nov 1936 - 1 Dec 1937:	Chief of Shipping Bureau, Sasebo Naval District
1 Dec 1936:	Promoted to *Rear-Admiral*
1 Dec 1937 - 15 Dec 1937:	Attached to Naval General Staff
21 Dec 1937:	Transferred to the reserve
5 Jan 1942 - 15 Jan 1942:	Recalled; Attached to Ryojun Guard District
15 Jan 1942 - 15 Nov 1942:	Commander, Ryojun Area Base Force
15 Nov 1942 - 21 Dec 1942:	Attached to Naval General Staff
21 Dec 1942:	Demobilized

Rear-Admiral **Shizuka NAKAMURA** (1 Feb 1860 - 18 Jun 1936)
23 May 1900 - 6 Jul 1901:	Chief of Bureau 3, Naval General Staff
6 Jul 1901 - 28 Dec 1903:	Aide-de-Camp to the Crown Prince
28 Dec 1903 - 12 Jan 1905:	Chief of Staff, 3rd Fleet
12 Jan 1905 - 14 Mar 1906:	Commandant, Torpedo Training Center
14 Mar 1906 - 21 Jun 1906:	Attached to the Department of the Navy
21 Jun 1906 - 21 Oct 1907:	Naval Attache, China
22 Nov 1906:	Promoted to *Rear-Admiral*
21 Oct 1907 - 15 May 1908:	Unassigned

15 May 1908 - 28 Aug 1908:	Commander, Sasebo Torpedo Corps
28 Aug 1908 - 2 Mar 1909:	Unassigned
2 Mar 1909:	Transferred to the reserve

Vice-Admiral (Paymaster) **Teisuke NAKAMURA** (21 Aug 1891 - 12 Dec 1953)
1 Nov 1942:	Promoted to *Rear-Admiral (Paymaster)*
1 Nov 1942 - 10 Jun 1945:	Paymaster-General, Maizuru Naval District
10 Jun 1945 - 15 Nov 1945:	Paymaster-General, Sasebo Naval District
1 Nov 1945:	Promoted to *Vice-Admiral (Paymaster)*

Vice-Admiral **Todomu NAKAMURA** (15 Aug 1892 - 1 Sep 1972)
15 Nov 1940:	Promoted to *Rear-Admiral*
15 Nov 1940 - 1 Oct 1941:	Chief of Aircraft Bureau, Sasebo Navy Yard
1 Oct 1941 - 20 Nov 1941:	Commander, 21st Air Arsenal
20 Nov 1941 - 10 Dec 1941:	Attached to Yokosuka Naval District
10 Dec 1941 - 15 Oct 1942:	Chief of Aircraft Bureau, Air Technical Arsenal
15 Oct 1942 - 1 Nov 1942:	Attached to Naval Air Command
1 Nov 1942 - 15 Jun 1944:	Chief of Bureau 2, Naval Air Command
1 Nov 1943:	Promoted to *Vice-Admiral*
1 Nov 1943 - 15 Jan 1944:	Chief of Bureau 3, Naval Air Command
15 Jun 1944 - 1 Nov 1945:	Commander, 21st Air Arsenal

Vice-Admiral **Toshihisa NAKAMURA** (16 Feb 1890 - 19 Mar 1972)
15 Nov 1938:	Promoted to *Rear-Admiral*
15 Nov 1938 - 15 Dec 1938:	Attached to Naval General Staff
15 Dec 1938 - 10 Oct 1939:	Chief of Staff, Kure Naval District
10 Oct 1939 - 5 Nov 1939:	Staff Officer, China Area Fleet
5 Nov 1939 - 5 Mar 1941:	Deputy Chief of Staff, China Area Fleet
5 Mar 1941 - 20 Mar 1941:	Attached to Naval General Staff
20 Mar 1941 - 10 Apr 1941:	Staff officer, Combined Fleet
10 Apr 1941 - 10 Mar 1942:	Chief of Staff, 3rd Fleet
10 Mar 1942 - 10 Oct 1942:	Chief of Staff, 2nd Southern Expeditionary Fleet
10 Apr 1942 - 10 Oct 1942:	Chief of Staff, Southwestern Area Fleet
10 Oct 1942 - 27 Oct 1942:	Attached to Naval General Staff
27 Oct 1942 - 30 Nov 1945:	Aide-de-Camp to the Emperor
1 Nov 1942:	Promoted to *Vice-Admiral*

Vice-Admiral **Viscount Kuranosuke NAKAMUTA** (24 Feb 1837 - 30 Mar 1916)
3 Nov 1871:	Promoted to *Rear-Admiral*
3 Nov 1871 - 17 Oct 1875:	Commandant of the Naval Academy
17 Oct 1875 - 28 Oct 1875:	Attached to the Department of the Navy
28 Oct 1875 - 5 Sep 1876:	Commander, West Area
5 Sep 1876 - 31 Oct 1877:	Adjutant, Department of the Navy

31 Oct 1877 - 18 Jan 1878:	Commandant of the Naval Academy
18 Jan 1878 - 4 Dec 1880:	Commander, Yokosuka Submarine Base
21 Nov 1878:	Promoted to *Vice-Admiral*
4 Dec 1880 - 26 Apr 1886:	Admiral Commanding, Tokai Naval District
16 Jun 1881 - 12 Oct 1882:	Vice Lord of the Navy
12 Oct 1882 - 29 Jun 1885:	Commandant, Naval Engineering Academy
26 Apr 1886 - 8 Mar 1889:	Admiral Commanding, Yokosuka Naval District, Member, Admirals Committee
8 Mar 1889 - 12 Dec 1892:	Admiral Commanding, Kure Naval District
12 Dec 1892 - 20 May 1893:	Commandant of the Naval College, Member, Admirals Committee
12 Dec 1892 - 17 Jul 1894:	Chief of the Naval General Staff, Member, Admirals Committee
17 Jul 1894 - 1 Feb 1900:	Navy Councillor
1 Feb 1900:	Transferred to the reserve

Rear-Admiral **Katsuji NAKANO** (20 Feb 1891 - 13 Jun 1944)

16 Oct 1943 - 13 Jun 1944:	Commander, 57th Submarine Chaser Division
13 Jun 1944:	Posthumously promoted to *Rear-Admiral*

Vice-Admiral **Naoe NAKANO** (16 Feb 1868 - 6 Jul 1960)

1 Dec 1913:	Promoted to *Rear-Admiral*
1 Dec 1913 - 17 Apr 1914:	Chief of Staff, Kure Naval District
17 Apr 1914 - 1 Oct 1915:	Chief of Bureau 1, Naval Shipbuilding Command
1 Oct 1915 - 1 Apr 1916:	Chief of Shipping Division, Department of the Navy
1 Apr 1916 - 1 Dec 1917:	Chief of Shipping Bureau, Department of the Navy
1 Dec 1917:	Promoted to *Vice-Admiral*
1 Dec 1917 - 6 Jun 1918:	Member, Admirals Committee
6 Jun 1918 - 18 Oct 1918:	Chief of Shipping Bureau, Department of the Navy
18 Oct 1918 - 10 Sep 1919:	C-in-C, Training Fleet
10 Sep 1919 - 8 Nov 1919:	Member, Admirals Committee
8 Nov 1919 - 1 Oct 1920:	Commander, Kure Navy Yard
1 Oct 1920 - 1 Dec 1921:	Commander, Ryojun Guard District
1 Dec 1921 - 27 Jul 1922:	Commander, 2nd Escort Flotilla
27 Jul 1922 - 1 Dec 1922:	C-in-C, 3rd Fleet
1 Dec 1922 - 1 Jun 1923:	C-in-C, 2nd Fleet
1 Jun 1923 - 1 Dec 1923:	Member, Admirals Committee
1 Dec 1923 - 25 Feb 1924:	Unassigned
25 Feb 1924:	Transferred to the reserve

Rear-Admiral **Sadao NAKANO** (18 Aug 1893 - 24 Jun 1983)

1 Apr 1943 - 20 Apr 1944:	Chief Engineer Officer, Kure Naval District

5 Apr 1943 - 20 Apr 1944:	Chief of Shipping Bureau, Kure Naval District
1 May 1943:	Promoted to *Rear-Admiral*
20 Apr 1944 - 1 May 1944:	Staff officer, 1st Southern Expeditionary Fleet
1 May 1944 - 15 Jun 1945:	Chief of 101st Supply Bureau
15 Jun 1945 - 10 Aug 1945:	Attached to Yokosuka Naval District
10 Aug 1945 - 15 Sep 1945:	Chief of Bureau 3, Kinki Area Supervisor Office, Department of Military Supply

Rear-Admiral (Paymaster) **Shigaharu NAKANO** (5 Jan 1876 - 10 Nov 1960)

25 May 1923 - 18 Sep 1925:	Chief of Accounting Bureau, Kure Navy Yard
1 Dec 1923:	Promoted to *Rear-Admiral (Paymaster)*
18 Sep 1925 - 1 Dec 1925:	Attached to Naval General Staff
15 Dec 1925:	Transferred to the reserve

Vice-Admiral (Surgeon) **Taro NAKANO** (11 Mar 1887 - 16 Oct 1954)

15 Nov 1935:	Promoted to *Rear-Admiral (Surgeon)*
15 Nov 1935 - 21 Sep 1936:	Director, Beppu Naval Hospital
21 Sep 1936 - 15 Nov 1938:	Director, Sasebo Naval Hospital, Chief Surgeon, Sasebo Naval District
15 Nov 1938 - 1 Mar 1939:	Director, Kure Naval Hospital, Chief Surgeon, Kure Naval District
1 Mar 1939 - 15 Nov 1939:	Director, Yokosuka Naval Hospital, Chief Surgeon, Yokosuka Naval District
15 Nov 1939:	Promoted to *Vice-Admiral (Surgeon)*
15 Nov 1939 - 15 Oct 1941:	Chief of Naval Medical Service
15 Oct 1941 - 11 Mar 1942:	Attached to Naval General Staff
12 Mar 1942:	Transferred to the reserve

Rear-Admiral **Hachiro NAKAO** (15 Aug 1891 - 22 Sep 1944)

17 Jul 1943 - 22 Sep 1944:	Captain, Oiler *"Shiriya"*
22 Sep 1944:	Posthumously promoted to *Rear-Admiral*

Rear-Admiral **Kanefusa NAKAO** (21 Jul 1885 - 12 Dec 1949)

15 Nov 1932 - 15 Nov 1933:	Chief of Shipping Bureau, Kure Naval District
1 Dec 1932:	Promoted to *Rear-Admiral*
15 Nov 1933 - 11 Dec 1933:	Attached to Naval General Staff
15 Dec 1933:	Transferred to the reserve

Rear-Admiral **Kumataro NAKAO** (20 Oct 1901 - 16 May 1945)

1 Dec 1943 - 16 May 1945:	Staff officer, 5th Escort Flotilla
16 May 1945:	Posthumously promoted to *Rear-Admiral*

Rear-Admiral (Surgeon) **Taichiro NAKAO** (3 Oct 1861 - ?)
1 Dec 1913 - 1 Dec 1914:	Staff officer, Medical Bureau, Department of the Navy
1 Dec 1914:	Promoted to *General (Surgeon)*
1 Dec 1914 - 1 Feb 1915:	Attached to the Department of the Navy
1 Feb 1915 - 1 Dec 1915:	Unassigned
1 Dec 1915:	Transferred to the reserve
23 Sep 1919:	Redesignated *Rear-Admiral (Surgeon)*

Vice-Admiral **Yu NAKAO** (12 Sep 1856 - 10 Dec 1926)
12 Jan 1905 - 14 Jun 1905:	Chief of Staff, Yokosuka Naval District
14 Jun 1905:	Promoted to *Rear-Admiral*
14 Jun 1905 - 20 Dec 1905:	C-in-C, 4th Fleet
20 Dec 1905 - 22 Nov 1906:	C-in-C, 2nd Fleet
22 Nov 1906 - 28 Aug 1908:	Commander, Sasebo Harbor
28 Aug 1908 - 1 Dec 1911:	Chief of Naval Hydrography Command
1 Dec 1910:	Promoted to *Vice-Admiral*
1 Dec 1911 - 1 Dec 1912:	Unassigned
1 Dec 1912:	Transferred to the reserve

Rear-Admiral **Nobuki NAKAOKI** (1 Jan 1895 - 5 Nov 1943)
1 Dec 1942 - 5 Nov 1943:	Captain, Heavy Cruiser *"Atago"*
5 Nov 1943:	Posthumously promoted to *Rear-Admiral*

Rear-Admiral **Noboru NAKASE** (6 Mar 1896 - 17 Sep 1983)
25 Dec 1943 - 25 Feb 1945:	Captain, Battleship *"Ise"*
15 Oct 1944:	Promoted to *Rear-Admiral*
25 Feb 1945 - 7 Mar 1945:	Attached to Kure Naval District
7 Mar 1945 - 15 Apr 1945:	Attached to Naval General Staff
15 Apr 1945 - 1 Oct 1945:	Chief of Bureau 3, Naval General Staff

Rear-Admiral **Kyujiro NAKASUGI** (28 Feb 1886 - 15 Nov 1980)
1 Feb 1937 - 1 Dec 1937:	Chief of Section 11, Bureau 4, Naval General Staff
1 Dec 1937:	Promoted to *Rear-Admiral*
1 Dec 1937 - 16 Dec 1940:	Staff officer, Joint General Staff
21 Dec 1940:	Transferred to the reserve
1 Dec 1943 - 1 Mar 1945:	Recalled; Attached to Decipher Group, Naval General Staff
1 Mar 1945:	Demobilized

Rear-Admiral **Seiki NAKATSU** (23 Apr 1895 - 30 Jun 1944)
20 Sep 1943 - 30 Jun 1944:	Captain, Minelayer *"Tsugaru"*
30 Jun 1944:	Posthumously promoted to *Rear-Admiral*

Rear-Admiral **Eiichi NAKAYA** (23 Sep 1899 - 25 Oct 1944)
1 Apr 1944 - 25 Oct 1944:   Chief Engineer Officer, Battleship *"Fuso"*
25 Oct 1944:   Posthumously promoted to *Rear-Admiral*

Rear-Admiral **Tatsujiro NAKAYA** (12 May 1884 - 9 Nov 1969)
1 Dec 1930:   Promoted to *Rear-Admiral*
1 Dec 1930 - 1 Apr 1931:   Attached to Naval Shipbuilding Command
1 Apr 1931 - 15 Nov 1932:   Chief of Explosives Bureau, Navy Powder Yard
15 Nov 1932 - 10 Dec 1932: Attached to Naval Shipbuilding Command
15 Dec 1932:   Transferred to the reserve

Rear-Admiral **Michimoto NAKAYAMA** (12 Feb 1887 - 8 Nov 1979)
15 Nov 1935 - 1 Dec 1936:   Commander, Kure Defense Force
1 Dec 1936:   Promoted to *Rear-Admiral*
1 Dec 1936 - 15 Dec 1936:   Attached to Naval General Staff
22 Dec 1936:   Transferred to the reserve

Rear-Admiral **Nagaaki NAKAYAMA** (14 Jun 1855 - 13 Jan 1935)
12 Jan 1904 - 12 Mar 1907: Commander, Maizuru Harbor
2 Nov 1905:   Promoted to *Rear-Admiral*
12 Mar 1907 - 15 May 1908: Commander, Yokosuka Harbor
15 May 1908 - 31 May 1909: Unassigned
31 May 1909:   Transferred to the reserve

Rear-Admiral **Tomonobu NAKAYAMA** (13 Jun 1882 - 6 Jul 1937)
10 Nov 1923 - 1 Dec 1927:   Commander, Yokosuka Harbor
1 Dec 1927:   Promoted to *Rear-Admiral*
1 Dec 1927 - 15 Dec 1927:   Attached to Yokosuka Naval District
25 Dec 1927:   Transferred to the reserve

Vice-Admiral **Shigetsugu NAKAZATO** (28 Aug 1871 - 21 Jan 1945)
1 Dec 1913 - 13 Dec 1915:   Chief of Bureau 3, Naval General Staff
13 Dec 1915 - 1 Dec 1916:   Captain, Armored Cruiser *"Kasuga"*
1 Dec 1916 - 15 Aug 1918:   Captain, Armored Cruiser *"Iwate"*
15 Aug 1918 - 4 Sep 1918:   Attached to Naval General Staff
4 Sep 1918 - 1 Dec 1921:   Chief of Bureau 2, Naval General Staff
1 Dec 1918:   Promoted to *Rear-Admiral*
1 Dec 1921 - 11 Jun 1924:   Chief of Supply Bureau, Department of the Navy
1 Dec 1922:   Promoted to *Vice-Admiral*
11 Jun 1924 - 4 Oct 1924:   Attached to Naval General Staff
4 Oct 1924 - 1 Jun 1925:   Admiral Commanding, Maizuru Naval District
1 Jun 1925 - 15 Jun 1925:   Attached to Naval General Staff
19 Jun 1925:   Transferred to the reserve

Vice-Admiral **Tasuku NAKAZAWA** (28 Jun 1894 - 22 Dec 1977)
25 Jul 1941 - 6 Nov 1942:	Chief of Staff, 5th Fleet
1 Nov 1942:	Promoted to *Rear-Admiral*
6 Nov 1942 - 10 Dec 1942:	Attached to Naval General Staff
10 Dec 1942 - 15 Jun 1943:	Chief of Naval Personnel, Department of the Navy
15 Jun 1943 - 5 Dec 1944:	Chief of Bureau 1, Naval General Staff
5 Dec 1944 - 20 Dec 1944:	Staff officer, 2nd Air Fleet
20 Dec 1944 - 5 Feb 1945:	Commander, 21st Air Flotilla
5 Feb 1945 - 10 May 1945:	Commander, Taiwan Air Division
10 May 1945 - 15 Jun 1945:	Chief of Staff, 1st Air Fleet
10 May - Nov 1945:	Chief of Staff, Takao Guard District
1 Nov 1945:	Promoted to *Vice-Admiral*

Rear-Admiral **Takashi NAMIKAWA** (6 Jan 1897 - 1 Mar 1989)
10 Oct 1943 - 15 Sep 1944:	Chief of Research Bureau, 1st Navy Fuel Yard
1 Nov 1943:	Promoted to *Rear-Admiral*
15 Sep 1944 - 1 Nov 1945:	Commander, 2nd Navy Fuel Yard

Rear-Admiral **Kikuo NANBA** (27 Sep 1895 - 9 Feb 1969)
1 Apr 1944 - 1 Nov 1945:	Commander, 12th Air Arsenal
15 Oct 1944:	Promoted to *Rear-Admiral*

Rear-Admiral (Paymaster) **Chuzo NANBU** (15 Apr 1894 - 26 Nov 1968)
25 Oct 1943 - Oct 1945:	Paymaster-General, 2nd Southern Expeditionary Fleet, Chief of 102nd Accounting Bureau
1 May 1945:	Promoted to *Rear-Admiral (Paymaster)*

Rear-Admiral **Jiro NANGO** (21 Dec 1876 - 5 Mar 1951)
1 Dec 1922:	Promoted to *Rear-Admiral*
1 Dec 1922 - 1 Dec 1923:	Commander, Sasebo Defense Force
1 Dec 1923 - 10 Dec 1923:	Attached to Naval General Staff
10 Dec 1923 - 25 Feb 1924:	Unassigned
25 Feb 1924:	Transferred to the reserve

Rear-Admiral **Danichi NANRI** (7 Dec 1869 - 28 Jan 1931)
1 Dec 1917:	Promoted to *Rear-Admiral*
1 Dec 1917 - 4 Sep 1918:	Chief of Ordnance Bureau, Yokosuka Navy Yard
4 Sep 1918 - 1 Dec 1920:	Commander, Maizuru Navy Yard
1 Dec 1920 - 10 Dec 1920:	Attached to Maizuru Naval District
10 Dec 1920 - 1 Aug 1921:	Unassigned
1 Aug 1921:	Transferred to the reserve

Rear-Admiral (Paymaster) **Masaji NANRI** (4 Aug 1888 - 18 Nov 1965)
15 Nov 1935 - 1 Dec 1937: Chief of Section 3, Supply Bureau, Department of the Navy
1 Dec 1937: Promoted to *Rear-Admiral*
1 Dec 1937 - 15 Dec 1937: Attached to Naval General Staff
21 Dec 1937: Transferred to the reserve

Rear-Admiral **Toshihide NANRI** (4 Jul 1885 - 12 Oct 1952)
15 Nov 1932 - 1 Jul 1936: Commander of Naval Facilities, Maizuru Guard District
15 Nov 1933: Promoted to *Rear-Admiral*
1 Jul 1936 - 1 Dec 1936: Commander, Maizuru Navy Yard
1 Dec 1936 - 15 Dec 1936: Attached to Naval General Staff
22 Dec 1936: Transferred to the reserve

Rear-Admiral **Hachiro NAOTSUKA** (20 Oct 1888 - 21 Sep 1942)
20 Jul 1942 - 21 Sep 1942: Commander, 58th Submarine Chaser Division
21 Sep 1942: Posthumously promoted to *Rear-Admiral*

Rear-Admiral **Shogo NARAHARA** (31 Mar 1898 - 19 Jul 1944)
1 May 1944 - 19 Jul 1944: Commander, 7th Submarine Division
19 Jul 1944: Posthumously promoted to *Rear-Admiral*

Rear-Admiral **Jiro NARITA** (15 Nov 1888 - 3 Jul 1974)
15 Aug 1935 - 15 Dec 1936: Chief of Ordnance Bureau, Sasebo Navy Yard
1 Dec 1936: Promoted to *Rear-Admiral*
21 Dec 1936: Transferred to the reserve

Rear-Admiral **Katsuro NARITA** (29 Nov 1960 - 27 Dec 1943)
22 Nov 1904 - 20 Apr 1907: Commandant, Gunnery Training Center
12 Mar 1907: Promoted to *Rear-Admiral*
20 Apr 1907 - 10 Aug 1907: Commandant, Naval Gunnery School
10 Aug 1907 - 28 Aug 1908: Attached to Department of the Navy
28 Aug 1908 - 27 Aug 1909: Unassigned
27 Aug 1909: Transferred to the reserve

Rear-Admiral **Moichi NARITA** (? - 11 Nov 1942)
10 Apr 1942 - 11 Nov 1942: Captain, Light Cruiser *"Oi"*
11 Nov 1942: Posthumously promoted to *Rear-Admiral*

Rear-Admiral **Hakaru NARUKAWA** (20 Oct 1859 - 26 Jan 1919)
14 Jun 1905 - 4 Nov 1905: Captain, Auxiliary Tanker *"Nihon-maru"*
4 Nov 1905 - 27 Dec 1906: Unassigned

30 Nov 1906:	Promoted to *Rear-Admiral*
27 Dec 1906:	Transferred to the reserve

Rear-Admiral **Seiji NARUSE** (26 Dec 1893 - 29 Jan 1960)

1 Apr 1943 - 15 Feb 1945:	Chief of Torpedo Bureau, Air Technical Arsenal
1 May 1944:	Promoted to *Rear-Admiral*
15 Feb 1945 - 30 Sep 1945:	Chief of Torpedo Bureau, 1st Technical Arsenal

Vice-Admiral **Baron Tokioki NASHIBA** (19 Aug 1850 - 24 Oct 1928)

7 Jul 1903:	Promoted to *Rear-Admiral*
7 Jul 1903 - 5 Sep 1903:	Commander, Kure Harbor
5 Sep 1903 - 28 Dec 1903:	C-in-C, Readiness Fleet
28 Dec 1903 - 12 Jan 1905:	C-in-C, 1st Fleet, Commander, 1st Escort Flotilla
12 Jan 1905 - 4 Nov 1905:	C-in-C, Ryojun Naval District Fleet
4 Nov 1905 - 12 Dec 1905:	Unassigned
12 Dec 1905 - 28 May 1906:	Commander, Yokosuka Harbor
28 May 1906 - 22 Nov 1906:	Commander, Sasebo Harbor
22 Nov 1906 - 23 Mar 1907:	Commander, Mako Guard District
23 Mar 1907:	Promoted to *Vice-Admiral*
23 Mar 1907 - 8 May 1907:	Member, Admirals Committee
8 May 1907 - 31 Oct 1907:	Unassigned
31 Oct 1907:	Transferred to the reserve

Admiral **Matahachiro NAWA** (22 Dec 1863 - 12 Jan 1928)

18 Dec 1907 - 23 May 1910:	Chief of Bureau 4, Naval General Staff
28 Aug 1908:	Promoted to *Rear-Admiral*
23 May 1910 - 20 Apr 1912:	Chief of Staff, Kure Naval District
20 Apr 1912 - 25 Mar 1914:	C-in-C, 3rd Fleet
1 Dec 1912:	Promoted to *Vice-Admiral*
25 Mar 1914 - 5 Feb 1915:	Member, Admirals Committee
22 Apr 1914 - 5 Feb 1915:	Chief of Naval Training Command
5 Feb 1915 - 13 Dec 1915:	C-in-C, 2nd Fleet
13 Dec 1915 - 1 Dec 1917:	Admiral Commanding, Maizuru Naval District
1 Dec 1917 - 24 Aug 1920:	Admiral Commanding, Yokosuka Naval District, Member, Admirals Committee
2 Jul 1918:	Promoted to *Admiral*
24 Aug 1920 - 10 Dec 1922:	Navy Councillor
10 Dec 1922 - 31 Mar 1923:	Unassigned
31 Mar 1923:	Transferred to the reserve

Vice-Admiral **Takeshi NAWA** (28 Nov 1892 - 22 Jun 1972)

15 Nov 1939 - 15 Oct 1941:	Chief of Electronics Bureau, Kure Navy Yard

15 Nov 1940:	Promoted to *Rear-Admiral*
15 Oct 1941 - 1 Jul 1943:	Chief of Bureau 3, Naval Shipbuilding Command
1 Jul 1943 - 10 Jul 1943:	Attached to Technical Research Department
10 Jul 1943 - 15 Feb 1945:	Chief of Radio Research Bureau, Technical Research Department
1 May 1944:	Promoted to *Vice-Admiral*
15 Feb 1945 - 20 Nov 1945:	Chief of Radio and Communications Bureaus, 2nd Technical Arsenal

Rear-Admiral **Kazutaka NIIMI** (18 Oct 1889 - 23 Feb 1944)

28 Oct 1943 - 23 Feb 1944:	Commander of Minesweepers, Oiler *"Ogura-maru No. 3"*
23 Feb 1944:	Posthumously promoted to *Rear-Admiral*

Vice-Admiral **Masaichi NIIMI** (4 Feb 1887 - 2 Feb 1993)

15 Nov 1935:	Promoted to *Rear-Admiral*
15 Nov 1935 - 1 Apr 1936:	Chief of Staff, Kure Naval District
1 Apr 1936 - 1 Dec 1936:	Chief of Staff, 2nd Fleet
1 Dec 1936 - 1 Dec 1937:	Attached to Naval General Staff
1 Dec 1937 - 15 Nov 1939:	Chief of Naval Training Bureau, Department of the Navy
15 Nov 1939:	Promoted to *Vice-Admiral*
15 Nov 1939 - 4 Apr 1941:	Commandant of the Naval Academy
4 Apr 1941 - 14 Jul 1942:	C-in-C, 2nd China Expeditionary Fleet
14 Jul 1942 - 1 Dec 1932:	Admiral Commanding, Maizuru Naval District
1 Dec 1943 - 15 Mar 1944:	Attached to Naval General Staff
20 Mar 1944:	Transferred to the reserve

Vice-Admiral **Yoshiyuki NIIYAMA** (1 Jul 1885 - 17 Feb 1954)

30 Nov 1929 - 1 Dec 1931:	Commander, Sasebo Defense Force
1 Dec 1930:	Promoted to *Rear-Admiral*
1 Dec 1931 - 15 Nov 1933:	Chief of Staff, Sasebo Naval District
15 Nov 1933 - 15 Nov 1934:	Commander, Mako Guard District
15 Nov 1934:	Promoted to *Vice-Admiral*
15 Nov 1934 - 25 Mar 1935:	Attached to Naval General Staff
30 Mar 1935:	Transferred to the reserve

Rear-Admiral **Ichiro NIJIMA** (3 Oct 1954 - 8 Feb 1922)

10 May 1905 - 2 Feb 1906:	Chief of Staff, Kure Naval District
2 Nov 1905:	Promoted to *Rear-Admiral*
2 Feb 1906 - 7 Apr 1906:	Chief of Staff, Sasebo Naval District
7 Apr 1906 - 14 Feb 1907:	Unassigned
14 Feb 1907:	Transferred to the reserve

Rear-Admiral **Nobuo NIJIMA** (1 Oct 1896 - 30 Apr 1981)
27 Jul 1942 - 5 May 1945:	Adjutant, Naval General Staff
1 May 1945:	Promoted to *Rear-Admiral*
5 May 1945 - 20 Oct 1945:	Commander, Chinkai Sailors Corps
10 Jul 1945 - 20 Oct 1945:	Commander, Chinkai Combined Marine Force

Vice-Admiral **Yukitake NIKAIDO** (20 Feb 1889 - 7 Apr 1978)
1 Jun 1934 - 20 Sep 1939:	Chief of Steel Bureau, Kure Navy Yard
1 Dec 1936:	Promoted to *Rear-Admiral*
20 Sep 1939 - 15 Nov 1940:	Commander, Maizuru Navy Yard
15 Nov 1940:	Promoted to *Vice-Admiral*
15 Nov 1940 - 1 Nov 1942:	Chief of Technical Research Department
1 Nov 1942 - 1 Dec 1943:	Commander, Yokosuka Navy Yard
1 Dec 1943 - 15 Dec 1943:	Attached to Naval General Staff
20 Dec 1943:	Transferred to the reserve

Rear-Admiral **Teizo NIPPA** (15 May 1890 - 13 Mar 1967)
11 Aug 1941 - 20 May 1942:	Commander, Maizuru Sailors Corps
15 Oct 1941:	Promoted to *Rear-Admiral*
20 Nov 1941 - 20 May 1942:	Commander, Maizuru Guard Force
20 May 1942 - 25 Nov 1942:	Attached to Ominato Guard District
25 Nov 1942 - 1 Jan 1944:	Commander, Chishima Area Base Force
1 Jan 1944 - 5 Feb 1944:	Attached to Naval General Staff
5 Feb 1944 - 10 Apr 1944:	Commander, Sasebo Defense Flotilla
10 Apr 1944 - 20 Jan 1945:	Commander, 4th Maritime Escort Force, Commander, Okinawa Area Auxiliary Base
20 Jan 1945 - 1 May 1945:	Commander, Sasebo Guard Force
1 May 1945 - 15 May 1945:	Attached to Naval General Staff
21 May 1945:	Transferred to the reserve
15 Jul 1945 - 5 Oct 1945:	Recalled; Chief of Transport Bureau, Maizuru Naval District

Vice-Admiral (Surgeon) **Isao NISHI** (7 Feb 1869 - 27 Mar 1948)
13 Dec 1915 - 1 Jun 1919:	Director, Sasebo Naval Hospital, Chief Surgeon, Sasebo Naval District
1 Dec 1917:	Promoted to *General (Surgeon)*
1 Jun 1919 - 1 Dec 1919:	Unassigned
23 Sep 1919:	Redesignated *Rear-Admiral (Surgeon)*
1 Dec 1919 - 1 Dec 1922:	Commandant, Navy Medical School
1 Jun 1922:	Promoted to *Vice-Admiral (Surgeon)*
1 Dec 1922 - 10 Dec 1922:	Attached to Naval General Staff
10 Dec 1922 - 31 Mar 1923:	Unassigned
31 Mar 1923:	Transferred to the reserve

Vice-Admiral **Baron Shinrokuro NISHI** (28 Sep 1860 - 16 Oct 1933)
26 May 1908 - 1 Dec 1912:	Aide-de-Camp to the Emperor
28 Aug 1908:	Promoted to *Rear-Admiral*
1 Dec 1912 - 14 Apr 1913:	Member, Admirals Committee
14 Apr 1913 - 1 Dec 1913:	Commander, Mako Guard District
25 Sep 1913:	Promoted to *Vice-Admiral*
1 Dec 1913 - 1 Dec 1914:	Unassigned
1 Dec 1914:	Transferred to the reserve

Rear-Admiral **Yoshikatsu NISHI** (3 Aug 1882 - 11 Mar 1933)
20 May 1926 - 30 Nov 1929:	Chief of Supply Bureau, Sasebo Naval District
1 Dec 1926:	Promoted to *Rear-Admiral*
30 Nov 1929 - 1 May 1930:	Attached to Naval General Staff
10 May 1930:	Transferred to the reserve

Rear-Admiral **Heishiro NISHIDA** (13 Oct 1894 - 28 Jan 1948)
1 Apr 1943 - 25 May 1944:	Chief of Fire Bureau, Air Technical Arsenal
1 May 1944:	Promoted to *Rear-Admiral*
25 May 1944 - 1 Nov 1945:	Chief of Ordnance Bureau, Sasebo Navy Yard

Vice-Admiral **Shoji NISHIMURA** (30 Nov 1889 - 25 Oct 1944)
1 Nov 1940 - 20 Jun 1942:	Commander, 4th Destroyer Flotilla
15 Nov 1940:	Promoted to *Rear-Admiral*
20 Jun 1942 - 25 Jun 1942:	Staff officer, Combined Fleet
25 Jun 1942 - 25 Mar 1944:	Commander, 7th Battleship Flotilla
1 Nov 1943:	Promoted to *Vice-Admiral*
25 Mar 1944 - 10 Sep 1944:	Attached to Naval General Staff
10 Sep 1944 - 25 Oct 1944:	Commander, 2nd Battleship Flotilla

Rear-Admiral **Kozo NISHINA** (4 Dec 1895 - 29 Apr 1979)
10 Aug 1942 - 11 Nov 1943:	Chief of Merchant Naval Section, Administration Bureau, Naval Shipbuilding Command
1 Nov 1943:	Promoted to *Rear-Admiral*
11 Nov 1943 - 15 Nov 1943:	Staff officer, 6th (Submarine) Fleet
15 Nov 1943 - 21 Dec 1944:	Chief of Staff, 6th (Submarine) Fleet
1 Apr 1944 - 25 Apr 1944:	Commander, 30th Submarine Base Force
21 Dec 1944 - 15 Sep 1945:	Commander, 11th Submarine Flotilla

Vice-Admiral (Paymaster) **Sadaichi NISHINO** (19 Jun 1892 - 14 Jan 1968)
15 Oct 1941:	Promoted to *Rear-Admiral (Paymaster)*
15 Oct 1941 - 1 Nov 1942:	Chief of Accounting Bureau, Kure Navy Yard
1 Nov 1942 - 10 Dec 1944:	Chief of Accounting Bureau, Naval Air Command

10 Dec 1944 - Oct 1945:	Paymaster-General, Yokosuka Naval District
1 May 1945:	Promoted to *Vice-Admiral (Paymaster)*

Vice-Admiral **Hidehiko NISHIO** (12 Jan 1893 - 14 May 1961)
1 Aug 1941 - 21 Jan 1943:	Chief of Administration Bureau, Naval Facility Command
15 Oct 1941:	Promoted to *Rear-Admiral*
21 Jan 1943 - 1 Feb 1943:	Staff officer, Southeastern Area Fleet
1 Feb 1943 - 1 Sep 1943:	Deputy Chief of Staff, Southeastern Area Fleet
1 Sep 1943 - 20 Sep 1943:	Attached to Naval General Staff
20 Sep 1943 - 1 Mar 1944:	Deputy Chief of Staff, Southwestern Area Fleet
1 Mar 1944 - 1 Nov 1944:	Chief of Staff, Southwestern Area Fleet, Chief of Staff, 13th Air Fleet
15 Oct 1944:	Promoted to *Vice-Admiral*
1 Nov 1944 - 11 Dec 1944:	Attached to Naval General Staff
11 Dec 1944 - 25 Aug 1945:	Chief of Staff, Maritime Escort Fleet
25 Aug 1945 - 30 Sep 1945:	Attached to Naval General Staff

Rear-Admiral **Shiro NISHIO** (23 Oct 1886 - 3 Nov 1952)
14 Feb 1929 - 10 Jun 1933:	Chief of Mine Research Bureau, Yokosuka Navy Yard
10 Jun 1933 - 15 Nov 1934:	Attached to Naval General Staff
15 Nov 1934:	Promoted to *Rear-Admiral*
15 Nov 1934 - 15 Nov 1935:	Attached to Yokosuka Naval District
15 Nov 1935 - 10 Dec 1935:	Attached to Naval General Staff
14 Dec 1925:	Transferred to the reserve

Rear-Admiral **Yujiro NISHIO** (17 Sep 1868 - 10 May 1939)
1 Dec 1916 - 1 Jun 1919:	Chief of Bureau 3, Naval Technical Command
1 Dec 1917:	Promoted to *Rear-Admiral*
1 Jun 1919 - 2 Mar 1920:	Unassigned
2 Mar 1920:	Transferred to the reserve

Rear-Admiral **Kiichiro NISHIOKA** (2 Feb 1893 - 25 Feb 1957)
1 Oct 1942 - 1 Jun 1944:	Commander, 51st Air Arsenal
1 May 1944:	Promoted to *Rear-Admiral*
1 Jun 1944 - 20 Dec 1944:	Chief of Supply Bureau, 11th Air Arsenal
20 Dec 1944 - 1 Nov 1945:	Commander, 1st Air Arsenal

Rear-Admiral **Shigeyasu NISHIOKA** (20 Feb 1891 - 28 May 1963)
15 Jan 1944 - 5 May 1945:	Staff officer, Maritime Escort Fleet
1 May 1944:	Promoted to *Rear-Admiral*
5 Aug 1944 - 5 May 1945:	Commander, Anti-Submarine Training Unit
5 May 1945 - 15 Sep 1945:	Commander, 51st Escort Flotilla

Rear-Admiral **Sanechika NISHIYAMA** (21 Sep 1860 - 19 Mar 1915)
1 Dec 1909 - 28 Sep 1910:	Chief of Naval Staff, Government of Taiwan
28 Sep 1910 - 12 Jul 1912:	Unassigned
12 Jul 1912:	Promoted to *Rear-Admiral*
12 Jul 1912:	Transferred to the reserve

Rear-Admiral **Yasukichi NISHIYAMA** (20 Dec 1863 - 19 Oct 1913)
5 May 1910 - 16 Jan 1911:	Captain, Battlecruiser *"Kurama"*, Executive Officer, Yokosuka Navy Yard
16 Jan 1911 - 15 Feb 1913:	Unassigned
15 Feb 1913:	Promoted to *Rear-Admiral*
15 Feb 1913:	Transferred to the reserve

Rear-Admiral **Katsuyuki NISHIZAKI** (7 Apr 1881 - 14 Oct 1949)
1 Dec 1927:	Promoted to *Rear-Admiral*
1 Dec 1927 - 1 Mar 1928:	Attached to Naval Shipbuilding Command
1 Mar 1928 - 1 Dec 1931:	Chief of Bureau 2, Naval Shipbuilding Command
1 Dec 1931 - 15 Dec 1931:	Attached to Naval Shipbuilding Command
21 Dec 1931:	Transferred to the reserve

Rear-Admiral **Shigenobu NISHIZAWA** (14 Mar 1894 - 14 May 1966)
1 Feb 1944 - 1 May 1945:	Chief of Submarine Bureau, Yokosuka Navy Yard
15 Oct 1944:	Promoted to *Rear-Admiral*
1 May 1945 - 1 Jul 1945:	Attached to Kure Naval District
1 Jul 1945 - 20 Sep 1945:	Chief of Ship Repair Bureau, Naval Shipbuilding Command

Rear-Admiral **Shigeharu NITTA** (13 May 1889 - 5 Apr 1982)
15 Oct 1940:	Promoted to *Rear-Admiral*
15 Oct 1940 - 10 Sep 1941:	Attached to Technical Research Department
10 Sep 1941 - 1 May 1943:	Chief of Scientific Research Bureau, Technical Research Department
1 May 1943 - 1 Apr 1944:	Chief of Chemical Research Bureau, Technical Research Department
1 Apr 1944 - 30 May 1944:	Attached to Naval General Staff
31 May 1944:	Transferred to the reserve

Rear-Admiral **Yoshio NITTA** (25 Mar 1879 - 23 Sep 1970)
15 Apr 1925 - 20 May 1926:	Chief of Supply Bureau, Sasebo Naval District
20 May 1926 - 1 Dec 1927:	Instructor, Naval College
1 Dec 1926:	Promoted to *Rear-Admiral*
1 Dec 1927 - 15 Dec 1927:	Attached to Naval General Staff
25 Dec 1927:	Transferred to the reserve

Rear-Admiral **Noritada NIWA** (Mar 1859 - 4 Jan 1944)
26 May 1908 - 28 Aug 1908:	Chief of Bureau 2, Naval Shipbuilding Command
28 Aug 1908:	Promoted to *Rear-Admiral*
28 Aug 1908 - 27 Aug 1909:	Unassigned
27 Aug 1909:	Transferred to the reserve

Vice-Admiral **Shozo NIWATA** (29 Sep 1889 - 9 Apr 1980)
15 Dec 1937 - 15 Nov 1939:	Chief of Shipbuilding Bureau, Sasebo Navy Yard
15 Nov 1938:	Promoted to *Rear-Admiral*
15 Nov 1939 - 15 Sep 1942:	Chief of Shipbuilding Bureau, Kure Navy Yard
15 Sep 1942 - 15 Dec 1942:	Attached to Bureau 4, Naval Shipbuilding Command
1 Nov 1942:	Promoted to *Vice-Admiral*
21 Dec 1942:	Transferred to the reserve

Vice-Admiral **Shigeoki NOBETA** (19 Feb 1883 - 28 Feb 1952)
10 Dec 1928 - 1 Dec 1930:	Commandant, Submarine School
1 Dec 1930:	Promoted to *Rear-Admiral*
1 Dec 1930 - 15 Nov 1932:	Commander, 2nd Submarine Flotilla
15 Nov 1932 - 1 Apr 1933:	Chief of Bureau 5, Naval Shipbuilding Command
1 Apr 1933 - 15 Nov 1934:	Chief of Bureau 6, Naval Shipbuilding Command
15 Nov 1934:	Promoted to *Vice-Admiral*
15 Nov 1934 - 10 Dec 1934:	Attached to Naval Shipbuilding Command
15 Dec 1934:	Transferred to the reserve

Rear-Admiral **Yasuji NOBUTANI** (10 Nov 1890 - 18 Mar 1950)
8 Oct 1943 - 10 Mar 1945:	Chief of Navigation Research Bureau, Yokosuka Navy Yard
1 Nov 1943:	Promoted to *Rear-Admiral*
10 Mar 1945 - 15 Sep 1945:	Chief of Examination Bureau, Yokosuka Navy Yard

Rear-Admiral **Kenzo NODA** (2 Nov 1886 - 8 Oct 1943)
25 Jan 1943 - 8 Oct 1943:	Chief of Traffic Control, 1st Maritime Escort Force
8 Oct 1943:	Posthumously promoted to *Rear-Admiral*

Vice-Admiral **Kiyoshi NODA** (6 Jul 1887 - 29 Mar 1974)
28 Jul 1934 - 15 Dec 1938:	Chief of Public Relations Bureau, Department of the Navy
15 Nov 1934:	Promoted to *Rear-Admiral*
15 Nov 1938:	Promoted to *Vice-Admiral*
21 Dec 1938:	Transferred to the reserve

Vice-Admiral **Tsuruo NODA** (24 Jan 1875 - 9 Jan 1936)
1 Apr 1919 - 1 Dec 1922: Chief of Steel Bureau, Kure Navy Yard
1 Apr 1921: Promoted to *Rear-Admiral*
1 Dec 1922 - 1 Apr 1923: Commander, Ordnance Arsenal
1 Apr 1923 - 7 Dec 1925: Chief of Technical Research Department
1 Dec 1925: Promoted to *Vice-Admiral*
9 Dec 1925: Transferred to the reserve

Rear-Admiral **Gosaburo NOGUCHI** (25 Apr 1902 - 27 Oct 1944)
28 Mar 1944: Chief Engineer Officer, Heavy Cruiser *"Chokai"*
27 Oct 1944: Posthumously promoted to *Rear-Admiral*

Rear-Admiral **Okikuni NOGUCHI** (4 Aug 1871 - 28 Dec 1942)
1 Apr 1916 - 1 Dec 1917: Chief Engineer Officer, 3rd Fleet
1 Dec 1917 - 1 Apr 1918: Attached to Yokosuka Naval District
1 Apr 1918 - 1 Jun 1919: Staff officer, Engineering Bureau, Department of the Navy
1 Jun 1919: Promoted to *Rear-Admiral*
1 Jun 1919 - 2 Mar 1920: Unassigned
2 Mar 1920: Transferred to the reserve

Rear-Admiral **Rokuro NOGUCHI** (4 Nov 1899 - 25 Oct 1944)
20 Sep 1944 - 25 Oct 1944: Chief Engineer Officer, 1st Task Fleet, Chief Engineer Officer, 3rd Fleet
25 Oct 1944: Posthumously promoted to *Rear-Admiral*

Admiral **Kaneo NOMAGUCHI** (14 Feb 1866 - 24 Dec 1943)
1 Dec 1909: Promoted to *Rear-Admiral*
1 Dec 1909 - 11 Mar 1911: Chief of Staff, 1st Fleet
11 Mar 1911 - 21 Sep 1911: Chief of Staff, Sasebo Naval District
21 Sep 1911 - 20 Apr 1912: Commandant, Naval Gunnery School
20 Apr 1912 - 10 Jan 1913: Chief of Staff, Kure Naval District
10 Jan 1913 - 17 Apr 1914: Chief, Bureau of Naval Affairs, Department of the Navy, Member, Admirals Committee
17 Apr 1914 - 13 Dec 1915: Commander, Kure Navy Yard
29 May 1914: Promoted to *Vice-Admiral*
13 Dec 1915 - 1 Dec 1916: Commander, 6th Escort Flotilla
1 Dec 1916 - 1 Dec 1918: Commandant of the Naval Academy
1 Dec 1918 - 1 Dec 1919: Admiral Commanding, Maizuru Naval District
1 Dec 1919 - 1 Dec 1920: C-in-C, 3rd Fleet
16 Aug 1920: Promoted to *Admiral*
1 Dec 1920 - 1 Apr 1923: Chief of Naval Training Command, Member, Admirals Committee

1 Apr 1923 - 15 May 1923:	Navy Councillor
15 May 1923 - 5 Feb 1924:	Admiral Commanding, Yokosuka Naval District, Member, Admirals Committee
5 Feb 1924 - 10 Mar 1924:	Navy Councillor
20 Mar 1924:	Transferred to the reserve

Rear-Admiral **Kanetomo NOMAGUCHI** (? - 11 Jul 1943)

20 Oct 1941 - 11 Jul 1943:	Commander, 5th Destroyer Division
11 Jul 1943:	Posthumously promoted to *Rear-Admiral*

Rear-Admiral **Saburo NOMIYA** (28 Apr 1891 - 3 Oct 1950)

20 Aug 1941 - 25 Aug 1942:	Chief Engineer Officer, China Area Fleet
1 May 1942:	Promoted to *Rear-Admiral*
25 Aug 1942 - 20 Apr 1943:	Chief of Supply Bureau, Maizuru Naval District
20 Apr 1943 - 20 May 1944:	Commander, 5th Navy Fuel Yard
20 May 1944 - 26 Jun 1944:	Staff officer, 2nd Southern Expeditionary Fleet
26 Jun 1944 - Oct 1945:	Commander, 102nd Navy Fuel Yard

Rear-Admiral **Tameki NOMOTO** (29 Aug 1894 - 19 Dec 1987)

1 Sep 1944 - 15 Dec 1944:	Commander, 11th Combined Air Division, Commander, Kasumigaura Air Division
15 Oct 1944:	Promoted to *Rear-Admiral*
15 Dec 1944 - 15 Sep 1945:	Commander, 903rd Air Division

Vice-Admiral **Tsunaakira NOMOTO** (15 Feb 1858 - 7 Dec 1922)

12 Mar 1907:	Promoted to *Rear-Admiral*
12 Mar 1907 - 15 May 1908:	Commander, Yokosuka Torpedo Corps
15 May 1908 - 10 Dec 1908:	C-in-C, 2nd Fleet
10 Dec 1908 - 4 Mar 1909:	C-in-C, Kure Reserve Fleet
4 Mar 1909 - 1 Dec 1909:	Unassigned
1 Dec 1909 - 16 Jul 1910:	C-in-C, Yokosuka Reserve Fleet
16 Jul 1910 - 1 Dec 1911:	C-in-C, 1st Fleet
1 Dec 1911:	Promoted to *Vice-Admiral*
1 Dec 1911 - 1 Oct 1912:	Commander, Takeshiki Guard District
1 Oct 1912 - 31 Mar 1913:	Unassigned
31 Mar 1913:	Transferred to the reserve

Rear-Admiral **Fusajiro NOMURA** (7 Dec 1869 - 11 Jan 1941)

30 Jun 1915 - 1 Dec 1916:	Commander, Sasebo Sailors Corps, Captain, Battleship *"Okinoshima"*
1 Dec 1916:	Promoted to *Rear-Admiral*
1 Dec 1916 - 1 Dec 1917:	Unassigned
1 Dec 1917:	Transferred to the reserve

Admiral **Kichisaburo NOMURA** (16 Dec 1877 - 8 May 1964)
1 Jun 1922:	Promoted to *Rear-Admiral*
1 Jun 1922 - 15 Sep 1923:	Chief of Bureau 3, Naval General Staff
15 Sep 1923 - 20 Apr 1925:	C-in-C, 1st Expeditionary Fleet
20 Apr 1925 - 18 Sep 1925:	Attached to Naval General Staff
18 Sep 1925 - 26 Jul 1926:	Chief of Naval Training Bureau, Department of the Navy
26 Jul 1926 - 10 Dec 1928:	Deputy Chief of the Naval General Staff
1 Dec 1926:	Promoted to *Vice-Admiral*
10 Dec 1928 - 1 Feb 1929:	Attached to Naval General Staff
1 Feb 1929 - 15 Jan 1930:	C-in-C, Training Fleet
15 Jan 1930 - 11 Jun 1930:	Attached to Naval General Staff
11 Jun 1930 - 1 Dec 1931:	Admiral Commanding, Kure Naval District
1 Dec 1931 - 2 Feb 1932:	Admiral Commanding, Yokosuka Naval District, Member, Admirals Committee
2 Feb 1932 - 28 Jun 1932:	C-in-C, 3rd Fleet
28 Jun 1932 - 10 Oct 1932:	Navy Councillor
10 Oct 1932 - 15 Nov 1933:	Admiral Commanding, Yokosuka Naval District, Member, Admirals Committee
1 Mar 1933:	Promoted to *Admiral*
15 Nov 1933 - 6 Apr 1937:	Navy Councillor
6 Apr 1937:	Transferred to the reserve
25 Sep 1939 - 16 Jan 1940:	Minister of Foreign Affairs
27 Nov 1940 - 20 Aug 1942:	Extraordinary Ambassador to the USA

Rear-Admiral **Motoji NOMURA** (11 Oct 1896 - 4 Feb 1970)
15 Feb 1945 - 7 Jul 1945:	Chief of Pyrotechnical Bureau, 1st Technical Arsenal
1 May 1945:	Promoted to *Rear-Admiral*
7 Jul 1945 - 20 Sep 1945:	Chief of 1st Production Bureau, 3rd Navy Powder Yard

Admiral **Naokuni NOMURA** (15 May 1885 - 12 Dec 1973)
15 Nov 1933 - 15 Nov 1934:	Commandant, Submarine School
15 Nov 1934:	Promoted to *Rear-Admiral*
15 Nov 1934 - 15 Nov 1935:	Commander, 2nd Submarine Flotilla
15 Nov 1935 - 16 Nov 1936:	Chief of Staff, Combined Fleet, Chief of Staff, 1st Fleet
16 Nov 1936 - 1 Dec 1936:	Attached to Naval General Staff
1 Dec 1936 - 25 Apr 1938:	Chief of Bureau 3, Naval General Staff
25 Apr 1938 - 26 Oct 1939:	Naval Attache, China, Chief of Naval Special Task Office
15 Nov 1938:	Promoted to *Vice-Admiral*
26 Oct 1939 - 15 Nov 1939:	Attached to Naval General Staff
15 Nov 1939 - 30 Sep 1940:	C-in-C, 3rd China Expeditionary Fleet

30 Sep 1940 - 9 Aug 1943:	Naval Attache, Berlin
9 Aug 1943 - 20 Oct 1943:	Navy Councillor
20 Oct 1943 - 17 Jul 1944:	Admiral Commanding, Kure Naval District
1 Mar 1944:	Promoted to *Admiral*
17 Jul 1944 - 22 Jul 1944:	Minister of the Navy
22 Jul 1944 - 2 Aug 1944:	Navy Councillor
2 Aug 1944 - 15 Sep 1944:	Admiral Commanding, Yokosuka Naval District, Member, Admirals Committee
2 Aug 1944 - 1 May 1945:	C-in-C, Maritime Escort Fleet
1 May 1945 - 10 Oct 1945:	Navy Councillor

Rear-Admiral **Shozo NOMURA** (20 Apr 1889 - 15 Mar 1960)

15 Nov 1935 - 1 Dec 1936:	Chief Engineer Officer, Combined Fleet, Chief Engineer Officer, 1st Fleet
1 Dec 1936:	Promoted to *Rear-Admiral*
1 Dec 1936 - 15 Nov 1938:	Chief of Research Bureau, Navy Fuel Yard
15 Nov 1938 - 30 Aug 1939:	Attached to Kure Naval District
30 Aug 1939 - 15 Dec 1939:	Attached to Naval General Staff
21 Dec 1939:	Transferred to the reserve

Rear-Admiral **Tomekichi NOMURA** (10 May 1896 - 27 Apr 1980)

5 Dec 1943 - 1 Mar 1945:	Captain, Battleship *"Hyuga"*
15 Oct 1944:	Promoted to *Rear-Admiral*
1 Mar 1945 - 15 Mar 1945:	Attached to Naval General Staff
15 Mar 1945 - 5 Sep 1945:	Chief of Bureau 4, Naval General Staff, Commander, 1st Combined Communications Unit, Chief of Communications Bureau, Joint General Staff
5 Sep 1945 - 30 Nov 1945:	Attached to Naval General Staff

Vice-Admiral **Sueo NONAKA** (26 Mar 1874 - ?)

1 Dec 1914 - 13 Aug 1923:	Chief of Shipbuilding Bureau, Kure Navy Yard
1 Dec 1919:	Promoted to *Rear-Admiral*
13 Aug 1923 - 1 Dec 1923:	Attached to Naval Shipbuilding Command
1 Dec 1923:	Promoted to *Vice-Admiral*
5 Dec 1923:	Transferred to the reserve

Rear-Admiral **Saiji NORIMITSU** (12 May 1897 - 25 Oct 1944)

7 Jan 1944 - 25 Oct 1944:	Captain, Heavy Cruiser *"Chikuma"*
25 Oct 1944:	Posthumously promoted to *Rear-Admiral*

Rear-Admiral **Kojuro NOZAKI** (2 Nov 1872 - 24 May 1946)

1 Dec 1919:	Promoted to *Rear-Admiral*

1 Dec 1919 - 1 Apr 1922:	Commander, Southern Islands Defense Force
1 Apr 1922 - 1 Dec 1922:	Member, Admirals Committee
1 Dec 1922 - 31 Mar 1923:	Unassigned
31 Mar 1923:	Transferred to the reserve

Vice-Admiral **Mitsuzo NUNOME** (17 Aug 1868 - 1 Feb 1945)

1 Dec 1916:	Promoted to *Rear-Admiral*
1 Dec 1916 - 1 Oct 1920:	Chief of Naval Hydrographic Command
1 Oct 1920 - 1 Dec 1921:	Commander, Ominato Guard District
1 Dec 1920:	Promoted to *Vice-Admiral*
1 Dec 1921 - 10 Apr 1922:	Member, Admirals Committee
10 Apr 1922 - 31 Mar 1923:	Unassigned
31 Mar 1923:	Transferred to the reserve

Rear-Admiral **Sango OBANA** (5 Mar 1864 - 29 Jun 1937)

2 Sep 1911 - 1 Dec 1912:	Commander, Kure Torpedo Corps
1 Dec 1911:	Promoted to *Rear-Admiral*
1 Dec 1912 - 31 May 1913:	Unassigned
31 May 1913:	Transferred to the reserve

Vice-Admiral **Aiki OBATA** (4 Jan 1892 - 2 May 1955)

15 Nov 1939:	Promoted to *Rear-Admiral*
15 Nov 1939 - 15 Nov 1940:	Instructor, Naval College
15 Nov 1940 - 1 Apr 1941:	Attached to Yokosuka Naval District
1 Apr 1941 - 1 Oct 1942:	Branch Chief, Air Technical Arsenal
1 Oct 1942 - 25 Oct 1943:	Commander, 2nd Navy Fuel Yard
1 May 1943:	Promoted to *Vice-Admiral*
25 Oct 1943 - 1 May 1945:	Commander, 1st Navy Fuel Yard
1 May 1945 - 26 Aug 1945:	Attached to the Bureau of Naval Affairs, Department of the Navy
26 Aug 1945 - 15 Sep 1945:	Attached to Naval Air Command

Rear-Admiral **Bunzaburo OBATA** (10 Sep 1863 - 1957)

6 Mar 1908 - 21 Nov 1910:	Chief of Shipbuilding Bureau, Yokosuka Navy Yard
10 Dec 1908:	Promoted to *General (Constructor)*
21 Nov 1910 - 4 Aug 1911:	Unassigned
4 Aug 1911 - 5 Jun 1913:	Attached to Bureau 3, Naval Shipbuilding Command
5 Jun 1913:	Transferred to the reserve
23 Sep 1919:	Redesignated *Rear-Admiral*

Rear-Admiral **Chozaemon OBATA** (10 Dec 1893 - 18 Dec 1948)

1 Sep 1942 - 19 Oct 1943:	Chief of Staff, 2nd China Expeditionary Fleet, Commander, Hong Kong Area Base Force

1 Nov 1942:	Promoted to *Rear-Admiral*
19 Oct 1943 - 1 Nov 1943:	Attached to Yokosuka Naval District
1 Nov 1943 - 25 Oct 1945:	Commandant, Yokosuka Naval Gunnery School

Vice-Admiral (Judge) **Yoshizumi OBATA** (15 Apr 1884 - 16 Sep 1957)

8 Apr 1936 - 1 Apr 1941:	Prosecutor, Tokyo Court Martial
30 Sep 1936:	Promoted to 2nd *Grade Official*
31 Mar 1941:	Promoted to 1st *Grade Official*
1 Apr 1941 - 1 Nov 1944:	Chief of Navy Legal Bureau, Department of the Navy
1 Apr 1942:	Redesignated *Vice-Admiral (Judge)*
1 Nov 1944 - 15 Mar 1945:	Attached to Naval General Staff
20 Mar 1945:	Transferred to the reserve

Rear-Admiral **Sueo OBAYASHI** (8 Mar 1895 - 13 Apr 1983)

10 Dec 1942 - 1 Jul 1943:	Captain, Battleship *"Hyuga"*
1 May 1943:	Promoted to *Rear-Admiral*
1 Jul 1943 - 1 Feb 1944:	Commander, 51st Air Flotilla
1 Feb 1944 - 1 Oct 1944:	Commander, 3rd Carrier Flotilla
15 Feb 1944 - 29 Mar 1944:	Commander, 653rd Air Division
1 Oct 1944 - 15 Nov 1944:	Chief of Staff, 1st Task Fleet, Chief of Staff, 3rd Fleet
15 Nov 1944 - 10 Dec 1944:	Attached to Naval General Staff
10 Dec 1944 - 10 Feb 1945:	Commander, 1st Carrier Flotilla
10 Feb 1945 - 20 Mar 1945:	Attached to Naval General Staff
20 Mar 1945 - 30 Sep 1945:	Commander, 1st Special Attack Flotilla

Rear-Admiral (Surgeon) **Kumao OBO** (16 Mar 1879 - 16 Jun 1935)

1 Dec 1922 - 10 Nov 1925:	Chief of Bureau 2, Sasebo Naval Hospital
10 Nov 1925 - 5 Dec 1925:	Attached to Sasebo Naval District
1 Dec 1925:	Promoted to *Rear-Admiral (Surgeon)*
16 Dec 1925:	Transferred to the reserve

Rear-Admiral **Kohei OCHI** (3 Feb 1889 - 25 Jun 1968)

1 Dec 1936 - 1 Dec 1937:	Captain, Battlecruiser *"Hiei"*
1 Dec 1937:	Promoted to *Rear-Admiral*
1 Dec 1937 - 15 Dec 1937:	Attached to Naval General Staff
21 Dec 1937:	Transferred to the reserve

Rear-Admiral **Katsuji ODA** (29 Jul 1897 - 27 Mar 1973)

1 Dec 1944 - 1 Nov 1945:	Chief of Shipbuilding Bureau, Maizuru Navy Yard
1 May 1945:	Promoted to *Rear-Admiral*

Rear-Admiral (Surgeon) **Kazuaki ODA** (15 Nov 1896 - ?)
10 Jan 1945 - 10 Oct 1945:   Chief of 2nd Production Bureau, 1st Medical Depot
10 Oct 1945 - 30 Nov 1945:   Director, Beppu Naval Hospital
1 Nov 1945:   Promoted to *Rear-Admiral (Surgeon)*

Rear-Admiral **Kiyozo ODA**   (15 Jun 1863 - 25 Apr 1912)
18 Jan 1911 - 25 Apr 1912:   Chief of Torpedo Bureau, Kure Navy Yard
12 Apr 1911:   Promoted to *Rear-Admiral*

Rear-Admiral **Tamekiyo ODA**   (18 Nov 1893 - 17 Feb 1944)
15 Oct 1943 - 17 Feb 1944:   Captain, Training Cruiser *"Katori"*
17 Feb 1944:   Posthumously promoted to *Rear-Admiral*

Rear-Admiral **Toru ODA**   (15 Nov 1847 - 2 Feb 1915)
22 Mar 1899 - 7 Jun 1900:   Captain, Protected Cruiser *"Takachiho"*
7 Jun 1900 - 1 Nov 1900:   Unassigned
1 Nov 1900:   Promoted to *Rear-Admiral*
1 Nov 1900:   Transferred to the reserve

Rear-Admiral (Judge) **Tsuneo ODAGAKI** (29 Jan 1893 - 19 Feb 1985)
1 Nov 1942:   Promoted to *Rear-Admiral (Judge)*
1 Nov 1942 - 1 Nov 1944:   Chief Judge, Kure Naval District
1 Nov 1944 - 5 Nov 1945:   Chief Judge, Yokosuka Naval District

Rear-Admiral (Surgeon) **Shokichi ODAJIMA** (13 Dec 1897 - 8 Jul 1944)
5 Mar 1944 - 8 Jul 1944:   Chief Surgeon, Central Pacific Area Fleet,
   Chief Surgeon, 14th Air Fleet
8 Jul 1944:   Posthumously promoted to *Rear-Admiral (Surgeon)*

General (Ordnance) **Genzaburo ODATE** (22 Jan 1866 - 4 Feb 1914)
18 Jan 1911 - 1 Dec 1913:   Chief of Ordnance Bureau, Yokosuka Navy Yard
3 Feb 1912:   Promoted to *General (Ordnance)*
1 Dec 1913 - 4 Feb 1914:   Unassigned

Rear-Admiral **Toshihiko ODAWARA** (22 Oct 1899 - 25 Jan 1945)
7 Aug 1944 - 8 Jan 1945:   Chief of Staff, 1st Air Fleet
8 Jan 1945 - 15 Jan 1945:   Deputy Chief of Staff, 1st Air Fleet
15 Jan 1945:   Posthumously promoted to *Rear-Admiral*

Rear-Admiral **Ryokichi ODERA** (3 Feb 1877 - 30 Nov 1969)
1 Dec 1923 - 15 Apr 1925:   Commander, Sasebo Sailors Corps
1 Dec 1924:   Promoted to *Rear-Admiral*
15 Apr 1925 - 1 Jul 1925:   Attached to Naval General Staff

1 Jul 1925 - 16 Dec 1925:	Unassigned
16 Dec 1925:	Transferred to the reserve

Rear-Admiral **Ranji OE** (18 Aug 1897 - 23 Oct 1944)
26 Dec 1943 - 23 Oct 1944:	Captain, Heavy Cruiser *"Maya"*
23 Oct 1944:	Posthumously promoted to *Rear-Admiral*

Rear-Admiral **Shuzo OE** (19 Jan 1896 - 16 Feb 1974)
11 Sep 1944 - 15 Jun 1945:	Deputy Chief of Staff, Sasebo Naval District, Chief of Shipbuilding Bureau, Sasebo Naval District
15 Oct 1944:	Promoted to *Rear-Admiral*
15 Jun 1945 - 1 Nov 1945:	Commander, Ominato Naval Facility

Vice-Admiral **Naganari OGASAWARA** (20 Nov 1867 - 20 Sep 1958)
1 Apr 1914 - 12 Apr 1915:	Secretary to the Crown Prince
1 Dec 1914:	Promoted to *Rear-Admiral*
12 Apr 1915 - 1 Dec 1918:	Attached to the Ministry of the Imperial Household
1 Dec 1918:	Promoted to *Vice-Admiral*
1 Dec 1918 - 1 Apr 1921:	Unassigned
1 Apr 1921:	Transferred to the reserve

Rear-Admiral **Koreyoshi OGATA** (26 Jul 1850 - 13 Nov 1914)
14 May 1898:	Promoted to *Rear-Admiral*
14 May 1898 - 12 Jan 1900:	Admiral Commanding, Sasebo Naval District
17 Jun 1899 - 12 Jan 1900:	C-in-C, Sasebo Naval District Fleet
12 Jan 1900 - 31 May 1902:	Unassigned
31 May 1902:	Transferred to the reserve

Vice-Admiral **Masaki OGATA** (4 Nov 1892 - 3 May 1944)
20 Aug 1941 - 10 Apr 1942:	Staff officer, 3rd China Expeditionary Fleet
15 Oct 1941:	Promoted to *Rear-Admiral*
10 Apr 1942 - 1 Nov 1942:	Staff officer, China Area Fleet
1 Nov 1942 - 2 Dec 1942:	Attached to Naval General Staff
2 Dec 1942 - 15 Nov 1943:	Chief of Staff, Sasebo Naval District
15 Nov 1943 - 3 May 1944:	Chief of Staff, 9th Fleet
10 Dec 1943 - 25 Mar 1944:	Commander, 2nd Naval Base Force, Commander, 8th Construction Bureau
3 May 1944:	Posthumously promoted to *Vice-Admiral*

Rear-Admiral **Tsutomu OGATA** (15 Oct 1891 - 4 Jan 1948)
1 Jul 1942 - 10 May 1945:	Commander, Yokosuka Defense Force
20 Jul 1944 - 10 May 1945:	Commander, 21st Transport Division

1 May 1945:	Promoted to *Rear-Admiral*
10 May 1945 - 15 Sep 1945:	Chief of Mine Research Bureau, Yokosuka Navy Yard

Rear-Admiral (Surgeon) **Junkichi OGAWA** (27 Apr 1893 - 17 Nov 1970)

1 Oct 1942 - 15 Nov 1944:	Director, Iwakuni Naval Hospital
1 May 1943:	Promoted to *Rear-Admiral (Surgeon)*
15 Nov 1944 - 9 Dec 1944:	Attached to Kainan Guard District
9 Dec 1944 - Oct 1945:	Chief of Health Bureau, Kainan I Naval Special Task Office

Rear-Admiral **Kanji OGAWA** (10 Sep 1893 - 23 Jan 1973)

15 May 1942 - 1 Dec 1942:	Chief of Bureau 3, Naval General Staff
1 Nov 1942:	Promoted to *Rear-Admiral*
1 Dec 1942 - 7 Mar 1944:	Attached to Bureau of Naval Affairs, Department of the Navy
16 Dec 1943 - 20 Jan 1945:	Director, Total Warfare Research Laboratory
7 Mar 1944 - 15 Apr 1944:	Chief Instructor, Naval College, Chief of Research Bureau, Naval College
20 Jan 1945 - 10 Feb 1945:	Staff officer, China Area Fleet
10 Feb 1945 - Oct 1945:	Deputy Chief of Staff, China Area Fleet

Rear-Admiral **Nobuki OGAWA** (12 Nov 1895 - 24 Feb 1944)

22 Dec 1943 - 24 Feb 1944:	Commander of Traffic Control, 2nd Maritime Escort Force
24 Feb 1944:	Posthumously promoted to *Rear-Admiral*

Vice-Admiral (Surgeon) **Ryu OGAWA** (17 Apr 1878 - 22 Feb 1932)

1 Dec 1924:	Promoted to *Rear-Admiral (Surgeon)*
1 Dec 1924 - 27 Apr 1925:	Chief of Bureau 1, Yokosuka Naval Hospital
27 Apr 1925 - 1 Dec 1925:	Director, Sasebo Naval Hospital, Chief Surgeon, Sasebo Naval District
1 Dec 1925 - 30 Nov 1929:	Commandant, Navy Medical School
10 Dec 1928:	Promoted to *Vice-Admiral (Surgeon)*
30 Nov 1929 - 22 Feb 1932:	Chief of Naval Medical Service

Rear-Admiral **Tokuichi OGAWA** (10 Nov 1893 - 17 Apr 1954)

15 Apr 1943 - 1 May 1944:	Chief of 101st Supply Bureau
1 May 1943:	Promoted to *Rear-Admiral*
1 May 1944 - 20 May 1944:	Attached to Kure Naval District
20 May 1944 - Oct 1945:	Commander, 5th Navy Fuel Yard

Rear-Admiral **Genzaburo OGI** (1 Oct 1863 - 25 Feb 1932)
4 Mar 1909 - 1 Dec 1909: Chief of Staff, Sasebo Naval District
1 Dec 1909: Promoted to *Rear-Admiral*
1 Dec 1909 - 1 Dec 1910: Chief of Staff, Ryojun Naval District
1 Dec 1910 - 1 Dec 1912: Unassigned
1 Dec 1912: Transferred to the reserve

Rear-Admiral (Judge) **Takejiro OGIWARA** (10 Feb 1889 - 16 Mar 1967)
1 Apr 1941 - 1 Nov 1942: Chief Judge, Yokosuka Naval District
1 Apr 1942: Promoted to *Rear-Admiral (Judge)*
1 Nov 1942 - 15 Dec 1944: Attached to Naval General Staff
20 Dec 1944: Transferred to the reserve

Vice-Admiral **Byoichiro OGURA** (21 Jul 1853 - 23 Dec 1928)
28 Dec 1903 - 12 Jan 1905: Chief of Staff, Yokosuka Naval District
6 Jun 1904: Promoted to *Rear-Admiral*
12 Jan 1905 - 21 Jan 1905: Commander, Special Command
21 Jan 1905 - 14 Jun 1905: C-in-C, Special Task Fleet
14 Jun 1905 - 20 Dec 1905: C-in-C, 1st Fleet
20 Dec 1905 - 28 Aug 1908: Chief of Naval Personnel
20 Dec 1905 - 10 Dec 1908: Member, Admirals Committee
28 Aug 1908: Promoted to *Vice-Admiral*
10 Dec 1908 - 10 Dec 1909: Unassigned
10 Dec 1909: Transferred to the reserve

Rear-Admiral **Shinji OGURA** (4 Jan 1893 - 7 Aug 1975)
15 Jul 1943 - 20 Sep 1944: Naval Attache, Thailand
1 May 1944: Promoted to *Rear-Admiral*
20 Sep 1944 - 15 Nov 1944: Attached to Naval General Staff
15 Nov 1944 - 15 Nov 1945: Chief of Personnel, Maizuru Naval District

Rear-Admiral **Sotokichi OGURA** (18 Jun 1892 - 24 Sep 1944)
21 Dec 1943 - 24 Sep 1944: Commander, Kanton Guard Force
24 Sep 1944: Posthumously promoted to *Rear-Admiral*

Rear-Admiral **Taizo OGURA** (10 Mar 1883 - 27 Dec 1939)
13 May 1927 - 10 Dec 1928: Attached to Yokosuka Naval District
10 Dec 1928: Promoted to *Rear-Admiral*
10 Dec 1928 - 20 Dec 1928: Attached to Naval General Staff
25 Dec 1928: Transferred to the reserve

Rear-Admiral **Tozaburo OGURA** (1 Jun 1900 - 13 Apr 1944)
15 Apr 1943 - 13 Apr 1944: Instructor, Yokosuka Naval Gunnery School,

	Instructor, Tateyama Naval Gunnery School
13 Apr 1944:	Posthumously promoted to *Rear-Admiral*

Vice-Admiral **Yoshiaki OGURA** (2 Sep 1878 - 23 Nov 1949)
1 Jun 1923 - 1 Dec 1926:	Chief of Bureau 2, Naval Shipbuilding Command
1 Dec 1923:	Promoted to *Rear-Admiral*
1 Dec 1926 - 25 Mar 1927:	Commander, Hiro Navy Yard
25 Mar 1927 - 1 Dec 1927:	Commander, Yokosuka Navy Yard
1 Dec 1927:	Promoted to *Vice-Admiral*
1 Dec 1927 - 15 Dec 1927:	Attached to Naval General Staff
25 Dec 1927:	Transferred to the reserve

Admiral **Kozaburo OGURI** (4 Aug 1868 - 27 Oct 1944)
1 Dec 1912 - 17 Apr 1914:	Chief of Bureau 1, Naval Shipbuilding Command
24 May 1913:	Promoted to *Rear-Admiral*
17 Apr 1914 - 29 May 1914:	Unassigned
29 May 1914 - 15 Aug 1914:	Attached to Department of the Navy
15 Aug 1915 - 25 Dec 1915:	Naval Attache, United Kingdom
25 Dec 1915 - 23 Jun 1916:	Supervisor for Construction & Ordnance, Naval Shipbuilding Command
23 Jun 1916 - 7 Feb 1917:	Chief, Bureau of Naval Affairs, Department of the Navy, Member, Admirals Committee
7 Feb 1917 - 12 Dec 1917:	C-in-C, 1st Special Task Fleet
1 Jun 1917:	Promoted to *Vice-Admiral*
12 Dec 1917 - 8 Nov 1919:	Commander, Kure Navy Yard
8 Nov 1919 - 1 Dec 1920:	Member, Admirals Committee
1 Dec 1920 - 1 Dec 1921:	C-in-C, 3rd Fleet
1 Dec 1921 - 1 Apr 1923:	Admiral Commanding, Maizuru Naval District
1 Apr 1923 - 1 Dec 1923:	Member, Admirals Committee
3 Aug 1923:	Promoted to *Admiral*
1 Dec 1923 - 25 Feb 1924:	Unassigned
25 Feb 1924:	Transferred to the reserve

Rear-Admiral **Shinichi OGURI** (26 Oct 1881 - 29 Dec 1957)
10 Dec 1928:	Promoted to *Rear-Admiral*
10 Dec 1928 - 1 Dec 1931:	Chief of Torpedo Bureau, Kure Navy Yard
1 Dec 1931 - 20 May 1932:	Attached to Naval General Staff
31 May 1932:	Transferred to the reserve

Rear-Admiral **Hideo OGURO** (20 Jul 1868 - 26 Jan 1938)
29 May 1914 - 13 Dec 1915:	Chief of Survey Section, Naval Hydrographic Command

13 Dec 1915:	Promoted to *Rear-Admiral*
13 Dec 1915 - 1 Dec 1916:	Unassigned
1 Dec 1916:	Transferred to the reserve

Vice-Admiral **Sei OHASHI** (10 Oct 1870 - 5 Aug 1946)

1 Dec 1913 - 13 Dec 1915:	Chief Engineer Officer, 2nd Fleet
13 Dec 1915:	Promoted to *Rear-Admiral*
13 Dec 1915 - 1 Apr 1916:	Attached to Naval Shipbuilding Command
1 Apr 1916 - 1 Dec 1917:	Chief Engineer Officer, Kure Naval District
1 Dec 1917 - 1 Dec 1918:	Chief Engineer Officer, 1st Fleet
1 Sep 1918 - 1 Dec 1918:	Chief Engineer Officer, Combined Fleet
1 Dec 1918 - 1 Dec 1919:	Chief Engineer Officer, Yokosuka Naval District
1 Dec 1919 - 1 Dec 1920:	Attached to Kure Naval District
1 Dec 1920:	Promoted to *Vice-Admiral*
1 Dec 1920 - 10 Jan 1921:	Attached to Naval Shipbuilding Command
10 Jan 1921 - 1 Aug 1922:	Chief of Hiro Branch, Kure Navy Yard
1 Aug 1922 - 1 Dec 1922:	Attached to Naval Shipbuilding Command
1 Dec 1922 - 31 Mar 1923:	Unassigned
31 Mar 1923:	Transferred to the reserve

Rear-Admiral **Tatsuo OHASHI** (31 Aug 1891 - 20 Jul 1969)

1 Mar 1944 - 15 Jan 1945:	Chief of Traffic Control, 1st Maritime Escort Force
15 Oct 1944:	Promoted to *Rear-Admiral*
15 Jan 1945 - 10 Jun 1945:	Chief of Moji Branch, Shipping Guard Division, Joint General Staff
20 May 1945 - 20 Sep 1945:	Commander, Moji Harbor Guard Force

Rear-Admiral **Goichi OIE** (17 Feb 1897 - 2 Aug 1944)

1 Mar 1944 - 2 Aug 1944:	Commander, 56th Guard Force
2 Aug 1944:	Posthumously promoted to *Rear-Admiral*

Admiral **Koshiro OIKAWA** (8 Feb 1883 - 9 May 1958)

10 Dec 1928:	Promoted to *Rear-Admiral*
10 Dec 1928 - 18 Jun 1930:	Chief of Staff, Kure Naval District
18 Jun 1930 - 15 Nov 1932:	Chief of Bureau 1, Naval General Staff
15 Nov 1932 - 3 Oct 1933:	Commander, 1st Air Flotilla
3 Oct 1933 - 15 Nov 1935:	Commandant of the Naval Academy
15 Nov 1933:	Promoted to *Vice-Admiral*
15 Nov 1935 - 2 Dec 1935:	Attached to Naval General Staff
2 Dec 1935 - 1 Dec 1936:	C-in-C, 3rd Fleet
1 Dec 1936 - 25 Apr 1938:	Chief of Naval Air Command
25 Apr 1938 - 15 Nov 1939:	C-in-C, 3rd Fleet
25 Apr 1938 - 1 May 1940:	C-in-C, China Area Fleet

15 Nov 1939:	Promoted to *Admiral*
1 May 1940 - 5 Sep 1940:	Admiral Commanding, Yokosuka Naval District, Member, Admirals Committee
5 Sep 1940 - 18 Oct 1941:	Minister of the Navy
18 Oct 1941 - 2 Aug 1944:	Navy Councillor
10 Oct 1942 - 15 Nov 1943:	Commandant of the Naval College
15 Nov 1943 - 2 Aug 1944:	C-in-C, Maritime Escort Fleet, Navy Councillor
2 Aug 1944 - 29 May 1945:	Chief of the Naval General Staff
29 May 1945 - 5 Sep 1945:	Navy Councillor

Rear-Admiral **Kyuma OINOUE** (8 Apr 1858 - 15 Feb 1920)

7 Jan 1905 - 12 Dec 1905:	Commander, Yokosuka Harbor
12 Dec 1905 - 30 Nov 1906:	Unassigned
30 Nov 1906:	Promoted to *Rear-Admiral*
30 Nov 1906:	Transferred to the reserve

Vice-Admiral (Surgeon) **Shigekichi OISHI** (17 Jan 1869 - 29 Dec 1946)

1 Dec 1916 - 1 Dec 1917:	Chief Surgeon, 1st Fleet
1 Oct 1917 - 1 Dec 1917:	Chief Surgeon, Combined Fleet
1 Dec 1917:	Promoted to *General (Surgeon)*
1 Dec 1917 - 1 Jun 1919:	Director, Kure Naval Hospital Chief Surgeon, Kure Naval District
1 Jun 1919 - 1 Dec 1921:	Director, Yokosuka Naval Hospital Chief Surgeon, Yokosuka Naval District
23 Sep 1919:	Redesignated *Rear-Admiral (Surgeon)*
1 Dec 1921:	Promoted to *Vice-Admiral (Surgeon)*
1 Dec 1921 - 10 Apr 1922:	Attached to Naval General Staff
10 Apr 1922 - 31 Mar 1923:	Transferred to the reserve

Rear-Admiral **Shokichi OISHI** (1 Oct 1876 - 2 May 1938)

1 Dec 1921:	Promoted to *Rear-Admiral*
1 Dec 1921 - 1 Apr 1923:	Chief of Bureau 2, Naval Training Command
1 Apr 1923 - 1 Jun 1923:	Attached to Naval General Staff
1 Jun 1923 - 5 Feb 1924:	Commander, Ominato Guard District
5 Feb 1924 - 10 Mar 1924:	Member, Admirals Committee
20 Mar 1924:	Transferred to the reserve

Vice-Admiral **Arata OKA** (16 Jul 1890 - 23 Mar 1958)

1 Sep 1938 - 15 Nov 1939:	Chief of Staff, 4th Fleet
15 Nov 1938:	Promoted to *Rear-Admiral*
15 Nov 1939 - 1 Dec 1940:	Chief of Staff, Yokosuka Naval District
1 Dec 1940 - 15 Oct 1941:	Attached to Bureau of Naval Affairs, Department of the Navy

15 Oct 1941 - 1 Nov 1941:	Acting Chief of Total Warfare Resarch Laboratory
1 Nov 1941 - 15 Nov 1941:	Staff officer, China Area Fleet
15 Nov 1941 - 20 Aug 1943:	Military Representative, Shanghai
1 Nov 1942:	Promoted to *Vice-Admiral*
20 Aug 1943 - 20 Sep 1943:	Attached to Naval General Staff
20 Sep 1943 - 15 Aug 1944:	C-in-C, 3rd Southern Expeditionary Fleet
15 Aug 1944 - 1 Nov 1944:	Attached to Naval General Staff
1 Nov 1944 - 15 Nov 1945:	Commander, Osaka Guard District

Rear-Admiral **Iwao OKA** (1 Mar 1902 - 4 Aug 1944)
4 Aug 1944: Posthumously promoted to *Rear-Admiral*

Vice-Admiral **Takazumi OKA** (11 Feb 1890 - 4 Dec 1973)

10 Oct 1939 - 15 Oct 1940:	Chief of Bureau 3, Naval General Staff
15 Nov 1939:	Promoted to *Rear-Admiral*
15 Oct 1940 - 1 Aug 1944:	Chief of Naval Affairs Bureau
1 Nov 1942:	Promoted to *Vice-Admiral*
18 Jul 1944 - 5 Aug 1944:	Deputy Minister of the Navy, Member, Admirals Committee
5 Aug 1944 - 9 Sep 1944:	Attached to Naval General Staff
9 Sep 1944 - 20 Apr 1945:	Commander, Chinkai Guard District
20 Apr 1945 - 15 Jun 1945:	Attached to Naval General Staff
20 Jun 1945:	Transferred to the reserve

Rear-Admiral (Paymaster) **Yasuzo OKA** (30 Jul 1891 - 1 Apr 1965)

25 Sep 1943 - 21 May 1945:	Chief of 1st Accounting Bureau, Paymaster-General, China Area Fleet, Chief of 1st Supply Bureau
1 May 1944:	Promoted to *Rear-Admiral (Paymaster)*
21 May 1945 - 10 Jun 1945:	Attached to Naval General Staff
10 Jun 1945 - 15 Nov 1945:	Paymaster-General, Osaka Guard District

Rear-Admiral **Jisaku OKADA** (13 Aug 1893 - 5 Jun 1942)
15 Sep 1941 - 5 Jun 1942: Captain, Aircraft Carrier *"Kaga"*
5 Jun 1942: Posthumously promoted to *Rear-Admiral*

Admiral **Keisuke OKADA** (21 Jan 1868 - 10 Oct 1952)

1 Dec 1913:	Promoted to *Rear-Admiral*
1 Dec 1913 - 18 Aug 1914:	Chief of Ordnance Bureau, Sasebo Navy Yard
18 Aug 1914 - 1 Dec 1914:	C-in-C, 2nd Fleet
1 Dec 1914 - 1 Apr 1915:	Commander, 1st Destroyer Flotilla
1 Apr 1915 - 1 Oct 1915:	Commander, 3rd Destroyer Flotilla
1 Oct 1915 - 13 Dec 1915:	Chief of Bureaus 2 & 3, Naval Technical Command

13 Dec 1915 - 1 Dec 1917:	Chief of Naval Personnel
1 Dec 1917:	Promoted to *Vice-Admiral*
1 Dec 1917 - 4 Sep 1918:	Commander, Sasebo Navy Yard
4 Sep 1918 - 18 Oct 1918:	Member, Admirals Committee
18 Oct 1918 - 1 Oct 1920:	Chief of Shipping Bureau, Department of the Navy
1 Oct 1920 - 25 May 1923:	Chief of Naval Shipbuilding Command
11 Oct 1920 - 11 Jun 1924:	Member, Admirals Committee
25 May 1923 - 11 Jun 1924:	Deputy Minister of the Navy
11 Jun 1924:	Promoted to *Admiral*
11 Jun 1924 - 1 Dec 1924:	Navy Councillor
1 Dec 1924 - 10 Dec 1926:	C-in-C, Combined Fleet, C-in-C, 1st Fleet
10 Dec 1926 - 20 Apr 1927:	Admiral Commanding, Yokosuka Naval District, Member, Admirals Committee
20 Apr 1927 - 2 Jul 1929:	Minister of the Navy
2 Jul 1929 - 26 May 1932:	Navy Councillor
26 May 1932 - 9 Jan 1933:	Minister of the Navy
21 Jan 1933:	Transferred to the reserve
8 Jul 1934 - 9 Mar 1936:	Prime Minister

Rear-Admiral **Mitsuyoshi OKADA** (16 Aug 1869 - 12 Dec 1927)

29 May 1914 - 1 Dec 1918:	Commander, Yokosuka Sailors Corps
1 Dec 1918:	Promoted to *Rear-Admiral*
1 Dec 1918 - 1 Aug 1919:	Unassigned
1 Aug 1919:	Transferred to the reserve

Rear-Admiral **Shunichi OKADA** (10 May 1887 - 24 Dec 1943)

29 May 1933 - 15 Nov 1934:	Attached to Yokosuka Naval District
15 Nov 1934:	Promoted to *Rear-Admiral*
15 Nov 1934 - 10 Dec 1934:	Attached to Naval General Staff
15 Dec 1934:	Transferred to the reserve

Rear-Admiral **Tametsugu OKADA** (19 Feb 1895 - 3 Sep 1947)

16 Feb 1943 - 17 Nov 1943:	Captain, Aircraft Carrier *"Shokaku"*
1 Nov 1943:	Promoted to *Rear-Admiral*
17 Nov 1943 - 30 Nov 1943:	Attached to Naval General Staff
30 Nov 1943 - 10 Mar 1945:	Chief of Staff, 4th Southern Expeditionary Fleet
10 Jan 1945 - 9 Jun 1945:	Commander, 104th Construction Bureau
10 Mar 1945 - 9 Jun 1945:	Commander, 25th Auxiliary Base Force
9 Jun 1945 - 20 Jul 1945:	Attached to Naval General Staff
20 Jul 1945 - 15 Oct 1945:	Deputy Chief of Staff, Kure Naval District
15 Oct 1945 - 30 Nov 1945:	Chief of Staff, Kure Naval District

Rear-Admiral **Ikuo OKAMOTO** (10 Jun 1881 - 22 Dec 1949)
1 Dec 1927:	Promoted to *Rear-Admiral*
1 Dec 1927 - 10 Dec 1928:	Commander, 1st Destroyer Flotilla
10 Dec 1928 - 30 Nov 1929:	Commander, 2nd Destroyer Flotilla
30 Nov 1929 - 1 Oct 1930:	Attached to Naval General Staff
10 Oct 1930:	Transferred to the reserve

Rear-Admiral **Yoshisuke OKAMOTO** (8 Oct 1897 - 27 Nov 1942)
1 Jul 1942 - 27 Nov 1942:	Commander, 12th Submarine Division
27 Nov 1942:	Posthumously promoted to *Rear-Admiral*

Rear-Admiral **Hidejiro OKAMURA** (10 May 1877 - 13 Feb 1947)
1 Dec 1922:	Promoted to *Rear-Admiral*
31 Mar 1923:	Transferred to the reserve

Rear-Admiral **Jun OKAMURA** (4 Dec 1896 - 21 Jun 1976)
20 Feb 1943 - 15 Sep 1944:	Chief of Aircraft Bureau, 11th Air Arsenal
1 May 1944:	Promoted to *Rear-Admiral*
15 Sep 1944 - 10 Nov 1945:	Commander, Takaza Navy Yard

Vice-Admiral **Masao OKAMURA** (25 Jan 1888 - 31 Jul 1945)
10 Mar 1939 - 15 Nov 1939:	Commander, 2nd Harbor
15 Nov 1939:	Promoted to *Rear-Admiral*
15 Nov 1939 - 15 Dec 1939:	Attached to Kure Naval District
21 Dec 1939:	Transferred to the reserve
25 Sep 1942 - 1 Oct 1942:	Recalled; Attached to Kure Naval District
1 Oct 1942 - 22 Sep 1943:	Chief of Takamatsu Area Personnel Bureau
22 Sep 1943 - 27 Sep 1943:	Attached to Kure Naval District
27 Sep 1943 - 1 Oct 1943:	Attached to Yokosuka Naval District
1 Oct 1943 - 10 Jan 1945:	Commander, 18th Guard Force
10 Jan 1945 - 31 Jul 1945:	Chief of Manoqwari Branch, 104th Construction Bureau
31 Jul 1945:	Posthumously promoted to *Vice-Admiral*

Rear-Admiral (Judge) **Sanji OKAMURA** (3 Dec 1893 - 16 Sep 1961)
15 Apr 1944 - 1 Nov 1944:	Chief Judge, Osaka Guard District
15 Oct 1944:	Promoted to *Rear-Admiral (Judge)*
1 Nov 1944 - 5 Nov 1945:	Chief Judge, Maizuru Naval District

Rear-Admiral **Fujimatsu OKANO** (21 Mar 1868 - 25 Mar 1931)
13 Dec 1915:	Promoted to *Rear-Admiral*
13 Dec 1915 - 1 Apr 1917:	Chief of Ordnance Bureau, Sasebo Navy Yard
1 Apr 1917 - 1 Dec 1917:	Commander, 4th Destroyer Flotilla

1 Dec 1917 - 1 Dec 1918:	Unassigned
1 Dec 1918:	Transferred to the reserve

Rear-Admiral **Ikkan OKANO** (20 Jan 1886 - 6 Jan 1945)

25 May 1943 - 6 Jan 1945:	Commander of Minesweepers, "Nichiei-maru" Convoy
6 Jan 1945:	Posthumously promoted to *Rear-Admiral*

Rear-Admiral **Tokuo OKANO** (2 Apr 1893 - 1 May 1946)

14 Jul 1942 - 1 Nov 1942:	Chief Engineer Officer, 3rd Fleet
1 Nov 1942:	Promoted to *Rear-Admiral*
1 Nov 1942 - 10 Nov 1942:	Attached to Naval General Staff
10 Nov 1942 - 20 Oct 1943:	Commander, 2nd Naval Facility
20 Oct 1943 - 22 Oct 1943:	Attached to Naval General Staff
22 Oct 1943 - 27 Dec 1944:	Chief Supervisor for Construction & Ordnance, Naval Shipbuilding Command
27 Dec 1944 - 10 Jun 1945:	Supervisor for Construction & Ordnance, Naval Shipbuilding Command, Supervisor for Ordnance, Naval Air Command
10 Jun 1945 - 6 Sep 1945:	Attached to Naval General Staff
6 Sep 1945:	Transferred to the reserve

Vice-Admiral **Denshichi OKAWACHI** (2 Sep 1886 - 13 Feb 1958)

16 Nov 1936 - 25 Apr 1938:	Commander, Shanghai Marine Force
1 Dec 1936:	Promoted to *Rear-Admiral*
25 Apr 1938 - 6 Sep 1940:	Commandant, Naval Gunnery School
6 Sep 1940 - 1 Oct 1940:	Staff officer, China Area Fleet
1 Oct 1940 - 16 Mar 1942:	Chief of Staff, China Area Fleet
15 Nov 1940:	Promoted to *Vice-Admiral*
16 Mar 1942 - 14 Jul 1942:	Attached to Naval General Staff
14 Jul 1942 - 20 Sep 1943:	C-in-C, 1st Southern Expeditionary Fleet
20 Sep 1943 - 1 Dec 1943:	Attached to Naval General Staff
1 Dec 1943 - 1 Apr 1944:	Admiral Commanding, Maizuru Naval District
1 Apr 1944 - 20 Apr 1944:	Attached to Naval General Staff
20 Apr 1944 - 5 Aug 1944:	Chief of Naval Radar Command
5 Aug 1944 - 22 Oct 1944:	Commandant of the Naval Academy
22 Oct 1944 - 1 Nov 1944:	Staff officer, Combined Fleet
1 Nov 1944 - 8 Jan 1945:	C-in-C, 13th Air Fleet
1 Nov 1944 - Sep 1945:	C-in-C, Southwest Area Fleet, C-in-C, 3rd Southern Expeditionary Fleet

Vice-Admiral **Teigo OKAZAKI** (2 Sep 1871 - 15 Jul 1942)

1 Jun 1919 - 1 Dec 1920:	Chief Engineer Officer, Sasebo Naval District

1 Dec 1919:	Promoted to *Rear-Admiral*
1 Dec 1920 - 1 Sep 1921:	Chief of Bureau 3, Naval Training Command
1 Sep 1921 - 1 Dec 1922:	Commander, Maizuru Navy Yard
1 Dec 1922 - 25 Jul 1924:	Commander, Sasebo Navy Yard
1 Dec 1923:	Promoted to *Vice-Admiral*
25 Jul 1924 - 15 Apr 1925:	Commandant, Naval Engineering Academy
15 Apr 1925 - 1 Jul 1925:	Attached to Naval General Staff
1 Jul 1925 - 16 Dec 1925:	Unassigned
16 Dec 1925:	Transferred to the reserve

Rear-Admiral **Harukichi OKI** (4 May 1859 - 17 Nov 1922)

27 Jun 1905 - 10 Apr 1911:	Chief of Engine Construction Bureau, Sasebo Navy Yard
24 Nov 1906:	Promoted to *General (Constructor)*
10 Apr 1911 - 10 Apr 1912:	Unassigned
10 Apr 1912:	Transferred to the reserve
23 Sep 1919:	Redesignated *Rear-Admiral*

Rear-Admiral **Tadashi OKI** (5 Feb 1861 - 5 Sep 1932)

3 Feb 1909 - 1 Dec 1909:	Chief Engineer Officer, Ryojun Naval District
1 Dec 1909 - 1 Dec 1911:	Unassigned
1 Dec 1911:	Promoted to *Rear-Admiral*
1 Dec 1911:	Transferred to the reserve

Rear-Admiral **Itaru OKIMOTO** (3 Apr 1888 - ?)

1 Dec 1930 - 15 Nov 1935:	Supervisor for Construction & Ordnance, Naval Shipbuilding Command
15 Nov 1935:	Promoted to *Rear-Admiral*
15 Nov 1935 - 10 Dec 1935:	Attached to Naval General Staff
14 Dec 1935:	Transferred to the reserve

Vice-Admiral **Nobukazu OKU** (22 Dec 1889 - 11 Feb 1943)

15 Nov 1935 - 15 Nov 1938:	Chief of Personnel Bureau, Kure Naval District
15 Nov 1938:	Promoted to *Rear-Admiral*
15 Nov 1938 - 10 Jan 1942:	Chief Supervisor for Construction & Ordnance, Naval Shipbuilding Command
15 Mar 1940 - 20 Nov 1941:	Commander, Hanshin Naval Force
10 Jan 1942 - 15 Jan 1942:	Attached to Naval General Staff
15 Jan 1942 - 2 Dec 1942:	Commander, 10th Base Force
1 May 1942:	Promoted to *Vice-Admiral*
2 Dec 1942 - 11 Feb 1943:	Attached to Naval General Staff

Rear-Admiral **Hiroshi OKUBO** (? - 30 Nov 1943)
22 Jul 1943 - 30 Nov 1943: Commander, 33rd Minesweeper Division
30 Nov 1943: Posthumously promoted to *Rear-Admiral*

Rear-Admiral **Hokizo OKUBO** (16 Aug 1854 - 14 Dec 1931)
2 Nov 1905: Promoted to *Rear-Admiral*
2 Nov 1905 - 1 Oct 1906: Commander, Dairen Bay Defense Force
1 Oct 1906 - 12 Mar 1907: Unassigned
12 Mar 1907 - 15 May 1908: Commander, Ominato Guard District
15 May 1908 - 28 Aug 1908: Commander, Yokosuka Torpedo Corps
28 Aug 1908 - 27 Aug 1909: Unassigned
27 Aug 1909: Transferred to the reserve

Rear-Admiral (Surgeon) **Shin OKUBO** (25 Apr 1895 - 1 Apr 1944)
3 May 1943 - 1 Apr 1944: Chief Surgeon, Combined Fleet
1 Apr 1944: Posthumously promoted to *Rear-Admiral (Surgeon)*

Vice-Admiral **Tatsu OKUBO** (22 Apr 1871 - 4 Feb 1941)
1 Dec 1918: Promoted to *General (Constructor)*
1 Dec 1918 - 10 Jun 1922: Chief of Shipbuilding Bureau, Yokosuka Naval District
23 Sep 1919: Redesignated *Rear-Admiral*
10 Jun 1922 - 1 Dec 1922: Attached to Naval Shipbuilding Command
1 Dec 1922: Promoted to *Vice-Admiral*
1 Dec 1922 - 31 Mar 1932: Unassigned
31 Mar 1923: Transferred to the reserve

Rear-Admiral **Kikuji OKUDA** (4 Feb 1894 - 4 Nov 1939)
15 Dec 1938 - 4 Nov 1939: Commander, 13th Air Division
4 Nov 1939: Posthumously promoted to *Rear-Admiral*

Vice-Admiral **Masakichi OKUMA** (30 Jan 1888 - 15 Jun 1943)
1 Dec 1936: Promoted to *Rear-Admiral*
1 Dec 1936 - 1 Dec 1937: Commander, 5th Destroyer Flotilla
1 Dec 1937 - 15 Nov 1938: Commander, 2nd Destroyer Flotilla
15 Nov 1938 - 15 Nov 1939: Commander, 8th Escort Flotilla
15 Nov 1939 - 1 May 1940: Attached to Sasebo Naval District
1 May 1940 - 1 Nov 1940: Commander, 5th Escort Flotilla
1 Nov 1940 - 15 Nov 1940: Attached to Naval General Staff
15 Nov 1940: Promoted to *Vice-Admiral*
15 Nov 1940 - 15 Sep 1942: Admiral Commanding, Ominato Guard District
15 Sep 1942 - 15 Oct 1942: Attached to Naval General Staff
20 Oct 1942: Transferred to the reserve

Rear-Admiral **Yuzuru OKUMA** (15 Feb 1897 - 15 Aug 1956)
19 Oct 1943 - Oct 1945:	Commander, Hong Kong Area Base Force, Chief of Staff, 2nd China Expeditionary Fleet
1 May 1944:	Promoted to *Rear-Admiral*

Rear-Admiral **Mamoru OKUMIYA** (7 Oct 1860 - 7 Jan 1933)
12 Apr 1911:	Promoted to *Rear-Admiral*
12 Apr 1911 - 1 Dec 1911:	Commander, Yokosuka Torpedo Corps
1 Dec 1911 - 1 Dec 1912:	Unassigned
1 Dec 1912:	Transferred to the reserve

Rear-Admiral **Toshio OKUMURA** (7 Feb 1893 - 12 Jul 1978)
25 Oct 1943 - Oct 1945:	Chief of 8th Facility Bureau
15 Oct 1944:	Promoted to *Rear-Admiral*

Rear-Admiral **Tomesaburo OKURA** (21 Apr 1894 - 4 Dec 1943)
27 Sep 1943 - 4 Dec 1943:	Captain, Aircraft Carrier *"Chuyo"*
4 Dec 1943:	Posthumously promoted to *Rear-Admiral*

Vice-Admiral (Paymaster) **Bunpei OMATSUZAWA** (2 Nov 1893 - 13 Jul 1976)
20 Oct 1942 - 1 May 1945:	Chief of Accounting Bureau, Hikari Navy Yard
1 Nov 1942:	Promoted to *Rear-Admiral (Paymaster)*
1 May 1945 - 21 May 1945:	Staff officer, China Area Fleet
21 May 1945 - 15 Jul 1946:	Chief of 1st Accounting Bureau, Paymaster-General, China Area Fleet
1 Nov 1945:	Promoted to *Vice-Admiral (Paymaster)*

Rear-Admiral **Heishiro OMI** (29 Apr 1876 - 2 Dec 1953)
20 Nov 1920 - 20 Nov 1921:	Captain, Battlecruiser *"Haruna"*
20 Nov 1921 - 1 Dec 1921:	Attached to Yokosuka Naval District
1 Dec 1921:	Promoted to *Rear-Admiral*
1 Dec 1921 - 31 Mar 1923:	Unassigned
31 Mar 1923:	Transferred to the reserve

Vice-Admiral **Naotaro OMINATO** (1 Jul 1879 - 27 Apr 1958)
1 Dec 1925:	Promoted to *Rear-Admiral*
1 Dec 1925 - 1 Nov 1926:	Chief of Staff, Combined Fleet, Chief of Staff, 1st Fleet
1 Nov 1926 - 1 Dec 1926:	Attached to Yokosuka Naval District
1 Dec 1926 - 1 Dec 1927:	Commandant, Naval Gunnery School
1 Dec 1927 - 10 Dec 1928:	Commander, 3rd Escort Flotilla
10 Dec 1928 - 10 Jun 1930:	Chief of Naval Training Bureau, Department of the Navy

30 Nov 1929:	Promoted to *Vice-Admiral*
10 Jun 1930 - 1 Dec 1931:	Commandant of the Naval Academy
1 Dec 1931 - 1 Dec 1932:	Admiral Commanding, Maizuru Guard District
1 Dec 1932 - 10 Dec 1932:	Attached to Naval General Staff
15 Dec 1932:	Transferred to the reserve

Vice-Admiral **Sentaro OMORI** (3 Oct 1892 - 24 Dec 1974)

15 Oct 1940 - 5 Nov 1942:	Commander, 1st Destroyer Flotilla
15 Nov 1940:	Promoted to *Rear-Admiral*
5 Nov 1942 - 10 Nov 1942:	Attached to Naval General Staff
10 Nov 1942 - 25 Nov 1943:	Commander, 5th Cruiser Flotilla
25 Nov 1943 - 13 Sep 1944:	Commandant, Torpedo School
1 May 1944:	Promoted to *Vice-Admiral*
13 Sep 1944 - 10 Aug 1945:	Chief of Special Attack Division, Department of the Navy
10 Aug 1945 - 20 Aug 1945:	Staff officer, Supreme Navy HQ
20 Aug 1945 - 15 Sep 1945:	C-in-C, 7th Fleet
15 Sep 1945 - 10 Oct 1945:	Attached to Naval General Staff

Rear-Admiral **Jiro ONISHI** (1 May 1885 - 17 Apr 1953)

15 Nov 1932 - 15 Nov 1934:	Commander, Yokosuka Air Division
15 Nov 1933:	Promoted to *Rear-Admiral*
15 Nov 1934 - 15 Nov 1935:	Commander, Kure Guard Flotilla
15 Nov 1935 - 28 Mar 1936:	Attached to Naval General Staff
30 Mar 1936:	Transferred to the reserve

Rear-Admiral **Keiichi ONISHI** (30 Dec 1893 - 21 May 1945)

20 Aug 1944 - 15 Mar 1945:	Chief of Bureau 4, Naval General Staff
15 Oct 1944:	Promoted to *Rear-Admiral*
15 Mar 1945 - 21 May 1945:	Attached to Naval General Staff

Vice-Admiral **Shinzo ONISHI** (17 Jul 1892 - 21 Jan 1988)

11 Aug 1941 - 5 Jun 1942:	Commander, 7th Submarine Flotilla
15 Oct 1941:	Promoted to *Rear-Admiral*
5 Jun 1942 - 14 Jul 1942:	Attached to Naval General Staff
14 Jul 1942 - 29 Mar 1943:	Chief of Staff, 8th Fleet
29 Mar 1943 - 11 Jun 1943:	Attached to Naval General Staff
11 Jun 1943 - 10 Sep 1944:	Chief of Staff, Kure Naval District
10 Sep 1944 - 5 May 1945:	Chief of Naval Training Bureau, Department of the Navy
15 Oct 1944:	Promoted to *Vice-Admiral*
5 May 1945 - 15 Oct 1945:	Deputy Commandant of the Naval Academy

Vice-Admiral **Takijiro ONISHI** (2 Jun 1891 - 16 Aug 1945)
19 Oct 1939 - 1 Nov 1940:	Commander, 2nd Combined Air Division
15 Nov 1939:	Promoted to *Rear-Admiral*
1 Nov 1940 - 15 Jan 1941:	Commander, 1st Combined Air Division
15 Jan 1941 - 10 Feb 1942:	Chief of Staff, 11th Air Fleet
10 Feb 1942 - 20 Mar 1942:	Attached to Naval Air Command
20 Mar 1942 - 1 Nov 1943:	Chief of Administration Bureau, Naval Air Command
1 May 1943:	Promoted to *Vice-Admiral*
1 Nov 1943 - 5 Oct 1944:	Chief of Administration Bureau, Warplane Agency, Department of Military Supply
5 Oct 1944 - 20 Oct 1944:	Staff officer, Southwestern Area Fleet
20 Oct 1944 - 10 May 1945:	C-in-C, 1st Air Fleet
10 May 1945 - 19 May 1945:	Attached to Naval General Staff
19 May 1945 - 16 Aug 1945:	Deputy Chief of the Naval General Staff

Rear-Admiral **Tetsuo ONITSUKA** (11 Jan 1898 - 3 May 1944)
1 Feb 1944 - 3 May 1944:	Commander, 90th Guard Force
3 May 1944:	Posthumously promoted to *Rear-Admiral*

Vice-Admiral **Hiroshi ONO** (31 Mar 1883 - 6 Oct 1956)
30 Nov 1929:	Promoted to *Rear-Admiral*
30 Nov 1929 - 1 Dec 1931:	Commandant, Naval Gunnery School
1 Dec 1931 - 15 Nov 1932:	Commander, 1st Submarine Flotilla
15 Nov 1932 - 15 Nov 1933:	Commander, Ominato Guard District
15 Nov 1933 - 15 Nov 1934:	Commander, 1st Escort Flotilla
15 Nov 1934:	Promoted to *Vice-Admiral*
15 Nov 1934 - 15 Nov 1935:	Commander, Mako Guard District
15 Nov 1935 - 28 Mar 1936:	Attached to Naval General Staff
30 Mar 1936:	Transferred to the reserve

Vice-Admiral **Ichiro ONO** (23 Jan 1890 - 8 Dec 1973)
25 Apr 1938 - 15 Dec 1938:	Captain, Aircraft Carrier *"Kaga"*
15 Nov 1938:	Promoted to *Rear-Admiral*
15 Dec 1938 - 15 Oct 1940:	Commander, Kasumigaura Air Division
15 Oct 1940 - 1 Sep 1941:	Commander, Amoi Area Base Force
1 Sep 1941 - 25 Sep 1941:	Attached to Yokosuka Naval District
25 Sep 1941 - 1 Oct 1941:	Attached to Sasebo Naval District
1 Oct 1941 - 15 Jan 1942:	Commander, Oshima Area Auxiliary Base Force
15 Jan 1942 - 14 Feb 1942:	Attached to Yokosuka Naval District
14 Feb 1942 - 1 Jun 1943:	Commander, Shanghai Area Auxiliary Base Force, Commander, Shanghai Marine Force
1 May 1942:	Promoted to *Vice-Admiral*

1 Jun 1943 - 10 Aug 1943:	Attached to Naval General Staff
10 Aug 1943 - 20 Aug 1943:	Staff officer, China Area Fleet
20 Aug 1943 - 20 Mar 1944:	Commander, Yosuko Area Base Force
20 Mar 1944 - 1 Apr 1944:	Attached to Naval General Staff
1 Apr 1944 - 1 Nov 1944:	Commander, Osaka Guard District
1 Nov 1944 - 15 Dec 1944:	Attached to Naval General Staff
20 Dec 1944:	Transferred to the reserve

Rear-Admiral **Iori ONO** (3 Jul 1892 - 4 Apr 1947)

20 Sep 1940 - 23 Jan 1942:	Chief of Supply Bureau, Maizuru Naval District
15 Nov 1940:	Promoted to *Rear-Admiral*
23 Jan 1942 - 1 Mar 1944:	Chief Supervisor for Construction & Ordnance, Naval Shipbuilding Command
1 Mar 1944 - 15 Mar 1944:	Attached to Naval General Staff
20 Mar 1944:	Transferred to the reserve

Rear-Admiral **Itaru ONO** (30 Jun 1901 - 16 May 1945)

? - 16 May 1945:	Executive Officer, Heavy Cruiser *"Haguro"*
16 May 1945:	Posthumously promoted to *Rear-Admiral*

Rear-Admiral **Koro ONO** (16 Oct 1898 - 8 Jun 1943)

10 Jan 1943 - 1 Jun 1943:	Executive Officer, Battleship *"Mutsu"*
1 Jun 1943 - 8 Jun 1943:	Staff officer, Combined Fleet
8 Jun 1943:	Posthumously promoted to *Rear-Admiral*

Rear-Admiral **Tadashi ONO** (20 Dec 1888 - 16 Dec 1973)

15 Nov 1939:	Promoted to *Rear-Admiral*
15 Nov 1939 - 15 Nov 1940:	Chief of Research Bureau, Navy Fuel Yard
15 Nov 1940 - 23 Jan 1942:	Supervisor for Construction & Ordnance, Naval Shipbuilding Command
23 Jan 1942 - 29 Jan 1942:	Attached to Naval General Staff
30 Jan 1942:	Transferred to the reserve

Rear-Admiral **Takeji ONO** (1 Oct 1894 - 18 Dec 1976)

7 Sep 1943 - 25 Jan 1944:	Captain, Battleship *"Yamato"*
1 Nov 1943:	Promoted to *Rear-Admiral*
25 Jan 1944 - 2 Mar 1944:	Attached to Naval General Staff
2 Mar 1944 - 15 Apr 1945:	Chief of Bureau 3, Naval General Staff
15 Apr 1945 - 7 May 1945:	Attached to Naval General Staff
7 May 1945 - 24 Nov 1945:	Chief of Naval Personnel

Vice-Admiral **Tokusaburo ONO** (19 May 1882 - 1 May 1956)

10 Dec 1928:	Promoted to *Rear-Admiral*

10 Dec 1928 - 1 Dec 1931:	Chief of Engine Construction Bureau, Yokosuka Navy Yard
1 Dec 1931 - 15 Nov 1932:	Commander, Hiro Navy Yard
15 Nov 1932 - 15 Nov 1934:	Commandant, Naval Engineering School
15 Nov 1933:	Promoted to *Vice-Admiral*
15 Nov 1934 - 25 Mar 1945:	Attached to Naval General Staff
30 Mar 1935:	Transferred to the reserve

Rear-Admiral **Toshihiko ONO** (2 Dec 1885 - 18 Aug 1971)

1 Dec 1931 - 15 Nov 1933:	Chief of Engine Construction Bureau, Sasebo Navy Yard
15 Nov 1933:	Promoted to *Rear-Admiral*
15 Nov 1933 - 11 Dec 1933:	Attached to Naval Shipbuilding Command
15 Dec 1933:	Transferred to the reserve

Vice-Admiral **Yaichi ONO** (26 Feb 1884 - 6 Apr 1939)

8 Feb 1929 - 1 Dec 1931:	Captain, Armored Cruiser *"Kasuga"*
1 Dec 1931:	Promoted to *Rear-Admiral*
1 Dec 1931 - 1 Dec 1932:	Attached to Naval General Staff
1 Dec 1932 - 15 Nov 1935:	Chief of Naval Hydrographic Command
15 Nov 1935:	Promoted to *Vice-Admiral*
15 Nov 1935 - 10 Dec 1935:	Attached to Naval General Staff
14 Dec 1935:	Transferred to the reserve

Rear-Admiral **Yutaka ONO** (12 Jun 1889 - ?)

1 Dec 1936 - 7 Sep 1937:	Chief Engineer Officer, 3rd Fleet
7 Sep 1937 - 13 Sep 1937:	Attached to Sasebo Naval District
13 Sep 1937 - 15 Nov 1939:	Attached to Kure Naval District
15 Nov 1939:	Promoted to *Rear-Admiral*
15 Nov 1939 - 15 Dec 1939:	Attached to Naval General Staff
21 Dec 1939:	Transferred to the reserve

Vice-Admiral **Hiromu ONODERA** (15 Apr 1883 - 13 Jan 1961)

1 Dec 1924 - 30 Nov 1929:	Chief of Engine Construction Bureau, Kure Navy Yard
1 Dec 1927:	Promoted to *Rear-Admiral*
30 Nov 1929 - 1 Dec 1931:	Supervisor for Construction & Ordnance, Naval Shipbuilding Command
1 Dec 1931 - 10 May 1934:	Commandant, Naval Engineering Academy
1 Dec 1932:	Promoted to *Vice-Admiral*
10 May 1934 - 2 Dec 1935:	Chief of Supply Bureau, Department of the Navy
2 Dec 1935 - 15 Dec 1935:	Attached to Naval General Staff
22 Dec 1935:	Transferred to the reserve

Rear-Admiral **Satoru ONOMOTO** (17 Jul 1882 - 19 Feb 1943)
1 Dec 1927 - 10 Dec 1928:	Commandant, Submarine School
10 Dec 1928:	Promoted to *Rear-Admiral*
10 Dec 1928 - 1 Dec 1930:	Commander, 1st Submarine Flotilla
1 Dec 1930 - 20 Mar 1931:	Attached to Naval General Staff
31 Mar 1931:	Transferred to the reserve

Vice-Admiral **Tomomichi ONOMOTO** (28 Dec 1850 - 3 Jan 1925)
14 May 1898:	Promoted to *Rear-Admiral*
14 May 1898 - 20 May 1900:	Commander, Takeshiki Guard District
20 May 1900 - 23 Sep 1903:	Chief of Shipping Bureau, Sasebo Naval District
23 Sep 1903 - 14 Feb 1905:	Commander, Mako Guard District
12 Jan 1905:	Promoted to *Vice-Admiral*
14 Feb 1905 - 14 Feb 1907:	Unassigned
14 Feb 1907:	Transferred to the reserve

Vice-Admiral (Surgeon) **Yasuzo ONUKI** (9 Jun 1877 - 13 Jan 1950)
1 Dec 1923:	Promoted to *Rear-Admiral (Surgeon)*
1 Dec 1923 - 27 Apr 1925:	Director, Sasebo Naval Hospital, Chief Surgeon, Sasebo Naval District
27 Apr 1925 - 1 Dec 1927:	Director, Yokosuka Naval Hospital, Chief Surgeon, Yokosuka Naval District
1 Dec 1927:	Promoted to *Vice-Admiral (Surgeon)*
1 Dec 1927 - 30 Nov 1929:	Chief of Naval Medical Service
30 Nov 1929 - 10 Jun 1930:	Attached to Naval General Staff
20 Jun 1930:	Transferred to the reserve

Rear-Admiral **Ryutaro ONUMA** (1 May 1871 - 20 Apr 1935)
13 Dec 1915 - 1 Jun 1919:	Chief Engineer Officer, Maizuru Naval District
1 Jun 1919:	Promoted to *Rear-Admiral*
1 Jun 1919 - 2 Mar 1920:	Unassigned
2 Mar 1920:	Transferred to the reserve

Rear-Admiral (Surgeon) **Tsuneji ORIMO** (10 Apr 1879 - 9 Mar 1956)
1 Dec 1925 - 10 Dec 1928:	Director, Kamekawa Naval Hospital
10 Dec 1928:	Promoted to *Rear-Admiral (Surgeon)*
10 Dec 1928 - 30 Nov 1929:	Director, Sasebo Naval Hospital, Chief Surgeon, Sasebo Naval District
30 Nov 1929 - 15 Dec 1929:	Attached to Naval General Staff
25 Dec 1929:	Transferred to the reserve

Rear-Admiral **Tsuneo ORITA** (11 Feb 1900 - 7 Jun 1944)
1 Apr 1944 - 7 Jun 1944:	Commander, 32nd Destroyer Division
7 Jun 1944:	Posthumously promoted to *Rear-Admiral*

Vice-Admiral (Surgeon) **Katsuyoshi OSADA** (11 Dec 1888 - 2 Feb 1939)
15 Nov 1933 - 15 Nov 1934:	Chief of Medical Bureau, Kure Navy Yard
15 Nov 1934:	Promoted to *Rear-Admiral (Surgeon)*
15 Nov 1934 - 1 Dec 1937:	Chief Instructor, Navy Medical School
1 Dec 1937 - 15 Dec 1938:	Director, Yokosuka Naval Hospital, Chief Surgeon, Yokosuka Naval District
15 Nov 1938:	Promoted to *Vice-Admiral (Surgeon)*
21 Dec 1938:	Transferred to the reserve

Rear-Admiral (Paymaster) **Masayoshi OSADA** (1 Aug 1884 - ?)
30 Nov 1929 - 10 Oct 1933:	Chief of Accounting Bureau, Kure Navy Yard
1 Dec 1932:	Promoted to *Rear-Admiral (Paymaster)*
10 Oct 1933 - 15 Nov 1934:	Paymaster-General, Yokosuka Naval District
15 Nov 1934 - 10 Dec 1934:	Attached to Naval General Staff
15 Dec 1934:	Transferred to the reserve

Rear-Admiral **Kishichiro OSAWA** (9 Oct 1867 - 11 Aug 1936)
10 Jan 1913 - 1 Dec 1913:	Chief of Staff, Kure Naval District
24 May 1913:	Promoted to *Rear-Admiral*
1 Dec 1913 - 25 Mar 1914:	Unassigned
25 Mar 1914 - 8 Aug 1914:	Commander, Sasebo Torpedo Group
8 Aug 1914 - 18 Aug 1914:	Acting C-in-C, 2nd Fleet
18 Aug 1914 - 1 Dec 1914:	Chief of Staff, Yokosuka Naval District
1 Dec 1914 - 1 Dec 1915:	Unassigned
1 Dec 1915:	Transferred to the reserve

Rear-Admiral **Kenshiro OSHIMA** (20 Mar 1889 - 9 Mar 1938)
15 Nov 1937 - 9 Mar 1938:	Captain, Battlecruiser *"Haruna"*
9 Mar 1938:	Posthumously promoted to *Rear-Admiral*

Rear-Admiral **Masatake OSHIMA** (2 Oct 1865 - 23 Jan 1945)
1 Oct 1915 - 13 Dec 1915:	Commander, Maizuru Sailors Corps, Captain, Battleship *"Mishima"*
13 Dec 1915:	Promoted to *Rear-Admiral*
13 Dec 1915 - 1 Dec 1916:	Unassigned
1 Dec 1916:	Transferred to the reserve

Rear-Admiral **Shiro OSHIMA** (4 Jan 1886 - 6 Feb 1954)
20 Apr 1938 - 15 Dec 1938:	Commander, Sasebo Defense Flotilla
15 Nov 1938:	Promoted to *Rear-Admiral*
15 Dec 1938 - 2 Oct 1939:	Attached to Sasebo Naval District
2 Oct 1939 - 15 Nov 1939:	Commander, 1st Combined Marine Force
15 Nov 1939 - 10 Apr 1941:	Commander, Seito Area Base Force

10 Apr 1941 - 1 Nov 1941:	Commander, Sasebo Defense Flotilla
1 Nov 1941 - 15 Dec 1941:	Attached to Naval General Staff
22 Dec 1941:	Transferred to the reserve

Vice-Admiral (Surgeon) **Tomiji OSUGA** (28 Jun 1893 - 29 May 1983)

15 Nov 1940 - 22 Sep 1941:	Chief Surgeon, Combined Fleet
22 Sep 1941 - 1 Nov 1942:	Attached to Yokosuka Naval District
15 Oct 1941:	Promoted to *Rear-Admiral (Surgeon)*
1 Nov 1942 - 10 Jul 1943:	Chief Instructor, Navy Medical School
10 Jul 1943 - 5 Feb 1945:	Chief of Research Bureau, Navy Medical School
5 Feb 1945 - 1 Nov 1945:	Chief of Medical Bureau, Yokosuka Navy Yard
1 May 1945:	Promoted to *Vice-Admiral (Surgeon)*
1 Nov 1945 - 30 Nov 1945:	Attached to Yokosuka Naval District

Vice-Admiral **Morikazu OSUGI** (11 Mar 1892 - 28 Aug 1948)

10 Apr 1942 - 21 Jun 1943:	Chief Instructor, Naval Academy
1 May 1942:	Promoted to *Rear-Admiral*
21 Jun 1943 - 3 Dec 1943:	Commander, 10th Escort Flotilla
3 Dec 1943 - 10 Jan 1944:	Staff officer, Combined Fleet
10 Jan 1944 - 26 Jan 1944:	Staff officer, 2nd Southern Expeditionary Fleet
26 Jan 1944 - Oct 1945:	Commander, 23rd Special Naval Base Force
1 May 1945:	Promoted to *Vice-Admiral*

Admiral **Baron Mineo OSUMI** (1 May 1876 - 5 Feb 1941)

1 Mar 1919 - 1 Oct 1921:	Naval Attache, France
1 Dec 1920:	Promoted to *Rear-Admiral*
1 Oct 1921 - 10 Jan 1922:	Attached to Naval General Staff
10 Jan 1922 - 1 May 1922:	Attached to Yokosuka Naval District
1 May 1922 - 1 Dec 1923:	Chief of the Naval Affairs Bureau, Department of the Navy
1 Dec 1923 - 1 Dec 1924:	Commander, 3rd Escort Flotilla
1 Dec 1924:	Promoted to *Vice-Admiral*
1 Dec 1924 - 15 Apr 1925:	Attached to Naval General Staff
15 Apr 1925 - 10 Dec 1928:	Deputy Minister of the Navy, Member, Admirals Committee
10 Dec 1928 - 11 Nov 1929:	C-in-C, 2nd Fleet
11 Nov 1929 - 1 Dec 1931:	Admiral Commanding, Yokosuka Naval District, Member, Admirals Committee
1 Apr 1931:	Promoted to *Admiral*
1 Dec 1931 - 13 Dec 1931:	Navy Councillor
13 Dec 1931 - 26 May 1932:	Minister of the Navy
26 May 1932 - 9 Jan 1933:	Navy Councillor
9 Jan 1933 - 9 Mar 1936:	Minister of the Navy
9 Mar 1936 - 5 Feb 1941:	Navy Councillor

Rear-Admiral (Paymaster) **Ichiro OTA** (29 May 1880 - ?)
1 Dec 1923 - 13 Apr 1927:	Chief of Accounting Section, Yokosuka Navy Yard
1 Dec 1926:	Promoted to *Rear-Admiral (Paymaster)*
13 Apr 1927 - 30 Nov 1929:	Paymaster-General, Yokosuka Naval District
30 Nov 1929 - 15 Dec 1929:	Attached to Yokosuka Naval District
25 Dec 1929:	Transferred to the reserve

Vice-Admiral **Minoru OTA** (7 Apr 1891 - 13 Jun 1945)
10 Aug 1942 - 11 Nov 1942:	Commander, 2nd Sasebo Sailors Corps
1 Nov 1942:	Promoted to *Rear-Admiral*
11 Nov 1942 - 20 Nov 1942:	Staff officer, 8th Fleet
20 Nov 1942 - 1 Dec 1943:	Commander, 8th Combined Marine Force
1 Dec 1943 - 10 Feb 1944:	Commander, 14th Auxiliary Base Force
10 Feb 1944 - 20 Mar 1944:	Attached to Naval General Staff
20 Mar 1944 - 20 Jan 1945:	Commander, Sasebo Guard Force, Commander, Sasebo Sailors Corps
20 Jan 1945 - 25 Feb 1945:	Commander, 4th Maritime Escort Force
20 Jan 1945 - 13 Jun 1945:	Commander, Okinawa Naval Base Force
13 Jun 1945:	Posthumously promoted to *Vice-Admiral*

Rear-Admiral **Morizane OTA** (5 Feb 1858 - 10 Aug 1940)
17 Feb 1904 - 9 Sep 1905:	Staff officer, Joint General Staff
9 Sep 1905 - 20 Dec 1905:	Executive Officer, Light Cruiser *"Soya"*
20 Dec 1905 - 30 Nov 1906:	Unassigned
30 Nov 1906:	Promoted to *Rear-Admiral*
30 Nov 1906:	Transferred to the reserve

Rear-Admiral **Nobunosuke OTA** (28 Nov 1897 - 11 Feb 1943)
26 Aug 1942 - 11 Feb 1943:	Commander, 1st Submarine Division
11 Feb 1943:	Posthumously promoted to *Rear-Admiral*

Rear-Admiral **Shichihei OTA** (16 Jun 1883 - 16 Jun 1941)
30 Nov 1929:	Promoted to *Rear-Admiral*
30 Nov 1929 - 1 Dec 1931:	Chief of Shipping Bureau, Sasebo Naval District
1 Dec 1931 - 15 Dec 1931:	Attached to Naval General Staff
21 Dec 1931:	Transferred to the reserve

Vice-Admiral **Taiji OTA** (15 Jan 1887 - 12 Feb 1960)
1 Dec 1936:	Promoted to *Rear-Admiral*
1 Dec 1936 - 15 Nov 1938:	Chief of Personnel Bureau, Yokosuka Naval District
15 Nov 1938 - 20 Jan 1939:	Attached to Naval General Staff
20 Jan 1939 - 15 Nov 1939:	Commander, 4th Auxiliary Base Force
15 Nov 1939 - 1 Jul 1940:	Attached to Naval General Staff

1 Jul 1940 - 7 May 1941:	Chief of Communication Office, Asian Development Agency
15 Nov 1940:	Promoted to *Vice-Admiral*
7 May 1941 - 1 Nov 1942:	Chief of Central China Communication Office, Asian Development Agency
1 Nov 1942 - 1 Dec 1942:	Attached to Naval General Staff
1 Dec 1942 - 20 Sep 1943:	C-in-C, 3rd Southern Expeditionary Fleet
20 Sep 1943 - 25 Jan 1944:	Attached to Naval General Staff
31 Jan 1944:	Transferred to the reserve

Rear-Admiral **Tomio OTA** (17 Sep 1880 - ?)

20 May 1926 - 15 Nov 1926:	Chief Engineer Officer, Combined Fleet, Chief Engineer Officer, 1st Fleet
15 Nov 1926 - 1 Dec 1927:	Chief Engineer Officer, Yokosuka Naval District
1 Dec 1927:	Promoted to *Rear-Admiral*
1 Dec 1927 - 15 Dec 1927:	Attached to Yokosuka Naval District
25 Dec 1927:	Transferred to the reserve

Rear-Admiral (Surgeon) **Yataro OTA** (23 Jan 1859 - 24 Dec 1935)

13 Dec 1905 - 9 Oct 1907:	Director, Ryojun Naval Hospital, Chief Surgeon, Ryojun Naval District
9 Oct 1907 - 9 Apr 1910:	Director, Sasebo Naval Hospital, Chief Surgeon, Sasebo Naval District
28 Aug 1908:	Promoted to *General (Surgeon)*
9 Apr 1910 - 17 Apr 1911:	Unassigned
17 Apr 1911:	Transferred to the reserve
23 Sep 1919:	Redesignated *Rear-Admiral (Surgeon)*

Vice-Admiral **Tomisaburo OTAGAKI** (3 Sep 1883 - 15 Oct 1956)

15 Nov 1933:	Promoted to *Rear-Admiral*
15 Nov 1933 - 1 Mar 1934:	Commander, Kure Defense Force
1 Mar 1934 - 1 Apr 1934:	Attached to Yokosuka Naval District
1 Apr 1934 - 15 Nov 1935:	Commandant, Navigation School
15 Nov 1935 - 1 Dec 1937:	Chief of Naval Hydrographic Command
1 Dec 1937:	Promoted to *Vice-Admiral*
1 Dec 1937 - 15 Dec 1937:	Attached to Naval General Staff
21 Dec 1937:	Transferred to the reserve

Rear-Admiral (Surgeon) **Hajime OTAGAWA** (17 Dec 1895 - 6 Oct 1945)

11 May 1945 - 6 Oct 1945:	Chief of Medical Bureau, Navy Powder Yard
6 Oct 1945:	Posthumously promoted to *Rear-Admiral (Surgeon)*

Rear-Admiral **Toshio OTAKE** (25 Jun 1896 - 27 Jan 1942)
11 Aug 1941 - 27 Jan 1942: Commander, 20th Submarine Division
27 Jan 1942: Posthumously promoted to *Rear-Admiral*

Vice-Admiral **Koshiro OTANI** (20 Jul 1872 - 24 Jun 1937)
1 Dec 1920: Promoted to *Rear-Admiral*
1 Dec 1920 - 1 Dec 1921: Commander, 3rd Destroyer Flotilla
1 Dec 1921 - 1 Dec 1922: Commander, 1st Destroyer Flotilla
1 Dec 1922 - 1 Jun 1923: Commander, Ominato Guard District
1 Jun 1923 - 1 Dec 1924: Commandant, Torpedo School
1 Dec 1924: Promoted to *Vice-Admiral*
1 Dec 1924 - 10 Dec 1926: Commandant of the Naval College
10 Dec 1926 - 16 May 1928: Admiral Commanding, Maizuru Naval District
16 May 1928 - 10 Dec 1928: C-in-C, 2nd Fleet
10 Dec 1928 - 11 Nov 1929: Admiral Commanding, Kure Naval District
11 Nov 1929 - 10 Jun 1930: Attached to Naval General Staff
20 Jun 1930: Transferred to the reserve

Rear-Admiral **Shiro OTANI** (Mar 1883 - 15 Oct 1943)
1 Dec 1927 - 10 Dec 1928: Chief of Supply Bureau, Kure Naval District
10 Dec 1928: Promoted to *Rear-Admiral*
10 Dec 1928 - 20 Dec 1928: Attached to Naval General Staff
25 Dec 1928: Transferred to the reserve

Rear-Admiral **Toru OTAWARA** (17 Nov 1876 - 23 May 1943)
23 Jul 1920 - 20 Jul 1921: Commander, Interim Defense Force
20 Jul 1921 - 1 Jun 1922: Attached to Yokosuka Naval District
1 Jun 1922 - 1 May 1923: Unassigned
30 Apr 1923: Promoted to *Rear-Admiral*
1 May 1923: Transferred to the reserve

Vice-Admiral **Miki OTSUKA** (17 May 1891 - 18 Jul 1945)
26 Dec 1943 - 3 Mar 1945: Captain, Seaplane Tender *"Kiyokawa-maru"*
15 Oct 1944: Promoted to *Rear-Admiral*
3 Mar 1945 - 28 Apr 1945: Attached to Yokosuka Naval District
28 Apr 1945 - 18 Jul 1945: Captain, Battleship *"Nagato"*
18 Jul 1945: Posthumously promoted to *Vice-Admiral*

Vice-Admiral (Paymaster) **Takeo OTSUKA** (10 Aug 1882 - 29 Jul 1968)
1 Dec 1932 - 10 Oct 1935: Chief of Coalmining Bureau, Navy Fuel Yard
15 Nov 1934: Promoted to *Rear-Admiral (Paymaster)*
10 Oct 1935 - 1 Dec 1937: Chief of Supply Bureau, Yokosuka Naval District
1 Dec 1937 - 12 Apr 1939: Commandant, Navy Paymaster Academy

15 Nov 1938:	Promoted to *Vice-Admiral (Paymaster)*
12 Apr 1939 - 1 Aug 1939:	Attached to Naval General Staff
10 Aug 1939:	Transferred to the reserve

Rear-Admiral **Aishichi OUCHI** (27 Nov 1874 - 9 Jan 1949)
1 Jun 1919 - 13 Aug 1923:	Chief of Engine Construction Bureau, Sasebo Navy Yard
1 Dec 1921:	Promoted to *Rear-Admiral*
13 Aug 1923 - 1 Dec 1923:	Attached to Naval Shipbuilding Command
1 Dec 1923 - 25 Feb 1924:	Unassigned
25 Feb 1924:	Transferred to the reserve

Rear-Admiral **Morishige OUCHIDA** (20 Sep 1871 - 24 Mar 1943)
20 Nov 1919 - 20 Nov 1920:	Captain, Battleship *"Yamashiro"*
20 Nov 1920 - 1 Dec 1920:	Attached to Yokosuka Naval District
1 Dec 1920:	Promoted to *Rear-Admiral*
1 Dec 1920 - 1 Aug 1921:	Unassigned
1 Aug 1921:	Transferred to the reserve

Rear-Admiral **Noboru OWADA** (6 Oct 1893 - 30 Sep 1960)
19 Mar 1943 - 17 Nov 1943:	Chief of Staff, 5th Fleet
1 May 1943:	Promoted to *Rear-Admiral*
17 Nov 1943 - 4 Dec 1943:	Staff officer, Southeastern Area Fleet
4 Dec 1943 - 20 Mar 1945:	Commander, 7th Submarine Flotilla
20 Mar 1945 - 15 Oct 1945:	Commander, 10th Special Attack Flotilla
?:	Acting C-in-C, 6th (Submarine) Fleet

Rear-Admiral **Yoshinosuke OWADA** (20 Apr 1886 - 17 Jul 1954)
15 Nov 1935:	Promoted to *Rear-Admiral*
15 Nov 1935 - 1 Dec 1937:	Commander, 2nd Submarine Flotilla
1 Dec 1937 - 1 Feb 1938:	Attached to Naval General Staff
1 Feb 1938 - 15 Nov 1938:	Commander, Yokosuka Defense Flotilla
15 Nov 1938 - 15 Dec 1938:	Attached to Naval General Staff
21 Dec 1938:	Transferred to the reserve
15 Sep 1941 - 1 Oct 1941:	Reactivated; Attached to Chinkai Guard District
1 Oct 1941 - 10 Aug 1942:	Commander, Chinkai Guard District
10 Aug 1942 - 1 Sep 1942:	Attached to Naval General Staff
1 Sep 1942:	Demobilized

Rear-Admiral **Shizuo OYAGI** (23 Jan 1897 - 15 Sep 1980)
1 May 1944:	Promoted to *Rear-Admiral*
1 May 1944 - 15 Sep 1945:	Attached to Technical Research Department

Rear-Admiral **Takanosuke OYAMA** (5 Aug 1869 - 10 Jun 1938)
1 Dec 1914 - 1 Dec 1918:	Chief of Personnel Bureau, Yokosuka Naval District
1 Dec 1918:	Promoted to *Rear-Admiral*
1 Dec 1918 - 1 Aug 1919:	Unassigned
1 Aug 1919:	Transferred to the reserve

Rear-Admiral **Tomasu OYAMA** (28 Nov 1875 - 5 Sep 1977)
20 Dec 1921 - 30 Sep 1922:	Attached to Bureau 1, Naval Shipbuilding Command
30 Sep 1922 - 31 Mar 1923:	Unassigned
1 Dec 1922:	Promoted to *Rear-Admiral*
31 Mar 1923:	Transferred to the reserve

Vice-Admiral **Shigezo OYAMADA** (23 Dec 1876 - 14 Jul 1935)
10 Nov 1922 - 1 Sep 1924:	Chief of Personnel Bureau, Kure Naval District
1 Dec 1923:	Promoted to *Rear-Admiral*
1 Sep 1924 - 5 Dec 1927:	Aide-de-Camp to the Emperor
1 Dec 1927:	Promoted to *Vice-Admiral*
5 Dec 1927 - 15 Mar 1928:	Attached to Naval General Staff
25 Mar 1928:	Transferred to the reserve

Rear-Admiral **Toshiharu OZAKI** (22 Feb 1900 - 25 Oct 1944)
? - 25 Oct 1944:	Executive Officer, Battleship *"Yamashiro"*
25 Oct 1944:	Posthumously promoted to *Rear-Admiral*

Vice-Admiral **Jisaburo OZAWA** (2 Oct 1886 - 9 Nov 1966)
1 Dec 1936:	Promoted to *Rear-Admiral*
1 Dec 1936 - 18 Feb 1937:	Instructor, Naval College
18 Feb 1937 - 15 Nov 1937:	Chief of Staff, Combined Fleet, Chief of Staff, 1st Fleet
15 Nov 1937 - 15 Nov 1938:	Commander, 8th Escort Flotilla
15 Nov 1938 - 15 Nov 1939:	Commandant, Torpedo School
15 Nov 1939 - 1 Nov 1940:	Commander, 1st Air Flotilla
1 Nov 1940 - 6 Sep 1941:	Commander, 3rd Escort Flotilla
15 Nov 1940:	Promoted to *Vice-Admiral*
6 Sep 1941 - 18 Oct 1941:	Commandant of the Naval College
18 Oct 1941 - 14 Jul 1942:	C-in-C, Southern Expeditionary Fleet
14 Jul 1942 - 14 Jul 1942:	C-in-C, 1st Southern Expeditionary Fleet
14 Jul 1942 - 11 Nov 1942:	Attached to Naval General Staff
11 Nov 1942 - 15 Nov 1944:	C-in-C, 3rd Fleet
1 Mar 1944 - 15 Nov 1944:	C-in-C, 1st Task Fleet
15 Nov 1944 - 18 Nov 1944:	Attached to Naval General Staff
18 Nov 1944 - 19 May 1945:	Deputy Chief of the Naval General Staff, Commandant of the Naval College

19 May 1945 - 29 May 1945:	Attached to Naval General Staff
29 May 1945 - 25 Aug 1945:	C-in-C, Maritime Escort Fleet
29 May 1945 - 10 Oct 1945:	C-in-C, Naval Supreme HQ, C-in-C, Combined Fleet

Rear-Admiral **Kakusuke OZAWA** (20 Jun 1886 - 19 Mar 1945)
1 Jun 1944 - 15 Mar 1945:	Commander, Fukuoka Air Division
15 Mar 1945 - 19 Mar 1945:	Attached to Sasebo Naval District
19 Mar 1945:	Posthumously promoted to *Rear-Admiral*

Vice-Admiral **Senkichi OZAWA** (21 Dec 1889 - 27 Oct 1976)
15 Nov 1938:	Promoted to *Rear-Admiral*
15 Nov 1938 - 15 Oct 1941:	Chief of Bureau 3, Naval Shipbuilding Command
15 Oct 1941 - 10 Mar 1944:	Commander, Maizuru Navy Yard
1 Nov 1942:	Promoted to *Vice-Admiral*
10 Mar 1944 - 19 Mar 1944:	Attached to Naval General Staff
20 Mar 1944:	Transferred to the reserve

Rear-Admiral **Masaharu OZOEGAWA** (13 Jan 1880 - 18 Dec 1961)
22 Aug 1925 - 1 Dec 1926:	Captain, Battleship *"Nagato"*
1 Dec 1926:	Promoted to *Rear-Admiral*
1 Dec 1926 - 20 Mar 1927:	Atttached to Yokosuka Naval District
20 Mar 1927 - 10 Apr 1927:	Unassigned
10 Apr 1927:	Transferred to the reserve

Rear-Admiral **Tokusaburo OZUMI** (30 Apr 1890 - 6 Oct 1970)
1 Dec 1939 - 10 Sep 1941:	Chief of Personnel Bureau, Maizuru Naval District
15 Nov 1940:	Promoted to *Rear-Admiral*
10 Sep 1941 - 10 Oct 1943:	Chief of Supply Bureau, Sasebo Naval District
10 Oct 1943 - 15 Oct 1943:	Attached to Naval General Staff
16 Oct 1943:	Transferred to the reserve

Rear-Admiral **Jungo RAI** (1 Jun 1897 - ?)
1 Oct 1942 - 10 Nov 1945:	Chief of Torpedo Research Bureau, Kure Navy Yard
1 Nov 1943 - 20 Jan 1944:	Chief of Torpedo Bureau, Kure Navy Yard
1 May 1944:	Promoted to *Rear-Admiral*

General (Ordnance) **Masatake RINOIE** (28 Sep 1857 - 26 Feb 1913)
10 Nov 1903 - 12 Jan 1909:	Chief of Ordnance Bureau, Maizuru Navy Yard
10 Dec 1908:	Promoted to *General (Ordnance)*

Rear-Admiral **Jiro SABA** (27 Oct 1893 - 27 Jan 1974)
15 Oct 1942 - 1 Aug 1945:	Chief of Aircraft Bureau, Air Technical Arsenal

1 Nov 1942:	Promoted to *Rear-Admiral*
1 Aug 1945 - 15 Oct 1945:	Chief of Bureau 2, Naval Air Command
5 Sep 1945 - 15 Oct 1945:	Chief of Bureau 7 Naval Air Command

Rear-Admiral **Kenichi SADA** (13 Jul 1886 - 27 Jun 1949)
15 Nov 1934:	Promoted to *Rear-Admiral*
15 Nov 1934 - 15 Dec 1934:	Commander, Sasebo Defense Force
15 Dec 1934 - 15 Nov 1935:	Commander, Sasebo Defense Flotilla
15 Nov 1935 - 28 Mar 1936:	Attached to Naval General Staff
30 Mar 1936:	Transferred to the reserve

Rear-Admiral **Jinshichi SAEKI** (27 Aug 1892 - 7 Mar 1988)
10 Oct 1943 - 15 Jun 1944:	Attached to Bureau 1 Naval Air Command
1 May 1944:	Promoted to *Rear-Admiral*
15 Jun 1944 - 1 Aug 1945:	Chief of Bureau 2, Naval Air Command
1 Aug 1945 - 30 Sep 1945:	Chief of Aircraft Bureau, 1st Technical Arsenal

Rear-Admiral (Paymaster) **Kiyoshi SAGARA** (25 Dec 1866 - ?)
1 Dec 1914 - 13 Dec 1915:	Paymaster-General, Maizuru Naval District
13 Dec 1915:	Promoted to *General (Paymaster)*
13 Dec 1915 - 1 Dec 1916:	Commandant, Naval Paymaster Academy
1 Dec 1916 - 1 Dec 1918:	Paymaster-General, Yokosuka Naval District
1 Dec 1918 - 1 Aug 1919:	Unassigned
1 Aug 1919:	Transferred to the reserve
23 Sep 1919:	Redesignated *Rear-Admiral (Paymaster)*

Rear-Admiral **Tatsuo SAGARA** (6 May 1884 - 27 Apr 1945)
10 Dec 1928 - 15 May 1931:	Commander, Sasebo Sailors Corps
15 May 1931 - 1 Dec 1931:	Attached to Sasebo Naval District
1 Dec 1931:	Promoted to *Rear-Admiral*
1 Dec 1931 - 15 Dec 1931:	Attached to Naval General Staff
21 Dec 1931:	Transferred to the reserve

Fleet Admiral **Marquis Tsugumichi SAIGO** (4 May 1843 - 18 Jul 1902)
28 Jul 1871:	Promoted to *Major-General*
28 Jul 1871 - 4 Dec 1871:	Director, Ministry of the Armed Forces
4 Dec 1871 - 27 Feb 1872:	Deputy Lord of the Armed Forces
27 Feb 1872 - 2 Jul 1873:	Deputy Lord of the Army
9 Mar 1872 - 9 Aug 1872:	Deputy Commander, Guard Force
2 Jul 1873 - 14 Feb 1877:	Vice Lord of the Army
4 Apr 1874:	Promoted to *Lieutenant-General*
14 Feb 1877 - 26 Nov 1877:	Acting Lord of the Army
26 Nov 1877 - 18 Apr 1878:	Commander, Guard Force

18 Apr 1878 - 24 May 1878:	Envoy Extraordinary
24 May 1878 - 24 Dec 1878:	Lord of Education
24 Dec 1878 - 21 Oct 1881:	Lord of the Army
21 Oct 1881 - 1 Feb 1884:	Lord of Commerce and Agriculture
1 Feb 1884 - 22 Dec 1885:	Lord of the Army
22 Dec 1885 - 17 May 1890:	Minister of the Navy
17 May 1890 - 1 Jun 1891:	Minister of the Interior
1 Jun 1891 - 28 Jan 1892:	Unassigned
28 Jan 1892 - 30 Jun 1892:	Councillor of the Royal Court
30 Jun 1892 - 20 Nov 1892:	Unassigned
20 Nov 1892 - 11 Mar 1893:	Chairman of the National Foundation
11 Mar 1893 - 8 Nov 1898:	Minister of the Navy
3 Oct 1894:	Promoted to *Admiral*
9 Oct 1894 - 7 Mar 1895:	Acting Minister of the Army
20 Jan 1898:	Appointed *Fleet Admiral*
8 Nov 1898 - 19 Oct 1900:	Minister of the Interior

Vice-Admiral **Yoshikatsu SAIO** (1 Oct 1889 - 7 Jun 1986)

15 Nov 1939:	Promoted to *Rear-Admiral*
15 Nov 1939 - 15 Nov 1940:	Attached to Technical Research Department
15 Nov 1940 - 15 Jun 1942:	Chief of Ordnance Bureau, Yokosuka Navy Yard
15 Jun 1942 - 8 Jul 1942:	Attached to Naval Shipbuilding Command
8 Jul 1942 - 1 Jun 1943:	Attached to Yokosuka Naval District
1 Jun 1943 - 10 Aug 1945:	Commander, Suzuka Navy Yard
1 Nov 1943:	Promoted to *Vice-Admiral*
10 Aug 1945 - 6 Sep 1945:	Attached to Naval Shipbuilding Command

General (Surgeon) **Ariki SAITO** (27 Apr 1857 - 2 Jan 1918)

9 Apr 1910 - 1 Dec 1911:	Director, Sasebo Naval Hospital, Chief Surgeon, Sasebo Naval District
1 Dec 1910:	Promoted to *General (Surgeon)*
1 Dec 1911 - 1 Dec 1912:	Unassigned
1 Dec 1912:	Transferred to the reserve

Rear-Admiral **Eisho SAITO** (6 May 1892 - 9 Mar 1954)

6 Jul 1944 - Oct 1945:	Commander, 105th Air Base Force
15 Oct 1944:	Promoted to *Rear-Admiral*

Rear-Admiral **Fumine SAITO** (7 Dec 1895 - ?)

15 Feb 1943 - 20 May 1944:	Attached to Yokosuka Navy Yard
1 May 1943:	Promoted to *Rear-Admiral*
20 May 1944 - 1 Nov 1945:	Chief of Engine Construction Bureau, Kure Navy Yard

Vice-Admiral **Hanroku SAITO** (16 Jun 1869 - ?)
1 Dec 1916:	Promoted to *Rear-Admiral*
1 Dec 1916 - 1 Dec 1917:	Chief of Staff, Sasebo Naval District
1 Dec 1917 - 1 Dec 1918:	Chief of Staff, 1st Fleet
1 Sep 1918 - 1 Dec 1918:	Chief of Staff, Combined Fleet
1 Dec 1918 - 1 Dec 1920:	Commandant, Torpedo School
1 Dec 1920:	Promoted to *Vice-Admiral*
1 Dec 1920 - 1 May 1921:	Commander, 2nd Escort Flotilla
1 May 1921 - 15 Apr 1922:	C-in-C, Training Fleet
15 Apr 1922 - 27 Jul 1922:	Member, Admirals Committee
27 Jul 1922 - 1 Dec 1922:	Commander, 2nd Escort Flotilla
1 Dec 1922 - 1 Apr 1923:	Member, Admirals Committee
1 Apr 1923 - 1 Jun 1923:	Admiral Commanding, Maizuru Naval District
1 Jun 1923 - 5 Feb 1924:	Admiral Commanding, Sasebo Naval District
5 Feb 1924 - 1 Apr 1924:	Member, Admirals Committee
1 Apr 1924 - 1 Dec 1924:	Attached to Naval General Staff
1 Dec 1924 - 18 Sep 1925:	C-in-C, 2nd Fleet
18 Sep 1925 - 1 Dec 1925:	Attached to Naval General Staff
16 Dec 1925:	Transferred to the reserve

Rear-Admiral **Jiro SAITO** (28 Feb 1887 - 26 Jan 1937)
1 Dec 1936:	Promoted to *Rear-Admiral*
1 Dec 1936 - 26 Jan 1937:	Commander, 1st Destroyer Flotilla

Vice-Admiral **Koshi SAITO** (28 Mar 1860 - 30 Oct 1927)
7 Apr 1906 - 21 Oct 1907:	Chief of Staff, Sasebo Naval District
22 Nov 1906:	Promoted to *Rear-Admiral*
21 Oct 1907 - 1 Mar 1909:	Chief of Bureau 1, Naval General Staff
1 Mar 1909 - 1 Dec 1909:	C-in-C, Kure Reserve Fleet
1 Dec 1909 - 17 Apr 1911:	Unassigned
17 Apr 1911:	Promoted to *Vice-Admiral*
17 Apr 1911:	Transferred to the reserve

Rear-Admiral (Engineer) **Koshiro SAITO** (6 Oct 1873 - 16 Mar 1944)
8 Apr 1919 - 20 Nov 1919:	Chief Engineer Officer, 3rd Fleet
20 Nov 1919 - 1 Dec 1919:	Attached to Kure Naval District
1 Dec 1919:	Promoted to *Rear-Admiral*
1 Dec 1919 - 1 Aug 1920:	Unassigned
1 Aug 1920:	Transferred to the reserve

Admiral **Viscount Makoto SAITO** (27 Oct 1858 - 26 Feb 1936)
10 Nov 1898 - 7 Jan 1906:	Deputy Minister of the Navy, Member, Admirals Committee

20 May 1900:	Promoted to *Rear-Admiral*
20 May 1900 - 25 Oct 1900:	Chief, Bureau of Naval Affairs
3 Feb 1904 - 20 Dec 1905:	Chief, Bureau of Naval Affairs
6 Jun 1904:	Promoted to *Vice-Admiral*
7 Jan 1905 - 7 Nov 1905:	Chief of Naval Training Command
7 Jan 1905 - 7 Jan 1906:	Chief of Naval Shipbuilding Command
7 Jan 1906 - 16 Apr 1914:	Minister of the Navy
16 Oct 1912:	Promoted to *Admiral*
16 Apr 1914 - 11 May 1914:	Unassigned
11 May 1914:	Transferred to the reserve

Vice-Admiral **Makoto SAITO** (8 Sep 1877 - ?)

1 Mar 1919 - 10 Jan 1921:	Attached to Kure Naval District
1 Dec 1920:	Promoted to *Rear-Admiral*
10 Jan 1921 - 1 Aug 1922:	Chief of Engine Construction Bureau, Hiro Branch, Kure Navy Yard
1 Aug 1922 - 1 Apr 1923:	Commander, Hiro Branch, Kure Navy Yard
1 Apr 1923 - 13 Aug 1923:	Commander, Hiro Navy Yard
13 Aug 1923 - 1 Dec 1925:	Chief of Bureau 5, Naval Shipbuilding Command
1 Dec 1924:	Promoted to *Vice-Admiral*
1 Dec 1925 - 5 Dec 1925:	Attached to Naval Shipbuilding Command
16 Dec 1925:	Transferred to the reserve

Rear-Admiral **Rokuro SAITO** (9 Sep 1893 - 7 Feb 1982)

15 Oct 1939 - 1 Nov 1942:	Chief of Shipbuilding Bureau, Maizuru Navy Yard
1 Nov 1942:	Promoted to *Rear-Admiral*
1 Nov 1942 - 15 Dec 1942:	Attached to Naval Shipbuilding Command
21 Dec 1942:	Transferred to the reserve

Vice-Admiral **Shichigoro SAITO** (12 Dec 1869 - 23 Jul 1926)

1 Dec 1917 - 1 Dec 1918:	Chief of Staff, 3rd Fleet
1 Dec 1918:	Promoted to *Rear-Admiral*
1 Dec 1918 - 1 Dec 1920:	Chief of Staff, Kure Naval District
1 Dec 1920 - 1 Dec 1922:	Chief of Bureau 1, Naval General Staff
1 Dec 1922:	Promoted to *Vice-Admiral*
1 Dec 1922 - 1 Jun 1923:	Commander, 5th Escort Flotilla
1 Jun 1923 - 10 Apr 1924:	C-in-C, Training Fleet
10 Apr 1924 - 23 Jul 1926:	Deputy Chief of the Naval General Staff

Rear-Admiral **Taizo SAITO** (16 Apr 1896 - 17 Mar 1945)

30 Nov 1942 - 1 Feb 1945:	Captain, Minelayer "*Wakataka*"
1 Feb 1945 - 17 Mar 1945:	Attached to Yokosuka Naval District
17 Mar 1945:	Posthumously promoted to *Rear-Admiral*

Rear-Admiral (Paymaster) **Yoshitaro SAITO** (20 Aug 1869 - 9 Apr 1925)
1 Dec 1921:	Promoted to *Rear-Admiral (Paymaster)*
1 Dec 1921 - 10 Nov 1922:	Chief of Coalmining Bureau, Navy Fuel Yard
10 Nov 1922 - 1 Dec 1922:	Attached to Kure Naval District
1 Dec 1922 - 31 Mar 1923:	Unassigned
31 Mar 1923:	Transferred to the reserve

Rear-Admiral **Seizo SAKABE** (31 Aug 1886 - 12 Jul 1942)
15 Nov 1935 - 1 Dec 1936:	Attached to Yokosuka Naval District
1 Dec 1937:	Promoted to *Rear-Admiral*
1 Dec 1937 - 15 Dec 1937:	Attached to Naval General Staff
21 Dec 1937:	Transferred to the reserve

Rear-Admiral **Tomihei SAKAGAMI** (1 Apr 1895 - Nov 1980)
10 Mar 1944 - 1 Apr 1945:	Chief of Administration Bureau, Yokosuka Navy Yard
15 Oct 1944:	Promoted to *Rear-Admiral*
1 Apr 1945 - 5 May 1945:	Attached to Naval General Staff
5 May 1945 - 22 Jun 1945:	Chief of Section 4, Supply Bureau, Department of the Navy
22 Jun 1945 - 15 Sep 1945:	Attached to Yokosuka Naval District

Rear-Admiral **Rokuzo SAKAGUCHI** (12 May 1892 - ?)
15 Nov 1940 - 15 May 1942:	Supervisor for Construction & Ordnance, Naval Shipbuilding Command
15 May 1942 - 14 Nov 1942:	Attached to Bureau 5, Naval Shipbuilding Command
1 Nov 1942:	Promoted to *Rear-Admiral*
16 Nov 1942:	Transferred to the reserve

Rear-Admiral **Mokichi SAKAI** (14 May 1890 - 15 Feb 1980)
15 Nov 1939:	Promoted to *Rear-Admiral*
15 Nov 1939 - 1 Aug 1940:	Naval Representative, Taihoku
1 Aug 1940 - 1 Nov 1941:	Chief Supervisor, Taihoku
1 Nov 1941 - 22 Nov 1941:	Attached to Naval General Staff
24 Nov 1941:	Transferred to the reserve

Rear-Admiral **Tadatoshi SAKAI** (12 May 1857 - 8 Feb 1943)
13 Feb 1905 - 21 Nov 1905:	Commander, Genzan Defense Force
23 Sep 1905:	Promoted to *Rear-Admiral*
21 Nov 1905 - 30 Nov 1906:	Unassigned
30 Nov 1906:	Transferred to the reserve

Rear-Admiral **Shigematsu SAKAIBARA** (28 Dec 1894 - 19 Jun 1947)
10 Dec 1942 - Oct 1945:	Commander, 65th Naval Guard Force
15 Oct 1944:	Promoted to *Rear-Admiral*

Vice-Admiral **Munetaka SAKAMAKI** (9 Jan 1894 - 24 Apr 1969)
19 Oct 1939 - 12 Sep 1941:	Chief of Training Bureau, Naval Air Command
15 Nov 1940:	Promoted to *Rear-Admiral*
12 Sep 1941 - 25 Jan 1942:	Attached to Naval General Staff
25 Jan 1942 - 10 Feb 1942:	Staff officer, 11th Air Fleet
10 Feb 1942 - 24 Dec 1942:	Chief of Staff, 11th Air Fleet
24 Dec 1942 - 15 Jan 1943:	Attached to Naval General Staff
15 Jan 1943 - 10 May 1943:	Commander, 50th Air Flotilla
10 May 1943 - 22 May 1943:	Staff officer, 3rd Fleet
22 May 1943 - 1 Sep 1943:	Commander, 2nd Carrier Flotilla
1 Sep 1943 - 9 Apr 1944:	Commander, 26th Carrier Flotilla
1 Nov 1943:	Promoted to *Vice-Admiral*
9 Apr 1944 - 7 Oct 1944:	Attached to Naval General Staff
7 Oct 1944 - 26 Aug 1945:	Chief of Administration Bureau, Warplane Agency, Department of Military Supply
26 Aug 1945 - 25 Sep 1945:	Attached to Naval Air Command

Vice-Admiral **Hajime SAKAMOTO** (12 Oct 1859 - 21 Nov 1948)
22 Nov 1906 - 28 Aug 1908:	Chief of Naval Hydrographic Command
12 Mar 1907:	Promoted to *Rear-Admiral*
28 Aug 1908 - 9 Apr 1910:	Commander, Maizuru Navy Yard
9 Apr 1910 - 1 Dec 1912:	Commander, Yokosuka Navy Yard
5 Jun 1911:	Promoted to *Vice-Admiral*
1 Dec 1912 - 1 Apr 1914:	Admiral Commanding, Ryojun Naval District
1 Apr 1914 - 17 Apr 1914:	Member, Admirals Committee
17 Apr 1914 - 13 Dec 1915:	Admiral Commanding, Maizuru Naval District
13 Dec 1915 - 1 Apr 1916:	Member, Admirals Committee
1 Apr 1916 - 1 Dec 1916:	Unassigned
1 Dec 1916:	Transferred to the reserve

Vice-Admiral **Ikuta SAKAMOTO** (17 Jun 1887 - 26 Jan 1974)
1 Aug 1936 - 1 Dec 1936:	Commander, 3rd Destroyer Flotilla
1 Dec 1936:	Promoted to *Rear-Admiral*
1 Dec 1936 - 1 Dec 1937:	Commander, 2nd Destroyer Flotilla
1 Dec 1937 - 20 Apr 1938:	Commander, Kure Guard Flotilla
20 Apr 1938 - 15 Nov 1939:	Commander, Sasebo Sailors Corps
15 Nov 1939 - 1 Sep 1941:	Commandant, Torpedo School
15 Nov 1940:	Promoted to *Vice-Admiral*
1 Sep 1941 - 15 Sep 1942:	Admiral Commanding, Chinkai Guard District

15 Sep 1942 - 15 Dec 1942:	Attached to Naval General Staff
21 Dec 1942:	Transferred to the reserve

Rear-Admiral **Noritoshi SAKAMOTO** (26 Feb 1870 - 25 Aug 1918)
13 Dec 1915 - 1 Nov 1916:	Chief of Bureau 3, Naval General Staff
1 Nov 1916 - 11 Jul 1918:	Adjutant, Naval General Staff
11 Jul 1918 - 25 Aug 1918:	Unassigned
10 Aug 1918:	Promoted to *Rear-Admiral*

Rear-Admiral (Apothecary) **Sataro SAKAMOTO** (17 Aug 1888 - 17 Feb 1972)
1 Dec 1932 - 1 Dec 1936:	Staff officer, Medical Bureau, Department of the Navy
1 Dec 1936:	Promoted to *Rear-Admiral (Apothecary)*
1 Dec 1936 - 15 Mar 1937:	Attached to Naval General Staff
25 Mar 1937:	Transferred to the reserve

Rear-Admiral **Teiji SAKAMOTO** (25 Mar 1880 - 16 Jan 1974)
1 Dec 1924:	Promoted to *Rear-Admiral*
1 Dec 1924 - 1 Jun 1925:	Attached to Naval General Staff
1 Jun 1925 - 20 Oct 1925:	Attached to Yokosuka Naval District
20 Oct 1925 - 1 Dec 1926:	Commander, 2nd Destroyer Flotilla
1 Dec 1926 - 20 Mar 1927:	Attached to Yokosuka Naval District
20 Mar 1927 - 10 Apr 1927:	Unassigned
10 Apr 1927:	Transferred to the reserve

Vice-Admiral **Baron Toshiatsu SAKAMOTO** (25 Oct 1858 - 17 Mar 1941)
20 May 1900 - 3 Feb 1904:	Commandant of the Naval College
27 May 1902:	Promoted to *Rear-Admiral*
3 Feb 1904 - 2 Nov 1905:	Chief of Staff, Sasebo Naval District
2 Nov 1905 - 28 Aug 1908:	Commandant of the Naval College
13 Nov 1905:	Promoted to *Vice-Admiral*
2 Feb 1906 - 22 Nov 1906:	Chief of Naval Training Command, Member, Admirals Committee
28 Aug 1908 - 1 Dec 1912:	Chief of Naval Training Command, Member, Admirals Committee
1 Dec 1912 - 31 May 1913:	Unassigned
31 May 1913:	Transferred to the reserve

Vice-Admiral **Tsuneyoshi SAKANO** (1 Dec 1884 - 21 Sep 1971)
15 Nov 1927 - 1 Apr 1931:	Naval Attache, USA
1 Dec 1930:	Promoted to *Rear-Admiral*
1 Apr 1931 - 20 May 1932:	Chief of Bureau 3, Naval General Staff
20 May 1932 - 6 Jun 1932:	Staff officer, 3rd Fleet

6 Jun 1932 - 20 May 1933:	C-in-C, 1st Expeditionary Fleet
20 May 1933 - 15 Nov 1933:	Commander, 11th Escort Flotilla
15 Nov 1933 - 14 May 1934:	Attached to Naval General Staff
14 May 1934 - 10 Dec 1934:	Chief of Public Relations Bureau, Department of the Navy
15 Nov 1934:	Promoted to *Vice-Admiral*
15 Dec 1934:	Transferred to the reserve

Rear-Admiral **Yoshito SAKATA** (23 Jul 1897 - 31 Mar 1945)

10 Oct 1944 - 31 Mar 1945:	Commander, Matsushima Air Division
31 Mar 1945:	Posthumously promoted to *Rear-Admiral*

Rear-Admiral **Kazuo SAKAYA** (15 Nov 1877 - 31 Jan 1940)

20 Nov 1923 - 15 Mar 1928:	Supervisor for Construction, Naval Shipbuilding Command
1 Dec 1927:	Promoted to *Rear-Admiral*
25 Mar 1928:	Transferred to the reserve

Rear-Admiral **Shakao SAKIYAMA** (28 Aug 1892 - 7 Jun 1942)

1 Nov 1940 - 7 Jun 1942:	Captain, Heavy Cruiser *"Mikuma"*
7 Jun 1942:	Posthumously promoted to *Rear-Admiral*

Vice-Admiral **Seizo SAKONJI** (27 Jun 1879 - 30 Aug 1969)

1 Dec 1924:	Promoted to *Rear-Admiral*
1 Dec 1924 - 1 Dec 1926:	Chief of Naval Personnel, Department of the Navy
1 Dec 1926 - 25 Mar 1927:	Attached to Naval General Staff
25 Mar 1927 - 6 Sep 1929:	Chief, Bureau of Naval Affairs, Department of the Navy
10 Dec 1928:	Promoted to *Vice-Admiral*
6 Sep 1929 - 12 Nov 1929:	Attached to Naval General Staff
12 Nov 1929 - 1 Oct 1930:	Assistant to the Plenipotentiary, London Conference
1 Oct 1930 - 1 Oct 1931:	C-in-C, Training Fleet
1 Oct 1931 - 1 Dec 1931:	Attached to Naval General Staff
1 Dec 1931 - 1 Jun 1932:	Deputy Minister of the Navy, Member, Admirals Committee
1 Jun 1932 - 11 Jun 1932:	Member, Admirals Committee
11 Jun 1932 - 28 Jun 1932:	Attached to Naval General Staff
28 Jun 1932 - 1 Dec 1932:	C-in-C, 3rd Fleet
1 Dec 1932 - 15 Nov 1933:	Admiral Commanding, Sasebo Naval District
15 Nov 1933 - 26 Mar 1934:	Attached to Naval General Staff
31 Mar 1934:	Transferred to the reserve

Vice-Admiral **Naomasa SAKONJO** (6 Jun 1890 - 21 Jan 1948)
1 Sep 1941 - 15 Jul 1943:	Naval Attache, Thailand
15 Oct 1941:	Promoted to *Rear-Admiral*
15 Jul 1943 - 10 Sep 1943:	Attached to Naval General Staff
10 Sep 1943 - 16 Sep 1943:	Staff officer, Southwestern Area Fleet
16 Sep 1943 - 15 Nov 1944:	Commander, 16th Cruiser Flotilla
15 Nov 1944 - 1 Dec 1944:	Attached to Naval General Staff
1 Dec 1944 - 15 Dec 1944:	Staff officer, China Area Fleet
15 Dec 1944 - Oct 1945:	Chief of Staff, China Area Fleet

Vice-Admiral (Paymaster) **Kotaro SAKURA** (9 Jun 1866 - 13 Jan 1920)
1 Dec 1913:	Promoted to *General (Paymaster)*
1 Dec 1913 - 8 Aug 1914:	Commandant, Maval Paymaster Academy
8 Aug 1914 - 1 Dec 1917:	Paymaster-General, Sasebo Naval District
1 Dec 1917 - 1 Dec 1918:	Unassigned
1 Dec 1918:	Promoted to *General (Paymaster), Senior grade*
1 Dec 1918:	Transferred to the reserve
23 Sep 1919:	Redesignated *Vice-Admiral (Paymaster)*

Rear-Admiral **Takeo SAKURA** (21 Jan 1888 - 29 Sep 1940)
1 Dec 1936 - 20 Apr 1938:	Commander, Sasebo Sailors Corps
1 Dec 1937:	Promoted to *Rear-Admiral*
20 Apr 1938 - 15 Dec 1938:	Attached to Naval General Staff
21 Dec 1938:	Transferred to the reserve

Rear-Admiral **Kikunozo SAKURAI** (6 Jun 1848 - 27 Nov 1912)
1 Nov 1900 - 1 Jun 1901:	Commandant, Naval Gunnery School
1 Jun 1901 - 1 Jul 1901:	Unassigned
1 Jul 1901:	Promoted to *Rear-Admiral*
1 Jul 1901:	Transferred to the reserve

Rear-Admiral **Masumi SAKURAI** (6 Nov 1872 - 17 Mar 1951)
10 Sep 1919 - 1 Aug 1922:	Chief of Torpedo Bureau, Kure Navy Yard
1 Dec 1920:	Promoted to *Rear-Admiral*
1 Aug 1922 - 1 Dec 1922:	Attached to Yokosuka Naval District
1 Dec 1922 - 31 Mar 1923:	Unassigned
31 Mar 1923:	Transferred to the reserve

Vice-Admiral **Tadatake SAKURAI** (27 Dec 1887 - 16 Mar 1945)
15 Nov 1935 - 1 Oct 1937:	Chief of Aircraft Bureau, Air Arsenal
1 Dec 1936:	Promoted to *Rear-Admiral*
1 Oct 1937 - 1 Jun 1938:	Attached to Naval Air Command
1 Jun 1938 - 1 Aug 1941:	Attached to Bureau of Naval Affairs, Department of the Navy

15 Nov 1940:	Promoted to *Vice-Admiral*
1 Aug 1941 - 20 Nov 1941:	Attached to Naval General Staff
20 Nov 1941 - 1 Dec 1942:	Commander, 21st Air Arsenal
1 Dec 1942 - 21 Dec 1942:	Attached to Naval General Staff
22 Dec 1942:	Transferred to the reserve

Rear-Admiral (Surgeon) **Tokuichi SAKURAI** (20 Dec 1896 - ?)

5 Nov 1943 - 8 Jan 1945:	Chief Medical Officer, 13th Air Fleet
5 Nov 1943 - Oct 1945:	Chief Medical Officer, Southwestern Area Fleet
15 Aug 1944 - Oct 1945:	Chief Medical Officer, 2nd Southern Expeditionary Fleet
1 May 1945:	Promoted to *Rear-Admiral (Surgeon)*

Admiral **Baron Kazunori SAMEJIMA** (10 May 1845 - 14 Oct 1910)

17 Dec 1894:	Promoted to *Rear-Admiral*
17 Dec 1894 - 16 Feb 1895:	C-in-C, Readiness Fleet
16 Feb 1895 - 16 Nov 1895:	C-in-C, West Fleet
16 Nov 1895 - 5 Nov 1896:	C-in-C, Readiness Fleet
5 Nov 1896 - 1 Feb 1898:	Commandant of the Naval College, Member, Admirals Committee
8 Oct 1897:	Promoted to *Vice-Admiral*
1 Feb 1898 - 19 Jan 1899:	Admiral Commanding, Yokosuka Naval District, Member, Admirals Committee
19 Jan 1899 - 20 May 1900:	C-in-C, Readiness Fleet
20 May 1900 - 2 Feb 1906:	Admiral Commanding, Sasebo Naval District
13 Nov 1905:	Promoted to *Admiral*
2 Feb 1906 - 14 Feb 1907:	Unassigned
14 Feb 1907:	Transferred to the reserve

Vice-Admiral **Tomoshige SAMEJIMA** (8 Apr 1889 - 13 Sep 1966)

1 Dec 1937:	Promoted to *Rear-Admiral*
1 Dec 1937 - 1 Aug 1938:	Commander, 4th Air Flotilla
1 Aug 1938 - 1 Sep 1938:	Commander, 13th Escort Flotilla
1 Sep 1938 - 20 Oct 1939:	Commander, 2nd Air Flotilla
20 Oct 1939 - 15 Nov 1939:	Attached to Naval General Staff
15 Nov 1939 - 26 Oct 1942:	Chief Naval Aide-de Camp to the Emperor
15 Oct 1941:	Promoted to *Vice-Admiral*
26 Oct 1942 - 1 Apr 1943:	C-in-C, 4th Fleet
1 Apr 1943 - Oct 1945:	C-in-C, 8th Fleet

Rear-Admiral **Yuji SANADA** (24 Nov 1901 - 25 Nov 1944)

15 Oct 1943 - 25 Nov 1944:	Executive Officer, Heavy Cruiser *"Kumano"*
25 Nov 1944:	Posthumously promoted to *Rear-Admiral*

Vice-Admiral (Surgeon) **Viscount Yasuzumi SANEYOSHI** (20 Mar 1848 - 1 Mar 1932)
6 Aug 1892:	Promoted to *General (Surgeon)*
6 Aug 1892 - 1 Apr 1897:	Chairman, Health Committee
1 Apr 1897 - 11 Feb 1904:	Chief of Naval Medical Service
11 Feb 1904 - 13 Dec 1905:	Chief of Medical Bureau, Joint General Staff
13 Dec 1905:	Transferred to the reserve
23 Sep 1919:	Redesignated *Vice-Admiral (Surgeon)*

Rear-Admiral (Paymaster) **Renzaburo SANO** (19 Mar 1868 - 9 Apr 1945)
1 Dec 1917 - 1 Jun 1919:	Paymaster-General, Maizuru Naval District
1 Jun 1919:	Promoted to *General (Paymaster)*
1 Jun 1919 - 2 Mar 1920:	Unassigned
23 Sep 1919:	Redesignated *Rear-Admiral (Paymaster)*
2 Mar 1920:	Transferred to the reserve

Rear-Admiral **Tsuneha SANO** (3 Jul 1871 - 25 Jan 1956)
1 Dec 1917 - 1 Dec 1919:	Captain, Battlecruiser *"Haruna"*
1 Dec 1919:	Promoted to *Rear-Admiral*
1 Dec 1919 - 1 Aug 1920:	Unassigned
1 Aug 1920:	Transferred to the reserve

Rear-Admiral (Paymaster) **Yoshisue SANO** (20 Aug 1888 - 28 Jul 1954)
15 Nov 1938 - 15 Nov 1939:	Paymaster-General, Maizuru Naval District
15 Nov 1939:	Promoted to *Rear-Admiral*
15 Nov 1939 - 15 Dec 1939:	Attached to Naval General Staff
21 Dec 1939:	Transferred to the reserve

Vice-Admiral (Paymaster) **Yuji SANO** (22 May 1869 - 9 Apr 1940)
1 Dec 1916:	Promoted to *General (Paymaster)*
1 Dec 1916 - 1 Dec 1919:	Commandant, Naval Paymaster Academy
23 Sep 1919:	Redesignated *Rear-Admiral (Paymaster)*
1 Dec 1919 - 1 Dec 1922:	Paymaster-General, Kure Naval District
1 Dec 1921:	Promoted to *Vice-Admiral (Paymaster)*
1 Dec 1922 - 10 Dec 1922:	Attached to Naval General Staff
10 Dec 1922 - 31 Mar 1923:	Unassigned
31 Mar 1923:	Transferred to the reserve

Rear-Admiral **Kiyoshi SASAGAWA** (5 Mar 1898 - 30 Jul 1977)
1 Sep 1943 - 15 Oct 1945:	Chief of Steel Group, Administration Bureau, Naval Shipbuilding Command
1 May 1944:	Promoted to *Rear-Admiral*
10 Feb 1945 - 15 Oct 1945:	Chief of Material Research Bureau, Department of Technical Research

Rear-Admiral **Hankyu SASAKI** (1 Jan 1896 - 6 Oct 1971)
25 Aug 1944 - 21 Dec 1944: Staff officer, 6th (Submarine) Fleet
15 Oct 1944: Promoted to *Rear-Admiral*
21 Dec 1944 - 15 Sep 1945: Chief of Staff, 6th (Submarine) Fleet
15 Sep 1945 - 30 Sep 1945: Attached to Kure Naval District

Vice-Admiral (Paymaster) **Juzo SASAKI** (1 Feb 1885 - 8 Dec 1951)
1 Dec 1932: Promoted to *Rear-Admiral (Paymaster)*
1 Dec 1932 - 15 Nov 1934: Paymaster-General, Sasebo Naval District
15 Nov 1934 - 15 Nov 1935: Paymaster-General, Yokosuka Naval District
15 Nov 1935 - 1 Dec 1937: Commandant, Naval Paymaster Academy
1 Dec 1936: Promoted to *Vice-Admiral (Paymaster)*
1 Dec 1937 - 15 Mar 1938: Attached to Naval General Staff
25 Mar 1938: Transferred to the reserve

Rear-Admiral **Kiyoyasu SASAKI** (12 Apr 1889 - 22 Dec 1982)
15 Nov 1938 - 10 Dec 1942: Chief of Electronic Research Bureau, Department of Technical Research
15 Nov 1939: Promoted to *Rear-Admiral*
10 Dec 1942 - 15 Dec 1942: Attached to Naval General Staff
21 Dec 1942: Transferred to the reserve

Rear-Admiral **Takanobu SASAKI** (4 Nov 1898 - 1 Apr 1945)
10 Jan 1943 - 20 Mar 1945: Executive Officer, 11th Naval Base Force
20 Mar 1945 - 1 Apr 1945: Attached to Yokosuka Naval District
1 Apr 1945: Posthumously promoted to *Rear-Admiral*

Rear-Admiral (Surgeon) **Masato SASANO** (30 Jan 1880 - 20 Apr 1936)
16 May 1927 - 15 Nov 1927: Director, Kasado-maru Naval Hospital
15 Nov 1927 - 15 Dec 1927: Attached to Naval General Staff
1 Dec 1927: Promoted to *Rear-Admiral (Surgeon)*
25 Dec 1927: Transferred to the reserve

General (Constructor) **Baron Sachu SASO** (15 Apr 1852 - 9 Oct 1905)
1 Apr 1897 - 20 May 1900: Chief of Shipbuilding Section, Bureau of Naval Affairs, Department of the Navy
28 Dec 1897: Promoted to *General (Constructor)*
20 May 1900 - 9 Oct 1905: Chief of Bureau 3, Naval Shipbuilding Command

Rear-Admiral **Hatsuki SASSA** (2 Mar 1882 - 8 Sep 1955)
1 Dec 1927 - 30 Nov 1929: Supervisor for Construction & Ordnance, Naval Shipbuilding Command
30 Nov 1929: Promoted to *Rear-Admiral*

30 Nov 1929 - 15 Dec 1929: Attached to Naval Shipbuilding Command
25 Dec 1929: Transferred to the reserve

Rear-Admiral (Surgeon) **Satoshi SATAKE** (16 Jan 1861 - 20 Jan 1938)
29 Jul 1908 - 1 Dec 1910: Executive Officer, Maizuru Naval Hospital
15 Sep 1910 - 1 Dec 1910: Chief of Bureau 1, Maizuru Naval Hospital
1 Dec 1910 - 1 Dec 1912: Unassigned
1 Dec 1912: Promoted to *General (Surgeon)*
1 Dec 1912: Transferred to the reserve
23 Sep 1919: Redesignated *Rear-Admiral (Surgeon)*

Vice-Admiral **Genzo SATO** (20 Jan 1890 - 14 Sep 1944)
31 Oct 1935 - 15 Nov 1940: Chief of Armaments Bureau, Air Arsenal
15 Nov 1939: Promoted to *Rear-Admiral*
15 Nov 1940 - 1 Nov 1942: Chief of Supply Bureau, Naval Air Command
1 Nov 1942 - 15 Apr 1943: Chief of Bureau 1, Naval Air Command
15 Apr 1943 - 1 May 1943: Staff officer, Southeastern Area Fleet
1 May 1943: Promoted to *Vice-Admiral*
1 May 1943 - 14 Sep 1944: Commander, Southeastern Area Air Depot

Vice-Admiral **Ichiro SATO** (28 Aug 1889 - 12 Apr 1958)
15 Nov 1934: Promoted to *Rear-Admiral*
15 Nov 1934 - 1 Apr 1936: Chief of Training Bureau, Naval Air Command
1 Apr 1936 - 1 Dec 1936: Chief of Staff, Kure Naval District
1 Dec 1936 - 15 Nov 1938: Chief Instructor, Naval College
15 Nov 1938: Promoted to *Vice-Admiral*
15 Nov 1938 - 15 Nov 1939: Commander, Ryojun Guard District
15 Nov 1939 - 1 Apr 1940: Attached to Naval General Staff
5 Apr 1940: Transferred to the reserve

Rear-Admiral **Kametaro SATO** (20 Feb 1859 - 26 Jul 1913)
28 Sep 1907 - 10 Dec 1908: Chief Engineer Officer, Ryojun Naval District
10 Dec 1908: Promoted to *Rear-Admiral*
10 Dec 1908 - 1 Dec 1909: Chief Engineer Officer, Sasebo Naval District
1 Dec 1909 - 17 Apr 1911: Unassigned
17 Apr 1911: Transferred to the reserve

Rear-Admiral **Katsuya SATO** (16 Apr 1895 - 10 Nov 1974)
25 Jun 1943 - 15 Aug 1944: Chief of Staff, Chinkai Guard District
1 May 1944: Promoted to *Rear-Admiral*
15 Aug 1944 - 20 Sep 1944: Attached to Naval General Staff
20 Sep 1944 - Oct 1945: Naval Attache, Thailand
14 Apr 1945 - 10 Aug 1945: Naval Attache, Burma
10 Aug 1945 - Oct 1945: Chief of Staff, 13th Naval Base Force

Rear-Admiral **Koichi SATO** (7 Sep 1884 - 30 Jul 1942)
20 Jun 1942 - 30 Jul 1942: Supervisor of Minesweepers, Transport Ship *"Kotoku-maru"*
30 Jul 1942: Posthumously promoted to *Rear-Admiral*

Vice-Admiral **Kozo SATO** (15 May 1871 - 23 Mar 1948)
13 Dec 1915 - 7 Feb 1917: Chief of Bureau 2, Naval Training Command
1 Dec 1916: Promoted to *Rear-Admiral*
7 Feb 1917 - 20 Jul 1919: C-in-C, 2nd Special Task Fleet
20 Jul 1919 - 10 Sep 1919: Member, Admirals Committee
10 Sep 1919 - 1 Dec 1921: Commandant, Naval Gunnery School
1 Dec 1920: Promoted to *Vice-Admiral*
1 Dec 1921 - 10 Dec 1922: Commander, Ominato Guard District
10 Dec 1922 - 31 Mar 1923: Unassigned
31 Mar 1923: Transferred to the reserve

Rear-Admiral **Kyosuke SATO** (17 Mar 1895 - 10 Aug 1976)
1 Apr 1941 - 10 May 1944: Chief of 2nd Production Bureau, Navy Powder Yard
1 Nov 1942: Promoted to *Rear-Admiral*
10 May 1944 - 1 Jun 1945: Chief of Chemical Research Bureau, Department of Technical Research
1 Jun 1945 - 5 Nov 1945: Commander, 3rd Navy Powder Yard

Rear-Admiral **Meijiro SATO** (6 Oct 1892 - 2 Mar 1986)
30 Sep 1943 - Oct 1945: Chief of 8th Supply Bureau
15 Oct 1944: Promoted to *Rear-Admiral*

Rear-Admiral **Minokichi SATO** (3 Apr 1879 - 3 Apr 1952)
1 Dec 1926 - 1 Dec 1927: Chief of Shipbuilding Bureau, Yokosuka Naval District
1 Dec 1927: Promoted to *Rear-Admiral*
1 Dec 1927 - 15 Dec 1927: Attached to Yokosuka Naval District
25 Dec 1927: Transferred to the reserve

Rear-Admiral **Namizo SATO** (6 Jul 1890 - 8 Apr 1947)
15 Nov 1939 - 1 Nov 1942: Chief of Mine Research Bureau, Yokosuka Navy Yard
15 Oct 1941: Promoted to *Rear-Admiral*
20 Oct 1941 - 20 Jan 1944: Commandant, Mine School
20 Jan 1944 - 8 Apr 1944: Staff officer, Maritime Escort Fleet
8 Apr 1944 - 15 Apr 1944: Commander, 5th Convoy HQ
15 Apr 1944 - 5 Dec 1944: Staff officer, Maritime Escort Fleet
5 Dec 1944 - 15 Dec 1944: Attached to Naval General Staff
20 Dec 1944: Transferred to the reserve

Rear-Admiral **Osamu SATO** (5 Dec 1886 - 5 Dec 1974)
1 Dec 1932 - 1 Dec 1936:	Naval Attache, China
15 Nov 1934:	Promoted to *Rear-Admiral*
1 Dec 1936 - 15 Dec 1937:	Attached to Naval General Staff
21 Dec 1937:	Transferred to the reserve
14 Oct 1943 - 25 Oct 1943:	Recalled; Attached to Naval General Staff
25 Oct 1943 - Oct 1945:	Naval Representative, Beijing

Vice-Admiral **Saburo SATO** (24 Jun 1885 - 19 Aug 1938)
1 Dec 1931:	Promoted to *Rear-Admiral*
1 Dec 1931 - 3 Oct 1933:	Commander, Kasumigaura Air Division
3 Oct 1933 - 15 Nov 1935:	Chief of Technical Bureau, Naval Air Command
1 Jun 1934 - 1 Nov 1934:	Chief of Administration Bureau, Naval Air Command
15 Nov 1935 - 1 Dec 1936:	Commander, 1st Air Flotilla
1 Dec 1936:	Promoted to *Vice-Admiral*
1 Dec 1936 - 1 Dec 1937:	Commandant of the Naval College
1 Dec 1937 - 19 Aug 1938:	Attached to Naval General Staff

Rear-Admiral **Seishiro SATO** (25 Oct 1886 - 7 Jul 1958)
15 Nov 1937 - 15 Dec 1937:	Attached to Naval General Staff
1 Dec 1937:	Promoted to *Rear-Admiral*
20 Dec 1937:	Transferred to the reserve

Rear-Admiral **Shiro SATO** (13 May 1893 - 16 Aug 1946)
25 Mar 1944 - 1 May 1944:	Chief of 8th Construction Bureau
25 Mar 1944 - Oct 1945:	Commander, 27th Naval Base Force
1 May 1944:	Promoted to *Rear-Admiral*

Rear-Admiral **Tadakazu SATO** (2 Mar 1888 - 24 Sep 1954)
15 Aug 1935 - 7 Sep 1938:	Chief of Administration Bureau, Sasebo Navy Yard
7 Sep 1938 - 15 Nov 1939:	Attached to Sasebo Naval District
15 Nov 1939:	Promoted to *Rear-Admiral*
15 Nov 1939 - 15 Dec 1939:	Attached to Naval General Staff
21 Dec 1939:	Transferred to the reserve

Vice-Admiral **Tetsutaro SATO** (13 Jul 1866 - 4 Mar 1942)
1 Dec 1912:	Promoted to *Rear-Admiral*
1 Dec 1912 - 1 Dec 1913:	Chief of Bureau 4, Naval General Staff
1 Dec 1913 - 17 Apr 1914:	Chief of Staff, 1st Fleet
17 Apr 1914 - 10 Aug 1915:	Chief of Bureau 1, Naval General Staff
10 Aug 1915 - 13 Dec 1915:	Deputy Chief of the Naval General Staff, Member, Admirals Committee

13 Dec 1915 - 16 Aug 1920:	Commandant of the Naval College
1 Dec 1916:	Promoted to *Vice-Admiral*
16 Aug 1920 - 1 Dec 1921:	Admiral Commanding, Maizuru Naval District
1 Dec 1921 - 10 Apr 1922:	Member, Admirals Committee
10 Apr 1922 - 31 Mar 1923:	Unassigned
31 Mar 1923:	Transferred to the reserve

Rear-Admiral **Torajiro SATO** (23 Oct 1892 - 12 Jul 1943)

12 Feb 1943 - 12 Jul 1943:	Captain, Light Cruiser *"Jintsu"*
12 Jul 1943:	Posthumously promoted to *Rear-Admiral*

Rear-Admiral **Toshimi SATO** (12 Jan 1892 - 17 Mar 1972)

5 Aug 1943 - 10 Jul 1945:	Commander, 51st Guard Force
1 May 1945:	Promoted to *Rear-Admiral*
10 Jul 1945 - 1 Aug 1945:	Commander, 1st Ominato Marine Force
1 Aug 1945 - 1 Nov 1945:	Chief of Transport Bureau, Ominato Guard District

Rear-Admiral **Tsutomu SATO** (3 Jun 1890 - 25 Aug 1980)

15 Nov 1940:	Promoted to *Rear-Admiral*
15 Nov 1940 - 11 Aug 1941:	Commander, 7th Submarine Flotilla
11 Aug 1941 - 15 Apr 1942:	Commander, 1st Submarine Flotilla
15 Apr 1942 - 11 Jun 1942:	Attached to Kure Naval District
11 Jun 1942 - 20 Nov 1943:	Commander, Kure Guard Force
20 Nov 1943 - 15 Dec 1943:	Attached to Naval General Staff
15 Dec 1943 - 20 Dec 1943:	Unassigned
20 Dec 1943 - 15 Apr 1944:	Attached to Naval General Staff
15 Apr 1944 - 9 Jan 1945:	Commander, 8th Convoy HQ
9 Jan 1945 - 9 Jun 1945:	Staff officer, Maritime Escort Fleet
9 Jun 1945 - 1 Sep 1945:	Attached to Naval General Staff

Vice-Admiral **Yasuo SATO** (31 Mar 1894 - 3 Mar 1943)

15 Aug 1940 - 10 Apr 1941:	Commander, 5th Destroyer Division
10 Apr 1941 - 15 Feb 1943:	Commander, 9th Destroyer Division
15 Feb 1943 - 3 Mar 1943:	Commander, 8th Destroyer Division
3 Mar 1943:	Posthumously promoted 2 grades to *Vice-Admiral*

Vice-Admiral **Kannojo SAWA** (20 Jan 1960 - 21 May 1947)

10 Nov 1903 - 1 Dec 1912:	Commander, Ordnance Arsenal
24 Dec 1905:	Promoted to *General (Ordnance)*
1 Dec 1912 - 15 Jan 1913:	Attached to Naval Shipbuilding Command
15 Jan 1913 - 25 Jul 1913:	Unassigned
25 Jul 1913:	Transferred to the reserve
23 Sep 1919:	Redesignated *Vice-Admiral*

Rear-Admiral **Masao SAWA** (20 Nov 1895 - 14 Nov 1942)
20 Aug 1941 - 14 Nov 1942: Captain, Heavy Cruiser *"Kinugasa"*
14 Nov 1942: Posthumously promoted to *Rear-Admiral*

Rear-Admiral **Ryokan SAWA** (5 Oct 1853 - 8 Oct 1923)
27 Dec 1897 - 13 Jun 1898: Captain, Ironclad *"Chinen"*
13 Jun 1898 - 27 Dec 1900: Unassigned
27 Dec 1900: Promoted to *Rear-Admiral*
27 Dec 1900: Transferred to the reserve

Vice-Admiral **Tatsu SAWA** (11 Jul 1892 - 15 Mar 1987)
15 Nov 1939 - 15 Oct 1941: Chief Instructor, Naval Engineering Academy
15 Nov 1940: Promoted to *Rear-Admiral*
15 Oct 1941 - 22 Feb 1943: Chief of Supply Bureau, Kure Naval District
22 Feb 1943 - 5 Mar 1943: Staff officer, 2nd Southern Expeditionary Fleet
5 Mar 1943 - 1 Apr 1944: Commander, 101st Navy Fuel Yard
1 Apr 1944 - 1 May 1944: Attached to Naval General Staff
1 May 1944: Promoted to *Vice-Admiral*
1 May 1944 - 1 May 1945: Commander, 3rd Navy Fuel Yard
1 May 1945 - 20 Jul 1945: Chief Supervisor for Construction & Ordnance, Naval Shipbuilding Command
20 Jul 1945 - 21 Jul 1945: Attached to Naval Shipbuilding Command
21 Jul 1945 - 6 Sep 1945: Unassigned

Vice-Admiral **Torao SAWADA** (27 Sep 1891 - 25 Jul 1958)
31 Jul 1941 - 3 Jan 1942: Chief of Staff, Southern Expeditionary Fleet
15 Oct 1941: Promoted to *Rear-Admiral*
3 Jan 1942 - 20 Jun 1942: Chief of Staff, 1st Southern Expeditionary Fleet
20 Jun 1942 - 29 Jul 1942: Attached to Naval Shipbuilding Command
29 Jul 1942 - 15 Nov 1944: Chief of Merchant Marine Bureau, Naval Shipbuilding Command
15 Oct 1944: Promoted to *Vice-Admiral*
15 Nov 1944 - 21 Nov 1944: Staff officer, China Area Fleet
21 Nov 1944 - Oct 1945: Commander, Yosuko Area Base Force

Admiral **Yorio SAWAMOTO** (15 Nov 1886 - 29 Jun 1965)
15 Nov 1934: Promoted to *Rear-Admiral*
15 Nov 1934 - 15 Mar 1935: Attached to Naval General Staff
15 Mar 1935 - 15 Nov 1935: Chief Instructor, Naval College
15 Nov 1935 - 15 Feb 1936: Attached to Naval Shipbuilding Command
15 Feb 1936 - 1 Dec 1937: Chief of Administration Bureau, Naval Shipbuilding Command
1 Dec 1937 - 15 Dec 1938: Commander, 7th Escort Flotilla

15 Nov 1938:	Promoted to *Vice-Admiral*
15 Dec 1938 - 1 Apr 1939:	Attached to Naval General Staff
1 Apr 1939 - 23 Dec 1939:	C-in-C, Training Fleet
23 Dec 1939 - 15 Oct 1940:	Commandant of the Naval College
15 Oct 1940 - 4 Apr 1941:	C-in-C, 2nd China Expeditionary Fleet
4 Apr 1941 - 17 Jul 1944:	Deputy Minister of the Navy, Member, Admirals Committee
11 Aug 1941 - 10 Sep 1941:	Chief of Naval Air Command
1 Mar 1944:	Promoted to *Admiral*
1 Mar 1944 - 17 Jul 1944:	Navy Councillor
17 Jul 1944 - 1 May 1945:	Admiral Commanding, Kure Naval District
1 May 1945 - 1 Sep 1945:	Navy Councillor
5 Sep 1945:	Transferred to the reserve

Rear-Admiral **Toyonari SAYAMA** (9 Sep 1864 - 28 Oct 1939)
1 Dec 1911:	Promoted to *Rear-Admiral*
1 Dec 1911 - 1 Dec 1913:	Commander, Maizuru Navy Yard
1 Dec 1913 - 1 Dec 1914:	Unassigned
1 Dec 1914:	Transferred to the reserve

Rear-Admiral **Tamesaburo SEGAWA** (26 May 1897 - 13 Jan 1979)
30 Jan 1945 - 30 Sep 1945:	Chief of Armaments Bureau, 2md Air Arsenal
1 May 1945:	Promoted to *Rear-Admiral*

Rear-Admiral **Ikuya SEKI** (10 Feb 1893 - 11 Aug 1980)
20 Jul 1944 - 1 Mar 1945:	Commander, Yokosuka 2nd Guard Force
15 Oct 1944:	Promoted to *Rear-Admiral*
1 Mar 1945 - 20 Jun 1945:	Commandant, Navy Weather School
20 Jun 1945 - 1 Nov 1945:	Commander, Ou Air Division

Rear-Admiral (Engineer) **Shigemitsu SEKI** (3 Oct 1875 - 9 Nov 1937)
1 Dec 1921 - 20 Nov 1922:	Chief Engineer Officer, Ominato Guard District
20 Nov 1922 - 1 Dec 1922:	Attached to Yokosuka Naval District
1 Dec 1922:	Promoted to *Rear-Admiral*
1 Dec 1922 - 31 Mar 1923:	Unassigned
31 Mar 1923:	Transferred to the reserve

Rear-Admiral (Engineer) **Shigetada SEKI** (22 Nov 1863 - 12 Mar 1945)
10 Dec 1908 - 12 Jul 1912:	Chief Engineer Officer, Maizuru Naval District
5 Jun 1911:	Promoted to *Rear-Admiral*
12 Jul 1912 - 31 Mar 1913:	Unassigned
31 Mar 1913:	Transferred to the reserve

Rear-Admiral **Shigetaka SEKI** (11 Jan 1870 - 1 Jan 1930)
11 Apr 1916 - 1 Dec 1916:	Captain, Battleship *"Iwami"*
1 Dec 1916 - 1 Dec 1917:	Unassigned
1 Dec 1917:	Promoted to *Rear-Admiral*
1 Dec 1917:	Transferred to the reserve

Rear-Admiral **Tateki SEKI** (15 Nov 1880 - 5 Dec 1934)
1 Dec 1923:	Promoted to *Rear-Admiral*
1 Dec 1923 - 19 Dec 1923:	Chief of Bureau 1, Naval General Staff, Chief of Bureau 2, Naval General Staff
19 Dec 1923 - 5 Feb 1924:	Chairman, Code Book Editor Committee
5 Feb 1924 - 1 Dec 1924:	Chief of Bureau 2, Naval General Staff
1 Dec 1924 - 1 Aug 1925:	Commander, Sasebo Defense Force
1 Aug 1925 - 1 Oct 1925:	Attached to Naval General Staff
1 Oct 1925 - 16 Dec 1925:	Unassigned
16 Dec 1925:	Transferred to the reserve

Rear-Admiral **Tei SEKI**   (10 Feb 1886 - 31 Jan 1944)
31 May 1943 - 31 Jan 1944:	Captain, Auxiliary Submarine Tender *"Yasukuni-maru"*
31 Jan 1944:	Posthumously promoted to *Rear-Admiral*

Rear-Admiral **Komakichi SEKIDA** (3 Jan 1875 - 5 Nov 1939)
1 Oct 1920 - 20 Nov 1921:	Chief of Section 1, Naval Hydrographic Command
20 Nov 1921 - 1 Dec 1921:	Attached to Naval General Staff
1 Dec 1921:	Promoted to *Rear-Admiral*
1 Dec 1921 - 31 Mar 1923:	Unassigned
31 Mar 1923:	Transferred to the reserve

Rear-Admiral **Gunpei SEKINE** (1 Aug 1886 - 25 Aug 1964)
16 Nov 1936 - 15 Nov 1938:	Chief of Public Relations Bureau, Department of the Navy
1 Dec 1936:	Promoted to *Rear-Admiral*
15 Nov 1938 - 15 Dec 1938:	Attached to Naval General Staff
21 Dec 1938:	Transferred to the reserve

Vice-Admiral **Kenkichi SEKINO** (19 Sep 1865 - 7 Jun 1947)
1 Dec 1912:	Promoted to *Rear-Admiral*
1 Dec 1912 - 22 Dec 1916:	Aide-de-Camp to the Emperor
1 Dec 1916:	Promoted to *Vice-Admiral*
22 Dec 1916 - 1 Jun 1917:	Member, Admirals Committee
1 Jun 1917 - 1 Jun 1918:	Unassigned
1 Jun 1918:	Transferred to the reserve

Rear-Admiral (Surgeon) **Eiichi SEKUZU** (22 Apr 1895 - 26 Dec 1954)
15 Oct 1943 - Oct 1945:	Director, 8th Naval Hospital
1 May 1944:	Promoted to *Rear-Admiral (Surgeon)*

Rear-Admiral **Kinji SENDA** (10 Aug 1896 - 22 Jan 1966)
7 Sep 1942 - 10 Mar 1944:	Instructor, Naval College
1 Nov 1943:	Promoted to *Rear-Admiral*
10 Mar 1944 - Oct 1945:	Chief of Staff, Kainan Guard District

Vice-Admiral **Sadatoshi SENDA** (22 Jul 1890 - 25 Dec 1944)
15 Mar 1941 - 1 Nov 1942:	Commander, Kasumigaura Air Division
1 May 1942:	Promoted to *Rear-Admiral*
1 Nov 1942 - 1 Mar 1944:	Commander, 14th Combined Air Division
1 Mar 1944 - 18 Apr 1944:	Attached to Naval General Staff
18 Apr 1944 - 1 May 1944:	Staff officer, 4th Southern Expeditionary Fleet
1 May 1944 - 25 Dec 1944:	Commander, 28th Auxiliary Base Force
25 Dec 1944:	Posthumously promoted to *Vice-Admiral*

Rear-Admiral **Michizo SENDO** (6 May 1895 - 25 Apr 1969)
22 May 1942 - 20 Sep 1945:	Professor, University of Tokyo
1 May 1943:	Promoted to *Rear-Admiral*

Vice-Admiral **Taketeru SENDO** (3 Sep 1864 - 11 Dec 1919)
1 Dec 1910:	Promoted to *Rear-Admiral*
1 Dec 1910 - 2 Sep 1911:	Commander, Chinkai Defense Force
2 Sep 1911 - 1 Apr 1913:	C-in-C, Kure Reserve Fleet
1 Apr 1913 - 1 Dec 1913:	C-in-C, Kure Naval District Fleet
1 Dec 1913 - 1 Dec 1914:	Unassigned
1 Dec 1914:	Promoted to *Vice-Admiral*
1 Dec 1914:	Transferred to the reserve

Vice-Admiral **Tomoyuki SENOO** (1 Aug 1891 - 5 Nov 1984)
15 Nov 1939:	Promoted to *Rear-Admiral*
15 Nov 1939 - 10 Jan 1940:	Chief of Section 1, Administration Bureau, Naval Shipbuilding Command
10 Jan 1940 - 1 Oct 1940:	Attached to Naval Shipbuilding Command
1 Oct 1940 - 1 Oct 1943:	Commander, Hikari Navy Yard
1 May 1943:	Promoted to *Vice-Admiral*
1 Oct 1943 - 1 Nov 1943:	Chief of the Shipping Agency, Department of the Navy
1 Nov 1943 - 21 Oct 1944:	Director-General of Sealift Agency, Department of Transport and Communication
21 Oct 1944 - 1 Nov 1944:	Attached to Naval General Staff

1 Nov 1944 - 1 May 1945:	Kanto Area Inspector, Department of Military Supply
1 May 1945 - 1 Nov 1945:	Commander, Kure Navy Yard

Rear-Admiral **Tesuku SERATA** (3 Oct 1856 - 1 Aug 1900)
21 May 1900:	Promoted to *Rear-Admiral*
21 May 1900 - 20 Jun 1900:	C-in-C, Kure Naval District Fleet
20 Jun 1900 - 4 Jul 1900:	Chief of Staff, Sasebo Naval District
4 Jul 1900 - 1 Aug 1900:	Unassigned

Rear-Admiral (Paymaster) **Masato SERIZAWA** (10 Nov 1880 - 9 Oct 1963)
30 Mar 1928 - 10 Dec 1928:	Paymaster-General, Maizuru Guard District
10 Dec 1928:	Promoted to *Rear-Admiral (Paymaster)*
10 Dec 1928 - 20 Dec 1928:	Attached to Naval General Staff
25 Dec 1928:	Transferred to the reserve

Rear-Admiral **Kikujiro SETO** (24 Sep 1867 - 6 Jan 1922)
9 Jun 1908 - 1 Dec 1913:	Chief of Steel Bureau, Kure Navy Yard
1 Dec 1912:	Promoted to *General (Ordnance)*
1 Dec 1913 - 1 Dec 1914:	Chief of Ordnance Bureau, Yokosuka Navy Yard
1 Dec 1914 - 1 Dec 1915:	Unassigned
1 Dec 1915:	Transferred to the reserve
23 Sep 1919:	Redesignated *Rear-Admiral*

Rear-Admiral **Yasuhide SETOYAMA** (10 Mar 1895 - 13 Oct 1943)
7 May 1943 - 13 Oct 1943:	Captain, Oiler *"Naruto"*
13 Oct 1943:	Posthumously promoted to *Rear-Admiral*

Rear-Admiral **Nihei SEZAKI** (9 Dec 1881 - 12 Aug 1961)
1 Apr 1928 - 1 Dec 1930:	Commander, Kure Sailors Corps
1 Dec 1930:	Promoted to *Rear-Admiral*
1 Dec 1930 - 15 Dec 1930:	Attached to Naval General Staff
13 Dec 1930:	Transferred to the reserve

Rear-Admiral **Ko SHIBANAI** (13 Mar 1876 - 10 Jun 1933)
1 Dec 1921 - 1 Dec 1922:	Chief of Ordnance Bureau, Maizuru Navy Yard
1 Dec 1922:	Promoted to *Rear-Admiral*
1 Dec 1922 - 10 Dec 1922:	Attached to Naval Shipbuilding Command
10 Dec 1922 - 31 Mar 1923:	Unassigned
31 Mar 1923:	Transferred to the reserve

Rear-Admiral **Hideo SHIBATA** (17 May 1875 - 17 Jan 1949)
20 May 1922 - 13 Aug 1923:	Staff officer, Engine Construction Bureau, Yokosuka Navy Yard

13 Aug 1923 - 1 Dec 1923:	Attached to Yokosuka Naval District
1 Dec 1923:	Promoted to *Rear-Admiral*
1 Dec 1923 - 15 Jan 1924:	Unassigned
15 Jan 1924:	Transferred to the reserve

Rear-Admiral (Surgeon) **Toshio SHIBATA** (10 May 1892 - 18 May 1950)

15 Nov 1940:	Promoted to *Rear-Admiral (Surgeon)*
15 Nov 1940 - 15 Oct 1941:	Chief Surgeon, China Area Fleet
15 Oct 1941 - 1 Oct 1942:	Attached to Kure Naval District
1 Oct 1942 - 1 Nov 1943:	Director, Minato Naval Hospital
1 Nov 1943 - 15 Dec 1943:	Attached to Naval General Staff
20 Dec 1943:	Transferred to the reserve

Rear-Admiral **Tsutomu SHIBATA** (11 Dec 1889 - 19 Jan 1942)

27 Dec 1941 - 19 Jan 1942:	Supervisor of Minesweepers, Oiler *"Akebono-maru"*
19 Jan 1942:	Posthumously promoted to *Rear-Admiral*

Vice-Admiral **Yaichiro SHIBATA** (1 Nov 1889 - 16 Jun 1981)

10 Mar 1939 - 8 Aug 1940:	Staff officer, 4th Fleet
15 Nov 1939:	Promoted to *Rear-Admiral*
8 Aug 1940 - 22 Aug 1940:	Attached to Naval General Staff
22 Aug 1940 - 1 May 1941:	Chief of Bureau 2, Planning Agency, Department of the Navy
1 May 1941 - 1 Nov 1942:	Chief of Bureau 6, Planning Agency, Department of the Navy
1 Nov 1942 - 22 Feb 1943:	Chief of Bureau 5, Planning Agency, Department of the Navy
22 Feb 1943 - 13 Mar 1943:	Staff officer, 2nd Southern Expeditionary Fleet
13 Mar 1943 - 30 Nov 1943:	Commander, 24th Naval Base Force
1 Nov 1943:	Promoted to *Vice-Admiral*
30 Nov 1943 - 1 Feb 1944:	Commander, 24th Auxiliary Naval Base Force
1 Feb 1944 - 10 Mar 1944:	Attached to Naval General Staff
10 Mar 1944 - 20 Dec 1944:	Commander, Tagajo Navy Yard
20 Dec 1944 - 6 Jan 1945:	Attached to Naval General Staff
6 Jan 1945 - 29 Jan 1945:	Staff officer, Southwestern Area Fleet
29 Jan 1945 - Sep 1945:	C-in-C, 2nd Southern Expeditionary Fleet

Rear-Admiral **Zenjiro SHIBATA** (14 Oct 1889 - 30 May 1944)

1 Feb 1944 - 30 May 1944:	Chief of Personnel Bureau, Takao Guard District
30 May 1944:	Posthumously promoted to *Rear-Admiral*

Rear-Admiral **Baron Masaki SHIBAYAMA** (13 Aug 1884 - 15 Mar 1952)

15 Nov 1934:	Promoted to *Rear-Admiral*

15 Nov 1934 - 1 Dec 1936:	Chief of Personnel Bureau, Yokosuka Naval District
1 Dec 1936 - 15 Dec 1936:	Attached to Naval General Staff
22 Dec 1936:	Transferred to the reserve

Rear-Admiral **Shiba SHIBAYAMA** (14 Jan 1883 - 17 Oct 1962)

10 Dec 1928 - 1 Dec 1931:	Chief of Personnel Bureau, Sasebo Naval District
1 Dec 1930:	Promoted to *Rear-Admiral*
1 Dec 1931 - 1 Dec 1932:	Commander, Yokosuka Defense Force
1 Dec 1932 - 10 Dec 1932:	Attached to Naval General Staff
15 Dec 1932:	Transferred to the reserve

Admiral **Baron Yahachi SHIBAYAMA** (13 Jul 1850 - 27 Jan 1924)

20 Dec 1893 - 13 Jul 1894:	Commandant of the Naval Academy
13 Jul 1894 - 8 Oct 1897:	Admiral Commanding, Sasebo Naval District
30 Jul 1894:	Promoted to *Rear-Admiral*
8 Oct 1897:	Promoted to *Vice-Admiral*
8 Oct 1897 - 19 Jan 1899:	C-in-C, Readiness Fleet
19 Jan 1899 - 20 May 1900:	Commandant of the Naval College, Member, Admirals College
20 May 1900 - 7 Jan 1905:	Admiral Commanding, Kure Naval District
7 Jan 1905 - 2 Feb 1906:	Admiral Commanding, Ryojun Naval District
13 Nov 1905:	Promoted to *Admiral*
2 Feb 1906 - 14 Feb 1907:	Unassigned
14 Feb 1907:	Transferred to the reserve

Vice-Admiral **Keiji SHIBAZAKI** (9 Apr 1894 - 25 Nov 1943)

25 Apr 1943 - 9 Jul 1943:	Commander, Kure Defense Flotilla
1 May 1943:	Promoted to *Rear-Admiral*
9 Jul 1943 - 20 Jul 1943 :	Staff officer, 4th Fleet
20 Jul 1943 - 25 Nov 1943:	Commander, 3rd Special Naval Base Force
25 Nov 1943:	Posthumously promoted to *Vice-Admiral*

Rear-Admiral **Kiyomi SHIBUYA** (27 Sep 1895 - 20 Feb 1985)

20 Dec 1944 - 28 Apr 1945:	Captain, Battleship *"Nagato"*
28 Apr 1945 - 20 May 1945:	Attached to Yokosuka Naval District
1 May 1945:	Promoted to *Rear-Admiral*
20 May 1945 - 5 Nov 1945:	Commander, 3rd Special Attack Flotilla

Vice-Admiral **Ryutaro SHIBUYA** (5 Apr 1887 - 8 Apr 1973)

2 Dec 1935 - 1 Dec 1937:	Chief of Engine Construction Bureau, Yokosuka Navy Yard
1 Dec 1936:	Promoted to *Rear-Admiral*
1 Dec 1937 - 15 Nov 1938:	Chief of Scientific Research Bureau, Technical Research Department

15 Nov 1938 - 1 Oct 1940:	Chief of Engine Construction Bureau, Kure Navy Yard
1 Oct 1940 - 20 Nov 1941:	Commander, Hiro Navy Yard
15 Nov 1940:	Promoted to *Vice-Admiral*
20 Nov 1941 - 15 Sep 1943:	Commander, Kure Navy Yard
15 Sep 1943 - 1 Oct 1943:	Attached to Naval General Staff
1 Oct 1943 - 18 Nov 1944:	Attached to Naval Shipbuilding Command
18 Nov 1944 - 1 Nov 1945:	Chief of Naval Shipbuilding Command, Member, Admirals Committee

Vice-Admiral **Shiro SHIBUYA** (18 Nov 1893 - 12 Jan 1945)

10 Sep 1944 - 15 Nov 1944:	Staff officer, Maritime Escort Fleet
15 Oct 1944:	Promoted to *Rear-Admiral*
15 Nov 1944 - 12 Jan 1945:	Commander, 101st Escort Flotilla
12 Jan 1945:	Posthumously promoted to *Vice-Admiral*

Rear-Admiral **Shusaku SHIBUYA** (19 Oct 1886 - 24 Jan 1942)

1 Sep 1941 - 24 Jan 1942:	Captain, Transport Ship *"Sumanoura-maru"*
24 Jan 1942:	Posthumously promoted to *Rear-Admiral*

Rear-Admiral **Kesaichi SHICHIDA** (22 Apr 1880 - 4 Jul 1956)

1 Dec 1925:	Promoted to *Rear-Admiral*
1 Dec 1925 - 20 Aug 1926:	?
20 Aug 1926 - 1 Dec 1927:	Commander, 2nd Submarine Flotilla
1 Dec 1927 - 10 Dec 1928:	Commander, Mako Guard District

Rear-Admiral **Atsuyuki SHIGEHISA** (28 Jan 1853 - 5 Aug 1926)

10 Nov 1903 - 12 Dec 1905:	Chief Engineer Officer, Kure Naval District
12 Dec 1905 - 14 Feb 1907:	Unassigned
26 Jan 1906:	Promoted to *Rear-Admiral*
14 Feb 1907:	Transferred to the reserve

Rear-Admiral **Giichi SHIGEMURA** (14 Feb 1875 - 31 Mar 1938)

20 Nov 1920 - 1 Dec 1921:	Chief Engineer Officer, 2nd Fleet
1 Dec 1920:	Promoted to *Rear-Admiral*
1 Dec 1921 - 20 Nov 1922:	Chief Engineer Officer, 1st Fleet
20 Nov 1922 - 1 Dec 1923:	Commander, Navy Fuel Yard
1 Dec 1923 - 10 Dec 1923:	Attached to Naval General Staff
10 Dec 1923 - 25 Feb 1924:	Unassigned
25 Feb 1924:	Transferred to the reserve

Rear-Admiral **Kazue SHIGENAGA** (2 Jan 1898 - 1 Mar 1964)

25 Jan 1944 - 20 Dec 1944:	Captain, Battleship *"Haruna"*
15 Oct 1944:	Promoted to *Rear-Admiral*

20 Dec 1944 - 10 Jan 1945:	Attached to Kure Naval District
10 Jan 1945 - 15 Jan 1945:	Attached to Takao Guard District
15 Jan 1945 - Oct 1945:	Deputy Chief of Staff, Takao Guard District
10 Apr 1945 - 15 Jun 1945:	Deputy Chief of Staff, 10th Area Army
15 Jun 1945 - Oct 1945:	Deputy Chief of Staff, 1st Air Fleet

Vice-Admiral **Nobujiro SHIGEOKA** (10 May 1879 - 16 Jan 1971)

1 Dec 1925 - 1 Dec 1927:	Commandant, Submarine School
1 Dec 1926:	Promoted to *Rear-Admiral*
1 Dec 1927 - 30 Nov 1929:	Commander, 2nd Submarine Flotilla
30 Nov 1929 - 10 Jun 1930:	Attached to Naval General Staff
10 Jun 1930 - 1 Dec 1930:	Chief of Bureau 5, Naval Shipbuilding Command
1 Dec 1930 - 1 Dec 1931:	Commandant, Submarine School
1 Dec 1931:	Promoted to *Vice-Admiral*
1 Dec 1931 - 15 Dec 1931:	Attached to Naval General Staff
21 Dec 1931:	Transferred to the reserve

Rear-Admiral (Surgeon) **Saburo SHIINA** (7 Jan 1894 - 18 Dec 1976)

1 Apr 1945 - 30 Nov 1945:	Director, Kamo Naval Hospital
1 May 1945:	Promoted to *Rear-Admiral (Surgeon)*

Vice-Admiral **Kosuke SHIKAMA** (26 Oct 1876 - 12 Dec 1937)

21 Feb 1917 - 1 Dec 1923:	Aide-de-Camp to the Emperor
1 Dec 1921:	Promoted to *Rear-Admiral*
1 Dec 1923 - 5 Feb 1924:	Attached to Naval General Staff
5 Feb 1924 - 1 Dec 1925:	Commander, Ominato Guard District
1 Dec 1925:	Promoted to *Vice-Admiral*
1 Dec 1925 - 5 Dec 1925:	Attached to Naval General Staff
16 Dec 1925:	Transferred to the reserve

Rear-Admiral **Koji SHIKATA** (15 Oct 1899 - 10 May 1945)

5 Oct 1944 - 10 Jan 1945:	Chief of Work Bureau, SW Area Air Depot
10 Jan 1945 - 10 May 1945:	Attached to Administration Bureau, Naval Air Command
10 May 1945:	Posthumously promoted to *Rear-Admiral*

Vice-Admiral **Kiyohide SHIMA** (25 Feb 1890 - 7 Nov 1973)

15 Nov 1939:	Promoted to *Rear-Admiral*
15 Nov 1939 - 15 Oct 1940:	Chief of Staff, Maizuru Naval District
15 Oct 1940 - 15 Nov 1940:	Staff officer, 4th Fleet
15 Nov 1940 - 14 Jul 1942:	Commander, 19th Minelayer Flotilla
14 Jul 1942 - 10 Sep 1942:	Attached to Naval General Staff
10 Sep 1942 - 3 Oct 1942:	Staff officer, Southwestern Area Fleet

3 Oct 1942 - 16 Sep 1943:	Commander, 16th Escort Flotilla
1 May 1943:	Promoted to *Vice-Admiral*
16 Sep 1943 - 15 Feb 1944:	Commandant, Yokosuka Naval Communications School
15 Feb 1944 - 5 Feb 1945:	C-in-C, 5th Fleet
5 Feb 1945 - 5 May 1945:	Attached to Naval General Staff
5 May 1945 - 10 May 1945:	Attached to Takao Guard District
10 May 1945 - 15 Jun 1945:	C-in-C, 1st Air Fleet
10 May 1945 - Oct 1945:	Commander, Takao Guard District

Rear-Admiral **Takeshi SHIMA** (28 Jan 1867 - 23 Jun 1940)

13 Dec 1915 - 1 Dec 1916:	Captain, Battlecruiser *"Kirishima"*
1 Dec 1916:	Promoted to *Rear-Admiral*
1 Dec 1916 - 1 Dec 1917:	Unassigned
1 Dec 1917:	Transferred to the reserve

Vice-Admiral **Yukichi SHIMA** (8 May 1881 - 12 Oct 1963)

1 Dec 1924 - 1 Dec 1925:	Chief of Staff, 2nd Fleet
1 Dec 1925:	Promoted to *Rear-Admiral*
1 Dec 1925 - 1 Dec 1927:	Chief of Staff, Sasebo Naval District
1 Dec 1927 - 30 Nov 1929:	Commander, Ominato Guard District
30 Nov 1929:	Promoted to *Vice-Admiral*
30 Nov 1929 - 10 Jun 1930:	Attached to Naval General Staff
15 Jun 1930:	Transferred to the reserve

Vice-Admiral (Judge) **Kiyoshi SHIMADA** (12 Aug 1894 - 29 Apr 1977)

1 Apr 1941 - 20 Nov 1945:	Promoted to *Rear-Admiral (Judge)*
1 Nov 1942:	Judge, High Court Martial
1 Nov 1944 - 20 Nov 1945:	Chief of Navy Legal Bureau
1 Nov 1945:	Promoted to *Vice-Admiral (Judge)*

Admiral **Shigetaro SHIMADA** (24 Sep 1883 - 7 Jun 1976)

30 Nov 1929:	Promoted to *Rear-Admiral*
30 Nov 1929 - 1 Dec 1930:	Chief of Staff, 2nd Fleet
1 Dec 1930 - 1 Dec 1931:	Chief of Staff, Combined Fleet, Chief of Staff, 1st Fleet
1 Dec 1931 - 2 Feb 1932:	Commandant, Submarine School
2 Feb 1932 - 28 Jun 1932:	Chief of Staff, 3rd Fleet
28 Jun 1932 - 1 Dec 1932:	Chief of Bureau 3, Naval General Staff
15 Nov 1932 - 2 Dec 1935:	Chief of Bureau 1, Naval General Staff
15 Nov 1934:	Promoted to *Vice-Admiral*
2 Dec 1935 - 1 Dec 1937:	Deputy Chief of the Naval General Staff
1 Dec 1937 - 15 Nov 1938:	C-in-C, 2nd Fleet

15 Nov 1938 - 15 Apr 1940:	Admiral Commanding, Kure Naval District
15 Apr 1940 - 1 May 1940:	Attached to Naval General Staff
1 May 1940 - 1 Sep 1941:	C-in-C, China Area Fleet
15 Nov 1940:	Promoted to *Admiral*
1 Sep 1941 - 18 Oct 1941:	Admiral Commanding, Yokosuka Naval District, Member, Admirals Committee
18 Oct 1941 - 17 Jul 1944:	Minister of the Navy
21 Feb 1944 - 2 Aug 1944:	Chief of the Naval General Staff
2 Aug 1944 - 20 Jan 1945:	Navy Councillor
20 Jan 1945:	Transferred to the reserve

Rear-Admiral **Tojiro SHIMADA** (20 Jun 1893 - 5 Oct 1966)

15 Apr 1943 - 4 Mar 1944:	Commander, 102nd Naval Facility
1 May 1943:	Promoted to *Rear-Admiral*
4 Mar 1944 - 15 Nov 1945:	Chief of Supply & Transport Bureaus, Kure Naval District

Rear-Admiral **Hisagoro SHIMAMOTO** (1 Apr 1895 - 15 Sep 1973)

22 Oct 1942 - 15 Nov 1943:	Chief of Staff, 6th (Submarine) Fleet
1 May 1943:	Promoted to *Rear-Admiral*
15 Nov 1943 - 23 Feb 1944:	Chief of Staff, Maritime Escort Fleet
23 Feb 1944 - 15 Jul 1944:	Deputy Chief of Staff, Maritime Escort Fleet
15 Jul 1944 - 27 Jul 1944:	Staff officer, 3rd Southern Expeditionary Fleet
27 Jul 1944 - 1 Nov 1944:	Chief of Staff, 3rd Southern Expeditionary Fleet
15 Aug 1944 - Oct 1945:	Deputy Chief of Staff, Southwestern Area Fleet
3 Jul 1945 - Oct 1945:	Deputy Chief of Staff, 14th Area Army

Rear-Admiral **Mantaro SHIMAMOTO** (20 Jan 1891 - 4 Jan 1974)

15 Nov 1939 - 8 Aug 1942:	Supervisor for Construction & Ordnance, Naval Shipbuilding Command
1 May 1942:	Promoted to *Rear-Admiral*
8 Aug 1942 - 5 Nov 1942:	Staff officer, Southwestern Area Fleet
5 Nov 1942 - 14 Nov 1942:	Attached to Naval General Staff
16 Nov 1942:	Transferred to the reserve

Fleet Admiral **Baron Hayao SHIMAMURA** (20 Sep 1858 - 8 Jan 1923)

27 Oct 1903 - 28 Dec 1903:	Chief of Staff, Readiness Fleet
28 Dec 1903 - 12 Jan 1905:	Chief of Staff, Combined Fleet, Chief of Staff, 1st Fleet
6 Jun 1904:	Promoted to *Rear-Admiral*
12 Jan 1905 - 12 Dec 1905:	C-in-C, 2nd Fleet
12 Dec 1905 - 20 Dec 1905:	C-in-C, 4th Fleet
20 Dec 1905 - 19 Nov 1906:	C-in-C, Training Fleet
19 Nov 1906 - 28 Aug 1908:	Commandant of the Naval Academy

28 Aug 1908:	Promoted to *Vice-Admiral*
28 Aug 1908 - 1 Dec 1909:	Commandant of the Naval College
1 Dec 1909 - 1 Dec 1911:	C-in-C, 2nd Fleet
1 Dec 1911 - 25 Mar 1914:	Admiral Commanding, Sasebo Naval District
25 Mar 1914 - 22 Apr 1914:	Chief of Naval Training Command, Member, Admirals Committee
22 Apr 1914 - 1 Dec 1920:	Chief of the Naval General Staff, Member, Admirals Committee
28 Aug 1915:	Promoted to *Admiral*
1 Dec 1920 - 8 Jan 1923:	Navy Councillor
8 Jan 1923:	Posthumously appointed *Fleet Admiral*

Vice-Admiral **Shosuke SHIMAMURA** (9 Jan 1885 - 30 Jul 1953)

15 Nov 1934:	Promoted to *Rear-Admiral*
15 Nov 1934 - 15 Nov 1935:	Commander, 5th Destroyer Flotilla
15 Nov 1935 - 1 Dec 1936:	Commander, 1st Submarine Flotilla
1 Dec 1936 - 22 Jan 1937:	Attached to Naval General Staff
22 Jan 1937 - 20 Oct 1937:	Commander, 10th Escort Flotilla
20 Oct 1937 - 1 Dec 1937:	Commander, 14th Escort Flotilla
1 Dec 1937 - 15 Nov 1938:	Commander, Ominato Guard District
15 Nov 1938:	Promoted to *Vice-Admiral*
15 Nov 1938 - 15 Dec 1939:	Attached to Naval General Staff
21 Dec 1939:	Transferred to the reserve

Rear-Admiral **Kanta SHIMANOUCHI** (11 Dec 1870 - 19 Sep 1940)

1 Dec 1919:	Promoted to *Rear-Admiral*
1 Dec 1919 - 1 Dec 1921:	Commander, 1st Destroyer Flotilla
1 Dec 1921 - 1 Aug 1922:	Member, Admirals Committee
1 Aug 1922 - 31 Mar 1923:	Unassigned
31 Mar 1923:	Transferred to the reserve

Rear-Admiral (Paymaster) **Renpei SHIMAZAKI** (24 Jan 1870 - 13 Nov 1937)

27 May 1914 - 1 Dec 1916:	Chief of Section 1, Accounting Bureau, Kure Naval District
1 Dec 1916 - 1 Dec 1917:	Unassigned
1 Dec 1917:	Promoted to *General (Paymaster)*
1 Dec 1917:	Transferred to the reserve
23 Sep 1919:	Redesignated *Rear-Admiral (Paymaster)*

Rear-Admiral **Shigekazu SHIMAZAKI** (9 Sep 1908 - 9 Jan 1945)

8 Jan 1945 - 9 Jan 1945:	Staff Officer, 3rd Air Fleet
9 Jan 1945:	Posthumously promoted 2 grades to *Rear-Admiral*

Rear-Admiral (Surgeon) **Tadashi SHIMAZAKI** (6 Feb 1894 - ?)
28 Nov 1944 - Oct 1945:	Director, 103rd Naval Hospital
1 May 1945:	Promoted to *Rear-Admiral (Surgeon)*

Vice-Admiral **Toshio SHIMAZAKI** (7 Jan 1896 - 21 Nov 1944)
17 Jul 1943 - 21 Nov 1944:	Captain, Battleship *"Kongo"*
15 Oct 1944:	Promoted to *Rear-Admiral*
21 Nov 1944:	Posthumously promoted to *Vice-Admiral*

Rear-Admiral **Yoshitada SHIMAZAKI** (5 May 1851 - 2 Feb 1905)
6 Jul 1901:	Promoted to *Rear-Admiral*
6 Jul 1901 - 7 Jul 1903:	Chief of Reserve Bureau, Sasebo Naval District
7 Jul 1903 - 2 Feb 1905:	Unassigned

Rear-Admiral (Paymaster) **Izuo SHIMAZU** (8 May 1893 - 22 Apr 1970)
10 Jun 1944 - Oct 1945:	Chief of 102nd Supply Bureau
1 May 1945:	Promoted to *Rear-Admiral (Paymaster)*

Rear-Admiral (Paymaster) **Soji SHIMAZU** (15 May 1895 - 15 Feb 1977)
1 Apr 1945 - 1 Oct 1945:	Chief Instructor, Naval Paymaster Academy
1 May 1945:	Promoted to *Rear-Admiral (Paymaster)*
1 Oct 1945 - 15 Oct 1945:	Attached to Department of the Navy

Rear-Admiral **Tadashige SHIMAZU** (20 Oct 1886 - 9 Apr 1968)
10 Dec 1928 - 10 Jul 1931:	Naval Attache, United Kingdom
10 Jul 1931 - 10 Dec 1935:	Attached to Naval General Staff
15 Nov 1935:	Promoted to *Rear-Admiral*
14 Dec 1935:	Transferred to the reserve

Vice-Admiral **Fumio SHIMIZU** (26 Mar 1894 - 22 Mar 1965)
14 Jul 1942 - 27 Aug 1943:	Chief of Bureau 1, Naval Shipbuilding Command
1 Nov 1942:	Promoted to *Rear-Admiral*
27 Aug 1943 - 1 Nov 1943:	Attached to Naval Shipbuilding Command
1 Nov 1943 - 20 Nov 1945:	Commander, Toyokawa Navy Yard
1 May 1944:	Promoted to *Vice-Admiral*

Rear-Admiral **Iwao SHIMIZU**   (23 Jan 1890 - 2 Mar 1942)
5 Sep 1941 - 2 Mar 1942:	Captain, Aircraft Transport *"Kamogawa-maru"*
2 Mar 1942:	Posthumously promoted to *Rear-Admiral*

Vice-Admiral **Mitsumi SHIMIZU** (16 Mar 1888 - 5 May 1971)
31 Oct 1935 - 16 Nov 1936:	Chief of Staff, Sasebo Naval District
15 Nov 1935:	Promoted to *Rear-Admiral*

16 Nov 1936 - 1 Dec 1936:	Attached to Naval General Staff
1 Dec 1936 - 15 Dec 1938:	Chief of Naval Personnel
15 Dec 1938 - 20 May 1939:	Commander, 7th Escort Flotilla
20 May 1939 - 15 Nov 1939:	Commander, 6th Escort Flotilla
15 Nov 1939:	Promoted to *Vice-Admiral*
15 Nov 1939 - 1 Jun 1940:	Attached to Naval General Staff
1 Jun 1940 - 20 Sep 1940:	C-in-C, Training Fleet
20 Sep 1940 - 30 Sep 1940:	Attached to Naval General Staff
30 Sep 1940 - 5 Jul 1941:	C-in-C, 3rd China Expeditionary Fleet
5 Jul 1941 - 21 Jul 1941:	Attached to Naval General Staff
21 Jul 1941 - 16 Mar 1942:	C-in-C, 6th (Submarine) Fleet
16 Mar 1942 - 14 Jul 1942:	Attached to Naval General Staff
14 Jul 1942 - 20 Oct 1943:	C-in-C, 1st Fleet
20 Oct 1943 - 19 Feb 1944:	Attached to Naval General Staff
21 Feb 1944:	Transferred to the reserve

Rear-Admiral **Ryutaro SHIMIZU** (24 Nov 1885 - 17 Feb 1944)

29 Nov 1943 - 17 Feb 1944:	Commander of Minesweepers, Ammunition Ship *"Nichiro-maru"*
17 Feb 1944:	Posthumously promoted to *Rear-Admiral*

Rear-Admiral **Taro SHIMIZU** (18 Apr 1899 - 5 Mar 1944)

31 Dec 1943 - 5 Mar 1944:	Commander, 34th Submarine Division
5 Mar 1944:	Posthumously promoted to *Rear-Admiral*

Rear-Admiral (Apothecary) **Tatsuta SHIMIZU** (27 Apr 1892 - 23 Feb 1961)

15 Dec 1936 - 3 Jun 1942:	Instructor, Navy Medical School
15 Oct 1941:	Promoted to *Rear-Admiral (Apothecary)*
15 Oct 1941 - 3 Jun 1942:	Attached to Yokosuka Naval District
3 Jun 1942 - 15 Aug 1942:	Attached to Naval General Staff
25 Aug 1942:	Transferred to the reserve

Vice-Admiral **Tokuichi SHIMIZU** (13 Mar 1876 - ?)

1 Dec 1921:	Promoted to *Rear-Admiral*
1 Dec 1921 - 1 Dec 1923:	Attached to Naval Shipbuilding Command
1 Dec 1923 - 20 Dec 1924:	Chief Engineer Officer, Yokosuka Naval District
20 Dec 1924 - 15 Apr 1925:	Chief of Shipping Bureau, Yokosuka Naval District
15 Apr 1925 - 10 Dec 1928:	Commandant of the Navy Engineering Academy
1 Dec 1925:	Promoted to *Vice-Admiral*
10 Dec 1928 - 30 Nov 1929:	Chief of Supply Bureau, Department of the Navy
30 Nov 1929 - 10 Jun 1930:	Attached to Naval General Staff
20 Jun 1930:	Transferred to the reserve

Rear-Admiral **Toshio SHIMIZU** (27 Sep 1895 - 30 Nov 1942)
31 Aug 1942 - 30 Nov 1942:	Commander, 31st Destroyer Division
30 Nov 1942:	Posthumously promoted to *Rear-Admiral*

Vice-Admiral (Paymaster) **Usuke SHIMIZU** (27 Mar 1867 - 17 Nov 1924)
8 Aug 1914 - 13 Dec 1915:	Commandant of the Naval Paymaster Academy
1 Dec 1914:	Promoted to *General (Paymaster)*
13 Dec 1915 - 1 Dec 1916:	Paymaster-General, Yokosuka Naval District
1 Dec 1916 - 1 Dec 1919:	Paymaster-General, Kure Naval District
23 Sep 1919:	Redesignated *Rear-Admiral (Paymaster)*
1 Dec 1919 - 10 Dec 1919:	Attached to Department of the Navy
10 Dec 1919 - 1 Aug 1920:	Unassigned
1 Aug 1920:	Promoted to *Vice-Admiral (Paymaster)*
1 Aug 1920:	Transferred to the reserve

Rear-Admiral **Eitaro SHIMODAIRA** (19 Jan 1869 - 13 May 1933)
1 Nov 1917 - 1 Dec 1917:	Captain, Battleship *"Hyuga"*
1 Dec 1917:	Promoted to *Rear-Admiral*
1 Dec 1917 - 1 Dec 1918:	Unassigned
1 Dec 1918:	Transferred to the reserve

Vice-Admiral **Katsumi SHIMOMURA** (2 Jan 1891 - ?)
15 Nov 1939:	Promoted to *Rear-Admiral*
15 Nov 1939 - 10 Sep 1941:	Chief of Supply Bureau, Sasebo Naval District
10 Sep 1941 - 5 Nov 1941:	Attached to Naval General Staff
5 Nov 1941 - 15 Nov 1942:	Chief of Bureau 6, Naval Shipbuilding Command
15 Nov 1942 - 25 Nov 1942:	Staff officer, 2nd Southern Expeditionary Fleet
25 Nov 1942 - 26 Jan 1944:	Commander, 23rd Naval Base Force
1 May 1943:	Promoted to *Vice-Admiral*
26 Jan 1944 - 15 Mar 1944:	Attached to Naval General Staff
20 Mar 1944:	Transferred to the reserve

Vice-Admiral **Nobutaro SHIMOMURA** (19 Sep 1867 - 7 Feb 1947)
1 Dec 1917:	Promoted to *Rear-Admiral*
1 Dec 1917 - 10 Nov 1918:	Chief of Staff, Sasebo Naval District
10 Nov 1918 - 1 Dec 1921:	Chief of Bureau 1, Naval Training Command
1 Dec 1921:	Promoted to *Vice-Admiral*
1 Dec 1921 - 10 Apr 1922:	Member, Admirals Committee
10 Apr 1922 - 31 Mar 1923:	Unassigned
31 Mar 1923:	Transferred to the reserve

Vice-Admiral **Shosuke SHIMOMURA** (9 Jan 1885 - 30 Jul 1953)
15 Nov 1934:	Promoted to *Rear-Admiral*

15 Nov 1934 - 15 Nov 1935:	Commander, 5th Destroyer Flotilla
15 Nov 1935 - 1 Dec 1936:	Commander, 1st Submarine Flotilla
1 Dec 1936 - 22 Jan 1937:	Attached to Naval General Staff
22 Jan 1937 - 20 Oct 1937:	Commander, 10th Escort Flotilla
20 Oct 1937 - 1 Dec 1937:	Commander, 14th Escort Flotilla
1 Dec 1937 - 15 Nov 1938:	Commander, Ominato Guard District
15 Nov 1938:	Promoted to *Vice-Admiral*
15 Nov 1938 - 15 Dec 1939:	Attached to Naval General Staff
21 Dec 1939:	Transferred to the reserve

Rear-Admiral **Saneuji SHINJO** (16 Sep 1876 - 24 Jul 1937)
1 Aug 1923 - 1 Dec 1923:	Attached to Bureau 4, Naval Shipbuilding Command
1 Dec 1923:	Promoted to *Rear-Admiral*
1 Dec 1923 - 25 Feb 1924:	Unassigned
25 Feb 1924:	Transferred to the reserve

Rear-Admiral **Shuji SHINKI** (12 Nov 1899 - 8 Jul 1944)
1 Mar 1944 - 8 Jul 1944:	Staff officer, 5th Construction Bureau
8 Jul 1944:	Posthumously promoted to *Rear-Admiral*

Vice-Admiral **Katsukiyo SHINODA** (27 May 1895 - 25 Oct 1944)
6 May 1944 - 25 Oct 1944:	Captain, Battleship *"Yamashiro"*
15 Oct 1944:	Promoted to *Rear-Admiral*
25 Oct 1944:	Posthumously promoted to *Vice-Admiral*

Rear-Admiral **Kiyohiko SHINODA** (13 Dec 1893 - 8 Jan 1945)
10 Dec 1944:	Traffic Control Officer, 1st Escort Fleet
8 Jan 1945:	Posthumously promoted to *Rear-Admiral*

Rear-Admiral **Tarohachi SHINODA** (19 Mar 1895 - 29 Nov 1949)
1 Oct 1944 - Oct 1945:	Commander, Malaya Air Division
1 May 1945:	Promoted to *Rear-Admiral*

Rear-Admiral **Shinsuke SHINOZAKI** (20 Oct 1870 - 18 Nov 1951)
1 Dec 1918 - 10 Nov 1922:	Chief of Personnel, Yokosuka Naval District
1 Dec 1920:	Promoted to *Rear-Admiral*
10 Nov 1922 - 1 Apr 1923:	Attached to Yokosuka Naval District
1 Apr 1923 - 1 May 1923:	Unassigned
1 May 1923:	Transferred to the reserve

Rear-Admiral (Surgeon) **Choei SHIOMI** (14 Aug 1880 - ?)
1 Sep 1924 - 30 Nov 1929:	Instructor, Navy Medical School

30 Nov 1929:	Promoted to *Rear-Admiral (Surgeon)*
30 Nov 1929 - 15 Dec 1929:	Attached to Naval General Staff
25 Dec 1929:	Transferred to the reserve

Rear-Admiral **Wataro SHIOMI** (3 Mar 1885 - 25 Apr 1971)

5 Apr 1927 - 1 Dec 1927:	Supervisor for Construction & Ordnance, Naval Shipbuilding Command
1 Dec 1927:	Promoted to *Rear-Admiral*
1 Dec 1927 - 15 Dec 1927:	Attached to Naval Shipbuilding Command
25 Dec 1927:	Transferred to the reserve

Admiral **Koichi SHIOZAWA** (5 Mar 1883 - 17 Nov 1943)

1 Dec 1926 - 1 Jun 1929:	Naval Attache, United Kingdom
10 Dec 1928:	Promoted to *Rear-Admiral*
1 Jun 1929 - 15 Aug 1929:	Attached to Naval General Staff
15 Aug 1929 - 6 Sep 1929:	Staff officer, 2nd Fleet
6 Sep 1929 - 30 Nov 1929:	Chief of Staff, 2nd Fleet
30 Nov 1929 - 1 Dec 1930:	Chief of Staff, Combined Fleet, Chief of Staff, 1st Fleet
1 Dec 1930 - 6 Jun 1932:	C-in-C, 1st Expeditionary Fleet
6 Jun 1932 - 1 Oct 1932:	Attached to Naval General Staff
1 Oct 1932 - 1 Dec 1932:	Chief of Public Relations Bureau, Department of the Navy
1 Dec 1932 - 17 Jan 1934:	Commander, Chinkai Guard District
15 Nov 1933:	Promoted to *Vice-Admiral*
17 Jan 1934 - 2 Dec 1935:	Chief of Naval Air Command
2 Dec 1935 - 1 Dec 1936:	Admiral Commanding, Maizuru Naval District
1 Dec 1936 - 1 Dec 1937:	Admiral Commanding, Sasebo Naval District
1 Dec 1937 - 1 Feb 1938:	Attached to Naval General Staff
1 Feb 1938 - 15 Dec 1938:	C-in-C, 5th Fleet
15 Dec 1938 - 27 Jan 1939:	Attached to Naval General Staff
27 Jan 1939 - 30 Aug 1939:	Chief of Naval Shipbuilding Command, Member, Admirals Committee
30 Aug 1939 - 5 Sep 1940:	Navy Councillor
15 Nov 1939:	Promoted to *Admiral*
5 Sep 1940 - 10 Sep 1941:	Admiral Commanding, Yokosuka Naval District, Member, Admirals Committee
10 Sep 1941 - 17 Nov 1943:	Navy Councillor

Rear-Admiral **Masashichi SHIRAHAMA** (5 Dec 1898 - 8 Jun 1944)

25 Dec 1943 - 8 Jun 1944:	Commander, 27th Destroyer Division
8 Jun 1944:	Posthumously promoted to *Rear-Admiral*

Rear-Admiral **Yorikichi SHIRAI** (21 Jul 1872 - 11 May 1943)
25 Sep 1909 - 19 Jul 1916:	Chief of Shipbuilding Bureau, Sasebo Navy Yard
13 Dec 1915:	Promoted to *Rear-Admiral*
19 Jul 1916 - 19 Jul 1917:	Unassigned
19 Jul 1917:	Transferred to the reserve

Vice-Admiral **Kazutaka SHIRAISHI** (24 Oct 1892 - 16 Nov 1961)
30 Aug 1941 - 2 Jul 1943:	Chief of Staff, 2nd Fleet
15 Oct 1941:	Promoted to *Rear-Admiral*
2 Jul 1943 - 9 Aug 1943:	Attached to Naval General Staff
9 Aug 1943 - 6 Mar 1944:	Chief Instructor, Naval College
6 Mar 1944 - 25 Mar 1944:	Staff officer, 2nd Fleet
25 Mar 1944 - 21 Nov 1944:	Commander, 7th Cruiser Flotilla
15 Oct 1944:	Promoted to *Vice-Admiral*
21 Nov 1944 - 15 Dec 1944:	Attached to Naval General Staff
15 Dec 1944 - 2 May 1945:	Chief of Seamen Bureau, Sealift Agency, Department of Transport and Communication
2 May 1945 - 30 Sep 1945:	Attached to the Joint General Staff

Rear-Admiral **Naosuke SHIRAISHI** (23 Apr 1868 - 4 Nov 1945)
1 Dec 1916 - 1 Dec 1918:	Commander, Sasebo Harbor
1 Dec 1918:	Promoted to *Rear-Admiral*
1 Dec 1918 - 1 Aug 1919:	Unassigned
1 Aug 1919:	Transferred to the reserve

Rear-Admiral **Nobunari SHIRAISHI** (12 Oct 1880 - 9 Apr 1925)
18 Jul 1924 - 2 Mar 1925:	Attached to Naval General Staff
1 Dec 1924:	Promoted to *Rear-Admiral*
20 Mar 1925:	Transferred to the reserve

Vice-Admiral (Paymaster) **Kimitaro SHIRAKAMI** (14 Jan 1892 - 30 Sep 1956)
15 Nov 1940:	Promoted to *Rear-Admiral*
15 Nov 1940 - 15 Jan 1941:	Staff officer, China Area Fleet
15 Jan 1941 - 15 Oct 1941:	Chief of 1st Accounting Bureau
12 Apr 1941 - 30 May 1941:	Paymaster-General, China Area Fleet
15 Oct 1941 - 10 Jul 1943:	Chief of Supply Bureau, Yokosuka Naval District
10 Jul 1943 - 1 Oct 1943:	Attached to Yokosuka Naval District
1 Oct 1943 - 1 Apr 1945:	Chief of 1st Clothing & Food Depot
1 May 1944:	Promoted to *Vice-Admiral*
1 Apr 1945 - 16 Apr 1945:	Attached to Naval General Staff
20 Apr 1945:	Transferred to the reserve

Vice-Admiral **Kumazo SHIRANE** (2 Jan 1876 - 31 Aug 1939)
1 Dec 1921:	Promoted to *Rear-Admiral*
1 Dec 1921 - 1 Dec 1923:	Chief of Staff, 1st Fleet
1 Dec 1922 - 1 Dec 1923:	Chief of Staff, Combined Fleet
1 Dec 1923 - 10 Apr 1924:	Attached to Naval General Staff
10 Apr 1924 - 18 Sep 1925:	Chief of Naval Training Bureau
18 Sep 1925 - 1 Apr 1927:	Commandant of the Naval Academy
1 Dec 1925:	Promoted to *Vice-Admiral*
1 Apr 1927 - 15 Dec 1927:	Attached to Naval General Staff
22 Dec 1927:	Transferred to the reserve

Rear-Admiral **Teisuke SHIRANE** (10 Jan 1884 - 12 Oct 1953)
15 Nov 1932 - 15 Nov 1934:	Commander, Sasebo Defense Force
15 Nov 1933:	Promoted to *Rear-Admiral*
15 Nov 1934 - 10 Dec 1934:	Attached to Naval General Staff
15 Dec 1934:	Transferred to the reserve

Vice-Admiral **Kiyoshi SHIROYA** (13 Apr 1892 - 19 Nov 1972)
15 Nov 1939:	Promoted to *Rear-Admiral*
15 Nov 1939 - 15 Aug 1941:	Naval Representative, Beijing
15 Aug 1941 - 4 Oct 1941:	Attached to Naval General Staff
4 Oct 1941 - 15 Oct 1941:	Staff officer, China Area Fleet
15 Oct 1941 - 10 Feb 1943:	Naval Attache, China
10 Feb 1943 - 5 Mar 1943:	Attached to Naval General Staff
5 Mar 1943 - 15 Mar 1943:	Staff officer, 3rd Southern Expeditionary Fleet
15 Mar 1943 - 6 Oct 1944:	Commander, 32nd Naval Base Force
1 Nov 1943:	Promoted to *Vice-Admiral*
6 Oct 1944 - 15 Dec 1944:	Attached to Naval General Staff
20 Dec 1944:	Transferred to the reserve

Vice-Admiral (Paymaster) **Masaru SHISA** (6 Feb 1864 - 20 Mar 1928)
15 Aug 1908 - 1 Dec 1909:	Paymaster-General, Sasebo Naval District
10 Dec 1908:	Promoted to *General (Paymaster)*
1 Dec 1909 - 23 Mar 1911:	Unassigned
23 Mar 1911 - 1 Dec 1911:	Attached to Department of the Navy
1 Dec 1911 - 10 May 1912:	Unassigned
10 May 1912 - 25 May 1923:	Chief of Naval Accounting Bureau
29 May 1914:	Promoted to *General (Paymaster), Senior grade*
23 Sep 1919:	Redesignated *Vice-Admiral (Paymaster)*
25 May 1923 - 1 Jun 1923:	Attached to Naval General Staff
1 Jun 1923 - 1 Jul 1932:	Unassigned
1 Jul 1923:	Transferred to the reserve

Vice-Admiral **Yoshinobu SHISHIDO** (2 Jan 1887 - 7 Jan 1976)
15 Nov 1934 - 15 Dec 1936:	Commander, Kure Sailors Corps
1 Dec 1936:	Promoted to *Rear-Admiral*
15 Dec 1936 - 20 Dec 1937:	Attached to Naval General Staff
20 Dec 1937 - 25 Apr 1938:	Commander, 1st Combined Marine Force
25 Apr 1938 - 15 Nov 1939:	Commander, Shanghai Marine Force
15 Nov 1939 - 15 Nov 1940:	Attached to Kure Naval District
15 Nov 1940:	Promoted to *Vice-Admiral*
15 Nov 1940 - 16 Dec 1940:	Attached to Naval General Staff
16 Dec 1940 - 17 Jan 1941:	Unassigned
17 Jan 1941:	Transferred to the reserve

Rear-Admiral **Sadakichi SHITABO** (5 Jan 1889 - 17 Aug 1972)
15 Oct 1940 - 20 Apr 1941:	Commander, Kure Defense Flotilla
15 Nov 1940:	Promoted to *Rear-Admiral*
20 Apr 1941 - 15 May 1941:	Attached to Naval General Staff
15 May 1941 - 20 Mar 1942:	Chief of Bureau 2, Naval Hydrographic Command
15 May 1941 - 1 Dec 1943:	Chief of Bureau 3, Naval Hydrographic Command
15 Apr 1943 - 1 Dec 1943:	Chief of Weather Division, Department of the Navy
1 Dec 1943 - 15 Dec 1943:	Attached to Naval General Staff
15 Dec 1943 - 20 Dec 1943:	Unassigned
20 Dec 1943 - 20 Mar 1945:	Attached to Naval General Staff
20 Mar 1945 - 20 Oct 1945:	Commander, Osaka Sailors Corps
1 May 1945 - 20 May 1945:	Commander, Tanabe Sailors Corps

Rear-Admiral **Teiichiro SHITSUDA** (Oct 1868 - 9 Dec 1943)
20 May 1916 - 1 Dec 1916:	Captain, Battleship *"Yamashiro"*
1 Dec 1916:	Promoted to *Rear-Admiral*
1 Dec 1916 - 1 Dec 1917:	Unassigned
1 Dec 1917:	Transferred to the reserve

Rear-Admiral **Takeshi SHIWA** (1 Jan 1902 - 21 Sep 1944)
1 Sep 1944 - 21 Sep 1944:	Captain, Minelayer *"Katsuriki"*
21 Sep 1944:	Posthumously promoted to *Rear-Admiral*

Rear-Admiral **Kiijiro SHOJI** (19 Dec 1894 - 2 Nov 1943)
20 May 1943 - 2 Nov 1943:	Captain, Light Cruiser *"Sendai"*
2 Nov 1943:	Posthumously promoted to *Rear-Admiral*

Rear-Admiral **Yoshikichi SHOJI** (1 Mar 1891 - 12 Jun 1944)
1 Jun 1943 - 12 Jun 1944:	Traffic Control Officer, 2nd Maritime Escort Force
12 Jun 1944:	Posthumously promoted to *Rear-Admiral*

Rear-Admiral **Yoshimoto SHOJI** (27 Dec 1863 - 12 Mar 1928)
1 Dec 1910:	Promoted to *Rear-Admiral*
1 Dec 1910 - 21 Sep 1911:	Commandant, Naval Gunnery School
21 Sep 1911 - 6 Dec 1911:	Unassigned
6 Dec 1911 - 1 Dec 1912:	Chief of Staff, Ryojun Naval District
1 Dec 1912 - 31 May 1913:	Unassigned
31 May 1913:	Transferred to the reserve

Vice-Admiral **Daisuke SOEJIMA** (14 Feb 1890 - 19 Apr 1974)
1 Dec 1936 - 1 Feb 1938:	Commander, Yokosuka Sailors Corps
1 Dec 1937:	Promoted to *Rear-Admiral*
1 Feb 1938 - 15 Nov 1939:	Chief of Staff, Yokosuka Naval District
15 Nov 1939 - 1 Sep 1941:	Commander, Kanton Area Base Force
1 Sep 1941 - 20 Nov 1941:	Attached to Naval General Staff
15 Oct 1941:	Promoted to *Vice-Admiral*
20 Nov 1941 - 21 Jun 1943:	Chief of Naval Hydrographic Command
21 Jun 1943 - 25 Apr 1945:	C-in-C, 2nd China Expeditionary Fleet
25 Apr 1945 - 6 Sep 1945:	Attached to Naval General Staff

Vice-Admiral **Rokuro SOMA** (21 Dec 1889 - 30 Apr 1974)
15 Nov 1938:	Promoted to *Rear-Admiral*
15 Nov 1938 - 15 Nov 1940:	Chief of Ordnance Bureau, Sasebo Navy Yard
15 Nov 1940 - 21 Apr 1941:	Chief of Gunnery Bureau, Kure Navy Yard
21 Apr 1941 - 1 Nov 1943:	Commander, Toyokawa Navy Yard
1 Nov 1942:	Promoted to *Vice-Admiral*
1 Nov 1943 - 1 Nov 1945:	Commander, Sasebo Navy Yard

Rear-Admiral **Shinshiro SOMA** (21 Feb 1892 - 23 Mar 1962)
15 Mar 1945 - 8 May 1945:	Attached to Kure Naval District
1 May 1945:	Promoted to *Rear-Admiral*
8 May 1945 - 1 Jun 1945:	Staff officer, 51st Escort Flotilla
1 Jun 1945 - 15 Jul 1945:	Chief of Transport Bureau, Maizuru Naval District
15 Jul 1945 - Oct 1945:	Commander, Mako Area Base Force

Rear-Admiral **Akira SONE** (22 Jan 1896 - 8 Oct 1971)
25 Sep 1943 - 11 Sep 1944:	Chief of Staff, Maizuru Naval District
1 May 1944:	Promoted to *Rear-Admiral*
11 Sep 1944 - 25 Sep 1944:	Chief of Supply Bureau, Maizuru Naval District
25 Sep 1944 - 1 Apr 1945:	Commander, 1st Transport Flotilla
1 Apr 1945 - 20 Sep 1945:	Chief of Weather Division, Department of the Navy
20 Sep 1945 - 29 Nov 1945:	Chief of Bureau 2, Naval Hydrographic Command

Rear-Admiral **Minoru SONODA** (4 Apr 1884 - 8 Oct 1937)
1 Dec 1932:	Promoted to *Rear-Admiral*
1 Dec 1932 - 15 Nov 1933:	Chief Instructor, Naval College
15 Nov 1933 - 20 Sep 1934:	Chief of Staff, Yokosuka Naval District
20 Sep 1934 - 15 Mar 1935:	Chief of Naval Training Bureau
15 Mar 1935 - 15 Feb 1936:	Attached to Naval General Staff
15 Feb 1936 - 1 Jul 1936:	Unassigned
1 Jul 1936:	Transferred to the reserve

Vice-Admiral **Shigeru SONODA** (7 Jul 1887 - 7 Feb 1940)
1 Dec 1936:	Promoted to *Rear-Admiral*
1 Dec 1936 - 1 Dec 1937:	Commander, Yokosuka Defense Flotilla
1 Dec 1937 - 15 Dec 1938:	Commander, 1st Auxiliary Base Force
15 Dec 1938 - 1 Nov 1939:	Attached to Naval General Staff
1 Nov 1939 - 7 Feb 1940:	Attached to Yokosuka Naval District
7 Feb 1940:	Posthumously promoted to *Vice-Admiral*

Rear-Admiral **Hitoshi SONOYAMA** (12 Oct 1901 - 6 Feb 1944)
1 Nov 1942 - 6 Feb 1944:	Commander, 752nd Air Division
6 Feb 1944:	Posthumously promoted to *Rear-Admiral*

Rear-Admiral **Tanetsugu SOSA** (7 Jan 1878 - 14 Apr 1960)
20 Nov 1922 - 1 Dec 1923:	Commander, Sasebo Sailors Corps
1 Dec 1922:	Promoted to *Rear-Admiral*
1 Dec 1923 - 20 Dec 1923:	Attached to Naval General Staff
20 Dec 1923 - 25 Feb 1924:	Unassigned
25 Feb 1924:	Transferred to the reserve

Rear-Admiral **Minoru SUDA** (10 Oct 1885 - 3 Nov 1964)
15 Nov 1935:	Promoted to *Rear-Admiral*
15 Nov 1935 - 1 Dec 1936:	Chief of Mining Bureau, Navy Fuel Yard
1 Dec 1936 - 15 Nov 1938:	Chief of Supply Bueau, Sasebo Naval District
15 Nov 1938 - 15 Dec 1938:	Attached to Naval General Staff
21 Dec 1938:	Transferred to the reserve

Vice-Admiral (Surgeon) **Iwao SUDO** (1 Oct 1891 - 28 Dec 1944)
20 Jan 1943 - 10 Mar 1944:	Director, Nobi Naval Hospital
1 May 1943:	Promoted to *Rear-Admiral (Surgeon)*
10 Mar 1944 - 25 Mar 1944:	Staff officer, 1st Southern Expeditionary Fleet
25 Mar 1944 - 16 Dec 1944:	Director, 101st Naval Hospital
16 Dec 1944 - 28 Dec 1944:	Attached to Yokosuka Naval District
28 Dec 1944:	Posthumously promoted to *Vice-Admiral (Surgeon)*

Rear-Admiral **Yoshiki SUEHIRO** (6 Feb 1894 - 28 Sep 1964)
1 Jun 1943 - 5 Aug 1945:	Chief of Radio Bureau, Numazu Navy Yard
1 May 1944:	Promoted to *Rear-Admiral*
5 Aug 1945 - 10 Aug 1945:	Attached to Naval Shipbuilding Command
10 Aug 1945 - 15 Sep 1945:	Chief of Administration Section, Tohoku Area Supervisory Office, Department of Military Supply

Rear-Admiral **Kojiro SUETSUGU** (17 Oct 1873 - 6 Oct 1940)
1 Dec 1917 - 20 Nov 1919:	Chief Engineer Officer, Ryojun Guard District
20 Nov 1919 - 1 Dec 1919:	Attached to Sasebo Naval District
1 Dec 1919:	Promoted to *Rear-Admiral*
1 Dec 1919 - 1 Aug 1920:	Unassigned
1 Aug 1920:	Transferred to the reserve

Admiral **Nobumasa SUETSUGU** (30 Jun 1880 - 29 Dec 1944)
1 Dec 1922 - 1 Dec 1923:	Chief of Bureau 1, Naval General Staff
1 Dec 1923:	Promoted to *Rear-Admiral*
1 Dec 1923 - 1 Dec 1925:	Commander, 1st Submarine Flotilla
1 Dec 1925 - 26 Jul 1926:	Instructor, Naval College
26 Jul 1926 - 10 Dec 1928:	Chief of Naval Training Bureau
1 Dec 1927:	Promoted to *Vice-Admiral*
10 Dec 1928 - 10 Jun 1930:	Deputy Chief of the Naval General Staff
10 Jun 1930 - 1 Dec 1930:	Attached to Naval General Staff
1 Dec 1930 - 1 Dec 1931:	Admiral Commanding, Maizuru Naval District
1 Dec 1931 - 15 Nov 1933:	C-in-C, 2nd Fleet
15 Nov 1933 - 15 Nov 1934:	C-in-C, Combined Fleet, C-in-C, 1st Fleet
1 Mar 1934:	Promoted to *Admiral*
15 Nov 1934 - 2 Dec 1935:	Admiral Commanding, Yokosuka Naval District, Member, Admirals Committee
2 Dec 1935 - 15 Oct 1937:	Navy Councillor
15 Oct 1937:	Transferred to the reserve

Rear-Admiral **Kyosuke SUETSUNE** (27 Jan 1881 - 1 Jan 1960)
3 Jun 1925 - 1 Dec 1926:	Chief of Scientific Research Bureau, Technical Research Department
1 Dec 1926:	Promoted to *Rear-Admiral*
1 Dec 1926 - 20 Mar 1927:	Attached to Naval General Staff
20 Mar 1927 - 10 Apr 1927:	Unassigned
10 Apr 1927:	Transferred to the reserve

Vice-Admiral **Hikojiro SUGA** (4 Mar 1889 - 5 Feb 1941)
22 Nov 1937 - 5 Feb 1941:	Staff officer, China Area Fleet

15 Nov 1939: Promoted to *Rear-Admiral*
5 Feb 1941: Posthumously promoted to *Vice-Admiral*

Rear-Admiral (Surgeon) **Minoru SUGA** (28 Oct 1887 - 7 Oct 1949)
1 Dec 1931 - 15 Nov 1934: Chief of Bureau 1, Kure Naval Hospital
15 Nov 1934: Promoted to *Rear-Admiral (Surgeon)*
15 Nov 1934 - 10 Dec 1934: Attached to Naval General Staff
15 Dec 1934: Transferred to the reserve

Rear-Admiral **Shujiro SUGANUMA** (15 Dec 1876 - 26 Dec 1963)
12 Nov 1920 - 1 Jun 1923: Chief of Personnel Bureau, Sasebo Naval District
1 Dec 1922: Promoted to *Rear-Admiral*
1 Jun 1923 - 15 Jun 1923: Attached to Naval General Staff
1 Jul 1923: Transferred to the reserve

Vice-Admiral (Surgeon) **Naoki SUGATA** (1 Apr 1893 - 28 Dec 1975)
15 Nov 1940: Promoted to *Rear-Admiral (Surgeon)*
15 Nov 1940 - 15 Oct 1941: Attached to Kure Naval District
15 Oct 1941 - 1 Nov 1944: Chief of Medical Bureau, Kure Navy Yard
1 May 1944: Promoted to *Vice-Admiral (Surgeon)*
1 Nov 1944 - 15 Oct 1945: Director, Maizuru Naval Hospital,
Chief Surgeon, Maizuru Naval District

Vice-Admiral (Surgeon) **Sahei SUGAWARA** (17 Mar 1885 - 17 Jul 1969)
15 Nov 1933 - 15 Nov 1934: Director, Minato Naval Hospital
15 Nov 1934: Promoted to *Rear-Admiral (Surgeon)*
15 Nov 1934 - 15 Nov 1935: Director, Sasebo Naval Hospital,
Chief Surgeon, Sasebo Naval District
15 Nov 1935 - 15 Nov 1938: Director, Kure Naval Hospital,
Chief Surgeon, Kure Naval District
15 Nov 1938: Promoted to *Vice-Admiral (Surgeon)*
15 Nov 1938 - 15 Dec 1938: Attached to Naval General Staff
21 Dec 1938: Transferred to the reserve

Vice-Admiral **Masato SUGI** (13 Aug 1880 - 19 Nov 1951)
1 Dec 1925: Promoted to *Rear-Admiral*
1 Dec 1925 - 5 Apr 1927: Chief of Bureau 5, Naval Shipbuilding Command
5 Apr 1927 - 10 Dec 1928: Chief of Bureau 4, Naval Shipbuilding Command
10 Dec 1928 - 1 Dec 1931: Commander, Kure Navy Yard
30 Nov 1929: Promoted to *Vice-Admiral*
1 Dec 1931 - 1 Jun 1932: Chief of Supply Bureau
1 Jun 1932 - 10 May 1934: Chief of Naval Shipbuilding Command
10 May 1934 - 25 Mar 1935: Attached to Naval General Staff
30 Mar 1935: Transferred to the reserve

Rear-Admiral **Toma SUGI** (2 Mar 1900 - 21 Nov 1944)
1 Sep 1943 - 21 Nov 1944:	Staff officer, 3rd Escort Flotilla
21 Nov 1944:	Posthumously promoted to *Rear-Admiral*

Rear-Admiral **Michio SUGIMOTO** (2 Jan 1891 - 18 Dec 1943)
25 May 1943 - 18 Dec 1943:	Commander of Minesweeping, Auxiliary Oiler *"Kenyo-maru"*
18 Dec 1943:	Posthumously promoted to *Rear-Admiral*

Rear-Admiral **Osamu SUGIMOTO** (17 Aug 1891 - 21 Jul 1978)
15 Nov 1939 - 10 Dec 1941:	Chief of Aircraft Bureau, Air Technical Arsenal
15 Oct 1941:	Promoted to *Rear-Admiral*
10 Dec 1941 - 15 Dec 1941:	Attached to Naval General Staff
22 Dec 1941:	Transferred to the reserve

Vice-Admiral (Surgeon) **Toyomatsu SUGIMOTO** (30 Oct 1892 - 27 Aug 1970)
15 Oct 1941 - 1 Nov 1942:	Chief Surgeon, China Area Fleet
1 Nov 1942:	Promoted to *Rear-Admiral (Surgeon)*
1 Nov 1942 - 25 Oct 1943:	Director, Ureshino Naval Hospital
25 Oct 1943 - 1 Nov 1944:	Director, Beppu Naval Hospital
1 Nov 1944 - 1 Nov 1945:	Chief of Medical Bureau, Kure Naval Yard
1 May 1945:	Promoted to *Vice-Admiral (Surgeon)*

Vice-Admiral **Ushie SUGIMOTO** (12 May 1894 - 12 Jun 1945)
1 Feb 1944 - 15 Jun 1944:	Commander, 62nd Air Flotilla
1 May 1944:	Promoted to *Rear-Admiral*
15 Jun 1944 - 27 Oct 1944:	Chief of Staff, 2nd Air Fleet
27 Oct 1944 - 12 Jun 1945:	Commander, 26th Air Flotilla
12 Jun 1945:	Posthumously promoted to *Vice-Admiral*

Rear-Admiral **Yutaka SUGIMOTO** (13 Apr 1897 - 29 Jul 1944)
15 Mar 1944 - 29 Jul 1944:	Commander, 54th Guard Force
29 Jul 1944:	Posthumously promoted to *Rear-Admiral*

Vice-Admiral **Teijiro SUGISAKA** (15 Feb 1884 - 22 Jun 1950)
6 Jun 1932 - 15 Nov 1933:	Commander, Shanghai Marine Force
1 Dec 1932:	Promoted to *Rear-Admiral*
15 Nov 1933 - 2 Dec 1935:	Commander, 11th Escort Flotilla
2 Dec 1935 - 16 Mar 1936:	Attached to Naval General Staff
16 Mar 1936 - 1 Dec 1936:	Commander, Ominato Guard District
1 Dec 1936:	Promoted to *Vice-Admiral*
1 Dec 1936 - 15 Mar 1937:	Attached to Naval General Staff
25 Mar 1937:	Transferred to the reserve

Vice-Admiral **Kaju SUGIURA** (5 May 1896 - 16 May 1945)
1 Dec 1943 - 16 May 1945:	Captain, Heavy Cruiser *"Haguro"*
1 May 1945:	Promoted to *Rear-Admiral*
16 May 1945:	Posthumously promoted to *Vice-Admiral*

Rear-Admiral **Keizaburo SUGIURA** (15 Apr 1899 - 19 Aug 1944)
24 Apr 1944 - 19 Aug 1944:	Captain, Auxiliary Oiler *"Hayasui"*
19 Aug 1944:	Posthumously promoted to *Rear-Admiral*

Rear-Admiral **Masao SUGIURA** (30 Sep 1881 - ?)
1 Nov 1926 - 20 Aug 1927:	Captain, Battleship *"Fuso"*
20 Aug 1927 - 15 Dec 1927:	Attached to Yokosuka Naval District
1 Dec 1927:	Promoted to *Rear-Admiral*
25 Dec 1927:	Transferred to the reserve

Rear-Admiral **Kinsaku SUGIYAMA** (10 Oct 1892 - ?)
1 Apr 1939 - 15 Nov 1940:	Chief of Air Engine Bureau, Air Technical Arsenal
15 Nov 1939:	Promoted to *Rear-Admiral*
15 Nov 1940 - 16 Dec 1940:	Attached to Naval Air Command
21 Dec 1940:	Transferred to the reserve

Vice-Admiral **Rokuzo SUGIYAMA** (4 Jan 1890 - 6 Jun 1947)
16 Nov 1936 - 25 Apr 1938:	Chief of Staff, 3rd Fleet
1 Dec 1936:	Promoted to *Rear-Admiral*
20 Oct 1937 - 25 Apr 1938:	Chief of Staff, China Area Fleet
25 Apr 1938 - 15 Dec 1938:	Attached to Naval General Staff
15 Dec 1938 - 15 Nov 1939:	Commander, 11th Escort Flotilla
15 Nov 1939 - 1 Feb 1940:	Attached to Yokosuka Naval District
1 Feb 1940 - 15 Mar 1940:	Commander, Yokosuka Guard Flotilla
15 Mar 1940 - 1 May 1940:	Attached to Yokosuka Naval District
1 May 1940 - 15 Nov 1940:	Commander, 18th Escort Flotilla
15 Nov 1940:	Promoted to *Vice-Admiral*
15 Nov 1940 - 1 Apr 1941:	Attached to Yokosuka Naval District
1 Apr 1941 - 5 Jul 1941:	Commandant, Mine School
5 Jul 1941 - 26 Dec 1941:	C-in-C, 3rd China Expeditionary Fleet
26 Dec 1941 - 3 Jan 1942:	Attached to Naval General Staff
3 Jan 1942 - 1 Dec 1942:	C-in-C, 3rd Southern Expeditionary Fleet
1 Dec 1942 - 15 Apr 1943:	Attached to Naval General Staff
15 Apr 1943 - 4 Nov 1944:	Chief of Naval Shipbuilding Command, Member, Admirals Committee
5 Aug 1944 - 4 Nov 1944:	Chief of Naval Radar Command
4 Nov 1944 - 15 Nov 1945:	Admiral Commanding, Sasebo Naval District

Vice-Admiral **Toshisuke SUGIYAMA** (9 May 1886 - 14 Dec 1946)
15 Nov 1934 - 1 Dec 1936:	Commander, Yokosuka Air Division
15 Nov 1935:	Promoted to *Rear-Admiral*
1 Dec 1936 - 1 Oct 1937:	Chief of Technical Bureau, Naval Air Command
1 Oct 1937 - 17 Jan 1938:	Chief Supervisor for Construction & Ordnance, Naval Shipbuilding Command
17 Jan 1938 - 15 Nov 1939:	Chief Supervisor, Nagoya
15 Nov 1939:	Promoted to *Vice-Admiral*
15 Nov 1939 - 21 May 1940:	Director, Air Technical Arsenal
21 May 1940 - 16 Dec 1940:	Attached to Naval General Staff
21 Dec 1940:	Transferred to the reserve

Vice-Admiral **Tamazo SUKIGARA** (23 Sep 1889 - 18 Jan 1955)
1 Dec 1937:	Promoted to *Rear-Admiral*
1 Dec 1937 - 20 Jun 1938:	Commander, 3rd Submarine Flotilla
20 Jun 1938 - 15 Sep 1938:	Attached to Naval General Staff
15 Sep 1938 - 15 Nov 1939:	Commander, 2nd Auxiliary Base Force
15 Nov 1939 - 1 Dec 1939:	Attached to Maizuru Guard District
1 Dec 1939 - 1 May 1940:	Attached to Maizuru Naval District
1 May 1940 - 15 Nov 1940:	Commander, 5th Submarine Flotilla
15 Nov 1940 - 15 Apr 1941:	Attached to Naval General Staff
15 Apr 1941 - 1 May 1941:	Staff officer, 6th (Submarine) Fleet
1 May 1941 - 11 Aug 1941:	Commander, 1st Submarine Flotilla
11 Aug 1941 - 20 Sep 1941:	Attached to Naval General Staff
20 Sep 1941 - 1 Oct 1941:	Attached to Sasebo Naval District
1 Oct 1941 - 20 May 1942:	Commander, Rashin Auxiliary Naval Base Force
15 Oct 1941:	Promoted to *Vice-Admiral*
20 May 1942 - 1 Sep 1942:	Commander, Rashin Area Naval Base Force
1 Sep 1942 - 15 Dec 1942:	Attached to Naval General Staff
21 Dec 1942:	Transferred to the reserve
15 May 1944 - 20 Mar 1945:	Recalled; Chief of Shipping Protection Division, Joint General Staff
20 Mar 1945 - 1 Sep 1945:	Attached to Naval General Staff
1 Sep 1945:	Demobilized

Rear-Admiral **Sashichi SUMI** (24 Feb 1883 - 5 Sep 1981)
1 Dec 1931 - 15 Nov 1933:	Chief of Mining Bureau, Navy Fuel Yard
1 Dec 1932:	Promoted to *Rear-Admiral*
15 Nov 1933 - 11 Dec 1933:	Attached to Naval General Staff
15 Dec 1933:	Transferred to the reserve

Rear-Admiral **Toshio SUMIDA** (14 Mar 1879 - 17 Jan 1935)
1 Apr 1923 - 1 Aug 1925:	Instructor, Naval College

1 Aug 1925 - 1 Oct 1925:	Attached to Naval General Staff
1 Oct 1925 - 16 Dec 1925:	Unassigned
1 Dec 1925:	Promoted to *Rear-Admiral*
16 Dec 1925:	Transferred to the reserve

Rear-Admiral **Michio SUMIKAWA** (5 Aug 1896 - 18 Jun 1977)

15 Aug 1943 - 23 Dec 1943:	Executive Officer, Aircraft Carrier *"Taiho"*
1 Nov 1943:	Promoted to *Rear-Admiral*
23 Dec 1943 - 6 Jan 1944:	Staff officer, 4th Fleet
6 Jan 1944 - 30 Mar 1944:	Chief of Staff, 4th Fleet
30 Mar 1944 - Oct 1945	Commander, 22nd Air Flotilla
12 Aug 1944 - Oct 1945:	Chief of Staff, 4th Fleet

Vice-Admiral **Naoji SUMIKI** (9 Jun 1890 - ?)

1 Aug 1942 - 18 Aug 1943:	Chief of Construction Bureau, Yokosuka Naval District
1 Nov 1942:	Promoted to *Rear-Admiral*
18 Aug 1943 - 20 Sep 1944:	Chief of Facilities Bureau, Yokosuka Naval District
20 Sep 1944 - 1 Oct 1944:	Staff officer, 2nd Southern Expeditionary Fleet
1 Oct 1944 - 1 Nov 1945:	Chief of 102nd Facilities Bureau
1 Nov 1945:	Promoted to *Vice-Admiral*

Vice-Admiral **Tokutaro SUMIYAMA** (1 May 1886 - 30 Nov 1962)

15 Nov 1932 - 15 Nov 1934:	Chief of Staff, Kure Naval District
1 Dec 1932:	Promoted to *Rear-Admiral*
15 Nov 1934 - 15 Nov 1935:	Commander, 8th Escort Flotilla
15 Nov 1935 - 2 Dec 1935:	Attached to Naval General Staff
2 Dec 1935 - 1 Dec 1937:	Chief of Naval Training Bureau
1 Dec 1936:	Promoted to *Vice-Admiral*
1 Dec 1937 - 30 Aug 1939:	Commandant of the Naval Academy
30 Aug 1939 - 6 Sep 1940:	Deputy Minister of the Navy, Member, Admirals Committee
6 Sep 1940 - 15 Oct 1940:	Attached to Naval General Staff
15 Oct 1940 - 20 Nov 1941:	Admiral Commanding, Sasebo Naval District
20 Nov 1941 - 14 Mar 1942:	Navy Councillor
20 Mar 1942:	Transferred to the reserve

Rear-Admiral (Surgeon) **Masato SUNABORI** (25 Aug 1876 - 20 Mar 1955)

11 Jun 1923 - 1 Dec 1924:	Chief Surgeon, Naval Academy
1 Dec 1924:	Promoted to *Rear-Admiral*
1 Dec 1924 - 2 Mar 1925:	Attached to Naval General Staff
20 Mar 1925:	Transferred to the reserve

Vice-Admiral **Kaneo SUNAGAWA** (1887 - 5 Mar 1948)
15 Nov 1935:	Promoted to *Rear-Admiral*
15 Nov 1935 - 1 Dec 1937:	Chief of Bureau 2, Naval Shipbuilding Command
1 Dec 1937 - 15 Nov 1939:	Commander, Sasebo Navy Yard
15 Nov 1939:	Promoted to *Vice-Admiral*
15 Nov 1939 - 20 Nov 1941:	Commander, Kure Navy Yard
20 Nov 1941 - 15 Dec 1942:	Commander, Kainan Guard District
15 Dec 1942 - 15 Mar 1943:	Attached to Naval General Staff
20 Mar 1943:	Transferred to the reserve

Rear-Admiral **Koguma SUWA** (11 Aug 1873 - 15 Jun 1940)
6 Apr 1921 - 1 Dec 1923:	Supervisor of Construction & Ordnance, Naval Shipbuilding Command
1 Dec 1923:	Promoted to *Rear-Admiral*
1 Dec 1923 - 10 Dec 1923:	Attached to Naval Shipbuilding Command
10 Dec 1923 - 25 Feb 1924:	Unassigned
25 Feb 1924:	Transferred to the reserve

Rear-Admiral **Chozo SUZUKI** (25 Apr 1890 - 13 Jun 1952)
15 Nov 1939 - 10 Dec 1942:	Chief of Gunnery Research Bureau, Kure Navy Yard
15 Oct 1941:	Promoted to *Rear-Admiral*
10 Dec 1942 - 24 Jan 1944:	Staff officer, 2nd Southern Expeditionary Fleet
24 Jan 1944 - 15 Mar 1944:	Commander, 25th Naval Base Force
15 Mar 1944 - 20 Mar 1944:	Staff officer, China Area Fleet
20 Mar 1944 - 18 Aug 1944:	Commander, Shanghai Special Naval Landing Force
18 Aug 1944 - 10 Dec 1944:	Attached to Kure Naval District
10 Dec 1944 - 15 Dec 1944:	Attached to Naval General Staff
20 Dec 1944:	Transferred to the reserve

Vice-Admiral **Giichi SUZUKI** (13 May 1882 - 6 Feb 1982)
18 Jun 1930 - 1 Dec 1931:	Chief of Staff, Kure Naval District
1 Dec 1930:	Promoted to *Rear-Admiral*
1 Dec 1931 - 15 Nov 1932:	Commander, Sasebo Defense Force
15 Nov 1932 - 20 May 1933:	Commander, 3rd Escort Flotilla
20 May 1933 - 15 Nov 1933:	Commander, 7th Escort Flotilla
15 Nov 1933 - 11 Dec 1933:	Attached to Sasebo Naval District
11 Dec 1933 - 15 Nov 1934:	Commander, Sasebo Guard Flotilla
15 Nov 1934:	Promoted to *Vice-Admiral*
15 Nov 1934 - 25 Mar 1935:	Attached to Naval General Staff
30 Mar 1935:	Transferred to the reserve

Rear-Admiral (Paymaster) **Hisashi SUZUKI** (2 Sep 1894 - 7 Mar 1975)
10 Sep 1943 - 1 Apr 1945:	Chief of 101st Accounting Bureau
1 May 1944:	Promoted to *Rear-Admiral (Paymaster)*
6 May 1944 - 13 Apr 1945:	Paymaster-General, 1st Southern Expeditionary Fleet
8 Jan 1945 - 13 Apr 1945:	Paymaster-General, 13th Air Fleet
5 Feb 1945 - 13 Apr 1945:	Paymaster-General, 10th Area Fleet
13 Apr 1945 - Oct 1945:	Chief of 101st Accounting Bureau

Vice-Admiral **Hisatake SUZUKI** (23 Apr 1889 - 17 Jan 1948)
1 Dec 1937 - 15 Nov 1938:	Chief Engineer Officer, Combined Fleet, Chief Engineer Officer, 1st Fleet
15 Nov 1938:	Promoted to *Rear-Admiral*
15 Nov 1938 - 10 Sep 1941:	Chief of Scientific Research Bureau, Technical Research Department
10 Sep 1941 - 20 Jun 1943:	Commandant, Naval Engineering School
5 Nov 1941 - 15 Dec 1941:	Commandant, Naval Construction School
1 Nov 1942:	Promoted to *Vice-Admiral*
20 Jun 1943 - 24 Jun 1943:	Attached to Naval General Staff
25 Jun 1943:	Transferred to the reserve

Vice-Admiral **Kakuji SUZUKI** (1 Jan 1887 - 7 Feb 1944)
15 Nov 1933 - 25 Oct 1935:	Chief of Shipbuilding Bureau, Sasebo Navy Yard
15 Nov 1934:	Promoted to *Rear-Admiral*
25 Oct 1935 - 1 Dec 1936:	Chief of Shipbuilding Research Bureau, Technical Research Department
1 Dec 1936 - 15 Nov 1938:	Chief of Shipbuilding Bureau, Yokosuka Navy Yard
15 Nov 1938:	Promoted to *Vice-Admiral*
15 Nov 1938 - 15 Dec 1938:	Attached to Naval Shipbuilding Command
21 Dec 1938:	Transferred to the reserve

Vice-Admiral (Surgeon) **Kannosuke SUZUKI** (6 Feb 1875 - 22 Apr 1925)
1 Dec 1921:	Promoted to *Rear-Admiral (Surgeon)*
1 Dec 1921 - 1 Dec 1922:	Director, Maizuru Naval Hospital, Chief Surgeon, Maizuru Naval Hospital
1 Dec 1922 - 1 Dec 1924:	Commandant, Navy Medical School
1 Dec 1924 - 22 Apr 1925:	Director, Yokosuka Naval Hospital, Chief Surgeon, Yokosuka Naval Hospital
22 Apr 1925:	Posthumously promoted to *Vice-Admiral (Surgeon)*

Admiral **Baron Kantaro SUZUKI** (24 Dec 1867 - 17 Apr 1948)
24 May 1913:	Promoted to *Rear-Admiral*
24 May 1913 - 10 Aug 1913:	Commander, Maizuru Torpedo Group
10 Aug 1913 - 15 Nov 1913:	C-in-C, 2nd Fleet

15 Nov 1913 - 1 Dec 1913:	Commander, Maizuru Torpedo Group
1 Dec 1913 - 23 May 1914:	Chief of Naval Personnel
17 Apr 1914 - 1 Sep 1917:	Deputy Minister of the Navy, Member, Admirals Committee
21 Feb 1916 - 23 Jun 1916:	Chief, Bureau of Naval Affairs, Department of the Navy
1 Jun 1917:	Promoted to *Vice-Admiral*
1 Sep 1917 - 18 Oct 1918:	C-in-C, Training Fleet
18 Oct 1918 - 1 Dec 1918:	Member, Admirals Committee
1 Dec 1918 - 1 Dec 1920:	Commandant of the Naval Academy
1 Dec 1920 - 1 Dec 1921:	C-in-C, 2nd Fleet
1 Dec 1921 - 27 Jul 1922:	C-in-C, 3rd Fleet
27 Jul 1922 - 27 Jan 1924:	Admiral Commanding, Kure Naval District
3 Aug 1923:	Promoted to *Admiral*
27 Jan 1924 - 1 Dec 1924:	C-in-C, Combined Fleet, C-in-C, 1st Fleet
1 Dec 1924 - 15 Apr 1925:	Navy Councillor
15 Apr 1925 - 22 Jan 1929:	Chief of the Naval General Staff, Member, Admirals Committee
22 Jan 1929:	Transferred to the reserve

Rear-Admiral **Kasuke SUZUKI** (2 Dec 1885 - 10 May 1978)

15 Nov 1934 - 15 Nov 1935:	Chief of Shipping Bureau, Sasebo Naval District
15 Nov 1935:	Promoted to *Rear-Admiral*
15 Nov 1935 - 10 Dec 1935:	Attached to Naval General Staff
14 Dec 1935:	Transferred to the reserve

Vice-Admiral **Keiji SUZUKI** (13 Jan 1875 - 29 Sep 1930)

1 Dec 1918 - 1 Dec 1921:	Chief of Shipbuilding Bureau, Maizuru Navy Yard
1 Dec 1921:	Promoted to *Rear-Admiral*
1 Dec 1921 - 10 Jun 1922:	Attached to Naval Shipbuilding Command
10 Jun 1922 - 13 Aug 1923:	Chief of Shipbuilding Bureau, Yokosuka Navy Yard
13 Aug 1923 - 5 Apr 1927:	Chief of Bureau 4, Naval Shipbuilding Command
1 Dec 1925:	Promoted to *Vice-Admiral*
5 Apr 1927 - 16 May 1928:	Chief of Bureau 3, Naval Shipbuilding Command
16 May 1928 - 20 Dec 1928:	Attached to Naval Shipbuilding Command
25 Dec 1928:	Transferred to the reserve

Rear-Admiral **Kiyoshi SUZUKI** (28 May 1885 - 12 May 1942)

1 Aug 1941 - 12 May 1942:	Commander, 14th Minesweeper Division
12 May 1942:	Posthumously promoted to *Rear-Admiral*

Vice-Admiral (Surgeon) **Konosuke SUZUKI** (12 Jul 1854 - 20 Aug 1945)
29 Nov 1900:	Promoted to *General (Surgeon)*
29 Nov 1900 - 10 Nov 1903:	Director, Yokosuka Naval Hospital, Chief of Medical Bureau, Yokosuka Naval District
10 Nov 1903 - 7 Jan 1905:	Director, Kure Naval Hospital, Chief Surgeon, Kure Naval District
7 Jan 1905 - 13 Dec 1905:	Director, Ryojun Naval Hospital, Chief Surgeon, Ryojun Naval District
13 Dec 1905 - 14 Feb 1907:	Unassigned
14 Feb 1907:	Transferred to the reserve
23 Sep 1919:	Redesignated *Vice-Admiral (Surgeon)*

Rear-Admiral **Kozo SUZUKI** (26 Dec 1885 - 23 Sep 1944)
17 Mar 1943 - 23 Sep 1944:	Commander, 45th Minesweeper Division
23 Sep 1944:	Posthumously promoted to *Rear-Admiral*

Vice-Admiral (Surgeon) **Shigemichi SUZUKI** (26 Jul 1857 - 16 Mar 1926)
19 Jan 1904 - 14 Jun 1905:	Staff medical officer, 1st Fleet
12 Jan 1905:	Promoted to *General (Surgeon)*
14 Jun 1905 - 24 Jun 1905:	Staff medical officer, Combined Fleet
24 Jun 1905 - 20 Dec 1905:	Attached to Joint General Staff
20 Dec 1905 - 4 Jan 1906:	Attached to Department of the Navy
4 Jan 1906 - 20 Apr 1912:	Director, Yokosuka Naval Hospital, Chief Surgeon, Yokosuka Naval District
20 Apr 1912 - 31 Mar 1913:	Unassigned
31 Mar 1913:	Transferred to the reserve
23 Sep 1919:	Redesignated *Vice-Admiral (Surgeon)*

Rear-Admiral **Shigetomo SUZUKI** (1 Feb 1883 - 1 May 1930)
1 May 1929 - 13 Dec 1929:	Chief Engineer Officer, 2nd Fleet
13 Dec 1929 - 1 May 1930:	Attached to Kure Naval District
1 May 1930:	Posthumously promoted to *Rear-Admiral*

Rear-Admiral **Shinji SUZUKI** (1 Sep 1888 - 18 Dec 1968)
1 Dec 1936:	Promoted to *Rear-Admiral*
1 Dec 1936 - 1 Dec 1937:	Commander, Sasebo Defense Flotilla
1 Dec 1937 - 20 Apr 1938:	Commander, Sasebo Guard Flotilla
20 Apr 1938 - 25 Apr 1938:	Attached to Naval General Staff
25 Apr 1938 - 15 Dec 1938:	Commander, 1st Combined Marine Force
15 Dec 1938 - 15 Dec 1939:	Attached to Naval General Staff
21 Dec 1939:	Transferred to the reserve
6 Oct 1941 - 15 Oct 1941:	Recalled; Attached to Sasebo Naval District
15 Oct 1941 - 15 Jan 1942:	Commander, Sasebo Guard Flotilla

15 Jan 1942 - 2 Feb 1942:	Attached to Sasebo Naval District
2 Feb 1942 - 6 Jan 1943:	Commandant, Tateyama Naval Gunnery School
6 Jan 1943 - 20 Mar 1943:	Attached to Naval General Staff
20 Mar 1943:	Demobilized

Rear-Admiral **Tomizo SUZUKI** (2 Apr 1868 - 7 Jun 1945)
1 Apr 1913 - 29 May 1914:	Chief of Bureau 2, Naval Shipbuilding Command
29 May 1914 - 28 Aug 1914:	Unassigned
28 Aug 1914 - 1 Dec 1914:	Attached to Sasebo Naval District
1 Dec 1914 - 1 Dec 1915:	Unassigned
1 Dec 1915:	Promoted to *Rear-Admiral*
1 Dec 1915:	Transferred to the reserve

Vice-Admiral (Paymaster) **Toru SUZUKI** (30 Jan 1890 - 1 Jul 1960)
1 Dec 1937:	Promoted to *Rear-Admiral*
1 Dec 1937 - 15 Nov 1939:	Chief of Supply Bureau, Yokosuka Naval District
15 Nov 1939 - 15 Oct 1941:	Paymaster-General, Yokosuka Naval District
15 Oct 1941:	Promoted to *Vice-Admiral*
15 Oct 1941 - 15 Dec 1941:	Attached to Naval General Staff
22 Dec 1941:	Transferred to the reserve

Rear-Admiral **Tsukasa SUZUKI** (1 Jan 1895 - 11 Feb 1986)
13 Oct 1944 - 1 Dec 1944:	Attached to Administration Bureau, Naval Air Command
15 Oct 1944:	Promoted to *Rear-Admiral*
1 Dec 1944 - 1 Nov 1945:	Commander, 22nd Air Arsenal

Rear-Admiral (Paymaster) **Tsuneji SUZUKI** (10 Apr 1890 - 29 Jun 1982)
15 Nov 1940 - 15 Oct 1941:	Paymaster-General, Mako Guard District
15 Oct 1941:	Promoted to *Rear-Admiral*
15 Oct 1941 - 10 Oct 1943:	Chief of Accounting Bureau, Sasebo Navy Yard
10 Oct 1943 - 20 Oct 1943:	Attached to Naval General Staff
25 Oct 1943:	Transferred to the reserve

Rear-Admiral **Yasuatsu SUZUKI** (14 Sep 1899 - 11 Nov 1944)
31 May 1943 - 11 Nov 1944:	Captain, Destroyer *"Wakatsuki"*
11 Nov 1944:	Posthumously promoted to *Rear-Admiral*

Vice-Admiral **Yoshio SUZUKI** (15 Nov 1890 - 21 Nov 1944)
1 Nov 1939 - 30 Aug 1941:	Chief of Staff, 2nd Fleet
15 Nov 1939:	Promoted to *Rear-Admiral*
30 Aug 1941 - 6 Sep 1941:	Attached to Naval General Staff
6 Sep 1941 - 19 Jul 1943:	Chief of Bureau 2, Naval General Staff

1 May 1943:	Promoted to *Vice-Admiral*
19 Jul 1943 - 22 Jul 1943:	Staff officer, 3rd Fleet
22 Jul 1943 - 21 Nov 1944:	Commander, 3rd Battleship Flotilla

Vice-Admiral (Surgeon) **Yuzo SUZUKI** (15 Jul 1868 - 8 Aug 1925)

1 Dec 1916 - 1 Dec 1917:	Director, Kure Naval Hospital, Chief Surgeon, Kure Naval District
1 Jun 1917:	Promoted to *General (Surgeon)*
1 Dec 1917 - 1 Dec 1919:	Commandant, Navy Medical School
23 Sep 1919:	Redesignated *Rear-Admiral (Surgeon)*
1 Dec 1919 - 1 Dec 1923:	Chief of Naval Medical Service
1 Dec 1921:	Promoted to *Vice-Admiral (Surgeon)*
1 Dec 1923 - 10 Dec 1923:	Attached to Naval General Staff
10 Dec 1923 - 25 Feb 1924:	Unassigned
25 Feb 1924:	Transferred to the reserve

Rear-Admiral **Hiroyoshi TABATA** (1 Jan 1886 - 21 Jul 1968)

15 Nov 1933 - 15 Nov 1934:	Chief of Personnel Bureau, Sasebo Naval District
15 Nov 1934:	Promoted to *Rear-Admiral*
15 Nov 1934 - 1 Mar 1935:	Chief of Staff, Sasebo Naval District
1 Mar 1935 - 1 Dec 1936:	Commandant, Naval Gunnery School
1 Dec 1936 - 15 Mar 1937:	Attached to Naval General Staff
25 Mar 1937:	Transferred to the reserve

Rear-Admiral **Meijiro TACHI** (15 Apr 1882 - 27 Apr 1933)

20 Aug 1926 - 1 Dec 1927:	Commander, Kure Defense Force
1 Dec 1926:	Promoted to *Rear-Admiral*
1 Dec 1927 - 10 Dec 1928:	Commander, 2nd Destroyer Flotilla
10 Dec 1928 - 15 Mar 1929:	Attached to Naval General Staff
25 Mar 1929:	Transferred to the reserve

Rear-Admiral **Hajime TACHIBANA** (7 Dec 1882 - 31 Oct 1966)

1 Dec 1930 - 1 Dec 1932:	Commander, Kure Harbor
1 Dec 1932:	Promoted to *Rear-Admiral*
1 Dec 1932 - 10 Dec 1932:	Attached to Naval General Staff
15 Dec 1932:	Transferred to the reserve

Rear-Admiral **Saijiro TACHIBANA** (2 Dec 1885 - 11 Jun 1960)

15 Nov 1935 - 1 Dec 1936:	Chief Engineer Officer, Kure Naval District
1 Dec 1936:	Promoted to *Rear-Admiral*
1 Dec 1936 - 25 Oct 1937:	Chief of Shipbuilding Bureau, Kure Naval District
25 Oct 1937 - 15 Nov 1938:	Chief Supervisor for Construction & Ordnance, Naval Shipbuilding Command

15 Nov 1938 - 15 Dec 1938:	Attached to Naval General Staff
21 Dec 1938:	Transferred to the reserve

Rear-Admiral **Norimasa TADA** (18 Mar 1885 - 17 Dec 1965)
1 Apr 1932 - 15 Nov 1935:	Chief of Scientific Bureau, Air Arsenal
1 Dec 1932:	Promoted to *Rear-Admiral*
15 Nov 1935 - 10 Dec 1935:	Attached to Naval General Staff
14 Dec 1935:	Transferred to the reserve

Vice-Admiral **Rikizo TADA** (16 Aug 1893 - 29 Mar 1977)
21 May 1940 - 1 Nov 1942:	Chief of Technical Bureau Naval Air Command
15 Oct 1941:	Promoted to *Rear-Admiral*
1 Nov 1942 - 1 Nov 1943:	Chief of Bureau 3, Naval Air Command
1 Nov 1943 - 9 Feb 1944:	Chief of Bureau 4, Naval Air Command
1 Nov 1943 - 15 May 1945:	Chief of Bureau 2, Warplane Agency, Department of Military Supply
15 Oct 1944:	Promoted to *Vice-Admiral*
15 May 1945 - 1 Nov 1945:	Commander, 1st Technical Air Arsenal

Vice-Admiral **Takeo TADA** (7 Oct 1890 - 3 Mar 1953)
8 Aug 1940 - 20 Aug 1941:	Staff officer, 3rd China Expeditionary Fleet
15 Nov 1940:	Promoted to *Rear-Admiral*
20 Aug 1941 - 1 Sep 1941:	Attached to Naval General Staff
1 Sep 1941 - 1 Sep 1942:	Commander, 21st Air Flotilla
1 Sep 1942 - 30 Sep 1942:	Attached to Naval General Staff
30 Sep 1942 - 10 Oct 1942:	Staff officer, Southwestern Area Fleet
10 Oct 1942 - 1 Mar 1944:	Chief of Staff, Southwestern Area Fleet
	Chief of Staff, 2nd Southern Expeditionary Fleet
20 Sep 1943 - 1 Mar 1944:	Chief of Staff, 13th Air Fleet
1 Nov 1943:	Promoted to *Vice-Admiral*
1 Mar 1944 - 15 Mar 1944:	Attached to Naval Air Command
15 Mar 1944 - 1 Aug 1944:	Chief of Administration Bureau, Naval Air Command
1 Aug 1944 - 15 May 1945:	Chief, Bureau of Naval Affairs, Department of the Navy, Member, Admirals Committee
15 May 1945 - 1 Nov 1945:	Deputy Minister of the Navy, Member, Admirals Committee

Rear-Admiral **Shigenobu TADAKI** (? - 6 Feb 1944)
15 Jun 1943 - 6 Feb 1944:	Chief of 2nd Branch, Southeastern Area Air Depot
6 Feb 1944:	Posthumously promoted to *Rear-Admiral*

Vice-Admiral **Hiromi TADOKORO** (24 Jul 1869 - 19 Jan 1924)
29 May 1914 - 1 Dec 1914:	Chief of Naval Staff, Taiwan Government
1 Dec 1914:	Promoted to *Rear-Admiral*
1 Dec 1914 - 1 Dec 1916:	Chief of Staff, Sasebo Naval District
1 Dec 1916 - 7 Feb 1917:	Commander, 1st Destroyer Flotilla
7 Feb 1917 - 10 Nov 1918:	Commander, 3rd Destroyer Flotilla
10 Nov 1918 - 1 Dec 1918:	Member, Admirals Committee
1 Dec 1918:	Promoted to *Vice-Admiral*
1 Dec 1918 - 1 Dec 1919:	Commander, Chinkai Guard District
1 Dec 1919 - 1 Aug 1920:	Member, Admirals Committee
1 Aug 1920 - 1 Apr 1921:	Unassigned
1 Apr 1921:	Transferred to the reserve

Vice-Admiral (Surgeon) **Sukezo TAGAWA** (22 Jul 1888 - 14 Oct 1974)
15 Nov 1938:	Promoted to *Rear-Admiral (Surgeon)*
15 Nov 1938 - 15 Nov 1939:	Chief Surgeon, Combined Fleet, Chief Surgeon, 1st Fleet
15 Nov 1939 - 15 Nov 1940:	Director, Sasebo Naval Hospital, Chief Surgeon, Sasebo Naval District
15 Nov 1940 - 15 Oct 1941:	Chief Instructor, Navy Medical School
15 Oct 1941 - 1 Nov 1942:	Director, Kure Naval Hospital, Chief Surgeon, Kure Naval District
1 Nov 1942:	Promoted to *Vice-Admiral (Surgeon)*
1 Nov 1942 - 15 Dec 1942:	Attached to Naval General Staff
21 Dec 1942:	Transferred to the reserve

Rear-Admiral **Hisamori TAGUCHI** (20 Jul 1872 - 22 Nov 1946)
10 Nov 1918 - 20 Nov 1920:	Chief of Staff, Maizuru Naval District
20 Nov 1920 - 1 Dec 1921:	Chief of Staff, 3rd Fleet
1 Dec 1920:	Promoted to *Rear-Admiral*
1 Dec 1921 - 1 Aug 1922:	Attached to Yokosuka Naval District
1 Aug 1922 - 31 Mar 1923:	Unassigned
31 Mar 1923:	Transferred to the reserve

Rear-Admiral **Taro TAGUCHI** (13 Apr 1897 - 9 Feb 1971)
6 Jan 1945 - 3 Aug 1945:	Chief of Section 1, Bureau 1, Naval General Staff
1 May 1945:	Promoted to *Rear-Admiral*
3 Aug 1945 - 10 Oct 1945:	Commander, 32nd Air Flotilla

Rear-Admiral **Hozo TAHARA** (1 Dec 1892 - 2 Dec 1979)
20 Oct 1943 - 1 Nov 1944:	Commander, 2nd Naval Facility
1 May 1944:	Promoted to *Rear-Admiral*
1 Nov 1944 - 25 Oct 1945:	Chief of Administration Bureau, Sasebo Navy Yard

Rear-Admiral **Susumu TAHARA** (24 Jul 1889 - 6 Dec 1974)
26 Dec 1943 - 11 Nov 1944:	Commander, Yokosuka Marine Force
15 Oct 1944:	Promoted to *Rear-Admiral*
11 Nov 1944 - 5 Feb 1945:	Attached to Yokosuka Naval District
5 Feb 1945 - 20 Mar 1945:	Commander, Osaka Sailors Corps
20 Mar 1945 - 26 Mar 1945:	Attached to Osaka Guard District
26 Mar 1945 - 10 May 1945:	Attached to Yokosuka Naval District
10 May 1945 - 20 Sep 1945:	Commander, Saiki Defense Force
20 Sep 1945:	Demobilized

Rear-Admiral **Hideo TAJIMA** (? - 14 Jul 1943)
1 Jul 1941 - 14 Jul 1943:	Commander, Yokosuka Communications Unit
14 Jul 1943:	Posthumously promoted to *Rear-Admiral*

Vice-Admiral **Tadatsugu TAJIRI** (23 Nov 1874 - ?)
12 Nov 1920 - 6 Apr 1921:	Commander, Yokosuka Air Division
1 Dec 1920:	Promoted to *Rear-Admiral*
6 Apr 1921 - 1 Nov 1922:	Commander, Temporary Flying Training Center
1 Nov 1922 - 6 Nov 1923:	Commander, Kasumigaura Air Division
6 Nov 1923 - 20 Dec 1924:	Commander, Mako Guard District
1 Dec 1924:	Promoted to *Vice-Admiral*
20 Dec 1924 - 2 Mar 1925:	Attached to Naval General Staff
20 Mar 1925:	Transferred to the reserve

Rear-Admiral **Toshiro TAJIRI** (18 Sep 1882 - 27 Jan 1935)
1 Dec 1930 - 1 Dec 1932:	Commander, Yokosuka Harbor
1 Dec 1932:	Promoted to *Rear-Admiral*
1 Dec 1932 - 10 Dec 1932:	Attached to Naval General Staff
15 Dec 1932:	Transferred to the reserve

Rear-Admiral **Sakae TAKADA** (20 Jan 1896 - 17 Jul 1973)
10 Feb 1945 - 10 Nov 1945:	Deputy Chief of Staff, Osaka Guard District
1 May 1945:	Promoted to *Rear-Admiral*
10 Nov 1945 - 30 Nov 1945:	Chief of Personnel Bureau, Osaka Guard District

Vice-Admiral **Satoshi TAKADA** (1 Jan 1895 - 10 Mar 1945)
20 Mar 1944 - 5 May 1944:	Staff officer, Combined Air Unit Group
1 May 1944:	Promoted to *Rear-Admiral*
5 May 1944 - 1 Sep 1944:	Instructor, Otake Sailors Corps
1 Sep 1944 - 10 Mar 1945:	Commander, Yasuura Sailors Corps
10 Mar 1945:	Posthumously promoted to *Vice-Admiral*

Rear-Admiral **Toshitane TAKADA** (15 Jan 1895 - 25 Oct 1987)
20 Sep 1944 - 10 May 1945:	Deputy Chief of Staff, Combined Fleet
15 Oct 1944:	Promoted to *Rear-Admiral*
25 Apr 1945 - 10 May 1945:	Deputy Chief of Staff, Supreme Navy HQ
10 May 1945 - 15 May 1945:	Attached to Naval General Staff
15 May 1945 - 20 Oct 1945:	Deputy Chief, Bureau of Naval Affairs, Department of the Navy
15 May 1945 - 1 Sep 1945:	Chief of Shipping Safety Command, Department of the Navy
15 May 1945 - 15 Sep 1945:	Chief of Chemical Warfare Division, Department of the Navy
27 May 1945 - 1 Oct 1945:	Chief of Bureau 2, Naval General Staff, Chief of Readiness Bureau, Joint General Staff
20 Oct 1945 - 30 Nov 1945:	Attached to Department of the Navy

Rear-Admiral **Eijiro TAKAGI** (29 Dec 1851 - 2 Jun 1904)
28 Feb 1897 - 1 Jul 1903:	Chief of Survey Section, Naval Hydrographic Command
1 Jul 1903 - 2 Jun 1904:	Unassigned
1 Jun 1904:	Promoted to *Rear-Admiral*

Rear-Admiral **Shichitaro TAKAGI** (5 Apr 1869 - 6 Nov 1933)
13 Dec 1915:	Promoted to *Rear-Admiral*
13 Dec 1915 - 1 Apr 1916:	Chief of Staff, 3rd Fleet
1 Apr 1916 - 1 Dec 1916:	Commander, 2nd Destroyer Flotilla
1 Dec 1916 - 1 Dec 1917:	Unassigned
1 Dec 1917:	Transferred to the reserve

Rear-Admiral **Sokichi TAKAGI** (10 Nov 1893 - 27 Jul 1979)
10 Jun 1942 - 25 Sep 1943:	Chief of Staff, Maizuru Naval District
1 May 1943:	Promoted to *Rear-Admiral*
25 Sep 1943 - 1 Mar 1944:	Attached to Naval General Staff
1 Mar 1944 - 10 Sep 1944:	Chief of Naval Training Bureau
10 Sep 1944 - 15 Sep 1945:	Attached to Naval General Staff

Rear-Admiral **Sukekazu TAKAGI** (6 Jul 1963 - 8 Feb 1920)
28 Aug 1908:	Promoted to *Rear-Admiral*
28 Aug 1908 - 1 Dec 1908:	Commander, Maizuru Harbor
1 Dec 1908 - 1 Dec 1911:	C-in-C, Maizuru Reserve Fleet
1 Dec 1911 - 1 Dec 1912:	Unassigned
1 Dec 1912:	Transferred to the reserve

Rear-Admiral **Tachisaburo TAKAGI** (28 Mar 1855 - 15 Mar 1925)
29 Jun 1912 - 1 Dec 1913:	Chief of Engine Construction Bureau, Yokosuka Navy Yard
1 Dec 1913 - 1 Mar 1914:	Unassigned
1 Mar 1914:	Promoted to *General (Constructor)*
1 Mar 1914:	Transferred to the reserve
23 Sep 1919:	Redesignated *Rear-Admiral*

Vice-Admiral (Surgeon) **Takashi TAKAGI** (23 Sep 1886 - 9 Nov 1963)
15 Nov 1938:	Promoted to *Rear-Admiral (Surgeon)*
15 Nov 1938 - 1 Mar 1939:	Chief of Bureau 1, Yokosuka Navy Hospital
1 Mar 1939 - 15 Nov 1939:	Director, Beppu Naval Hospital
15 Nov 1939 - 15 Oct 1941:	Director, Kure Naval Hospital, Chief Surgeon, Kure Naval District
15 Oct 1941 - 1 Nov 1943:	Director, Yokosuka Naval Hospital, Chief Surgeon, Yokosuka Naval District
1 Nov 1942:	Promoted to *Vice-Admiral (Surgeon)*
1 Nov 1943 - 25 Jan 1944:	Attached to Naval General Staff
31 Jan 1944:	Transferred to the reserve

Admiral **Takeo TAKAGI** (25 Jan 1892 - 8 Jul 1944)
15 Nov 1938:	Promoted to *Rear-Admiral*
15 Nov 1938 - 1 Nov 1939:	Chief of Staff, 2nd Fleet
1 Nov 1939 - 15 Nov 1939:	Attached to Naval General Staff
15 Nov 1939 - 6 Sep 1941:	Chief of Bureau 2, Naval General Staff
6 Sep 1941 - 10 Nov 1942:	Commander, 5th Cruiser Flotilla
1 May 1942:	Promoted to *Vice-Admiral*
10 Nov 1942 - 20 Nov 1942:	Attached to Naval General Staff
20 Nov 1942 - 1 Apr 1943:	Commander, Mako Guard District
1 Apr 1943 - 1 Jun 1943:	Commander, Takao Guard District
1 Jun 1943 - 21 Jun 1943:	Attached to Naval General Staff
21 Jun 1943 - 8 Jul 1944:	C-in-C, 6th (Submarine) Fleet
8 Jul 1944:	Posthumously promoted to *Admiral*

Rear-Admiral **Toshio TAKAGI** (? - 23 Oct 1944)
8 Jul 1944 - 23 Oct 1944:	Chief Engineer Officer, Heavy Cruiser *"Maya"*
23 Oct 1944:	Posthumously promoted to *Rear-Admiral*

Rear-Admiral **Jiro TAKAHARA** (30 Sep 1887 - ?)
15 Nov 1934 - 15 Nov 1935:	Chief of Engine Construction Bureau, Hiro Navy Yard
15 Nov 1935:	Promoted to *Rear-Admiral*
15 Nov 1935 - 1 Dec 1936:	Chief of Engine Construction Bureau, Kure Navy Yard

1 Dec 1936 - 15 Dec 1936:	Attached to Naval Shipbuilding Command
22 Dec 1936:	Transferred to the reserve

Rear-Admiral **Hideo TAKAHASHI** (23 Jan 1888 - 8 Aug 1959)
15 Nov 1934 - 11 Sep 1935:	Captain, Battleship *"Hyuga"*
11 Sep 1935 - 1 Dec 1936:	Attached to Kure Naval District
1 Dec 1936:	Promoted to *Rear-Admiral*
1 Dec 1936 - 15 Dec 1936:	Attached to Naval General Staff
22 Dec 1936:	Transferred to the reserve

Vice-Admiral **Ibo TAKAHASHI** (20 Apr 1888 - 18 Mar 1947)
15 Nov 1935:	Promoted to *Rear-Admiral*
15 Nov 1935 - 15 Nov 1937:	Chief of Bureau 2, Naval General Staff
15 Nov 1937 - 15 Nov 1939:	Chief of Staff, Combined Fleet, Chief of Staff, 1st Fleet
15 Nov 1939:	Promoted to *Vice-Admiral*
15 Nov 1939 - 27 Feb 1941:	Commander, Mako Guard District
27 Feb 1941 - 10 Apr 1941:	Attached to Naval General Staff
10 Apr 1941 - 10 Mar 1942:	C-in-C, 3rd Fleet
10 Mar 1942 - 15 Sep 1942:	C-in-C, 2nd Southern Expeditionary Fleet
10 Apr 1942 - 15 Sep 1942:	C-in-C, Southwest Area Fleet
15 Sep 1942 - 10 Nov 1942:	Attached to Naval General Staff
10 Nov 1942 - 21 Jun 1943:	Admiral Commanding, Kure Naval District
21 Jun 1943 - 15 Dec 1944:	Attached to Naval General Staff
20 Dec 1944:	Transferred to the reserve

Vice-Admiral **Ichimatsu TAKAHASHI** (30 Jan 1890 - 4 Aug 1944)
10 Oct 1943 - 25 Jun 1944:	Commander, Rashin Naval Area Base Force
1 May 1944:	Promoted to *Rear-Admiral*
25 Jun 1944 - 8 Jul 1944:	Staff officer, Maritime Escort Fleet
8 Jul 1944 - 4 Aug 1944:	Commander, 2nd Maritime Escort Force
4 Aug 1944:	Posthumously promoted to *Vice-Admiral*

Rear-Admiral **Jutaro TAKAHASHI** (15 Jan 1879 - 8 Apr 1945)
1 Dec 1924:	Promoted to *Rear-Admiral*
1 Dec 1924 - 1 Dec 1925:	Chief Instructor, Naval College
1 Dec 1925 - 1 Dec 1926:	Commandant, Naval Gunnery School
1 Dec 1926 - 1 Dec 1927:	Commander, 1st Destroyer Flotilla
1 Dec 1927 - 15 Mar 1928:	Attached to Naval General Staff
25 Mar 1928:	Transferred to the reserve

Rear-Admiral **Kameshiro TAKAHASHI** (13 Aug 1900 - 25 Oct 1944)
25 Mar 1944 - 25 Oct 1944:	Commander, 4th Destroyer Division
25 Oct 1944:	Posthumously promoted to *Rear-Admiral*

Rear-Admiral (Surgeon) **Michimaro TAKAHASHI** (9 Aug 1879 - 17 Jan 1934)
1 Dec 1927 - 30 Nov 1929:	Chief Instructor, Navy Medical School
10 Dec 1928:	Promoted to *Rear-Admiral*
30 Nov 1929 - 10 Jun 1930:	Attached to Naval General Staff
20 Jun 1930:	Transferred to the reserve

Rear-Admiral **Nobukichi TAKAHASHI** (7 Apr 1897 - 16 May 1945)
15 May 1945 - 16 May 1945:	Commander, Indochina Air Division
16 May 1945:	Posthumously promoted to *Rear-Admiral*

Rear-Admiral **Ritsuto TAKAHASHI** (25 Aug 1880 - 3 May 1953)
1 Dec 1924:	Promoted to *Rear-Admiral*
1 Dec 1924 - 1 Dec 1925:	Commander, 1st Destroyer Flotilla
1 Dec 1925 - 10 Mar 1926:	Instructor, Naval College
10 Mar 1926 - 1 Dec 1926:	Commander, 1st Submarine Flotilla
1 Dec 1926 - 1 Dec 1927:	Commandant, Torpedo School
1 Dec 1927 - 15 Dec 1927:	Attached to Naval General Staff
25 Dec 1927:	Transferred to the reserve

Rear-Admiral **Ryoji TAKAHASHI** (14 Jul 1878 - 3 Jun 1931)
1 Apr 1923 - 20 Oct 1923:	Commander, Kure Harbor
20 Oct 1923 - 5 Sep 1925:	Attached to Yokosuka Naval District
5 Sep 1925 - 16 Dec 1925:	Unassigned
1 Dec 1925:	Promoted to *Rear-Admiral*
16 Dec 1925:	Transferred to the reserve

Admiral **Sankichi TAKAHASHI** (24 Aug 1882 - 15 Jun 1966)
1 Dec 1925:	Promoted to *Rear-Admiral*
1 Dec 1925 - 1 Nov 1926:	Chief of Bureau 2, Naval General Staff
1 Nov 1926 - 1 Dec 1927:	Chief of Staff, Combined Fleet, Chief of Staff, 1st Fleet
1 Dec 1927 - 1 Apr 1928:	Attached to Naval General Staff
1 Apr 1928 - 10 Dec 1928:	Commander, 1st Air Flotilla
10 Dec 1928 - 1 Apr 1929:	Attached to Naval General Staff
1 Apr 1929 - 30 Nov 1929:	Commander, 1st Air Flotilla
30 Nov 1929:	Promoted to *Vice-Admiral*
30 Nov 1929 - 8 Feb 1932:	Commandant of the Naval College
8 Feb 1932 - 15 Nov 1933:	Deputy Chief of the Naval General Staff
15 Nov 1933 - 15 Nov 1934:	C-in-C, 2nd Fleet
15 Nov 1934 - 1 Dec 1936:	C-in-C, Combined Fleet, C-in-C, 1st Fleet
1 Apr 1936:	Promoted to *Admiral*
1 Dec 1936 - 1 Apr 1939:	Navy Councillor
5 Apr 1939:	Transferred to the reserve

Rear-Admiral **Setsuo TAKAHASHI** (3 Feb 1878 - 1 Apr 1971)
1 Dec 1923:	Promoted to *Rear-Admiral*
1 Dec 1923 - 1 Dec 1924:	Commander, Sasebo Defense Force
1 Dec 1924 - 2 Mar 1925:	Attached to Naval General Staff
20 Mar 1925:	Transferred to the reserve

Vice-Admiral (Paymaster) **Shiro TAKAHASHI** (15 Dec 1886 - 9 Dec 1957)
1 Dec 1936:	Promoted to *Rear-Admiral (Paymaster)*
1 Dec 1936 - 12 Apr 1939:	Chief of Accounting Bureau, Naval Shipbuilding Command
12 Apr 1939 - 15 Oct 1941:	Paymaster-General, Kure Naval District
15 Nov 1940:	Promoted to *Vice-Admiral (Paymaster)*
15 Oct 1941 - 22 Nov 1941:	Attached to Naval General Staff
24 Nov 1941:	Transferred to the reserve

Rear-Admiral **Yuji TAKAHASHI** (17 Apr 1896 - 2 Apr 1986)
1 Sep 1944 - 20 Jun 1945:	Commandant, Radar School
15 Oct 1944:	Promoted to *Rear-Admiral*
20 Jun 1945 - 1 Nov 1945:	Commander, Kanto Air Division

Rear-Admiral (Surgeon) **Yutaka TAKAHASHI** (23 Oct 1893 - 16 Jul 1959)
22 Sep 1941 - 1 Nov 1942:	Chief of Medical Bureau, Hikari Navy Yard
1 Nov 1942:	Promoted to *Rear-Admiral (Surgeon)*
1 Nov 1942 - 1 Nov 1943:	Attached to Yokosuka Naval District
1 Nov 1943 - 5 Feb 1945:	Chief of Medical Bureau, Yokosuka Navy Yard
5 Feb 1945 - 30 Sep 1945:	Director, Minato Naval Hospital
30 Sep 1945 - 10 Oct 1945:	Attached to Yokosuka Naval District

Vice-Admiral **Tamotsu TAKAMA** (25 Sep 1893 - 10 Jan 1980)
20 Aug 1941 - 20 Jun 1942:	Captain, Battleship *"Haruna"*
1 May 1942:	Promoted to *Rear-Admiral*
20 Jun 1942 - 20 Jul 1943:	Commander, 4th Destroyer Flotilla
20 Jul 1943 - 15 Dec 1943:	Commander, 2nd Destroyer Flotilla
15 Dec 1943 - 1 Jul 1945:	Commander, 11th Destroyer Flotilla
1 Jul 1945 - 10 Nov 1945:	Attached to Naval General Staff
1 Nov 1945:	Promoted to *Vice-Admiral*

Rear-Admiral (Paymaster) **Chozo TAKAMATSU** (1 Jul 1884 - 12 Jan 1955)
1 Dec 1930 - 1 Dec 1932:	Paymaster-General, Combined Fleet, Paymaster-General, 1st Fleet
1 Dec 1932:	Promoted to *Rear-Admiral (Paymaster)*
1 Dec 1932 - 15 Nov 1934:	Chief of Supply Bureau, Yokosuka Naval District
15 Nov 1934 - 10 Dec 1934:	Attached to Naval General Staff
15 Dec 1934:	Transferred to the reserve

Rear-Admiral (Surgeon) **Takashi TAKAMIYA** (15 May 1877 - 20 Feb 1944)
1 Apr 1923 - 10 Nov 1923:	Director, Maizuru Guard District Naval Hospital, Chief Surgeon, Maizuru Guard District
10 Nov 1923 - 1 Dec 1923:	Attached to Yokosuka Naval District
1 Dec 1923:	Promoted to *Rear-Admiral (Surgeon)*
1 Dec 1923 - 25 Feb 1924:	Unassigned
25 Feb 1924:	Transferred to the reserve

Rear-Admiral **Jun TAKANO** (19 Sep 1882 - 27 Jun 1961)
1 Dec 1931 - 15 Nov 1932:	Chief of Shipbuilding Bureau, Kure Naval District
15 Nov 1932 - 10 Dec 1932:	Attached to Naval General Staff
1 Dec 1932:	Promoted to *Rear-Admiral*
15 Dec 1932:	Transferred to the reserve

Admiral **Takeshi TAKARABE** (7 Apr 1867 - 13 Jan 1949)
10 Dec 1908 - 1 Dec 1909:	Chief of Staff, 1st Fleet
1 Dec 1909:	Promoted to *Rear-Admiral*
1 Dec 1909 - 17 Apr 1914:	Deputy Minister of the Navy, Member, Admirals Committee
1 Dec 1913:	Promoted to *Vice-Admiral*
17 Apr 1914 - 11 May 1914:	Member, Admirals Committee
11 May 1914 - 5 Feb 1915:	Unassigned
5 Feb 1915 - 13 Dec 1915:	C-in-C, 3rd Fleet
13 Dec 1915 - 1 Dec 1916:	Commander, Ryojun Guard District
1 Dec 1916 - 1 Dec 1917:	Member, Admirals Committee
1 Dec 1917 - 1 Dec 1918:	Admiral Commanding, Maizuru Naval District
1 Dec 1918 - 27 Jul 1922:	Admiral Commanding, Sasebo Naval District
25 Nov 1919:	Promoted to *Admiral*
27 Jul 1922 - 15 May 1923:	Admiral Commanding, Yokosuka Naval District, Member, Admirals Committee
15 May 1923 - 7 Jan 1924:	Minister of the Navy
7 Jan 1924 - 11 Jun 1924:	Navy Councillor
11 Jun 1924 - 20 Apr 1927:	Minister of the Navy
20 Apr 1927 - 2 Jul 1929:	Navy Councillor
2 Jul 1929 - 3 Oct 1930:	Minister of the Navy
3 Oct 1930 - 7 Apr 1932:	Navy Councillor
7 Apr 1932:	Transferred to the reserve

Rear-Admiral **Chikateru TAKASAKI** (1 Oct 1880 - 7 Mar 1952)
20 Oct 1925 - 1 Dec 1926:	Captain, Battleship *"Hyuga"*
1 Dec 1926:	Promoted to *Rear-Admiral*
1 Dec 1926 - 20 Mar 1927:	Attached to Naval General Staff
20 Mar 1927 - 10 Apr 1927:	Unassigned
10 Apr 1927:	Transferred to the reserve

Rear-Admiral **Takeo TAKASAKI** (31 Mar 1888 - 18 Jun 1955)
26 Jan 1937 - 1 Dec 1937:	Captain, Battleship *"Fuso"*
1 Dec 1937:	Promoted to *Rear-Admiral*
1 Dec 1937 - 15 Dec 1937:	Attached to Naval General Staff
21 Dec 1937:	Transferred to the reserve

Rear-Admiral **Sanji TAKASHIMA** (8 Sep 1894 - 2 Jul 1944)
1 Mar 1944 - 2 Jul 1944:	Commander, 55th Guard Force
10 Mar 1944 - 2 Jul 1944:	Commander, 5th Transport Force
2 Jul 1944:	Posthumously promoted to *Rear-Admiral*

Vice-Admiral **Sanjiro TAKASU** (6 Jan 1889 - 14 Nov 1973)
1 Dec 1937:	Promoted to *Rear-Admiral*
1 Dec 1937 - 15 Nov 1939:	Commander, 2nd Submarine Flotilla
15 Nov 1939 - 5 Jul 1941:	Commandant, Submarine School
5 Jul 1941 - 1 Nov 1942:	Chief of Bureau 7, Naval Shipbuilding Command
15 Oct 1941:	Promoted to *Vice-Admiral*
1 Nov 1942 - 15 Mar 1943:	Attached to Naval General Staff
30 Mar 1943:	Transferred to the reserve

Admiral **Shiro TAKASU** (27 Oct 1884 - 2 Sep 1944)
15 Nov 1933 - 15 Nov 1934:	Chief of Staff, 3rd Fleet
15 Nov 1934:	Promoted to *Rear-Admiral*
15 Nov 1934 - 1 Dec 1936:	Chief of Bureau 3, Naval General Staff
1 Dec 1936 - 1 Dec 1937:	Commander, 1st Air Flotilla
1 Dec 1937 - 1 Aug 1938:	C-in-C, Training Fleet
1 Aug 1938 - 15 Nov 1938:	Commander, Manchuria Expeditionary Force
15 Nov 1938:	Promoted to *Vice-Admiral*
15 Nov 1938 - 29 Sep 1939:	Commandant of the Naval College
29 Sep 1939 - 15 Nov 1939:	C-in-C, 5th Fleet
15 Nov 1939 - 15 Oct 1940:	C-in-C, 2nd China Expeditionary Fleet
15 Oct 1940 - 15 Nov 1940:	Attached to Naval General Staff
15 Nov 1940 - 11 Aug 1941:	C-in-C, 4th Fleet
11 Aug 1941 - 14 Jul 1942:	C-in-C, 1st Fleet
14 Jul 1942 - 15 Sep 1942:	Attached to Naval General Staff
15 Sep 1942 - 15 Apr 1943:	C-in-C, 2nd Southern Expeditionary Fleet
15 Sep 1942 - 18 Jun 1944:	C-in-C, Southwest Area Fleet
20 Sep 1943 - 18 Jun 1944:	C-in-C, 13th Air Fleet
1 Mar 1944:	Promoted to *Admiral*
31 Mar 1944 - 3 May 1944:	Acting C-in-C, Combined Fleet
18 Jun 1944 - 2 Sep 1944:	Navy Councillor

Vice-Admiral (Surgeon) **Shinichiro TAKASUGI** (21 Jan 1880 - 25 Apr 1958)
10 Dec 1928:	Promoted to *Rear-Admiral (Surgeon)*
10 Dec 1928 - 30 Nov 1929:	Director, Kure Naval Hospital, Chief Surgeon, Kure Naval District
30 Nov 1929 - 25 Feb 1932:	Director, Yokosuka Naval Hospital, Chief Surgeon, Yokosuka Naval District
25 Feb 1932 - 15 Nov 1934:	Commandant, Navy Medical School
15 Nov 1933:	Promoted to *Vice-Admiral (Surgeon)*
15 Nov 1934 - 15 Nov 1939:	Chief of Naval Medical Service
15 Nov 1939 - 15 Mar 1940:	Attached to Naval General Staff
21 Mar 1940:	Transferred to the reserve

Vice-Admiral (Surgeon) **Rokuro TAKATA** (7 Apr 1887 - 18 Apr 1943)
25 Oct 1942 - 10 Nov 1942:	Staff officer, Combined Fleet
1 Nov 1942:	Promoted to *Rear-Admiral (Surgeon)*
10 Nov 1942 - 18 Apr 1943:	Chief Surgeon, Combined Fleet
18 Apr 1943:	Posthumously promoted to *Vice-Admiral (Surgeon)*

Rear-Admiral **Kanichi TAKATSUGI** (5 Nov 1893 - 16 Apr 1984)
10 Jul 1944 - 5 May 1945:	Commander, Hyakurihara Air Division
1 May 1945:	Promoted to *Rear-Admiral*
5 May 1945 - 15 Sep 1945:	Commander, 53rd Air Flotilla

Rear-Admiral **Seigo TAKATSUKA** (11 Dec 1888 - 11 Oct 1962)
15 Nov 1939:	Promoted to *Rear-Admiral*
15 Nov 1939 - 15 Nov 1940:	Commander, Sasebo Defense Flotilla
15 Nov 1940 - 20 Oct 1941:	Commander, 5th Submarine Flotilla
20 Oct 1941 - 2 Feb 1942:	Attached to Sasebo Naval District
2 Feb 1942 - 10 Sep 1942:	Commander, Kure Defense Flotilla
10 Sep 1942 - 10 Oct 1942:	Attached to Naval General Staff
15 Oct 1942:	Transferred to the reserve

Vice-Admiral **Gihachi TAKAYANAGI** (17 Apr 1891 - 29 Dec 1973)
1 Nov 1941 - 17 Dec 1942:	Captain, Battleship *"Yamato"*
1 May 1942:	Promoted to *Rear-Admiral*
17 Dec 1942 - 6 Jan 1943:	Attached to Yokosuka Naval District
6 Jan 1943 - 25 Feb 1944:	Chief of Staff, 1st Fleet
25 Feb 1944 - 20 Dec 1944:	Commander, Kure Training Flotilla
25 Feb 1944 - 5 May 1945:	Deputy Commandant of the Naval Academy, Chief Instructor, Naval Academy
1 May 1945:	Promoted to *Vice-Admiral*
5 May 1945 - 20 Aug 1945:	Chief of Naval Training Bureau
27 May 1945 - 20 Aug 1945:	Chief of Training Division, Joint General Staff

20 Aug 1945 - 15 Oct 1945:	Deputy Chief of the Naval General Staff
15 Oct 1945 - 20 Nov 1945:	Attached to Department of the Navy

Rear-Admiral **Chuji TAKEBAYASHI** (7 Mar 1898 - 12 May 1942)

15 Mar 1941 - 12 May 1942:	Commander, Shoei-maru Naval Facility
12 May 1942:	Posthumously promoted to *Rear-Admiral*

Vice-Admiral **Hideo TAKEDA** (16 Nov 1863 - 16 Feb 1942)

1 Dec 1909:	Promoted to *Rear-Admiral*
1 Dec 1909 - 15 Apr 1911:	Commander, Navy Briquette Yard
1 Dec 1910 - 1 Dec 1913:	Chief of Bureau 3, Naval Training Command
1 Dec 1913:	Promoted to *Vice-Admiral*
1 Dec 1913 - 1 Apr 1914:	Commandant, Naval Engineer Academy
1 Apr 1914 - 20 Jun 1914:	Unassigned
20 Jun 1914:	Transferred to the reserve

Rear-Admiral **Isamu TAKEDA** (31 Jul 1893 - 14 Nov 1970)

25 Apr 1943 - 15 Oct 1943:	Chief of Staff, Shanghai Special Area Base Force
1 May 1943:	Promoted to *Rear-Admiral*
15 Oct 1943 - 1 Nov 1943:	Staff officer, 8th Fleet
1 Nov 1943 - Oct 1945:	Commander, 1st Auxiliary Base Force

Rear-Admiral (Surgeon) **Masamori TAKEDA** (11 Feb 1864 - 24 Jul 1931)

20 Apr 1912 - 1 Dec 1912:	Director, Ryojun Naval Hospital, Chief Surgeon, Ryojun Naval District
1 Dec 1912:	Promoted to *General (Surgeon)*
1 Dec 1912 - 31 May 1913:	Unassigned
31 May 1913:	Transferred to the reserve
23 Sep 1919:	Redesigated *Rear-Admiral (Surgeon)*

Vice-Admiral **Moriji TAKEDA** (2 Apr 1889 - 27 Feb 1973)

15 Dec 1937 - 15 Nov 1939:	Commander, Kure Sailors Corps
15 Nov 1938:	Promoted to *Rear-Admiral*
15 Nov 1939 - 15 Sep 1941:	Commander, Shanghai Marine Force
15 Sep 1941 - 15 Oct 1941:	Attached to Kure Naval District
15 Oct 1941 - 10 Mar 1942:	Commander, 24th Cruiser Flotilla
10 Mar 1942 - 20 Mar 1942:	Attached to Kure Naval District
20 Mar 1942 - 10 Apr 1942:	Commander, 3rd Auxiliary Base Force
10 Apr 1942 - 15 Jun 1942:	Commander, 3rd Naval Base Force
1 May 1942:	Promoted to *Vice-Admiral*
15 Jun 1942 - 15 Jul 1943:	Commander, 4th Auxiliary Base Force, Commander, 2nd Maritime Escort Force
15 Jul 1943 - 6 Sep 1943:	Attached to Naval General Staff
10 Sep 1943:	Transferred to the reserve

Rear-Admiral **Rokukichi TAKEDA** (20 Jan 1886 - 24 Mar 1972)
1 Mar 1944 - Oct 1945:	Commander, 31st Air Division
15 Oct 1944:	Promoted to *Rear-Admiral*

Rear-Admiral **Tadayuki TAKEDA** (12 Oct 1881 - 22 Apr 1973)
1 Nov 1927 - 1 Dec 1931:	Chief of Administration Bureau, Kure Navy Yard
1 Dec 1931:	Promoted to *Rear-Admiral*
1 Dec 1931 - 15 Dec 1931:	Attached to Naval General Staff
21 Dec 1931:	Transferred to the reserve

Rear-Admiral **Kuichiro TAKEHARA** (7 Oct 1885 - 14 Jan 1944)
15 Oct 1943 - 14 Jan 1944:	Commander of Minesweeping, Auxiliary Oiler *"Nihon-maru"*
14 Jan 1944:	Posthumously promoted to *Rear-Admiral*

Vice-Admiral (Paymaster) **Daisuke TAKEI** (25 Apr 1887 - 30 Mar 1972)
1 Nov 1929 - 1 Nov 1934:	Chief of Section 2, Administration Bureau, Naval Shipbuilding Command
15 Nov 1933:	Promoted to *Rear-Admiral (Paymaster)*
1 Nov 1934 - 15 Nov 1934:	Attached to Naval General Staff
15 Nov 1934 - 15 Nov 1935:	Paymaster-General Sasebo Naval District
15 Nov 1935 - 15 Dec 1937:	Paymaster-General Yokosuka Naval District
1 Dec 1937:	Promoted to *Vice-Admiral (Paymaster)*
15 Dec 1937 - 2 May 1938:	Attached to Naval General Staff
2 May 1938 - 1 Jun 1943:	Chief of Naval Accounting Bureau, Department of the Navy
1 Jun 1943 - 8 Apr 1944:	Attached to Naval General Staff
10 Apr 1944:	Transferred to the reserve

Rear-Admiral (Surgeon) **Hiizu TAKEI** (11 Sep 1898 - 5 Jan 1944)
15 Dec 1943 - 5 Jan 1944:	Chief Surgeon, 3rd Southern Expeditionary Fleet
5 Jan 1944:	Posthumously promoted to *Rear-Admiral (Surgeon)*

Rear-Admiral (Surgeon) **Mitsuzumi TAKEI** (5 Jan 1881 - 20 Sep 1953)
1 Feb 1928 - 1 Nov 1928:	Staff officer, Training Fleet
1 Nov 1928 - 15 Sep 1929:	Attached to Naval General Staff
10 Dec 1928:	Promoted to *Rear-Admiral (Surgeon)*
30 Sep 1929:	Transferred to the reserve

Rear-Admiral **Taro TAKEISHI** (5 Feb 1885 - 16 Sep 1933)
30 Nov 1929 - 15 Sep 1933:	Chief of Ordnance Bureau, Sasebo Navy Yard
1 Dec 1932:	Promoted to *Rear-Admiral*
15 Sep 1933 - 16 Sep 1933:	Attached to Sasebo Naval District

Vice-Admiral (Surgeon) **Shinpei TAKEMASA** (29 Nov 1890 - 7 Jun 1966)
15 Nov 1938 - 15 Nov 1939:	Chief Surgeon, China Area Fleet, Chief Surgeon, 3rd Fleet
15 Nov 1939:	Promoted to *Rear-Admiral (Surgeon)*
15 Nov 1939 - 1 Nov 1942:	Chief of Medical Bureau, Yokosuka Navy Yard
1 Nov 1942 - 1 Nov 1944:	Director, Maizuru Naval Hospital, Chief Surgeon, Maizuru Naval District
1 Nov 1943:	Promoted to *Vice-Admiral (Surgeon)*
1 Nov 1944 - 15 Mar 1945:	Director, Totsuka Naval Hospital
15 Mar 1945 - 16 Apr 1945:	Attached to Naval General Staff
20 Apr 1945:	Transferred to the reserve

Rear-Admiral **Kazu TAKEMITSU** (1 Jan 1878 - 10 May 1974)
20 Nov 1921 - 1 Dec 1922:	Captain, Battlecruiser *"Kongo"*
1 Dec 1922:	Promoted to *Rear-Admiral*
1 Dec 1922 - 5 Feb 1924:	Attached to Naval General Staff
25 Feb 1924:	Transferred to the reserve

Rear-Admiral **Kotaro TAKEMURA** (16 Apr 1879 - 29 Mar 1948)
1 May 1923 - 1 Dec 1923:	Chief of Engine Research Bureau, Hiro Navy Yard
1 Dec 1923:	Promoted to *Rear-Admiral*
1 Dec 1923 - 1 Dec 1924:	Instructor, Naval College
1 Dec 1924 - 2 Mar 1925:	Attached to Naval General Staff
20 Mar 1925:	Transferred to the reserve

Vice-Admiral **Ryuzo TAKENAKA** (22 Mar 1891 - 29 Jan 1972)
10 Apr 1941 - 25 Jan 1943:	Commander, 23rd Air Flotilla
15 Oct 1941:	Promoted to *Rear-Admiral*
25 Jan 1943 - 25 Feb 1943:	Attached to Yokosuka Naval District
25 Feb 1943 - 1 Nov 1945:	Branch Chief, Air Technical Arsenal
1 May 1945:	Promoted to *Vice-Admiral*

Rear-Admiral **Makito TAKENOUCHI** (13 Jul 1890 - ?)
1 May 1941 - 10 Mar 1943:	Commander, 1st Navy Powder Yard
15 Oct 1941:	Promoted to *Rear-Admiral*
10 Mar 1943 - 15 Mar 1943:	Attached to Naval General Staff
20 Mar 1943:	Transferred to the reserve

Rear-Admiral **Kenji TAKEOKA** (11 Dec 1889 - 8 May 1974)
1 Apr 1937 - 15 Nov 1938:	Chief of Supply Bureau, Maizuru Guard District
15 Nov 1938:	Promoted to *Rear-Admiral*
15 Nov 1938 - 15 Dec 1938:	Attached to Naval General Staff
21 Dec 1938:	Transferred to the reserve

15 Apr 1944 - 22 May 1944:	Recalled; Attached to Naval General Staff
22 May 1944 - Oct 1945:	Chief of Western Branch, Southern Islands Agency

Rear-Admiral **Eigoro TAKESHITA** (14 Nov 1889 - 19 Oct 1945)

1 Sep 1943 - 19 Oct 1945:	Staff officer, 102nd Supply Bureau
19 Oct 1945:	Posthumously promoted to *Rear-Admiral*

Admiral **Isamu TAKESHITA** (4 Dec 1869 - 1 Jul 1946)

1 Dec 1912 - 1 Dec 1913:	Chief of Staff, 1st Fleet
24 May 1913:	Promoted to *Rear-Admiral*
1 Dec 1913 - 10 Aug 1915:	Chief of Bureau 4, Naval General Staff
10 Aug 1915 - 1 Dec 1916:	Chief of Bureau 1, Naval General Staff
1 Dec 1916 - 30 May 1917:	Commander, 2nd Escort Flotilla
30 May 1917 - 12 Dec 1917:	Member, Admirals Committee
1 Jun 1917:	Promoted to *Vice-Admiral*
12 Dec 1917 - 13 Jun 1918:	C-in-C, 1st Special Task Fleet
13 Jun 1918 - 13 Sep 1920:	Deputy Chief of the Naval General Staff, Member, Admirals Committee
13 Sep 1920 - 10 May 1922:	Naval Attache, League of Nations
10 May 1922 - 27 Jul 1922:	Member, Admirals Committee
27 Jul 1922 - 27 Jan 1924:	C-in-C, 1st Fleet
1 Dec 1922 - 27 Jan 1924:	C-in-C, Combined Fleet
3 Aug 1923:	Promoted to *Admiral*
27 Jan 1924 - 15 Apr 1925:	Admiral Commanding, Kure Naval District
15 Apr 1925 - 11 Nov 1929:	Navy Councillor
11 Nov 1929:	Transferred to the reserve

Rear-Admiral **Nobutoyo TAKESHITA** (23 May 1898 - 19 Oct 1944)

1 Oct 1944 - 19 Oct 1944:	Commander, 36th Guard Force
19 Oct 1944:	Posthumously promoted to *Rear-Admiral*

Rear-Admiral **Shigeri TAKESHITA** (21 Nov 1885 - 16 Jul 1944)

15 Jul 1943 - 16 Jul 1944:	Traffic Control Officer, 1st Maritime Escort Force
16 Jul 1944:	Posthumously promoted to *Rear-Admiral*

Rear-Admiral **Kanichi TAKETOMI** (28 Dec 1878 - 6 Dec 1960)

20 Jan 1923 - 20 Nov 1923:	Captain, Battleship *"Settsu"*
20 Nov 1923 - 10 Dec 1923:	Attached to Kure Naval District
1 Dec 1923:	Promoted to *Rear-Admiral*
10 Dec 1923 - 25 Feb 1924:	Unassigned
25 Feb 1924:	Transferred to the reserve

Vice-Admiral **Kunikane TAKETOMI** (9 Nov 1852 - 17 Feb 1931)
12 Jan 1905:	Promoted to *Rear-Admiral*
12 Jan 1905 - 14 Jun 1905:	C-in-C, 3rd Fleet, Commander, 5th Escort Flotilla
14 Jun 1905 - 13 Nov 1905:	C-in-C, 4th Fleet
13 Nov 1905 - 20 Dec 1905:	C-in-C, 3rd Fleet, Commander, 6th Escort Flotilla
20 Dec 1905 - 22 Nov 1906:	C-in-C, South China Fleet
22 Nov 1906 - 15 May 1908:	Chief, Bureau of Naval Affairs, Department of the Navy, Member, Admirals Committee
15 May 1908 - 28 Aug 1908:	Commander, Ominato Guard District
28 Aug 1908 - 27 Aug 1909:	Unassigned
27 Aug 1909:	Promoted to *Vice-Admiral*
27 Aug 1909:	Transferred to the reserve

Rear-Admiral **Kunishige TAKETOMI** (15 Mar 1885 - 12 Sep 1953)
1 Dec 1930 - 10 Dec 1935:	Attached to Naval General Staff
15 Nov 1935:	Promoted to *Rear-Admiral*
14 Dec 1935:	Transferred to the reserve

Rear-Admiral **Heitaro TAKEUCHI** (18 Dec 1862 - 21 Dec 1933)
27 Dec 1907:	Promoted to *Rear-Admiral*
27 Dec 1907 - 23 May 1910:	Chief of Staff, Kure Naval District
23 May 1910 - 19 Sep 1910:	Attached to Naval General Staff
19 Sep 1910 - 19 Jan 1911:	Unassigned
19 Jan 1911:	Transferred to the reserve

Rear-Admiral **Jiro TAKEUCHI** (22 Sep 1867 - 21 Jan 1925)
6 May 1914 - 1 Dec 1915:	Captain, Battlecruiser *"Tsukuba"*
1 Dec 1915:	Promoted to *Rear-Admiral*
1 Dec 1915:	Transferred to the reserve

Rear-Admiral **Kaoru TAKEUCHI** (22 Sep 1896 - 18 Jan 1971)
10 Jul 1942 - 1 Oct 1945:	Chief of Section 5, Bureau 3, Naval General Staff
1 May 1945:	Promoted to *Rear-Admiral*
1 Oct 1945 - 30 Nov 1945:	Attached to Department of the Navy

Vice-Admiral **Shigetoshi TAKEUCHI** (19 Nov 1871 - 3 Mar 1951)
1 Dec 1918:	Promoted to *Rear-Admiral*
1 Dec 1918 - 30 Mar 1920:	Attached to Naval General Staff
30 Mar 1920 - 15 Nov 1921:	Chief of Staff, Yokosuka Naval District
15 Nov 1921 - 1 Dec 1921:	Commander, 5th Escort Flotilla
1 Dec 1921 - 24 Apr 1922:	Commander, 6th Escort Flotilla

24 Apr 1922 - 1 Sep 1922:	Unassigned
1 Sep 1922 - 1 Dec 1922:	Attached to Naval General Staff
1 Dec 1922:	Promoted to *Vice-Admiral*
1 Dec 1922 - 31 Mar 1923:	Unassigned
31 Mar 1923:	Transferred to the reserve

Rear-Admiral **Yasutami TAKEUCHI** (15 Jul 1882 - 21 Mar 1944)

10 Dec 1928:	Promoted to *Rear-Admiral*
10 Dec 1928 - 30 Nov 1929:	Chief of Shipbuilding Bureau, Yokosuka Naval District
30 Nov 1929 - 1 Dec 1930:	Chief of Oil Bureau, Navy Fuel Yard
1 Dec 1930 - 15 Dec 1930:	Attached to Naval General Staff
24 Dec 1930:	Transferred to the reserve

Rear-Admiral (Engineer) **Yutaka TAKEUCHI** (5 Mar 1877 - 3 Apr 1958)

1 Dec 1921:	Promoted to *Rear-Admiral*
1 Dec 1921 - 1 Dec 1922:	Chief Engineer Officer, 3rd Fleet
1 Dec 1922 - 10 Dec 1922:	Attached to Naval General Staff
10 Dec 1922 - 31 Mar 1923:	Unassigned
31 Mar 1923:	Transferred to the reserve

Rear-Admiral **Tomokazu TAKIGAWA** (22 Jul 1859 - 12 Feb 1923)

22 Nov 1906:	Promoted to *Rear-Admiral*
22 Nov 1906 - 28 Aug 1908:	Chief of Staff, Ryojun Naval District
28 Aug 1908 - 27 Aug 1909:	Unassigned
27 Aug 1909:	Transferred to the reserve

Rear-Admiral **Yoshio TAKITA** (8 Oct 1880 - 20 Nov 1960)

1 Dec 1926 - 10 Dec 1928:	Commander, Sasebo Sailors Corps
10 Dec 1928:	Promoted to *Rear-Admiral*
10 Dec 1928 - 20 Dec 1928:	Attached to Naval General Staff
25 Dec 1928:	Transferred to the reserve

Rear-Admiral **Tomejiro TAMAKI** (31 Aug 1896 - 21 Jun 1943)

1 May 1942 - 21 Jun 1943:	Commander, 7th Submarine Division
21 Jun 1943:	Posthumously promoted to *Rear-Admiral*

Rear-Admiral (Apothecary) **Yuzo TAMAMUSHI** (26 Sep 1890 - Jun 1981)

1 Dec 1936 - 15 Nov 1938:	Instructor, Navy Medical School
15 Nov 1938:	Promoted to *Rear-Admiral (Apothecary)*
15 Nov 1938 - 21 Dec 1938:	Attached to Naval General Staff
21 Dec 1938:	Transferred to the reserve

Vice-Admiral **Chikataka TAMARI** (3 Oct 1853 - 24 Aug 1916)
7 Jan 1905 - 22 Nov 1906:	Chief of Staff, Ryojun Naval District
2 Nov 1905:	Promoted to *Rear-Admiral*
22 Nov 1906 - 28 Aug 1908:	C-in-C, South China Fleet
28 Aug 1908 - 1 Dec 1909:	Commander, Ominato Guard District
1 Dec 1909:	Promoted to *Vice-Admiral*
1 Dec 1909 - 1 Dec 1910:	Commander, Mako Guard District
1 Dec 1910 - 1 Dec 1911:	Unassigned
1 Dec 1911:	Transferred to the reserve

Rear-Admiral **Toshiharu TAMASHIRO** (22 Nov 1885 - 16 Aug 1944)
6 May 1944 - 16 Aug 1944:	Commander, 48th Minesweeper Division
16 Aug 1944:	Posthumously promoted to *Rear-Admiral*

Vice-Admiral **Akira TAMAZAWA** (25 Mar 1881 - 26 Jul 1961)
1 Dec 1927:	Promoted to *Rear-Admiral*
1 Dec 1927 - 1 Dec 1930:	Chief of Shipbuilding Bureau, Kure Navy Yard
1 Dec 1930 - 1 Apr 1933:	Chief of Bureau 3, Naval Shipbuilding Command
1 Dec 1932:	Promoted to *Vice-Admiral*
1 Apr 1933 - 5 Apr 1934:	Chief of Bureau 4, Naval Shipbuilding Command
5 Apr 1934 - 10 Dec 1934:	Attached to Naval Shipbuilding Command
15 Dec 1934:	Transferred to the reserve

Vice-Admiral (Paymaster) **Hiroatsu TAMEMOTO** (24 Oct 1893 - 29 Jun 1959)
30 May 1941 - 26 Dec 1941:	Paymaster-General, China Area Fleet
15 Oct 1941:	Promoted to *Rear-Admiral (Paymaster)*
15 Oct 1941 - 10 Apr 1942:	Chief of 1st Accounting Bureau, Chief of 1st Supply Bureau
10 Apr 1942 - 1 Nov 1942:	Chief of Shanghai Area Transport Bureau
1 Nov 1942 - 1 May 1943:	Paymaster-General, Yokosuka Naval District
1 May 1943 - 15 May 1943:	Attached to Accounting Bureau, Naval Shipbuilding Command
15 May 1943 - 1 Nov 1945:	Chief of Accounting Bureau, Naval Shipbuilding Command
1 May 1945:	Promoted to *Vice-Admiral (Paymaster)*
1 Nov 1945 - 30 Nov 1945:	Attached to Department of the Navy

Rear-Admiral (Surgeon) **Akira TAMURA** (12 Mar 1897 - 16 Jun 1944)
10 Oct 1942 - 16 Jun 1944:	Chief of Bureau 1, Kure Naval Hospital
16 Jun 1944:	Posthumously promoted to *Rear-Admiral (Surgeon)*

Rear-Admiral **Viscount Hiroaki TAMURA** (29 Nov 1875 - 13 Jan 1945)
1 Dec 1924:	Promoted to *Rear-Admiral*
1 Dec 1924 - 22 Aug 1925:	Commander, Yokosuka Defense Force

22 Aug 1925 - 20 Oct 1925:	Attached to Naval General Staff
20 Oct 1925 - 16 Dec 1925:	Unassigned
16 Dec 1925:	Transferred to the reserve

Rear-Admiral **Ryukichi TAMURA** (4 Nov 1890 - 16 Mar 1948)

10 Feb 1944 - Oct 1945:	Commander, 14th Naval Base Force, Commander, 83rd Guard Force
1 May 1944:	Promoted to *Rear-Admiral*

Rear-Admiral **Saburo TAMURA** (3 Nov 1901 - 17 Mar 1945)

17 Mar 1945:	Posthumously promoted to *Rear-Admiral*

Vice-Admiral **Suguru TAMURA** (7 Oct 1888 - 25 Feb 1967)

15 Nov 1940:	Promoted to *Rear-Admiral*
15 Nov 1940 - 10 Jan 1942:	Chief of Ordnance Bureau, Sasebo Navy Yard
10 Jan 1942 - 1 Oct 1943:	Chief Supervisor for Construction & Ordnance, Naval Shipbuilding Command
1 Oct 1943 - 1 Nov 1945:	Commander, Hikari Navy Yard
1 May 1944:	Promoted to *Vice-Admiral*

Rear-Admiral (Engineer) **Ototetsu TANABE** (28 Jul 1860 - 3 Dec 1932)

12 Dec 1905 - 10 Dec 1920:	Chief Engineer Officer, Kure Naval District
13 Mar 1907:	Promoted to *Rear-Admiral*
10 Dec 1908 - 10 Dec 1909:	Unassigned
10 Dec 1909:	Transferred to the reserve

Vice-Admiral (Surgeon) **Yutaka TANABE** (1 Mar 1893 - 21 Jul 1950)

22 Sep 1941 - 1 Nov 1943:	Chief of Medical Bureau, Sasebo Navy Yard
15 Oct 1941:	Promoted to *Rear-Admiral (Surgeon)*
1 Nov 1943 - 5 Feb 1945:	Director, Minato Naval Hospital
5 Feb 1945 - 1 Apr 1945:	Director, Kamo Naval Hospital
1 Apr 1945 - 1 Oct 1945:	Commandant, Kamo Navy Sanitary School
1 May 1945:	Promoted to *Vice-Admiral (Surgeon)*
1 Oct 1945 - 5 Oct 1945:	Attached to Kure Naval District

Vice-Admiral (Surgeon) **Asazo TANAKA** (9 May 1885 - 15 Dec 1955)

1 Dec 1932 - 15 Nov 1933:	Chief Surgeon, Combined Fleet, Chief Surgeon, 1st Fleet
15 Nov 1933:	Promoted to *Rear-Admiral (Surgeon)*
15 Nov 1933 - 15 Nov 1934:	Chief of Bureau 2, Yokosuka Naval Hospital
15 Nov 1934 - 15 Nov 1935:	Director, Kure Naval Hospital, Chief Surgeon, Kure Naval District
15 Nov 1935 - 1 Dec 1937:	Director, Yokosuka Naval Hospital, Chief Surgeon, Yokosuka Naval District

1 Dec 1937:	Promoted to *Vice-Admiral (Surgeon)*
1 Dec 1937 - 15 Nov 1939:	Commandant, Navy Medical School
15 Nov 1939 - 15 Mar 1940:	Attached to Naval General Staff
21 Mar 1940:	Transferred to the reserve

Vice-Admiral (Surgeon) **Higotaro TANAKA** (1 Mar 1885 - 31 Jan 1949)
15 Nov 1935:	Promoted to *Rear-Admiral (Surgeon)*
15 Nov 1935 - 1 Dec 1937:	Instructor, Navy Medical School
1 Dec 1937 - 15 Nov 1938:	Chief Instructor, Navy Medical School
15 Nov 1938 - 15 Nov 1939:	Director, Sasebo Naval Hospital, Chief Surgeon, Sasebo Naval District
15 Nov 1939:	Promoted to *Vice-Admiral (Surgeon)*
15 Nov 1939 - 15 Oct 1941:	Commandant, Navy Medical School
15 Oct 1941 - 25 Oct 1943:	Chief of Naval Medical Service
25 Oct 1943 - 19 Feb 1944:	Attached to Naval General Staff
21 Feb 1944:	Transferred to the reserve

Rear-Admiral **Hiroshi TANAKA** (7 Nov 1885 - 29 Jan 1942)
1 Apr 1932 - 1 Jun 1934:	Chief of Steel Bureau, Kure Navy Yard
1 Jun 1934 - 15 Nov 1934:	Attached to Kure Naval District
15 Nov 1934:	Promoted to *Rear-Admiral*
15 Nov 1934 - 10 Dec 1934:	Attached to Naval Shipbuilding Command
15 Dec 1934:	Transferred to the reserve

Rear-Admiral **Isamu TANAKA** (18 Sep 1881 - 10 Nov 1935)
2 Feb 1925 - 1 Dec 1926:	Chief of Naval Personnel, Kure Naval District
1 Dec 1926:	Promoted to *Rear-Admiral*
1 Dec 1926 - 1 Mar 1927:	Attached to Kure Naval District
1 Mar 1927 - 20 Mar 1927:	Attached to Naval General Staff
20 Mar 1927 - 10 Apr 1927:	Unassigned
10 Apr 1927:	Transferred to the reserve

Rear-Admiral **Jo TANAKA** (28 Oct 1898 - 25 Oct 1944)
6 Jun 1944 - 25 Oct 1944:	Captain, Heavy Cruiser *"Chokai"*
25 Oct 1944:	Posthumously promoted to *Rear-Admiral*

Rear-Admiral **Kikumatsu TANAKA** (27 Jan 1895 - 7 Oct 1964)
10 Mar 1943 - 1 Nov 1944:	Chief of Naval Personnel, Kure Naval District
1 May 1943:	Promoted to *Rear-Admiral*
1 Nov 1944 - 17 Nov 1944:	Staff officer, 2nd Southern Expeditionary Fleet
17 Nov 1944 - Oct 1945:	Commander, 21st Naval Base Force
1 Aug 1945 - Oct 1945:	Commander of Naval Land Units, Surabaya Naval Base

Vice-Admiral **Kotaro TANAKA** (26 Mar 1868 - 9 Nov 1939)
1 Dec 1917:	Promoted to *Rear-Admiral*
1 Dec 1917 - 27 Jan 1919:	Instructor, Naval College
27 Jan 1919 - 8 Nov 1919:	Staff officer, Vladivostok Expeditionary Army
8 Nov 1919 - 1 Jun 1922:	Chief of Bureau 3, Naval General Staff
1 Jun 1922:	Promoted to *Vice-Admiral*
1 Jun 1922 - 1 Oct 1922:	Member, Admirals Committee
1 Oct 1922 - 31 Mar 1923:	Unassigned
31 Mar 1923:	Transferred to the reserve

Rear-Admiral **Minoru TANAKA** (4 Jun 1894 - 27 Sep 1977)
1 Apr 1944 - 15 Sep 1944:	Commander, Takaza Navy Yard
1 May 1944:	Promoted to *Rear-Admiral*
15 Sep 1944 - 25 Nov 1944:	Commander, 101st Air Flotilla
25 Nov 1944 - 20 Jul 1945:	Chief of Staff, 101st Air Flotilla
20 Jul 1945 - 10 Oct 1945:	Commander, 31st Air Arsenal

Vice-Admiral **Morihide TANAKA** (4 Aug 1866 - ?)
1 Dec 1912:	Promoted to *Rear-Admiral*
1 Dec 1912 - 1 Dec 1913:	Chief of Ordnance Bureau, Sasebo Navy Yard
1 Dec 1913 - 13 Dec 1915:	Commander, Maizuru Navy Yard
13 Dec 1915 - 1 Dec 1916:	Commander, Sasebo Navy Yard
1 Dec 1916:	Promoted to *Vice-Admiral*
1 Dec 1916 - 4 Nov 1918:	Commander, Yokosuka Navy Yard
10 Nov 1918:	Transferred to the reserve

Vice-Admiral **Raizo TANAKA** (27 Apr 1892 - 9 Jul 1969)
1 May 1941 - 15 Sep 1941:	Commander, 6th Submarine Flotilla
15 Sep 1941 - 29 Dec 1942:	Commander, 2nd Destroyer Flotilla
15 Oct 1941:	Promoted to *Rear-Admiral*
29 Dec 1942 - 5 Feb 1943:	Attached to Naval General Staff
5 Feb 1943 - 1 Oct 1943:	Commander, Maizuru Guard Force
1 Oct 1943 - Oct 1945:	Commander, 13th Auxiliary Naval Base Force
15 Oct 1944:	Promoted to *Vice-Admiral*

Rear-Admiral (Surgeon) **Takehito TANAKA** (11 Oct 1873 - 7 Jun 1923)
24 Apr 1920 - 7 Jun 1923:	Chief Surgeon, Naval Academy
7 Jun 1923:	Posthumously promoted to *Rear-Admiral (Surgeon)*

Rear-Admiral (Engineer) **Tatsuo TANAKA** (27 May 1877 - 28 Mar 1946)
1 Oct 1920 - 1 Dec 1921:	Supervisor for Construction & Ordnance, Naval Shipbuilding Command
1 Dec 1921:	Promoted to *Rear-Admiral*

1 Dec 1921 - 10 Dec 1921:	Attached to Yokosuka Naval District
10 Dec 1921 - 6 May 1922:	Unassigned
6 May 1922:	Transferred to the reserve

Rear-Admiral **Tatsuzo TANAKA** (24 Jul 1877 - 11 Nov 1926)
1 Apr 1923 - 1 Aug 1925:	Chief of Aircraft Bureau, Hiro Navy Yard
1 Dec 1923:	Promoted to *Rear-Admiral*
1 Aug 1925 - 11 Nov 1926:	Chief of Ordnance Bureau, Yokosuka Navy Yard

Rear-Admiral **Yasuro TANAKA** (5 Oct 1893 - 30 Nov 1966)
1 May 1943:	Promoted to *Rear-Admiral*
1 May 1943 - 1 Feb 1944:	Chief of Torpedo Bureau, Kawatana Navy Yard
1 Feb 1944 - 15 Oct 1945:	Chief of Bureau 3, Naval Air Command
9 Feb 1944 - 25 May 1944:	Chief of Bureau 4, Naval Air Command
23 Dec 1944 - 1 Mar 1945:	Chief of Bureau 2, Naval Air Command
1 Mar 1945 - 15 Oct 1945:	Chief of Bureau 4, Naval Air Command

Rear-Admiral **Hitoshi TANAMACHI** (17 Aug 1903 - 13 Jun 1945)
5 Apr 1945 - 13 Jun 1945:	Staff officer, Combined Fleet
13 Jun 1945:	Posthumously promoted to *Rear-Admiral*

Rear-Admiral (Paymaster) **Isokichi TANAMACHI** (18 Apr 1875 - 11 Jan 1940)
1 Dec 1924 - 20 Nov 1925:	Chief of Coal Mining Bureau, Navy Fuel Yard
20 Nov 1925 - 1 Dec 1925:	Attached to Naval General Staff
1 Dec 1925:	Promoted to *Rear-Admiral*
16 Dec 1925:	Transferred to the reserve

Rear-Admiral **Sakae TANEDA** (31 Aug 1890 - 1 Mar 1987)
15 Nov 1940:	Promoted to *Rear-Admiral*
15 Nov 1940 - 21 Apr 1941:	Chief of Oil Bureau, Navy Fuel Yard
21 Apr 1941 - 1 Oct 1941:	Chief of Oil Refining Bureau, 3rd Navy Fuel Yard
1 Oct 1941 - 25 Oct 1941:	Attached to Naval General Staff
27 Oct 1941:	Transferred to the reserve

Vice-Admiral **Uhachiro TANEDA** (8 Dec 1863 - 20 Nov 1932)
10 Nov 1903 - 18 Jan 1911:	Chief of Ordnance Bureau, Yokosuka Navy Yard
26 Feb 1909:	Promoted to *General (Ordnance)*
18 Jan 1911 - 1 Dec 1914:	Chief of Gunnery Bureau, Kure Navy Yard
1 Dec 1914:	Promoted to *General (Ordnance), Senior grade*
1 Dec 1914 - 1 Nov 1915:	Commander, Navy Ordnance Arsenal
1 Nov 1915 - 1 Oct 1920:	Chief of Bureau 1, Naval Technical Command
23 Sep 1919:	Redesignated *Vice-Admiral*
1 Dec 1919 - 12 Nov 1920:	Chief of Bureau 6, Naval Technical Command

1 Oct 1920 - 12 Nov 1920:	Chief of Bureau 6, Naval Shipbuilding Command
1 Oct 1920 - 1 Dec 1921:	Chief of Bureau 1, Naval Shipbuilding Command
1 Dec 1921 - 10 Apr 1922:	Attached to Naval Shipbuilding Command
10 Apr 1922 - 31 Mar 1923:	Unassigned
31 Mar 1923:	Transferred to the reserve

Rear-Admiral **Kunji TANGE** (23 Nov 1885 - 6 May 1962)

15 Nov 1935:	Promoted to *Rear-Admiral*
15 Nov 1935 - 16 Nov 1936:	Chief of Shipbuilding Bureau, Sasebo Naval District
16 Nov 1936 - 15 Dec 1936:	Attached to Naval General Staff
22 Dec 1936:	Transferred to the reserve

Rear-Admiral **Keikichiro TANI** (24 Apr 1895 - ?)

15 Nov 1939 - 1 Jul 1943:	Chief of Communications Research Bureau, Yokosuka Navy Yard
1 Nov 1942:	Promoted to *Rear-Admiral*
1 Jul 1943 - 15 Feb 1945:	Attached to Technical Research Department
15 Feb 1945 - 20 Oct 1945:	Attached to 2nd Technical Arsenal

Admiral **Naomi TANIGUCHI** (17 Mar 1870 - 30 Oct 1941)

1 Dec 1917:	Promoted to *Rear-Admiral*
1 Dec 1917 - 1 Dec 1920:	Chief of Naval Personnel, Department of the Navy
1 Dec 1920 - 1 Aug 1921:	Commander, Mako Guard District
1 Aug 1921 - 15 Apr 1922:	Member, Admirals Committee
1 Dec 1921:	Promoted to *Vice-Admiral*
15 Apr 1922 - 1 Mar 1923:	C-in-C, Training Fleet
1 Mar 1923 - 1 Apr 1923:	Member, Admirals Committee
1 Apr 1923 - 18 Sep 1925:	Commandant of the Naval Academy
18 Sep 1925 - 10 Dec 1926:	C-in-C, 2nd Fleet
10 Dec 1926 - 10 Dec 1928:	Admiral Commanding, Kure Naval District
2 Apr 1928:	Promoted to *Admiral*
10 Dec 1928 - 11 Nov 1929:	C-in-C, Combined Fleet, C-in-C, 1st Fleet
11 Nov 1929 - 11 Jun 1930:	Admiral Commanding, Kure Naval District
11 Jun 1930 - 2 Feb 1932:	Chief of the Naval General Staff, Member, Admirals Committee
2 Feb 1932 - 1 Sep 1933:	Navy Councillor
1 Sep 1933:	Transferred to the reserve

Vice-Admiral **Yoshisada TANIGUCHI** (23 May 1880 - 2 Sep 1964)

1 Sep 1924 - 1 Dec 1927:	Chief of Gunnery Bureau, Kure Navy Yard
1 Dec 1925:	Promoted to *Rear-Admiral*

1 Dec 1927 - 30 Nov 1929:	Commander, Sasebo Navy Yard
30 Nov 1929:	Promoted to *Vice-Admiral*
30 Nov 1929 - 15 Dec 1929:	Attached to Naval General Staff
25 Dec 1929:	Transferred to the reserve

Rear-Admiral **Tamotsu TANII** (6 Nov 1899 - 21 Nov 1944)

18 Dec 1943 - 21 Nov 1944:	Commander, 17th Destroyer Division
21 Nov 1944:	Posthumously promoted to *Rear-Admiral*

Rear-Admiral **Keizo TANIMOTO** (20 Jul 1894 - 27 Jul 1980)

10 Aug 1944 - 10 Oct 1945:	Commander, Maizuru Guard Force
1 May 1945:	Promoted to *Rear-Admiral*
20 Jul 1945 - 10 Oct 1945:	Commander, Maizuru Combined Marine Force

Vice-Admiral **Umataro TANIMOTO** (20 Apr 1886 - 11 Nov 1942)

15 Nov 1934:	Promoted to *Rear-Admiral*
15 Nov 1934 - 15 Nov 1935:	Chief of Staff, Kure Naval District
15 Nov 1935 - 1 Dec 1936:	Commander, 8th Escort Flotilla
1 Dec 1936 - 1 Dec 1937:	Commander, 11th Escort Flotilla
1 Dec 1937 - 1 Aug 1938:	Commander, Manchuria Expeditionary Force
1 Aug 1938 - 1 Apr 1939:	C-in-C, Training Fleet
15 Oct 1938:	Promoted to *Vice-Admiral*
1 Apr 1939 - 15 Nov 1939:	Attached to Naval General Staff
15 Nov 1939 - 15 Nov 1940:	C-in-C, 1st China Expeditionary Fleet
15 Nov 1940 - 10 Apr 1941:	Attached to Naval General Staff
10 Apr 1941 - 20 Nov 1941:	Commander, Kainan Guard District
20 Nov 1941 - 11 Nov 1942:	Admiral Commanding, Sasebo Naval District

Vice-Admiral **Toyotaro TANIMURA** (2 Nov 1885 - 28 Mar 1972)

1 Sep 1933 - 15 Nov 1934:	Chief of Ordnance Bureau, Yokosuka Navy Yard
15 Nov 1933:	Promoted to *Rear-Admiral*
15 Nov 1934 - 15 Nov 1940:	Chief of Bureau 1, Naval Shipbuilding Command
1 Dec 1937:	Promoted to *Vice-Admiral*
25 Mar 1938 - 15 Nov 1938:	Chief of Bureau 6, Naval Shipbuilding Command
15 Nov 1940 - 15 Mar 1941:	Attached to Naval Shipbuilding Command
20 Mar:	Transferred to the reserve

Rear-Admiral **Hiroo TANJI** (15 Dec 1853 - 8 Jan 1917)

24 May 1902 - 2 Nov 1905:	Commander, Maizuru Sailors Corps
2 Nov 1905:	Promoted to *Rear-Admiral*
2 Nov 1905 - 30 Nov 1906:	Unassigned
30 Nov 1906:	Transferred to the reserve

Vice-Admiral (Paymaster) **Toshio TANNAWA** (1 Oct 1883 - 14 Dec 1970)
13 Apr 1927 - 30 Nov 1929:	Chief of Accounting Bureau, Kure Navy Yard
10 Dec 1928:	Promoted to *Rear-Admiral (Paymaster)*
30 Nov 1929 - 1 Dec 1932:	Paymaster-General, Sasebo Naval District
1 Dec 1932 - 1 Dec 1933:	Paymaster-General, Kure Naval District
15 Nov 1933:	Promoted to *Vice- Admiral (Paymaster)*
1 Dec 1933 - 26 Mar 1934:	Attached to Naval General Staff
31 Mar 1934:	Transferred to the reserve

Rear-Admiral **Katsutaro TAOKA** (6 Sep 1882 - 1 Sep 1956)
1 Dec 1926:	Promoted to *Rear-Admiral*
1 Dec 1926 - 1 Dec 1927:	Commander, Sasebo Defense Force
1 Dec 1927 - 15 Dec 1927:	Attached to Naval General Staff
25 Dec 1927:	Transferred to the reserve

Rear-Admiral **Sohei TASHIRO** (8 Jan 1891 - 9 Dec 1943)
15 Oct 1941:	Promoted to *Rear-Admiral*
15 Oct 1941 - 15 Nov 1942:	Commander, Sasebo Defense Flotilla
15 Nov 1942 - 6 Nov 1943:	Chief of Bureau 6, Naval Shipbuilding Command
6 Nov 1943 - 9 Dec 1943:	Attached to Naval Shipbuilding Command

Rear-Admiral (Surgeon) **Itaru TATENO** (1 Aug 1875 - 24 Feb 1960)
15 Apr 1922 - 1 Dec 1923:	Chief of Bureau 1, Yokosuka Naval Hospital
1 Dec 1922:	Promoted to *Rear-Admiral (Surgeon)*
1 Dec 1923 - 1 Dec 1924:	Director, Yokosuka Naval Hospital, Chief Surgeon, Yokosuka Naval District
1 Dec 1924 - 1 Jun 1925:	Attached to Naval General Staff
1 Jun 1925 - 16 Dec 1925:	Unassigned
16 Dec 1925:	Transferred to the reserve

Vice-Admiral **Tokujiro TATENO** (16 Feb 1879 - 31 Jan 1936)
1 Apr 1923 - 16 Dec 1924:	Chief of Supply Bureau, Kure Naval District
1 Dec 1924:	Promoted to *Rear-Admiral*
16 Dec 1924 - 1 Dec 1926:	Chief of Staff, Kure Naval District
1 Dec 1926 - 1 Dec 1927:	Commander, 3rd Escort Flotilla
1 Dec 1927 - 30 Nov 1929:	Commander, Yokosuka Navy Yard
10 Dec 1928:	Promoted to *Vice-Admiral*
30 Nov 1929 - 10 Jun 1930:	Attached to Naval General Staff
20 Jun 1930:	Transferred to the reserve

Rear-Admiral **Yoshioki TAWARA** (28 Aug 1894 - 5 May 1944)
25 Dec 1943 - 5 May 1944:	Captain, Battleship *"Yamashiro"*
1 May 1944:	Promoted to *Rear-Admiral*

Vice-Admiral **Minoru TAYUI** (20 Jan 1890 - 28 Jun 1977)
1 Dec 1937:	Promoted to *Rear-Admiral*
1 Dec 1937 - 1 Feb 1938:	Chief of Staff, Yokosuka Naval District
1 Feb 1938 - 15 Dec 1938:	Chief of Staff, 5th Fleet
15 Dec 1938 - 10 Jan 1939:	Attached to Naval General Staff
10 Jan 1939 - 2 Oct 1939:	Naval Attache, Manchurai
2 Oct 1939 - 15 Nov 1939:	Attached to Naval General Staff
15 Nov 1939 - 15 Nov 1940:	Commander, 6th Escort Flotilla
15 Nov 1940 - 1 Mar 1942:	Commandant, Navigation School
15 Oct 1941:	Promoted to *Vice-Admiral*
1 Mar 1942 - 16 Mar 1942:	Staff officer, China Area Fleet
16 Mar 1942 - 1 Sep 1943:	Chief of Staff, China Area Fleet
1 Sep 1943 - 20 Sep 1943:	Attached to Naval General Staff
20 Sep 1943 - 13 Jan 1945:	C-in-C, 1st Southern Expeditionary Fleet
8 Jan 1945 - 13 Jan 1945:	C-in-C, 13th Air Fleet
13 Jan 1945 - 1 Mar 1945:	Attached to Naval General Staff
1 Mar 1945 - 15 Nov 1945:	Admiral Commanding, Maizuru Naval District
10 Jul 1945 - 25 Aug 1945:	C-in-C, 1st Escort Fleet
15 Nov 1945 - 30 Nov 1945:	Attached to Department of the Navy

Rear-Admiral **Einojo TERADA** (? - 13 Jan 1943)
15 Sep 1941 - 13 Jan 1943:	Commander, 53rd Guard Force
13 Jan 1943:	Posthumously promoted to *Rear-Admiral*

Rear-Admiral **Kokichi TERADA** (11 Aug 1886 - 24 Jun 1963)
27 Aug 1937 - 15 Dec 1938:	Commander, 3rd Air Flotilla
1 Dec 1937:	Promoted to *Rear-Admiral*
15 Dec 1938 - 1 Dec 1939:	Attached to Naval General Staff
1 Dec 1939 - 1 Nov 1940:	Commander, 12th Combined Air Division
1 Nov 1940 - 16 Dec 1940:	Attached to Naval General Staff
21 Dec 1940:	Transferred to the reserve

Rear-Admiral **Suketsugu TERADA** (14 Jul 1888 - 6 Aug 1962)
4 Nov 1939 - 6 Jan 1940:	Attached to Naval General Staff
15 Nov 1939:	Promoted to *Rear-Admiral*
6 Jan 1940 - 1 Jun 1943:	Staff officer, China Area Fleet
1 Jun 1943 - 25 Jun 1943:	Attached to Naval General Staff
25 Jun 1943:	Demobilized

Vice-Admiral **Izo TERAGAKI** (28 Jan 1857 - 1 Jun 1938)
14 Jun 1905 - 22 Nov 1906:	Chief of Staff, Yokosuka Naval District
2 Nov 1905:	Promoted to *Rear-Admiral*
22 Nov 1906 - 15 May 1908:	C-in-C, 2nd Fleet

15 May 1908 - 28 Aug 1908:	Commander, Maizuru Torpedo Corps
28 Aug 1908 - 24 Dec 1908:	C-in-C, South China Fleet
24 Dec 1908 - 1 Dec 1910:	C-in-C, 3rd Fleet
1 Dec 1909:	Promoted to *Vice-Admiral*
1 Dec 1910 - 25 Sep 1911:	Commander, Takeshiki Guard District
25 Sep 1911 - 25 Sep 1912:	Unassigned
25 Sep 1912:	Transferred to the reserve

Rear-Admiral **Keizo TERAGAKI** (1 Jan 1891 - 20 Apr 1943)

27 Nov 1942 - 20 Apr 1943:	Commander, 4th Patrol Boat Division
20 Apr 1943:	Posthumously promoted to *Rear-Admiral*

Vice-Admiral **Ken TERAJIMA** (23 Sep 1882 - 30 Jul 1972)

1 Dec 1927:	Promoted to *Rear-Admiral*
1 Dec 1927 - 10 Dec 1928:	Chief of Staff, 2nd Fleet
10 Dec 1928 - 30 Nov 1929:	Chief of Staff, Combined Fleet, Chief of Staff, 1st Fleet
30 Nov 1929 - 10 Jun 1930:	Attached to Naval General Staff
10 Jun 1930 - 16 Jun 1932:	Chief of Naval Training Bureau, Department of the Navy
12 May 1932 - 15 Sep 1933:	Chief, Bureau of Naval Affairs, Department of the Navy, Member, Admirals Committee
1 Dec 1932:	Promoted to *Vice-Admiral*
15 Sep 1933 - 3 Oct 1933:	C-in-C, Training Fleet
3 Oct 1933 - 26 Mar 1934:	Attached to Naval General Staff
31 Mar 1934:	Transferred to the reserve

Rear-Admiral (Surgeon) **Masafumi TERAKADO** (20 Sep 1899 - 7 Apr 1945)

10 Dec 1944 - 7 Apr 1945:	Chief Surgeon, 2nd Fleet
7 Apr 1945:	Posthumously promoted to *Rear-Admiral (Surgeon)*

Rear-Admiral **Takeji TERAMOTO** (25 Feb 1884 - 2 Dec 1958)

1 Dec 1931 - 1 Dec 1932:	Attached to Naval Training Bureau, Department of the Navy
1 Dec 1932:	Promoted to *Rear-Admiral*
1 Dec 1932 - 11 Dec 1933:	Attached to Naval General Staff
15 Dec 1933:	Transferred to the reserve

Rear-Admiral **Heigo TERAOKA** (7 Jul 1877 - 25 Jul 1977)

1 Dec 1923:	Promoted to *Rear-Admiral*
1 Dec 1923 - 2 Feb 1925:	Chief of Staff, Yokosuka Naval District
2 Feb 1925 - 20 Apr 1925:	Attached to Naval General Staff

20 Apr 1925 - 1 Dec 1925:	Commander, 3rd Escort Flotilla
1 Dec 1925 - 15 Sep 1926:	Attached to Naval General Staff
15 Sep 1926 - 10 Apr 1927:	Unassigned
10 Apr 1927:	Transferred to the reserve

Vice-Admiral **Kinpei TERAOKA** (13 Mar 1891 - 2 May 1984)

15 Nov 1939:	Promoted to *Rear-Admiral*
15 Nov 1939 - 1 Dec 1939:	Staff officer, 2nd China Expeditionary Fleet
1 Dec 1939 - 15 Nov 1940:	Commander, 3rd Combined Air Division
15 Nov 1940 - 25 Mar 1941:	Chief Instructor, Naval Academy
25 Mar 1941 - 14 Jan 1944:	Staff officer, China Area Fleet
1 Nov 1943:	Promoted to *Vice-Admiral*
14 Jan 1944 - 19 Feb 1944:	Attached to Naval General Staff
19 Feb 1944 - 7 Aug 1944:	Chief of Air Training Units HQ, Commander, 11th Combined Air Division
7 Aug 1944 - 20 Oct 1944:	C-in-C, 1st Air Fleet
20 Oct 1944 - 11 Nov 1944:	Attached to Naval General Staff
11 Nov 1944 - 26 Aug 1945:	C-in-C, 3rd Air Fleet
26 Aug 1945 - 15 Sep 1945:	Attached to Naval General Staff
15 Sep 1945:	Transferred to the reserve

Rear-Admiral **Sakae TERAYAMA** (10 Apr 1894 - 17 Oct 1965)

30 Apr 1944 - 15 Jan 1945:	Chief Engineer Officer, Combined Fleet
1 May 1944:	Promoted to *Rear-Admiral*
15 Jan 1945 - 1 Mar 1945:	Commandant, Naval Engineering School
1 Mar 1945 - 15 May 1945:	Commandant, Yokosuka Naval Engineering School
15 May 1945 - 20 May 1945:	Attached to Yokosuka Naval District
20 May 1945 - 10 Jun 1945:	Attached to Naval Shipbuilding Command
10 Jun 1945 - 10 Aug 1945:	Supervisor for Construction, Naval Shipbuilding Command, Supervisor for Ordnance, Naval Air Command
10 Aug 1945 - 1 Nov 1945:	Chief of Nagasaki Branch, Kyushu Area Supervisor Office, Department of Military Supply
1 Nov 1945 - 20 Nov 1945:	Attached to Sasebo Naval District

Rear-Admiral **Goro TEZUKA** (5 Mar 1891 - 7 Oct 1943)

24 Jul 1943 - 7 Oct 1943:	Commander, 4th Harbor
7 Oct 1943:	Posthumously promoted to *Rear-Admiral*

Admiral **Sojiro TOCHINAI** (8 Jun 1866 - 12 Jul 1932)

1 Dec 1909:	Promoted to *Rear-Admiral*
1 Dec 1909 - 20 Apr 1912:	Chief, Bureau of Naval Affairs, Member, Admirals Committee

20 Apr 1912 - 1 May 1913:	C-in-C, Training Fleet
1 May 1913 - 24 May 1913:	Attached to Yokosuka Naval District
24 May 1913 - 1 Dec 1913:	Commander, Ominato Guard District
1 Dec 1913 - 18 Aug 1914:	Commander, Yokosuka Navy Yard
29 May 1914:	Promoted to *Vice-Admiral*
18 Aug 1914 - 1 Oct 1914:	C-in-C, 2nd Fleet
1 Oct 1914 - 1 Dec 1914:	C-in-C, 1st Fleet
1 Dec 1914 - 6 Aug 1915:	Commander, 4th Escort Flotilla
6 Aug 1915 - 13 Dec 1915:	Commander, 3rd Escort Flotilla
13 Dec 1915 - 1 Sep 1917:	Chief of Naval Technical Command, Member, Admirals Committee
1 Sep 1917 - 24 Aug 1920:	Deputy Minister of the Navy, Chief of Construction Bureau, Department of the Navy
12 Dec 1917 - 24 Aug 1920:	Member, Admirals Committee
16 Aug 1920:	Promoted to *Admiral*
24 Aug 1920 - 31 Oct 1920:	C-in-C, Combined Fleet
24 Aug 1920 - 27 Jul 1922:	C-in-C, 1st Fleet
1 May 1921 - 31 Oct 1921:	C-in-C, Combined Fleet
27 Jul 1922 - 1 Jun 1923:	Admiral Commanding, Sasebo Naval District
1 Jun 1923 - 1 Dec 1923:	Navy Councillor
1 Dec 1923 - 25 Feb 1924:	Unassigned
25 Feb 1924:	Transferred to the reserve

Rear-Admiral **Isao TODO** (5 Sep 1884 - 4 May 1942)
12 Aug 1941 - 4 May 1942:	Captain, Auxiliary Minelayer *"Kinjo-maru"*
4 May 1942:	Posthumously promoted to *Rear-Admiral*

Rear-Admiral **Ichiro TOGAMI** (? - 6 Jan 1943)
20 May 1942 - 6 Jan 1943:	Captain, Submarine *"I-3"*
6 Jan 1943:	Posthumously promoted 2 grades to *Rear-Admiral*

Vice-Admiral **Takamoto TOGARI** (17 May 1887 - 5 Feb 1959)
1 Dec 1930 - 25 Jan 1936:	Naval Attache, France
15 Nov 1935:	Promoted to *Rear-Admiral*
25 Jan 1936 - 1 Jun 1936:	Attached to Naval General Staff
1 Jun 1936 - 1 Dec 1936:	Commander, 3rd Air Flotilla
1 Dec 1936 - 15 Dec 1938:	Chief of Staff, Kure Naval District
15 Dec 1938 - 15 Dec 1939:	Attached to Naval General Staff
15 Nov 1939:	Promoted to *Vice-Admiral*
21 Dec 1939:	Transferred to the reserve
10 Nov 1941 - 20 Nov 1941:	Recalled; Staff officer, Southern Expeditionary Fleet
20 Nov 1941 - 4 Dec 1942:	Commander, 11th Naval Base Force

4 Dec 1942 - 21 Dec 1942:   Attached to Naval General Staff
21 Dec 1942:   Demobilized

Fleet Admiral **Marquis Heihachiro TOGO** (22 Dec 1847 - 30 May 1934)
16 Feb 1895:   Promoted to *Rear-Admiral*
16 Feb 1895 - 16 Nov 1895:   C-in-C, Readiness Fleet
16 Nov 1895 - 19 Jan 1899:   Member, Admirals Committee
23 Mar 1896 - 5 Nov 1896:   Commandant of the Naval College
1 Feb 1898 - 19 Jan 1899:   Commandant of the Naval College
14 May 1898:   Promoted to *Vice-Admiral*
19 Jan 1899 - 20 May 1900:   Admiral Commanding, Sasebo Naval District
20 May 1900 - 1 Oct 1901:   C-in-C, Readiness Fleet
1 Oct 1901 - 19 Oct 1903:   Admiral Commanding, Maizuru Naval District
19 Oct 1903 - 28 Dec 1903:   C-in-C, Readiness Fleet
28 Dec 1903 - 20 Dec 1905:   C-in-C, Combined Fleet,
                             C-in-C, 1st Fleet
6 Jun 1904:   Promoted to *Admiral*
20 Dec 1905 - 1 Dec 1909:   Chief of the Naval General Staff,
                             Member, Admirals Committee
1 Dec 1909 - 30 May 1934:   Navy Councillor
21 Apr 1913:   Appointed *Fleet Admiral*

Rear-Admiral **Jiro TOGO**   (24 May 1892 - 23 Dec 1947)
1 Apr 1945 - 30 Nov 1945:   Chief of Yamaguchi Area Personnel Bureau
1 May 1945:   Promoted to *Rear-Admiral*

Vice-Admiral **Kichitaro TOGO**   (14 Dec 1866 - 26 Oct 1942)
18 Jun 1912 - 1 Dec 1913:   Attached to Naval General Staff
1 Dec 1912:   Promoted to *Rear-Admiral*
1 Dec 1913 - 1 Dec 1914:   Commandant, Naval Gunnery School
1 Dec 1914 - 6 Aug 1915:   Commander, 1st Escort Flotilla
6 Aug 1915 - 1 Dec 1916:   Commander, Southern Island Defense Force
1 Dec 1916:   Promoted to *Vice-Admiral*
1 Dec 1916 - 1 Dec 1918:   Commander, Chinkai Guard District
1 Dec 1918 - 1 Dec 1919:   Member, Admirals Committee
1 Dec 1919 - 1 Aug 1920:   Unassigned
1 Aug 1920:   Transferred to the reserve

Vice-Admiral **Masamichi TOGO** (1 Mar 1852 - 4 Jan 1906)
24 May 1902:   Promoted to *Rear-Admiral*
24 May 1902 - 28 Dec 1903:   Commandant of the Naval Academy
28 Dec 1903 - 13 Nov 1905:   C-in-C, 3rd Fleet,
                             Commander, 6th Escort Flotilla
13 Nov 1905 - 12 Dec 1905:   C-in-C, 4th Fleet

30 Nov 1905: Promoted to *Vice-Admiral*
12 Dec 1905 - 4 Jan 1906: Member, Admirals Committee

Rear-Admiral **Minoru TOGO** (10 Sep 1890 - 22 Apr 1962)
1 Nov 1943: Promoted to *Rear-Admiral*
1 Nov 1943 - 15 Nov 1943: Attached to Yokosuka Naval District
15 Nov 1943 - 15 Dec 1943: Attached to Naval General Staff
15 Dec 1943 - 20 Dec 1943: Unassigned
20 Dec 1943 - 1 Aug 1945: Attached to Naval General Staff
1 Aug 1945: Demobilized

Rear-Admiral **Seinosuke TOGO** (15 Feb 1866 - 22 Jan 1942)
1 Dec 1912: Promoted to *Rear-Admiral*
1 Dec 1912 - 1 Apr 1913: Chief of Staff, Maizuru Naval District
1 Apr 1913 - 1 Dec 1913: Unassigned
1 Dec 1913: Transferred to the reserve

Rear-Admiral **Meiji TOJO** (15 Dec 1871 - 7 May 1932)
6 Nov 1916 - 18 Oct 1918: Chief of Staff, Ominato Guard District
20 Aug 1919 - 1 Dec 1919: Attached to the Government of Korea
1 Dec 1919: Promoted to *Rear-Admiral*
1 Dec 1919 - 1 Aug 1920: Unassigned
1 Aug 1920: Transferred to the reserve

Rear-Admiral **Yuzo TOKAI** (14 Mar 1877 - 3 Jul 1950)
1 Dec 1921 - 1 Apr 1923: Chief of Shipbuilding Bureau, Maizuru Navy Yard
1 Apr 1923 - 1 Dec 1923: Attached to Bureau 4, Naval Shipbuilding Command
1 Dec 1923: Promoted to *Rear-Admiral*
1 Dec 1923 - 25 Feb 1924: Unassigned
25 Feb 1924: Transferred to the reserve

General (Paymaster) **Yutaka TOKI** (18 Dec 1847 - 5 Aug 1907)
30 Jun 1899 - 30 Jun 1901: Chief of Navy Legal Bureau, Department of the Navy
30 Jun 1901: Promoted to *General (Paymaster)*
30 Jun 1901: Transferred to the reserve

Rear-Admiral (Paymaster) **Gonzo TOKITA** (22 Aug 1897 - 19 Mar 1981)
10 Jul 1944 - Nov 1945: Paymaster-General, Kainan Guard District
1 Nov 1945: Promoted to *Rear-Admiral (Paymaster)*

Rear-Admiral **Shigeki TOKITO** (23 Mar 1893 - 12 Apr 1946)
1 Nov 1942:	Promoted to *Rear-Admiral*
1 Nov 1942 - 20 Apr 1943:	Commander, Oppama Air Division
20 Apr 1943 - 1 May 1943:	Staff officer, Southwestern Area Fleet
1 May 1943 - 12 Apr 1944:	Commander, SW Area Air Depot
12 Apr 1944 - 25 Apr 1944:	Attached to Naval Shipbuilding Command
25 Apr 1944 - 10 Mar 1945:	Chief Supervisor for Construction & Ordnance, Naval Shipbuilding Command
10 Mar 1945 - 15 Mar 1945:	Attached to Naval Air Command
20 Mar 1945:	Transferred to the reserve

Rear Admiral **Saburo TOKITSU** (11 Sep 1892 - 18 Feb 1972)
25 Aug 1942 - 1 May 1943:	Attached to Hikari Navy Yard
1 Nov 1942:	Promoted to *Rear-Admiral*
1 May 1943 - 5 Dec 1943:	Chief of Engine Construction Bureau, Hikari Navy Yard
5 Dec 1943 - 16 Sep 1944:	Chief Supervisor for Construction & Ordnance, Naval Shipbuilding Command
16 Sep 1944 - 20 Apr 1945:	Commander, Hiro Navy Yard
20 Apr 1945 - 15 Oct 1945:	Chief of Bureau 5, Naval Shipbuilding Command
15 Oct 1945 - 25 Oct 1945:	Attached to Department of the Navy

Rear-Admiral **Morie TOKIWA** (8 Dec 1881 - 8 Aug 1971)
1 Dec 1925 - 1 Dec 1927:	Chief of Supply Bureau, Kure Naval District
1 Dec 1926:	Promoted to *Rear-Admiral*
1 Dec 1927 - 15 Dec 1927:	Attached to Naval General Staff
25 Dec 1927:	Transferred to the reserve

Rear-Admiral **Shuji TOKIWA** (28 Dec 1877 - 6 Nov 1943)
1 Jul 1925 - 15 Mar 1929:	Chief of Engine Construction Bureau, Sasebo Navy Yard
1 Dec 1926:	Promoted to *Rear-Admiral*
15 Mar 1929 - 22 Mar 1929:	Attached to Naval Shipbuilding Command
25 Mar 1929:	Transferred to the reserve

Rear-Admiral **Inosuke TOKUDA** (11 Apr 1880 - 17 Feb 1975)
5 Apr 1927 - 1 Dec 1927:	Supervisor for Construction & Ordnance, Naval Shipbuilding Command
1 Dec 1927:	Promoted to *Rear-Admiral*
1 Dec 1927 - 15 Dec 1927:	Attached to Naval General Staff
25 Dec 1927:	Transferred to the reserve

Vice-Admiral **Viscount Takesada TOKUGAWA** (12 Oct 1888 - 29 Nov 1957)
1 Dec 1936 - 1 Nov 1942:	Chief of Shipbuilding Research Bureau, Technical Research Department
15 Nov 1938:	Promoted to *Rear-Admiral*
1 Nov 1942:	Promoted to *Vice-Admiral*
1 Nov 1942 - 20 Dec 1944:	Chief of Technical Research Department
20 Dec 1944 - 16 Apr 1945:	Attached to Naval Shipbuilding Command
20 Apr 1945:	Transferred to the reserve

Rear-Admiral **Takenobu TOKUHISA** (22 Jul 1852 - 13 Jul 1913)
18 Jan 1904 - 12 Dec 1905:	Commander, Kure Sailors Corps
12 Dec 1905:	Promoted to *Rear-Admiral*
12 Dec 1905:	Transferred to the reserve

Rear-Admiral (Paymaster) **Akira TOKUNAGA** (16 Nov 1869 - 14 Oct 1927)
1 Jun 1919 - 10 Dec 1921:	Chief of Accounting Bureau, Yokosuka Navy Yard
1 Dec 1921:	Promoted to *Rear-Admiral (Paymaster)*
10 Dec 1921 - 31 Mar 1923:	Unassigned
31 Mar 1923:	Transferred to the reserve

Vice-Admiral **Sakae TOKUNAGA** (27 Jul 1891 - 2 Oct 1974)
15 Oct 1940 - 4 Apr 1941:	Attached to Naval General Staff
15 Nov 1940:	Promoted to *Rear-Admiral*
4 Apr 1941 - 20 Nov 1942:	Chief of Naval Training Bureau, Department of the Navy
20 Nov 1942 - 29 Nov 1942:	Staff officer, 8th Fleet
29 Nov 1942 - 8 Nov 1943:	Commander, 8th Auxiliary Base Force
1 Nov 1943:	Promoted to *Vice-Admiral*
8 Nov 1943 - 1 Dec 1943:	Attached to Naval General Staff
1 Dec 1943 - 20 Dec 1944:	Commander, Yokosuka Navy Yard
20 Dec 1944 - 1 Nov 1945:	Chief of Technical Research Department

Rear-Admiral **Ryo TOMA** (16 Jul 1897 - 25 Oct 1944)
10 Apr 1944 - 25 Oct 1944:	Captain, Heavy Cruiser *"Mogami"*
25 Oct 1944:	Posthumously promoted to *Rear-Admiral*

Rear-Admiral **Mitsuyoshi TOMARI** (11 Nov 1897 - 16 Jan 1944)
12 Dec 1943 - 16 Jan 1943:	Commander, 61st Destroyer Division
16 Jan 1944:	Posthumously promoted to *Rear-Admiral*

Rear-Admiral (Apothecary) **Toshio TOMARU** (14 Mar 1894 - 21 Apr 1954)
1 May 1943:	Promoted to *Rear-Admiral (Apothecary)*
1 May 1943 - 15 Nov 1943:	Chief of 1st Production Bureau, Navy Medical Depot

15 Nov 1943 - 20 Jun 1944:	Commander, Navy Medical Depot
20 Jun 1944 - 20 Oct 1945:	Commander, 2nd Navy Medical Depot

Rear-Admiral (Paymaster) **Nobuzo TOMATSU** (25 Apr 1896 - 28 Dec 1980)
15 Feb 1945 - 30 Sep 1945:	Chief of Accounting Bureau, 1st Technical Arsenal
1 May 1945:	Promoted to *Rear-Admiral (Paymaster)*
30 Sep 1945 - 30 Nov 1945:	Chief of Supply Bureau, Yokosuka Naval District

Vice-Admiral (Surgeon) **Bunzo TOMATSURI** (8 Oct 1859 - 30 Jan 1935)
24 Nov 1906 - 20 Apr 1912:	Director, Maizuru Naval Hospital, Chief Surgeon, Maizuru Naval District
1 Apr 1910:	Promoted to *Rear-Admiral (Surgeon)*
20 Apr 1912 - 1 Dec 1917:	Director, Yokosuka Naval Hospital, Chief Surgeon, Yokosuka Naval District
13 Dec 1915:	Promoted to *Vice-Admiral (Surgeon)*
1 Dec 1917 - 1 Dec 1918:	Unassigned
1 Dec 1918:	Transferred to the reserve

Rear-Admiral **Fujitaro TOMIKAWA** (3 Oct 1885 - 27 Aug 1952)
30 Nov 1929 - 15 Nov 1933:	Chief of Electronic Research Bureau, Kure Navy Yard
15 Nov 1933:	Promoted to *Rear-Admiral*
15 Nov 1933 - 11 Dec 1933:	Attached to Naval Shipbuilding Command
15 Dec 1933:	Transferred to the reserve

Rear-Admiral **Shozo TOMINAGA** (2 Feb 1894 - 15 Apr 1981)
1 Mar 1944 - 9 Sep 1944:	Chief of Administration Bureau, Southwestern Area Fleet Civil Government
1 May 1944:	Promoted to *Rear-Admiral*
9 Sep 1944 - 1 Nov 1944:	Attached to Naval General Staff
1 Nov 1944 - 30 Nov 1945:	Chief of Personnel Bureau, Kure Naval District

Rear-Admiral **Aijiro TOMIOKA** (21 Feb 1884 - 16 Oct 1929)
10 Dec 1928 - 16 Oct 1929:	Chief of Supply Bureau, Kure Naval District
16 Oct 1929:	Posthumously promoted to *Rear-Admiral*

Rear-Admiral (Engineer) **Nobujiro TOMIOKA** (2 Dec 1865 - 2 Jan 1928)
1 Dec 1910 - 1 Dec 1911:	Chief Engineer Officer, 1st Fleet
1 Dec 1911:	Promoted to *Rear-Admiral*
1 Dec 1911 - 1 Dec 1912:	Chief Engineer Officer, Yokosuka Naval District
1 Dec 1912 - 31 May 1913:	Unassigned
31 May 1913:	Transferred to the reserve

Rear-Admiral **Baron Sadatoshi TOMIOKA** (8 Mar 1897 - 7 Dec 1970)
1 Sep 1943 - 6 Apr 1944:	Deputy Chief of Staff, Southeastern Area Fleet
1 Nov 1943:	Promoted to *Rear-Admiral*
6 Apr 1944 - 7 Nov 1944:	Chief of Staff, Southeastern Area Fleet, Chief of Staff, 11th Air Fleet
7 Nov 1944 - 5 Dec 1944:	Attached to Naval General Staff
5 Dec 1944 - 1 Oct 1945:	Chief of Bureau 1, Naval General Staff
1 Oct 1945 - 30 Nov 1945:	Attached to Department of the Navy

Vice-Admiral **Baron Sadayasu TOMIOKA** (5 Nov 1854 - 1 Jul 1917)
12 Apr 1903 - 28 Dec 1903:	Chief of Bureau 1, Naval General Staff
7 Jul 1903:	Promoted to *Rear-Admiral*
28 Dec 1903 - 19 Nov 1906:	Commandant of the Naval Academy
19 Nov 1906 - 21 Oct 1907:	C-in-C, Training Fleet
12 Mar 1907:	Promoted to *Vice-Admiral*
21 Oct 1907 - 28 Aug 1908:	Commander, Takeshiki Guard District
28 Aug 1908 - 1 Dec 1910:	Admiral Commanding, Ryojun Naval District
1 Dec 1910 - 1 Dec 1911:	Unassigned
1 Dec 1911:	Transferred to the reserve

Rear-Admiral **Sutezo TOMITA** (25 Aug 1901 - 15 Jul 1945)
15 May 1945 - 15 Jul 1945:	Commander, 52nd Minesweeper Division
15 Jul 1945:	Posthumously promoted to *Rear-Admiral*

Rear-Admiral **Kenichiro TOMONAGA** (23 Jan 1892 - 13 Feb 1954)
1 Dec 1937 - 15 Nov 1939:	Chief of Engine Construction Bureau, Sasebo Navy Yard
15 Nov 1938:	Promoted to *Rear-Admiral*
15 Nov 1939 - 16 Feb 1940:	Attached to Naval Shipbuilding Command
21 Feb 1940:	Transferred to the reserve

Rear-Admiral **Kiyoshi TOMONARI** (12 Nov 1899 - 19 Jun 1944)
1 Sep 1943 - 19 Jun 1944:	Executive Officer, Aircraft Carrier "Shokaku"
19 Jun 1944:	Posthumously promoted to *Rear-Admiral*

Rear-Admiral **Saichiro TOMONARI** (27 Nov 1887 - 16 Oct 1962)
15 Nov 1940:	Promoted to *Rear-Admiral*
15 Nov 1940 - 15 Sep 1942:	Chief of Personnel Bureau, Yokosuka Naval District
15 Sep 1942 - 15 Feb 1943:	Commander, 5th Naval Base Force
15 Feb 1943 - 20 Jul 1943:	Commander, 3rd Naval Base Force
20 Jul 1943 - 6 Sep 1943:	Attached to Naval General Staff
10 Sep 1943:	Transferred to the reserve

Rear-Admiral **Kurakichi TONAMI** (8 Oct 1863 - 11 Mar 1937)
1 Oct 1910 - 1 Dec 1911:	Adjutant to the Governor of Korea
1 Dec 1910:	Promoted to *Rear-Admiral*
1 Dec 1911 - 29 Jun 1912:	Attached to Department of the Navy
29 Jun 1912 - 31 Mar 1913:	Unassigned
31 Mar 1913:	Transferred to the reserve

Rear-Admiral (Engineer) **Tatsusaburo TONAMI** (17 Feb 1868 - 23 Mar 1939)
13 Dec 1915 - 1 Apr 1921:	Commander, Navy Briquette Yard
1 Jun 1917:	Promoted to *Rear-Admiral*
1 Apr 1921 - 1 Aug 1921:	Attached to Bureau 5, Naval Shipbuilding Command
1 Aug 1921 - 1 Apr 1922:	Unassigned
1 Apr 1922:	Transferred to the reserve

Rear-Admiral **Senzaburo TONOMURA** (7 Apr 1890 - 25 Feb 1944)
6 Sep 1943 - 25 Feb 1944:	Commander of Minesweeping, Auxiliary Oiler *"Nissho-maru"*
25 Feb 1944:	Posthumously promoted to *Rear-Admiral*

Rear-Admiral **Shinichi TORIGOE** (6 Apr 1894 - 8 Nov 1972)
20 Nov 1941 - 13 Aug 1943:	Chief of Staff, Osaka Guard District
1 May 1943:	Promoted to *Rear-Admiral*
13 Aug 1943 - 27 Aug 1943:	Staff officer, 1st Southern Expeditionary Fleet
27 Aug 1943 - 16 Aug 1944:	Chief of Staff, 1st Southern Expeditionary Fleet
16 Aug 1944 - 25 Sep 1944:	Attached to Naval General Staff
25 Sep 1944 - 30 Nov 1945:	Chief of Supply Bureau, Maizuru Naval District
10 Jul 1945 - 25 Aug 1945:	Chief of Staff, 1st Escort Fleet

Rear-Admiral (Paymaster) **Shinichi TORII** (30 Dec 1892 - 25 Apr 1957)
10 Sep 1943 - 20 Sep 1944:	Chief of Supply Bureau, Naval Facilities Command
1 May 1944:	Promoted to *Rear-Admiral (Paymaster)*
20 Sep 1944 - 15 Oct 1945:	Chief of Facilities Bureau, Ominato Guard District

Rear-Admiral **Iwajiro TORIN** (8 Nov 1880 - 15 Sep 1949)
10 Dec 1928:	Promoted to *Rear-Admiral*
10 Dec 1928 - 5 Mar 1929:	Attached to Yokosuka Naval District
5 Mar 1929 - 5 Jun 1930:	Chief of Yokosuka Sailors Corps
5 Jun 1930 - 10 Jun 1930:	Attached to Yokosuka Naval District
20 Jun 1930:	Transferred to the reserve

Rear-Admiral **Yasuzo TORISAKI** (2 Oct 1878 - 20 Feb 1929)
10 Nov 1922 - 1 Dec 1923:	Captain, Battleship *"Yamashiro"*

1 Dec 1923:	Promoted to *Rear-Admiral*
1 Dec 1923 - 10 Dec 1923:	Attached to Yokosuka Naval District
10 Dec 1923 - 25 Feb 1924:	Unassigned
25 Feb 1924:	Transferred to the reserve

General (Paymaster) **Yoriji TORIYAMA** (6 Aug 1862 - 20 Jun 1916)

1 Apr 1910 - 1 Dec 1912:	Paymaster-General, Maizuru Naval District
1 Dec 1912:	Promoted to *General (Paymaster)*
1 Dec 1912 - 31 May 1913:	Unassigned
31 May 1913:	Transferred to the reserve

Rear-Admiral **Yuzo TORIYAMA** (19 Sep 1892 - 27 Jul 1971)

5 Apr 1945 - Oct 1945:	Commander, 101st Naval Facility
1 May 1945:	Promoted to *Rear-Admiral*

Vice-Admiral **Tamaki TOSU** (1 Dec 1877 - 21 May 1949)

1 Dec 1921:	Promoted to *Rear-Admiral*
1 Dec 1921 - 25 May 1922:	Chief of Staff, Yokosuka Naval District
25 May 1922 - 5 Feb 1924:	Naval Attache, United Kingdom
5 Feb 1924 - 1 Dec 1925:	Chief of Bureau 1, Naval General Staff
20 Oct 1925 - 1 Dec 1925:	Chief of Bureau 2, Naval General Staff
1 Dec 1925:	Promoted to *Vice-Admiral*
1 Dec 1925 - 1 Dec 1926:	Commander, 5th Escort Flotilla
1 Dec 1926 - 1 Apr 1927:	Attached to Naval General Staff
1 Apr 1927 - 10 Dec 1928:	Commandant of the Naval Academy
10 Dec 1928 - 11 Nov 1929:	Admiral Commanding, Maizuru Guard District
11 Nov 1929 - 1 Dec 1930:	Admiral Commanding, Sasebo Naval District
1 Dec 1930 - 20 Mar 1931:	Attached to Naval General Staff
31 Mar 1931:	Transferred to the reserve

Rear-Admiral (Surgeon) **Kankai TOTSUKA** (11 Nov 1855 - 21 Jan 1932)

15 Apr 1901 - 27 May 1902:	Commandant, Navy Medical School
27 May 1902:	Promoted to *General (Surgeon)*
27 May 1902 - 13 Dec 1905:	Director, Sasebo Naval Hospital
10 Nov 1902 - 13 Dec 1905:	Chief Surgeon, Sasebo Naval District
13 Dec 1905 - 14 Feb 1907:	Unassigned
14 Feb 1907:	Transferred to the reserve
23 Sep 1919:	Redesignated *Rear-Admiral (Surgeon)*

Vice-Admiral **Michitaro TOTSUKA** (21 Apr 1890 - 6 Mar 1966)

11 Jul 1937 - 15 Dec 1938:	Commander, 1st Combined Air Division
1 Dec 1937:	Promoted to *Rear-Admiral*
15 Dec 1938 - 20 Oct 1939:	Commander, Yokosuka Air Division

20 Oct 1939 - 1 Nov 1940:	Commander, 2nd Air Flotilla
1 Nov 1940 - 10 Apr 1941:	Commander, 1st Air Flotilla
10 Apr 1941 - 18 May 1943:	Commander, 11th Combined Air Division
15 Oct 1941:	Promoted to *Vice-Admiral*
1 Feb 1943 - 18 May 1943:	Chief of Air Training Units HQ
18 May 1943 - 15 Sep 1944:	C-in-C, 12th Air Fleet
5 Aug 1943 - 15 Sep 1944:	C-in-C, Northeast Area Fleet
15 Sep 1944 - 1 May 1945:	Chief of Naval Air Command
1 May 1945 - 20 Nov 1945:	Admiral Commanding, Yokosuka Naval District, Member, Admirals Committee

Rear-Admiral **Takehiko TOTSUKA** (13 Jun 1896 - 6 Apr 1982)

10 Nov 1942 - 20 Sep 1945:	Chief of Pyrotechnical Bureau, Toyokawa Navy Yard
1 May 1945:	Promoted to *Rear-Admiral*

Rear-Admiral **Kiyoharu TOYAMA** (29 Aug 1889 - 25 Aug 1941)

15 Nov 1938 - 25 Aug 1941:	Chief of Submarine Bureau, Kure Navy Yard
25 Aug 1941:	Posthumously promoted to *Rear-Admiral*

Rear-Admiral (Surgeon) **Minoru TOYODA** (14 Jan 1890 - 16 Aug 1975)

15 Aug 1935 - 1 Dec 1936:	Director, Maizuru Guard District Naval Hospital, Chief Surgeon, Maizuru Guard District
1 Dec 1936:	Promoted to *Rear-Admiral (Surgeon)*
1 Dec 1936 - 15 Nov 1938:	Director, Beppu Naval Hospital
15 Nov 1938 - 15 Nov 1939:	Attached to Yokosuka Naval District
15 Nov 1939 - 15 Dec 1939:	Attached to Naval General Staff
20 Dec 1939:	Transferred to the reserve

Admiral **Soemu TOYODA** (22 May 1885 - 22 Sep 1957)

1 Dec 1931:	Promoted to *Rear-Admiral*
1 Dec 1931 - 15 Sep 1933:	Chief of Bureau 2, Naval General Staff
10 Oct 1932 - 23 Feb 1933:	Chief of Bureau 4, Naval General Staff
15 Sep 1933 - 15 Mar 1935:	Chief of Staff, Combined Fleet, Chief of Staff, 1st Fleet
15 Mar 1935 - 2 Dec 1935:	Chief of Naval Training Bureau, Department of the Navy
15 Nov 1935:	Promoted to *Vice-Admiral*
2 Dec 1935 - 20 Oct 1937:	Chief, Bureau of Naval Affairs, Department of the Navy, Member, Admirals Committee
20 Oct 1937 - 15 Nov 1938:	C-in-C, 4th Fleet
15 Nov 1938 - 21 Oct 1939:	C-in-C, 2nd Fleet

21 Oct 1939 - 18 Sep 1941:	Chief of Naval Shipbuilding Command, Member, Admirals Committee
18 Sep 1941:	Promoted to *Admiral*
18 Sep 1941 - 10 Nov 1942:	Admiral Commanding, Kure Naval District
10 Nov 1942 - 21 Apr 1943:	Navy Councillor
21 Apr 1943 - 3 May 1944:	Admiral Commanding, Yokosuka Naval District, Member, Admirals Committee
3 May 1944 - 29 May 1945:	C-in-C, Combined Fleet
25 Apr 1945 - 29 May 1945:	Supreme C-in-C of the Navy
1 May 1945 - 29 May 1945:	C-in-C, Maritime Escort Fleet
29 May 1945 - 15 Oct 1945:	Chief of the Naval General Staff

Admiral **Teijiro TOYODA** (7 Aug 1885 - 21 Nov 1961)

1 Dec 1930:	Promoted to *Rear-Admiral*
1 Dec 1930 - 10 Oct 1931:	Chief of Staff, Yokosuka Naval District
10 Oct 1931 - 2 Nov 1931:	Attached to Naval General Staff
2 Nov 1931 - 12 May 1932:	Chief, Bureau of Naval Affairs, Department of the Navy, Member, Admirals Committee
12 May 1932 - 15 Nov 1932:	Attached to Naval Air Command
15 Nov 1932 - 10 May 1934:	Commander, Hiro Navy Yard
10 May 1934 - 15 Feb 1936:	Chief of Administration Bureau, Naval Shipbuilding Command
15 Nov 1935:	Promoted to *Vice-Admiral*
15 Feb 1936 - 1 Dec 1937:	Commander, Kure Navy Yard
1 Dec 1937 - 15 Nov 1938:	Admiral Commanding, Sasebo Naval District
15 Nov 1938 - 1 Oct 1940:	Chief of Naval Air Command
30 Aug 1939 - 21 Oct 1939:	Chief of Naval Shipbuilding Command, Member, Admirals Committee
6 Sep 1940 - 4 Apr 1941:	Deputy Minister of the Navy, Member, Admirals Committee
4 Apr 1941:	Promoted to *Admiral*
4 Apr 1941:	Transferred to the reserve
4 Apr 1941 - 18 Jul 1941:	Minister of Commerce & Industry
18 Jul 1941 - 18 Oct 1941:	Minister of Foreign Affairs
7 Apr 1945 - 17 Aug 1945:	Minister of Military Supply

Rear-Admiral (Paymaster) **Seitaro TOYOSHIMA** (5 Jan 1873 - ?)

1 Dec 1919 - 10 Nov 1922:	Chief of Accounting Bureau, Maizuru Navy Yard
10 Nov 1922 - 1 Dec 1922:	Attached to Maizuru Naval District
1 Dec 1922:	Promoted to *Rear-Admiral*
1 Dec 1922 - 31 Mar 1923:	Unassigned
31 Mar 1923:	Transferred to the reserve

Surgeon (General) **Hidekata TOYOZUMI** (1 Nov 1945 - 5 Jan 1900)
22 Mar 1899 - 5 Jan 1900:	Commandant, Navy Medical School
4 Jan 1900:	Promoted to *Surgeon (General)*

Rear-Admiral **Kikuji TSUCHIDA** (7 Jul 1889 - 8 Jun 1953)
1 Dec 1936 - 1 Dec 1937:	Chief Engineer Officer, 2nd Fleet
1 Dec 1937 - 15 Nov 1938:	Chief Engineer Officer, Yokosuka Naval District
15 Nov 1938:	Promoted to *Rear-Admiral*
15 Nov 1938 - 15 Nov 1940:	Chief of Shipbuilding Bureau, Yokosuka Naval District
15 Nov 1940 - 15 Dec 1940:	Attached to Naval General Staff
21 Dec 1940:	Transferred to the reserve

Vice-Admiral **Baron Mitsukane TSUCHIYA** (3 Nov 1864 - 20 Mar 1925)
16 Jul 1910 - 1 Dec 1911:	Chief of Staff, Yokosuka Naval District
1 Dec 1911:	Promoted to *Rear-Admiral*
1 Dec 1911 - 24 Mar 1913:	Commander, Maizuru Torpedo Corps
24 Mar 1913 - 25 May 1913:	Commander, Maizuru Torpedo Group
25 May 1913 - 1 Dec 1913:	Commander, Kure Torpedo Group
1 Dec 1913 - 25 Mar 1914:	C-in-C, Kure Naval District Fleet
25 Mar 1914 - 5 Feb 1915:	C-in-C, 3rd Fleet
5 Feb 1915 - 1 May 1915:	Attached to Naval General Staff
1 May 1915 - 13 Dec 1915:	Commander, 1st Destroyer Flotilla
13 Dec 1915:	Promoted to *Vice-Admiral*
13 Dec 1915 - 1 Apr 1916:	Commander, 2nd Destroyer Flotilla
1 Apr 1916 - 1 Dec 1917:	Commander, Ominato Guard District
1 Dec 1917 - 1 Jun 1919:	Member, Admirals Committee
1 Jun 1919 - 2 Mar 1920:	Unassigned
2 Mar 1920:	Transferred to the reserve

Vice-Admiral **Tamotsu TSUCHIYA** (15 Mar 1859 - 23 Jul 1946)
26 May 1908 - 10 Dec 1908:	Chief of Staff, Sasebo Naval District
28 Aug 1908:	Promoted to *Rear-Admiral*
10 Dec 1908 - 11 Mar 1911:	Chief of Naval Personnel
11 Mar 1911 - 1 Dec 1911:	C-in-C, Yokosuka Reserve Fleet
1 Dec 1911 - 9 Jul 1912:	C-in-C, 1st Fleet
9 Jul 1912 - 24 May 1913:	Commander, Ominato Guard District
1 Dec 1912:	Promoted to *Vice-Admiral*
24 May 1913 - 1 Dec 1913:	Unassigned
1 Dec 1913:	Transferred to the reserve

Rear-Admiral **Tetsuzo TSUCHIYAMA** (1 Aug 1864 - 11 Feb 1941)
1 Dec 1912:	Promoted to *Rear-Admiral*

1 Dec 1912 - 1 Dec 1913:	Commander, Sasebo Navy Yard
1 Dec 1913 - 27 Sep 1914:	C-in-C, 1st Fleet
27 Sep 1914 - 1 Oct 1914:	Attached to Sasebo Naval District
1 Oct 1914 - 1 Dec 1914:	C-in-C, 1st Fleet
1 Dec 1914 - 1 Dec 1915:	Unassigned
1 Dec 1915:	Transferred to the reserve

Rear-Admiral **Katsuji TSUDA** (19 Feb 1890 - 14 Feb 1947)

15 Nov 1939 - 15 Nov 1940:	Chief Engineer Officer, Combined Fleet, Chief Engineer Officer, 1st Fleet
15 Nov 1940:	Promoted to *Rear-Admiral*
15 Nov 1940 - 15 Oct 1941:	Instructor, Naval College
15 Oct 1941 - 15 Dec 1941:	Chief of Shipbuilding Bureau, Yokosuka Naval District
15 Dec 1941 - 5 Oct 1942:	Commander, 103rd Naval Facility
5 Oct 1942 - 1 Nov 1942:	Attached to Kure Naval District
1 Nov 1942 - 5 Apr 1943:	Chief of Shipbuilding Bureau, Kure Naval District
5 Apr 1943 - 15 Apr 1943:	Attached to Naval General Staff
20 Apr 1943:	Transferred to the reserve

Vice-Admiral **Shizue TSUDA** (1 Apr 1883 - 13 Sep 1964)

30 Nov 1929:	Promoted to *Rear-Admiral*
30 Nov 1929 - 21 May 1930:	Attached to Naval General Staff
21 May 1930 - 20 Apr 1933:	C-in-C, 2nd Expeditionary Fleet
20 Apr 1933 - 1 Sep 1933:	Commander, Ryojun Guard District
1 Sep 1933 - 15 Nov 1934:	Chief of Bureau 3, Naval General Staff
15 Nov 1934:	Promoted to *Vice-Admiral*
15 Nov 1934 - 15 Nov 1935:	C-in-C, Manchuria Expeditionary Force
15 Nov 1935 - 28 Mar 1936:	Attached to Naval General Staff
30 Mar 1936:	Transferred to the reserve

Rear-Admiral **Masayasu TSUJI** (10 May 1892 - 8 Jul 1944)

20 May 1944 - 8 Jul 1944:	Chief of Northern Branch, Southern Island Agency
8 Jul 1944:	Posthumously promoted to *Rear-Admiral*

Vice-Admiral **Takehisa TSUJIMURA** (7 Mar 1893 - 8 Jul 1944)

15 Nov 1939 - 15 Jun 1942:	Chief of Ordnance Bureau, Maizuru Navy Yard
15 Oct 1941:	Promoted to *Rear-Admiral*
15 Jun 1942 - 1 Oct 1943:	Chief of Ordnance Bureau, Yokosuka Navy Yard
1 Oct 1943 - 1 Mar 1944:	Commander, 5th Naval Base Force
1 Mar 1944 - 8 Jul 1944:	Commander, 5th Auxiliary Naval Base Force, Commander, 2nd Maritime Escort Force
8 Jul 1944:	Posthumously promoted to *Vice-Admiral*

Rear-Admiral **Mori TSUKAHARA** (10 Sep 1893 - 27 Aug 1984)
15 Oct 1942 - 1 Nov 1943:	Chief of Bureau 2, Technological Agency, Department of the Navy
1 May 1943:	Promoted to *Rear-Admiral*
1 Nov 1943 - 14 Oct 1944:	Chief of Productivity Bureau, Technological Agency, Department of the Navy
14 Oct 1944:	Transferred to the reserve

Admiral **Nishizo TSUKAHARA** (3 Apr 1887 - 10 Jan 1966)
1 Nov 1934 - 1 Dec 1937:	Chief of Administration Bureau, Naval Air Command
15 Nov 1935:	Promoted to *Rear-Admiral*
1 Dec 1937 - 15 Dec 1937:	Commander, 2nd Air Flotilla
15 Dec 1937 - 15 Dec 1938:	Commander, 2nd Combined Air Division
15 Dec 1938 - 19 Oct 1939:	Commander, 1st Combined Air Division
19 Oct 1939 - 15 Apr 1940:	Attached to Naval General Staff
15 Nov 1939:	Promoted to *Vice-Admiral*
15 Apr 1940 - 1 Sep 1941:	Commander, Chinkai Guard District
1 Sep 1941 - 10 Sep 1941:	Attached to Naval General Staff
10 Sep 1941 - 1 Oct 1942:	C-in-C, 11th Air Fleet
1 Oct 1942 - 1 Dec 1942:	Attached to Naval General Staff
1 Dec 1942 - 15 Sep 1944:	Chief of Naval Air Command
1 Mar 1944 - 29 Jul 1944:	Deputy Chief of the Naval General Staff
1 Mar 1944 - 15 Sep 1944:	Navy Councillor
15 Sep 1944 - 1 May 1945:	Admiral Commanding, Yokosuka Naval District, Member, Admirals Committee
1 May 1945 - 10 Oct 1945:	Navy Councillor
15 May 1945:	Promoted to *Admiral*

Rear-Admiral **Naoshi TSUKAMOTO** (27 Sep 1876 - 17 Jul 1930)
1 Aug 1922 - 1 Dec 1925:	Chief of Torpedo Bureau, Kure Navy Yard
1 Dec 1924:	Promoted to *Rear-Admiral*
1 Dec 1925 - 5 Dec 1925:	Attached to Naval Shipbuilding Command
16 Dec 1925:	Transferred to the reserve

Rear-Admiral **Kiyotomo TSUKIYAMA** (20 May 1864 - ?)
12 Apr 1911 - 1 Dec 1912:	Technical Inspector, Yokosuka Navy Yard
1 Dec 1912 - 31 Mar 1913:	Unassigned
31 Mar 1913:	Promoted to *Rear-Admiral*
31 Mar 1913:	Transferred to the reserve

Rear-Admiral **Jiro TSUKUDO** (12 May 1877 - 3 Nov 1944)
20 Nov 1919 - 10 Nov 1922:	Chief of Personnel Bureau, Kure Naval District

1 Dec 1921:	Promoted to *Rear-Admiral*
10 Nov 1922 - 1 Dec 1923:	Commander, Kure Defense Force
1 Dec 1923 - 10 Dec 1923:	Attached to Naval General Staff
10 Dec 1923 - 25 Feb 1924:	Unassigned
25 Feb 1924:	Transferred to the reserve

Vice-Admiral **Hidematsu TSUNODA** (12 Feb 1850 - 13 Dec 1905)

15 Aug 1895:	Promoted to *Rear-Admiral*
15 Aug 1895 - 1 Apr 1896:	Deputy Chief of Staff, Government of Taiwan, Chief of Navy Bureau, Government of Taiwan
1 Apr 1896 - 1 Nov 1897:	Chief of Bureau of Naval Affairs, Government of Taiwan
1 Nov 1897 - 27 Dec 1897:	Chief of Naval Staff, Government of Taiwan
27 Dec 1897 - 14 May 1898:	Admiral Commanding, Sasebo Naval District
14 May 1898 - 19 Jan 1899:	Admiral Commanding, Kure Naval District
19 Jan 1899 - 20 May 1900:	C-in-C, Readiness Fleet
20 May 1900:	Promoted to *Vice-Admiral*
20 May 1900 - 3 Jul 1901:	Chief of Naval Shipbuilding Command
20 May 1900 - 1 Oct 1901:	Member, Admirals Committee
1 Oct 1901 - 26 Jul 1902:	C-in-C, Readiness Fleet
26 Jul 1902 - 28 Dec 1903:	Unassigned
28 Dec 1903 - 13 Dec 1905:	Commander, Takeshiki Guard District

Rear-Admiral **Nobukichi TSURUOKA** (1 Jan 1894 - 2 Oct 1984)

17 May 1943 - 23 Feb 1944:	Captain, Battleship *"Fuso"*
1 Nov 1943:	Promoted to *Rear-Admiral*
23 Feb 1944 - 8 Apr 1944:	Attached to Naval General Staff
8 Apr 1944 - 1 Jun 1944:	Commander, 3rd Convoy HQ
1 Jun 1944 - 1 Dec 1944:	Chief of Supply Bureau, Kure Naval District
1 Dec 1944 - 15 Aug 1945:	Commander, 31st Escort Flotilla
15 Aug 1945 - 25 Sep 1945:	Chief of Submarine Bureau, Kure Naval District

General (Surgeon) **Shikakichi TSURUTA** (23 Dec 1857 - 6 Dec 1914)

19 Jan 1904 - 13 Dec 1905:	Director, Maizuru Naval Hospital, Chief Surgeon, Maizuru Naval District
2 Nov 1905:	Promoted to *General (Surgeon)*
13 Dec 1905 - 1 Dec 1910:	Director, Kure Naval Hospital, Chief Surgeon, Kure Naval District
1 Dec 1910 - 1 Dec 1911:	Unassigned
1 Dec 1911:	Transferred to the reserve

Rear-Admiral (Surgeon) **Takashi TSUTOMI** (3 Aug 1894 - ?)

17 Nov 1944 - 22 Oct 1945:	Director, Kirishima Naval Hospital
1 May 1945:	Promoted to *Rear-Admiral (Surgeon)*

Rear-Admiral (Paymaster) **Kyoji TSUTSUMI** (2 Feb 1894 - 19 Nov 1975)
15 Mar 1943 - 20 Nov 1944:	Chief of Accounting Bureau, Air Technical Arsenal
1 May 1944:	Promoted to *Rear-Admiral (Paymaster)*
20 Nov 1944 - 10 Dec 1944:	Attached to Naval Air Command
10 Dec 1944 - 15 Nov 1945:	Chief of Accounting Bureau, Naval Air Command
15 Nov 1945 - 29 Nov 1945:	Attached to Department of the Navy

Vice-Admiral **Ishichi TSUZUKI** (10 Jan 1888 - 5 Nov 1974)
15 Nov 1933 - 1 Dec 1936:	Chief of Engine Construction Bureau, Sasebo Navy Yard
15 Nov 1935:	Promoted to *Rear-Admiral*
1 Dec 1936 - 15 Nov 1938:	Chief of Engine Construction Bureau, Kure Navy Yard
15 Nov 1938 - 15 Nov 1939:	Commander, Hiro Navy Yard
15 Nov 1939:	Promoted to *Vice-Admiral*
15 Nov 1939 - 15 Nov 1940:	Chief of Technical Research Department
15 Nov 1940 - 1 Nov 1942:	Commander, Yokosuka Navy Yard
1 Nov 1942 - 10 Nov 1942:	Attached to Naval General Staff
16 Nov 1942:	Transferred to the reserve

Rear-Admiral (Surgeon) **Masao TSUZUKI** (20 Oct 1892 - 5 Apr 1961)
8 Jun 1933 - 21 Dec 1939:	Instructor, Navy Medical School
15 Nov 1939:	Promoted to *Rear-Admiral (Surgeon)*
21 Dec 1939:	Transferred to the reserve

Rear-Admiral **Teiichi TSUZUKI** (1 Mar 1896 - 7 Aug 1945)
5 May 1944 - 7 Aug 1945:	Chief of Administration Bureau, Toyokawa Navy Yard
7 Aug 1945:	Posthumously promoted to *Rear-Admiral*

Vice-Admiral **Kosaburo UCHIDA** (1 Jul 1872 - 29 Nov 1954)
10 Jun 1919 - 20 Nov 1920:	Chief of Staff, 3rd Fleet
20 Nov 1920 - 1 Dec 1922:	Chief of Staff, Maizuru Naval District
1 Dec 1920:	Promoted to *Rear-Admiral*
1 Dec 1922 - 1 Jun 1923:	Attached to Naval General Staff
1 Jun 1923 - 1 Dec 1924:	Chief of Naval Hydrographic Command
1 Dec 1924:	Promoted to *Vice-Admiral*
1 Dec 1924 - 2 Mar 1925:	Attached to Naval General Staff
20 Mar 1925:	Transferred to the reserve

Vice-Admiral **Baron Masatoshi UCHIDA** (15 Mar 1851 - 11 May 1922)
22 May 1900:	Promoted to *Rear-Admiral*
22 May 1900 - 6 Jul 1901:	Commander, Sasebo Harbor

6 Jul 1901 - 26 Jul 1902:	C-in-C, Readiness Fleet
26 Jul 1902 - 5 Sep 1903:	Chief of Shipping Bureau, Kure Naval District
5 Sep 1903 - 13 Nov 1905:	Commander, Kure Harbor
13 Nov 1905:	Promoted to *Vice-Admiral*
13 Nov 1905 - 9 Feb 1906:	Unassigned
9 Feb 1906:	Transferred to the reserve

Rear-Admiral **Shigoro UCHIDA** (26 Mar 1898 - 18 Aug 1944)

1 Apr 1944 - 18 Aug 1944:	Chief of Administration Bureau, Southeast Area Air Depot
18 Aug 1944:	Posthumously promoted to *Rear-Admiral*

Rear-Admiral **Shinichi UCHINO** (? - 7 Apr 1945)

20 Jan 1944 - 7 Apr 1945:	Executive Officer, Light Cruiser *"Yahagi"*
7 Apr 1945:	Posthumously promoted to *Rear-Admiral*

Rear-Admiral **Giemon UEDA** (2 Oct 1888 - 4 Oct 1945)

15 Nov 1939 - 21 Apr 1941:	Chief of Coalmining Bureau, Navy Fuel Yard
15 Nov 1940:	Promoted to *Rear-Admiral*
21 Apr 1941 - 1 Apr 1943:	Commander, 4th Navy Fuel Yard
1 Apr 1943 - 20 Jun 1943:	Attached to Naval General Staff
25 Jun 1943:	Transferred to the reserve

Rear-Admiral (Surgeon) **Harujiro UEDA** (8 Mar 1883 - 1 Jan 1940)

1 May 1928 - 30 Nov 1929:	Chief Surgeon, 2nd Fleet
30 Nov 1929 - 15 Nov 1932:	Chief of Medical Section, Technical Research Department
15 Nov 1932 - 10 Dec 1932:	Attached to Naval General Staff
1 Dec 1932:	Promoted to *Rear-Admiral (Surgeon)*
15 Dec 1932:	Transferred to the reserve

Rear-Admiral **Kijichi UEDA** (3 Jul 1877 - 26 Dec 1963)

20 Nov 1921 - 1 Jul 1922:	Captain, Battlecruiser *"Haruna"*
1 Jul 1922 - 1 Dec 1922:	Attached to Yokosuka Naval District
1 Dec 1922:	Promoted to *Rear-Admiral*
1 Dec 1922 - 31 Mar 1923:	Unassigned
31 Mar 1923:	Transferred to the reserve

Vice-Admiral **Muneshige UEDA** (15 Aug 1884 - 26 Jan 1939)

1 Dec 1927 - 1 Dec 1930:	Instructor, Naval College
30 Nov 1929:	Promoted to *Rear-Admiral*
1 Dec 1930 - 25 Oct 1933:	Chief of Scientific Research Bureau, Technical Research Department

25 Oct 1933 - 10 May 1934:	Commander, Navy Fuel Yard
10 May 1934 - 2 Dec 1935:	Commandant, Naval Engineering Academy
15 Nov 1934:	Promoted to *Vice-Admiral*
2 Dec 1935 - 1 Dec 1936:	Chief of Supply Bureau, Department of the Navy
1 Dec 1936 - 26 Jan 1939:	Chief of Naval Shipbuilding Command, Member, Admirals Committee

Vice-Admiral **Yoshitake UEDA** (6 May 1878 - 21 Feb 1957)

1 Apr 1923 - 1 Jun 1925:	Attached to Technical Research Department
1 Dec 1924:	Promoted to *Rear-Admiral*
1 Jun 1925 - 25 Mar 1927:	Chief of Aircraft Research Bureau, Technical Research Department
25 Mar 1927 - 1 Dec 1927:	Commander, Hiro Navy Yard
1 Dec 1927 - 10 Dec 1928:	Chief of Technical Bureau, Naval Air Command
10 Dec 1928:	Promoted to *Vice-Admiral*
10 Dec 1928 - 10 Apr 1929:	Attached to Naval General Staff
15 Apr 1929:	Transferred to the reserve

Rear-Admiral (Surgeon) **Junnosuke UEHARA** (30 May 1891 - 2 Dec 1947)

15 Nov 1939 - 1 Apr 1940:	Chief of Bureau 1, Yokosuka Naval Hospital
1 Apr 1940 - 15 Nov 1940:	Attached to Yokosuka Naval District
15 Nov 1940:	Promoted to *Rear-Admiral (Surgeon)*
15 Nov 1940 - 16 Dec 1940:	Attached to Naval General Staff
21 Dec 1940:	Transferred to the reserve

Rear-Admiral **Shinjiro UEHARA** (10 May 1860 - 19 Mar 1918)

22 Nov 1906 - 27 Dec 1907:	Chief of Staff, Kure Naval District
12 Mar 1907:	Promoted to *Rear-Admiral*
27 Dec 1907 - 15 May 1908:	Member, Admirals Committee
15 May 1908 - 31 May 1909:	Unassigned
31 May 1909:	Transferred to the reserve

Rear-Admiral **Yoshio UEHARA** (1 Mar 1896 - 21 Jan 1982)

10 Apr 1943 - 20 Dec 1944:	Chief of Section 1, Administration Bureau, Naval Shipbuilding Command
15 Oct 1944:	Promoted to *Rear-Admiral*
20 Dec 1944 - 30 Nov 1945:	Chief of Administration Bureau, Naval Shipbuilding Command

Rear-Admiral **Toma UEMATSU** (30 Apr 1883 - 22 Aug 1948)

1 Dec 1931:	Promoted to *Rear-Admiral*
1 Dec 1931 - 4 Feb 1932:	Commander, 2nd Destroyer Flotilla
4 Feb 1932 - 1 Jun 1932:	Staff officer, 3rd Fleet

1 Jun 1932 - 6 Jun 1932:	Commander, Shanghai Marine Force
6 Jun 1932 - 28 Jun 1932:	Attached to Naval General Staff
28 Jun 1932 - 15 Nov 1933:	Commandant, Submarine School
15 Nov 1933 - 26 Mar 1934:	Attached to Naval General Staff
31 Mar 1934:	Transferred to the reserve

Vice-Admiral **Nagataka UEMURA** (7 Jul 1849 - 27 Jan 1931)

5 Jul 1901:	Promoted to *Rear-Admiral*
5 Jul 1901 - 7 Jan 1905:	Commander, Yokosuka Harbor
7 Jan 1905 - 13 Jun 1905:	Commander, Ryojun Harbor
13 Jun 1905 - 20 Dec 1905:	Commander, Mako Guard District
13 Nov 1905:	Promoted to *Vice-Admiral*
20 Dec 1905 - 24 Feb 1907:	Unassigned
24 Feb 1907:	Transferred to the reserve

Rear-Admiral **Nobuo UEMURA** (16 Jun 1877 - 16 Dec 1965)

10 Nov 1922 - 1 Dec 1924:	Chief of Personnel Bureau, Yokosuka Naval District
1 Dec 1922:	Promoted to *Rear-Admiral*
1 Dec 1924 - 1 Dec 1925:	Chief of Naval Hydrographic Command
1 Dec 1925 - 5 Dec 1925:	Attached to Naval General Staff
22 Dec 1925:	Transferred to the reserve

Vice-Admiral **Shigeo UEMURA** (28 Feb 1883 - 19 Mar 1966)

1 Feb 1927 - 10 Dec 1928:	Chief of Personnel Bureau, Yokosuka Naval District
1 Dec 1927:	Promoted to *Rear-Admiral*
10 Dec 1928 - 1 Feb 1929:	Attached to Yokosuka Naval District
1 Feb 1929 - 30 Nov 1929:	Attached to Naval General Staff
30 Nov 1929 - 1 Dec 1930:	Chief of Staff, Yokosuka Naval District
1 Dec 1930 - 1 Dec 1932:	Chief of Naval Hydrographic Command
1 Dec 1932:	Promoted to *Vice-Admiral*
1 Dec 1932 - 10 Dec 1932:	Attached to Naval General Staff
15 Dec 1932:	Transferred to the reserve

Rear-Admiral **Tsunekichi UEMURA** (28 Apr 1868 - 21 Nov 1922)

1 Dec 1913:	Promoted to *Rear-Admiral*
1 Dec 1913 - 1 Dec 1914:	Commander, Ominato Guard District
1 Dec 1914 - 13 Dec 1915:	Chief of Naval Hydrographic Command
13 Dec 1915 - 1 Dec 1916:	Unassigned
1 Dec 1916:	Transferred to the reserve

Vice-Admiral **Gonta UENO** (4 Jul 1895 - 31 Mar 1944)

5 Sep 1943 - 31 Mar 1944:	Chief Engineer Officer, Combined Fleet
1 Nov 1943:	Promoted to *Rear-Admiral*
31 Mar 1944:	Posthumously promoted to *Vice-Admiral*

Rear-Admiral **Count Masao UENO** (16 Jul 1890 - 16 Feb 1965)
12 Apr 1943 - 10 Oct 1943:	Commander, 11th Submarine Base Force
10 Oct 1943 - 15 Nov 1943:	Attached to Yokosuka Naval District
1 Nov 1943:	Promoted to *Rear-Admiral*
15 Nov 1943 - 15 Dec 1943:	Attached to Naval General Staff
20 Dec 1943:	Transferred to the reserve

Vice-Admiral **Kanji UGAKI** (23 Jan 1889 - 27 Sep 1974)
10 Oct 1939 - 20 Aug 1941:	Chief of Staff, Kure Naval District
15 Nov 1939:	Promoted to *Rear-Admiral*
20 Aug 1941 - 1 Sep 1941:	Attached to Naval General Staff
1 Sep 1941 - 19 Feb 1943:	Chief of Staff, Kainan Guard District
19 Feb 1943 - 10 Mar 1943:	Attached to Yokosuka Naval District
10 Mar 1943 - 1 May 1943:	Commandant, Navy Communications School
1 May 1943:	Promoted to *Vice-Admiral*
1 May 1943 - 25 Aug 1943:	Commandant, Yokosuka Navy Communications School
25 Aug 1943 - 1 Sep 1943:	Staff officer, China Area Fleet
1 Sep 1943 - 15 Dec 1944:	Chief of Staff, China Area Fleet
15 Dec 1944 - 15 Mar 1945:	Attached to Naval General Staff
15 Mar 1945 - 15 Nov 1945:	C-in-C, 12th Air Fleet, Commander, Ominato Guard District
15 Nov 1945 - 30 Nov 1945:	Attached to Department of the Navy

Vice-Admiral **Matome UGAKI** (15 Feb 1890 - 15 Aug 1945)
15 Nov 1938:	Promoted to *Rear-Admiral*
15 Nov 1938 - 15 Dec 1938:	Attached to Naval General Staff
15 Dec 1938 - 10 Apr 1941:	Chief of Bureau 1, Naval General Staff
10 Apr 1941 - 1 Aug 1941:	Commander, 8th Escort Flotilla
1 Aug 1941 - 16 Aug 1941:	Chief of Staff, 1st Fleet
1 Aug 1941 - 22 May 1943:	Chief of Staff, Combined Fleet
1 Nov 1942:	Promoted to *Vice-Admiral*
22 May 1943 - 25 Feb 1944:	Attached to Naval General Staff
25 Feb 1944 - 15 Nov 1944:	Commander, 1st Battleship Flotilla
15 Nov 1944 - 10 Feb 1945:	Attached to Naval General Staff
10 Feb 1945 - 15 Aug 1945:	C-in-C, 5th Air Fleet

Vice-Admiral **Wataru UGAWA** (30 Dec 1879 - 16 Dec 1977)
1 Sep 1924 - 2 Feb 1925:	Chief of Personnel Bureau, Kure Naval District
1 Dec 1924:	Promoted to *Rear-Admiral*
2 Feb 1925 - 1 Dec 1927:	Chief of Staff, Yokosuka Naval District
1 Dec 1927 - 10 Dec 1928:	C-in-C, 1st Expeditionary Fleet
10 Dec 1928:	Promoted to *Vice-Admiral*

10 Dec 1928 - 30 Nov 1929:	Commander, 5th Escort Flotilla
30 Nov 1929 - 10 Jun 1930:	Attached to Naval General Staff
20 Jun 1930:	Transferred to the reserve

Rear-Admiral **Chikaharu UJIIE** (5 Sep 1885 - 17 Jan 1967)

15 Nov 1934 - 1 Dec 1936:	Chief of Shipbuilding Bureau, Yokosuka Naval District
15 Nov 1935:	Promoted to *Rear-Admiral*
1 Dec 1936 - 15 Dec 1936:	Attached to Naval General Staff
22 Dec 1936:	Transferred to the reserve

Rear-Admiral (Surgeon) **Kojiro UJIIE** (30 Mar 1881 - 27 Feb 1947)

10 Dec 1928 - 30 Nov 1929:	Director, Maizuru Guard District Naval Hospital, Chief Surgeon, Maizuru Guard District
30 Nov 1929:	Promoted to *Rear-Admiral (Surgeon)*
30 Nov 1929 - 1 Dec 1930:	Director, Kure Naval Hospital, Chief Surgeon, Kure Naval District
1 Dec 1930 - 15 Dec 1930:	Attached to Naval General Staff
24 Dec 1930:	Transferred to the reserve

Vice-Admiral **Nagaaki UJIIE** (30 Apr 1886 - 1 Oct 1951)

30 Nov 1929 - 1 Jun 1932:	Chief of Engine Construction Bureau, Kure Navy Yard
1 Dec 1931:	Promoted to *Rear-Admiral*
1 Jun 1932 - 1 Apr 1933:	Chief of Bureau 4, Naval Shipbuilding Command
1 Apr 1933 - 5 Apr 1934:	Chief of Bureau 5, Naval Shipbuilding Command
5 Apr 1934 - 15 Nov 1935:	Commander, Sasebo Navy Yard
15 Nov 1935 - 1 Dec 1936:	Chief of Technical Research Department
1 Dec 1936:	Promoted to *Vice-Admiral*
1 Dec 1936 - 30 Aug 1939:	Chief of Supply Bureau, Department of the Navy
30 Aug 1939 - 16 Dec 1940:	Attached to Naval General Staff
21 Dec 1940:	Transferred to the reserve

Vice-Admiral **Hidehiko UKITA** (12 Jul 1889 - 21 Jun 1984)

15 Nov 1935 - 1 Dec 1937:	Commandant, Submarine School
1 Dec 1936:	Promoted to *Rear-Admiral*
1 Dec 1937 - 25 Mar 1938:	Chief of Bureau 6, Naval Shipbuilding Command
25 Mar 1938 - 5 Jul 1941:	Chief of Bureau 7, Naval Shipbuilding Command
15 Nov 1940:	Promoted to *Vice-Admiral*
5 Jul 1941 - 15 Jan 1942:	Admiral Commanding, Ryojun Guard District
15 Jan 1942 - 25 Aug 1942:	Attached to Naval General Staff
1 Sep 1942:	Transferred to the reserve

Rear-Admiral **Masayoshi UMEBAYASHI** (23 Aug 1893 - 4 Aug 1966)
1 Apr 1942 - 25 Oct 1943:	Chief of Administration Bureau, Technical Research Department
1 Nov 1942:	Promoted to *Rear-Admiral*
25 Oct 1943 - 10 Nov 1943:	Attached to Administration Bureau, Naval Facilities Command
10 Nov 1943 - 1 Oct 1944:	Chief of 102nd Facility Bureau
1 Oct 1944 - 15 Jul 1945:	Commandant, Numazu Naval Construction School
15 Jul 1945 - 6 Sep 1945:	Attached to Naval General Staff

Rear-Admiral **Kaoru UMETANI** (10 Apr 1897 - 11 Jul 1963)
1 May 1945:	Promoted to *Rear-Admiral*
1 May 1945 - 15 Nov 1945:	Commander, 41st Air Arsenal

Rear-Admiral **Sekizo UNO** (17 Jun 1884 - 25 Jan 1935)
15 Nov 1933:	Promoted to *Rear-Admiral*
15 Nov 1933 - 15 Nov 1934:	Commander, Shanghai Marine Force
15 Nov 1934 - 25 Jan 1935:	Commandant, Naval Gunnery School

Rear-Admiral **Rokuzo UNOIKE** (17 Feb 1888 - 29 May 1973)
15 Nov 1940 - 1 Aug 1945:	Attached to Section 1, Training Bureau, Department of the Navy
15 Oct 1941:	Promoted to *Rear-Admiral*
1 Aug 1945:	Demobilized

Rear-Admiral **Jisaku UOZUMI** (23 Aug 1892 - 20 May 1963)
20 Oct 1942 - 1 Dec 1943:	Captain, Heavy Cruiser *"Haguro"*
1 Nov 1943:	Promoted to *Rear-Admiral*
1 Dec 1943 - 8 Jul 1944:	Commander, Kure Defense Flotilla
8 Jul 1944 - 22 Jul 1944:	Attached to Naval General Staff
22 Jul 1944 - 4 Aug 1944:	Staff officer, 1st Southern Expeditionary Fleet
4 Aug 1944 - 20 Feb 1945:	Commander, 8th Submarine Flotilla
4 Aug 1945 - Oct 1945:	Commander, 15th Auxiliary Naval Base Force

Rear-Admiral **Kakuzo URANO** (18 Jan 1898 - ?)
15 Sep 1944 - 20 Nov 1945:	Commander, Hamana Sailors Corps
1 May 1945:	Promoted to *Rear-Admiral*

Admiral **Baron Sotokichi URYU** (2 Jan 1857 - 11 Nov 1937)
21 May 1900:	Promoted to *Rear-Admiral*
21 May 1900 - 10 Apr 1902:	Chief of Bureau 1, Naval General Staff
10 Apr 1902 - 28 Dec 1903:	C-in-C, Readiness Fleet

28 Dec 1903 - 20 Dec 1905:	C-in-C, 2nd Fleet, Commander, 4th Escort Flotilla
6 Jun 1904:	Promoted to *Vice-Admiral*
20 Dec 1905 - 22 Nov 1906:	Commander, Takeshiki Guard District
22 Nov 1906 - 1 Mar 1909:	Admiral Commanding, Sasebo Naval District
1 Mar 1909 - 1 Dec 1909:	Member, Admirals Committee
1 Dec 1909 - 1 Dec 1912:	Admiral Commanding, Yokosuka Naval District, Member, Admirals Committee
16 Oct 1912:	Promoted to *Admiral*
1 Dec 1912 - 31 May 1913:	Unassigned
31 May 1913:	Transferred to the reserve

Rear-Admiral **Tomoyoshi USAGAWA** (19 Sep 1877 - 10 Oct 1950)

1 Dec 1922:	Promoted to *Rear-Admiral*
1 Dec 1922 - 1 Feb 1923:	Attached to Naval General Staff
1 Feb 1923 - 1 Dec 1923:	Chief of Staff, Yokosuka Naval District
1 Dec 1923 - 2 Mar 1925:	Attached to Naval General Staff
20 Mar 1925:	Transferred to the reserve

Rear-Admiral **Juzaburo USHIDA** (8 May 1865 - 22 Mar 1935)

1 Dec 1911:	Promoted to *Rear-Admiral*
1 Dec 1911 - 1 Dec 1912:	Chief of Staff, Maizuru Naval District
1 Dec 1912 - 31 May 1913:	Unassigned
31 May 1913:	Transferred to the reserve

Rear-Admiral (Surgeon) **Shigetsune USHIKUBO** (20 Apr 1896 - Oct 1975)

20 Nov 1943 - 25 Jun 1945:	Chief of Medical Bureau, Maizuru Navy Yard
1 May 1945:	Promoted to *Rear-Admiral (Surgeon)*
25 Jun 1945 - 22 Oct 1945:	Director, Osaka Naval Hospital, Chief Surgeon, Osaka Guard District
22 Oct 1945 - 20 Nov 1945:	Attached to Department of the Navy
20 Nov 1945 - 30 Nov 1945:	Attached to Sasebo Naval District

Vice-Admiral **Fukusaku USHIMARU** (3 Feb 1882 - Aug 1956)

1 Dec 1925:	Promoted to *Rear-Admiral*
1 Dec 1925 - 10 Dec 1928:	Chief of Engine Construction Bureau, Yokosuka Naval District
10 Dec 1928 - 1 Jun 1932:	Chief of Bureau 4, Naval Shipbuilding Command
1 Dec 1930:	Promoted to *Vice-Admiral*
1 Jun 1932 - 10 May 1934:	Chief of Supply Bureau, Department of the Navy
10 May 1934 - 27 Dec 1935:	Attached to Naval General Staff
28 Dec 1935:	Transferred to the reserve

Rear-Admiral **Fujimasa USHIO** (2 May 1893 - 24 Dec 1953)
15 Aug 1944 - 15 Jul 1945:	Commandant, Hofu Naval Communication School
15 Oct 1944:	Promoted to *Rear-Admiral*
15 Jul 1945 - 15 Sep 1945:	Commandant, Navy Radar School

Rear-Admiral (Surgeon) **Hiroshi USUI** (1 Oct 1862 - 29 Sep 1945)
1 Dec 1913:	Promoted to *General (Surgeon)*
1 Dec 1913 - 1 Dec 1916:	Director, Kure Naval Hospital, Chief Surgeon, Kure Naval District
1 Dec 1916 - 1 Dec 1917:	Unassigned
1 Dec 1917:	Transferred to the reserve
23 Sep 1919:	Redesignated *Rear-Admiral (Surgeon)*

Vice-Admiral **Kuni USUI** (22 Nov 1881 - 17 Mar 1965)
1 Dec 1926:	Promoted to *Rear-Admiral*
1 Dec 1926 - 5 Apr 1927:	Attached to Naval General Staff
5 Apr 1927 - 10 Dec 1928:	Chief of Training Bureau, Naval Air Command
10 Dec 1928 - 1 Dec 1930:	Chief of Technical Bureau, Naval Air Command
8 Oct 1929 - 1 Nov 1929:	Chief of Training Bureau, Naval Air Command
1 Dec 1930 - 1 Dec 1931:	Commander, Hiro Navy Yard
1 Dec 1931:	Promoted to *Vice-Admiral*
1 Dec 1931 - 15 Dec 1931:	Attached to Naval General Staff
21 Dec 1931:	Transferred to the reserve

Rear-Admiral (Paymaster) **Shozo USUI** (? - 3 May 1944)
15 Nov 1943 - 3 May 1944:	Paymaster-General, 9th Fleet
3 May 1944:	Posthumously promoted to *Rear-Admiral (Paymaster)*

Rear-Admiral (Paymaster) **Heizo UTO** (18 Feb 1872 - ?)
1 Dec 1919 - 1 Apr 1921:	Commander, Navy Coal Mining Yard
1 Dec 1920:	Promoted to *Rear-Admiral (Paymaster)*
1 Apr 1921 - 1 Dec 1921:	Chief of Coal Mining Bureau, Navy Fuel Yard
1 Dec 1921 - 10 Nov 1922:	Paymaster-General, Sasebo Naval District
10 Nov 1922 - 1 Dec 1923:	Attached to Yokosuka Naval District
1 Dec 1923 - 31 Mar 1923:	Unassigned
31 Mar 1923:	Transferred to the reserve

Rear-Admiral (Paymaster) **Kanae UTSUNOMIYA** (12 Aug 1864 - 19 Apr 1934)
1 Dec 1912 - 8 Aug 1914:	Paymaster-General, Kure Naval District
1 Dec 1913:	Promoted to *General (Paymaster)*
8 Aug 1914 - 7 Aug 1915:	Unassigned

7 Aug 1915:	Transferred to the reserve
23 Sep 1919:	Redesignated *Rear-Admiral (Paymaster)*

Vice-Admiral **Keizo UWANO** (20 Dec 1891 - 25 Sep 1985)
15 Nov 1940 - 17 Nov 1942:	Commander, Yokosuka Air Division
15 Oct 1941:	Promoted to *Rear-Admiral*
17 Nov 1942 - 5 May 1944:	Commander, 25th Air Flotilla
5 May 1944 - 15 May 1944:	Staff officer, 1st Air Fleet
15 May 1944 - 15 Nov 1944:	Commander, 61st Air Flotilla
15 Oct 1944:	Promoted to *Vice-Admiral*
15 Nov 1944 - 10 Mar 1945:	Attached to Naval General Staff
10 Mar 1945 - 10 Aug 1945:	Chief Supervisor for Construction & Ordnance, Naval Shipbuilding Command
10 Jun 1945 - 15 Sep 1945:	Chief, Tokai & Hokuriku Tohoku Navy Office

Vice-Admiral **Hideho WADA** (2 Jan 1886 - 3 Apr 1972)
1 Apr 1932 - 3 Oct 1933:	Chief of Aircraft Bureau, Air Arsenal
1 Dec 1932:	Promoted to *Rear-Admiral*
3 Oct 1933 - 1 Jun 1934:	Commander, Kasumigaura Air Division
1 Jun 1934 - 15 Nov 1935:	Commander, 1st Air Flotilla
15 Nov 1935 - 1 Dec 1936:	Commander, Ryojun Guard District
1 Dec 1936:	Promoted to *Vice-Admiral*
1 Dec 1936 - 15 Dec 1937:	Attached to Naval General Staff
21 Dec 1937:	Transferred to the reserve

Rear-Admiral **Kenkichi WADA** (15 Mar 1880 - 16 Nov 1939)
1 Dec 1924 - 22 Aug 1925:	Captain, Battleship *"Ise"*
22 Aug 1925 - 20 Oct 1925:	Attached to Naval General Staff
20 Oct 1925 - 16 Dec 1925:	Unassigned
1 Dec 1925:	Promoted to *Rear-Admiral*

Vice-Admiral **Kensuke WADA** (28 Oct 1861 - 20 Oct 1939)
28 Aug 1908:	Promoted to *Rear-Admiral*
28 Aug 1908 - 9 Apr 1910:	Commander, Yokosuka Navy Yard
9 Apr 1910 - 1 Dec 1911:	Chief of Staff, Maizuru Naval District
1 Dec 1911 - 9 Jul 1912:	C-in-C, Sasebo Reserve Fleet
9 Jul 1912 - 1 Dec 1912:	Chief of Staff, Yokosuka Naval District
1 Dec 1912 - 31 May 1913:	Unassigned
31 May 1913:	Promoted to *Vice-Admiral*
31 May 1913:	Transferred to the reserve

Vice-Admiral **Misao WADA** (6 Dec 1889 - 19 Nov 1981)
1 Oct 1937 - 21 May 1940:	Chief of Technical Bureau, Naval Air Command

1 Dec 1937:	Promoted to *Rear-Admiral*
21 May 1940 - 15 May 1945:	Commander, Air Technical Arsenal
15 Oct 1941:	Promoted to *Vice-Admiral*
15 May 1945 - 1 Nov 1945:	Chief of Naval Air Command

Vice-Admiral **Nobufusa WADA** (1 Nov 1882 - 26 Jan 1967)
30 Nov 1929:	Promoted to *Rear-Admiral*
30 Nov 1929 - 15 Nov 1932:	Chief of Naval Facility, Maizuru Guard District
15 Nov 1932 - 15 Nov 1934:	Chief of Bureau 1, Naval Shipbuilding Command
15 Nov 1934:	Promoted to *Vice-Admiral*
15 Nov 1934 - 10 Dec 1934:	Attached to Naval Shipbuilding Command
15 Dec 1934:	Transferred to the reserve

Rear-Admiral **Seizo WADA** (16 Aug 1883 - 29 Mar 1943)
1 Dec 1941 - 29 Mar 1943:	Commander of Minesweeping, Auxiliary Cable Ship *"Yamabato-maru"*
29 Mar 1943:	Posthumously promoted to *Rear-Admiral*

Vice-Admiral **Senzo WADA** (29 Sep 1884 - 29 Sep 1974)
1 Apr 1933 - 15 Nov 1934:	Commander, Sasebo Sailors Corps
15 Nov 1933:	Promoted to *Rear-Admiral*
15 Nov 1934 - 15 Nov 1935:	Commander, Sasebo Guard Flotilla
15 Nov 1935 - 1 Dec 1937:	Commander, Mako Guard District
1 Dec 1937:	Promoted to *Vice-Admiral*
1 Dec 1937 - 15 Mar 1938:	Attached to Naval General Staff
25 Mar 1938:	Transferred to the reserve

Rear-Admiral **Sumihisa WADA** (30 Jan 1897 - 6 Feb 1944)
1 Jul 1943 - 6 Feb 1944:	Commander, 6th Communications Unit
6 Feb 1944:	Posthumously promoted to *Rear-Admiral*

Rear-Admiral **Tetsujiro WADA** (31 Jan 1904 - 29 Oct 1945)
15 Nov 1944 - 29 Oct 1945:	Commander, 153rd Air Division
29 Oct 1945:	Posthumously promoted to *Rear-Admiral*

Rear-Admiral **Yushiro WADA** (3 Nov 1901 - 3 May 1944)
27 Jan 1944 - 3 May 1944:	Staff Officer, 9th Fleet
3 May 1944:	Posthumously promoted to *Rear-Admiral*

Vice-Admiral **Seisaku WAKABAYASHI** (1 Mar 1889 - 27 Jan 1968)
15 Nov 1939:	Promoted to *Rear-Admiral*
15 Nov 1939 - 1 Nov 1940:	Commander, 4th Submarine Flotilla
1 Nov 1940 - 22 Nov 1940:	Staff officer, 4th Fleet

22 Nov 1940 - 19 Dec 1941:	Attached to Naval General Staff
19 Dec 1941 - 1 Jan 1942:	Chief of Seamen Bureau, Shipping Agency, Department of the Navy
1 Jan 1942 - 15 Jul 1943:	Commandant, Seamen Training Center
1 May 1943:	Promoted to *Vice-Admiral*
15 Jul 1943 - 19 Feb 1944:	Commander, 4th Auxiliary Naval Base Force, Commander, 2nd Maritime Escort Force
19 Feb 1944 - 20 Oct 1944:	Attached to Naval General Staff
20 Oct 1944 - 15 Sep 1945:	Commandant, Shimizu Merchant Marine College

Rear-Admiral **Shigekichi WAKAO** (5 Aug 1879 - 25 Jan 1947)

1 Dec 1925 - 15 Nov 1926:	Chief Engineer Officer, Sasebo Naval District
15 Nov 1926 - 20 Mar 1927:	Attached to Naval General Staff
1 Dec 1926:	Promoted to *Rear-Admiral*
25 Mar 1927:	Transferred to the reserve

Vice-Admiral (Surgeon) **Yoshiho WAKAO** (1 Aug 1886 - 29 Jan 1955)

15 Nov 1938:	Promoted to *Rear-Admiral (Surgeon)*
15 Nov 1938 - 15 Nov 1940:	Chief Instructor, Navy Medical School
15 Nov 1940 - 1 Nov 1943:	Director, Sasebo Naval Hospital, Chief Surgeon, Sasebo Naval District
1 Nov 1942:	Promoted to *Vice-Admiral (Surgeon)*
1 Nov 1943 - 22 Oct 1945:	Director, Yokosuka Naval Hospital, Chief Surgeon, Yokosuka Naval District

Rear-Admiral **Ryuzo WAKATSUKI** (16 Jul 1900 - 25 Jan 1944)

15 Nov 1943 - 25 Jan 1944:	Staff Officer, 9th Fleet
25 Jan 1944:	Posthumously promoted to *Rear-Admiral*

Rear-Admiral **Kanae WAKI** (5 Jul 1887 - 22 Feb 1960)

1 Dec 1936:	Promoted to *Rear-Admiral*
1 Dec 1936 - 15 Nov 1939:	Chief of Supply Bureau, Kure Naval District
15 Nov 1939 - 15 Mar 1940:	Attached to Naval General Staff
21 Mar 1940:	Transferred to the reserve

Rear-Admiral **Johei WAKISAKA** (27 Dec 1888 - 6 Feb 1944)

25 Sep 1943 - 6 Feb 1944:	Commander, 16th Minesweeper Division
6 Feb 1944:	Posthumously promoted to *Rear-Admiral*

Rear-Admiral **Kiichiro WAKITA** (1 Oct 1898 - 25 Nov 1944)

15 Jul 1944 - 25 Nov 1944:	Commander, 41st Destroyer Division
25 Nov 1944:	Posthumously promoted to *Rear-Admiral*

Vice-Admiral **Hoichi WANAMI** (2 Nov 1883 - 2 Jan 1975)
1 Dec 1931:	Promoted to *Rear-Admiral*
1 Dec 1931 - 15 Nov 1932:	Chief of Bureau 5, Naval Shipbuilding Command
15 Nov 1932 - 15 Nov 1934:	Commander, 2nd Submarine Flotilla
15 Nov 1934 - 15 Nov 1935:	Commandant, Submarine School
15 Nov 1935:	Promoted to *Vice-Admiral*
15 Nov 1935 - 28 Mar 1936:	Attached to Naval General Staff
30 Mar 1936:	Transferred to the reserve

Rear-Admiral **Isaburo WATANABE** (6 Feb 1895 - ?)
15 Sep 1944 - 1 May 1945:	Chief of Research Bureau, 1st Navy Fuel Yard
15 Oct 1944:	Promoted to *Rear-Admiral*
1 May 1945 - 1 Nov 1945:	Commander, 3rd Navy Fuel Yard

Rear-Admiral **Kanzaburo WATANABE** (12 Mar 1883 - 4 Aug 1964)
10 Oct 1932 - 1 Dec 1934:	Chief of Torpedo Bureau, Kure Navy Yard
15 Nov 1934:	Promoted to *Rear-Admiral*
1 Dec 1934 - 15 Dec 1934:	Attached to Naval Shipbuilding Command
22 Dec 1934:	Transferred to the reserve

Rear-Admiral **Mizuhiko WATANABE** (6 Jan 1894 - 19 Apr 1985)
1 Nov 1942:	Promoted to *Rear-Admiral*
1 Nov 1942 - 24 Dec 1942:	Attached to Naval General Staff
24 Dec 1942 - 10 Oct 1943:	Chief of Research Bureau, 1st Navy Fuel Yard
10 Oct 1943 - 15 Jun 1945:	Naval Representative, Shonan
15 Jun 1945 - 30 Sep 1945:	Chief of 101st Supply Bureau, Chief of Transport Bureau, Singapore

Rear-Admiral **Ryukichi WATANABE** (15 Oct 1893 - 22 Jun 1950)
15 Nov 1940 - 1 Dec 1944:	Chief of Shipbuilding Bureau, Yokosuka Navy Yard
15 Oct 1941:	Promoted to *Rear-Admiral*
1 Dec 1944 - 16 Apr 1945:	Attached to Bureau 4, Naval Shipbuilding Command
20 Apr 1945:	Transferred to the reserve

Rear-Admiral **Saburo WATANABE** (15 Sep 1883 - 21 Jan 1945)
22 Sep 1943 - 21 Jan 1945:	Captain, Motor Torpedo Boat Tender *"Shuri-maru"*
21 Jan 1945:	Posthumously promoted to *Rear-Admiral*

Rear-Admiral (Paymaster) **Sasuke WATANABE** (25 Aug 1891 - 15 Jun 1965)
15 Nov 1940 - 15 Oct 1941:	Paymaster-General, Ominato Guard District
15 Oct 1941:	Promoted to *Rear-Admiral*
15 Oct 1941 - 1 Apr 1943:	Chief of Accounting Bureau, 2nd Navy Fuel Yard

1 Apr 1943 - 20 Jun 1943:	Attached to Naval General Staff
25 Jun 1943:	Transferred to the reserve

Rear-Admiral **Seishichi WATANABE** (22 Feb 1893 - 15 Feb 1948)

20 Jan 1943 - 1 Jul 1943:	Staff officer, 3rd Southern Expeditionary Fleet
1 May 1943:	Promoted to *Rear-Admiral*
1 Jul 1943 - 9 Jul 1943:	Attached to Naval General Staff
9 Jul 1943 - 1 Dec 1943:	Commander, Kure Defense Flotilla
1 Dec 1943 - 15 Apr 1944:	Chief of Bureau 3, Naval Hydrographic Command
1 Dec 1943 - 1 Apr 1945:	Chief of Weather Section, Department of the Navy
1 Apr 1945 - 10 Apr 1945:	Attached to Ominato Guard District
10 Apr 1945 - 20 Sep 1945:	Commander, 104th Escort Flotilla

Rear-Admiral **Takeo WATANABE** (26 Jun 1890 - 1970)

15 Oct 1935 - 15 Nov 1939:	Supervisor for Construction & Ordnance, Naval Shipbuilding Command
15 Nov 1939:	Promoted to *Rear-Admiral*
15 Nov 1939 - 15 Dec 1939:	Attached to Naval Shipbuilding Command
21 Dec 1939:	Transferred to the reserve

Rear-Admiral **Dr. Takeshi WATANABE** (26 Sep 1892 - 4 Sep 1977)

1 Oct 1942 - 10 Jun 1944:	Chief of Bomb Bureau, Hikari Navy Yard
1 Nov 1942:	Promoted to *Rear-Admiral*
10 Jun 1944 - 24 Jun 1944:	Attached to Naval Shipbuilding Command
26 Jun 1944:	Transferred to the reserve

Rear-Admiral **Tamaki WATANABE** (27 Jan 1879 - 5 Jun 1947)

1 Dec 1924:	Promoted to *Rear-Admiral*
1 Dec 1924 - 20 Oct 1925:	Chief of Administration Bureau, Naval Shipbuilding Command
20 Oct 1925 - 1 Dec 1925:	Attached to Naval Shipbuilding Command
16 Dec 1925:	Transferred to the reserve

Rear-Admiral **Tsutomu WATANABE** (16 Sep 1884 - 8 Feb 1945)

20 May 1943 - 8 Feb 1945:	Captain, Gunboat *"Eifuku-maru"*
8 Feb 1945:	Posthumously promoted to *Rear-Admiral*

Rear-Admiral **Yasumasa WATANABE** (8 Jun 1899 - 18 Dec 1943)

20 Aug 1943 - 18 Dec 1943:	Commander, 1st Destroyer Division
18 Dec 1943:	Posthumously promoted to *Rear-Admiral*

Vice-Admiral **Tokutaro WAZUMI** (21 Jul 1890 - 26 May 1982)

1 Dec 1937 - 15 Nov 1938:	Chief Engineer Officer, 2nd Fleet

15 Nov 1938 - 15 Nov 1939:	Chief Engineer Officer, China Area Fleet, Chief Engineer Officer, 3rd Fleet
15 Nov 1939:	Promoted to *Rear-Admiral*
15 Nov 1939 - 15 Nov 1940:	Chief of Mining Bureau, Navy Fuel Yard
15 Nov 1940 - 1 Apr 1941:	Attached to Yokosuka Naval District
1 Apr 1941 - 5 Nov 1941:	Commandant, Naval Construction School
5 Nov 1941 - 5 Mar 1943:	Commander, 101st Navy Fuel Yard
5 Mar 1943 - 15 Mar 1943:	Attached to Naval General Staff
15 Mar 1943 - 15 Feb 1944:	Commandant, Naval Construction School
1 Nov 1943:	Promoted to *Vice-Admiral*
15 Feb 1944 - 20 Dec 1944:	Commander, 1st Air Arsenal
20 Dec 1944 - 10 Aug 1945:	Chief Supervisor for Construction & Ordnance, Naval Shipbuilding Command
10 Aug 1945 - 15 Oct 1945:	Kyushu Area Inspector, Department of Military Supply

Vice-Admiral (Surgeon) **Tatsusaburo YABE** (10 Mar 1863 - 29 Mar 1924)

1 Dec 1911:	Promoted to *General (Surgeon)*
1 Dec 1911 - 13 Dec 1915:	Director, Sasebo Naval Hospital, Chief Surgeon, Sasebo Naval District
13 Dec 1915 - 1 Dec 1917:	Commandant, Navy Medical School
1 Dec 1917:	Promoted to *General (Surgeon), Senior grade*
1 Dec 1917 - 1 Jun 1919:	Director, Yokosuka Naval Hospital, Chief Surgeon, Yokosuka Naval District
1 Jun 1919 - 2 Mar 1920:	Unassigned
23 Sep 1919:	Redesignated *Vice-Admiral (Surgeon)*
2 Mar 1920:	Transferred to the reserve

Rear-Admiral (Engineer) **Masatsume YAGASAKI** (5 Jun 1895 - 11 Sep 1961)

1 May 1943:	Promoted to *Rear-Admiral*
1 May 1943 - 1 Dec 1944:	Attached to Bureau 4, Naval Shipbuilding Command
1 Dec 1944 - 15 Oct 1945:	Chief of Shipbuilding Bureau, Yokosuka Navy Yard

Rear-Admiral **Hidetsuna YAGI** (12 Oct 1892 - 15 Mar 1943)

21 Apr 1941 - 8 Dec 1941:	Chief of Administration Bureau, Kure Navy Yard
8 Dec 1941 - 1 Nov 1942:	Attached to Administration Bureau, Naval Shipbuilding Command
1 Nov 1942:	Promoted to *Rear-Admiral*
1 Nov 1942 - 15 Mar 1943:	Attached to Naval General Staff

Rear-Admiral **Kyugo YAGI** (? - 6 Apr 1945)

11 Mar 1945 - 6 Apr 1945:	Commander, 2nd Patrol Boat Division
6 Apr 1945:	Posthumously promoted to *Rear-Admiral*

Vice-Admiral **Junkichi YAJIMA** (29 Oct 1865 - 15 May 1924)
1 Dec 1911:	Promoted to *Rear-Admiral*
1 Dec 1911 - 1 Dec 1914:	Commandant, Torpedo School
1 Dec 1914 - 1 Dec 1915:	Unassigned
1 Dec 1915:	Promoted to *Vice-Admiral*
1 Dec 1915:	Transferred to the reserve

Rear-Admiral **Takeo YAJIMA** (22 Jun 1881 - 12 Sep 1938)
1 Dec 1927 - 1 Dec 1931:	Chief of Ordnance Bureau, Yokosuka Navy Yard
10 Dec 1928:	Promoted to *Rear-Admiral*
1 Dec 1931 - 10 Dec 1931:	Attached to Naval General Staff
21 Dec 1931:	Transferred to the reserve

Rear-Admiral (Surgeon) **Gunji YAKABE** (15 Aug 1895 - 21 Jan 1977)
1 Nov 1942 - 15 Nov 1943:	Chief Medical Officer, China Area Fleet
1 May 1943:	Promoted to *Rear-Admiral (Surgeon)*
15 Nov 1943 - 10 Mar 1944:	Attached to Yokosuka Naval District
10 Mar 1944 - 23 May 1945:	Director, Nobi Naval Hospital
23 May 1945 - 11 Sep 1945:	Chief Medical Officer, Navy Supreme HQ, Chief Medical Officer, Combined Fleet
11 Sep 1945 - 10 Oct 1945:	Attached to Naval General Staff
10 Oct 1945 - 25 Oct 1945:	Chief of Medical Bureau, Technical Research Department
25 Oct 1945 - 30 Nov 1945:	Attached to Department of the Navy

Rear-Admiral **Chuji YAMADA** (11 Nov 1883 - 7 Jul 1971)
3 Oct 1933 - 1 Dec 1936:	Chief of Flight Research Bureau, Air Arsenal
15 Nov 1934:	Promoted to *Rear-Admiral*
1 Dec 1936 - 15 Dec 1936:	Attached to Naval General Staff
22 Dec 1936:	Transferred to the reserve

Vice-Admiral (Engineer) **Einosuke YAMADA** (9 Dec 1867 - 24 Sep 1922)
12 Jul 1912:	Promoted to *Rear-Admiral*
12 Jul 1912 - 1 Apr 1913:	Chief Engineer Officer, Maizuru Naval District
1 Apr 1913 - 1 Dec 1913:	Attached to Naval Shipbuilding Command
1 Dec 1913 - 1 Jul 1916:	Chief of Engine Construction Bureau, Kure Navy Yard
1 Jul 1916 - 1 Jun 1917:	Chief of Engine Construction Bureau, Yokosuka Navy Yard
1 Jun 1917:	Promoted to *Vice-Admiral*
1 Jun 1917 - 1 Jun 1918:	Unassigned
1 Jun 1918:	Transferred to the reserve

Vice-Admiral **Hikohachi YAMADA** (29 Feb 1855 - 28 Jan 1942)

6 Jun 1904:	Promoted to *Rear-Admiral*
6 Jun 1904 - 31 Jan 1905:	Commander, 5th Escort Flotilla
6 Jun 1904 - 20 Dec 1905:	C-in-C, 3rd Fleet
31 Jan 1905 - 20 Dec 1905:	Commander, 7th Escort Flotilla
20 Dec 1905 - 22 Nov 1906:	C-in-C, 1st Fleet
22 Nov 1906 - 12 Mar 1907:	Commander, Sasebo Torpedo Corps
12 Mar 1907 - 28 Aug 1908:	Commander, Kure Torpedo Corps
28 Aug 1908:	Promoted to *Vice-Admiral*
28 Aug 1908 - 1 Dec 1909:	C-in-C, 1st Fleet
1 Dec 1909 - 1 Dec 1910:	Commander, Takeshiki Guard District
1 Dec 1910 - 1 Dec 1912:	Commander, Ryojun Guard District
1 Dec 1912 - 29 May 1914:	Admiral Commanding, Yokosuka Naval District
1 Dec 1912 - 1 Mar 1915:	Member, Admirals Committee
1 Mar 1915:	Transferred to the reserve

Rear-Admiral **Kiyoshi YAMADA** (14 Mar 1890 - 26 Oct 1945)

1 Dec 1937:	Promoted to *Rear-Admiral*
1 Dec 1937 - 15 Nov 1940:	Chief Supervisor for Construction & Ordnance, Naval Shipbuilding Command
15 Nov 1940 - 16 Dec 1940:	Attached to Naval General Staff
21 Dec 1940:	Transferred to the reserve

Rear-Admiral **Kogoro YAMADA** (10 Sep 1889 - 23 Jul 1982)

10 Mar 1929 - 15 Nov 1938:	Staff officer, Technical Research Department
15 Nov 1938:	Promoted to *Rear-Admiral*
15 Nov 1938 - 15 Dec 1938:	Attached to Naval Shipbuilding Command
21 Dec 1938:	Transferred to the reserve

Rear-Admiral **Masaoki YAMADA** (24 Jun 1881 - 29 Oct 1956)

1 Dec 1924 - 1 Dec 1926:	Supervisor for Construction & Ordnance, Naval Shipbuilding Command
1 Dec 1926:	Promoted to *Rear-Admiral*
1 Dec 1926 - 20 Mar 1927:	Attached to Naval General Staff
20 Mar 1927 - 10 Apr 1927:	Unassigned
10 Apr 1927:	Transferred to the reserve

Vice-Admiral **Michiyuki YAMADA** (18 Dec 1893 - 6 Feb 1944)

1 Nov 1942:	Promoted to *Rear-Admiral*
1 Nov 1942 - 20 Jan 1943:	Commander, Kasumigaura Air Division
20 Jan 1943 - 6 Feb 1944:	Commander, 24th Air Flotilla
6 Feb 1944:	Posthumously promoted to *Vice-Admiral*

Rear-Admiral **Mitsuru YAMADA** (15 Dec 1889 - 6 May 1970)
9 May 1938 - 1 Nov 1939:	Chief of Division 3, Resource Control Bureau, Department of Commerce and Industry
15 Nov 1938:	Promoted to *Rear-Admiral*
1 Nov 1939 - 15 Nov 1939:	Staff officer, 3rd Fleet
15 Nov 1939 - 15 Nov 1940:	Commander, 13th Escort Flotilla
15 Nov 1940 - 15 Oct 1941:	Naval Attache, Manchuria
15 Oct 1941 - 13 Dec 1941:	Attached to Naval General Staff
15 Dec 1941:	Transferred to the reserve

Rear-Admiral **Naranosuke YAMADA** (20 May 1865 - 14 Nov 1926)
9 Jul 1912 - 8 Aug 1914:	Commander, Chinkai Defense Force
1 Dec 1912:	Promoted to *Rear-Admiral*
8 Aug 1914 - 1 Dec 1914:	C-in-C, Maizuru Naval District Fleet
1 Dec 1914 - 1 Dec 1915:	Unassigned
1 Dec 1915:	Transferred to the reserve

Vice-Admiral **Sadayoshi YAMADA** (26 Nov 1892 - 16 Nov 1971)
20 Sep 1941 - 20 Mar 1942:	Attached to Naval General Staff
15 Oct 1941:	Promoted to *Rear-Admiral*
20 Mar 1942 - 1 Apr 1942:	Staff officer, 11th Air Fleet
1 Apr 1942 - 17 Nov 1942:	Commander, 25th Air Flotilla
17 Nov 1942 - 20 Nov 1942:	Attached to Naval General Staff
20 Nov 1942 - 23 Nov 1942:	Staff officer, 3rd Fleet
23 Nov 1942 - 6 Dec 1943:	Chief of Staff, 3rd Fleet
6 Dec 1943 - 15 Mar 1944:	Commander, Yokosuka Air Division
15 Mar 1944 - 15 Nov 1944:	Commander, 51st Air Flotilla
15 Oct 1944:	Promoted to *Vice-Admiral*
15 Nov 1944 - 25 Nov 1944:	Attached to Naval General Staff
25 Nov 1944 - 20 Jul 1945:	Commander, 101st Air Flotilla
20 Jul 1945 - 24 Aug 1945:	Attached to Naval General Staff
24 Aug 1945 - 26 Aug 1945:	Staff officer, Supreme Naval HQ
26 Aug 1945 - 1 Oct 1945:	C-in-C, 3rd Air Fleet
1 Oct 1945 - 15 Oct 1945:	Attached to Department of the Navy

Vice-Admiral **Saku YAMADA** (10 May 1866 - 12 Feb 1940)
1 Dec 1914 - 1 Dec 1918:	Chief of Shipbuilding Bureau, Yokosuka Navy Yard
13 Dec 1915:	Promoted to *General (Constructor)*
1 Dec 1918 - 1 Oct 1920:	Chief of Bureau 4, Naval Technical Command
23 Sep 1919:	Redesignated *Rear-Admiral*
1 Oct 1920 - 1 Dec 1920:	Chief of Bureau 4, Naval Shipbuilding Command
1 Dec 1920:	Promoted to *Vice-Admiral*
1 Dec 1920 - 10 Dec 1920:	Attached to Naval Shipbuilding Command

10 Dec 1920 - 1 Jun 1921:	Unassigned
1 Jun 1921:	Transferred to the reserve

Rear-Admiral **Seiji YAMADA** (11 Feb 1901 - 26 Aug 1944)
15 Nov 1938 - 26 Aug 1944:	Supervisor for Construction, Naval Shipbuilding Command
26 Aug 1944:	Posthumously promoted to *Rear-Admiral*

Rear-Admiral **Seizo YAMADA** (15 Dec 1889 - 7 Jun 1990)
12 Oct 1942 - Oct 1945:	Commander, 2nd Harbor
1 May 1945:	Promoted to *Rear-Admiral*

Rear-Admiral **Takashi YAMADA** (1 Oct 1899 - 12 Jul 1944)
7 Apr 1944 - 12 Jul 1944:	Commander, 34th Submarine Division
12 Jul 1944:	Posthumously promoted to *Rear-Admiral*

Rear-Admiral **Takeji YAMADA** (21 Mar 1899 - 17 Jul 1944)
2 May 1943 - 17 Jul 1944:	Captain, Auxiliary Oiler *"Kyodo Maru No. 36"*
17 Jul 1944:	Posthumously promoted to *Rear-Admiral*

Rear-Admiral **Yuji YAMADA** (17 Oct 1895 - 28 Aug 1942)
11 Aug 1941 - 28 Aug 1942:	Commander, 20th Destroyer Division
28 Aug 1942:	Posthumously promoted to *Rear-Admiral*

Rear-Admiral **Yusuke YAMADA** (22 Feb 1899 - 13 Nov 1942)
6 Apr 1942 - 13 Nov 1942:	Commander, 6th Destroyer Division
13 Nov 1942:	Posthumously promoted to *Rear-Admiral*

Vice-Admiral **Nobuji YAMAGA** (7 May 1887 - 4 Nov 1954)
15 Nov 1933:	Promoted to *Rear-Admiral*
15 Nov 1933 - 15 Nov 1935:	Chief of Research Bureau, Navy Powder Yard
15 Nov 1935 - 1 Dec 1937:	Commander, Navy Powder Yard
1 Dec 1937:	Promoted to *Vice-Admiral*
1 Dec 1937 - 15 Dec 1937:	Attached to Naval Shipbuilding Command
21 Dec 1937:	Transferred to the reserve

Vice-Admiral **Bunzo YAMAGATA** (16 Dec 1862 - 8 Sep 1930)
1 Dec 1911:	Promoted to *Rear-Admiral*
1 Dec 1911 - 1 Dec 1913:	Adjutant, Governor of Korea
1 Dec 1913 - 1 Nov 1914:	C-in-C, Sasebo Naval District Fleet
1 Nov 1914 - 1 Dec 1914:	Attached to Sasebo Naval District
1 Dec 1914 - 1 Dec 1915:	Unassigned
1 Dec 1915:	Promoted to *Vice-Admiral*
1 Dec 1915:	Transferred to the reserve

Rear-Admiral **Masaji YAMAGATA** (6 Feb 1893 - 6 Feb 1944)
14 Sep 1943 - 6 Feb 1944: Commander, 61st Guard Force,
6 Feb 1944: Posthumously promoted to *Rear-Admiral*

Admiral **Seigo YAMAGATA** (15 Feb 1891 - 17 Mar 1945)
15 Jul 1938 - 1 Dec 1938: Attached to Naval Air Command
15 Nov 1938: Promoted to *Rear-Admiral*
1 Dec 1938 - 15 Dec 1938: Staff officer, 5th Fleet
15 Dec 1938 - 1 Dec 1939: Commander, 3rd Combined Air Division
1 Dec 1939 - 20 Mar 1942: Chief of Administration Bureau, Naval Air Command
20 Mar 1942 - 1 Apr 1942: Staff officer, 11th Air Fleet
1 Apr 1942 - 25 Feb 1943: Commander, 26th Air Flotilla
1 May 1942: Promoted to *Vice-Admiral*
25 Feb 1943 - 10 Jun 1943: Attached to Naval General Staff
10 Jun 1943 - 30 Nov 1943: Commander, Takao Guard District
30 Nov 1943 - 10 Mar 1945: C-in-C, 4th Southern Expeditionary Fleet
10 Mar 1945 - 17 Mar 1945: Attached to Naval General Staff
17 Mar 1945: Posthumously promoted to *Admiral*

Rear-Admiral **Shosuke YAMAGATA** (? - 11 Jan 1945)
7 Apr 1943 - 11 Jan 1945: Commander, 8th Harbor, Commander, 8th Communications Unit
11 Jan 1945: Posthumously promoted to *Rear-Admiral*

Rear-Admiral **Bunjiro YAMAGUCHI** (5 Feb 1896 - 3 Jan 1948)
13 Aug 1943 - 26 Feb 1945: Chief of Staff, Osaka Guard District
1 Nov 1943: Promoted to *Rear-Admiral*
26 Feb 1945 - 6 Sep 1945: Attached to Naval General Staff

Rear-Admiral **Chonan YAMAGUCHI** (15 Aug 1883 - 14 Nov 1942)
1 Dec 1931 - 15 Nov 1933: Chief of Personnel, Yokosuka Naval District
1 Dec 1932: Promoted to *Rear-Admiral*
15 Nov 1933 - 11 Dec 1933: Attached to Yokosuka Naval District
11 Dec 1933 - 15 Nov 1934: Commander, Yokosuka Guard Flotilla
15 Nov 1934 - 7 Oct 1935: Commander, Ominato Guard District
7 Oct 1935 - 1 Jul 1936: Attached to Naval General Staff
1 Jul 1936 - 22 Dec 1936: Unassigned
22 Dec 1936: Transferred to the reserve

Rear-Admiral **Denichi YAMAGUCHI** (1 Apr 1879 - 30 Dec 1947)
1 Dec 1918 - 1 Sep 1922: Captain, Battleship *"Fuji"*
1 Sep 1922 - 1 Apr 1923: Attached to Yokosuka Naval District

1 Dec 1922:	Promoted to *Rear-Admiral*
1 Apr 1923 - 1 May 1923:	Unassigned
1 May 1923:	Transferred to the reserve

Vice-Admiral **Ei YAMAGUCHI** (13 May 1867 - 20 Jan 1945)
1 Dec 1917:	Promoted to *Rear-Admiral*
1 Dec 1917 - 1 Oct 1920:	Member, Admirals Committee
1 Oct 1920 - 1 Dec 1921:	Chief of Supply Bureau, Department of the Navy
1 Dec 1921:	Promoted to *Vice-Admiral*
1 Dec 1921 - 10 Apr 1922:	Member, Admirals Committee
10 Apr 1922 - 31 Mar 1923:	Unassigned
31 Mar 1923:	Transferred to the reserve

Vice-Admiral **Gisaburo YAMAGUCHI** (26 Nov 1889 - 13 Dec 1972)
15 Nov 1939:	Promoted to *Rear-Admiral*
15 Nov 1939 - 10 Oct 1941:	Commandant, Navy Communications School
10 Oct 1941 - 2 Dec 1942:	Chief of Staff, Sasebo Naval District
2 Dec 1942 - 25 Nov 1943:	Commander, 10th Naval Base Force
1 Nov 1943:	Promoted to *Vice-Admiral*
25 Nov 1943 - 15 Jan 1944:	Attached to Naval General Staff
15 Jan 1944 - 20 Apr 1945:	Commander, Ryojun Area Base Force
20 Apr 1945 - 15 Nov 1945:	Commander, Chinkai Guard District
15 Nov 1945 - 30 Nov 1945:	Attached to Department of the Navy

Rear-Admiral (Paymaster) **Hajime YAMAGUCHI** (10 Apr 1891 - 27 Dec 1943)
10 Jul 1941 - 15 Mar 1943:	Chief of Accounting Bureau, Air Technical Arsenal
1 Nov 1942:	Promoted to *Rear-Admiral (Paymaster)*
15 Mar 1943 - 27 Dec 1943:	Commander, 2nd Air Arsenal

Vice-Admiral **Jihei YAMAGUCHI** (20 Aug 1891 - 19 Mar 1985)
20 Apr 1942 - 21 Jan 1943:	Chief of Staff, 1st Southern Expeditionary Fleet
1 Nov 1942:	Promoted to *Rear-Admiral*
21 Jan 1943 - 15 Nov 1945:	Chief of Administration Bureau, Naval Facilities Command
1 Nov 1945:	Promoted to *Vice-Admiral*

Vice-Admiral **Kujuro YAMAGUCHI** (4 Dec 1865 - 24 Sep 1928)
24 May 1913:	Promoted to *Rear-Admiral*
24 May 1913 - 8 Aug 1914:	C-in-C, Maizuru Naval District Fleet
8 Aug 1914 - 1 Apr 1916:	Commander, Chinkai Defense Force
1 Apr 1916 - 1 Dec 1916:	Commander, Chinkai Guard District
1 Dec 1916 - 1 Dec 1917:	Commander, Sasebo Navy Yard
1 Jun 1917:	Promoted to *Vice-Admiral*

1 Dec 1917 - 1 Dec 1918:	Member, Admirals Committee
1 Dec 1918 - 1 Aug 1919:	Unassigned
1 Aug 1919:	Transferred to the reserve

Vice-Admiral **Masumi YAMAGUCHI** (14 Feb 1893 - 15 Aug 1974)

15 Nov 1939 - 15 Nov 1940:	Chief Engineer Officer, Kure Naval District
15 Nov 1940:	Promoted to *Rear-Admiral*
15 Nov 1940 - 1 Apr 1941:	Attached to Naval General Staff
1 Apr 1941 - 1 Nov 1942:	Chief of Division 2, Fuel Bureau, Department of Commerce & Industry
1 Nov 1942 - 1 Nov 1943:	Chief of Oil Division, Fuel Bureau, Department of Commerce & Industry
1 Nov 1943 - 1 Jul 1944:	Chief of Oil Division, Fuel Bureau, Department of Military Supply
1 May 1944:	Promoted to *Vice-Admiral*
1 Jul 1944 - 15 Sep 1944:	Commander, 2nd Navy Fuel Yard
15 Sep 1944 - 24 Sep 1944:	Attached to Naval General Staff
25 Sep 1944:	Transferred to the reserve

Rear-Admiral **Minoru YAMAGUCHI** (7 Nov 1887 - 13 Mar 1969)

15 Nov 1934 - 1 Dec 1936:	Commander, Interim Defense Force
1 Dec 1936:	Promoted to *Rear-Admiral*
1 Dec 1936 - 15 Dec 1936:	Attached to Naval General Staff
22 Dec 1936:	Transferred to the reserve

Rear-Admiral **Nobuichi YAMAGUCHI** (31 Aug 1882 - 1 Feb 1945)

15 Jun 1926 - 4 Dec 1928:	Chief of Section 1, Naval Hydrographic Command
4 Dec 1928 - 20 Dec 1928:	Attached to Naval General Staff
10 Dec 1928:	Promoted to *Rear-Admiral*
25 Dec 1928:	Transferred to the reserve

Vice-Admiral **Nobusuke YAMAGUCHI** (20 Jun 1892 - 7 Jun 1986)

15 Oct 1941:	Promoted to *Rear-Admiral*
15 Oct 1941 - 1 Jul 1943:	Chief of Electronics Bureau, Kure Navy Yard
1 Jul 1943 - 20 Dec 1944:	Chief of Bureau 3, Naval Shipbuilding Command
20 Dec 1944 - 1 May 1945:	Chief Supervisor for Construction & Ordnance, Naval Shipbuilding Command
1 May 1945:	Promoted to *Vice-Admiral*
1 May 1945 - 1 Nov 1945:	Commander, 1st Navy Fuel Yard

Rear-Admiral **Seishichi YAMAGUCHI** (2 May 1883 - 10 Apr 1949)

4 Dec 1928 - 1 Dec 1931:	Chief of Section 1, Naval Hydrographic Command
1 Dec 1931:	Promoted to *Rear-Admiral*

1 Dec 1931 - 20 Jul 1932: Attached to Naval General Staff
30 Jul 1932: Transferred to the reserve

Vice-Admiral **Tamon YAMAGUCHI** (17 Aug 1892 - 5 Jun 1942)
15 Nov 1938: Promoted to *Rear-Admiral*
15 Nov 1938 - 1 Dec 1938: Attached to Naval General Staff
1 Dec 1938 - 15 Dec 1938: Staff officer, 5th Fleet
15 Dec 1938 - 15 Nov 1939: Chief of Staff, 5th Fleet
15 Nov 1939 - 15 Jan 1940: Staff officer, 1st Fleet
15 Jan 1940 - 1 Nov 1940: Commander, 1st Combined Air Division
1 Nov 1940 - 5 Jun 1942: Commander, 2nd Carrier Flotilla
5 Jun 1942: Posthumously promoted to *Vice-Admiral*

Rear-Admiral **Dr. Tatsuya YAMAGUCHI** (23 Dec 1856 - 9 Apr 1927)
8 Oct 1897 - 13 Nov 1900: Commander, Yokosuka Submarine Yard
22 May 1900: Promoted to *General (Constructor)*
13 Nov 1900 - 5 Apr 1903: Unassigned
5 Apr 1903: Transferred to the reserve
23 Sep 1919: Redesignated *Rear-Admiral*

Rear-Admiral **Tokujiro YAMAGUCHI** (21 Sep 1878 - 28 Jan 1966)
1 Apr 1925 - 1 Dec 1927: Chief of Shipbuilding Bureau, Sasebo Navy Yard
1 Dec 1927: Promoted to *Rear-Admiral*
1 Dec 1927 - 15 Dec 1927: Attached to Naval Shipbuilding Command
25 Dec 1927: Transferred to the reserve

Vice-Admiral **Kazuyoshi YAMAJI** (13 Mar 1869 - 13 Mar 1963)
17 Apr 1914 - 1 Dec 1914: Chief of Staff, 1st Fleet
1 Dec 1914: Promoted to *Rear-Admiral*
1 Dec 1914 - 1 Dec 1916: Commandant, Naval Gunnery School
1 Dec 1916 - 13 Apr 1917: Commander, 4th Escort Flotilla
13 Apr 1917 - 12 Dec 1917: C-in-C, 3rd Special Task Fleet
12 Dec 1917 - 13 Jun 1918: Commander, 2nd Escort Flotilla
13 Jun 1918 - 1 Dec 1919: Commander, Mako Guard District
1 Dec 1918: Promoted to *Vice-Admiral*
1 Dec 1919 - 1 Dec 1920: Commander, 2nd Escort Flotilla
1 Dec 1920 - 1 Dec 1922: Commander, Chinkai Guard District
1 Dec 1922 - 10 Dec 1922: Member, Admirals Committee
10 Dec 1922 - 31 Mar 1923: Unassigned
31 Mar 1923: Transferred to the reserve

Rear-Admiral **Akira YAMAKI** (30 Apr 1896 - 28 Aug 1982)
1 Jun 1942 - 8 Feb 1945: Chief of Section 2, Bureau of Naval Affairs, Department of the Navy

15 Oct 1944:	Promoted to *Rear-Admiral*
8 Feb 1945 - 20 Mar 1945:	Deputy Chief of Staff, Takao Guard District
20 Mar 1945 - 24 Sep 1945:	Chief Instructor, Naval Academy
24 Sep 1945 - 30 Nov 1945:	Staff officer, Kure Naval District
30 Nov 1945 - 1 Dec 1945:	Chief of Personnel, Kure Naval District

Rear-Admiral **Kamenosuke YAMAMORI** (1 Nov 1895 - 25 Aug 1986)

10 Aug 1944 - 23 Oct 1944:	Captain, Aircraft Carrier *"Amagi"*
15 Oct 1944:	Promoted to *Rear-Admiral*
23 Oct 1944 - 20 Mar 1945:	Chief Instructor, Naval Academy
20 Mar 1945 - 10 Nov 1945:	Commander, Kyushu Air Division

Rear-Admiral **Chikao YAMAMOTO** (13 Oct 1896 - 4 Nov 1980)

20 Jan 1943 - 6 Jan 1945:	Chief of Section 1, Bureau 1, Naval General Staff
15 Oct 1944:	Promoted to *Rear-Admiral*
6 Jan 1945 - 10 Feb 1945:	Commander, 11th Air Flotilla
10 Feb 1945 - 15 Feb 1945:	Sraff officer, 5th Air Fleet
15 Feb 1945 - 1 Mar 1945:	Staff officer, Combined Fleet
1 Mar 1945 - 25 May 1945:	Chief of Staff, 10th Air Fleet
25 May 1945 - 10 Oct 1945:	Commander, 72nd Air Flotilla

Admiral **Eisuke YAMAMOTO** (15 May 1876 - 27 Jul 1962)

15 Mar 1920 - 1 Sep 1921:	Attached to Naval General Staff
1 Dec 1920:	Promoted to *Rear-Admiral*
1 Sep 1921 - 1 Dec 1922:	Chief of Bureau 2, Naval Shipbuilding Command
1 Dec 1922 - 1 Jun 1923:	Chief Instructor, Naval College
1 Jun 1923 - 1 Dec 1924:	Commandant of the Naval College
1 Dec 1924:	Promoted to *Vice-Admiral*
1 Dec 1924 - 1 Dec 1925:	Commander, 5th Escort Flotilla
1 Dec 1925 - 15 Jan 1926:	Attached to Naval General Staff
15 Jan 1926 - 1 Feb 1927:	C-in-C, Training Fleet
1 Feb 1927 - 5 Apr 1927:	Attached to Naval General Staff
5 Apr 1927 - 10 Dec 1928:	Chief of Naval Air Command
10 Dec 1928 - 11 Nov 1929:	Admiral Commanding, Yokosuka Naval District, Member, Admirals Committee
11 Nov 1929 - 1 Dec 1931:	C-in-C, Combined Fleet, C-in-C, 1st Fleet
1 Apr 1931:	Promoted to *Admiral*
1 Dec 1931 - 2 Feb 1932:	Navy Councillor
2 Feb 1932 - 10 Oct 1932:	Admiral Commanding, Yokosuka Naval District, Member, Admirals Committee
10 Oct 1932 - 28 Mar 1936:	Navy Councillor
30 Mar 1936:	Transferred to the reserve

Admiral **Count Gombei YAMAMOTO** (15 Oct 1852 - 9 Dec 1933)
8 Mar 1895:	Promoted to *Rear-Admiral*
8 Mar 1895 - 8 Nov 1898:	Chief, Bureau of Naval Affairs, Department of the Navy, Member, Admirals Committee
14 May 1898:	Promoted to *Vice-Admiral*
8 Nov 1898 - 7 Jan 1906:	Minister of the Navy
6 Jun 1904:	Promoted to *Admiral*
9 Jan 1906 - 20 Feb 1913:	Navy Councillor
20 Feb 1913 - 16 Apr 1914:	Prime Minister
16 Apr 1914 - 11 May 1914:	Unassigned
11 May 1914:	Transferred to the reserve

Rear-Admiral (Surgeon) **Hidetada YAMAMOTO** (10 Jun 1873 - 5 Mar 1940)
7 Jun 1921 - 1 Dec 1921:	Chief of Bureau 1, Kure Naval Hospital
1 Dec 1921:	Promoted to *Rear-Admiral*
1 Dec 1921 - 10 Dec 1921:	Attached to Kure Naval District
10 Dec 1921 - 31 Mar 1923:	Unassigned
31 Mar 1923:	Transferred to the reserve

Fleet Admiral **Isoroku YAMAMOTO** (4 Apr 1884 - 18 Apr 1943)
12 Nov 1929 - 1 Sep 1930:	Assistant to Plenipotentiary, London Conference
30 Nov 1929:	Promoted to *Rear-Admiral*
1 Sep 1930 - 1 Dec 1930:	Attached to Naval General Staff
1 Dec 1930 - 3 Oct 1933:	Chief of Technical Bureau, Naval Air Command
3 Oct 1933 - 1 Jun 1934:	Commander, 1st Carrier Flotilla
1 Jun 1934 - 7 Sep 1934:	Attached to Naval General Staff
7 Sep 1934 - 12 Feb 1935:	Representative for Preliminary Negotiation, London Conference
15 Nov 1934:	Promoted to *Vice-Admiral*
12 Feb 1935 - 2 Dec 1935:	Attached to Naval General Staff
2 Dec 1935 - 1 Dec 1936:	Chief of Naval Air Command
1 Dec 1936 - 30 Aug 1939:	Deputy Minister of the Navy
25 Apr 1938 - 15 Nov 1938:	Chief of Naval Air Command
30 Aug 1939 - 11 Aug 1941:	C-in-C, 1st Fleet
15 Nov 1940:	Promoted to *Admiral*
30 Aug 1939 - 18 Apr 1943:	C-in-C, Combined Fleet
18 Apr 1943:	Posthumously appointed *Fleet Admiral*

Rear-Admiral **Iwata YAMAMOTO** (15 May 1896 - 25 Oct 1944)
15 Dec 1943 - 25 Oct 1944:	Captain, Light Cruiser *"Tama"*
25 Oct 1944:	Posthumously promoted to *Rear-Admiral*

Rear-Admiral **Junpei YAMAMOTO** (15 Jul 1888 - 12 Jan 1956)
15 Nov 1939:	Promoted to *Rear-Admiral*
15 Nov 1939 - 15 Sep 1940:	Attached to Administration Bureau, Naval Air Command
15 Sep 1940 - 15 Oct 1941:	Chief Supervisor for Construction & Ordnance, Naval Shipbuilding Command
15 Oct 1941 - 22 Nov 1941:	Attached to Naval General Staff
24 Nov 1941:	Transferred to the reserve

General (Surgeon) **Kageyuki YAMAMOTO** (1853 - 27 Aug 1914)
10 Nov 1903 - 12 Jan 1905:	Director, Yokosuka Naval Hospital
1 Sep 1904:	Promoted to *General (Surgeon)*
12 Jan 1905 - 19 Dec 1905:	Director, Kure Naval Hospital
19 Dec 1905 - 24 Feb 1907:	Unassigned
24 Feb 1907:	Transferred to the reserve

Vice-Admiral **Kaizo YAMAMOTO** (15 Feb 1868 - 18 Apr 1958)
1 Dec 1916:	Promoted to *General (Constructor)*
1 Dec 1916 - 1 Oct 1920:	Attached to Naval Technical Command
23 Sep 1919:	Redesignated *Rear-Admiral*
1 Oct 1920 - 1 Dec 1920:	Attached to Naval Shipbuilding Command
1 Dec 1920 - 13 Aug 1923:	Chief of Bureau 4, Naval Shipbuilding Command
1 Dec 1921:	Promoted to *Vice-Admiral*
13 Aug 1923 - 1 Dec 1923:	Attached to Naval Shipbuilding Command
1 Dec 1923 - 25 Feb 1924:	Unassigned
25 Feb 1924:	Transferred to the reserve

Vice-Admiral (Paymaster) **Kameji YAMAMOTO** (16 Oct 1893 - 13 Aug 1945)
1 Apr 1943 - 25 Oct 1943:	Chief of 102nd Accounting Bureau
15 Apr 1943 - 25 Oct 1943:	Paymaster-General, 2nd Southern Expeditionary Fleet
1 May 1943:	Promoted to *Rear-Admiral (Paymaster)*
25 Oct 1943 - 13 Nov 1943:	Attached to Naval Shipbuilding Command
13 Nov 1943 - 2 Aug 1945:	Chief of Materiel Bureau, Naval Shipbuilding Command
2 Aug 1945 - 13 Aug 1945:	Attached to Naval Shipbuilding Command
13 Aug 1945:	Posthumously promoted to *Vice-Admiral (Paymaster)*

Vice-Admiral **Koki YAMAMOTO** (20 Apr 1887 - 24 Jan 1958)
1 Dec 1936:	Promoted to *Rear-Admiral*
1 Dec 1936 - 15 Nov 1938:	Chief of Ordnance Bureau, Yokosuka Navy Yard
15 Nov 1938 - 15 Nov 1940:	Chief of Bureau 2, Naval Shipbuilding Command

15 Nov 1940:	Promoted to *Vice-Admiral*
15 Nov 1940 - 27 Feb 1941:	Attached to Naval General Staff
27 Feb 1941 - 20 Nov 1942:	Admiral Commanding, Mako Guard District
20 Nov 1942 - 15 Mar 1943:	Attached to Naval General Staff
20 Mar 1943:	Transferred to the reserve

Vice-Admiral **Mikinosuke YAMAMOTO** (16 Oct 1883 - 5 May 1944)

16 May 1928 - 15 Nov 1932:	Chief of Shipbuilding Bureau, Yokosuka Navy Yard
10 Dec 1928:	Promoted to *Rear-Admiral*
15 Nov 1932 - 5 Apr 1934:	Commander, Sasebo Navy Yard
15 Nov 1933:	Promoted to *Vice-Admiral*
5 Apr 1934 - 1 Dec 1937:	Chief of Bureau 4, Naval Shipbuilding Command
1 Dec 1937 - 2 Feb 1938:	Attached to Naval Shipbuilding Command
3 Feb 1938:	Transferred to the reserve

Rear-Admiral (Engineer) **Naonori YAMAMOTO** (20 Mar 1860 - 2 Sep 1929)

10 Nov 1903 - 12 Dec 1905:	Chief Engineer Officer, Maizuru Naval District
2 Nov 1905:	Promoted to *General (Engineer)*
12 Dec 1905 - 30 Nov 1906:	Unassigned
26 Jan 1906:	Redesignated *Rear-Admiral (Engineer)*
30 Nov 1906:	Transferred to the reserve

Rear-Admiral **Shinjiro YAMAMOTO** (22 Dec 1877 - 28 Feb 1942)

6 Jan 1922 - 10 Dec 1923:	Attached to the Ministry of the Imperial Household
1 Dec 1922:	Promoted to *Rear-Admiral*
10 Dec 1923 - 25 Feb 1924:	Unassigned
25 Feb 1924:	Transferred to the reserve

Rear-Admiral (Paymaster) **Tohei YAMAMOTO** (? - 9 Mar 1945)

5 Sep 1943 - 9 Mar 1945:	Paymaster-General, 5th Fleet
9 Mar 1945:	Posthumously promoted to *Rear-Admiral (Paymaster)*

Vice-Admiral (Paymaster) **Ushinosuke YAMAMOTO** (6 Sep 1889 - 8 Feb 1976)

1 Jun 1936 - 12 Apr 1939:	Chief of Section 1, Accounting Bueau, Department of the Navy
15 Nov 1938:	Promoted to *Rear-Admiral (Paymaster)*
12 Apr 1939 - 10 Apr 1941:	Chief of Accounting Bureau, Yokosuka Navy Yard
10 Apr 1941 - 15 May 1943:	Chief of Accounting Bureau, Naval Shipbuilding Command
1 Nov 1942:	Promoted to *Vice-Admiral (Paymaster)*
15 May 1943 - 1 Jun 1943:	Attached to Naval General Staff
1 Jun 1943 - 30 Nov 1945:	Chief of Naval Accounting Bureau, Department of the Navy

Vice-Admiral (Engineer) **Yasujiro YAMAMOTO** (11 Sep 1861 - 16 Jun 1913)

28 Dec 1903 - 4 Nov 1905:	Chief Engineer Officer, Combined Fleet, Chief Engineer Officer, 1st Fleet
1 Sep 1904:	Promoted to *General (Engineer)*
4 Nov 1905 - 28 Aug 1908:	Commandant, Naval Engineering Academy
26 Jan 1906:	Redesignated *Rear-Admiral (Engineer)*
28 Aug 1908 - 1 Dec 1910:	Chief of Bureau 4, Naval Shipbuilding Command
16 Sep 1910:	Promoted to *Vice-Admiral (Engineer)*
1 Dec 1910 - 1 Dec 1911:	Unassigned
1 Dec 1911:	Transferred to the reserve

Rear-Admiral **Yoshio YAMAMOTO** (20 Jun 1898 - 28 Nov 1978)

14 Jul 1942 - 10 Jul 1945:	Chief of Section 1, Bureau of Naval Affairs, Department of the Navy
1 May 1945:	Promoted to *Rear-Admiral*
21 May 1945 - 10 Jul 1945:	Chief of Section 3, Bureau 2, Naval General Staff
10 Jul 1945 - 1 Sep 1945:	Attached to Naval General Staff
1 Sep 1945 - 30 Nov 1945:	Chief of Bureau of Naval Affairs, Department of the Navy

Rear-Admiral **Yuji YAMAMOTO** (17 Jan 1903 - 7 Apr 1945)

10 Aug 1944 - 7 Apr 1945:	Staff officer, 2nd Fleet
7 Apr 1945:	Posthumously promoted to *Rear-Admiral*

Vice-Admiral **Masayuki YAMANAKA** (11 Jan 1886 - 9 Jun 1951)

1 Dec 1930:	Promoted to *Rear-Admiral*
1 Dec 1930 - 15 Nov 1933:	Instructor, Naval College
15 Nov 1933 - 10 May 1934:	Chief of Scientific Research Bureau, Technical Research Department
10 May 1934 - 1 Dec 1936:	Commander, Navy Fuel Yard
15 Nov 1935:	Promoted to *Vice-Admiral*
1 Dec 1936 - 10 Jan 1938:	Attached to Naval General Staff
15 Jan 1938:	Transferred to the reserve

Vice-Admiral **Shibakichi YAMANAKA** (6 Feb 1870 - 21 Jun 1941)

1 Dec 1914:	Promoted to *Rear-Admiral*
1 Dec 1914 - 13 Dec 1915:	Chief of Staff, 1st Fleet
1 Nov 1915 - 13 Dec 1915:	Chief of Staff, Combined Fleet
13 Dec 1915 - 16 Jul 1917:	Chief of Staff, Kure Naval District
20 Mar 1916 - 16 Jul 1917:	C-in-C, Special Task Fleet
16 Jul 1917 - 18 Oct 1918:	Commander, 2nd Destroyer Flotilla
18 Oct 1918 - 4 Nov 1918:	Attached to Yokosuka Naval District
4 Nov 1918 - 1 Sep 1921:	Commander, Yokosuka Navy Yard
1 Dec 1918:	Promoted to *Vice-Admiral*

1 Sep 1921 - 1 Dec 1921:	Member, Admirals Committee
1 Dec 1921 - 8 Sep 1922:	Unassigned
8 Sep 1922:	Transferred to the reserve

Vice-Admiral **Tomojiro YAMANAKA** (10 Oct 1889 - 14 Feb 1986)

15 Oct 1941:	Promoted to *Rear-Admiral*
15 Oct 1941 - 5 Oct 1942:	Chief Instructor, Naval Engineering Academy
5 Oct 1942 - 25 Sep 1943:	Commander, 103rd Naval Facility
25 Sep 1943 - 10 Oct 1943:	Attached to Naval General Staff
10 Oct 1943 - 25 Feb 1944:	Supervisor for Construction & Ordnance, Naval Shipbuilding Command
25 Feb 1944 - 10 Dec 1944:	Chief of Toyama Detachment, Niigata Area Inspector Office, Department of Military Supply
10 Dec 1944 - 1 Mar 1945:	Attached to Yokosuka Naval District
1 Mar 1945 - 25 Aug 1945:	Commandant, Dainian Naval Engineering School
1 May 1945:	Promoted to *Vice-Admiral*
25 Aug 1945 - 15 Sep 1945:	Commander, 20th Combined Air Division

Admiral **Katsunoshin YAMANASHI** (26 Jul 1877 - 17 Dec 1967)

17 Aug 1921 - 25 May 1922:	Assistant to the Plenipotentiary, Washington Conference
1 Dec 1921:	Promoted to *Rear-Admiral*
25 May 1922 - 5 Sep 1923:	Chief of Staff, Yokosuka Naval District
5 Sep 1923 - 1 Dec 1924:	Chief of Naval Personnel, Department of the Navy
1 Dec 1924 - 15 Apr 1925:	Attached to Naval General Staff
15 Apr 1925 - 10 Dec 1926:	Commander, Yokosuka Navy Yard
1 Dec 1925:	Promoted to *Vice-Admiral*
10 Dec 1926 - 1 Feb 1929:	Chief of Naval Shipbuilding Command, Member, Admirals Committee
10 Dec 1928 - 10 Jun 1930:	Deputy Minister of the Navy, Member, Admirals Committee
10 Jun 1930 - 1 Dec 1930:	Attached to Naval General Staff
1 Dec 1930 - 1 Dec 1931:	Admiral Commanding, Sasebo Naval District
1 Dec 1931 - 1 Dec 1932:	Admiral Commanding, Kure Naval District
1 Apr 1932:	Promoted to *Admiral*
1 Dec 1932 - 6 Mar 1933:	Navy Councillor
11 Mar 1933:	Transferred to the reserve

Rear-Admiral (Surgeon) **Shuzo YAMANOUCHI** (4 Apr 1894 - ?)

1 Nov 1942:	Promoted to *Rear-Admiral (Surgeon)*
1 Nov 1942 - 10 Nov 1944:	Chief of Medical Bureau, Hikari Navy Yard
10 Nov 1944 - 14 Dec 1944:	Staff officer, 2nd Southern Expeditionary Fleet
14 Dec 1944 - 26 Jul 1946:	Director, 102nd Naval Hospital

Vice-Admiral **Toyokazu YAMAOKA** (5 Dec 1868 - 21 Jul 1926)

1 Dec 1917:	Promoted to *Rear-Admiral*
1 Dec 1917 - 15 Dec 1917:	Attached to Naval General Staff
15 Dec 1917 - 10 Aug 1918:	Commander, 7th Escort Flotilla
10 Aug 1918 - 9 Aug 1919:	C-in-C, China Expeditionary Fleet
9 Aug 1919 - 8 Nov 1919:	C-in-C, 1st Expeditionary Fleet
8 Nov 1919 - 1 Dec 1919:	Member, Admirals Committee
1 Dec 1919 - 25 Oct 1920:	Commander, 4th Escort Flotilla
25 Oct 1920 - 1 Dec 1921:	Member, Admirals Committee
1 Dec 1921:	Promoted to *Vice-Admiral*
1 Dec 1921 - 31 Mar 1923:	Unassigned
31 Mar 1923:	Transferred to the reserve

Vice-Admiral **Shigeaki YAMASAKI** (21 Jan 1893 - 28 Dec 1980)

15 Nov 1940:	Promoted to *Rear-Admiral*
15 Nov 1940 - 5 Feb 1942:	Commander, 2nd Submarine Flotilla
5 Feb 1942 - 15 Apr 1942:	Attached to Naval General Staff
15 Apr 1942 - 22 Oct 1942:	Commander, 1st Submarine Flotilla
22 Oct 1942 - 15 Sep 1943:	Attached to Naval General Staff
15 Sep 1943 - 10 Jul 1944:	Commandant, Submarine School
1 Dec 1943 - 10 Jul 1944:	Commander, Kure Submarine Flotilla
1 May 1944:	Promoted to *Vice-Admiral*
10 Jul 1944 - 15 Apr 1945:	Chief of Submarine Division, Department of the Navy
15 Apr 1945 - 20 Aug 1945:	Chief of Special Weapons Division, Department of the Navy
20 Aug 1945 - 20 Sep 1945:	Attached to Naval General Staff

Admiral **Baron Gentaro YAMASHITA** (30 Jul 1863 - 18 Feb 1931)

22 Nov 1906 - 10 Dec 1908:	Chief of Staff, 1st Fleet
28 Aug 1908:	Promoted to *Rear-Admiral*
8 Oct 1908 - 20 Nov 1908:	Chief of Staff, Combined Fleet
10 Dec 1908 - 4 Mar 1909:	Chief of Staff, Sasebo Naval District
4 Mar 1909 - 19 Jul 1909:	Chief of Bureau 1, Naval Shipbuilding Command
19 Jul 1909 - 23 Mar 1910:	Unassigned
23 Mar 1910 - 1 Dec 1910:	Chief of Bureau 1, Naval General Staff
1 Dec 1910 - 25 Mar 1914:	Commandant of the Naval Academy
1 Dec 1912:	Promoted to *Vice-Admiral*
25 Mar 1914 - 10 Aug 1915:	Deputy Chief of the Naval General Staff, Member, Admirals Committee
10 Aug 1915 - 1 Dec 1917:	Admiral Commanding, Sasebo Naval District
1 Dec 1917 - 1 Dec 1919:	C-in-C, 1st Fleet
2 Jul 1918:	Promoted to *Admiral*
1 Sep 1918 - 15 Oct 1918:	C-in-C, Combined Fleet

1 Jun 1919 - 28 Oct 1919:	C-in-C, Combined Fleet
1 Dec 1919 - 1 Dec 1920:	Navy Councillor
1 Dec 1920 - 15 Apr 1925:	Chief of the Naval General Staff, Member, Admirals Committee
15 Apr 1925 - 1 Jul 1928:	Navy Councillo
1 Jul 1928:	Transferred to the reserve

Vice-Admiral **Gihachiro YAMASHITA** (3 Feb 1879 - 10 Apr 1960)

20 Apr 1921 - 1 Dec 1923:	Chief Instructor, Naval Engineering Academy
1 Dec 1922:	Promoted to *Rear-Admiral*
1 Dec 1923 - 1 Dec 1924:	Chief Engineer Officer, Combined Fleet, Chief Engineer Officer, 1st Fleet
1 Dec 1924 - 10 Dec 1928:	Commander, Navy Fuel Yard
1 Dec 1926:	Promoted to *Vice-Admiral*
10 Dec 1928 - 30 Nov 1929:	Commandant, Naval Engineering Academy
30 Nov 1929 - 1 Dec 1931:	Chief of Supply Bureau, Department of the Navy
1 Dec 1931 - 22 Mar 1932:	Attached to Naval General Staff
31 Mar 1932:	Transferred to the reserve

Vice-Admiral **Kanemitsu YAMASHITA** (4 Sep 1883 - 30 Mar 1941)

1 Dec 1931:	Promoted to *Rear-Admiral*
1 Dec 1931 - 10 Oct 1932:	Chief of Torpedo Bureau, Kure Navy Yard
10 Oct 1932 - 10 May 1934:	Chief of Administration Bureau, Naval Shipbuilding Command
10 May 1934 - 15 Nov 1935:	Commander, Hiro Navy Yard
15 Nov 1935:	Promoted to *Vice-Admiral*
15 Nov 1935 - 10 Dec 1935:	Attached to Naval General Staff
15 Dec 1935:	Transferred to the reserve

Rear-Admiral (Surgeon) **Tomoyoshi YAMASHITA** (1 Apr 1882 - 8 Apr 1932)

1 Dec 1925 - 10 Dec 1928:	Director, Maizuru Guard District Naval Hospital, Chief Surgeon, Maizuru Guard District
10 Dec 1928:	Promoted to *Rear-Admiral (Surgeon)*
10 Dec 1928 - 20 Dec 1928:	Attached to Naval General Staff
25 Dec 1928:	Transferred to the reserve

Rear-Admiral **Tarozo YAMASUMI** (12 Oct 1865 - 7 May 1918)

22 May 1909 - 1 Dec 1910:	Chief of Survey Section, Naval Hydrographic Command
1 Dec 1910 - 1 Dec 1912:	Unassigned
1 Dec 1912:	Promoted to *Rear-Admiral*
1 Dec 1912:	Transferred to the reserve

Rear-Admiral **Matsujiro YAMATAKA** (3 Jul 1894 - 18 Oct 1944)
16 Sep 1944 - 18 Oct 1944:	Captain, Motor Vessel *"Shinko-maru"*
18 Oct 1944:	Posthumously promoted to *Rear-Admiral*

Vice-Admiral **Baron Masuji YAMAUCHI** (29 Mar 1860 - 18 Sep 1919)
25 May 1897 - 10 Nov 1903:	Commander, Kure Ordnance Arsenal
26 May 1902:	Promoted to *Rear-Admiral*
10 Nov 1903 - 2 Feb 1906:	Commander, Kure Navy Yard
13 Nov 1905:	Promoted to *Vice-Admiral*
2 Feb 1906 - 1 Dec 1909:	Admiral Commanding, Kure Naval District
1 Dec 1909 - 15 Jul 1910:	Unassigned
15 Jul 1910:	Transferred to the reserve

Vice-Admiral **Shiro YAMAUCHI** (5 Mar 1872 - 10 Nov 1923)
1 Dec 1919:	Promoted to *Rear-Admiral*
1 Dec 1919 - 12 Nov 1920:	Commander, Yokosuka Air Division
12 Nov 1920 - 1 Apr 1923:	Chief of Bureau 6, Naval Shipbuilding Command
1 Apr 1923 - 1 Jun 1923:	Chief of Bureau 2, Naval Shipbuilding Command
1 Jun 1923 - 6 Nov 1923:	Commander, Mako Guard District
10 Nov 1923:	Posthumously promoted to *Vice-Admiral*

Rear-Admiral **Teizo YAMAUCHI** (27 Jul 1900 - 25 Oct 1944)
25 Dec 1943 - 25 Oct 1944:	Executive Officer, Heavay Cruiser *"Chikuma"*
25 Oct 1944:	Posthumously promoted to *Rear-Admiral*

Rear-Admiral **Toyonaka YAMAUCHI** (30 May 1885 - 30 Oct 1952)
5 Dec 1927 - 1 Jun 1932:	Aide-de-Camp to the Emperor
1 Dec 1930:	Promoted to *Rear-Admiral*
1 Jun 1932 - 16 Jun 1932:	Attached to Naval General Staff
16 Jun 1932 - 15 Nov 1933:	Commander, Mako Guard District
15 Nov 1933 - 26 Mar 1934:	Attached to Naval General Staff
31 Mar 1934:	Transferred to the reserve

Admiral **Tanin YAMAYA** (4 Mar 1866 - 10 Sep 1940)
27 Dec 1907 - 1 Dec 1909:	Chief of Bureau 2, Naval General Staff
1 Dec 1909:	Promoted to *Rear-Admiral*
1 Dec 1909 - 1 Dec 1911:	Chief of Bureau 1, Naval Training Command, Chief of Bureau 2, Naval Training Command
25 Sep 1911 - 1 Dec 1911:	Commandant of the Naval College
1 Dec 1911 - 20 Apr 1912:	C-in-C, Maizuru Reserve Fleet
20 Apr 1912 - 1 Dec 1913:	Chief of Naval Personnel, Department of the Navy
1 Dec 1913:	Promoted to *Vice-Admiral*
1 Dec 1913 - 18 Aug 1914:	Commandant of the Naval College
18 Aug 1914 - 14 Sep 1914:	C-in-C, 1st Fleet

14 Sep 1914 - 1 Feb 1915:	Commander, 1st Southern Detachment
1 Feb 1915 - 6 Aug 1915:	Commander, 3rd Escort Flotilla
6 Aug 1915 - 25 Sep 1915:	Unassigned
25 Sep 1915 - 13 Jun 1918:	Member, Admirals Committee
13 Dec 1915 - 13 Jun 1918:	Deputy Chief of the Naval General Staff
13 Jun 1918 - 1 Dec 1919:	C-in-C, 2nd Fleet
25 Nov 1919:	Promoted to *Admiral*
1 Dec 1919 - 24 Aug 1920:	C-in-C, 1st Fleet
1 May 1920 - 24 Aug 1920:	C-in-C, Combined Fleet
24 Aug 1920 - 27 Jul 1922:	Admiral Commanding, Yokosuka Naval District, Member, Admirals Committee
27 Jul 1922 - 10 Dec 1922:	Navy Councillor
10 Dec 1922 - 31 Mar 1923:	Unassigned
31 Mar 1923:	Transferred to the reserve

General (Paymaster) **Hikonoshin YAMAZAKI** (13 May 1868 - 6 Oct 1918)

1 Dec 1914 - 13 Dec 1915:	Paymaster-General, 1st Fleet
1 Nov 1915 - 13 Dec 1915:	Paymaster-General, Combined Fleet
13 Dec 1915 - 24 Jul 1916:	Paymaster-General, Maizuru Naval District
24 Jul 1916 - 13 Sep 1916:	Attached to Yokosuka Naval District
13 Sep 1916 - 13 Sep 1917:	Unassigned
13 Sep 1917:	Promoted to *General (Paymaster)*
13 Sep 1917:	Transferred to the reserve

Vice-Admiral (Paymaster) **Hinata YAMAZAKI** (12 May 1870 - 21 May 1924)

1 Aug 1916 - 1 Dec 1917:	Paymaster-General, Maizuru Naval District
1 Dec 1917 - 1 Dec 1918:	Paymaster-General, Sasebo Naval District
1 Dec 1918:	Promoted to *General (Paymaster)*
1 Dec 1918 - 10 Nov 1922:	Paymaster-General, Yokosuka Naval District
23 Sep 1919:	Redesignated *Rear-Admiral (Paymaster)*
10 Nov 1922 - 31 Mar 1923:	Attached to Naval General Staff
1 Dec 1922:	Promoted to *Vice-Admiral (Paymaster)*
31 Mar 1923:	Transferred to the reserve

Rear-Admiral **Sukeichi YAMAZAKI** (7 Jul 1889 - 4 Aug 1943)

7 Aug 1942 - 3 May 1943:	Captain, Seaplane Tender *"Kamoi"*
3 May 1943 - 4 Aug 1943:	Attached to Sasebo Naval District
4 Aug 1943:	Posthumously promoted to *Rear-Admiral*

Rear-Admiral **Tsurunosuke YAMAZAKI** (4 Apr 1860 - 8 Dec 1932)

28 Sep 1907 - 15 Jun 1911:	Chief Engineer Officer, Yokosuka Naval District
10 Dec 1907 - 21 Feb 1908:	Commandant, Naval Engineering School
28 Aug 1908:	Promoted to *Rear-Admiral*

15 Jun 1911 - 15 Jun 1912: Unassigned
15 Jun 1912: Transferred to the reserve

Rear-Admiral **Teijiro YAMAZUMI** (15 Nov 1896 - 25 Jan 1976)
29 Mar 1943 - Oct 1945: Chief of Staff, 8th Fleet
1 May 1943: Promoted to *Rear-Admiral*

Vice-Admiral **Hiromitsu YANAGIHARA** (19 Mar 1889 - 31 Dec 1966)
10 Jun 1937 - 1 Apr 1941: Chief of Division 2, Fuel Bureau, Department of Commerce and Industry
1 Dec 1937: Promoted to *Rear-Admiral*
1 Apr 1941 - 21 Apr 1941: Attached to Naval General Staff
21 Apr 1941 - 25 Oct 1943: Commander, 1st Navy Fuel Yard
15 Oct 1941: Promoted to *Vice-Admiral*
25 Oct 1943 - 1 Oct 1944: Commandant, Naval Engineering Academy
1 Oct 1944 - 4 Dec 1944: Attached to Naval General Staff
5 Dec 1944: Transferred to the reserve

Rear-Admiral **Ryusaku YANAGIMOTO** (9 Jan 1894 - 5 Jun 1942)
6 Oct 1941 - 5 Jun 1942: Captain, Aircraft Carrier *"Soryu"*
5 Jun 1942: Posthumously promoted to *Rear-Admiral*

Rear-Admiral **Yoshitane YANAGIMURA** (26 Sep 1900 - 31 Mar 1944)
20 Feb 1944 - 31 Mar 1944: Staff officer, 22nd Air Flotilla
31 Mar 1944: Posthumously promoted to *Rear-Admiral*

Rear-Admiral **Kuranosuke YANAGISAWA** (20 Feb 1898 - 31 Mar 1944)
5 Oct 1943 - 31 Mar 1944: Staff officer, Combined Fleet
31 Mar 1944: Posthumously promoted to *Rear-Admiral*

Rear-Admiral **Sukefuyu YANAGISAWA** (1 Jan 1876 -23 Oct 1945)
1 Jun 1919 - 1 Dec 1921: Chief of Ordnance Bureau, Maizuru Navy Yard
1 Dec 1921: Promoted to *Rear-Admiral*
1 Dec 1921 - 10 Dec 1921: Attached to Maizuru Naval District
10 Dec 1921 - 24 Jan 1922: Unassigned
24 Jan 1922: Transferred to the reserve

Vice-Admiral **Hideo YANO** (1 Nov 1894 - 8 Jul 1944)
11 Aug 1941 - 10 Nov 1942: Captain, Battleship *"Nagato"*
1 Nov 1942: Attached to Naval General Staff
10 Nov 1942- 1 Dec 1942: Attached to Naval General Staff
1 Dec 1942 - 2 Mar 1944: Chief of Naval Intelligence (Bureau 3, Naval General Staff)

2 Mar 1944 - 4 Mar 1944:	Attached to Naval General Staff
4 Mar 1944 - 8 Jul 1944:	Chief of Staff, Central Pacific Area Fleet, Chief of Staff, 14th Air Fleet
8 Jul 1944:	Posthumously promoted to *Vice-Admiral*

Rear-Admiral (Paymaster) **Jotaro YANO** (4 Feb 1864 - 16 Sep 1922)

10 Nov 1903 - 26 Dec 1904:	Commandant, Navy Paymaster Training Center
26 Dec 1904 - 20 Dec 1906:	Accounting Supervisor for Construction & Ordnance, Naval Shipbuilding Command
20 Dec 1906 - 5 Oct 1909:	Attached to Naval General Staff
5 Oct 1909 - 17 Apr 1911:	Unassigned
17 Apr 1911:	Promoted to *General (Paymaster)*
17 Apr 1911:	Transferred to the reserve
23 Sep 1919:	Redesignated *Rear-Admiral (Paymaster)*

Rear-Admiral **Kanji YANO** (6 Dec 1900 - 25 Oct 1944)

25 Oct 1944:	Posthumously promoted to *Rear-Admiral*

Vice-Admiral **Shikazo YANO** (5 Aug 1893 - 24 Jan 1966)

10 Oct 1941 - 1 Nov 1942:	Chief of Staff, 4th Fleet
1 Nov 1942:	Promoted to *Rear-Admiral*
1 Nov 1942 - 20 Nov 1942:	Attached to Naval General Staff
20 Nov 1942 - 1 Mar 1944:	Chief of Naval Training Bureau, Department of the Navy
1 Mar 1944 - 20 Apr 1944:	Attached to Naval Shipbuilding Command
20 Apr 1944 - 20 Dec 1944:	Chief of Administration Bureau, Naval Radar Command
20 Dec 1944 - 10 May 1945:	Chief of Bureau 3, Naval Shipbuilding Command
20 Dec 1944 - 1 Mar 1945:	Chief of Bureau 4, Naval Air Command
1 Mar 1945 - 10 May 1945:	Chief of Bureau 5, Naval Air Command
10 May 1945 - 25 Jun 1945:	Deputy Chief of Staff, Supreme Naval HQ Deputy Chief of Staff, Combined Fleet
25 Jun 1945 - 25 Sep 1945:	Chief of Staff, Supreme Naval HQ Chief of Staff, Combined Fleet
25 Sep 1945 - 30 Nov 1945:	Attached to Department of the Navy
1 Nov 1945:	Promoted to *Vice-Admiral*

Rear-Admiral (Surgeon) **Tamaki YANO** (1 Dec 1880 - 17 Jun 1964)

1 Dec 1929 - 1 Dec 1932:	Director, Maizuru Guard District Naval Hospital, Chief Surgeon, Maizuru Guard District
1 Dec 1932:	Promoted to *Rear-Admiral (Surgeon)*
1 Dec 1932 - 10 Dec 1932:	Attached to Kure Naval District
15 Dec 1932:	Transferred to the reserve

Rear-Admiral **Umakichi YANO** (15 Feb 1880 - 18 Feb 1947)
1 Dec 1923 - 10 Jul 1925:	Commander, Kure Sailors Corps
10 Jul 1925 - 1 Sep 1925:	Attached to Kure Naval District
1 Sep 1925 - 16 Dec 1925:	Unassigned
1 Dec 1925:	Promoted to *Rear-Admiral*
16 Dec 1925:	Transferred to the reserve

Rear-Admiral (Surgeon) **Yoshio YANO** (15 Sep 1892 - 12 May 1975)
15 Nov 1939 - 22 Sep 1941:	Director, Minato Naval Hospital
22 Sep 1941 - 1 Nov 1943:	Attached to Sasebo Naval District
15 Oct 1941:	Promoted to *Rear-Admiral (Surgeon)*
1 Nov 1943 - 1 Nov 1944:	Chief of Medical Bureau, Sasebo Navy Yard
1 Nov 1944 - 15 Dec 1944:	Attached to Naval General Staff
20 Dec 1944:	Transferred to the reserve

Admiral **Baron Rokuro YASHIRO** (3 Jan 1860 - 30 Jun 1930)
12 Dec 1905 - 10 Dec 1908:	Naval Attache, Germany
27 Dec 1907:	Promoted to *Rear-Admiral*
10 Dec 1908 - 1 Dec 1909:	C-in-C, Yokosuka Reserve Fleet
1 Dec 1909 - 13 Jun 1910:	C-in-C, 1st Fleet
13 Jun 1910 - 16 Jul 1910:	Attached to Kure Naval District
16 Jul 1910 - 11 Mar 1911:	C-in-C, Training Fleet
11 Mar 1911 - 1 Dec 1911:	C-in-C, 2nd Fleet
1 Dec 1911:	Promoted to *Vice-Admiral*
1 Dec 1911 - 25 Sep 1913:	Commandant of the Naval College
25 Sep 1913 - 16 Apr 1914:	Admiral Commanding, Maizuru Naval District
16 Apr 1914 - 10 Aug 1915:	Minister of the Navy
10 Aug 1915 - 13 Dec 1915:	Unassigned
13 Dec 1915 - 1 Dec 1917:	C-in-C, 2nd Fleet
1 Dec 1917 - 1 Dec 1918:	Admiral Commanding, Sasebo Naval District
2 Jul 1918:	Promoted to *Admiral*
1 Dec 1918 - 25 Nov 1919:	Navy Councillor
25 Nov 1919 - 1 Aug 1920:	Unassigned
1 Aug 1920:	Transferred to the reserve

Vice-Admiral **Yasuo YASUBA** (23 Oct 1892 - 6 May 1976)
13 Aug 1941 - 1 Sep 1942:	Chief of Staff, 2nd China Expeditionary Fleet
15 Oct 1941:	Promoted to *Rear-Admiral*
10 Mar 1942 - 1 Sep 1942:	Commander, Hong Kong Naval Base Force
1 Sep 1942 - 15 Sep 1942:	Attached to Naval General Staff
15 Sep 1942 - 1 Feb 1944:	Chief of Bureau 2, Naval Shipbuilding Command
1 Feb 1944 - 15 Feb 1945:	Chief of Sonic Research Bureau, Technical Research Department

15 Feb 1945 - 30 Sep 1945:	Chief of Sonic Weapons Bureau, 2nd Technical Arsenal
1 May 1945:	Promoted to *Vice-Admiral*

Vice-Admiral **Yoshitatsu YASUDA** (1 Mar 1897 - 2 Jan 1943)

1 May 1942 - 2 Jan 1943:	Commander, Yokosuka 5th Marine Force
2 Jan 1943:	Posthumously promoted 2 grades to *Vice-Admiral*

Rear-Admiral **Kaneji YASUHARA** (15 Nov 1853 - 28 Jun 1926)

18 Jan 1904 - 11 Jul 1905:	Commander, Yokosuka Sailors Corps
11 Jul 1905 - 24 May 1906:	Unassigned
24 May 1906:	Promoted to *Rear-Admiral*
24 May 1906:	Transferred to the reserve

Vice-Admiral **Saburo YASUMI** (19 Dec 1880 - 20 Jan 1965)

1 Dec 1925:	Promoted to *Rear-Admiral*
1 Dec 1925 - 1 Dec 1926:	Commander, 1st Destroyer Flotilla
1 Dec 1926 - 1 Dec 1927:	Commander, 2nd Destroyer Flotilla
1 Dec 1927 - 12 Sep 1929:	Commandant, Torpedo School
12 Sep 1929 - 30 Nov 1929:	Attached to Yokosuka Naval District
30 Nov 1929 - 1 Mar 1931:	Commander, Ominato Guard District
1 Dec 1930:	Promoted to *Vice-Admiral*
1 Mar 1931 - 20 Mar 1931:	Attached to Naval General Staff
31 Mar 1931:	Transferred to the reserve

Rear-Admiral **Sukeichi YASUMURA** (12 Mar 1874 - 5 Jun 1951)

1 Dec 1921:	Promoted to *Rear-Admiral*
1 Dec 1921 - 1 Aug 1922:	Commander, Maizuru Sailors Corps
1 Aug 1922 - 1 Dec 1922:	Attached to Yokosuka Naval District
1 Dec 1922 - 31 Mar 1923:	Unassigned
31 Mar 1923:	Transferred to the reserve

Rear-Admiral **Shiro YASUTAKE** (12 Dec 1897 - 11 Sep 1942)

1 Sep 1941 - 11 Sep 1942:	Commander, 30th Destroyer Division
11 Sep 1942:	Posthumously promoted to *Rear-Admiral*

Rear-Admiral (Surgeon) **Kodo YASUYAMA** (12 Jun 1888 - 22 Dec 1958)

1 Oct 1942 - 15 Nov 1943:	Commander, Medical Depot
1 Nov 1942:	Promoted to *Rear-Admiral (Surgeon)*
15 Nov 1943 - 10 Mar 1944:	Staff officer, Navy Medical School
10 Mar 1944 - 10 Oct 1945:	Director, Omura Naval Hospital

Rear-Admiral **Arito YATSUGI** (7 Jan 1896 - 25 Jan 1952)
1 May 1945: Promoted to *Rear-Admiral*
1 May 1945 - 20 Sep 1945: Chief of Supply Bureau, Sasebo Naval District

Rear-Admiral **Hitoshi YATSUSHIRO** (6 Jun 1884 - 12 Aug 1963)
1 Nov 1926 - 15 Nov 1932: Chief of Shipbuilding Research Bureau, Technical Research Department
1 Dec 1931: Promoted to *Rear-Admiral*
15 Nov 1932 - 10 Dec 1932: Attached to Naval Shipbuilding Command
15 Dec 1932: Transferred to the reserve

Vice-Admiral **Sukeyoshi YATSUSHIRO** (1 Feb 1890 - 1 Feb 1942)
15 Nov 1940: Promoted to *Rear-Admiral*
15 Nov 1940 - 22 Nov 1940: Attached to Sasebo Naval District
22 Nov 1940 - 15 Jan 1941: Staff officer, 4th Fleet
15 Jan 1941 - 1 Feb 1942: Commander, 6th Auxiliary Naval Base Force
1 Feb 1942: Posthumously promoted to *Vice-Admiral*

Rear-Admiral **Mitsuji YODA** (25 Dec 1865 - 18 Feb 1926)
1 Dec 1911: Promoted to *Rear-Admiral*
1 Dec 1911 - 20 Apr 1912: Commander, Yokosuka Torpedo Corps
20 Apr 1912 - 1 Dec 1912: Chief of Ordnance Bureau, Sasebo Navy Yard
1 Dec 1912 - 24 May 1913: Unassigned
24 May 1913: Transferred to the reserve

Rear-Admiral **Joji YOKOCHI** (8 Dec 1878 - 5 Jan 1960)
10 Nov 1922 - 1 Dec 1923: Captain, Battlecruiser *"Hiei"*
1 Dec 1923: Promoted to *Rear-Admiral*
1 Dec 1923 - 5 Feb 1924: Attached to Naval General Staff
25 Feb 1924: Transferred to the reserve

Rear-Admiral (Surgeon) **Kimito YOKOCHI** (6 Aug 1868 - 18 Feb 1921)
1 Dec 1917 - 1 Dec 1918: Executive Officer, Yokosuka Naval Hospital
 Chief of Bureau 1, Yokosuka Naval Hospital
1 Dec 1918 - 1 Aug 1919: Unassigned
1 Aug 1919: Promoted to *General (Surgeon)*
1 Aug 1919: Transferred to the reserve
23 Sep 1919: Redesignated *Rear-Admiral (Surgeon)*

Rear-Admiral **Tadao YOKOI** (6 Mar 1895 - 10 Sep 1965)
2 Sep 1940 - 28 Dec 1943: Naval Attaché, Germany
21 Jul 1941 - 28 Dec 1943: Naval Attaché, Finland
1 Nov 1942: Promoted to *Rear-Admiral*

28 Dec 1943 - 1 Mar 1944:	Attached to Naval General Staff
1 Mar 1944 - 20 May 1945:	Chief of Staff, Yokosuka Naval District
20 May 1945 - 1 Jun 1945:	Commander, Tanabe Sailors Corps
1 Jun 1945 - 15 Nov 1945:	Commander, 6th Special Attack Flotilla

Rear-Admiral **Toshiyuki YOKOI** (11 Mar 1897 - 23 Dec 1969)

24 Oct 1944 - 10 Feb 1945:	Commander, 25th Air Flotilla
10 Feb 1945 - 10 Oct 1945:	Chief of Staff, 5th Air Fleet
1 May 1945:	Promoted to *Rear-Admiral*

Rear-Admiral **Ichihei YOKOKAWA** (24 Apr 1893 - 7 Jan 1979)

19 Dec 1942 - 1 Nov 1943:	Chief of Division 3, Aeronautics Bureau, Department of Commerce and Industry
1 May 1943:	Promoted to *Rear-Admiral*
1 Nov 1943 - 25 May 1944:	Commander, 26th Naval Base Force
25 May 1944 - 6 Sep 1945:	Attached to Naval General Staff

Rear-Admiral (Surgeon) **Seijiro YOKOKURA** (8 Aug 1895 - 31 Jul 1956)

1 Nov 1942 - 15 Mar 1945:	Instructor, Navy Medical School
1 May 1944:	Promoted to *Rear-Admiral (Surgeon)*
15 Mar 1945 - 1 Nov 1945:	Chief Instructor, Navy Medical School
1 Nov 1945 - 30 Nov 1945:	Attached to Yokosuka Naval District

Rear-Admiral (Paymaster) **Hoichi YOKOMI** (14 Nov 1877 - ?)

18 Sep 1925 - 15 Mar 1927:	Chief of Accounting Bureau, Kure Navy Yard
1 Dec 1926:	Promoted to *Rear-Admiral (Paymaster)*
15 Mar 1927 - 1 Dec 1927:	Paymaster-General, Sasebo Naval District
1 Dec 1927 - 15 Dec 1927:	Attached to Naval General Staff
25 Dec 1927:	Transferred to the reserve

Rear-Admiral **Hisashi YOKOO** (27 Oct 1874 - ?)

1 Dec 1921:	Promoted to *Rear-Admiral*
1 Dec 1921 - 10 Nov 1922:	Commander, Yokosuka Defense Force
10 Nov 1922 - 1 Dec 1922:	Attached to Yokosuka Naval District
1 Dec 1922 - 31 Mar 1923:	Unassigned
31 Mar 1923:	Transferred to the reserve

Vice-Admiral (Paymaster) **Iwao YOKOO** (12 Jul 1893 - 2 Feb 1977)

1 Oct 1940 - 20 Oct 1942:	Chief of Accounting Bureau, Hikari Navy Yard
15 Nov 1940:	Promoted to *Rear-Admiral (Paymaster)*
20 Oct 1942 - 10 Sep 1943:	Chief, 101st Accounting Bureau
10 Sep 1943 - 15 Sep 1943:	Attached to Yokosuka Naval District
15 Sep 1943 - 1 Oct 1943:	Attached to Naval General Staff

1 Oct 1943 - 6 Jan 1944:	Attached to Naval Shipbuilding Command
6 Jan 1944 - 10 Nov 1945:	Commander, 2nd Air Arsenal
1 May 1944:	Promoted to *Vice-Admiral (Paymaster)*

Rear-Admiral **Toshio YOKOTA** (22 Sep 1897 - 16 Jun 1975)
25 Mar 1942 - 20 Dec 1944:	Chief of Comp Bureau, 2nd Navy Fuel Yard
15 Oct 1944:	Promoted to *Rear-Admiral*
20 Dec 1944 - 20 Sep 1945:	Attached to Naval General Staff

Rear-Admiral **Katsumi YOKOTE** (25 Feb 1905 - 29 Nov 1944)
5 Nov 1944 - 29 Nov 1944:	Chief Gunnery Officer, Aircraft Carrier *"Shinano"*
29 Nov 1944:	Posthumously promoted to *Rear-Admiral*

Rear-Admiral **Ichiro YOKOYAMA** (1 Mar 1900 - 28 Jul 1993)
20 Jul 1944 - 20 May 1945:	Commander, Tokyo Guard Force
1 May 1945:	Promoted to *Rear-Admiral*
20 May 1945 - 15 Oct 1945:	Attached to Naval General Staff
15 Oct 1945 - 30 Nov 1945:	Attached to Department of the Navy

Rear-Admiral (Engineer) **Masayasu YOKOYAMA** (15 Oct 1859 - 21 Apr 1933)
22 Nov 1907 - 10 Dec 1928:	Chief Engineer Officer, Sasebo Naval District
28 Aug 1908:	Promoted to *Rear-Admiral*
10 Dec 1908 - 1 Dec 1909:	Chief Engineer Officer, Kure Naval District
1 Dec 1909 - 17 Apr 1911:	Unassigned
17 Apr 1911:	Transferred to the reserve

Rear-Admiral **Sugao YOKOYAMA** (28 Nov 1886 - 25 Oct 1957)
15 Nov 1933 - 15 Nov 1935:	Captain, Heavy Cruiser *"Ashigara"*
15 Nov 1935 - 1 Dec 1936:	Attached to Sasebo Naval District
1 Dec 1936:	Promoted to *Rear-Admiral*
1 Dec 1936 - 15 Dec 1936:	Attached to Naval General Staff
22 Dec 1936:	Transferred to the reserve

Rear-Admiral **Tokujiro YOKOYAMA** (19 Feb 1887 - 11 May 1945)
15 Aug 1943 - 11 May 1945:	Commander, 86th Guard Force
1 May 1944:	Promoted to *Rear-Admiral*

Rear-Admiral (Engineer) **Morinosuke YOKURA** (1 Dec 1877 - 23 Jun 1922)
17 Jun 1921 - 30 May 1922:	Chief of Bureau 3, Naval Shipbuilding Command
30 May 1922 - 23 Jun 1922:	Unassigned
23 Jun 1922:	Posthumously promoted to *Rear-Admiral*

Admiral **Mitsumasa YONAI** (2 Mar 1880 - 20 Apr 1948)
1 Dec 1925:	Promoted to *Rear-Admiral*
1 Dec 1925 - 1 Dec 1926:	Chief of Staff, 2nd Fleet
1 Dec 1926 - 10 Dec 1928:	Chief of Bureau 3, Naval General Staff
10 Dec 1928 - 1 Dec 1930:	C-in-C, 1st Expeditionary Fleet
1 Dec 1930:	Promoted to *Vice-Admiral*
1 Dec 1930 - 1 Dec 1932:	Commander, Chinkai Guard District
1 Dec 1932 - 15 Sep 1933:	C-in-C, 3rd Fleet
15 Sep 1933 - 15 Nov 1933:	Attached to Naval General Staff
15 Nov 1933 - 15 Nov 1934:	Admiral Commanding, Sasebo Naval District
15 Nov 1934 - 2 Dec 1935:	C-in-C, 2nd Fleet
2 Dec 1935 - 1 Dec 1936:	Admiral Commanding, Yokosuka Naval District, Member, Admirals Committee
1 Dec 1936 - 2 Feb 1937:	C-in-C, Combined Fleet, C-in-C, 1st Fleet
2 Feb 1937 - 30 Aug 1939:	Minister of the Navy
1 Apr 1937:	Promoted to *Admiral*
30 Aug 1939 - 16 Jan 1940:	Navy Councillor
16 Jan 1940:	Transferred to the reserve
16 Jan 1940 - 22 Jul 1940:	Prime Minister
22 Jul 1944 - 30 Nov 1945:	Recalled; Minister of the Navy

Vice-Admiral (Paymaster) **Tokutaro YONEHANA** (20 May 1891 - 22 May 1981)
15 Nov 1939 - 15 Nov 1940:	Paymaster-General, Combined Fleet, Paymaster-General, 1st Fleet
15 Nov 1940:	Promoted to *Rear-Admiral (Paymaster)*
15 Nov 1940 - 1 Nov 1942:	Paymaster-General, Maizuru Naval District
1 Nov 1942 - 15 Nov 1945:	Paymaster-General, Kure Naval District
1 May 1944:	Promoted to *Vice-Admiral (Paymaster)*

Vice-Admiral **Sueki YONEMURA** (13 Mar 1879 - 27 Dec 1941)
1 Dec 1925:	Promoted to *Rear-Admiral*
1 Dec 1925 - 1 Dec 1930:	Chief of Naval Hydrographic Command
30 Nov 1929:	Promoted to *Vice-Admiral*
1 Dec 1930 - 15 Dec 1930:	Attached to Naval General Staff
24 Dec 1930:	Transferred to the reserve

Rear-Admiral (Surgeon) **Hajime YOSHIDA** (10 Dec 1897 - 13 Nov 1971)
3 May 1943 - Nov 1945:	Chief Medical Officer, Southeast Area Fleet, Chief Medical Officer, 11th Air Fleet
15 Oct 1944:	Promoted to *Rear-Admiral (Surgeon)*

Vice-Admiral **Kiyokaze YOSHIDA** (5 May 1871 - 9 Apr 1950)
1 Dec 1912 - 1 Feb 1915:	Chief of Staff, 2nd Fleet
1 Feb 1915 - 4 Sep 1918:	Chief of Bureau 2, Naval General Staff
1 Dec 1916:	Promoted to *Rear-Admiral*
4 Sep 1918 - 1 Jul 1919:	Attached to Naval General Staff
1 Jul 1919 - 1 Dec 1919:	Commander, Yokosuka Air Division
1 Dec 1919 - 12 Jan 1920:	Attached to Naval General Staff
12 Jan 1920 - 4 Apr 1921:	C-in-C, 2nd Expeditionary Fleet
1 Dec 1920:	Promoted to *Vice-Admiral*
4 Apr 1921 - 1 Aug 1921:	Member, Admirals Committee
1 Aug 1921 - 26 Dec 1921:	Commander, Mako Guard District
26 Dec 1921 - 31 Mar 1923:	Unassigned
31 Mar 1923:	Transferred to the reserve

Vice-Admiral **Masujiro YOSHIDA** (28 Jun 1867 - 14 Mar 1942)
1 Dec 1916:	Promoted to *Rear-Admiral*
1 Dec 1916 - 1 Dec 1917:	Commander, Interim Southern Islands Defense Force
1 Dec 1917 - 13 Jun 1918:	Attached to Naval General Staff
13 Jun 1918 - 8 Nov 1919:	Chief of Bureau 3, Naval General Staff
8 Nov 1919 - 1 May 1922:	C-in-C, 1st Expeditionary Fleet
1 Dec 1920:	Promoted to *Vice-Admiral*
1 May 1922 - 1 Oct 1922:	Member, Admirals Committee
1 Oct 1922 - 31 Mat 1923:	Unassigned
31 Mar 1923:	Transferred to the reserve

Rear-Admiral **Sennosuke YOSHIDA** (30 Jan 1873 - ?)
15 Jun 1921 - 13 Aug 1923:	Chief of Engine Construction Bureau, Yokosuka Navy Yard
1 Dec 1921:	Promoted to *Rear-Admiral*
13 Aug 1923 - 1 Dec 1923:	Attached to Naval Shipbuilding Command
1 Dec 1923 - 25 Feb 1924:	Unassigned
25 Feb 1924:	Transferred to the reserve

Rear-Admiral **Shinichi YOSHIDA** (20 Jun 1885 - 18 Nov 1948)
1 Dec 1930 - 15 Nov 1934:	Chief of Submarine Bureau, Kure Navy Yard
15 Nov 1934:	Promoted to *Rear-Admiral*
15 Nov 1934 - 15 Nov 1935:	Chief of Shipping Bureau, Kure Naval District
15 Nov 1935 - 10 Dec 1935:	Attached to Naval General Staff
14 Dec 1935:	Transferred to the reserve

Rear-Admiral **Takeshi YOSHIDA** (8 Jan 1871 - 3 Jan 1942)
1 Dec 1916 - 10 Sep 1919:	Chief of Torpedo Bureau, Kure Navy Yard

10 Sep 1919 - 1 Dec 1919:	Attached to Yokosuka Naval District
1 Dec 1919:	Promoted to *Rear-Admiral*
1 Dec 1919 - 2 Aug 1920:	Unassigned
2 Aug 1920:	Transferred to the reserve

Rear-Admiral **Taro YOSHIDA** (4 Jan 1876 - 16 Feb 1947)

1 Dec 1921:	Promoted to *Rear-Admiral*
1 Dec 1921 - 1 Dec 1923:	Chief of Ordnance Bureau, Yokosuka Navy Yard
1 Dec 1923 - 20 Dec 1923:	Attached to Naval Shipbuilding Command
20 Dec 1923 - 22 Jan 1924:	Unassigned
22 Jan 1924:	Transferred to the reserve

Vice-Admiral (Engineer) **Teiichi YOSHIDA** (8 Aug 1852 - 7 Aug 1923)

17 Jun 1899 - 24 May 1902:	Chief of Engineering Bureau, Sasebo Naval District
22 May 1900:	Promoted to *General (Engineer)*
24 May 1902 - 10 Nov 1903:	Chief of Engineering Bureau, Yokosuka Naval District
10 Nov 1903 - 12 Dec 1905:	Chief Engineer Officer, Yokosuka Naval District
12 Dec 1905 - 24 Feb 1907:	Unassigned
26 Jan 1906:	Redesignated *Rear-Admiral (Engineer)*
8 Nov 1906:	Promoted to *Vice-Admiral (Engineer)*
24 Feb 1907:	Transferred to the reserve

General (Surgeon) **Teijun YOSHIDA** (24 Sep 1852 - 13 Jan 1913)

29 Nov 1900 - 27 May 1902:	Director, Sasebo Naval Hospital, Chief of Medical Bureau, Sasebo Naval District
4 Jul 1901:	Promoted to *General (Surgeon)*
27 May 1902 - 10 Nov 1903:	Director, Kure Naval Hospital, Chief of Medical Bureau, Kure Naval District
10 Nov 1903 - 10 Nov 1906:	Unassigned
10 Nov 1906:	Transferred to the reserve

Rear-Admiral **Tsunemitsu YOSHIDA** (15 Jun 1886 - 26 Feb 1947)

26 Jan 1937 - 15 Nov 1938:	Commander, 1st Destroyer Flotilla
1 Dec 1937:	Promoted to *Rear-Admiral*
15 Nov 1938 - 15 Dec 1939:	Attached to Naval General Staff
21 Dec 1939:	Transferred to the reserve
15 Sep 1941 - 1 Oct 1941:	Recalled; Attached to Maizuru Naval District
1 Oct 1941 - 10 Aug 1942:	Commander, Maizuru Defense Flotilla
10 Aug 1942 - 1 Sep 1942:	Attached to Naval General Staff
1 Sep 1942:	Unassigned

Admiral **Zengo YOSHIDA** (14 Feb 1885 - 14 Nov 1966)

30 Nov 1929:	Promoted to *Rear-Admiral*

30 Nov 1929 - 1 Dec 1931:	Chief of Bureau 2, Naval General Staff
1 Dec 1931 - 1 Sep 1933:	Chief of Staff, Combined Fleet, Chief of Staff, 1st Fleet
1 Sep 1933 - 15 Sep 1933:	Attached to Naval General Staff
15 Sep 1933 - 2 Dec 1935:	Chief, Bureau of Naval Affairs, Department of the Navy
15 Nov 1934:	Promoted to *Vice-Admiral*
2 Dec 1935 - 1 Feb 1936:	Attached to Naval General Staff
1 Feb 1936 - 1 Dec 1936:	C-in-C, Training Fleet
1 Dec 1936 - 1 Dec 1937:	C-in-C, 2nd Fleet
1 Dec 1937 - 30 Aug 1939:	C-in-C, Combined Fleet, C-in-C, 1st Fleet
30 Aug 1939 - 5 Sep 1940:	Minister of the Navy
5 Sep 1940 - 15 Nov 1940:	Attached to Naval General Staff
15 Nov 1940:	Promoted to *Admiral*
15 Nov 1940 - 10 Nov 1942:	Navy Councillor
10 Nov 1942 - 1 Dec 1943:	C-in-C, China Area Fleet
1 Dec 1943 - 3 May 1944:	Navy Councillor
14 Dec 1943 - 15 Mar 1944:	Commandant of the Naval College
3 May 1944 - 2 Aug 1944:	Admiral Commanding, Yokosuka Naval District, Member, Admirals Committee
2 Aug 1944 - 1 Jun 1945:	Navy Councillor
1 Jun 1945:	Transferred to the reserve

Grand Marshal Emperor **YOSHIHITO** (Taisho) (31 Aug 1879 - 25 Dec 1926)

30 Jul 1912 - 25 Dec 1926:	Supreme Commander-in-Chief of the Armed Forces

Rear-Admiral **Kazuo YOSHII** (20 Apr 1894 - ?)

15 Nov 1940 - 5 Aug 1945:	Chief of Shipbuilding Bureau, Sasebo Navy Yard
1 Nov 1942:	Promoted to *Rear-Admiral*
5 Aug 1945 - 1 Nov 1945:	Chief of Shipbuilding Bureau, Kure Navy Yard
1 Nov 1945 - 10 Nov 1945:	Attached to Kure Naval District

Rear-Admiral **Jutaro YOSHIJIMA** (25 Feb 1868 - 19 Mar 1929)

1 Oct 1915 - 1 Dec 1916:	Commander, 3rd Destroyer Flotilla
13 Dec 1915:	Promoted to *Rear-Admiral*
1 Dec 1916 - 1 Dec 1917:	Unassigned
1 Dec 1917:	Transferred to the reserve

Vice-Admiral (Surgeon) **Ikuzo YOSHIKAWA** (4 Apr 1871 - 11 May 1942)

1 Dec 1918 - 1 Jun 1919:	Director, Maizuru Naval Hospital, Chief Surgeon, Maizuru Naval District
1 Jun 1919:	Promoted to *General (Surgeon)*

1 Jun 1919 - 1 Dec 1923:	Director, Kure Naval Hospital, Chief Surgeon, Kure Naval District
23 Sep 1919:	Redesignated *Rear-Admiral (Surgeon*
1 Dec 1923:	Promoted to *Vice-Admiral (Surgeon)*
1 Dec 1923 - 10 Dec 1923:	Attached to Naval General Staff
10 Dec 1923 - 25 Feb 1924:	Unassigned
25 Feb 1924:	Transferred to the reserve

Rear-Admiral (Paymaster) **Sunao YOSHIKAWA** (20 Jan 1893 - 30 May 1963)

1 Nov 1942:	Promoted to *Rear-Admiral (Paymaster)*
1 Nov 1942 - 10 Jun 1945:	Paymaster-General, Osaka Guard District
10 Jun 1945 - 15 Nov 1945:	Paymaster-General, Maizuru Naval District

Vice-Admiral **Yasuhira YOSHIKAWA** (17 Nov 1873 - 1 Jan 1959)

1 Dec 1919:	Promoted to *Rear-Admiral*
1 Dec 1919 - 1 Dec 1920:	Chief of Staff, 2nd Fleet
1 Dec 1920 - 1 Dec 1922:	Commandant, Submarine School
1 Dec 1922 - 1 Apr 1923:	Chief of Bureau 7, Naval Shipbuilding Command
1 Apr 1923 - 13 Aug 1923:	Chief of Bureau 3, Naval Shipbuilding Command
13 Aug 1923 - 11 Jun 1924:	Commander, Kure Navy Yard
1 Dec 1923:	Promoted to *Vice-Admiral*
11 Jun 1924 - 10 Dec 1926:	Chief of Naval Shipbuilding Command, Member, Admirals Committee
10 Dec 1926 - 16 May 1928:	C-in-C, 2nd Fleet
16 May 1928 - 10 Dec 1928:	Admiral Commanding, Yokosuka Naval District, Member, Admirals Committee
10 Dec 1928 - 10 Mar 1929:	Attached to Naval General Staff
25 Mar 1929:	Transferred to the reserve

Rear-Admiral **Hiroshi YOSHIMATSU** (30 Mar 1903 - 21 Nov 1944)

20 Nov 1942 - 21 Nov 1944:	Deputy Commander & Chief Navigation Officer, Battlecruiser *"Kongo"*
21 Nov 1944:	Posthumously promoted to *Rear-Admiral*

Admiral **Motaro YOSHIMATSU** (7 Jan 1859 - 2 Feb 1935)

2 Nov 1905:	Promoted to *Rear-Admiral*
2 Nov 1905 - 2 Feb 1906:	Chief of Staff, Sasebo Naval District
2 Feb 1906 - 22 Nov 1906:	Chief of Staff, Kure Naval District
22 Nov 1906 - 21 Oct 1907:	C-in-C, 1st Fleet
21 Oct 1907 - 28 Aug 1908:	C-in-C, Training Fleet
28 Aug 1908 - 1 Dec 1910:	Commandant of the Naval Academy
1 Dec 1909:	Promoted to *Vice-Admiral*
1 Dec 1910 - 25 Sep 1911:	Commandant of the Naval College

25 Sep 1911 - 1 Dec 1911:	Commander, Takeshiki Guard District
1 Dec 1911 - 1 Dec 1912:	C-in-C, 2nd Fleet
1 Dec 1912 - 25 Mar 1914:	Chief of Naval Training Command, Department of the Navy, Member, Admirals Committee
25 Sep 1913 - 1 Dec 1913:	Commandant of the Naval College
25 Mar 1914 - 23 Sep 1915:	Admiral Commanding, Kure Naval District
23 Sep 1915 - 1 Dec 1917:	C-in-C, 1st Fleet
11 Nov 1915 - 13 Dec 1915:	C-in-C, Combined Fleet
1 Sep 1916 - 14 Oct 1916:	C-in-C, Combined Fleet
1 Dec 1916:	Promoted to *Admiral*
1 Oct 1917 - 22 Oct 1917:	C-in-C, Combined Fleet
22 Oct 1917 - 25 Nov 1919:	Navy Councillor
25 Nov 1919 - 1 Aug 1920:	Unassigned
1 Aug 1920:	Transferred to the reserve

Vice-Admiral **Kenkai YOSHIMI** (18 Nov 1864 - 29 Nov 1942)

15 Jan 1910 - 30 Apr 1912:	Chief of Ordnance Bureau, Sasebo Navy Yard
1 Dec 1911:	Promoted to *Rear-Admiral*
30 Apr 1912 - 1 Dec 1912:	Chief of Torpedo Bureau, Kure Navy Yard
1 Dec 1912 - 1 Dec 1914:	Commander, Navy Ordnance Arsenal
1 Dec 1914 - 1 Dec 1915:	Unassigned
1 Dec 1915:	Promoted to *Vice-Admiral*
1 Dec 1915:	Transferred to the reserve

Rear-Admiral **Nobuichi YOSHIMI** (22 May 1894 - 18 May 1988)

13 Jul 1943 - 25 Nov 1945:	Commander, 64th Guard Force
15 Oct 1944:	Promoted to *Rear-Admiral*

Rear-Admiral **Yusuke YOSHIMI** (? - 22 Dec 1941)

5 Sep 1941 - 22 Dec 1941:	Captain, Gunboat *"Zuiko-maru"*
22 Dec 1941:	Posthumously promoted to *Rear-Admiral*

Rear-Admiral (Paymaster) **Hiroshi YOSHIMURA** (14 May 1876 - 4 May 1945)

21 May 1920 - 1 Dec 1921:	Paymaster-General, 1st Fleet
1 May 1921 - 28 Oct 1921:	Paymaster-General, Combined Fleet
1 Dec 1921 - 20 Nov 1922:	Chief of Section 1, Accounting Bureau, Kure Naval District
20 Nov 1922 - 1 Dec 1922:	Attached to Kure Naval District
1 Dec 1922:	Promoted to *Rear-Admiral (Paymaster)*
1 Dec 1922 - 31 Mar 1923:	Unassigned
31 Mar 1923:	Transferred to the reserve

Rear-Admiral **Kishaku YOSHIMURA** (21 Sep 1900 - 8 Jun 1943)
1 Nov 1942 - 1 Jun 1943:	Chief Engineer Officer, Battleship *"Mutsu"*
1 Jun 1943 - 8 Jun 1943:	Staff officer, Combined Fleet
8 Jun 1943:	Posthumously promoted to *Rear-Admiral*

General (Surgeon) **Susumu YOSHIMURA** (25 Apr 1858 - 14 Nov 1912)
7 Jan 1905 - 19 Dec 1905:	Director, Kure Naval Hospital, Chief Surgeon, Kure Naval District
2 Nov 1905:	Promoted to *General (Surgeon)*
19 Dec 1905 - 9 Oct 1907:	Director, Sasebo Naval Hospital, Chief Surgeon, Sasebo Naval District
31 Oct 1907:	Transferred to the reserve

Rear-Admiral (Paymaster) **Takeo YOSHIMURA** (5 Nov 1890 - 18 Jan 1974)
7 Jan 1938 - 15 Nov 1940:	Supervisor, Osaka & Kobe
15 Nov 1939:	Promoted to *Rear-Admiral (Paymaster)*
15 Nov 1940 - 15 Oct 1941:	Paymaster-General, Sasebo Naval District
15 Oct 1941 - 1 Nov 1942:	Paymaster-General, Kure Naval District
1 Nov 1942 - 15 Dec 1942:	Attached to Naval General Staff
21 Dec 1942:	Transferred to the reserve

Rear-Admiral (Paymaster) **Umekichi YOSHIMURA** (3 Jan 1881 - 3 Jun 1947)
10 Dec 1928 - 30 Nov 1929:	Paymaster-General, Maizuru Naval District
30 Nov 1929:	Promoted to *Rear-Admiral (Paymaster)*
30 Nov 1929 - 15 Dec 1930:	Attached to Naval General Staff
25 Dec 1930:	Transferred to the reserve

Vice-Admiral **Muneo YOSHINARI** (10 Aug 1886 - 13 Apr 1959)
1 Dec 1931 - 5 Apr 1934:	Chief of Engine Construction Bureau, Yokosuka Navy Yard
15 Nov 1933:	Promoted to *Rear-Admiral*
5 Apr 1934 - 1 Dec 1936:	Chief of Bureau 5, Naval Shipbuilding Command
1 Dec 1936 - 1 Dec 1937:	Commander, Navy Fuel Yard
1 Dec 1937:	Promoted to *Vice-Admiral*
1 Dec 1937 - 15 Nov 1939:	Commander, Kure Navy Yard
15 Nov 1939 - 15 Dec 1939:	Attached to Naval General Staff
21 Dec 1939:	Transferred to the reserve

Rear-Admiral **Jinshiro YOSHINO** (1895 - 25 Jun 1982)
5 Sep 1944 - 1 Apr 1945:	Supervisor for Ordnance, Naval Air Command
1 Apr 1945 - 15 Sep 1945:	Attached to Naval Air Command
1 May 1945:	Promoted to *Rear-Admiral*

Vice-Admiral **Hansaku YOSHIOKA** (14 May 1869 - 19 Mar 1930)

1 Dec 1917:	Promoted to *Rear-Admiral*
1 Dec 1917 - 1 Dec 1919:	Chief of Bureau 2, Naval Training Command
1 Dec 1919 - 1 Dec 1921:	Chief of Staff, 1st Fleet
1 May 1920 - 5 Oct 1920:	Chief of Staff, Combined Fleet
1 May 1921 - 31 Oct 1921:	Chief of Staff, Combined Fleet
1 Dec 1921:	Promoted to *Vice-Admiral*
1 Dec 1921 - 1 Apr 1923:	Commandant, Naval Gunnery School
1 Apr 1923 - 1 Dec 1923:	Member, Admirals Committee
1 Dec 1923 - 25 Feb 1924:	Unassigned
25 Feb 1924:	Transferred to the reserve

Vice-Admiral **Yasusada YOSHIOKA** (25 Feb 1880 - 14 Sep 1953)

1 Dec 1926:	Promoted to *Rear-Admiral*
1 Dec 1926 - 30 Nov 1929:	Chief of Administration Bureau, Naval Shipbuilding Command
30 Nov 1929 - 1 Dec 1931:	Commander, Sasebo Navy Yard
1 Dec 1931:	Promoted to *Vice-Admiral*
1 Dec 1931 - 15 Oct 1933:	Commander, Navy Fuel Yard
15 Oct 1933 - 9 Nov 1933:	Attached to Naval General Staff
10 Nov 1933:	Transferred to the reserve

Rear-Admiral **Junzo YOSHITAKE** (23 Jan 1885 - 6 Feb 1945)

10 Dec 1928 - 1 Dec 1930:	Commander, Yokosuka Defense Force
1 Dec 1930:	Promoted to *Rear-Admiral*
1 Dec 1930 - 15 Dec 1930:	Attached to Naval General Staff
24 Dec 1930:	Transferred to the reserve

Rear-Admiral **Sadasuke YOSHITAKE** (25 Mar 1879 - 18 Feb 1945)

20 Nov 1922 - 1 Dec 1923:	Chief of Section 3, Supply Bureau, Department of the Navy
1 Dec 1923:	Promoted to *Rear-Admiral*
1 Dec 1923 - 10 Dec 1923:	Attached to Naval General Staff
10 Dec 1923 - 25 Feb 1924:	Unassigned
25 Feb 1924:	Transferred to the reserve

Rear-Admiral **Setsuzo YOSHITOMI** (4 Oct 1890 - 8 Apr 1979)

1 Nov 1940 - 10 Mar 1942:	Commander, 4th Submarine Flotilla
15 Nov 1940:	Promoted to *Rear-Admiral*
10 Mar 1942 - 25 May 1942:	Attached to Kure Naval District
25 May 1942 - 5 Jun 1942:	Staff officer, 4th Fleet
5 Jun 1942 - 12 Jan 1943:	Commander, 7th Submarine Flotilla
12 Jan 1943 - 5 Feb 1943:	Attached to Yokosuka Naval District

5 Feb 1943 - 27 Dec 1943:	Commander, Yokosuka Defense Flotilla
27 Dec 1943 - 25 Jan 1944:	Attached to Naval General Staff
25 Jan 1944 - 31 Jan 1944:	Unassigned
31 Jan 1944 - 15 Apr 1944:	Attached to Naval General Staff
15 Apr 1944 - 25 Dec 1944:	Commander, 5th Convoy HQ
25 Dec 1944 - 20 Mar 1945:	Staff officer, Maritime Escort Fleet
20 Mar 1945 - 10 Nov 1945:	Chief of Kobe Branch, Shipping Guard Division, Joint General Staff
1 May 1945 - 10 Oct 1045:	Commander, Kobe Harbor Guard Force

Rear-Admiral **Hidetoki YOSHIWARA** (11 Sep 1882 - 21 Apr 1968)

16 Mar 1929 - 1 Dec 1931:	Chief of Engine Construction Bureau, Sasebo Navy Yard
30 Nov 1929:	Promoted to *Rear-Admiral*
1 Dec 1931 - 15 Dec 1931:	Attached to Naval Shipbuilding Command
21 Dec 1931:	Transferred to the reserve

Rear-Admiral **Sakuzo YOSHIZAWA** (11 Mar 1879 - 17 Dec 1956)

1 Dec 1925 - 10 Dec 1928:	Chief of Heijo Mining Bureau, Navy Fuel Yard
1 Dec 1926:	Promoted to *Rear-Admiral*
10 Dec 1928 - 20 Dec 1928:	Attached to Naval General Staff
25 Dec 1928:	Transferred to the reserve

Rear-Admiral **Kensuke YOTSUMOTO** (21 May 1870 - 23 Oct 1927)

8 May 1917 - 20 Nov 1919:	Chief of Naval Personnel, Kure Naval District
20 Nov 1919 - 1 Dec 1919:	Attached to Kure Naval District
1 Dec 1919:	Promoted to *Rear-Admiral*
1 Dec 1919 - 1 Aug 1920:	Unassigned
1 Aug 1920:	Transferred to the reserve

Vice-Admiral **Shusei YUCHI** (2 May 1883 - 25 Apr 1940)

1 Dec 1926:	Promoted to *Rear-Admiral*
1 Dec 1926 - 10 Dec 1928:	Commander, 1st Submarine Flotilla
10 Dec 1928 - 30 Nov 1929:	Attached to Naval General Staff
30 Nov 1929 - 1 Dec 1930:	Commander, 3rd Escort Flotilla
1 Dec 1930 - 11 Jan 1932:	Commander, Mako Guard District
1 Dec 1931:	Promoted to *Vice-Admiral*
11 Jan 1932 - 22 Mar 1933:	Attached to Naval General Staff
31 Mar 1933:	Transferred to the reserve

Vice-Admiral (Engineer) **Teikan YUCHI** (8 Oct 1849 - 29 Jan 1927)

28 Dec 1897:	Promoted to *General (Engineer)*
28 Dec 1897 - 28 Dec 1903:	Commandant, Naval Engineering Academy
28 Dec 1903 - 2 May 1904:	Chief of Bureau 2, Naval Training Command

1 Feb 1904:	Promoted to *General (Engineer), Senior grade*
2 May 1904 - 25 Mar 1905:	Unassigned
25 Mar 1905 - 28 Apr 1906:	Chief of Bureau 2, Naval Training Command
26 Jan 1906:	Redesignated *Vice-Admiral (Engineer)*
28 Apr 1906:	Transferred to the reserve

Rear-Admiral (Judge) **Kikuo YUFU** (29 May 1897 - 6 Feb 1973)

6 Nov 1944 - 30 Nov 1945:	Prosecutor, High Court Martial
1 Nov 1945:	Promoted to *Rear-Admiral (Judge)*
20 Nov 1945 - 30 Nov 1945:	Chief Judge, Department of the Navy

Rear-Admiral (Paymaster) **Nobuo YUKIFUJI** (? - 25 Jan 1945)

1 Aug 1944 - 25 Jan 1945:	Paymaster-General, 2nd Air Fleet
25 Jan 1945:	Posthumously promoted to *Rear-Admiral*

Rear-Admiral **Katsumi YUKISHITA** (12 Mar 1887 - 27 May 1967)

15 Jul 1935 - 1 Dec 1936:	Chief of Supply Bureau, Kure Naval District
15 Nov 1935:	Promoted to *Rear-Admiral*
1 Dec 1936 - 1 Dec 1937:	Commander, Sasebo Guard Flotilla
1 Dec 1937 - 15 Dec 1937:	Attached to Naval General Staff
21 Dec 1937:	Transferred to the reserve
10 Jul 1941 - 19 Jul 1941:	Recalled; Attached to Naval General Staff
19 Jul 1941 - 5 May 1942:	Naval Attache, Chile
19 Jul 1942 - 19 Jun 1946:	Naval Attache, Argentina

Rear-Admiral **Kenzo YUTANI** (21 Mar 1878 - 24 Mar 1964)

1 Apr 1919 - 20 Nov 1922:	Technical Inspector, Yokosuka Navy Yard
20 Nov 1922 - 1 Dec 1922:	Attached to Yokosuka Naval District
1 Dec 1922:	Promoted to *Rear-Admiral*
1 Dec 1922 - 31 Mar 1923:	Unassigned
31 Mar 1923:	Transferred to the reserve

Marshal Emperor **HIROHITO**

Grand Marshal Emperor **MUTSUSHITO**

Marshal Emperor **YOSHIHITO**

Fleet Admiral Prince Takehito **ARISUGAWA**

Fleet Admiral Prince **Hiroyasu FUSHIMI**

Fleet Admiral Baron **Goro IJUIN**

Fleet Admiral **Viscount Yoshika INOUE**

Fleet Admiral **Count Sukeyuki ITO**

Fleet Admiral **Viscount Tomozaburo KATO**

Fleet Admiral **Mineichi KOGA**

Fleet Admiral **Osami NAGANO**

Fleet Admiral **Marquis Tsugumichi SAIGO**

Fleet Admiral **Baron Hayao SHIMAMURA**

Fleet Admiral **Marquis Heihachiro TOGO**

Fleet Admiral **Isoroku YAMAMOTO**

Admiral **Baron Shigeto DEWA**

Admiral **Gengo HYAKUTAKE**

Admiral **Shigeyoshi INOUE**

Admiral **Seiichi ITO**

Admiral **Count Sukenori KABAYAMA**

Admiral **Baron Hikonojo KAMIMURA**

Admiral **Baron Shichiro KATAOKA**

Admiral **Nobutake KONDO**

Admiral **Chuichi NAGUMO**

Admiral **Kichisaburo NOMURA**

Admiral **Naokuni NOMURA**

Admiral **Keisuke OKADA**

Admiral **Viscount Makoto SAITO**

Admiral **Baron Kazunori SAMEJIMA**

Admiral **Baron Yahachi SHIBAYAMA**

Admiral **Shigetaro SHIMADA**

Admiral **Baron Kantaro SUZUKI**

Admiral **Takeo TAKAGI**

Admiral **Nishizo TSUKAHARA**

Admiral **Baron Sotokichi URYU**

Admiral **Count Gombei YAMAMOTO**

Admiral **Tanin YAMAYA**

Admiral **Baron Rokuro YASHIRO**

Admiral **Mitsumasa YONAI**

Admiral **Zengo YOSHIDA**

Vice-Admiral **Saneyuki AKIYAMA**

Vice-Admiral **Marquis Tadashige DAIGO**

Vice-Admiral **Yasutaro EGASHIRA**

Vice-Admiral **Shigeru FUKUTOME**

Vice-Admiral **Aritomo GOTO**

Vice-Admiral **Boshiro HOSOGAYA**

Vice-Admiral **Rinosuke ICHIMARU**

Vice-Admiral **Baron Yoshitomo INOUE**

Vice-Admiral **Kakuji KAKUTA**

Vice-Admiral **Masatomi KIMURA**

Vice-Admiral **Marquis Teruhisa KOMATSU**

Vice-Admiral **Takeo KURITA**

Vice-Admiral **Gunichi MIKAWA**

Vice-Admiral **Sentaro OMORI**

Vice-Admiral **Jisaburo OZAWA**

Vice-Admiral **Kiyohide SHIMA**

Vice-Admiral **Raizo TANAKA**

Vice-Admiral **Tamon YAMAGUCHI**

Rear-Admiral **Toyo MITSUNOBU**

Rear-Admiral **Kikunozo SAKURAI**

ORDER OF BATTLE OF THE IMPERIAL JAPANESE NAVY, 1900 - 1945 MINISTRY OF THE NAVY

Minister of the Navy

8 Nov 1898 - 7 Jan 1906:	*Admiral* Count Gonbei Yamamoto
7 Jan 1906 - 16 Apr 1914:	*Admiral* Viscount Makoto Saito
16 Apr 1914 - 10 Aug 1915:	*Admiral* Rokuro Yashiro
10 Aug 1915 - 15 May 1923:	*Fleet Admiral* Viscount Tomozaburo Kato
15 May 1923 - 7 Jan 1924:	*Admiral* Takeshi Takarabe
7 Jan 1924 - 11 Jun 1924:	*Admiral* Kakuichi Murakami
11 Jun 1924 - 20 Apr 1927:	*Admiral* Takeshi Takarabe
20 Apr 1927 - 2 Jul 1929:	*Admiral* Keisuke Okada
2 Jul 1929 - 3 Oct 1930:	*Admiral* Takeshi Takarabe
3 Oct 1930 - 13 Dec 1931:	*Admiral* Baron Kiyokazu Abo
13 Dec 1931 - 26 May 1932:	*Admiral* Baron Mineo Osumi
26 May 1932 - 9 Jan 1933:	*Admiral* Keisuke Okada
9 Jan 1933 - 9 Mar 1936:	*Admiral* Baron Mineo Osumi
9 Mar 1936 - 2 Feb 1937:	*Fleet Admiral* Osami Nagano
2 Feb 1937 - 30 Aug 1939:	*Admiral* Mitsumasa Yonai
30 Aug 1939 - 5 Sep 1940:	*Admiral* Zengo Yoshida
5 Sep 1940 - 18 Oct 1941:	*Admiral* Koshiro Oikawa
18 Oct 1941 - 17 Jul 1944:	*Admiral* Shigetaro Shimada
17 Jul 1944 - 22 Jul 1944:	*Admiral* Naokuni Nomura
22 Jul 1944 - 30 Nov 1945:	*Admiral* Mitsumasa Yonai

Deputy Minister of the Navy

10 Nov 1898 - 7 Jan 1906:	*Admiral* Viscount Makoto Saito
7 Jan 1906 - 1 Dec 1909:	*Fleet Admiral* Viscount Tomozaburo Kato
1 Dec 1909 - 17 Apr 1914:	*Admiral* Takeshi Takarabe
17 Apr 1914 - 1 Sep 1917:	*Admiral* Baron Kantaro Suzuki
1 Sep 1917 - 16 Aug 1920:	*Admiral* Sojiro Tochinai
16 Aug 1920 - 25 May 1923:	*Admiral* Kenji Ide
25 May 1923 - 11 Jun 1924:	*Admiral* Keisuke Okada
11 Jun 1924 - 15 Apr 1925:	*Admiral* Baron Kiyokazu Abo
15 Apr 1925 - 10 Dec 1928:	*Admiral* Baron Mineo Osumi
10 Dec 1928 - 10 Jun 1930:	*Admiral* Katsunoshin Yamanashi
10 Jun 1930 - 1 Dec 1931:	*Admiral* Seizo Kobayashi
1 Dec 1931 - 1 Jun 1932:	*Vice-Admiral* Seizo Sakonji
1 Jun 1932 - 10 May 1934:	*Admiral* Hisanori Fujita
10 May 1934 - 1 Dec 1936:	*Admiral* Kiyoshi Hasegawa
1 Dec 1936 - 30 Aug 1939:	*Fleet Admiral* Isoroku Yamamoto
30 Aug 1939 - 5 Sep 1940:	*Vice-Admiral* Tokutaro Sumiyama

5 Sep 1940 - 4 Apr 1941:   *Admiral* Teijiro Toyoda
4 Apr 1941 - 18 Jul 1944:   *Admiral* Yorio Sawamoto
18 Jul 1944 - 5 Aug 1944:   *Vice-Admiral* Takazumi Oka
5 Aug 1944 - 15 May 1945:   *Admiral* Shigeyoshi Inoue
15 May 1945 - 20 Nov 1945:   *Vice-Admiral* Takeo Tada
20 Nov 1945 - 30 Nov 1945:   *Vice-Admiral* Hisashi Mita

Chief, Bureau of Naval Affairs
10 Nov 1898 - 20 May 1900:   *Vice-Admiral* Yoriyuki Morooka
20 May 1900 - 25 Oct 1900:   *Admiral* Viscount Makoto Saito
25 Oct 1900 - 29 Oct 1902:   *Admiral* Baron Hikonojo Kamimura
29 Oct 1902 - 27 Oct 1903:   *Admiral* Baron Shigeto Dewa
27 Oct 1903 - 3 Feb 1904:   *Vice-Admiral* Baron Tokutaro Nakamizo
3 Feb 1904 - 19 Dec 1905:   *Admiral* Viscount Makoto Saito
19 Dec 1905 - 22 Nov 1906:   *Fleet Admiral* Viscount Tomozaburo Kato
22 Nov 1906 - 15 May 1908:   *Vice-Admiral* Kunikane Taketomi
15 May 1908 - 1 Dec 1909:   *Vice-Admiral* Baron Tokutaro Nakamizo
1 Dec 1909 - 20 Apr 1912:   *Admiral* Sojiro Tochinai
20 Apr 1912 - 10 Jan 1913:   *Vice-Admiral* Yasutaro Egashira
10 Jan 1913 - 17 Apr 1914:   *Admiral* Kaneo Nomaguchi
17 Apr 1914 - 21 Feb 1916:   *Vice-Admiral* Saneyuki Akiyama
21 Feb 1916 - 23 Jun 1916:   *Admiral* Baron Kantaro Suzuki
23 Jun 1916 - 1 Dec 1916:   *Admiral* Kozaburo Oguri
1 Dec 1916 - 16 Aug 1920:   *Admiral* Kenji Ide
16 Aug 1920 - 1 May 1922:   *Vice-Admiral* Saburo Horiuchi
1 May 1922 - 1 Dec 1923:   *Admiral* Baron Mineo Osumi
1 Dec 1923 - 25 Mar 1927:   *Admiral* Seizo Kobayashi
25 Mar 1927 - 6 Sep 1929:   *Vice-Admiral* Seizo Sakonji
6 Sep 1929 - 2 Nov 1931:   *Vice-Admiral* Teikichi Hori
2 Nov 1931 - 12 May 1932:   *Admiral* Teijiro Toyoda
12 May 1932 - 15 Sep 1933:   *Vice-Admiral* Ken Terajima
15 Sep 1933 - 2 Dec 1935:   *Admiral* Zengo Yoshida
2 Dec 1935 - 20 Oct 1937:   *Admiral* Soemu Toyoda
20 Oct 1937 - 18 Oct 1939:   *Admiral* Shigeyoshi Inoue
18 Oct 1939 - 15 Oct 1940:   *Vice-Admiral* Katsuo Abe
15 Oct 1940 - 1 Aug 1944:   *Vice-Admiral* Takazumi Oka
1 Aug 1944 - 15 May 1945:   *Vice-Admiral* Takeo Tada
15 May 1945 - 17 Nov 1945:   *Vice-Admiral* Zenshiro Hoshina
17 Nov 1945 - 30 Nov 1945:   *Rear-Admiral* Yoshio Yamamoto

Chief, Naval Personnel Bureau
20 May 1900 - 3 Jul 1901:   *Vice-Admiral* Baron Masaaki Hashimoto
3 Jul 1901 - 28 Dec 1903:   *Admiral* Baron Sotaro Misu

28 Dec 1903 - 19 Dec 1905:	*Vice-Admiral* Baron Masaaki Hashimoto
19 Dec 1905 - 10 Dec 1908:	*Vice-Admiral* Byoichiro Ogura
10 Dec 1908 - 11 Mar 1911:	*Vice-Admiral* Tamotsu Tsuchiya
11 Mar 1911 - 20 Apr 1912:	*Vice-Admiral* Yasutaro Egashira
20 Apr 1912 - 1 Dec 1913:	*Admiral* Tanin Yamaya
1 Dec 1913 - 23 May 1914:	*Admiral* Baron Kantaro Suzuki
23 May 1914 - 13 Dec 1915:	*Vice-Admiral* Yaichi Mukai
13 Dec 1915 - 1 Dec 1917:	*Admiral* Keisuke Okada
1 Dec 1917 - 1 Oct 1920:	*Admiral* Naomi Taniguchi
1 Oct 1920 - 1 Feb 1923:	*Vice-Admiral* Shinzaburo Furukawa
1 Feb 1923 - 1 Dec 1924:	*Admiral* Katsunochin Yamanashi
1 Dec 1924 - 1 Dec 1926:	*Vice-Admiral* Seizo Sakonji
1 Dec 1926 - 10 Dec 1928:	*Admiral* Hisanori Fujita
10 Dec 1928 - 1 Dec 1930:	*Vice-Admiral* Hajime Matsushita
1 Dec 1930 - 15 Nov 1933:	*Vice-Admiral* Kiyoshi Anno
15 Nov 1933 - 1 Dec 1936:	*Vice-Admiral* Sonosuke Kobayashi
1 Dec 1936 - 15 Dec 1938:	*Vice-Admiral* Mitsumi Shimizu
15 Dec 1938 - 28 Nov 1940:	*Admiral* Seichi Ito
28 Nov 1940 - 10 Dec 1942:	*Vice-Admiral* Yoshimasa Nakahara
10 Dec 1942 - 15 Jun 1943:	*Vice-Admiral* Tasuku Nakazawa
15 Jun 1943 - 7 May 1945:	*Vice-Admiral* Hisashi Mito
7 May 1945 - 24 Nov 1945:	*Rear-Admiral* Takeji Ono
24 nov 1945 - 30 Nov 1945:	*Rear-Admiral* Iwao Kawai

Chief, Engineer Bureau

1 Apr 1916 - 1 Sep 1921:	*Vice-Admiral* (*Engineer*) Kiyojiro Ichikawa
1 Sep 1921 - 25 May 1923:	*Vice-Admiral* (*Engineer*) Zenya Funabashi
25 May 1923 - 20 Dec 1924:	*Vice-Admiral* (*Engineer*) Tamotsu Hiratsuka
20 Dec 1924:	POSITION ABOLISHED

Chief, Readiness Bureau

15 Nov 1940 - 1 Mar 1945:	*Vice-Admiral* Zenshiro Hoshina
1 Mar 1945:	POSITION ABOLISHED

Chief, Education Bureau

20 May 1900 - 3 Jul 1901:	*Vice-Admiral* Yoriyuki Morooka
3 Jul 1901 - 5 Sep 1903:	*Vice-Admiral* Yuju Matsunaga
5 Sep 1903 - 27 Oct 1903:	*Admiral* Baron Hikonojo Kamimura
27 Oct 1903 - 7 Feb 1905:	*Vice-Admiral* Shinichi Arima
7 Feb 1905 - 7 Nov 1905:	*Admiral* Viscount Makoto Saito
7 Nov 1905 - 2 Feb 1906:	*Admiral* Baron Sotaro Misu
2 Feb 1906 - 22 Nov 1906:	*Vice-Admiral* Baron Toshiatsu Sakamoto
22 Nov 1906 - 26 May 1908:	*Admiral* Baron Shigeto Dewa

26 May 1908 - 28 Aug 1908:   *Vice-Admiral* Shinichi Arima
28 Aug 1908 - 1 Dec 1912:   *Vice-Admiral* Baron Toshiatsu Sakamoto
1 Dec 1912 - 25 Mar 1914:   *Admiral* Motaro Yoshimatsu
25 Mar 1914 - 22 Apr 1914:   *Fleet Admiral* Baron Hayao Shimamura
22 Apr 1914 - 5 Feb 1915:   *Admiral* Matahachiro Nawa
5 Feb 1915 - 1 Dec 1916:   *Admiral* Baron Sadakichi Kato
1 Dec 1916 - 6 Apr 1917:   *Admiral* Ryokitsu Arima
6 Apr 1917 - 1 Dec 1919:   *Admiral* Kakuichi Murakami
1 Dec 1919 - 1 Dec 1920:   *Admiral* Ryokitsu Arima
1 Dec 1920 - 1 Apr 1923:   *Admiral* Kaneo Nomaguchi
1 Apr 1923 - 10 Apr 1924:   *Vice-Admiral* Shinzaburo Furukawa
10 Apr 1924 - 18 Sep 1925:   *Vice-Admiral* Kumazo Shirane
18 Sep 1925 - 26 Jul 1926:   *Admiral* Kichisaburo Nomura
26 Jul 1926 - 10 Dec 1928:   *Vice-Admiral* Nobumasa Suetsugu
10 Dec 1928 - 10 Jun 1930:   *Vice-Admiral* Naotaro Ominato
10 Jun 1930 - 16 Jun 1932:   *Vice-Admiral* Ken Terajima
16 Jun 1932 - 5 Nov 1933:   *Vice-Admiral* Akira Goto
5 Nov 1933 - 20 Sep 1934:   *Vice-Admiral* Kamesaburo Nakamura
20 Sep 1934 - 15 Mar 1935:   *Rear-Admiral* Minoru Sonoda
15 Mar 1935 - 2 Dec 1935:   *Admiral* Soemu Toyoda
2 Dec 1935 - 1 Dec 1937:   *Vice-Admiral* Tokutaro Sumiyama
1 Dec 1937 - 15 Nov 1939:   *Vice-Admiral* Masaichi Niimi
15 Nov 1939 - 4 Apr 1941:   *Vice-Admiral* Jinichi Kusaka
4 Apr 1941 - 20 Nov 1942:   *Vice-Admiral* Sakae Tokunaga
20 Nov 1942 - 1 Mar 1944:   *Vice-Admiral* Shikazo Yano
1 Mar 1944 - 9 Sep 1944:   *Rear-Admiral* Sokichi Takagi
9 Sep 1944 - 5 May 1945:   *Vice-Admiral* Shinzo Onishi
5 May 1945 - 20 Aug 1945:   *Vice-Admiral* Gihachi Takayanagi
20 Aug 1945 - 1 Oct 1945:   *Rear-Admiral* Kanae Kosaka

Chief, Naval Supply Bureau

1 Oct 1920 - 1 Dec 1921:   *Vice-Admiral* Ei Yamaguchi
1 Dec 1921 - 11 Jun 1924:   *Vice-Admiral* Shigetsugu Nakazato
11 Jun 1924 - 20 Dec 1924:   *Vice-Admiral* Eizaburo Fujiwara
20 Dec 1924 - 1 Aug 1925:   *Vice-Admiral* Tamotsu Hiratsuka
1 Aug 1925 - 10 Dec 1928:   *Vice-Admiral* Iwasaburo Ikeda
10 Dec 1928 - 30 Nov 1929:   *Vice-Admiral* Tokuichi Shimizu
30 Nov 1929 - 1 Dec 1931:   *Vice-Admiral* Gihachiro Yamashita
1 Dec 1931 - 1 Jun 1932:   *Vice-Admiral* Masato Sugi
1 Jun 1932 - 10 May 1934:   *Vice-Admiral* Fukusaku Ushimaru
10 May 1934 - 2 Dec 1935:   *Vice-Admiral* Hiromu Onodera
2 Dec 1935 - 1 Dec 1936:   *Vice-Admiral* Muneshige Ueda
1 Dec 1936 - 30 Aug 1939:   *Vice-Admiral* Nagaaki Ujiie

30 Aug 1939 - 25 Oct 1943:   *Vice-Admiral* Konomu Mishuku
25 Oct 1943 - 1 May 1945:   *Vice-Admiral* Shigeaki Nabeshima
1 May 1945 - 15 Nov 1945:   *Vice-Admiral* Kanichi Morita
15 Nov 1945 - 30 Nov 1945:   *Rear-Admiral* Jitsue Akishige

Chief, Medical Bureau
1 Apr 1897 - 13 Dec 1905:   *Surgeon-General* Yasuzumi Saneyoshi
13 Dec 1905 - 13 Dec 1915:   *Surgeon-General* Sosuke Kimura
13 Dec 1915 - 1 Dec 1919:   *Vice-Admiral (Surgeon)* Tadao Honda
1 Dec 1919 - 1 Dec 1923:   *Vice-Admiral (Surgeon)* Yuzo Suzuki
1 Dec 1923 - 1 Dec 1925:   *Vice-Admiral (Surgeon)* Isamu Hirano
1 Dec 1925 - 1 Dec 1927:   *Vice-Admiral (Surgeon)* Ryoshichiro Amamiya
1 Dec 1927 - 30 Nov 1929:   *Vice-Admiral (Surgeon)* Yasuzo Onuki
30 Nov 1929 - 25 Feb 1932:   *Vice-Admiral (Surgeon)* Ryu Ogawa
25 Feb 1932 - 15 Nov 1934:   *Vice-Admiral (Surgeon)* Naka Koda
15 Nov 1934 - 15 Nov 1939:   *Vice-Admiral (Surgeon)* Shinichiro Takasugi
15 Nov 1939 - 15 Oct 1941:   *Vice-Admiral (Surgeon)* Taro Nakano
15 Oct 1941 - 25 Oct 1943:   *Vice-Admiral (Surgeon)* Higotaro Tanaka
25 Oct 1943 - 29 Nov 1945:   *Vice-Admiral (Surgeon)* Nobuaki Hori
29 Nov 1945 - 30 Nov 1945:   *Captain (Surgeon)* Gen Arima

Chief, Accounting Bureau
5 Jun 1897 - 15 Aug 1908:   *Senior Paymaster-General* Keijiro Murakami
15 Aug 1908 - 10 May 1912:   *Paymaster-General* Kichinosuke Fukunaga
10 May 1912 - 25 May 1923:   *Vice-Admiral (Paymaster)* Masaru Shisa
25 May 1923 - 1 Aug 1925:   *Vice-Admiral (Paymaster)* Sadakichi Fukamizu
1 Aug 1925 - 13 Apr 1927:   *Vice-Admiral (Paymaster)* Shinjiro Nagayasu
13 Apr 1927 - 20 May 1933:   *Vice-Admiral (Paymaster)* Ryoichi Kato
20 May 1933 - 2 May 1938:   *Vice-Admiral (Paymaster)* Haruichi Murakami
2 May 1938 - 1 Jun 1943:   *Vice-Admiral (Paymaster)* Daisuke Takei
1 Jun 1943 - 30 Nov 1945:   *Vice-Admiral (Paymaster)* Ushinosuke Yamamoto

Chief, Legal Bureau
20 May 1900 - 30 May 1907:   *Rear-Admiral* Yutaka Toki
30 May 1907 - 30 Sep 1913:   *Admiral* Takeshi Takarabe
30 Sep 1913 - 16 Mar 1925:   Shigenari Uchida
16 Mar 1925 - 28 Mar 1936:   Saburo Yamada
28 Mar 1936 - 1 Apr 1941:   Shigeki Shiomi
1 Apr 1941 - 1 Nov 1944:   *Vice-Admiral (Judge)* Yoshizumi Obata
1 Nov 1944 - 20 Nov 1945:   *Vice-Admiral (Judge)* Kiyoshi Shimada
20 Nov 1945 - 30 Nov 1945:   *Rear-Admiral (Judge)* Kikuo Yufu

Chief, Naval Shipbuilding Command

20 May 1900 - 3 Jul 1901:	*Vice-Admiral* Hidematsu Tsunoda
3 Jul 1901 - 27 Oct 1903:	*Vice-Admiral* Shinichi Arima
27 Oct 1903 - 10 Jan 1906:	*Admiral* Viscount Makoto Saito
10 Jan 1906 - 22 Nov 1906:	*Fleet Admiral* Baron Goro Ijuin
22 Nov 1906 - 28 Aug 1908:	*Admiral* Shichiro Kataoka
28 Aug 1908 - 1 Dec 1913:	*Vice-Admiral* Kazu Matsumoto
1 Dec 1913 - 23 May 1914:	*Vice-Admiral* Suetaka Ijichi
23 May 1914 - 13 Dec 1915:	*Admiral* Kakuichi Murakami
13 Dec 1915 - 1 Sep 1917:	*Admiral* Sojiro Tochinai
1 Sep 1917 - 12 Dec 1917:	POST UNOCCUPIED
12 Dec 1917 - 1 Oct 1920:	*Vice-Admiral* Otojiro Ito
1 Oct 1920 - 25 May 1923:	*Admiral* Keisuke Okada
25 May 1923 - 11 Jun 1924:	*Admiral* Baron Kiyokazu Abo
11 Jun 1924 - 10 Dec 1926:	*Vice-Admiral* Yasuhira Yoshikawa
10 Dec 1926 - 10 Dec 1928:	*Admiral* Katsunoshin Yamanashi
10 Dec 1928 - 1 Feb 1929:	POST UNOCCUPIED
1 Feb 1929 - 10 Jun 1930:	*Admiral* Seizo Kobayashi
10 Jun 1930 - 1 Jun 1932:	*Admiral* Hisanori Fujita
1 Jun 1932 - 10 May 1934:	*Vice-Admiral* Masato Sugi
10 May 1934 - 16 Mar 1936:	*Admiral* Ryozo Nakamura
16 Mar 1936 - 1 Dec 1936:	*Admiral* Gengo Hyakutake
1 Dec 1936 - 27 Jan 1939:	*Vice-Admiral* Muneshige Ueda
27 Jan 1939 - 30 Aug 1939:	*Admiral* Koichi Shiozawa
30 Aug 1939 - 21 Oct 1939:	*Admiral* Teijiro Toyoda
21 Oct 1939 - 18 Sep 1941:	*Admiral* Soemu Toyoda
18 Sep 1941 - 15 Apr 1943:	*Vice-Admiral* Seiichi Iwamura
15 Apr 1943 - 4 Nov 1944:	*Vice-Admiral* Rokuzo Sugiyama
4 Nov 1944 - 18 Nov 1944:	*Admiral* Shigeyoshi Inoue
18 Nov 1944 - 30 Nov 1945:	*Vice-Admiral* Ryutaro Shibuya

Chief, Naval Air Command

5 Apr 1927 - 10 Dec 1928:	*Admiral* Eisuke Yamamoto
10 Dec 1928 - 10 Oct 1931:	*Vice-Admiral* Masataka Ando
10 Oct 1931 - 15 Nov 1933:	*Vice-Admiral* Shigeru Matsuyama
15 Nov 1933 - 17 Jan 1934:	*Admiral* Takayoshi Kato
17 Jan 1934 - 2 Dec 1935:	*Admiral* Koichi Shiozawa
2 Dec 1935 - 1 Dec 1936:	*Fleet Admiral* Isoroku Yamamoto
1 Dec 1936 - 25 Apr 1938:	*Admiral* Koshiro Oikawa
25 Apr 1938 - 15 Nov 1938:	*Fleet Admiral* Isoroku Yamamoto
15 Nov 1938 - 1 Oct 1940:	*Admiral* Teijiro Toyoda
1 Oct 1940 - 10 Sep 1941:	*Admiral* Shigeyoshi Inoue
10 Sep 1941 - 1 Dec 1942:	*Vice-Admiral* Eikichi Katagiri
1 Dec 1942 - 15 Sep 1944:	*Admiral* Nishizo Tsukahara

15 Sep 1944 - 1 May 1945: *Vice-Admiral* Michitaro Totsuka
1 May 1945 - 15 May 1945: *Admiral* Shigeyoshi Inoue
15 May 1945 - 30 Nov 1945: *Vice-Admiral* Misao Wada

HIGH COMMAND

Chief of the Naval High Command
25 Apr 1945 - 29 May 1945: *Admiral* Soemu Toyoda
29 May 1945 - 10 Oct 1945: *Admiral* Jisaburo Ozawa

Chief of the Naval General Staff
11 May 1895 - 20 Dec 1905: *Fleet Admiral* Count Sukeyuki Ito
20 Dec 1905 - 1 Dec 1909: *Fleet Admiral* Marquis Heihachiro Togo
1 Dec 1909 - 22 Apr 1914: *Fleet Admiral* Baron Goro Ijuin
22 Apr 1914 - 1 Dec 1920: *Fleet Admiral* Baron Hayao Shimamura
1 Dec 1920 - 15 Apr 1925: *Admiral* Baron Gentaro Yamashita
15 Apr 1925 - 22 Jan 1929: *Admiral* Baron Kantaro Suzuki
22 Jan 1929 - 11 Jun 1930: *Admiral* Hiroharu Kato
11 Jun 1930 - 2 Feb 1932: *Admiral* Naomi Taniguchi
2 Feb 1932 - 9 Apr 1941: *Fleet Admiral* Prince Hiroyasu Fushimi
9 Apr 1941 - 21 Feb 1944: *Fleet Admiral* Osami Nagano
21 Feb 1944 - 2 Aug 1944: *Admiral* Shigetaro Shimada
2 Aug 1944 - 29 May 1945: *Admiral* Koshiro Oikawa
29 May 1945 - 15 Oct 1945: *Admiral* Soemu Toyoda

Senior Deputy Chief of the Naval General Staff
1 Mar 1944 - 29 Jul 1944: *Admiral* Nishizo Tsukahara

Deputy Chief of the Naval General Staff
10 Nov 1898 - 17 Mar 1902: *Fleet Admiral* Baron Goro Ijuin
17 Mar 1902 - 29 Oct 1902: *Admiral* Baron Hikonojo Kamimura
29 Oct 1902 - 5 Sep 1903: *Admiral* Baron Shigeto Dewa
5 Sep 1903 - 22 Nov 1906: *Fleet Admiral* Baron Goro Ijuin
22 Nov 1906 - 1 Dec 1909: *Admiral* Baron Sotaro Misu
1 Dec 1909 - 25 Mar 1914: *Admiral* Koichi Fujii
25 Mar 1914 - 10 Aug 1915: *Admiral* Baron Gentaro Yamashita
10 Aug 1915 - 13 Dec 1915: *Vice-Admiral* Tetsutaro Sato
13 Dec 1915 - 13 Jun 1918: *Admiral* Tanin Yamaya
13 Jun 1918 - 13 Sep 1920: *Admiral* Isamu Takeshita
13 Sep 1920 - 1 May 1922: *Admiral* Baron Kiyokazu Abo
1 May 1922 - 1 Jun 1923: *Admiral* Hiroharu Kato
1 Jun 1923 - 5 Feb 1924: *Vice-Admiral* Saburo Horiuchi

5 Feb 1924 - 10 Apr 1924:
10 Apr 1924 - 23 Jul 1926: *Vice-Admiral* Shichigoro Saito
26 Jul 1926 - 10 Dec 1928: *Admiral* Kichisaburo Nomura
10 Dec 1928 - 10 Jun 1930: *Admiral* Nobumasa Suetsugu
10 Jun 1930 - 10 Oct 1931: *Fleet Admiral* Osami Nagano
10 Oct 1931 - 8 Feb 1932: *Admiral* Gengo Hyakutake
8 Feb 1932 - 15 Nov 1933: *Admiral* Sankichi Takahashi
15 Nov 1933 - 17 Jan 1934: *Vice-Admiral* Shigeru Matsuyama
17 Jan 1934 - 2 Dec 1935: *Admiral* Takayoshi Kato
2 Dec 1935 - 1 Dec 1937: *Admiral* Shigetaro Shimada
1 Dec 1937 - 21 Oct 1939: *Fleet Admiral* Mineichi Koga
21 Oct 1939 - 1 Sep 1941: *Admiral* Nobutake Kondo
1 Sep 1941 - 18 Nov 1944: *Admiral* Seiichi Ito
18 Nov 1944 - 29 May 1945: *Admiral* Jisaburo Ozawa
29 May 1945 - 20 Aug 1945: *Vice-Admiral* Takijiro Onishi
20 Aug 1945 - 15 Oct 1945: *Vice-Admiral* Gihachi Takayanagi

Chief of Bureau 1, Naval General Staff
10 Nov 1898 - 21 May 1900: *Admiral* Motaro Yoshimatsu
21 May 1900 - 10 Apr 1902: *Admiral* Baron Sotokichi Uryu
10 Apr 1902 - 12 Apr 1903:
12 Apr 1903 - 6 Jan 1904: *Vice-Admiral* Baron Sadayasu Tomioka
6 Jan 1904 - 2 Feb 1906: *Admiral* Baron Gentaro Yamashita
2 Feb 1906 - 21 Oct 1907: *Vice-Admiral* Reijiro Kawashima
21 Oct 1907 - 4 Mar 1909: *Vice-Admiral* Koshi Saito
4 Mar 1909 - 1 Dec 1909: *Vice-Admiral* Reijiro Kawashima
1 Dec 1909 - 23 Mar 1910:
23 Mar 1910 - 1 Dec 1910: *Admiral* Baron Gentaro Yamashita
1 Dec 1910 - 1 Dec 1912: *Admiral* Ryokitsu Arima
1 Dec 1912 - 17 Apr 1914: *Vice-Admiral* Saneyuki Akiyama
17 Apr 1914 - 10 Aug 1915: *Vice-Admiral* Tetsutaro Sato
10 Aug 1915 - 1 Dec 1916: *Admiral* Isamu Takeshita
1 Dec 1916 - 1 Dec 1920: *Admiral* Baron Kiyokazu Abo
1 Dec 1920 - 1 Dec 1922: *Vice-Admiral* Shichigoro Saito
1 Dec 1922 - 3 Dec 1923: *Admiral* Nobumasa Suetsugu
3 Dec 1923 - 5 Feb 1924: *Vice-Admiral* Kanjo Seki
5 Feb 1924 - 1 Dec 1925: *Vice-Admiral* Tamaki Tosu
1 Dec 1925 - 1 Dec 1927: *Vice-Admiral* Kanjiro Hara
1 Dec 1927 - 30 Nov 1929: *Admiral* Gengo Hyakutake
30 Nov 1929 - 18 Jun 1930: *Admiral* Takayoshi Kato
18 Jun 1930 - 15 Nov 1932: *Admiral* Koshiro Oikawa
15 Nov 1932 - 21 Feb 1935: *Admiral* Shigetaro Shimada
21 Feb 1935 - 6 Apr 1935: *Vice-Admiral* Kiyoshi Anno

6 Apr 1935 - 1 Aug 1935:
1 Aug 1935 - 2 Dec 1935: *Vice-Admiral* Kamezaburo Nakamura
2 Dec 1935 - 15 Dec 1938: *Admiral* Nobutake Kondo
15 Dec 1938 - 10 Apr 1941: *Vice-Admiral* Matome Ugaki
10 Apr 1941 - 15 Jun 1943: *Vice-Admiral* Shigeru Fukutome
15 Jun 1943 - 15 Dec 1944: *Vice-Admiral* Tasuku Nakazawa
15 Dec 1944 - 15 Oct 1945: *Rear-Admiral* Sadatoshi Tomioka

Chief of Bureau 2, Naval General Staff
7 Oct 1899 - 6 Apr 1901: *Vice-Admiral* Chikataka Tamari
6 Apr 1901 - 6 Jan 1904: *Admiral* Koichi Fujii
6 Jan 1904 - 27 Dec 1907: *Vice-Admiral* Etsutaro Mori
27 Dec 1907 - 1 Dec 1909: *Admiral* Tanin Yamaya
1 Dec 1909 - 1 Dec 1911: *Captain* Mantaro Takahashi
1 Dec 1911 - 17 Apr 1914: *Vice-Admiral* Kazuyoshi Yamaji
17 Apr 1914 - 27 May 1914:
27 May 1914 - 1 Dec 1914: *Vice-Admiral* Nobutaro Shimamura
1 Dec 1914 - 1 Feb 1915:
1 Feb 1915 - 4 Sep 1918: *Vice-Admiral* Kiyokaze Yoshida
4 Sep 1918 - 1 Dec 1921: *Vice-Admiral* Shigetsugu Nakazato
1 Dec 1921 - 1 Dec 1922: *Rear-Admiral* Shizen Komaki
1 Dec 1922 - 1 Dec 1923: *Vice-Admiral* Junichi Kiokawa
1 Dec 1923 - 1 Dec 1924: *Rear-Admiral* Kanjo Seki
1 Dec 1924 - 21 Oct 1925: *Vice-Admiral* Masataka Ando
21 Oct 1925 - 1 Dec 1925: *Vice-Admiral* Tamaki Tosu
1 Dec 1925 - 1 Nov 1926: *Admiral* Sankichi Takahashi
1 Nov 1926 - 1 Dec 1927: *Vice-Admiral* Eijiro Hamano
1 Dec 1927 - 12 Sep 1929: *Vice-Admiral* Shigeru Matsuyama
12 Sep 1929 - 30 Nov 1929:
30 Nov 1929 - 1 Dec 1931: *Admiral* Zengo Yoshida
1 Dec 1931 - 15 Sep 1933: *Admiral* Soemu Toyoda
15 Sep 1933 - 15 Nov 1935: *Fleet Admiral* Mineichi Koga
15 Nov 1935 - 15 Nov 1937: *Vice-Admiral* Ibo Takahashi
15 Nov 1937 - 15 Nov 1939: *Vice-Admiral* Gunichi Mikawa
15 Nov 1939 - 6 Sep 1941: *Admiral* Takeo Takagi
6 Sep 1941 - 19 Jul 1943: *Vice-Admiral* Yoshio Suzuki
19 Jul 1943 - 27 May 1945: *Rear-Admiral* Kameto Kuroshima
27 May 1945 - 15 Oct 1945: *Rear-Admiral* Toshitane Takada

Chief of Bureau 3, Naval General Staff
1 Dec 1897 - 23 May 1900: *Rear-Admiral* Kaneji Yasuhara
23 May 1900 - 6 Jul 1901: *Rear-Admiral* Shizuka Nakamura
6 Jul 1901 - 22 Apr 1902: *Rear-Admiral* Kitaro Endo

22 Apr 1902 - 21 Jan 1904:	*Rear-Admiral* Sukeuji Hosoya
21 Jan 1904 - 20 Dec 1905:	*Vice-Admiral* Yasutaro Egashira
20 Dec 1905 - 5 Nov 1906:	*Vice-Admiral* Keizaburo Moriyama
5 Nov 1906 - 23 Jan 1908:	*Vice-Admiral* Hiromi Tadokoro
23 Jan 1908 - 19 Mar 1910:	*Vice-Admiral* Kazuyoshi Yamaji
19 Mar 1910 - 1 Dec 1912:	*Rear-Admiral* Fusajiro Nomura
1 Dec 1912 - 1 Dec 1913:	*Admiral* Saburo Hyakutake
1 Dec 1913 - 25 Aug 1915:	*Vice-Admiral* Shigetsugu Nakazato
25 Aug 1915 - 13 Dec 1915:	*Admiral* Baron Kiyokazu Abo
13 Dec 1915 - 1 Nov 1916	*Rear-Admiral* Noritoshi Sakamoto
1 Nov 1916 - 13 Jun 1918:	*Vice-Admiral* keizaburo Moriyama
13 Jun 1918 - 8 Nov 1919:	*Vice-Admiral* Masujiro Yoshida
8 Nov 1919 - 1 Jun 1922:	*Vice-Admiral* Kotaro Tanaka
1 Jun 1922 - 15 Sep 1923:	*Admiral* Kichisaburo Nomura
15 Sep 1923 - 5 Feb 1924:	
5 Feb 1924 - 1 Dec 1924:	*Fleet Admiral* Osami Nagano
1 Dec 1924 - 1 Dec 1926:	*Admiral* Ryozo Nakamura
1 Dec 1926 - 10 Dec 1928:	*Admiral* Mitsumasa Yonai
10 Dec 1928 - 1 Apr 1931:	*Vice-Admiral* Togo Kono
1 Apr 1931 - 28 Jun 1932:	*Vice-Admiral* Tsuneyoshi Sakano
28 Jun 1932 - 15 Nov 1932:	*Admiral* Shigetaro Shimada
15 Nov 1932 - 1 Sep 1933:	*Fleet Admiral* Mineichi Koga
1 Sep 1933 - 15 Nov 1934:	*Vice-Admiral* Shizue Tsuda
15 Nov 1934 - 1 Dec 1936:	*Admiral* Shiro Takasu
1 Dec 1936 - 25 Apr 1938:	*Admiral* Naokuni Nomura
25 Apr 1938 - 10 Oct 1939:	*Vice-Admiral* Katsuo Abe
10 Oct 1939 - 15 Oct 1940:	*Vice-Admiral* Takazumi Oka
15 Oct 1940 - 15 May 1942:	*Vice-Admiral* Minoru Maeda
15 May 1942 - 1 Dec 1942:	*Rear-Admiral* Kanji Ogawa
1 Dec 1942 - 2 Mar 1944:	*Vice-Admiral* Hideo Yano
2 Mar 1944 - 2 Mar 1945:	*Rear-Admiral* Takeji Ono
2 Mar 1945 - 15 Oct 1945:	*Rear-Admiral* Noboru Nakase

Chief of Bureau 4, Naval General Staff

20 Dec 1905 - 18 Dec 1907:	*Vice-Admiral* Yasutaro Egashira
18 Dec 1907 - 22 May 1910:	*Admiral* Matahachiro Nawa
22 May 1910 - 9 Jul 1912:	*Admiral* Isamu Takeshita
9 Jul 1912 - 1 Dec 1912:	
1 Dec 1912 - 1 Dec 1913:	*Vice-Admiral* Tetsutaro Sato
1 Dec 1913 - 10 Aug 1915:	*Admiral* Isamu Takeshita
10 Aug 1915 - 13 Dec 1915:	
13 Dec 1915 - 1 Nov 1916:	*Vice-Admiral* Keizaburo Moriyama
1 Nov 1916 - 10 Oct 1932:	POSITION ABOLISHED

10 Oct 1932 - 23 Feb 1933:	*Admiral* Soemu Toyoda
23 Feb 1933 - 1 Dec 1936:	*Vice-Admiral* Masaichi Maeda
1 Dec 1936 - 15 Nov 1938:	*Vice-Admiral* Satoshi Furihata
15 Nov 1938 - 1 Jul 1941:	*Vice-Admiral* Torahiko Nakajima
1 Jul 1941 - 25 Jan 1943:	*Vice-Admiral* Shigeji Kaneko
25 Jan 1943 - 15 Feb 1944:	*Vice-Admiral* Chimaki Kono
15 Feb 1944 - 20 Aug 1944:	*Rear-Admiral* Kameto Kuroshima
20 Aug 1944 - 15 Mar 1945:	*Rear-Admiral* Keiichi Onishi
15 Mar 1945 - 5 Sep 1945:	*Rear-Admiral* Tomekichi Nomura

FLEETS

Commander-in-Chief of the Combined Fleet

28 Dec 1903 - 20 Dec 1905:	*Fleet Admiral* Marquis Heihachiro Togo
20 Dec 1905 - 8 Oct 1908:	UNIT DEMOBILIZED
8 Oct 1908 - 20 Nov 1908:	*Fleet Admiral* Baron Goro Ijuin
20 Nov 1908 - 1 Nov 1915:	UNIT DEMOBILIZED
1 Nov 1915 - 13 Dec 1915:	*Admiral* Motaro Yoshimatsu
13 Dec 1915 - 1 Sep 1916:	UNIT DEMOBILIZED
1 Sep 1916 - 14 Oct 1916:	*Admiral* Motaro Yoshimatsu
14 Oct 1916 - 1 Oct 1917:	UNIT DEMOBILIZED
1 Oct 1917 - 22 Oct 1917:	*Admiral* Motaro Yoshimatsu
22 Oct 1917 - 1 Sep 1918:	UNIT DEMOBILIZED
1 Sep 1918 - 15 Oct 1918:	*Admiral* Baron Gentaro Yamashita
15 Oct 1918 - 1 Jun 1919:	UNIT DEMOBILIZED
1 Jun 1919 - 28 Oct 1919:	*Admiral* Baron Gentaro Yamashita
28 Oct 1919 - 1 May 1920:	UNIT DEMOBILIZED
1 May 1920 - 24 Aug 1920:	*Admiral* Tanin Yamaya
24 Aug 1920 - 31 Oct 1920:	*Admiral* Sojiro Tochinai
31 Oct 1920 - 1 May 1921:	UNIT DEMOBILIZED
1 May 1921 - 31 Oct 1921:	*Admiral* Sojiro Tochinai
31 Oct 1931 - 1 Dec 1922:	UNIT DEMOBILIZED
1 Dec 1922 - 27 Jan 1924:	*Admiral* Isamu Takeshita
27 Jan 1924 - 1 Dec 1924:	*Admiral* Baron Kantaro Suzuki
1 Dec 1924 - 10 Dec 1926:	*Admiral* Keisuke Okada
10 Dec 1926 - 10 Dec 1928:	*Admiral* Hiroharu Kato
10 Dec 1928 - 11 Nov 1929:	*Admiral* Saburo Hyakutake
11 Nov 1929 - 1 Dec 1931:	*Admiral* Eisuke Yamamoto
1 Dec 1931 - 15 Nov 1933:	*Admiral* Seizo Kobayashi
15 Nov 1933 - 15 Nov 1934:	*Admiral* Nobumasa Suetsugu
15 Nov 1934 - 1 Dec 1936:	*Admiral* Sankichi Takahashi
1 Dec 1936 - 2 Feb 1937:	*Admiral* Mitsumasa Yonai

2 Feb 1937 - 1 Dec 1937:	*Fleet Admiral* Osami Nagano
1 Dec 1937 - 30 Aug 1939:	*Admiral* Zengo Yoshida
30 Aug 1939 - 18 Apr 1943:	*Fleet Admiral* Isoroku Yamamoto
18 Apr 1943 - 21 Apr 1943:	
21 Apr 1943 - 31 Mar 1944:	*Fleet Admiral* Mineichi Koga
31 Mar 1944 - 3 May 1944:	*Admiral* Shiro Takasu
3 May 1944 - 29 May 1945:	*Admiral* Soemu Toyoda
29 May 1945 - 10 Oct 1945:	*Admiral* Jisaburo Ozawa

Commander-in-Chief, Readiness Fleet

19 Jan 1899 - 20 May 1900:	*Admiral* Baron Kazunori Samejima
20 May 1900 - 1 Oct 1901:	*Fleet Admiral* Marquis Heihachiro Togo
1 Oct 1901 - 26 Jul 1902:	*Vice-Admiral* Hidematsu Tsunoda
26 Jul 1902 - 19 Oct 1903:	*Admiral* Baron Sonojo Hidaka
19 Oct 1903 - 28 Dec 1903:	*Fleet Admiral* Marquis Heihachiro Togo
28 Dec 1903:	UNIT DEMOBILIZED

Commander-in-Chief, 1st Fleet

28 Dec 1903 - 20 Dec 1905:	*Fleet Admiral* Marquis Heihachiro Togo
20 Dec 1905 - 22 Nov 1906:	*Admiral* Shichiro Kataoka
22 Nov 1906 - 26 May 1908:	*Vice-Admiral* Shinichi Arima
26 May 1908 - 1 Dec 1909:	*Fleet Admiral* Baron Goro Ijuin
1 Dec 1909 - 1 Dec 1911:	*Admiral* Baron Hikonojo Kamimura
1 Dec 1911 - 1 Dec 1913:	*Admiral* Baron Shigeto Dewa
1 Dec 1913 - 10 Aug 1915:	*Fleet Admiral* Viscount Tomozaburo Kato
10 Aug 1915 - 23 Sep 1915:	*Admiral* Koichi Fujii
23 Sep 1915 - 1 Dec 1917:	*Admiral* Motaro Yoshimatsu
1 Dec 1917 - 1 Dec 1919:	*Admiral* Baron Gentaro Yamashita
1 Dec 1919 - 24 Aug 1920:	*Admiral* Tanin Tamaya
24 Aug 1920 - 27 Jul 1922:	*Admiral* Sojrio Tochinai
27 Jul 1922 - 27 Jan 1924:	*Admiral* Isamu Takeshita
27 Jan 1924 - 1 Dec 1924:	*Admiral* Baron Kantaro Suzuki
1 Dec 1924 - 10 Dec 1926:	*Admiral* Keisuke Okada
10 Dec 1926 - 10 Dec 1928:	*Admiral* Hiroharu Kato
10 Dec 1928 - 11 Nov 1929:	*Admiral* Saburo Hyakutake
11 Nov 1929 - 1 Dec 1931:	*Admiral* Eisuke Yamamoto
1 Dec 1931 - 15 Nov 1933:	*Admiral* Seizo Kobayashi
15 Nov 1933 - 15 Nov 1934:	*Admiral* Nobumasa Suetsugu
15 Nov 1934 - 1 Dec 1936:	*Admiral* Sankichi Takahashi
1 Dec 1936 - 2 Feb 1937:	*Admiral* Mitsumasa Yonai
2 Feb 1937 - 1 Dec 1937:	*Fleet Admiral* Osami Nagano
1 Dec 1937 - 30 Aug 1939:	*Admiral* Zengo Yoshida
30 Aug 1939 - 11 Aug 1941:	*Fleet Admiral* Isoroku Yamamoto

11 Aug 1941 - 14 Jul 1942:   *Admiral* Shiro Takasu
14 Jul 1942 - 20 Oct 1943:   *Vice-Admiral* Mizumi Shimizu
20 Oct 1943 - 25 Feb 1944:   *Admiral* Chuichi Nagumo
25 Feb 1944:   UNIT DEMOBILIZED

Commander-in-Chief, 2nd Fleet
2 Oct 1903 - 20 Dec 1905:   *Admiral* Baron Hikonojo Kamimura
20 Dec 1905 - 22 Nov 1906:   *Admiral* Baron Shigeto Dewa
22 Nov 1906 - 26 May 1908:   *Fleet Admiral* Baron Goro Ijuin
26 May 1908 - 1 Dec 1909:   *Admiral* Baron Shigeto Dewa
1 Dec 1909 - 1 Dec 1911:   *Fleet Admiral* Baron Hayao Shimamura
1 Dec 1911 - 1 Dec 1912:   *Admiral* Motaro Yoshimatsu
1 Dec 1912 - 1 Dec 1913:   *Vice-Admiral* Suetaka Ijichi
1 Dec 1913 - 5 Feb 1915:   *Admiral* Baron Sadakichi Kato
5 Feb 1915 - 13 Dec 1915:   *Admiral* Matahachiro Nawa
13 Dec 1915 - 1 Dec 1917:   *Admiral* Baron Rokuro Yashiro
1 Dec 1917 - 13 Jun 1918:   *Fleet Admiral* Prince Yorihito Higashifushimi
13 Jun 1918 - 1 Dec 1919:   *Admiral* Tanin Yamaya
1 Dec 1919 - 1 Dec 1920:   *Fleet Admiral* Prince Hiroyasu Fushimi
1 Dec 1920 - 1 Dec 1921:   *Admiral* Baron Kantaro Suzuki
1 Dec 1921 - 1 Dec 1922:   UNIT DEMOBILIZED
1 Dec 1922 - 1 Jun 1923:   *Vice-Admiral* Naoe Nakano
1 Jun 1923 - 1 Dec 1924:   *Admiral* Hiroharu Kato
1 Dec 1924 - 16 Sep 1925:   *Vice-Admiral* Hanroku Saito
16 Sep 1925 - 10 Dec 1926:   *Admiral* Saburo Hyakutake
10 Dec 1926 - 16 May 1928:   *Vice-Admiral* Yasuhira Yoshikawa
16 May 1928 - 10 Dec 1928:   *Vice-Admiral* Koshiro Otani
10 Dec 1928 - 11 Nov 1929:   *Admiral* Baron Mineo Osumi
11 Nov 1929 - 1 Dec 1930:   *Vice-Admiral* Nobutaro Iida
1 Dec 1930 - 1 Dec 1931:   *Admiral* Ryozo Nakamura
1 Dec 1931 - 15 Nov 1933:   *Admiral* Nobumasa Suetsugu
15 Nov 1933 - 15 Nov 1934:   *Admiral* Sankichi Takahashi
15 Nov 1934 - 2 Dec 1935:   *Admiral* Mitsumasa Yonai
2 Dec 1935 - 1 Dec 1936:   *Admiral* Takayoshi Kato
1 Dec 1936 - 1 Dec 1937:   *Admiral* Zengo Yoshida
1 Dec 1937 - 15 Nov 1938:   *Admiral* Shigetaro Shimada
15 Nov 1938 - 21 Oct 1939:   *Admiral* Soemu Toyoda
21 Oct 1939 - 1 Sep 1941:   *Fleet Admiral* Mineichi Koga
1 Sep 1941 - 9 Aug 1943:   *Admiral* Nobutake Kondo
9 Aug 1943 - 23 Dec 1944:   *Vice-Admiral* Takeo Kurita
23 Dec 1944 - 20 Apr 1945:   *Admiral* Seiichi Ito
20 Apr 1945:   UNIT DEMOBILIZED

Commander-in-Chief, 3rd Fleet

28 Dec 1903 - 20 Dec 1905:	*Admiral* Shichiro Kataoka
20 Dec 1905 - 13 Dec 1915:	UNIT DEMOBILIZED
13 Dec 1915 - 6 Apr 1917:	*Admiral* Kakuichi Murakami
6 Apr 1917 - 1 Dec 1918:	*Admiral* Ryokitsu Arima
1 Dec 1918 - 1 Dec 1919:	*Admiral* Teijiro Kuroi
1 Dec 1919 - 1 Dec 1920:	*Admiral* Kaneo Nomaguchi
1 Dec 1920 - 1 Dec 1921:	*Admiral* Kozaburo Oguri
1 Dec 1921 - 27 Jul 1922:	*Admiral* Baron Kantaro Suzuki
27 Jul 1922 - 1 Dec 1922:	*Vice-Admiral* Naoe Nakano
1 Dec 1922 - 2 Feb 1932:	UNIT DEMOBILIZED
2 Feb 1932 - 28 Jun 1932:	*Admiral* Kichisaburo Nomura
28 Jun 1932 - 1 Dec 1932:	*Vice-Admiral* Seizo Sakonji
1 Dec 1932 - 15 Sep 1933:	*Admiral* Mitsumasa Yonai
15 Sep 1933 - 15 Nov 1934:	*Vice-Admiral* Shinjiro Imamura
15 Nov 1934 - 1 Dec 1935:	*Admiral* Gengo Hyakutake
1 Dec 1935 - 1 Dec 1936:	*Admiral* Koshiro Oikawa
1 Dec 1936 - 25 Apr 1938:	*Admiral* Kiyoshi Hasegawa
25 Apr 1938 - 15 Nov 1939:	*Admiral* Kosiro Oikawa
15 Nov 1939 - 10 Apr 1941:	UNIT DEMOBILIZED
10 Apr 1941 - 10 Mar 1942:	*Vice-Admiral* Ibo Takahashi
10 Mar 1942 - 14 Jul 1942:	UNIT DEMOBILIZED
14 Jul 1942 - 11 Nov 1942:	*Admiral* Chuichi Nagumo
11 Nov 1942 - 15 Nov 1944:	*Admiral* Jisaburo Ozawa
15 Nov 1944:	UNIT DEMOBILIZED

Commander-in-Chief, 4th Fleet

14 Jun 1905 - 20 Dec 1905:	*Admiral* Baron Shigeto Dewa
20 Dec 1905 - 20 Oct 1937:	UNIT DEMOBILIZED
20 Oct 1937 - 15 Nov 1938:	*Admiral* Soemu Toyoda
15 Nov 1938 - 15 Nov 1939:	*Vice-Admiral* Masaharu Hibino
15 Nov 1939 - 15 Nov 1940:	*Vice-Admiral* Eikichi Katagiri
15 Nov 1940 - 11 Aug 1941:	*Admiral* Shiro Takasu
11 Aug 1941 - 26 Oct 1942:	*Admiral* Shigeyoshi Inoue
26 Oct 1942 - 1 Apr 1943:	*Vice-Admiral* Tomoshige Samejima
1 Apr 1943 - 19 Feb 1944:	*Vice-Admiral* Masami Kobayashi
19 Feb 1944 - ? 1944:	*Vice-Admiral* Chichi Hara
? 1944:	UNIT DEMOBILIZED

Commander-in-Chief, 5th Fleet

1 Feb 1938 - 15 Dec 1938:	*Admiral* Koichi Shiozawa
15 Dec 1938 - 29 Sep 1939:	*Admiral* Nobutake Kondo
29 Sep 1939 - 15 Nov 1939:	*Admiral* Shiro Takasu

15 Nov 1939 - 25 Jul 1941:	UNIT DEMOBILIZED
25 Jul 1941 - 31 Mar 1943:	*Vice-Admiral* Boshiro Hosogaya
31 Mar 1943 - 15 Feb 1944:	*Vice-Admiral* Shiro Kawase
15 Feb 1944 - 5 Feb 1945:	*Vice-Admiral* Kiyohide Shima
5 Feb 1945:	UNIT DEMOBILIZED

Commander-in-Chief, 6th (Submarine) Fleet

15 Nov 1940 - 21 Jul 1941:	*Vice-Admiral* Noboru Hirata
21 Jul 1941 - 16 Mar 1942:	*Vice-Admiral* Mizumi Shimizu
16 Mar 1942 - 21 Jun 1943:	*Vice-Admiral* Marquis Teruhisa Komatsu
21 Jun 1943 - 10 Jul 1944:	*Vice-Admiral* Takeo Takagi
10 Jul 1944 - 1 May 1945:	*Vice-Admiral* Shigeyoshi Miwa
1 May 1945 - 15 Sep 1945:	*Vice-Admiral* Marquis Tadashige Daigo
15 Sep 1945:	UNIT DEMOBILIZED

Commander-in-Chief, 7th Fleet

15 Apr 1945 - 20 Aug 1945:	*Vice-Admiral* Fukuji Kishi
20 Aug 1945 - 15 Sep 1945:	*Vice-Admiral* Sentaro Omori
15 Sep 1945:	UNIT DEMOBILIZED

Commander-in-Chief, 8th Fleet

14 Jul 1942 - 1 Apr 1943:	*Vice-Admiral* Gunichi Mikawa
1 Apr 1943 - ? 1943:	*Vice-Admiral* Tomoshige Samejima
? 1943:	UNIT DEMOBILIZED

Commander-in-Chief, 9th Fleet

15 Nov 1943 - 10 Jul 1944:	*Admiral* Yoshikazu Endo
10 Jul 1944:	UNIT DEMOBILIZED

Commander-in-Chief, 10th Area Fleet

5 Feb 1945 - Sep 1945:	*Vice-Admiral* Shigeru Fukutome
Sep 1945:	UNIT DEMOBILIZED

Commander-in-Chief, 1st Escort Fleet

10 Dec 1944 - 10 Jul 1945:	*Vice-Admiral* Fukuji Kishi
10 Jul 1945 - 25 Aug 1945:	*Vice-Admiral* Minoru Tayui
25 Aug 1945:	UNIT DEMOBILIZED

Commander-in-Chief, 1st Task Fleet

1 Mar 1944 - 15 Nov 1944:	*Admiral* Jisaburo Ozawa
15 Nov 1944:	UNIT DEMOBILIZED

Commander-in-Chief, Maritime Escort Fleet
15 Nov 1943 - 15 Sep 1944: *Admiral* Koshiro Oikawa
15 Sep 1944 - 1 May 1945: *Admiral* Naokuni Nomura
1 May 1945 - 29 May 1945: *Admiral* Soemu Toyoda
29 May 1945 - 25 Aug 1945: *Admiral* Jisaburo Ozawa
25 Aug 1945: UNIT DEMOBILIZED

Commander-in-Chief, China Area Fleet
20 Oct 1937 - 25 Apr 1938: *Admiral* Kiyoshi Hasegawa
25 Apr 1938 - 1 May 1940: *Admiral* Koshiro Oikawa
1 May 1940 - 1 Sep 1941: *Admiral* Shigetaro Shimada
1 Sep 1941 - 10 Nov 1942: *Fleet Admiral* Mineichi Koga
10 Nov 1942 - 1 Dec 1943: *Admiral* Zengo Yoshida
1 Dec 1943 - 15 May 1945: *Admiral* Nobutake Kondo
15 May 1945 - Sep 1945: *Vice-Admiral* Ryozo Fukuda
Sep 1945: UNIT DEMOBILIZED

Commander-in-Chief, Northeastern Area Fleet
5 Aug 1943 - 15 Sep 1944: *Vice-Admiral* Michitaro Totsuka
15 Sep 1944 - 5 Dec 1944: *Vice-Admiral* Eiji Goto
5 Dec 1944: UNIT DEMOBILIZED

Commander-in-Chief, Southeastern Area Fleet
24 Dec 1942 - Sep 1945: *Vice-Admiral* Jinichi Kusaka
Sep 1945: UNIT DEMOBILIZED

Commander-in-Chief, Southwestern Area Fleet
10 Apr 1942 - 15 Sep 1942: *Vice-Admiral* Ibo Takahashi
15 Sep 1942 - 18 Jun 1944: *Admiral* Shiro Takasu
18 Jun 1944 - 1 Nov 1944: *Vice-Admiral* Gunichi Mikawa
1 Nov 1944 - Sep 1945: *Vice-Admiral* Denshichi Okawachi
Sep 1945: UNIT DEMOBILIZED

Commander-in-Chief, Central Pacific Area Fleet
4 Mar 1944 - 18 Jul 1944: *Admiral* Chuichi Nagumo
18 Jul 1944: UNIT DEMOBILIZED

Commander-in-Chief, Southern Expeditionary Fleet
31 Jul 1941 - 18 Oct 1941: *Vice-Admiral* Noboru Hirata
18 Oct 1941 - 3 Jan 1942: *Admiral* Jisaburo Ozawa
3 Jan 1942: UNIT DEMOBILIZED

Commander-in-Chief, 1ˢᵗ Southern Expeditionary Fleet
3 Jan 1942 - 14 Jul 1942:	*Admiral* Jisaburo Ozawa
14 Jul 1942 - 20 Sep 1943	*Vice-Admiral* Denshichi Okawachi
20 Sep 1943 - 13 Jan 1945:	*Vice-Admiral* Minoru Tayui
13 Jan 1945 - Sep 1945:	*Vice-Admiral* Shigeru Fukutome
Sep 1945:	UNIT DEMOBILIZED

Commander-in-Chief, 2ⁿᵈ Southern Expeditionary Fleet
10 Mar 1942 - 15 Sep 1942:	*Vice-Admiral* Ibo Takahashi
15 Sep 1942 - 15 Apr 1943:	*Admiral* Shiro Takasu
15 Apr 1943 - 3 Sep 1943:	*Vice-Admiral* Seiichi Iwamura
3 Sep 1943 - 18 Jun 1944:	*Vice-Admiral* Gunichi Mikawa
18 Jun 1944 - 29 Jan 1945:	*Vice-Admiral* Shiro Kawase
29 Jan 1945 - Sep 1945:	*Vice-Admiral* Yaichiro Shibata
Sep 1945:	UNIT DEMOBILIZED

Commander-in-Chief, 3ʳᵈ Southern Expeditionary Fleet
3 Jan 1942 - 1 Dec 1942:	*Vice-Admiral* Rokuzo Sugiyama
1 Dec 1942 - 20 Sep 1943:	*Vice-Admiral* Taiji Ota
20 Sep 1943 - 15 Aug 1944:	*Vice-Admiral* Arata Oka
15 Aug 1944 - 1 Nov 1944:	*Vice-Admiral* Gunichi Mikawa
1 Nov 1944 - Sep 1945:	*Vice-Admiral* Denshichi Okawachi
Sep 1945:	UNIT DEMOBILIZED

Commander-in-Chief, 4ᵗʰ Southern Expeditionary Fleet
30 Nov 1943 - 10 Mar 1945:	*Admiral* Seigo Yamagata
10 Mar 1945:	UNIT DEMOBILIZED

Commander-in-Chief, 1ˢᵗ China Expeditionary Fleet
15 Nov 1939 - 15 Nov 1940:	*Vice-Admiral* Umataro Tanimoto
15 Nov 1940 - 5 Jul 1941:	*Vice-Admiral* Boshiro Hosogaya
5 Jul 1941 - 14 Feb 1942:	*Vice-Admiral* Marquis Teruhisa Komatsu
14 Feb 1942 - 9 Mar 1943:	*Vice-Admiral* Kakusaburo Makita
9 Mar 1943 - 20 Aug 1943:	*Admiral* Yoshikazu Endo
20 Aug 1943:	UNIT DEMOBILIZED

Commander-in-Chief, 2ⁿᵈ China Expeditionary Fleet
15 Nov 1939 - 15 Oct 1940:	*Admiral* Shiro Takasu
15 Oct 1940 - 4 Apr 1941:	*Admiral* Yorio Sawamoto
4 Apr 1941 - 14 Jul 1942:	*Vice-Admiral* Masaichi Niimi
14 Jul 1942 - 21 Jun 1943:	*Vice-Admiral* Kiyoshi Hara
21 Jun 1943 - 25 Apr 1945:	*Vice-Admiral* Daisuke Soejima
25 Apr 1945 - Sep 1945:	*Vice-Admiral* Ruitaro Fujita
Sep 1945:	UNIT DEMOBILIZED

Commander-in-Chief, 3rd China Expeditionary Fleet
15 Nov 1939 - 30 Sep 1940:	*Admiral* Naokuni Nomura
30 Sep 1940 - 5 Jul 1941:	*Vice-Admiral* Mizumi Shimizu
5 Jul 1941 - 26 Dec 1941:	*Vice-Admiral* Rokuzo Sugiyama
26 Dec 1941 - 10 Apr 1942:	*Vice-Admiral* Shiro Kawase
10 Apr 1942:	UNIT DEMOBILIZED

AIR FLEETS

Commander-in-Chief, 1st Air Fleet
10 Apr 1941 - 14 Jul 1942:	*Admiral* Chuichi Nagumo
14 Jul 1942 - 1 Jul 1943:	UNIT DEMOBILIZED
1 Jul 1943 - 7 Aug 1944:	*Vice-Admiral* Sadamichi Kajioka
7 Aug 1944 - 20 Oct 1944:	*Vice-Admiral* Kinpei Teraoka
20 Oct 1944 - 10 May 1945:	*Vice-Admiral* Takijiro Onishi
10 May 1945 - 15 Jun 1945:	*Vice-Admiral* Kiyohide Shima
15 Jun 1945:	UNIT DEMOBILIZED

Commander-in-Chief, 2nd Air Fleet
15 Jun 1944 - 8 Jan 1945:	*Vice-Admiral* Shigeru Fukutome
8 Jan 1945:	UNIT DEMOBILIZED

Commander-in-Chief, 3rd Air Fleet
10 Jul 1944 - 17 Nov 1944:	*Vice-Admiral* Shunichi Kira
17 Nov 1944 - 26 Aug 1945:	*Vice-Admiral* Kinpei Teraoka
26 Aug 1945 - 15 Oct 1945:	*Vice-Admiral* Sadayoshi Yamada
15 Oct 1945:	UNIT DEMOBILIZED

Commander-in-Chief, 5th Air Fleet
10 Feb 1945 - 17 Aug 1945:	*Vice-Admiral* Matome Ugaki
17 Aug 1945 - 10 Oct 1945:	*Vice-Admiral* Ryunosuke Kusaka
10 Oct 1945:	UNIT DEMOBILIZED

Commander-in-Chief, 10th Air Fleet
1 Mar 1945 - 10 Oct 1945:	*Vice-Admiral* Minoru Maeda
10 Oct 1945:	UNIT DEMOBILIZED

Commander-in-Chief, 11th Air Fleet
15 Jan 1941 - 10 Sep 1941:	*Vice-Admiral* Eikichi Katagiri
10 Sep 1941 - 1 Oct 1942:	*Admiral* Nishizo Tsukahara
1 Oct 1942 - Sep 1945:	*Vice-Admiral* Jinichi Kusaka
Sep 1945:	UNIT DEMOBILIZED

Commander-in-Chief, 12th Air Fleet

18 May 1943 - 15 Sep 1944:   *Vice-Admiral* Michitaro Totsuka
15 Sep 1944 - 15 Mar 1945:   *Vice-Admiral* Eiji Goto
15 Mar 1945 - 30 Nov 1945:   *Vice-Admiral* Kanji Ugaki
30 Nov 1945:   UNIT DEMOBILIZED

Commander-in-Chief, 13th Air Fleet

20 Sep 1943 - 18 Jun 1944:   *Admiral* Shiro Takasu
18 Jun 1944 - 1 Nov 1944:   *Vice-Admiral* Gunichi Mikawa
1 Nov 1944 - 8 Jan 1945:   *Vice-Admiral* Denshichi Okawachi
8 Jan 1945 - 13 Jan 1945:   *Vice-Admiral* Minoru Tayui
13 Jan 1945 - Sep 1945:   *Vice-Admiral* Shigeru Fukutome
Sep 1945:   UNIT DEMOBILIZED

Commander-in-Chief, 14th Air Fleet

4 Mar 1944 - 18 Jul 1944:   *Admiral* Chuichi Nagumo
18 Jul 1944:   UNIT DEMOBILIZED

Commander-in-Chief, Combined Training Air Units HQ

1 Feb 1943 - 18 May 1943:   *Vice-Admiral* Michitaro Totsuka
18 May 1943 - 19 Feb 1944:   *Vice-Admiral* Chuichi Hara
19 Feb 1944 - 15 Aug 1944:   *Vice-Admiral* Kinpei Teraoka
15 Aug 1944 - 10 Jun 1945:   *Vice-Admiral* Sadaichi Matsunaga
10 Jun 1945:   UNIT DEMOBILIZED

NAVAL DISTRICTS

Admiral Commanding, Kure Naval District

26 Feb 1896 - 20 May 1900:   *Fleet Admiral* Viscount Yoshika Inoue
20 May 1900 - 6 Feb 1905:   *Admiral* Baron Yahachi Shibayama
6 Feb 1905 - 2 Feb 1906:   *Vice-Admiral* Shinichi Arima
2 Feb 1906 - 1 Dec 1909:   *Vice-Admiral* Baron Masuji Yamauchi
1 Dec 1909 - 1 Dec 1913:   *Fleet Admiral* Viscount Tomozaburo Kato
1 Dec 1913 - 25 Mar 1914:   *Vice-Admiral* Kazu Matsumoto
25 Mar 1914 - 23 Sep 1915:   *Admiral* Motaro Yoshimatsu
23 Sep 1915 - 1 Dec 1916:   *Vice-Admiral* Suetaka Ijichi
1 Dec 1916 - 1 Dec 1919:   *Admiral* Baron Sadakichi Kato
1 Dec 1919 - 27 Jul 1922:   *Admiral* Kakuichi Murakami
27 Jul 1922 - 27 Jan 1924:   *Admiral* Baron Kantaro Suzuki
27 Jan 1924 - 15 Apr 1925:   *Admiral* Isamu Takeshita
15 Apr 1925 - 10 Dec 1926:   *Admiral* Baron Kiyokazu Abo
10 Dec 1926 - 10 Dec 1928:   *Admiral* Saburo Hyakutake

10 Dec 1928 - 11 Nov 1929:   *Vice-Admiral* Koshiro Otani
11 Nov 1929 - 11 Jun 1930:   *Admiral* Saburo Hyakutake
11 Jun 1930 - 1 Dec 1931:   *Admiral* Kichisaburo Nomura
1 Dec 1931 - 1 Dec 1932:   *Admiral* Katsunoshin Yamanashi
1 Dec 1932 - 10 May 1934:   *Admiral* Ryozo Nakamura
10 May 1934 - 1 Dec 1936:   *Admiral* Hisanori Fujita
1 Dec 1936 - 15 Nov 1938:   *Admiral* Takayoshi Kato
15 Nov 1938 - 15 Apr 1940:   *Admiral* Shigetaro Shimada
15 Apr 1940 - 18 Sep 1941:   *Vice-Admiral* Masaharu Hibino
18 Sep 1941 - 10 Nov 1942:   *Admiral* Soemu Toyoda
10 Nov 1942 - 21 Jun 1943:   *Vice-Admiral* Ibo Takahashi
21 Jun 1943 - 20 Oct 1943:   *Admiral* Chuichi Nagumo
20 Oct 1943 - 17 Jul 1944:   *Admiral* Naokuni Nomura
17 Jul 1944 - 1 May 1945:   *Admiral* Yorio Sawamoto
1 May 1945 - 30 Nov 1945:   *Vice-Admiral* Masao Kanazawa

Chief of Staff, Kure Naval District

23 Mar 1899 - 6 Dec 1900:   *Captain* Isamu Yajima
6 Dec 1900 - 3 Feb 1904:   *Rear-Admiral* Hisamaro Oinoue
3 Feb 1904 - 10 May 1905:   *Vice-Admiral* Baron Tokutaro Nakamizo
10 May 1905 - 2 Feb 1906:   *Rear-Admiral* Ichiro Nijima
2 Feb 1906 - 22 Nov 1906:   *Admiral* Motaro Yoshimatsu
22 Nov 1906 - 27 Dec 1907:   *Rear-Admiral* Shinjiro Uehara
27 Dec 1907 - 22 May 1910:   *Rear-Admiral* Heitaro Takeuchi
22 May 1910 - 20 Apr 1912:   *Admiral* Matahichiro Nawa
20 Apr 1912 - 10 Jan 1913:   *Admiral* Kaneo Nomaguchi
10 Jan 1913 - 1 Dec 1913:   *Rear-Admiral* Kishichiro Osawa
1 Dec 1913 - 17 Apr 1914:   *Vice-Admiral* Naoe Nakano
17 Apr 1914 - 13 Dec 1915:   *Admiral* Kenji Ide
13 Dec 1915 - 13 Jul 1917:   *Vice-Admiral* Shibakichi Yamanaka
18 Jul 1917 - 1 Dec 1918:   *Vice-Admiral* Junichi Matsumura
1 Dec 1918 - 1 Dec 1920:   *Vice-Admiral* Shichigoro Saito
1 Dec 1920 - 1 Dec 1922:   *Vice-Admiral* Yoshimoto Masaki
1 Dec 1922 - 6 Nov 1923:   *Vice-Admiral* Naomoto Komatsu
6 Nov 1923 - 1 Dec 1924:   *Vice-Admiral* Naotaro Nagasawa
1 Dec 1924 - 16 Dec 1924:   *Rear-Admiral* Bekinari Kabayama
16 Dec 1924 - 1 Dec 1926:   *Vice-Admiral* Tokujiro Tateno
1 Dec 1926 - 10 Dec 1928:   *Vice-Admiral* Kiyohiro Ijichi
10 Dec 1928 - 10 Jun 1930:   *Admiral* Koshirō Oikawa
10 Jun 1930 - 1 Dec 1931:   *Vice-Admiral* Giichi Suzuki
1 Dec 1931 - 15 Nov 1932:   *Vice-Admiral* Choji Inoue
15 Nov 1932 - 15 Nov 1934:   *Vice-Admiral* Tokutaro Sumiyama
15 Nov 1934 - 15 Nov 1935:   *Vice-Admiral* Umataro Tanimoto

15 Nov 1935 - 1 Apr 1936:	*Vice-Admiral* Masaichi Niimi
1 Apr 1936 - 1 Dec 1936:	*Vice-Admiral* Ichiro Sato
1 Dec 1936 - 15 Dec 1938:	*Vice-Admiral* Takamoto Togari
15 Dec 1938 - 10 Oct 1939:	*Vice-Admiral* Toshihisa Nakamura
10 Oct 1939 - 20 Aug 1941:	*Vice-Admiral* Matome Ugaki
20 Aug 1941 - 6 Jan 1943:	*Vice-Admiral* Torahiko Nakajima
6 Jan 1943 - 11 Jun 1943:	*Vice-Admiral* Kengo Kobayashi
11 Jun 1943 - 9 Sep 1944:	*Vice-Admiral* Shinzo Onishi
10 Sep 1944 - 15 Oct 1945:	*Vice-Admiral* Shozo Hashimoto
15 Oct 1945 - 30 Nov 1945:	*Rear-Admiral* Tametsugu Okada

Admiral Commanding, Maizuru Naval District

1 Oct 1901 - 19 Oct 1903:	*Fleet Admiral* Marquis Heihachiro Togo
19 Oct 1903 - 28 Aug 1908:	*Admiral* Baron Sonojo Hidaka
28 Aug 1908 - 18 Jan 1911:	*Admiral* Shichiro Kataoka
18 Jan 1911 - 25 Sep 1913:	*Admiral* Baron Sotaro Misu
25 Sep 1913 - 17 Apr 1914:	*Admiral* Baron Rokuro Yashiro
17 Apr 1914 - 13 Dec 1915:	*Vice-Admiral* Hajime Sakamoto
13 Dec 1915 - 1 Dec 1917:	*Admiral* Matahachiro Nawa
1 Dec 1917 - 1 Dec 1918:	*Admiral* Takeshi Takarabe
1 Dec 1918 - 1 Dec 1919:	*Admiral* Kaneo Nomaguchi
1 Dec 1919 - 16 Aug 1920:	*Admiral* Teijro Kuroi
16 Aug 1920 - 1 Dec 1921:	*Vice-Admiral* Tetsutaro Sato
1 Dec 1921 - 1 Apr 1923:	*Admiral* Kozaburo Oguri
1 Apr 1923:	REDESIGNATED MAIZURU GUARD DISTRICT
1 Apr 1923 - 1 Jun 1923:	*Vice-Admiral* Hanroku Saito
1 Jun 1923 - 4 Oct 1924:	*Admiral* Saburo Hyakutake
4 Oct 1924 - 1 Jun 1925:	*Vice-Admiral* Shigetsugu Nakazato
1 Jun 1925 - 10 Dec 1926:	*Vice-Admiral* Shinzaburo Furukawa
10 Dec 1926 - 16 May 1928:	*Vice-Admiral* Koshiro Otani
16 May 1928 - 10 Dec 1928:	*Vice-Admiral* Nobutaro Iida
10 Dec 1928 - 11 Nov 1929:	*Vice-Admiral* Tamaki Tosu
11 Nov 1929 - 1 Dec 1930:	*Vice-Admiral* Junichi Kiyokawa
1 Dec 1930 - 1 Dec 1931:	*Admiral* Nobumasa Suetsugu
1 Dec 1931 - 1 Dec 1932:	*Vice-Admiral* Naotaro Ominato
1 Dec 1932 - 15 Sep 1933:	*Vice-Admiral* Shinjiro Imamura
15 Sep 1933 - 15 Nov 1934:	*Admiral* Gengo Hyakutake
15 Nov 1934 - 2 Dec 1935:	*Vice-Admiral* Hajime Matsushita
2 Dec 1935 - 1 Dec 1936:	*Admiral* Koichi Shiozawa
1 Dec 1936 - 1 Dec 1937:	*Vice-Admiral* Kamezaburo Nakamura
1 Dec 1937 - 15 Nov 1938:	*Vice-Admiral* Manbei Idemitsu
15 Nov 1938 - 15 Nov 1939:	*Vice-Admiral* Eikichi Katagiri
15 Nov 1939 - 15 Apr 1940:	*Vice-Admiral* Goro Hara

1 Dec 1939:	REDESIGNATED MAIZURU NAVAL DISTRICT
15 Apr 1940 - 14 Jul 1942:	*Vice-Admiral* Sonosuke Kobayashi
14 Jul 1942 - 1 Dec 1943:	*Vice-Admiral* Masaichi Niimi
1 Dec 1943 - 1 Apr 1944:	*Vice-Admiral* Denshichi Okawachi
1 Apr 1944 - 1 Mar 1945:	*Vice-Admiral* Kakusaburo Makita
1 Mar 1945 - 30 Nov 1945:	*Vice-Admiral* Minoru Tayui

Chief of Staff, Maizuru Naval District

1 Oct 1901 - 12 Mar 1902:	*Vice-Admiral* Baron Tokutaro Nakamizo
12 Mar 1902 - 10 May 1905:	*Rear-Admiral* Ichiro Nijima
10 May 1905 - 7 Apr 1906:	*Rear-Admiral* Shinjiro Uehara
7 Apr 1906 - 22 Nov 1906:	*Rear-Admiral* Arinobu Matsumoto
22 Nov 1906 - 15 May 1908:	*Vice-Admiral* Suetaka Ijichi
15 May 1908 - 9 Apr 1910:	*Admiral* Baron Sadakichi Kato
9 Apr 1910 - 1 Dec 1911:	*Vice-Admiral* Kensuke Wada
1 Dec 1911 - 1 Dec 1912:	*Rear-Admiral* Juzaburo Ushida
1 Dec 1912 - 1 Apr 1913:	*Rear-Admiral* Seinosuke Togo
1 Apr 1913 - 1 Dec 1913:	*Vice-Admiral* Tomojiro Chisaka
1 Dec 1913 - 1 Dec 1914:	*Vice-Admiral* Yasujiro Nagata
1 Dec 1914 - 1 Apr 1915:	*Rear-Admiral* Eitaro Kataoka
1 Apr 1915 - 1 Apr 1916:	*Rear-Admiral* Tokutaro Hiraga
1 Apr 1916 - 1 Dec 1917:	*Rear-Admiral* Yushichi Kanno
1 Dec 1917 - 25 Sep 1918:	*Rear-Admiral* Masaki Nakamura
25 Sep 1918 - 10 Nov 1918:	*Vice-Admiral* Kenzo Kobayashi
10 Nov 1918 - 10 Nov 1920:	*Rear-Admiral* Hisamori Taguchi
10 Nov 1920 - 1 Dec 1922:	*Vice-Admiral* Kosaburo Uchida
1 Dec 1922 - 1 Dec 1923:	*Vice-Admiral* Yukichi Shima
1 Dec 1923 - 1 Dec 1924:	*Rear-Admiral* Tanin Ikeda
1 Dec 1924 - 15 Apr 1925:	*Admiral* Zengo Yoshida
20 Nov 1925 - 1 Dec 1926:	*Vice-Admiral* Shigeru Matsuyama
1 Dec 1926 - 10 Dec 1928:	*Rear-Admiral* Shiba Shibayama
10 Dec 1928 - 1 May 1929:	*Vice-Admiral* Yutaka Arima
1 May 1929 - 1 Nov 1930:	*Vice-Admiral* Shigeru Kokuno
1 Nov 1930 - 1 Dec 1931:	*Vice-Admiral* Umataro Tanimoto
1 Dec 1931 - 15 Nov 1933:	*Rear-Admiral* Fuchina Iwaihara
15 Nov 1933 - 16 Nov 1936:	*Rear-Admiral* Shigekazu Nakamura
16 Nov 1936 - 25 Sep 1937:	*Vice-Admiral* Ichiro Ono
25 Sep 1937 - 22 Oct 1938:	*Vice-Admiral* Kanji Ugaki
22 Oct 1938 - 15 Nov 1939:	*Vice-Admiral* Morikazu Osugi
15 Nov 1939 - 15 Oct 1940:	*Vice-Admiral* Kiyohide Shima
15 Oct 1940 - 11 Aug 1941:	*Vice-Admiral* Naomasa Sakonjo
11 Aug 1941 - 10 Jun 1942:	*Rear-Admiral* Kiyoshi Hamada
10 Jun 1942 - 25 Sep 1943:	*Rear-Admiral* Sokichi Takagi

25 Sep 1943 - 11 Sep 1944:	*Rear-Admiral* Akira Sone
25 Sep 1944 - Sep 1945:	*Rear-Admiral* Shinichi Torigoe

Admiral Commanding, Sasebo Naval District

19 Jan 1899 - 20 May 1900:	*Fleet Admiral* Marquis Heihachiro Togo
20 May 1900 - 2 Feb 1906:	*Admiral* Baron Kazunori Samejima
2 Feb 1906 - 22 Nov 1906:	*Vice-Admiral* Shinichi Arima
22 Nov 1906 - 1 Mar 1909:	*Admiral* Baron Sotokichi Uryu
1 Mar 1909 - 1 Dec 1909:	*Vice-Admiral* Shinichi Arima
1 Dec 1909 - 1 Dec 1911:	*Admiral* Baron Shigeto Dewa
1 Dec 1911 - 25 Mar 1914:	*Fleet Admiral* Baron Hayao Shimamura
25 Mar 1914 - 10 Aug 1915:	*Admiral* Koichi Fujii
10 Aug 1915 - 1 Dec 1917:	*Admiral* Baron Gentaro Yamashita
1 Dec 1917 - 1 Dec 1918:	*Admiral* Baron Rokuro Yashiro
1 Dec 1918 - 27 Jul 1922:	*Admiral* Takeshi Takarabe
27 Jul 1922 - 1 Jun 1923:	*Admiral* Sojiro Tochinai
1 Jun 1923 - 5 Feb 1924:	*Vice-Admiral* Hanroku Saito
5 Feb 1924 - 15 Apr 1925:	*Fleet Admiral* Prince Hiroyasu Fushimi
15 Apr 1925 - 10 Dec 1926:	*Admiral* Saburo Hyakutake
10 Dec 1926 - 12 Oct 1928:	*Vice-Admiral* Shinzaburo Furukawa
12 Oct 1928 - 11 Nov 1929:	*Vice-Admiral* Nobutaro Iida
11 Nov 1929 - 1 Dec 1930:	*Vice-Admiral* Tamaki Tosu
1 Dec 1930 - 1 Dec 1931:	*Admiral* Katsunoshin Yamanashi
1 Dec 1931 - 1 Dec 1932:	*Admiral* Ryozo Nakamura
1 Dec 1932 - 15 Nov 1933:	*Vice-Admiral* Seizo Sakonji
15 Nov 1933 - 15 Nov 1934:	*Admiral* Mitsumasa Yonai
15 Nov 1934 - 2 Dec 1935:	*Vice-Admiral* Shinjiro Imamura
2 Dec 1935 - 16 Mar 1936:	*Admiral* Gengo Hyakutake
16 Mar 1936 - 1 Dec 1936:	*Vice-Admiral* Hajime Matsushita
1 Dec 1936 - 1 Dec 1937:	*Admiral* Koichi Shiozawa
1 Dec 1937 - 15 Nov 1938:	*Admiral* Teijiro Toyoda
15 Nov 1938 - 15 Nov 1939:	*Vice-Admiral* Kamezaburo Nakamura
15 Nov 1939 - 15 Oct 1940:	*Vice-Admiral* Noboru Hirata
15 Oct 1940 - 20 Nov 1941:	*Vice-Admiral* Tokutaro Sumiyama
20 Nov 1941 - 11 Nov 1942:	*Vice-Admiral* Umataro Tanimoto
11 Nov 1942 - 21 Jun 1943:	*Admiral* Chuichi Nagumo
21 Jun 1943 - 4 Nov 1944:	*Vice-Admiral* Marquis Teruhisa Komatsu
4 Nov 1944 - 30 Nov 1945:	*Vice-Admiral* Rokuzo Sugiyama

Chief of Staff, Sasebo Naval District

22 Mar 1899 - 19 Jun 1900:	*Rear-Admiral* Ichiro Nijima
19 Jun 1900 - 4 Jul 1900:	*Rear-Admiral* Tasuku Serata
4 Jul 1900 - 6 Jul 1901:	*Admiral* Motaro Yoshimatsu

6 Jul 1901 - 19 Oct 1903:	*Vice-Admiral* Hikohachi Yamada
21 Nov 1903 - 6 Jun 1904:	*Rear-Admiral* Shinjiro Uehara
6 Jun 1904 - 2 Nov 1905:	*Vice-Admiral* Baron Toshiatsu Sakamoto
2 Nov 1905 - 2 Feb 1906:	*Admiral* Motaro Yoshimatsu
2 Feb 1906 - 7 Apr 1906:	*Rear-Admiral* Ichiro Nijima
7 Apr 1906 - 21 Oct 1907:	*Vice-Admiral* Koshi Saito
21 Oct 1907 - 15 May 1908:	*Rear-Admiral* Genzaburo Ogi
15 May 1908 - 26 May 1908:	*Vice-Admiral* Baron Shinrokuro Nishi
26 May 1908 - 10 Dec 1908:	*Vice-Admiral* Tamotsu Tsuchiya
10 Dec 1908 - 4 Mar 1909:	*Admiral* Baron Gentaro Yamashita
4 Mar 1909 - 1 Dec 1909:	*Rear-Admiral* Genzaburo Ogi
1 Dec 1909 - 11 Mar 1911:	*Vice-Admiral* Yasutaro Egashira
11 Mar 1911 - 21 Sep 1911:	*Admiral* Kaneo Nomaguchi
21 Sep 1911 - 20 Apr 1912:	*Vice-Admiral* Rinroku Eguchi
20 Apr 1912 - 1 Dec 1913:	*Vice-Admiral* Otojiro Ito
1 Dec 1913 - 25 Mar 1914:	*Rear-Admiral* Ichitaro Nakajima
25 Mar 1914 - 1 Dec 1914:	*Vice-Admiral* Tomojiro Chisaka
1 Dec 1914 - 1 Dec 1916:	*Vice-Admiral* Hiromi Tadakoro
1 Dec 1916 - 1 Dec 1917:	*Vice-Admiral* Hanroku Saito
1 Dec 1917 - 10 Nov 1918:	*Vice-Admiral* Nobutaro Shimomura
10 Nov 1918 - 1 Dec 1919:	*Admiral* Saburo Hyakutake
1 Dec 1919 - 1 May 1922:	*Vice-Admiral* Kenzo Kobayashi
1 May 1922 - 1 Dec 1923:	*Rear-Admiral* Kametaro Muta
1 Dec 1923 - 1 Dec 1925:	*Vice-Admiral* Shiro Furukawa
1 Dec 1925 - 1 Dec 1927:	*Vice-Admiral* Yukichi Shima
1 Dec 1927 - 10 Dec 1928:	*Vice-Admiral* Togo Kawano
10 Dec 1928 - 1 Dec 1930:	*Vice-Admiral* Akira Fujiyoshi
1 Dec 1930 - 1 Dec 1931:	*Vice-Admiral* Giichiro Kawamura
1 Dec 1931 - 15 Nov 1933:	*Vice-Admiral* Yoshiyuki Niiyama
15 Nov 1933 - 15 Nov 1934:	*Vice-Admiral* Eikichi Katagiri
15 Nov 1934 - 1 Mar 1935:	*Rear-Admiral* Hiroyoshi Tabata
1 Mar 1935 - 31 Oct 1935:	*Vice-Admiral* Ibo Takahashi
31 Oct 1935 - 16 Nov 1936:	*Vice-Admiral* Mitsumi Shimizu
16 Nov 1936 - 1 Sep 1938:	*Vice-Admiral* Hidesaburo Koori
1 Sep 1938 - 15 Nov 1939:	*Vice-Admiral* Masami Kobayashi
15 Nov 1939 - 15 Oct 1940:	*Vice-Admiral* Kakuji Kakuta
15 Oct 1940 - 10 Oct 1941:	*Vice-Admiral* Shigenori Horiuchi
10 Oct 1941 - 2 Dec 1942:	*Vice-Admiral* Gisaburo Yamaguchi
2 Dec 1942 - 15 Nov 1943:	*Vice-Admiral* Masaki Ogata
15 Nov 1943 - 29 Jan 1945:	*Vice-Admiral* Shigeji Kaneko
29 Jan 1945 - 30 Nov 1945:	*Rear-Admiral* Keishi Ishii

Admiral Commanding, Yokosuka Naval District

19 Jan 1899 - 20 May:	*Vice-Admiral* Baron Norimichi Aiura
20 May 1900 - 20 Dec 1905:	*Fleet Admiral* Viscount Yoshika Inoue
20 Dec 1905 - 1 Dec 1909:	*Admiral* Baron Hikonojo Kamimura
1 Dec 1909 - 1 Dec 1912:	*Admiral* Baron Sotokichi Uryu
1 Dec 1912 - 23 May 1914:	*Vice-Admiral* Hikohachi Yamada
23 May 1914 - 23 Sep 1915:	*Vice-Admiral* Suetaka Ijichi
23 Sep 1915 - 1 Dec 1916:	*Admiral* Koichi Fujii
1 Dec 1916 - 1 Dec 1917:	*Fleet Admiral* Prince Yorihito Higashifushimi
1 Dec 1917 - 24 Aug 1920:	*Admiral* Matahachiro Nawa
24 Aug 1920 - 27 Jul 1922:	*Admiral* Tanin Yamaya
27 Jul 1922 - 15 May 1923:	*Admiral* Takeshi Takarabe
15 May 1923 - 5 Feb 1924:	*Admiral* Kaneo Nomaguchi
5 Feb 1924 - 1 Dec 1924:	*Vice-Admiral* Saburo Horiuchi
1 Dec 1924 - 10 Dec 1926:	*Admiral* Hiroharu Kato
10 Dec 1926 - 20 Apr 1927:	*Admiral* Keisuke Okada
20 Apr 1927 - 16 May 1928:	*Admiral* Baron Kiyokazu Abo
16 May 1928 - 10 Dec 1928:	*Vice-Admiral* Yasuhira Yoshikawa
10 Dec 1928 - 11 Nov 1929:	*Admiral* Eisuke Yamamoto
11 Nov 1929 - 1 Dec 1931:	*Admiral* Baron Mineo Osumi
1 Dec 1931 - 2 Feb 1932:	*Admiral* Kichisaburo Nomura
2 Feb 1932 - 10 Oct 1932:	*Admiral* Eisuke Yamamoto
10 Oct 1932 - 15 Nov 1933:	*Admiral* Kichisaburo Nomura
15 Nov 1933 - 15 Nov 1934:	*Fleet Admiral* Osami Nagano
15 Nov 1934 - 2 Dec 1935:	*Admiral* Nobumasa Suetsugu
2 Dec 1935 - 1 Dec 1936:	*Admiral* Mitsumasa Yonai
1 Dec 1936 - 25 Apr 1938:	*Admiral* Gengo Hyakutake
25 Apr 1938 - 1 May 1940:	*Admiral* Kiyoshi Hasegawa
1 May 1940 - 5 Sep 1940:	*Admiral* Koshiro Oikawa
5 Sep 1940 - 10 Sep 1941:	*Admiral* Koichi Shiozawa
10 Sep 1941 - 18 Oct 1941:	*Admiral* Shigetaro Shimada
18 Oct 1941 - 10 Nov 1942:	*Vice-Admiral* Noboru Hirata
10 Nov 1942 - 21 May 1943:	*Fleet Admiral* Mineichi Koga
21 May 1943 - 3 May 1944:	*Admiral* Soemu Toyoda
3 May 1944 - 2 Aug 1944:	*Admiral* Zengo Yoshida
2 Aug 1944 - 15 Sep 1944:	*Admiral* Naokuni Nomura
15 Sep 1944 - 1 May 1945:	*Admiral* Nishizo Tsukahara
1 May 1945 - 30 Nov 1945:	*Vice-Admiral* Michitaro Totsuka

Chief of Staff, Yokosuka Naval District

23 Mar 1899 - 6 Dec 1900:	*Vice-Admiral* Baron Yunoshin Kano
6 Dec 1900 - 18 Dec 1903:	*Vice-Admiral* Baron Shinkichi Mukaiyama
6 Jun 1904 - 14 Jun 1905:	*Vice-Admiral* Yu Nakao

14 Jun 1905 - 19 Nov 1906:	*Vice-Admiral* Izo Teragaki
19 Nov 1906 - 15 Nov 1907:	*Admiral* Koichi Fujii
15 Nov 1907 - 16 Jul 1910:	*Vice-Admiral* Kotaro Koizumi
16 Jul 1910 - 1 Dec 1911:	*Vice-Admiral* Baron Mitsukane Tsuchiya
1 Dec 1911 - 9 Jul 1912:	*Vice-Admiral* Tadamichi Kamaya
9 Jul 1912 - 1 Dec 1912:	*Vice-Admiral* Kensuke Wada
1 Dec 1912 - 1 Dec 1914:	*Vice-Admiral* Osuke Kamimura
1 Dec 1914 - 1 Dec 1916:	*Vice-Admiral* Takeshi Kimura
1 Dec 1916 - 1 Dec 1917:	*Vice-Admiral* Yasujiro Nagata
1 Dec 1917 - 10 Jul 1918:	*Vice-Admiral* Saburo Horiuchi
10 Jul 1918 - 1 Dec 1918:	*Vice-Admiral* Kajishiro Funakoshi
1 Dec 1918 - 10 Jun 1919:	*Admiral* Hiroharu Kato
10 Jun 1919 - 30 Mar 1920:	*Vice-Admiral* Shinzaburo Furukawa
30 Mar 1920 - 15 Nov 1921:	*Vice-Admiral* Shigetoshi Takeuchi
1 Dec 1921 - 25 May 1922:	*Vice-Admiral* Tamaki Tosu
25 May 1922 - 1 Feb 1923:	*Admiral* Katsunoshin Yamanashi
1 Feb 1923 - 1 Dec 1923:	*Rear-Admiral* Tomoyoshi Usagawa
1 Dec 1923 - 2 Feb 1925:	*Rear-Admiral* Heigo Teraoka
2 Feb 1925 - 1 Dec 1927:	*Vice-Admiral* Wataru Ugawa
1 Dec 1927 - 30 Nov 1929:	*Admiral* Kiyoshi Hasegawa
30 Nov 1929 - 1 Dec 1930:	*Vice-Admiral* Shigeo Uemura
1 Dec 1930 - 10 Oct 1931:	*Admiral* Teijiro Toyoda
10 Oct 1931 - 15 Nov 1933:	*Vice-Admiral* Kichijiro Hamada
15 Nov 1933 - 20 Sep 1934:	*Rear-Admiral* Minoru Sonoda
20 Sep 1934 - 15 Nov 1935:	*Rear-Admiral* Haruma Izawa
15 Nov 1935 - 16 Nov 1936:	*Admiral* Shigeyoshi Inoue
16 Nov 1936 - 1 Dec 1937:	*Vice-Admiral* Seiichi Iwamura
1 Dec 1937 - 1 Feb 1938:	*Vice-Admiral* Minoru Tayui
1 Feb 1938 - 15 Nov 1939:	*Vice-Admiral* Daisuke Soejima
15 Nov 1939 - 1 Dec 1940:	*Vice-Admiral* Arata Oka
1 Dec 1940 - 15 Oct 1941:	*Admiral* Yoshikazu Endo
15 Oct 1941 - 31 Dec 1941:	*Vice-Admiral* Masao Kanazawa
31 Dec 1941 - 1 Sep 1943:	*Vice-Admiral* Risaburo Fujita
1 Sep 1943 - 1 Mar 1944:	*Vice-Admiral* Sadaichi Matsunaga
1 Mar 1944 - 20 May 1945:	*Rear-Admiral* Tadao Yokoi
20 May 1945 - 30 Nov 1945:	*Rear-Admiral* Keizo Komura

GUARD DISTRICTS

Admiral Commanding, Chinkai Guard District

1 Apr 1916 - 1 Dec 1916:	*Vice-Admiral* Kujuro Yamaguchi
1 Dec 1916 - 1 Dec 1918:	*Vice-Admiral* Kichitaro Togo

1 Dec 1918 - 1 Dec 1919:	*Vice-Admiral* Hiromi Tadokoro
1 Dec 1919 - 1 Dec 1920:	*Vice-Admiral* Tomojiro Chisaka
1 Dec 1920 - 1 Dec 1922:	*Vice-Admiral* Kazuyoshi Yamaji
1 Dec 1922 - 1 Jun 1923:	*Admiral* Saburo Hyakutake
1 Jun 1923 - 5 Feb 1924:	*Vice-Admiral* Shozo Kuwashima
5 Feb 1924 - 15 Apr 1925:	*Vice-Admiral* Kikuo Matsumura
15 Apr 1925 - 1 Dec 1926:	*Vice-Admiral* Taro Inutsuka
1 Dec 1926 - 1 Dec 1927:	*Vice-Admiral* Naotaro Nagasawa
1 Dec 1927 - 1 Jul 1929:	*Vice-Admiral* Junichi Kiyokawa
1 Jul 1929 - 1 Dec 1930:	*Vice-Admiral* Kanjiro Hara
1 Dec 1930 - 1 Dec 1932:	*Admiral* Mitsumasa Yonai
1 Dec 1932 - 17 Jan 1934:	*Admiral* Koichi Shiozawa
17 Jan 1934 - 15 Nov 1934:	*Vice-Admiral* Hisao Ichimura
15 Nov 1934 - 16 Mar 1936:	*Vice-Admiral* Seizaburo Kobayashi
16 Mar 1936 - 1 Dec 1936:	*Vice-Admiral* Tsugumatsu Inoue
1 Dec 1936 - 1 Dec 1937:	*Vice-Admiral* Keitaro Hara
1 Dec 1937 - 15 Nov 1938:	*Vice-Admiral* Jugoro Arichi
15 Nov 1938 - 15 Apr 1940:	*Vice-Admiral* Sonosuke Kobayashi
15 Apr 1940 - 1 Sep 1941:	*Admiral* Nishizo Tsukahara
1 Sep 1941 - 15 Sep 1942:	*Vice-Admiral* Ikuta Sakamoto
15 Sep 1942 - 9 Sep 1944:	*Vice-Admiral* Eiji Goto
9 Sep 1944 - 20 Apr 1945:	*Vice-Admiral* Takazumi Oka
20 Apr 1945 - Sep 1945:	*Vice-Admiral* Gisaburo Yamaguchi

Chief of Staff, Chinkai Guard District

4 Apr 1916 - 1 Dec 1917:	*Rear-Admiral* Tsuneha Sano
1 Dec 1917 - 26 May 1919:	*Rear-Admiral* Heigo Teraoka
15 Jun 1921 - 10 Nov 1922:	*Rear-Admiral* Yasuzo Torisaki
10 Nov 1922 - 1 Dec 1924:	*Rear-Admiral* Chikateru Takasaki
1 Dec 1924 - 1 Dec 1926:	*Rear-Admiral* Naojiro Honshuku
1 Dec 1926 - 10 Dec 1928:	*Rear-Admiral* Sunao Matsuzaki
15 Nov 1930 - 15 Nov 1932:	*Rear-Admiral* Kentaro Kojima
15 Nov 1932 - 1 Nov 1934:	*Vice-Admiral* Yoshinobu Shishido
1 Nov 1934 - 1 Dec 1936:	*Rear-Admiral* Kohei Ochi
1 Dec 1936 - 1 Dec 1937:	*Rear-Admiral* Junichi Mizuno
1 Dec 1937 - 15 Nov 1939:	*Vice-Admiral* Sadaichi Matsunaga
15 Nov 1939 - 15 Nov 1940:	*Vice-Admiral* Tamotsu Takama
15 Nov 1940 - 25 Feb 1942:	*Rear-Admiral* Shigeki Ando
25 Feb 1942 - 25 Jun 1943:	*Rear-Admiral* Keiichi Onishi
25 Jun 1943 - 15 Aug 1944:	*Rear-Admiral* Katsuya Sato
15 Aug 1944 - 15 Apr 1945:	*Rear-Admiral* Chitoshi Ishizuka
15 Apr 1945 - 29 Nov 1945:	*Rear-Admiral* Haruo Katsuta

Admiral Commanding, Kainan Guard District

10 Apr 1941 - 20 Nov 1941: *Vice-Admiral* Umataro Tanimoto
20 Nov 1941 - 15 Dec 1942: *Vice-Admiral* Kaneo Sunagawa
15 Dec 1942 - 1 Oct 1943: *Vice-Admiral* Shiro Koike
1 Oct 1943 - 4 Nov 1944: *Vice-Admiral* Masukichi Matsuki
4 Nov 1944 - Sep 1945: *Vice-Admiral* Keijiro Goga

Chief of Staff, Kainan Guard District

10 Apr 1941 - 1 Sep 1941: *Vice-Admiral* Yasuo Inoue
1 Sep 1941 - 19 Feb 1943: *Vice-Admiral* Kanji Ugaki
19 Feb 1943 - 10 Mar 1944: *Vice-Admiral* Shinichi Ichise
10 Mar 1944 - Sep 1945: *Rear-Admiral* Kinji Senda

Admiral Commanding, Mako Guard District

4 Jul 1901 - 23 Sep 1903: *Vice-Admiral* Hikonojō Kamimura
23 Sep 1903 - 13 Jun 1905: *Vice-Admiral* Tomomichi Onomoto
13 Jun 1905 - 20 Dec 1905: *Vice-Admiral* Nagataka Uemura
20 Dec 1905 - 22 Nov 1906: *Vice-Admiral* Baron Masaaki Hashimoto
22 Nov 1906 - 12 Mar 1907: *Vice-Admiral* Baron Tokioki Nashiba
12 Mar 1907 - 1 Dec 1909: *Vice-Admiral* Baron Yunoshin Kano
1 Dec 1909 - 1 Dec 1910: *Vice-Admiral* Chikakata Tamari
1 Dec 1910 - 1 Dec 1911: *Vice-Admiral* Hikojiro Ijichi
1 Dec 1911 - 14 Apr 1913: *Vice-Admiral* Kotaro Koizumi
14 Apr 1913 - 1 Dec 1913: *Vice-Admiral* Baron Shinrokuro Nishi
1 Dec 1913 - 17 Dec 1914: *Vice-Admiral* Tadamichi Kamaya
17 Dec 1914 - 13 Dec 1915: *Vice-Admiral* Rinroku Eguchi
13 Dec 1915 - 1 Dec 1916: *Admiral* Teijiro Kuroi
1 Dec 1916 - 12 Dec 1917: *Vice-Admiral* Tatsuo Matsumura
12 Dec 1917 - 13 Jun 1918: *Vice-Admiral* Tomojiro Chisaka
13 Jun 1918 - 1 Dec 1919: *Vice-Admiral* Kazuyoshi Yamaji
1 Dec 1919 - 1 Dec 1920: *Rear-Admiral* Shigeushi Nakagawa
1 Dec 1920 - 1 Aug 1921: *Admiral* Naomi Taniguchi
1 Aug 1921 - 26 Dec 1921: *Vice-Admiral* Kiyokaze Yoshida
26 Dec 1921 - 1 Jun 1923: *Vice-Admiral* Hisatsune Iida
1 Jun 1923 - 6 Nov 1923: *Vice-Admiral* Shiro Yamauchi
6 Nov 1923 - 20 Dec 1924: *Vice-Admiral* Tadatsugu Tajiri
20 Dec 1924 - 1 Aug 1925: *Vice-Admiral* Eizaburo Fujiwara
1 Aug 1925 - 1 Dec 1927: *Vice-Admiral* Nobutaro Iida
1 Dec 1927 - 10 Dec 1928: *Rear-Admiral* Kesaichi Hitsuda
10 Dec 1928 - 1 Dec 1930: *Vice-Admiral* Eijiro Hamano
1 Dec 1930 - 11 Jan 1932: *Vice-Admiral* Shusei Yuchi
11 Jan 1932 - 18 Jun 1932: *Vice-Admiral* Akira Goto
18 Jun 1932 - 15 Nov 1933: *Rear-Admiral* Toyonaka Yamauchi

15 Nov 1933 - 15 Nov 1934:	*Vice-Admiral* Yoshiyuki Niyama
15 Nov 1934 - 15 Nov 1935:	*Vice-Admiral* Hiroshi Ono
15 Nov 1935 - 1 Dec 1937:	*Vice-Admiral* Senzo Wada
1 Dec 1937 - 15 Nov 1938:	*Vice-Admiral* Shunzo Mito
15 Nov 1938 - 15 Nov 1939:	*Vice-Admiral* Goro Hara
15 Nov 1939 - 27 Feb 1941:	*Vice-Admiral* Ibo Takahashi
27 Feb 1941 - 20 Nov 1942:	*Vice-Admiral* Koki Yamamoto
20 Nov 1942 - 1 Apr 1943:	*Admiral* Takeo Takagi

Chief of Staff, Mako Guard District

25 Dec 1904 - 14 Jun 1905:	*Vice-Admiral* Baron Shinrokuro Nishi
14 Jun 1905 - 10 May 1906:	*Vice-Admiral* Baron Mitsukane Tsuchiya
11 May 1906 - 5 Aug 1907:	*Rear-Admiral* Sango Obana
5 Aug 1907 - 28 Aug 1908:	*Rear-Admiral* Kanetane Imai
28 Aug 1908 - 11 Oct 1909:	*Rear-Admiral* Juntaro Hirose
8 Oct 1910 - 12 Jun 1911:	*Rear-Admiral* Yushichi Kanno
12 Jun 1911 - 20 Apr 1912:	*Rear-Admiral* Koki Hirose
20 Apr 1912 - 1 Dec 1913:	*Rear-Admiral* Eitaro Kataoka
1 Dec 1913 - 7 Aug 1914:	*Vice- Admiral* Kotaro Tanaka
7 Aug 1914 - 1 Sep 1915:	*Rear-Admiral* Shigeushi Nakagawa
1 Sep 1915 - 28 Jan 1916:	*Rear- Admiral* Moshiro Iwasaki
28 Jan 1916 - 1 Dec 1917:	*Rear- Admiral* Hisamori Taguchi
1 Dec 1918 - 26 Jul 1920:	*Rear-Admiral* Yoshitada Mikami
1 Mar 1923 - 1 Dec 1924:	*Rear-Admiral* Morie Tokiwa
1 Dec 1924 - 1 Apr 1925:	*Rear-Admiral* Shinichi Oguri
1 Jul 1926 - 15 Nov 1927:	*Rear-Admiral* Junzo Yoshitake
15 Nov 1927 - 30 Oct 1929:	*Rear-Admiral* Tadashi Kurata
20 Nov 1929 - 15 May 1931:	*Rear-Admiral* Seizaburo Mitsui
15 May 1931 - 1 Dec 1932:	*Vice- Admiral* Shunzo Mito
1 Dec 1932 - 1 Nov 1934:	*Rear-Admiral* Shinji Suzuki
1 Nov 1934 - 1 Dec 1936:	*Rear-Admiral* Tsuyoshi Kobata
1 Dec 1936 - 15 Dec 1938:	*Vice- Admiral* Shigeyoshi Miwa
15 Dec 1938 - 15 Nov 1939:	*Rear-Admiral* Raizo Tanaka
15 Nov 1939 - 10 May 1941:	*Rear-Admiral* Akira Matsuzaki
10 May 1941 - 1 Apr 1943:	*Vice- Admiral* Toshio Shimazaki

Admiral Commanding, Ominato Guard District

12 Dec 1905 - 12 Mar 1907:	*Vice-Admiral* Baron Heiji Mochihara
12 Mar 1907 - 15 May 1908:	*Rear-Admiral* Hokizo Okubo
15 May 1908 - 28 Aug 1908:	*Vice-Admiral* Kunikane Taketomi
28 Aug 1908 - 1 Dec 1909:	*Vice-Admiral* Chikakata Tamari
1 Dec 1909 - 1 Sep 1911:	*Vice-Admiral* Tokuya Kamiizumi
1 Sep 1911 - 9 Jul 1912:	*Vice-Admiral* Hideshiro Fujimoto

9 Jul 1912 - 24 May 1913:	*Vice-Admiral* Tamotsu Tsuchiya
24 May 1914 - 1 Dec 1913:	*Admiral* Sojiro Tochinai
1 Dec 1913 - 17 Dec 1914:	*Rear-Admiral* Tsunekichi Uemura
17 Dec 1914 - 1 Apr 1916:	*Rear-Admiral* Ichitaro Nakajima
1 Apr 1916 - 1 Dec 1917:	*Vice-Admiral* Baron Mitsukane Tsuchiya
1 Dec 1917 - 1 Dec 1919:	*Vice-Admiral* Toshitake Iwamura
1 Dec 1919 - 1 Oct 1920:	*Vice-Admiral* Keizaburo Moriyama
1 Oct 1920 - 1 Dec 1921:	*Vice-Admiral* Mitsuzo Nunome
1 Dec 1921 - 1 Dec 1922:	*Vice-Admiral* Kozo Sato
1 Dec 1922 - 1 Jun 1923:	*Vice-Admiral* Koshiro Otani
1 Jun 1923 - 5 Feb 1924:	*Rear-Admiral* Shokichi Oishi
5 Feb 1924 - 1 Dec 1925:	*Vice-Admiral* Kosuke Shikama
1 Dec 1925 - 1 Dec 1927:	*Vice-Admiral* Takashi Kanesaka
1 Dec 1927 - 30 Nov 1929:	*Vice-Admiral* Yukichi Shima
30 Nov 1929 - 1 Mar 1931:	*Vice-Admiral* Saburo Yasumi
1 Mar 1931 - 1 Dec 1931:	*Vice-Admiral* Kiyohiro Ijichi
1 Dec 1931 - 15 Nov 1932:	*Vice-Admiral* Togo Kawano
15 Nov 1932 - 15 Nov 1933:	*Vice-Admiral* Hiroshi Ono
15 Nov 1933 - 15 Nov 1934:	*Vice-Admiral* Choji Inoue
15 Nov 1934 - 7 Oct 1935:	*Rear-Admiral* Chonan Yamaguchi
7 Oct 1935 - 16 Mar 1936:	*Rear-Admiral* Katsuji Masaki
16 Mar 1936 - 1 Dec 1936:	*Vice-Admiral* Teijiro Sugisaka
1 Dec 1936 - 1 Dec 1937:	*Rear-Admiral* Haruma Izawa
1 Dec 1937 - 15 Nov 1938:	*Vice-Admiral* Shosuke Shimomura
15 Nov 1938 - 15 Nov 1940:	*Vice-Admiral* Shuichi Hoshino
15 Nov 1940 - 15 Sep 1942:	*Vice-Admiral* Masakichi Okuma
15 Sep 1942 - 1 Apr 1943:	*Vice-Admiral* Shiro Kawase
1 Apr 1943 - 15 Feb 1945:	*Vice-Admiral* Yasuo Inoue
15 Feb 1945 - 15 Mar 1945:	*Vice-Admiral* Eiji Goto
15 Mar 1945 - 30 Nov 1945:	*Vice-Admiral* Kanji Ugaki

Chief of Staff, Ominato Guard District

12 Dec 1905 - 22 Nov 1906:	*Rear-Admiral* Kiyozo Oda
22 Nov 1906 - 20 Feb 1908:	*Vice-Admiral* Junkichi Yajima
20 Feb 1908 - 7 Apr 1908:	*Vice-Admiral* Tadamichi Kamaya
7 Apr 1908 - 4 Mar 1909:	*Rear-Admiral* Shigetada Hideshima
4 Mar 1909 - 1 Dec 1910:	*Rear-Admiral* Tsunematsu Kondo
1 Dec 1910 - 22 Dec 1911:	*Vice-Admiral* Yasujiro Nagata
1 Apr 1913 - 27 May 1914:	*Rear-Admiral* Teiichiro Shitsuda
27 May 1914 - 17 Jul 1915:	*Rear-Admiral* Yushichi Kanno
17 Jul 1915 - 6 Nov 1916:	*Vice-Admiral* Kenzo Kobayashi
6 Nov 1916 - 18 Oct 1918:	*Rear-Admiral* Meiji Tojo
18 Oct 1918 - 2 Dec 1919:	*Rear-Admiral* Kanichi Taketomi

15 Mar 1922 - 6 Nov 1923:	*Rear-Admiral* Teiji Sakamoto
6 Nov 123 - 20 Aug 1926:	*Rear-Admiral* Kichisuke Komori
10 Dec 1928 - 1 Dec 1931:	*Rear-Admiral* Katsuji Masaki
1 Dec 1931 - 15 Nov 1933:	*Rear-Admiral* Tokujiro Yokoyama
15 Nov 1933 - 15 Nov 1935:	*Rear-Admiral* Takeo Sakura
15 Nov 1935 - 1 Apr 1937:	*Vice-Admiral* Jiro Matsunaga
1 Apr 1937 - 15 Dec 1938:	*Rear-Admiral* Namizo Sato
15 Dec 1938 - 28 Nov 1940:	*Rear-Admiral* Tokuji Mori
28 Nov 1940 - 10 Feb 1942:	*Rear-Admiral* Keishi Ishii
10 Feb 1940 - 1 Jul 1943:	*Vice-Admiral* Takeo Kaizuka
1 Jul 1943 - 30 Nov 1945:	*Rear-Admiral* Zensuke Kanome

Admiral Commanding, Osaka Guard District

20 Nov 1941 - 9 Mar 1943:	*Vice-Admiral* Masashi Kobayashi
9 Mar 1943 - 1 Apr 1944:	*Vice-Admiral* Kakusaburo Makita
1 Apr 1944 - 1 Nov 1944:	*Vice-Admiral* Ichiro Ono
1 Nov 1944 - 30 Nov 1945:	*Vice-Admiral* Arata Oka

Chief of Staff, Osaka Guard District

20 Nov 1941 - 13 Aug 1943:	*Rear-Admiral* Shinichi Torigoe
13 Aug 1943 - 26 Feb 1945:	*Rear-Admiral* Bunjiro Yamaguchi
26 Feb 1945 - 30 Nov 1945:	*Rear-Admiral* Akira Maysuzaki

Admiral Commanding, Ryojun Guard District

6 Feb 1905 - 2 Feb 1906:	*Admiral* Baron Yahachi Shibayama
2 Feb 1906 - 22 Nov 1906:	*Admiral* Baron Sotaro Misu
22 Nov 1906 - 28 Aug 1908:	*Vice-Admiral* Baron Masaaki Hashimoto
28 Aug 1908 - 1 Dec 1910:	*Vice-Admiral* Baron Sadayasu Tomioka
1 Dec 1910 - 1 Dec 1912:	*Vice-Admiral* Hikohachi Yamada
1 Dec 1912 - 1 Apr 1914:	*Vice-Admiral* Hajime Sakamoto
1 Apr 1914 - 13 Dec 1915:	*Vice-Admiral* Reijiro Kawashima
13 Dec 1915 - 1 Dec 1916:	*Admiral* Takeshi Takarabe
1 Dec 1916 - 1 Dec 1918:	*Admiral* Teijiro Kuroi
1 Dec 1918 - 1 Oct 1920:	*Vice-Admiral* Tatsuo Matsumura
1 Oct 1920 - 1 Dec 1921:	*Vice-Admiral* Naoe Nakano
1 Dec 1921 - 10 Dec 1922:	*Vice-Admiral* Kesataro Kawahara
10 Dec 1922 - 20 Apr 1933:	DISBANDED
20 Apr 1933 - 1 Jul 1933:	*Vice-Admiral* Shizue Tsuda
1 Jul 1933 - 15 Nov 1934:	*Vice-Admiral* Yurikazu Edahara
15 Nov 1934 - 15 Nov 1935:	*Vice-Admiral* Kichijiro Hamada
15 Nov 1935 - 1 Dec 1936:	*Admiral* Hideho Wada
1 Dec 1936 - 15 Nov 1938:	*Vice-Admiral* Masaichi Maeda
15 Nov 1938 - 15 Nov 1939:	*Vice-Admiral* Ichiro Sato

15 Nov 1939 - 15 Nov 1940: *Vice-Admiral* Boshiro Hosogaya
15 Nov 1940 - 5 Jul 1941: *Vice-Admiral* Teruhisa Komatsu
5 Jul 1941 - 5 Jan 1942: *Vice-Admiral* Hidehiko Ukita
5 Jan 1942: DISBANDED

Chief of Staff, Ryojun Guard District

7 Jan 1905 - 22 Nov 1906: *Vice-Admiral* Chikataka Tamari
22 Nov 1906 - 28 Aug 1908: *Rear-Admiral* Tomokazu Takigawa
28 Aug 1908 - 1 Dec 1909: *Vice-Admiral* Yasutaro Egashira
1 Dec 1909 - 1 Dec 1910: *Rear-Admiral* Genzaburo Ogi
1 Dec 1910 - 1 Dec 1911: *Vice-Admiral* Tadamichi Kamaya
1 Dec 1911 - 6 Dec 1911: *Rear-Admiral* Sukeshiro Hanabusa
6 Dec 1911 - 1 Dec 1912: *Rear-Admiral* Yoshimoto Shoji
1 Dec 1912 - 1 Dec 1913: *Rear-Admiral* Sadaichi Hiraoka
8 May 1914 - 11 May 1916: *Rear-Admiral* Masaki Nakamura
11 May 1916 - 1 Dec 1917: *Rear-Admiral* Kanshiro Haji
12 Feb 1918 - 10 Nov 1918: *Rear-Admiral* Kametaro Muta
20 Nov 1920 - 1 Apr 1922: *Rear-Admiral* Kenkichi Wada
1 Apr 1922 - 10 Nov 1922: *Vice-Admiral* Kiyohiro Ijichi
20 Apr 1933 - 15 Nov 1935: *Rear-Admiral* Hisoharu Kubota
15 Nov 1935 - 1 Dec 1937: *Vice-Admiral* Chuichi Hara
1 Dec 1937 - 15 Nov 1939: *Vice-Admiral* Shintaro Hashimoto
15 Nov 1939 - 1 Nov 1940: *Rear-Admiral* Isamu Takeda
1 Nov 1940 - 5 Jan 1942: *Rear-Admiral* Keizo Tanimoto
5 Jan 1942: DISBANDED

Admiral Commanding, Takao Guard District

1 Apr 1943 - 10 Jun 1943: *Admiral* Takeo Takagi
10 Jun 1943 - 30 Nov 1943: *Admiral* Seigo Yamagata
30 Nov 1943 - 10 May 1945: *Vice-Admiral* Ryozo Fukuda
10 May 1945 - 30 Nov 1945: *Vice-Admiral* Kiyohide Shima

Chief of Staff, Takao Guard District

1 Apr 1943 - 7 Jul 1943: *Vice-Admiral* Toshio Shimazaki
7 Jul 1943 - 15 Aug 1944: *Rear-Admiral* Chitoshi Ishizuka
15 Aug 1944 - 1 May 1945: *Rear-Admiral* Hiroshi Kurose
10 May 1945 - 30 Nov 1945: *Vice-Admiral* Tasuku Nakazawa

Admiral Commanding, Takeshiki Guard District

14 May 1898 - 20 May 1900: *Vice-Admiral* Tomomichi Onomoto
20 May 1900 - 26 Jul 1902: *Admiral* Baron Sonojo Hidaka
26 Jul 1902 - 28 Dec 1903: *Admiral* Baron Shichiro Kataoka
28 Dec 1903 - 13 Dec 1905: *Vice-Admiral* Hidematsu Tsunoda

20 Dec 1905 - 22 Nov 1906:	*Admiral* Baron Sotokichi Uryu
22 Nov 1906 - 21 Oct 1907:	*Vice-Admiral* Yoshigoro Ito
21 Oct 1907 - 28 Aug 1908:	*Vice-Admiral* Baron Sadayasu Tomioka
28 Aug 1908 - 1 Dec 1909:	*Vice-Admiral* Baron Shinkichi Mukaiyama
1 Dec 1909 - 1 Dec 1910:	*Vice-Admiral* Hikohachi Yamada
1 Dec 1910 - 25 Sep 1911:	*Vice-Admiral* Izo Teragaki
25 Sep 1911 - 1 Dec 1911:	*Admiral* Motaro Yoshimatsu
1 Dec 1911 - 1 Oct 1912:	*Vice-Admiral* Tsunaakira Nomoto
1 Oct 1912:	DISBANDED

Chief of Staff, Takeshiki Guard District

5 Jun 1902 - 12 Dec 1905:	*Vice-Admiral* Kotaro Koizumi
12 Dec 1905 - 22 Nov 1906:	*Admiral* Ryokitsu Arima
22 Nov 1906 - 28 Nov 1906:	*Rear-Admiral* Kiyozo Oda
28 Nov 1906 - 20 Nov 1908:	*Vice-Admiral* Rinroku Eguchi
20 Nov 1908 - 11 Oct 1909:	*Rear-Admiral* Kishichiro Osawa
11 Oct 1909 - 26 Oct 1910:	*Vice-Admiral* Takeshi Kimura
26 Oct 1910 - 16 Aug 1911:	*Vice-Admiral* Rokuro Kamaya
16 Aug 1911 - 1 Oct 1912:	
1 Oct 1912:	DISBANDED

Commandant of the Naval College

19 Jan 1899 - 20 May 1900:	*Admiral* Baron Yahachi Shibayama
20 May 1900 - 3 Feb 1904:	*Vice-Admiral* Baron Toshiatsu Sakamoto
3 Feb 1904 - 2 Nov 1905:	*Vice-Admiral* Baron Kaneyuki Kimotsuke
2 Nov 1905 - 28 Aug 1908:	*Vice-Admiral* Baron Toshiatsu Sakamoto
28 Aug 1908 - 1 Dec 1909:	*Fleet Admiral* Baron Hayao Shimamura
1 Dec 1909 - 1 Dec 1910:	*Vice-Admiral* Reijiro Kawashima
1 Dec 1910 - 25 Sep 1911:	*Admiral* Motaro Yoshimatsu
25 Sep 1911 - 1 Dec 1911:	*Admiral* Tanin Yamaya
1 Dec 1911 - 25 Sep 1913:	*Admiral* Baron Rokuro Yashiro
25 Sep 1913 - 1 Dec 1913:	*Admiral* Motaro Yoshimatsu
1 Dec 1913 - 22 Aug 1914:	*Admiral* Tanin Yamaya
22 Aug 1914 - 13 Dec 1915:	*Fleet Admiral* Prince Hiroyasu Fushimi
13 Dec 1915 - 10 Aug 1920:	*Vice-Admiral* Tetsutaro Sato
10 Aug 1920 - 1 May 1922:	*Admiral* Hiroharu Kato
1 May 1922 - 1 Jun 1923:	*Vice-Admiral* Saburo Horiuchi
1 Jun 1923 - 1 Dec 1924:	*Admiral* Eisuke Yamamoto
1 Dec 1924 - 1 Dec 1926:	*Vice-Admiral* Koshiro Otani
1 Dec 1926 - 30 Nov 1929:	*Admiral* Ryozo Nakamura
30 Nov 1929 - 8 Feb 1932:	*Admiral* Sankichi Takahashi
8 Feb 1932 - 1 Oct 1932:	*Admiral* Gengo Hyakutake
1 Oct 1932 - 1 Dec 1932:	

1 Dec 1932 - 15 Nov 1933:	*Admiral* Viscount Takayoshi Kato
15 Nov 1933 - 2 Dec 1935:	*Vice-Admiral* Tsugumatsu Inoue
2 Dec 1935 - 1 Dec 1936:	*Vice-Admiral* Kamezaburo Nakamura
1 Dec 1936 - 1 Dec 1937:	*Vice-Admiral* Saburo Sato
1 Dec 1937 - 15 Nov 1938:	*Vice-Admiral* Masaharu Hibino
15 Nov 1938 - 29 Sep 1939:	*Admiral* Shiro Takasu
29 Sep 1939 - 23 Dec 1939:	
23 Dec 1939 - 1 Nov 1940:	*Admiral* Yorio Sawamoto
1 Nov 1940 - 10 Apr 1941:	*Admiral* Chuichi Nagumo
10 Apr 1941 - 6 Sep 1941:	*Vice-Admiral* Kasuke Abe
6 Sep 1941 - 18 Oct 1941:	*Vice-Admiral* Jisaburo Ozawa
18 Oct 1941 - 1 Jun 1942:	*Admiral* Seiichi Ito
1 Jun 1942 - 15 Sep 1942:	*Vice-Admiral* Ayao Inagaki
15 Sep 1942 - 10 Oct 1942:	
10 Oct 1942 - 15 Nov 1943:	*Admiral* Koshiro Oikawa
15 Nov 1943 - 14 Dec 1943:	
14 Dec 1943 - 15 Mar 1944:	*Admiral* Zengo Yoshida
15 Mar 1944 - 18 Nov 1944:	*Admiral* Seiichi Ito
18 Nov 1944 - 29 May 1945:	*Vice-Admiral* Jisaburo Ozawa
29 May 1945:	POSITION ABOLISHED

Commandant of the Naval Academy

19 Jan 1899 - 24 May 1902:	*Vice-Admiral* Yoichi Kawahara
24 May 1902 - 28 Dec 1903:	*Vice-Admiral* Baron Masamichi Togo
28 Dec 1903 - 19 Nov 1906:	*Vice-Admiral* Baron Sadayasu Tomioka
19 Nov 1906 - 28 Aug 1908:	*Fleet Admiral* Baron Hayao Shimamura
28 Aug 1908 - 1 Dec 1910:	*Admiral* Motaro Yoshimatsu
1 Dec 1910 - 25 Mar 1914:	*Admiral* Baron Gentaro Yamashita
25 Mar 1914 - 1 Dec 1916:	*Admiral* Ryokitsu Arima
1 Dec 1916 - 1 Dec 1918:	*Admiral* Kaneo Nomaguchi
1 Dec 1918 - 1 Dec 1920:	*Admiral* Baron Kantaro Suzuki
1 Dec 1920 - 1 Apr 1923:	*Vice-Admiral* Tomojiro Chisaka
1 Apr 1923 - 8 Sep 1925:	*Admiral* Naomi Taniguchi
8 Sep 1925 - 1 Apr 1927:	*Vice-Admiral* Kumazo Shirane
1 Apr 1927 - 10 Dec 1928:	*Vice-Admiral* Tamaki Tosu
10 Dec 1928 - 10 Jun 1930:	*Fleet Admiral* Osami Nagano
10 Jun 1930 - 1 Dec 1931:	*Vice-Admiral* Naotaro Ominato
1 Dec 1931 - 3 Oct 1933:	*Vice-Admiral* Hajime Matsushita
3 Oct 1933 - 15 Nov 1935:	*Admiral* Koshiro Oikawa
15 Nov 1935 - 1 Dec 1937:	*Vice-Admiral* Manbei Idemitsu
1 Dec 1937 - 30 Aug 1939:	*Vice-Admiral* Tokutaro Sumiyama
30 Aug 1939 - 15 Nov 1939:	
15 Nov 1939 - 4 Apr 1941:	*Vice-Admiral* Masaichi Niimi
4 Apr 1941 - 1 Oct 1942:	*Vice-Admiral* Jinichi Kusaka

1 Oct 1942 - 26 Oct 1942:	
26 Oct 1942 - 5 Aug 1944:	*Admiral* Shigeyoshi Inoue
5 Aug 1944 - 4 Nov 1944:	*Vice-Admiral* Denshichi Okawachi
4 Nov 1944 - 15 Jan 1945:	*Vice-Admiral* Marquis Teruhisa Komatsu
15 Jan 1945 - 5 Oct 1945:	*Vice-Admiral* Takeo Kurita
5 Oct 1945:	POSITION ABOLISHED

Commandant, Naval Engineer Academy

28 Feb 1897 - 31 Dec 1903:	*Vice-Admiral (Engineer)* Teikan Yuchi
31 Dec 1903 - 4 Nov 1905:	*Rear-Admiral (Engineer)* Yoshimitsu Nagamine
4 Nov 1905 - 28 Aug 1908:	*Vice-Admiral (Engineer)* Yasujiro Yamamoto
28 Aug 1908 - 1 Dec 1910:	*Rear-Admiral (Engineer)* Yoshimitsu Nagamine
1 Dec 1910 - 1 Dec 1911:	*Rear-Admiral* Otomaru Gejo
1 Dec 1911 - 1 Dec 1913:	*Vice-Admiral (Engineer)* Kiyojiro Ichikawa
1 Dec 1913 - 1 Apr 1914:	*Vice-Admiral* Hideo Takeda
1 Apr 1914 - 1 Apr 1916:	*Vice-Admiral* Iwao Kamo
1 Apr 1916 - 1 Dec 1917:	*Vice-Admiral* Kosuke Kisaki
1 Dec 1917 - 1 Sep 1921:	*Vice-Admiral (Engineer)* Zenya Funabashi
1 Sep 1921 - 25 May 1923:	*Vice-Admiral (Engineer)* Tamotsu Hiratsuka
25 May 1923 - 25 Jul 1924:	*Vice-Admiral* Iwasaburo Ikeda
25 Jul 1924 - 15 Apr 1925:	*Vice-Admiral* Teigo Okazaki
15 Apr 1925 - 10 Dec 1928:	*Vice-Admiral* Tokuichi Shimizu
10 Dec 1928 - 30 Nov 1929:	*Vice-Admiral* Gihachiro Yamashita
30 Nov 1929 - 1 Dec 1931:	*Vice-Admiral* Takuma Kuroda
1 Dec 1931 - 10 May 1934:	*Vice-Admiral* Hiromu Onodera
10 May 1934 - 2 Dec 1935:	*Vice-Admiral* Muneshige Ueda
2 Dec 1935 - 15 Nov 1938:	*Vice-Admiral* Ichiro Kaneda
15 Nov 1938 - 20 Nov 1941:	*Vice-Admiral* Iwao Hiraoka
20 Nov 1941 - 25 Oct 1943:	*Vice-Admiral* Shigeaki Nabeshima
25 Oct 1943 - 1 Oct 1944:	*Vice-Admiral* Hiromitsu Yanagihara
1 Oct 1944 - 1 Oct 1945:	*Rear-Admiral* Tamenori Hidaka
1 Oct 1945:	POSITION ABOLISHED

Commandant, Naval Paymaster Academy

15 May 1899 - 22 Dec 1900:	*Paymaster General* Junnosuke Doi
22 Dec 1900 - 7 Jul 1903:	*Vice-Admiral (Paymaster)* Kichinosuke Fukunaga
7 Jul 1903 - 10 Nov 1903:	*Vice-Admiral (Paymaster)* Masaru Shisa
10 Nov 1903 - 29 Dec 1904:	*Rear-Admiral (Paymaster)* Jotaro Yano
29 Dec 1904 - 12 Jan 1905:	*Rear-Admiral (Paymaster)* Kanae Utsunomiya
12 Jan 1905 - 25 Jun 1905:	*Rear-Admiral (Paymaster)* Hachitaro Kato
25 Jun 1905 - 15 Aug 1908:	*Vice-Admiral (Paymaster)* Masaru Shisa
15 Aug 1908 - 7 Sep 1911:	*Rear-Admiral (Paymaster)* Kanae Utsunomiya
7 Sep 1911 - 1 Dec 1913:	*Rear-Admiral (Paymaster)* Tsunetaka Fujita

1 Dec 1913 - 8 Aug 1914:	*Vice-Admiral (Paymaster)* Kotaro Sakura
8 Aug 1914 - 13 Dec 1915:	*Vice-Admiral (Paymaster)* Usuke Shimizu
13 Dec 1915 - 1 Dec 1916:	*Rear-Admiral (Paymaster)* Kiyoshi Sagara
1 Dec 1916 - 1 Dec 1919:	*Vice-Admiral (Paymaster)* Yuji Sano
1 Dec 1919 - 25 May 1923:	*Vice-Admiral (Paymaster)* Sadakichi Fukamizu
25 May 1923 - 1 Dec 1924:	*Vice-Admiral (Paymaster)* Ryoichi Kato
1 Dec 1924 - 20 Oct 1925:	*Vice-Admiral (Paymaster)* Shinjiro Nagayasu
20 Oct 1925 - 13 Apr 1927:	*Vice-Admiral (Paymaster)* Mitsuyoshi Maki
13 Apr 1927 - 1 Dec 1931:	*Vice-Admiral (Paymaster)* Hitoshi Gyobu
1 Dec 1931 - 1 Dec 1932:	*Vice-Admiral (Paymaster)* Kiyonaga Iritani
1 Dec 1932 - 10 Oct 1933:	*Vice-Admiral (Paymaster)* Haruichi Murakami
10 Oct 1933 - 15 Nov 1935:	*Vice-Admiral (Paymaster)* Yasuo Ikebe
15 Nov 1935 - 1 Dec 1937:	*Vice-Admiral (Paymaster)* Juzo Sasaki
1 Dec 1937 - 12 Apr 1939:	*Vice-Admiral (Paymaster)* Takeo Otsuka
12 Apr 1939 - 10 Apr 1941:	*Vice-Admiral (Paymaster)* Takaichi Kanaya
10 Apr 1941 - 26 Mar 1942:	*Vice-Admiral (Paymaster)* Masuzo Honda
26 Mar 1942 - 1 Jun 1943:	*Vice-Admiral (Paymaster)* Kakutaro Kataoka
1 Jun 1943 - 10 Oct 1945:	*Vice-Admiral (Paymaster)* Itsuya Konno
10 Oct 1945:	POSITION ABOLISHED

Commandant, Naval Gunnery School

29 Sep 1899 - 1 Nov 1900:	*Captain* Isamu Takakura
1 Nov 1900 - 1 Jun 1901:	*Rear-Admiral* Kikunozo Sakurai
1 Jun 1901 - 22 Apr 1902:	*Captain* Sukeuji Hosotani
22 Apr 1902 - 25 Jun 1903:	*Rear-Admiral* Arinobu Matsumoto
25 Jun 1903 - 1 Oct 1903:	*Rear-Admiral* Mamoru Okumiya
1 Oct 1903 - 21 Nov 1903:	*Rear-Admiral* Shinjiro Uehara
21 Nov 1903 - 28 Dec 1903:	*Rear-Admiral* Mamoru Okumiya
28 Dec 1903 - 22 Nov 1904:	*Rear-Admiral* Kokichi Kimura
22 Nov 1904 - 10 Aug 1907:	*Rear-Admiral* Katsuro Narita
10 Aug 1907 - 28 Aug 1908:	*Rear-Admiral* Mamoru Okumiya
28 Aug 1908 - 20 Dec 1908:	*Captain* Takeo Sendo
20 Dec 1908 - 1 Dec 1910:	*Admiral* Ryokitsu Arima
1 Dec 1910 - 21 Sep 1911:	*Rear-Admiral* Yoshimoto Shoji
21 Sep 1911 - 20 Apr 1912:	*Admiral* Kaneo Nomaguchi
20 Apr 1912 - 1 Dec 1913:	*Vice-Admiral* Rinroku Eguchi
1 Dec 1913 - 1 Dec 1914:	*Vice-Admiral* Kichitaro Togo
1 Dec 1914 - 1 Dec 1916:	*Vice-Admiral* Kazuyoshi Yamaji
1 Dec 1916 - 9 Jan 1918:	*Admiral* Hiroharu Kato
9 Jan 1918 - 10 Jul 1918:	*Vice-Admiral* Kesataro Kawahara
10 Jul 1918 - 10 Sep 1919:	*Vice-Admiral* Saburo Horiuchi
10 Sep 1919 - 1 Dec 1921:	*Vice-Admiral* Kozo Sato
1 Dec 1921 - 1 Apr 1923:	*Vice-Admiral* Hansaku Yoshioka

1 Apr 1923 - 1 Dec 1923:	*Rear-Admiral* Bekinari Kabayama
1 Dec 1923 - 1 Dec 1925:	*Vice-Admiral* Takashi Kanesaka
1 Dec 1925 - 1 Dec 1926:	*Rear-Admiral* Jutaro Takahashi
1 Dec 1926 - 1 Dec 1927:	*Vice-Admiral* Naotaro Ominato
1 Dec 1927 - 30 Nov 1929:	*Rear-Admiral* Saburo Kanoe
10 Nov 1929 - 1 Dec 1931:	*Vice-Admiral* Hiroshi Ono
1 Dec 1931 - 15 Nov 1934:	*Vice-Admiral* Keitaro Hara
15 Nov 1934 - 25 Jan 1935:	*Rear-Admiral* Sekizo Uno
25 Jan 1935 - 1 Mar 1935:	
1 Mar 1935 - 1 Dec 1936:	*Rear-Admiral* Hiroyoshi Tabata
1 Dec 1936 - 1 Dec 1937:	*Vice-Admiral* Jinichi Kusaka
1 Dec 1937 - 25 Apr 1938:	*Vice-Admiral* Giichi Miyata
25 Apr 1938 - 1 Oct 1940:	*Vice-Admiral* Denshichi Okawachi
1 Oct 1940 - 15 Nov 1940:	
15 Nov 1940 - 17 Nov 1941:	*Vice-Admiral* Naosaburo Irifune
17 Nov 1941 - 15 Mar 1943:	*Vice-Admiral* Giichi Miyata
15 Mar 1943 - 1 Nov 1943:	*Vice-Admiral* Naosaburo Irifune
1 Nov 1943 - 15 Oct 1945:	*Rear-Admiral* Chozaemon Obata
15 Oct 1945:	POSITION ABOLISHED

Commandant, Tateyama Naval Gunnery School

1 Jun 1941 - 2 Feb 1942:	*Vice-Admiral* Koso Abe
2 Feb 1942 - 15 Dec 1942:	*Rear-Admiral* Shinji Suzuki
15 Dec 1942 - 6 Jan 1943:	
6 Jan 1943 - 27 Dec 1943:	*Rear-Admiral* Mitsuharu Matsuyama
27 Dec 1943 - 25 Apr 1945:	*Vice-Admiral* Koso Abe
25 Apr 1945:	POSITION ABOLISHED

Commandant, Naval Torpedo School

2 Mar 1899 - 1 Jun 1902:	*Captain* Zentaro Uchida
1 Jun 1902 - 27 Oct 1903:	*Captain* Tokunoshin Ida
27 Oct 1903 - 12 Jan 1904:	*Rear-Admiral* Kokichi Kimura
12 Jan 1904 - 24 Jan 1905:	*Captain* Ryoichi Araki
24 Jan 1905 - 14 Mar 1906:	*Rear-Admiral* Shizuka Nakamura
14 Mar 1906 - 28 Aug 1908:	*Rear-Admiral* Kokichi Kimura
28 Aug 1908 - 25 Sep 1908:	*Vice-Admiral* Takeichiro Kitakoga
25 Sep 1908 - 25 Jul 1910:	*Admiral* Keisuke Okada
25 Jul 1910 - 1 Dec 1911:	*Admiral* Baron Kantaro Suzuki
1 Dec 1911 - 1 Dec 1914:	*Vice-Admiral* Junkichi Yajima
1 Dec 1914 - 13 Dec 1915:	*Vice-Admiral* Etsutaro Mori
13 Dec 1915 - 1 Dec 1916:	*Rear-Admiral* Tsunematsu Kondo
1 Dec 1916 - 4 Sep 1918:	*Vice-Admiral* Kesataro Kawahara
4 Sep 1918 - 1 Dec 1918:	*Vice-Admiral* Saburo Horiuchi

1 Dec 1918 - 1 Dec 1920:	*Vice-Admiral* Hanroku Saito
1 Dec 1920 - 1 Dec 1921:	*Vice-Admiral* Yasuhira Yoshikawa
1 Dec 1921 - 1 Jun 1923:	*Vice-Admiral* Shozo Kuwashima
1 Jun 1923 - 1 Dec 1924:	*Vice-Admiral* Koshiro Otani
1 Dec 1924 - 20 Oct 1925:	*Vice-Admiral* Nobutaro Iida
20 Oct 1925 - 1 Dec 1926:	*Vice-Admiral* Naotaro Nagasawa
1 Dec 1926 - 1 Dec 1927:	*Rear-Admiral* Ritsuto Takahashi
1 Dec 1927 - 12 Sep 1929:	*Vice-Admiral* Saburo Yasumi
12 Sep 1929 - 1 Dec 1930:	*Vice-Admiral* Shigeru Matsuyama
1 Dec 1930 - 1 Dec 1932:	*Vice-Admiral* Hisao Ichimura
1 Dec 1932 - 15 Nov 1934:	*Rear-Admiral* Toshiu Higurashi
15 Nov 1934 - 1 Dec 1936:	*Vice-Admiral* Jugoro Arichi
1 Dec 1936 - 10 Mar 1937:	*Rear-Admiral* Taichi Miki
10 Mar 1937 - 15 Nov 1937:	*Vice-Admiral* Boshiro Hosogaya
15 Nov 1937 - 15 Nov 1938:	*Admiral* Chuichi Nagumo
15 Nov 1938 - 15 Nov 1939:	*Vice-Admiral* Jisaburo Ozawa
15 Nov 1939 - 1 Sep 1941:	*Vice-Admiral* Ikuta Sakamoto
1 Sep 1941 - 10 Jan 1942:	*Vice-Admiral* Shiro Kawase
10 Jan 1942 - 15 Mar 1943:	*Rear-Admiral* Taichi Miki
15 Mar 1943 - 25 Nov 1943:	*Vice-Admiral* Shintaro Hashimoto
25 Nov 1943 - 10 Aug 1945:	*Vice-Admiral* Sentaro Omori
10 Aug 1945 - 20 Nov 1945:	*Vice-Admiral* Tomiji Koyanagi
20 Nov 1945:	POSITION ABOLISHED

Commandant, Naval Navigation School

1 Apr 1934 - 15 Nov 1935:	*Vice-Admiral* Tomisaburo Otagaki
15 Nov 1935 - 1 Dec 1937:	*Vice-Admiral* Shiro Koike
1 Dec 1937 - 15 Nov 1940:	*Vice-Admiral* Shinichi Moizumi
15 Nov 1940 - 1 Mar 1942:	*Vice-Admiral* Minoru Tayui
1 Mar 1942 - 10 Apr 1942:	
10 Apr 1942 - 20 Apr 1943:	*Vice-Admiral* Kasuke Abe
20 Apr 1943 - 15 Sep 1943:	*Vice-Admiral* Gunichi Mikawa
15 Sep 1943 - 19 Dec 1944:	*Rear-Admiral* Kiyoshi Hamada
19 Dec 1944 - 1 May 1945:	*Vice-Admiral* Susumu Kimura
1 May 1945:	POSITION ABOLISHED

Commandant, Naval Weather School

1 Mar 1945 - 20 Jun 1945"	*Rear-Admiral* Ikuya Seki
20 Jun 1945:	POSITION ABOLISHED

Commandant, Naval Communication School

1 Jun 1930 - 1 Dec 1930:	*Vice-Admiral* Shigeru Matsuyama
1 Dec 1930 - 1 Dec 1932:	*Vice-Admiral* Hisao Ichimura
1 Dec 1932 - 15 Nov 1933:	*Rear-Admiral* Toshiu Higurashi

15 Nov 1933 - 1 Dec 1936:	*Vice-Admiral* Satoshi Furihata
1 Dec 1936 - 28 Jul 1937:	*Vice-Admiral* Boshiro Hosogaya
8 Jul 1937 - 1 Dec 1937:	
1 Dec 1937 - 15 Nov 1939:	*Vice-Admiral* Kakusaburo Makita
15 Nov 1939 - 10 Oct 1941:	*Vice-Admiral* Gisaburo Yamaguchi
10 Oct 1941 - 10 Mar 1943:	*Vice-Admiral* Satoshi Furihata
10 Mar 1943 - 16 Sep 1943:	*Vice-Admiral* Kanji Ugaki
16 Sep 1943 - 15 Feb 1944:	*Vice-Admiral* Kiyohide Shima
15 Feb 1944 - 20 Jul 1945:	*Vice-Admiral* Chimaki Kawano
20 Jul 1945:	POSITION ABOLISHED

Commandant, Hofu Naval Communication

1 May 1943 - 15 Aug 1944:	*Rear-Admiral* Hiroshi Kurose
15 Aug 1944 - 15 Jul 1945:	*Rear-Admiral* Fujimasa Ushio
15 Jul 1945 - 1 Oct 1945:	*Vice-Admiral* Masatomi Kimura
1 Oct 1945:	POSITION ABOLISHED

Commandant, Naval Radar School

1 Sep 1944 - 20 Jun 1945:	*Rear-Admiral* Yuji Takahashi
20 Jun 1945 - 15 Jul 1945:	
15 Jul 1945 - 15 Sep 1945:	*Rear-Admiral* Fujimasa Ushio
15 Sep 1945:	POSITION ABOLISHED

Commandant, Submarine School

15 Sep 1920 - 1 Dec 1921:	*Rear-Admiral* Tetsutaro Imaizumi
1 Dec 1921 - 1 Feb 1922:	*Rear-Admiral* Teisuke Fukuda
1 Feb 1922 - 1 Dec 1922:	*Vice-Admiral* Yasuhira Yoshikawa
1 Dec 1922 - 1 Oct 1923:	*Rear-Admiral* Tamisaburo Miyaji
1 Oct 1923 - 1 Dec 1924:	*Rear-Admiral* Torai Nakajo
1 Dec 1924 - 1 Dec 1925:	*Rear-Admiral* Koichi Kishii
1 Dec 1925 - 1 Dec 1927:	*Vice-Admiral* Nobujiro Shigeoka
1 Dec 1927 - 10 Dec 1928:	*Rear-Admiral* Satoru Onomoto
10 Dec 1928 - 1 Dec 1930:	*Vice-Admiral* Shigeoki Nobeta
1 Dec 1930 - 1 Dec 1931:	*Vice-Admiral* Nobujiro Shigeoka
1 Dec 1931 - 2 Feb 1932:	*Admiral* Shigetaro Shimada
1 Feb 1932 - 28 Jun 1932:	*Rear-Admiral* Kiyoshi Kitagawa
28 Jun 1932 - 15 Nov 1933:	*Rear-Admiral* Toma Uematsu
15 Nov 1933 - 15 Nov 1934:	*Admiral* Naokuni Nomura
15 Nov 1934 - 15 Nov 1935:	*Vice-Admiral* Hoichi Wanami
15 Nov 1935 - 1 Dec 1937:	*Vice-Admiral* Hidehiko Ukita
1 Dec 1937 - 15 Nov 1938:	*Vice-Admiral* Marquis Teruhisa Komatsu
15 Nov 1938 - 15 Nov 1939:	*Vice-Admiral* Yuzuru Kumaoka
15 Nov 1939 - 5 Jul 1941:	*Vice-Admiral* Sanjiro Takasu

5 Jul 1941 - 15 Sep 1943:	*Vice-Admiral* Shuichiro Higuchi
15 Sep 1943 - 23 Aug 1944:	*Vice-Admiral* Shigeaki Yamazaki
23 Aug 1944 - 1 May 1945:	*Vice-Admiral* Marquis Tadashige Daigo
1 May 1945 - 15 Sep 1945:	*Vice-Admiral* Hisashi Ichioka
15 Sep 1945:	POSITION ABOLISHED

Commandant, Anti-Submarine School

1 Apr 1941 - 5 Jul 1941:	*Vice-Admiral* Rokuzo Sugiyama
5 Jul 1941 - 20 Oct 1941:	
20 Oct 1941 - 20 Jan 1944:	*Rear-Admiral* Namizo Sato
20 Jan 1944 - 1 May 1945:	*Rear-Admiral* Shunsaku Nabeshima
1 May 1945 - 1 Jun 1945:	*Vice-Admiral* Chimaki Kawano
1 Jun 1945 - 15 Jul 1945:	*Vice-Admiral* Masatomi Kimura
15 Jul 1945:	POSITION ABOLISHED

Commandant, Naval Engineering School

20 Apr 1907 - 10 Dec 1907:	*Rear-Admiral (Engineer)* Teiichi Hirabe
10 Dec 1907 - 21 Feb 1908:	*Rear-Admiral* Tsurunosuke Yamazaki
21 Feb 1908 - 1 Dec 1911:	*Rear-Admiral (Engineer)* Shigeji Ito
1 Dec 1911 - 21 Jan 1913:	*Vice-Admiral* Iwao Kamo
21 Jan 1913 - 25 Jun 1928:	POSITION ABOLISHED
25 Jun 1928 - 10 Dec 1928:	*Vice-Admiral* Nobuta Kishimoto
10 Dec 1928 - 15 Nov 1932:	*Vice-Admiral* Toyotaro Murata
15 Nov 1932 - 15 Nov 1934:	*Vice-Admiral* Tokusaburo Ono
15 Nov 1934 - 1 Dec 1936:	*Vice-Admiral* Hiroshi Kawahara
1 Dec 1936 - 15 Nov 1939:	*Vice-Admiral* Hikokichi Asakuma
15 Nov 1939 - 10 Sep 1941:	*Vice-Admiral* Shizuka Gosho
10 Sep 1941 - 20 Jun 1943:	*Vice-Admiral* Hisatake Suzuki
20 Jun 1943 - 10 May 1944:	*Vice-Admiral* Isao Akasaka
10 May 1944 - 26 Jun 1944:	
26 Jun 1944 - 15 Jan 1945:	*Vice-Admiral* Kanichi Morita
15 Jan 1945 - 20 May 1945:	*Rear-Admiral* Sakae Terayama
20 May 1945:	POSITION ABOLISHED

Commandant, Dainan Naval Engineering School

1 Mar 1945 - 25 Aug 1945:	*Vice-Admiral* Tomojiro Yamanaka
25 Aug 1945 - 5 Nov 1945:	*Rear-Admiral* Masa Kitagawa
5 Nov 1945:	POSITION ABOLISHED

Commandant, Naval Construction School

1 Apr 1941 - 5 Nov 1941:	*Vice-Admiral* Tokutaro Wazumi
5 Nov 1941 - 15 Dec 1941:	*Vice-Admiral* Hisatake Suzuki
15 Dec 1941 - 15 Mar 1943:	*Vice-Admiral* Hikokichi Asakuma
15 Mar 1943 - 15 Feb 1944:	*Vice-Admiral* Tokutaro Wazumi

15 Feb 1944 - 15 Oct 1945:   *Rear-Admiral* Taizo Mihara
15 Oct 1945:   POSITION ABOLISHED

Commandant, Numazu Naval Construction School
1 Jun 1944 - 1 Oct 1944:   *Rear-Admiral* Masao Aoki
1 Oct 1944 - 15 Jul 1945:   *Rear-Admiral* Masayoshi Umebayashi
15 Jul 1945:   POSITION ABOLISHED

Commandant, Navy Medical School
22 Dec 1899 - 2 Mar 1900:   *Vice-Admiral (Surgeon)* Sosuke Kimura
2 Mar 1900 - 20 May 1900:   *General (Surgeon)* Teijun Yoshida
20 May 1900 - 15 Apr 1901:   *Vice-Admiral (Surgeon)* Sosuke Kimura
15 Apr 1901 - 27 May 1902:   *Rear-Admiral (Surgeon)* Kankai Totsuka
27 May 1902 - 9 Aug 1902:   *Rear-Admiral (Surgeon)* Shikakichi Tsuruta
9 Aug 1902 - 4 Jan 1906:   *Vice-Admiral (Surgeon)* Sosuke Kimura
4 Jan 1906 - 13 Dec 1915:   *Vice-Admiral (Surgeon)* Tadao Honda
13 Dec 1915 - 1 Dec 1917:   *Vice-Admiral (Surgeon)* Tatsusaburo Yabe
1 Dec 1917 - 1 Dec 1919:   *Vice-Admiral (Surgeon)* Yuzo Suzuki
1 Dec 1919 - 1 Dec 1922:   *Vice-Admiral (Surgeon)* Isao Nishi
1 Dec 1922 - 1 Dec 1924:   *Vice-Admiral (Surgeon)* Kannosuke Suzuki
1 Dec 1924 - 1 Dec 1925:   *Vice-Admiral (Surgeon)* Ryoshichiro Amamiya
1 Dec 1925 - 30 Nov 1929:   *Vice-Admiral (Surgeon)* Ryu Ogawa
30 Nov 1929 - 25 Feb 1932:   *Vice-Admiral (Surgeon)* Naka Koda
25 Feb 1932 - 15 Nov 1934:   *Vice-Admiral (Surgeon)* Shinichiro Takasugi
15 Nov 1934 - 1 Dec 1937:   *Vice-Admiral (Surgeon)* Yoshihiro Mukoyama
1 Dec 1937 - 15 Nov 1939:   *Vice-Admiral (Surgeon)* Asazo Tanaka
15 Nov 1939 - 15 Oct 1941:   *Vice-Admiral (Surgeon)* Higotaro Tanaka
15 Oct 1941 - 25 Oct 1943:   *Vice-Admiral (Surgeon)* Nobuaki Hori
25 Oct 1943 - 1 Nov 1945:   *Vice-Admiral (Surgeon)* Yoshiharu Kanbayashi
1 Nov 1945:   POSITION ABOLISHED

Commandant, Kamo Naval Sanitary School
1 Apr 1945 - 1 Oct 1945:   *Vice-Admiral (Surgeon)* Yutaka Tanabe
1 Oct 1945:   POSITION ABOLISHED

Commandant, Totsuka Naval Sanitary School
1 Apr 1945 - 11 Sep 1945:   *Rear-Admiral (Surgeon)* Izumi Kanai
11 Sep 1945:   POSITION ABOLISHED

MAJOR SHIPS OF THE IMPERIAL JAPANESE NAVY, 1900 - 1945
AIRCRAFT CARRIERS

Aircraft carrier *"Akagi"*
Laid down in 1920, originally intended as a battlecruiser. Converted to an aircraft carrier in 1923 and launched in 1925. Badly damaged by air attacks at the battle of Midway, and scuttled on 5 June 1942

Army carrier *"Akitsu-maru"*
Laid down in 1939 and launched in 1941. Originally built as a liner, and converted to an escort aircraft carrier. Sunk by a US submarine on 15 November 1944.

Unryu class Aircraft carrier *"Amagi"*
Laid down in 1942 and launched in 1943. Sunk by air attack at Kure Naval Base on July 27 1945. Refloated and scrapped in 1946.

Merchant carrier *"Chigusa-maru"*
Laid down and launched in 1944. Never completed, but survived the war and refitted as a merchant ship.

Chitose class Aircraft carrier *"Chitose"*
Laid down in 1934 and launched in 1936 as a seaplane tender. Converted as a light aircraft carrier in 1943. Lost in action at the Battle of Leyte Gulf on 25 October 1944.

Chitose class Aircraft carrier *"Chiyoda"*
Laid down in 1934 and launched in 1936 as a seaplane tender. Converted as a light aircraft carrier in 1943. Lost in action at the Battle of Leyte Gulf on 25 October 1944.

Taiyo class Aircraft carrier *"Chuyo"*
Laid down in 1938 and launched in 1939. Torpedoed and sunk by a USN submarine on 4 December 1943

Aircraft carrier *"Hiryu"*
Laid down in 1937 and launched in 1939. Badly damaged by air attacks at the battle of Midway, and scuttled on 5 June 1942.

Junyo class Aircraft carrier *"Hiyo"*
Laid down in 1939 and launched in 1941. Sunk by torpedo bombers on 21 June 1944, during the Battle of the Philippine Sea.

Hosho class Aircraft carrier *"Hosho"*
Laid down in 1919 and launched in 1921. Decommissioned in 1946, and scrapped the following year.

Aircraft carrier *"Ibuki"*
Laid down in 1942 and launched in 1943 as a heavy cruiser. Work began in 1944 for conversion to a light aircraft carrier, but was never completed and never entered into service. Scrapped in 1947.

Junyo class Aircraft carrier *"Junyo"*
Laid down in 1939 and launched in 1941. Damaged by torpedoes in December 1944, but survived the war, and was scrapped in 1947.

Aircraft carrier *"Kaga"*
Laid down in 1920 and launched in 1921 as a battleship. Converted to an aircraft carrier during 1922 - 1923. Crippled by US air attacks at the battle of Midway on 4 June 1942 and scuttled

Aircraft carrier *"Kaiyo"*
Launched in 1938 as a liner, converted to an escort carrier in 1943. Damaged by bombs in July 1945 and beached to prevent sinking. Refloated and scrapped in 1946.

Unryu class Aircraft carrier *"Katsuragi"*
Laid down in 1942 and launched in 1943. Survived the war and was decommissioned in April 1946 and scrapped at the end of that year.

Army carrier *"Kumano-maru"*
Laid down in 1943 and launched in 1945. Survived the war, and after 1947 converted to a merchant ship.

Army carrier *"Nigitsu-maru"*
Laid down in 1941 and launched in 1942. Originally built as a liner, and converted to an escort aircraft carrier. Torpedoed and sunk on 12 January 1944.

Merchant carrier *"Otakisan-maru"*
Laid down in 1944 and launched in 1945. While still incomplete, hit a mine and sunk on 25 August 1945. Hulk scrapped in 1948.

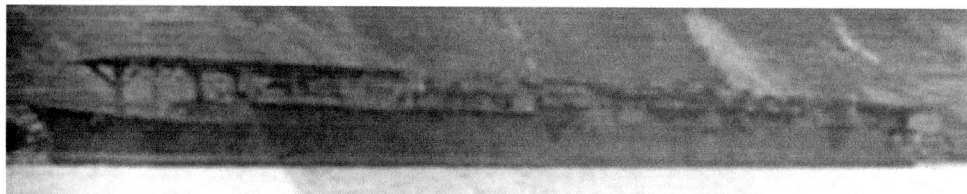

Aircraft carrier *"Ryuho"*
Laid down in 1929 and launched in 1933 as a submarine tender. Converted to a light aircraft carrier in 1942. Badly damaged by bombs off Kure in March 1945 and left unrepaired. Scrapped in 1946.

Aircraft carrier *"Ryujo"*
Laid down in 1929 and launched in 1931. Sunk by dive bombers and torpedo bombers on 24 August 1942, off Guadalcanal.

Merchant carrier *"Shimane-maru"*
Laid down and launched in 1944. Sunk in an air attack on 24 July 1945, in the port of Takamatsu. Hulk scrapped in 1948.

Aircraft carrier *"Shinano"*
Laid down in 1940, originally designed as a battleship. Refitted as an aircraft carrier and launched in 1944. Sunk by a US submarine on 29 November 1944.

Aircraft carrier *"Shinyo"*
Built in Germany in 1934 as an ocean liner. Trapped in Japan at the outbreak of the war, purchased by Japan and converted to an escort carrier. Sunk by a US submarine in the Yellow Sea, on 17 November 1944

Zuiho class Aircraft carrier *"Shoho"*
Laid down in 1934 as a submarine tender and converted to an aircraft carrier during 1940 - 1942. Sunk by air attack in the Coral Sea on 7 May 1942.

Shokaku class Aircraft carrier *"Shokaku"*
Laid down in 1937 and launched in 1939. Torpedoed and sunk on 19 June 1944 in the Battle of the Philippine Sea.

Aircraft carrier *"Soryu"*
Laid down in 1934 and launched in 1935. Crippled by US air attacks at the battle of Midway on 4 June 1942 and scuttled.

Aircraft carrier *"Taiho"*
Laid down in 1941 and launched in 1943. Sunk in the Battle of the Philippine Sea on 19 June 1944.

Taiyo class Aircraft carrier *"Taiyo"*
Laid down and launched in 1940. Sunk by a USN submarine off Cape Bolinao, Luzon on 18 August 1944.

Unryu class Aircraft carrier *"Unryu"*
Laid down in 1942 and launched in 1943. Torpedoed and sunk by a US submarine on December 19, 1944 in the East China Sea.

Taiyo class Aircraft carrier *"Unyo"*
Laid down in 1938 and launched in 1939. Sunk (torpedoed) by a USN submarine on 17 September 1944

Merchant carrier *"Yamashiro-maru"*
Laid down and launched in 1944. Sunk in an air attack, in Yokohama, on 17 February 1945.

Zuiho class Aircraft carrier *"Zuiho"*
Laid down as an oiler in 1934 and converted to an aircraft carrier in 1940. Sunk by air attack in the Battle of Cape Engaño on 25 October 1944.

Shokaku class Aircraft carrier *"Zuikaku"*
Laid down in 1938 and launched in 1939. Sunk by air attack in the Battle of Cape Engaño on 25 October 1944.

BATTLESHIPS/BATTLECRUISERS

Satsuma class Battleship *"Aki"*
Laid down in 1906 and launched 1907. Decommissioned under the terms of the Washington Naval Treaty in 1923 and sunk by gunfire in 1924, being used as a target ship.

Battleship *"Asahi"*
Laid down in 1897 and launched in 1899. Reclassed as a 1st-class Coastal defence ship in 1921 and disarmed in 1922, but retained as a training ship. Served at various times as a submarine tender, floating barracks, transport, and repair vessel. Lost in action (torpedoed) on 26 May 1942.

Ironclad *"Chinen"*
Laid down in Chinese Navy in 1881 and launched 1882. Captured by the Imperial Japanese Navy in 1895 and renamed. Retired in 1911 and broken up in 1912.

Fuji class Battleship *"Fuji"*
Laid down in 1894 and launched in 1896. Disarmed and stricken from the navy list in 1922, but retained as a floating barracks. Retired in 1945 and broken up in 1948.

Ironclad *"Fuso"*
Laid down in 1875 and launched in 1877. Sank after a collision in 1897 but refloated in 1898 and reclassed as a Second-Class Battleship. Reclassed as a 2nd-Class Coastal Defense Vessel in 1905. Retired in 1908 and broken up for scrap in 1910.

Fuso class Battleship *"Fuso"*
Laid down in 1912 and launched 1914. Sunk in action, 25 October 1944.

Kongo class Battlecruiser *"Haruna"*
Laid down in 1912 and launched 1913. Sunk by bombers at Kure Naval Base, on 28 July 1945. Later raised and scrapped.

Shikishima class Battleship *"Hatsuse"*
Laid down in 1897 and launched in 1898. Lost in action (mined) on 15 May 1904.

Ironclad *"Heien"*
Laid down in Chinese Navy in 1883 and launched in 1890. Captured by the Imperial Japanese Navy in 1895 and renamed. Lost in action (mined) on 18 September 1904.

Kongo class Ironclad *"Hiei"*
Laid down in 1875 and launched in 1877. Retired in 1911.

Kongo class Battlecruiser *"Hiei"*
Laid down in 1911 and launched 1912. Hit by shells and torpedoes during the Battle of Guadalcanal, and sank on 13 November 1942.

Battleship *"Hizen"*
Laid down by the Imperial Russian Navy in 1899 and launched in 1900. Sunk in action in 1904, salvaged by the Japanese Navy in 1905 and renamed. Decommissioned in 1923 and sunk as a target ship on 20 September, 1924.

Ise class Battleship *"Hyuga"*
Laid down in 1915 and launched 1917. Badly damaged by bombers, the vessel was run aground by her crew to prevent sinking, on 27 July 1945. Scrapped during 1946 - 1947.

Ibuki class Battlecruiser *"Ibuki"*
Laid down and launched in 1907. Decommissioned and scrapped under the terms of the Washington Naval Treaty in 1923.

Battleship *"Iki"*
Laid down by the Imperial Russian Navy in 1895 and launched in 1898. Captured by the Japanese Navy in 1905 and renamed. Reclassed as a First-class Coastal Defense Vessel and used as a gunnery training vessel. Decommissioned and sunk as a target ship on 3 October, 1915.

Tsukuba class Battlecruiser *"Ikoma"*
Laid down in 1905 and launched in 1906. Decommissioned in 1923, and broken up the following year.

Ise class Battleship *"Ise"*
Laid down in 1915 and launched 1916. Sunk by bombers off Kure, on 28 July 1945. Scrapped during 1946 - 1947.

Battleship *"Iwami"*
Laid down by the Imperial Russian Navy in 1900 and launched in 1902. Captured by the Japanese Navy in 1905 and renamed. Decommissioned in 1923 and sunk as a target ship on 10 July, 1924.

Kashima class Battleship *"Kashima"*
Laid down in 1904 and launched 1905. Decommissioned under the terms of the Washington Naval Treaty in 1923 and scrapped the following year.

Kashima class Battleship *"Katori"*
Laid down in 1904 and launched 1905. Decommissioned under the terms of the Washington Naval Treaty in 1923 and scrapped the following year.

Settsu class Battleship *"Kawachi"*
Laid down in 1909 and launched 1910. Exploded and sank while anchored in Tokuyama Bay, on 12 July 1918. The hulk was later raised and scrapped.

Kongo class Battlecruiser *"Kirishima"*
Laid down in 1912 and launched 1913. Badly damaged by shelling from USN vessels during the Battle of Guadalcanal, and scuttled on 15 November 1942.

Kongo class Ironclad *"Kongo"*
Laid down in 1875 and launched in 1877. Retired in 1909.

Kongo class Battlecruiser *"Kongo"*
Laid down in 1911 and launched 1912. Torpedoed and sunk in the Formosa Strait, on 21 November 1944.

Ibuki class Battlecruiser *"Kurama"*
Laid down in 1905 and launched 1907. Decommissioned and scrapped under the terms of the Washington Naval Treaty in 1923.

Battleship *"Mikasa"*
Laid down in 1899 and launched in 1900. Sunk following an accidental fire and magazine eAircraft carrierplosion in 1905, but refloated in 1906. Subsequently reclassed as a 2nd class battleship, then a 3rd class battleship, and finally a 1st-class Coastal defence ship in 1921. Decomissioned in 1923, and in 1925 designated a memorial. Restored in 1961, and still on display in Yokosuka Harbor today.

Battleship *"Mishima"*
Laid down by the Imperial Russian Navy in 1892 and launched in 1894. Captured by the Japanese Navy in 1905 and renamed. Reclassed as a submarine tender in 1921, and decommissioned in 1935. Sunk as a target ship in September 1936.

Yamato class Battleship *"Musashi"*
Laid down in 1938 and launched 1940. Sank on 24 October 1944 following 17 bomb and 19 torpedo hits.

Nagato class Battleship *"Mutsu"*
Laid down in 1918 and launched 1920. Sunk on 8 June 1943 following an ammunition magazine explosion.

Nagato class Battleship *"Nagato"*
Laid down in 1917 and launched 1919. Survived the war, but was sunk at Bikini Atoll during an atomic bomb test on 25 July 1946.

Battleship *"Okinoshima"*
Laid down by the Imperial Russian Navy in 1894 and launched in 1896. Captured by the Japanese Navy in 1905 and renamed. Reclassed as a submarine tender in 1921, and decommissioned in 1922. Sold as scrap in 1924 and preserved as a memorial ship. Scrapped in 1939.

Battleship *"Sagami"*
Laid down by the Imperial Russian Navy in 1895 and launched in 1898. Captured by the Japanese Navy in 1905 and renamed. In 1912 reclassed as a 1st-class Coastal Defense Vessel. Returned to the Russian Navy in 1916, and sunk by German mines on 4 January, 1917.

Satsuma class Battleship *"**Satsuma**"*
Laid down in 1905 and launched 1906. Decommissioned under the terms of the Washington Naval Treaty in 1923 and sunk by gunfire the following year, being used as a target ship.

Settsu class Battleship *"**Settsu**"*
Laid down in 1909 and launched 1911. Disarmed under the terms of the Washington Naval Treaty in 1922 and stricken from the Navy list in 1924. Converted to a target ship in 1924, and used as such until 24 July 1945, when it was sunk by US bombers at Etajima. The hulk was raised and scrapped in 1947.

Shikishima class Battleship *"**Shikishima**"*
Laid down in 1897 and launched in 1898. Reclassed in 1921 as a 1st-class Coastal Defense Vessel, and disarmed in 1922, but retained as a training vessel for submarine crews. Stricken from the navy list in 1926, but used as a floating barracks and training center until 1945. Broken up in 1948.

Battleship *"Suwo"*
Laid down by the Imperial Russian Navy in 1898 and launched in 1900. Sunk in action in 1904, salvaged by the Japanese Navy in 1905 and renamed. Reclassed as a 1st-class Coastal Defense Vessel in 1908. Disarmed in 1922, and broken up for scrap in 1946.

Battleship *"Tango"*
Laid down by the Imperial Russian Navy in 1892 and launched in 1894. Scuttled in 1904, salvaged by the Japanese Navy in 1905 and renamed. In 1912 reclassed as a 1st-class Coastal Defense Vessel. Returned to the Russian Navy in 1916, and captured by the British during the Russian Cvil War. Broken up in 1923.

Tsukuba class Battlecruiser *"Tsukuba"*
Laid down and launched in 1905, completed in 1907. Exploded and sank in the port of Yokosuka on 14 January, 1917.

Fuso class Battleship *"Yamashiro"*
Laid down in 1913 and launched 1915. Sunk in action, 25 October 1944.

Yamato class Battleship *"Yamato"*
Laid down in 1937 and launched 1940. Exploded and sank on 7 April 1945, having been hit by 10 torpedoes and 7 bombs.

Fuji class Battleship *"Yashima"*
Laid down in 1894 and launched in 1896. Lost in action (mined) on 15 May 1904.

CRUISERS

Nagara class Light cruiser *"Abukuma"*
Laid down in 1921 and launched in 1923. Sunk by US bombers on 26 October 1944, in the Mindanao Sea.

Armoured cruiser *"Adzuma"*
Laid down in 1898 and launched in 1899. Reclassified in 1921 as a 1st class Coastal Defense Vessel, and as a practice auxiliary vessel in 1942. Removed from the Navy list in 1944, and broken up for scrap the following year.

Agano class Light cruiser *"Agano"*
Laid down in 1940 and launched in 1941. Sunk by a US submarine off Truk, on 15 February 1944.

Suma class Protected cruiser *"Akashi"*
Laid down in 1894 and launched in 1897. Reclassified in 1921 as a 2nd class Coastal Defense Vessel and removed from the Navy list in 1928. Sunk as a target for dive bombers on 3 August 1930.

Protected cruiser *"Akitsushima"*
Laid down in 1890 and launched in 1892. Reclassified in 1912 as a 2nd class Coastal Defense Vessel, and redesignated a training vessel in 1921. Scrapped in 1927.

Aoba class Heavy cruiser *"Aoba"*
Laid down in 1924 and launched in 1926. Damaged by US torpedoes and bombs, reclassified as a reserve vessel in December 1944, and as a floating anti-aircraft battery in April 1945. Sunk by US bombers in Kure harbor, on 28 July 1945.

Asama class Armoured cruiser *"Asama"*
Laid down in 1896 and launched in 1898. Reclassified in 1921 as a 1st class Coastal Defense Vessel, and as a Coastal Defense Vessel in 1931. Redesignated as an auxiliary training vessel in 1942, it survived World War II and was scrapped in 1947.

Myoko class Heavy cruiser *"Ashigara"*
Laid down in 1925 and launched in 1928. Sunk by British submarines on June 8 1945, south of Singapore.

Armoured Cruiser *"Aso"*
Laid down in 1900 and launched in 1903 as part of the Imperial Russian Navy. Sunk by Japanese ships on 8 December 1904, but raised after the Russo-Japanese War and claimed by the Imperial Japanese Navy as a war prize. Repaired, recommissioned and renamed, the vessel was later (1920) reclassified as a minelayer. Removed from the Navy list in 1931, and sunk as target for shells, torpedoes and bombs, on 4 August 1932.

Takao class Heavy cruiser *"**Atago**"*
Laid down in 1927 and launched in 1930. Torpedoed by a US submarine and sunk on 23 October 1944, during the Battle of the Palawan Passage.

Chikuma class Protected cruiser *"**Chikuma**"*
Laid down in 1909 and launched in 1911. After 1924, used as a training ship until being removed from the Navy list in 1931. Sunk as a target ship in 1935.

Tone class Heavy cruiser *"**Chikuma**"*
Laid down in 1935 and launched in 1938. Sunk by US torpedo bombers during Battle of Leyte Gulf, on 25 October 1944.

Chitose class Armoured cruiser *"Chitose"*
Laid down in 1897 and launched in 1898. Reclassified in 1921 as a 2nd class Coastal Defense Vessel, and removed from the Navy list in 1928. Scuttled off Kochi, on 19 July 1931.

Armoured cruiser *"Chiyoda"*
Laid down in 1888 and launched in 1890. Reclassified in 1912 as a 2nd class Coastal Defense Vessel, and in 1921 downgraded to a torpedo depot ship. Decommissioned in 1927 and used as target practice, sinking on 5 August 1927.

Takao class Heavy cruiser *"Chokai"*
Laid down in 1928 and launched in 1931. Badly damaged by torpedoes and bombs during the Battle of Leyte Gulf, and scuttled on 25 October 1944.

Furutaka class Heavy cruiser *"**Furutaka**"*
Laid down in 1922 and launched in 1925. Sunk by US warships on 12 October 1942, during the Battle of Cape Esperance.

Myoko class Heavy cruiser *"**Haguro**"*
Laid down in 1925 and launched in 1928. Sunk by gunfire and torpedoes from British warships on 16 June 1945, in the Indian Ocean.

Matsushima class Protected cruiser *"**Hashidate**"*
Laid down in 1888 and launched in 1891. Reclassified in 1912 as a 2nd class Coastal Defense Vessel, and removed from the Navy list in 1922. Scrapped in 1927.

Chikuma class Protected cruiser *"Hirado"*
Laid down in 1910 and launched in 1911. Transferred to the reserve in 1933, and removed from the Navy list in 1940. The hulk was scrapped in 1947.

Light Cruiser *"Ioshima"*
Laid down in 1931 and launched in 1935 as part of the Chinese Navy. Sunk by Japanese bombers in September 1937, and salvaged in 1938 and claimed by the Imperial Japanese Navy as a war prize. Refitted as a cruiser in 1944, and sunk by a US submarine on 19 September 1944.

Nagara class Light cruiser *"Isuzu"*
Laid down in 1920 and launched in 1921. Torpedoed by US submarines in the Java Sea, and sank on 7 April 1945.

Matsushima class Protected cruiser *"Itsukushima"*
Laid down in 1888 and launched in 1889. Reclassified in 1912 as a 2nd class Coastal Defense Vessel, and later used as a submarine tender. Reclassified as a training hulk in 1920, and scrapped in 1926.

Izumo class Armoured cruiser *"Iwate"*
Laid down in 1898 and launched in 1900. Reclassified in 1921 as a 1st class Coastal Defense Vessel, but re-armed and reactivated as a 1st class cruiser in 1942. Sunk in Kure harbor, by US bombers, on 26 July 1945. Raised and scrapped in 1947.

Protected cruiser *"Izumi"*
Laid down in 1881 and launched in 1883. Downgraded from a 2nd class to a 3rd class Protected Cruiser in 1898. Scrapped in 1912.

Izumo class Armoured cruiser *"Izumo"*
Laid down in 1898 and launched in 1899. Reclassified in 1921 as a Coastal Defense Vessel, but re-armed and reactivated as a 1st class cruiser in 1942. Sunk in Kure harbor, by US bombers, on 24 July 1945. The hulk was raised and broken up in 1947.

Sendai class Light cruiser *"Jintsu"*
Laid down in 1922 and launched in 1923. Sunk in the Solomon Islands on 13 July 1943, after being shelled by Allied cruisers.

Furutaka class Heavy cruiser *"Kako"*
Laid down in 1922 and launched in 1925. Sunk by a US submarine off Savo Island, on 10 August 1942.

Chitose class Armoured cruiser *"Kasagi"*
Laid down in 1897 and launched in 1898. Ran aground and wrecked in the Tsugaru Strait, on 10 August 1916. Struck from the Navy list in November of the same year.

Katori class Training cruiser *"Kashii"*
Laid down in 1940 and launched in 1941. Sunk by torpedoes and bombs in the South China Sea, on 12 January 1945.

Katori class Training cruiser *"Kashima"*
Laid down in 1938 and launched in 1939. Survived the war, and was removed from the Navy list on 5 October 1945. Used as a troop transport vessel in 1946, and scrapped in 1947.

Kasuga class Armoured cruiser *"Kasuga"*
Laid down and launched in 1902. Reclassified in 1921 as a 1st class Coastal Defense Vessel, and later used as a training vessel. Survived until near the end of World War II, when it was sunk at Yokosuka on 18 July 1945 in an air raid.

Katori class Training cruiser *"Katori"*
Laid down in 1938 and launched in 1939. Sunk with all hands by naval gunfire on 17 February 1944, off Truk.

Nagara class Light cruiser *"Kinu"*
Laid down in 1921 and launched in 1922. Sunk by US bombers on 26 October 1944, southwest of Luzon (Philippines).

Aoba class Heavy cruiser *"Kinugasa"*
Laid down in 1924 and launched in 1926. Sunk by US bombers during the Battle of Guadalcanal on 13 November 1942.

Kuma class Light cruiser *"Kiso"*
Laid down in 1919 and launched in 1920. Badly damaged by US carrier-based bombers, and sank of Cavite (Philippines) on 20 October 1944. Salvaged in 1955 and broken up for scrap.

Kuma class Light cruiser *"Kitakami"*
Laid down in 1919 and launched in 1920. Converted in 1942 into a fast troop transport, and in 1944 as a human torpedo carrier. Survived the war, and was scrapped during 1946 - 1947.

Kuma class Light cruiser *"Kuma"*
Laid down in 1918 and launched in 1919. Sunk off Penang by a British submarine, on 11 January 1944.

Mogami class Heavy cruiser *"Kumano"*
Laid down in 1934 and launched in 1936. Sunk by US bombers at Santa Cruz harbor (Philippines) while undergoing repair for torpedo damage, on 25 November 1944.

Matsushima class Protected cruiser *"Matsushima"*
Laid down in 1888 and launched in 1890. Sank on 30 April 1908, off Taiwan, due to an accidental explosion in an ammunition locker.

Takao class Heavy cruiser *"Maya"*
Laid down in 1928 and launched in 1930. Sunk by a US submarine on 23 October 1944, during the Battle of Leyte Gulf.

Mogami class Heavy cruiser *"Mikuma"*
Laid down in 1931 and launched in 1934. Sunk by US dive bombers in theBattle of Midway, on 6 June 1942.

Yodo class Light Cruiser *"Mogami"*
Laid down in 1907 and launched in 1908. Reclassified as a 1st class gunboat in 1912, and scrapped in 1928.

Mogami class Heavy cruiser *"Mogami"*
Laid down in 1931 and launched in 1934. Damaged by torpedoes and bombs on several occasions during 1942 - 1944 and repaired/refitted each time. Crippled by US torpedo bombers and scuttled on 25 October 1944 in the Surigao Strait.

Myoko class Heavy cruiser *"Myoko"*
Laid down in 1924 and launched in 1927. Damaged by a submarine-fired torpedo in December 1944 and reclassified as a floating anti-aircraft battery. Survived the remainder of the war, and was scuttled on 8 June 1946.

Myoko class Heavy cruiser *"Nachi"*
Laid down in 1924 and launched in 1927. Sunk by US bombers in Manila Bay, on 5 November 1944.

Nagara class Light cruiser *"Nagara"*
Laid down in 1920 and launched in 1921. Torpedoed in the East China Sea by a US submarine, and sank on 7 August 1944.

Sendai class Light cruiser *"Naka"*
Laid down in 1922 and launched in 1925. Sunk by US torpedo bombers on 18 February 1944, off the island of Truk.

Naniwa class Protected cruiser *"Naniwa"*
Laid down in 1884 and launched in 1885. Ran aground and sank on 26 July 1912, in the Kurile Islands.

Nagara class Light cruiser *"Natori"*
Laid down in 1920 and launched in 1922. Sunk by a US submarine in the Philippines Sea on 18 August 1944.

Tsushima class Protected cruiser *"Niitaka"*
Laid down and launched in 1902. Reclassified in 1921 as a 2nd class Coastal Defense Vessel. Ran aground and sank in a typhoon on 26 August 1922 off Sakhalin Island.

Kasuga class Armoured cruiser *"**Nisshin**"*
Laid down in 1902 and launched in 1903. Partially disarmed in 1923 in accordance with the terms of the Washington Naval Treaty, and used as a transport and training vessel. Scuttled in 1936, but later raised and used for gunnery target practice, sinking on 18 January 1942.

Agano class Light cruiser *"**Noshiro**"*
Laid down in 1941 and launched in 1942. Sunk by US dive bombers during fighting in the Philippines, on 26 October 1944.

Kuma class Light cruiser *"**Oi**"*
Laid down in 1919 and launched in 1920. Converted in 1942 into a fast troop transport. Torpedoed by a US submarine and sank in the South China Sea on 19 July 1944.

Protected cruiser *"Otowa"*
Laid down and launched in 1903. Ran aground in July 1917, and despite efforts to save the ship, broke apart and sank on 10 August 1917.

Oyodo class Light cruiser *"Oyodo"*
Laid down in 1941 and launched in 1942. Sunk by US torpedo bombers at Kure Naval Base, on 28 July 1945. Raised in 1947, and broken up for scrap the following year.

Protected cruiser *"Saien"*
Laid down in 1880 and launched in 1883 as the Chinese vessel *'Jiyuan"*. Captured by the Imperial Japanese Navy during the Battle of Weihaiwei in 1895. Reclassified as a 3rd class Coastal Defense Vessel in November 1904 and sank off Port Arthur on 30 November 1904, after hitting a mine.

Agano class Light cruiser *"Sakawa"*
Laid down in 1942 and launched in 1944. The vessel never saw action and was removed from the Navy list on 5 October 1945. Sunk in an atomic bomb test at Bikini Atoll, on 2 July 1946.

Sendai class Light cruiser *"Sendai"*
Laid down in 1922 and launched in 1923. Sunk by US warships in the Java Sea, on 3 November 1943.

Light Cruiser *"Soya"*
Laid down in 1898 and launched in 1899 as part of the Imperial Russian Navy. Badly damaged during the Russo-Japanese War, the vessel was scuttled on 9 February 1904. Raised after the war and claimed by the Imperial Japanese Navy as a war prize. Repaired, recommissioned and renamed, and used primarily as a training ship. The vessel was returned to the Russian Navy in 1916.

Suma class Protected cruiser *"Suma"*
Laid down in 1892 and launched in 1895. Reclassified in 1921 as a 2nd class Coastal Defense Vessel and removed from the Navy list in 1923. Broken up for scrap in 1928.

Protected cruiser *"Suzuya"*
Laid down in 1898 and launched in 1900 as part of the Imperial Russian Navy. Badly damaged during the Russo-Japanese War, the vessel was scuttled in 1904. Raised after the war and claimed by the Imperial Japanese Navy as a war prize, repaired, recommissioned and renamed. Reclassified in 1912 as a 2nd class Coastal Defense Vessel, and scrapped the following year.

Mogami class Heavy cruiser *"Suzuya"*
Laid down in 1933 and launched in 1934. Sunk by US torpedo bombers during the Battle of Leyte Gulf, on 25 October 1944.

Naniwa class Protected cruiser *"Takachiho"*
Laid down in 1884 and launched in 1885. Torpedoed and sunk by a German torpedo boat in Chinese waters, on 14 October 1914 during the Battle of Tsingtao

Takao class Heavy cruiser *"Takao"*
Laid down in 1927 and launched in 1930. Badly damaged by torpedoes during the Battle of Leyte Gulf in October 1944, and reclassified as a floating anti-aircraft battery at Johor, Singapore. Partially destroyed by limpet mines in July 1945, and surrendered to the British in September 1945. Sunk as a target ship on 19 October 1946.

Protected cruiser *"Takasago"*
Laid down in 1896 and launched in 1897. Struck a mine and sank off Port Arthur, during the Russo-Japanese War, on 13 December 1904.

Kuma class Light cruiser *"Tama"*
Laid down in 1918 and launched in 1920. Sunk with all hands on 20 October 1944, after being torpedoed by a US submarine off Luzon.

Tenryu class Light cruiser *"Tatsuta"*
Laid down in 1917 and launched in 1918. Sunk en route to Saipan by a US submarine, on 13 March 1944.

Tenryu class Light cruiser *"Tenryu"*
Laid down in 1917 and launched in 1918. Sunk off New Guinea by a US submarine, on 19 December 1942

Asama class Armoured cruiser *"Tokiwa"*
Laid down and launched in 1898. Reclassified in 1921 as a 1st class Coastal Defense Vessel, then converted to a minelayer in 1922. Badly damaged by a US air attack whilst at harbor in Ominato port, on 9 August 1945, and beached to prevent sinking. Scrapped after the war.

Heavy Cruiser *"Tone"*
Laid down in 1905 and launched in 1907. Removed from the Navy list in 1931, and sunk as a target ship for bombers on 30 April 1933.

Tone class Heavy cruiser *"Tone"*
Laid down in 1934 and launched in 1937. Sunk by US bombers at Kure Naval Base, on 24 July 1945. Raised and scrapped during 1947 - 1948.

Protected cruiser *"Tsugaru"*
Laid down in 1895 and launched in 1899 as part of the Imperial Russian Navy. Sunk by Japanese artillery on 8 December 1904. Raised after the war and claimed by the Imperial Japanese Navy as a war prize, repaired, recommissioned and renamed. Reclassified as a minelayer in 1920, but removed from the Navy list in 1922. Scuttled on 27 May 1924.

Tsushima class Protected cruiser *"Tsushima"*
Laid down in 1901 and launched in 1902. Reclassified in 1921 as a 2nd class Coastal Defense Vessel. Partially disarmed in 1930, and removed from the Navy list in 1936. Redesignated a training hulk in 1939, and destroyed as a torpedo target in 1944.

Chikuma class Protected cruiser *"Yahagi"*
Laid down in 1910 and launched in 1911. Transferred to the reserve in 1924 and used as a training vessel. Removed from the Navy list in 1940, and used as a floating barracks for submarine crews. Scrapped in 1947.

Agano class Light cruiser *"Yahagi"*
Laid down in 1941 and launched in 1942. Sunk on 7 April 1945 by US aircraft south of Kyushu.

Armoured cruiser *"Yakumo"*
Laid down in 1898 and launched in 1899. Reclassified in 1921 as a Coastal Defense Vessel, but re-armed and reactivated as a 1st class cruiser in 1942. Survived the war, and scrapped in 1947.

Light Cruiser *"Yasoshima"*
Laid down in 1930 and launched in 1931 as part of the Chinese Navy. Sunk by Japanese bombers in September 1937, and salvaged in June 1938 and claimed by the Imperial Japanese Navy as a war prize. Refitted as a cruiser in 1944, and sunk by US torpedo bombers on 25 November 1944, off Luzon.

Yodo class Light Cruiser *"Yodo"*
Laid down in 1906 and launched in 1907. Reclassified as a 1st class gunboat in 1912, and later used as an auxiliary vessel until 1940 when it was decommissioned. Broken up for scrap in 1945.

Protected cruiser *"Yoshino"*
Laid down and launched in 1892. Sank in the Yellow Sea on 15 May 1904, following a collision with the armored cruiser *"Kasuga"*.

Light cruiser *"Yubari"*
Laid down in 1922 and launched in 1923. Sunk by a US submarine on 28 April 1944, off Palau.

Nagara class Light cruiser *"Yura"*
Laid down in 1920 and launched in 1922. Badly damaged by US bombers, and scuttled by torpedoes on 25 October 1942, off Guadalcanal.